Lecture Notes in Computer Sc   T0230334

Commenced Publication in 1973
Founding and Former Series Editors:
Gerhard Goos, Juris Hartmanis, and Jan van Leeuwen

Louis Goubin   Mitsuru Matsui (Eds.)

Cryptographic Hardware and Embedded Systems – CHES 2006

8th International Workshop
Yokohama, Japan, October 10-13, 2006
Proceedings

 Springer

Volume Editors

Louis Goubin
PRiSM Laboratory, Versailles St.-Quentin-en-Yvelines University
45 avenue des États-Unis, 78035 Versailles, France
E-mail: louis.goubin@prism.uvsq.fr

Mitsuru Matsui
Mitsubishi Electric Corporation, Information Technology R&D Center
5-1-1 Ofuna Kamakura, Kanagawa 247-8501, Japan
E-mail: matsui.mitsuru@ab.mitsubishielectric.co.jp

Library of Congress Control Number: 2006933431

CR Subject Classification (1998): E.3, C.2, C.3, B.7, G.2.1, D.4.6, K.6.5, F.2.1, J.2

LNCS Sublibrary: SL 4 – Security and Cryptology

ISSN   0302-9743
ISBN-10   3-540-46559-6 Springer Berlin Heidelberg New York
ISBN-13   978-3-540-46559-1 Springer Berlin Heidelberg New York

Springer is a part of Springer Science+Business Media

springer.com

Typesetting: Camera-ready by author, data conversion by Scientific Publishing Services, Chennai, India
Printed on acid-free paper   SPIN: 11894063   06/3142   5 4 3 2 1 0

Preface

These are the proceedings of the Eighth Workshop on Cryptographic Hardware and Embedded Systems (CHES 2006) held in Yokohama, Japan, October 10-13, 2006. The CHES workshop has been sponsored by the International Association for Cryptographic Research (IACR) since 2004. The first and the second CHES workshops were held in Worcester in 1999 and 2000, respectively, followed by Paris in 2001, San Francisco Bay Area in 2002, Cologne in 2003, Boston in 2004 and Edinburgh in 2005. This is the first CHES workshop held in Asia.

This year, a total of 112 paper submissions were received. The review process was therefore a delicate and challenging task for the Program Committee members. Each paper was carefully read by at least three reviewers, and submissions with a Program Committee member as a (co-)author by at least five reviewers. The review process concluded with a two week Web discussion process which resulted in 32 papers being selected for presentation. Unfortunately, there were a number of good papers that could not be included in the program due to a lack of space. We would like to thank all the authors who submitted papers to CHES 2006.

In addition to regular presentations, we were very fortunate to have in the program three excellent invited talks given by Kazumaro Aoki (NTT) on "Integer Factoring Utilizing PC Cluster," Ari Juels (RSA Labs) on "The Outer Limits of RFID Security" and Ahmad Sadeghi (Ruhr University Bochum) on "Challenges for Trusted Computing." The program also included a rump session, chaired by Christof Paar, featuring informal presentations on recent results.

We are very grateful to the Program Committee members and to the external reviewers for their hard work. Special thanks are also due to the members of the Local Committee: Akashi Satoh (Secretary - IBM Japan Ltd.), Toru Akishita (Sony Corporation), Tetsuya Izu (Fujitsu Laboratories Ltd.), Masanobu Koike (Toshiba Solutions Corporation), Natsume Matsuzaki (Matsushita Electric Industrial Co., Ltd.), Shiho Moriai (Sony Computer Entertainment Inc.), Sumio Morioka (NEC Corporation), Hanae Nozaki (Toshiba Corporation), Kenji Ohkuma (IPA), Katsuyuki Okeya (Hitachi Ltd.), Shunsuke Ota (Hitachi Ltd.), Yasuyuki Sakai (Mitsubishi Electric Corporation), Junji Shikata (Yokohama National University), Daisuke Suzuki (Mitsubishi Electric Corporation), Yukiyasu Tsunoo (NEC Corporation), Takanari Ueno (IPA), Takashi Watanabe (Hitachi Ltd.) and Atsuhiro Yamagishi (IPA), for their strong support.

Special thanks go to Tsutomu Matsumoto, the General Chair and local organizer for his extensive efforts to bring the workshop to the beautiful historic city of Yokohama, Japan. The Publicity Chair Çetin Kaya Koç was always very helpful and patient at all stages of the organization. Jens-Peter Kaps helped us as our dedicated webmaster for maintaining the Web review system.

We would also thank the corporate financial supporters, Cryptography Research, Inc., RSA Security Japan Ltd., Fujitsu Limited, IBM Corporation, Information Technology Promotion Agency, Japan (IPA), Initiative for Research on Information Security, Mitsubishi Electric Corporation, NTT Corporation, Renesas Technology Corp., Toshiba Corporation and Yokohama National University. Obviously CHES2006 was not possible without these supporters.

Lastly we would like to thank the CHES Steering Committee members for their hearty support and for giving us the honor of serving at such a prestigious conference.

October 2006   Louis Goubin
                                                       Mitsuru Matsui

8th Workshop on Cryptographic Hardware and Embedded Systems

October 10 – 13, 2006, Yokohama, Japan
http://www.chesworkshop.org/

Organizing Committee

- Tsutomu Matsumoto (General Chair), Yokohama National University, Japan
- Çetin Kaya Koç (Publicity Chair), Oregon State University, USA
- Louis Goubin (Program Co-chair), Versailles St-Quentin-en-Yvelines University, France
- Mitsuru Matsui (Program Co-chair), Mitsubishi Electric Corporation, Japan

Program Committee

- Mehdi-Laurent Akkar, Texas Instruments, France
- Jean-Sébastien Coron, University of Luxembourg, Luxembourg
- Nicolas T. Courtois, Gemalto, France
- Joan Daemen, ST Microelectronics, Belgium
- Pierre-Alain Fouque, ENS, Paris, France
- Jim Goodman, ATI Technologies, Canada
- Helena Handschuh, Spansion, France
- Tetsuya Izu, Fujitsu Laboratories Ltd., Japan
- Marc Joye, Thomson R&D, France
- Seungjoo Kim, Sungkyunkwan University, South Korea
- Çetin Kaya Koç, Oregon State University, USA
- Pil Joong Lee, Postech, South Korea
- Frédéric Muller, HSBC, France
- Katsuyuki Okeya, Hitachi, Japan
- Elisabeth Oswald, Graz University of Technology, Austria
- Christof Paar, Ruhr-Universität Bochum, Germany
- Josyula R. Rao, IBM T.J. Watson Research Center, USA
- Erkay Savaş, Sabanci University, Turkey
- Werner Schindler, Bundesamt für Sicherheit in der Informationstechnik, Germany
- Nigel Smart, University of Bristol, UK
- François-Xavier Standaert, Université Catholique de Louvain-la-Neuve, Belgium
- Berk Sunar, Worcester Polytechnic Institute, USA
- Frédéric Valette, DGA/CELAR, France
- Ingrid Verbauwhede, Katholieke Universiteit Leuven, Belgium
- Colin Walter, Comodo CA, UK
- Sung-Ming Yen, National Central University, Taiwan

Steering Committee

- Marc Joye, Thomson R&D, France
- Çetin Kaya Koç, Oregon State University, USA
- Christof Paar, Ruhr-Universität Bochum, Germany
- Jean-Jacques Quisquater, Université Catholique de Louvain, Belgium
- Josyula R. Rao, IBM T.J. Watson Research Center, USA
- Berk Sunar, Worcester Polytechnic Institute, USA
- Colin D. Walter, Comodo Research Lab, UK

External Referees

- Onur Acıiçmez
- Manfred Aigner
- Toru Akishita
- Frédéric Amiel
- Cédric Archambeau
- Lejla Batina
- Kamel Bentahar
- Guido Bertoni
- Régis Bévan
- Arnaud Boscher
- Donald R. Brown
- Cécile Canovas
- Chien-Ning Chen
- Benoît
    Chevallier-Mames
- Jessy Clédière
- Eric Dahmen
- Yasin Demirbas
- Loïc Duflot
- Takashi Endo
- Pooya Farshim
- Benoît Feix
- Kris Gaj
- Christophe Giraud
- Aline Gouget
- Rob Granger
- Johann Großschädl
- Jorge Guajardo
- Frank Guerkaynak
- Tim Güneysu
- Adnan Gutub
- DongGuk Han
- Christoph Herbst
- Yong Ho Hwang
- Kouichi Itoh
- Tetsuya Izu
- Charanjit Jutla
- Jin Ho Kim
- Tae Hyun Kim
- Young Hwan Kim
- Thorsten Kleinjung
- Sandeep Kumar
- Noboru Kunihiro
- Sébastien
    Kunz-Jacques
- Eun Jeong Kwon
- Soonhak Kwon
- Kerstin Lemke-Rust
- Wei-Chih Lien
- Manfred Lochter
- François Macé
- Pascal Manet
- Stefan Mangard
- Marian Margraf
- Gwenaëlle Martinet
- John McNeill
- Nele Mentens
- Guerric Meurice de
    Dormale
- Andrew Moss
- Francis Olivier
- Berna Örs
- Dan Page
- Jung Hyung Park
- Fabrice Pautot
- Eric Peeters
- Jan Pelzl
- Thomas Peyrin
- Thomas Popp
- Axel Poschmann
- Emmanuel Prouff
- Jean-Luc Rainard
- Arash
    Reyhani-Masoleh
- Francisco
    Rodriguez-Henriquez
- Kazuo Sakiyama
- Gökay Saldamlı
- Akashi Satoh
- Sven Schäge
- Daniel Schepers
- Kai Schramm
- Jae Woo Seo
- Jong Hoon Shin
- Alexei Tchoulkine
- Alexandre F. Tenca
- Stefan Tillich
- Elena Trichina
- Pim Tuyls
- François Vacherand
- Camille Vuillaume
- Takashi Watanabe
- Jun Yajima
- Yeon Hyeong Yang
- Hirotaka Yoshida
- Masayuki Yoshino
- Dae Hyun Yum

Previous CHES Workshop Proceedings

- **CHES 1999:** Çetin K. Koç and Christof Paar (Editors). *Cryptographic Hardware and Embedded Systems*, vol. 1717 of *Lecture Notes in Computer Science*, Springer, 1999.
- **CHES 2000:** Çetin K. Koç and Christof Paar (Editors). *Cryptographic Hardware and Embedded Systems*, vol. 1965 of *Lecture Notes in Computer Science*, Springer, 2000.
- **CHES 2001:** Çetin K. Koç, David Naccache, and Christof Paar (Editors). *Cryptographic Hardware and Embedded Systems*, vol. 2162 of *Lecture Notes in Computer Science*, Springer, 2001.
- **CHES 2002:** Burton S. Kaliski, Çetin K. Koç, and Christof Paar (Editors). *Cryptographic Hardware and Embedded Systems*, vol. 2523 of *Lecture Notes in Computer Science*, Springer, 2002.
- **CHES 2003:** Colin D. Walter, Çetin K. Koç, and Christof Paar (Editors). *Cryptographic Hardware and Embedded Systems*, vol. 2779 of *Lecture Notes in Computer Science*, Springer, 2003.
- **CHES 2004:** Marc Joye and Jean-Jacques Quisquater (Editors). *Cryptographic Hardware and Embedded Systems*, vol. 3156 of *Lecture Notes in Computer Science*, Springer, 2004.
- **CHES 2005:** Josyula R. Rao and Berk Sunar (Editors). *Cryptographic Hardware and Embedded Systems*, vol. 3659 of *Lecture Notes in Computer Science*, Springer, 2005.

Table of Contents

Special Purpose Hardware

Efficient Algorithms for Embedded Processors

Side Channels II

Invited Talk II

Hardware Attacks and Countermeasures II

Efficient Hardware I

Trusted Computing

Side Channels III

Hardware Attacks and Countermeasures III

Invited Talk III

Efficient Hardware II

Template Attacks in Principal Subspaces

C. Archambeau, E. Peeters, F.-X. Standaert, and J.-J. Quisquater

UCL Crypto Group - Université catholique de Louvain
Place du Levant 3, B-1348 Louvain-la-Neuve, Belgium
{archambeau, peeters, standaert, jjq}@dice.ucl.ac.be

Abstract. Side-channel attacks are a serious threat to implementations of cryptographic algorithms. Secret information is recovered based on power consumption, electromagnetic emanations or any other form of physical information leakage. Template attacks are probabilistic side-channel attacks, which assume a Gaussian noise model. Using the maximum likelihood principle enables us to reveal (part of) the secret for each set of recordings (i.e., leakage trace). In practice, however, the major concerns are (i) how to select the points of interest of the traces, (ii) how to choose the minimal distance between these points, and (iii) how many points of interest are needed for attacking. So far, only heuristics were provided. In this work, we propose to perform template attacks in the principal subspace of the traces. This new type of attack addresses all practical issues in principled way and automatically. The approach is validated by attacking stream ciphers such as RC4. We also report analysis results of template style attacks against an FPGA implementation of AES Rijndael. Roughly, the template attack we carried out requires five time less encrypted messages than the best reported correlation attack against similar block cipher implementations.

1 Introduction

Since their first public appearance in 1996 [6], side-channel attacks have been intensively studied by the cryptographic community. The basic principle is to monitor one (or more) unintentional channels that leak from a device such as a smart card and to match these observations with a key-dependent leakage prediction. This channel is usually monitored thanks to an oscilloscope that samples a continuous analog signal and turns it into a discrete digitalized sequence. This sequence is often referred to as a trace.

Recently, a probabilistic side-channel attack, called the Template Attack (TA), was introduced [2]. This attack was originally mounted to target stream ciphers implementation. In this context, the attacker can only observe a single use of the key, usually during the initialization step of the cipher. As it is not possible to generate different leakages from the same secret key (e.g., corresponding to different plaintexts), TAs were purposed for a more efficient way of retrieving information from side-channel traces.

There are three main reasons that make TAs more efficient than previous approaches to exploit side-channel leakages. First, TAs usually require a profiling step, in order to build a (probabilistic) noise model of the side-channel

L. Goubin and M. Matsui (Eds.): CHES 2006, LNCS 4249, pp. 1–14, 2006.

that can be used to capture the secret information leaked by a running device. Second, TAs usually exploit multivariate statistics to characterize the dependencies between the different time instant in the traces. Finally, TAs use maximum likelihood as similarity measure, that can capture any type of dependency (if the probabilistic model is found to be adequate), whereas, for example correlation analysis only captures linear dependencies [1]. In general, the cost of these improvements is a reduction of the adversarial flexibility. For example, Hamming weight leakage models can generally be used for any CMOS devices while template attacks profile the leakage function for one particular device.

TA relies on the hypothesis that leakage information is located in the variability of the leakage traces. In order to recover the secret, one has thus to focus at the time instants where the variability is maximal. However, in practice it is not clear how many and which moments exactly are important. The attacks are therefore based on heuristics, which specify these quantities according to some prior belief. For example, it is common to force the successive, relevant time instants to be one clock cycle distant.

The main contribution of this work is that we take TA a step further. Instead of applying TA directly, we first transform the leakage traces such that we are able to select the relevant features (i.e. transformed time instants) and their number automatically. Meanwhile, we do not need to determine a specific feature interdistance. Of course, when performing TA after transformation, we still take the correlations between the features into account. Now, in order to find a suitable transformation consider again ordinary TA. It is assumed that the secret information leakage is mainly hidden in the local variability of the mean traces. If this hypothesis is valid, it would be more appropriate to take the optimal linear combination of the relevant time samples and perform TA in the principal subspace of the mean traces. We call this approach principal subspace-based TA (PSTA). A principal subspace can be viewed as a lower dimensional subspace embedded in the data space[1] where each coordinate axis successively indicates the direction in which the data have maximal variability (or variance).

A standard statistical tool for finding the principal subspace of a data set is principal component analysis (PCA) [5]. PCA performs an eigendecomposition of the empirical data covariance matrix in order to identify, both, the principal directions (eigenvectors) and the variance (eigenvalues) associated to each one of them. However, practical issues may arise in the context of PSTA, as the dimension of the traces is much larger, (typically $\mathcal{O}(10^5)$) than the number of traces (typically $\mathcal{O}(10^3)$). Therefore, we propose to use a variant of PCA that is more suitable in this situation (see Section 3.1 for further details).

An attractive feature of PSTA is that the projected traces are aligned with the directions of maximal variance. These directions are nothing else than a weighted sum of all the time instants, the weights being determined such that the data variability is preserved after projection. So, in contrast to TA, which selects a relevant subset of time instants according to a heuristic, PSTA determines first the optimal (in terms of maximal variance) linear combination of these time

---

[1] Here, the data space is the space in which the leakage traces live.

instants. In other words, there is no need to determine an interdistance between the time samples anymore as the irrelevant ones will be assigned a small weight. Furthermore, based on the value of the eigenvalues, one can determine which (the largest) and how many directions are relevant. In order to validate our approach, we finally apply the described techniques to two implementation cases. First we target an implementation of RC4, similar to the one in [3] as a typical context where template attacks are necessary. The, we target an FPGA implementation of the AES Rijndael. For this purpose, we suggest an adaptation of template attacks that allow characterizing the leakage traces of block ciphers. We finally compare the obtained results with previously reported and observe a significant improvement of the attacks efficiency (which is, again, to be traded with less flexibility than previous attacks).

2   Template Attacks

In this section, the underlying principle of Template Attacks (TA) is first presented. Next, we introduce principal subspace TA (PSTA). In this approach, (linear) dimensionality reduction techniques [5,4] are used to select automatically the most relevant features and their number. In this context, features can be understood as weighted sums of the most relevant trace samples. In addition, both the computational requirements as well as the prohibitive memory usage of standard TA are reduced in a principled way.

2.1   Templates

Suppose that P_k traces of a given operation O_k were recorded. The traces $\{\mathbf{t}_{p_k}\}_{p_k=1}^{P_k}$ are N-dimensional time vectors. In TA a Gaussian noise model is considered [2], meaning that $\{\mathbf{t}_{p_k}\}_{p_k=1}^{P_k}$ are assumed to be drawn from the multivariate Gaussian distribution $\mathcal{N}(\cdot|\boldsymbol{\mu}_k, \boldsymbol{\Sigma}_k)$, which is defined as follows:

$$\mathcal{N}(\mathbf{t}|\boldsymbol{\mu}_k, \boldsymbol{\Sigma}_k) = (2\pi)^{-\frac{N}{2}}|\boldsymbol{\Sigma}_k|^{-\frac{1}{2}}\exp\left\{-\frac{1}{2}(\mathbf{t}-\boldsymbol{\mu}_k)^{\mathrm{T}}\boldsymbol{\Sigma}_k^{-1}(\mathbf{t}-\boldsymbol{\mu}_k)\right\}. \tag{1}$$

Note that the mean $\boldsymbol{\mu}_k$ and the covariance matrix $\boldsymbol{\Sigma}_k$ specify completely the noise distribution associated to the operation O_k. Constructing the templates consists then in estimating the sets of parameters $\{\boldsymbol{\mu}_k\}_{k=1}^{K}$ and $\{\boldsymbol{\Sigma}_k\}_{k=1}^{K}$.

A standard approach is to use the maximum likelihood principle. In this approach, we seek for the parameters that maximize the likelihood of the observations (traces) under the chosen noise model. Maximizing the likelihood is equivalent to maximizing the log-likelihood, which is given by

$$\log\mathcal{L}_k \equiv \log\prod_{p=1}^{P_k}p(\mathbf{t}_{p_k}|O_k) = \sum_{p_k=1}^{P_k}\log\mathcal{N}(\mathbf{t}_{p_k}|\boldsymbol{\mu}_k, \boldsymbol{\Sigma}_k) \tag{2}$$

where $p(\mathbf{t}_{p_k}|O_k)$ is the probability of observing trace $\mathbf{t}_{p_k}$ if we assume that operation O_k was performed on the device. Direct maximization of (2) is straightforward and leads to the following estimates:

$$\hat{\boldsymbol{\mu}}_k = \frac{1}{P_k} \sum_{p_k=1}^{P_k} \mathbf{t}_{p_k}, \quad \widehat{\boldsymbol{\Sigma}}_k = \frac{1}{P_k} \sum_{p_k=1}^{P_k} (\mathbf{t}_{p_k} - \hat{\boldsymbol{\mu}}_k)(\mathbf{t}_{p_k} - \hat{\boldsymbol{\mu}}_k)^{\mathrm{T}}. \tag{3}$$

Note that these quantities correspond respectively to the empirical mean and the empirical covariance matrix associated to the observations $\{\mathbf{t}_{p_k}\}_{p_k=1}^{P_k}$.

2.2   Attack

Assume that the set of possible operations that can be performed on the device is $\{O_k\}_{k=1}^{K}$. In order to determine to which operation a new trace $\mathbf{t}_{\mathrm{new}}$ (for example measured on a different device than the one on which the templates were constructed) corresponds, we apply Bayes' rule. This leads to the following classification rule:

$$\hat{O}_k = \underset{O_k}{\operatorname{argmax}} \; \hat{P}(O_k|\mathbf{t}_{\mathrm{new}}) = \underset{O_k}{\operatorname{argmax}} \; \hat{p}(\mathbf{t}_{\mathrm{new}}|O_k)P(O_k), \tag{4}$$

where $\hat{p}(\mathbf{t}_{\mathrm{new}}|O_k) = \mathcal{N}(\mathbf{t}_{\mathrm{new}}|\hat{\boldsymbol{\mu}}_k, \widehat{\boldsymbol{\Sigma}}_k)$ and $P(O_k)$ is the prior probability that operation O_k was performed. Thus, the classification rule assigns $\mathbf{t}_{\mathrm{new}}$ to the operation O_k with the highest posterior probability. Note that when the operations are equiprobable $P(O_k)$ equals $1/K$.

3   Template Attacks in Principal Subspaces

In practice, the number of samples N per trace is very large, typically $\mathcal{O}(10^5)$ as it depends on the sampling rate of the recording device. A high sampling rate is usually mandatory in order to retain the frequency content of the side-channel. This leads to excessive computational loads and a prohibitively large memory usage. Furthermore, it is expected that only a limited number of time samples are relevant for TA.

Several attempts were made to address these practical issues. Chari, *et al.* [2] select time samples showing the largest difference between the mean traces $\{\boldsymbol{\mu}_k\}_{k=1}^{K}$. Rechberger and Oswald [8] used a similar method; their selection rule is based on the cumulative difference between the mean traces. In addition, the traces are pre-processed by a Fast Fourier Transform (FFT) in order to remove high frequency noise. Another, simple rule is to select the points (after pre-processing) where the the largest variance of the mean traces occur. All these approaches assume that the relevant samples are the ones with the highest variability. However, they only provide heuristics and are therefore by no means optimal. Furthermore, they require to chose an arbitrary minimum distance between successive points (for example the clock cycle) in order to avoid redundancy and there is no satisfactory rule to determine how many such samples are needed to attack optimally.

Another, more systematic approach, which also relies on the data variability, is to select the relevant points based on principal component analysis (PCA) (see for example [5,4]). PCA is a standard statistical tool for dimensionality reduction. It looks for a linear transformation that projects high-dimensional data into a low-dimensional subspace while preserving the data variance (i.e., it minimizes the mean squared reconstruction error). In order to minimize the loss of relevant information, PCA works in two steps. First, it looks for a rotation of the original axes such that the new coordinate system indicates the successive directions in which the data have maximal variance. Second, it only retains the M most important directions in order to reduce the dimensionality. It assumes therefore that the variability in the discarded directions corresponds to noise. An example is shown in Appendix A.

3.1 Trace Principal Subspaces

Consider a set N-dimensional observations $\{\mathbf{t}_k\}_{k=1}^{K}$, which are the empirical mean traces associated to the set of operation $\{O_k\}_{k=1}^{K}$. PCA looks for the first principal directions $\{\mathbf{w}_m\}_{m=1}^{M}$ such that $N \geq M$ and which form an orthonormal basis of the M-dimensional subspace capturing maximal variance of $\{\mathbf{t}_k\}_{k=1}^{K}$. It can be shown [5] that the principal directions are the eigenvectors of the empirical covariance matrix, which is given by

$$\bar{\mathbf{S}} = \frac{1}{K} \sum_{k=1}^{K} (\mathbf{t}_k - \bar{\mathbf{t}})(\mathbf{t}_k - \bar{\mathbf{t}})^{\mathrm{T}}. \tag{5}$$

The quantity $\bar{\mathbf{t}} = \sum_{k=1}^{K} \mathbf{t}_k$ is the average of the mean traces.

In TA, N is typically $\mathcal{O}(10^5)$, meaning that $\bar{\mathbf{S}} \in \mathbb{R}^{N \times N}$ is beyond computation capabilities. Furthermore, the total number of mean traces K is much smaller than N. Matrix $\bar{\mathbf{S}}$ is of rank $K - 1$ (or less) and has therefore only $K - 1$ eigenvectors. Fortunately, one can compute the first $K - 1$ eigenvectors without having to compute the complete covariance matrix $\bar{\mathbf{S}}$ [4].

Let $\mathbf{T} = (\mathbf{t}_1 - \bar{\mathbf{t}}, \dots, \mathbf{t}_K - \bar{\mathbf{t}}) \in \mathbb{R}^{N \times K}$ be the matrix of the centered mean traces. By definition the empirical covariance matrix is given by $\frac{1}{K}\mathbf{T}\mathbf{T}^{\mathrm{T}}$. Let us denote the matrix of eigenvectors and eigenvalues of $\frac{1}{K}\mathbf{T}^{\mathrm{T}}\mathbf{T}$ by respectively $\mathbf{U}$ and $\boldsymbol{\Delta}$, the latter being diagonal. We have $(\frac{1}{K}\mathbf{T}^{\mathrm{T}}\mathbf{T})\mathbf{U} = \mathbf{U}\boldsymbol{\Delta}$. Left multiplying both sides by $\mathbf{T}$ and rearranging leads to

$$\bar{\mathbf{S}}(\mathbf{T}\mathbf{U}) = (\mathbf{T}\mathbf{U})\boldsymbol{\Delta}. \tag{6}$$

From this expression, we see that $\mathbf{T}\mathbf{U}$ is the matrix of the K eigenvectors of $\bar{\mathbf{S}}$. In order to form an orthonormal basis, they need to be normalized. The normalized principal directions are given by

$$\mathbf{V} = \frac{1}{\sqrt{K}}(\mathbf{T}\mathbf{U})\boldsymbol{\Delta}^{-\frac{1}{2}}. \tag{7}$$

The principal directions $\{\mathbf{w}_m\}_{m=1}^{M}$ are the columns of $\mathbf{V}$ corresponding to the M largest eigenvalues of $\boldsymbol{\Delta}$. Subsequently, we will denote these eigenvalues by the diagonal matrix $\boldsymbol{\Lambda} \in \mathbb{R}^{M \times M}$ and the corresponding matrix of principal directions by $\mathbf{W} \in \mathbb{R}^{N \times M}$.

As discussed above, PCA can be performed when the number of data vectors is (much) lower than their dimension. Still, one may question the pertinence of the solution, as a subspace of dimensionality $K - 1$ goes exactly through K points. However, the solution found by PCA makes sense if the intrinsic dimension of the data manifold is much lower than number of observations. In other words, the solution is valid if most of the relevant information can be summarized in very few principal directions. Fortunately, this is the case in the context of Template Attacks (see Section 4). Note that the same problematic arises in Computer Vision in the context of automatic face recognition. Here, the very high dimensional vectors are the face images. The principal characteristics are then found by following a similar approach, which is known as *eigenfaces* [12].

3.2 Principal Subspace Based Templates

In the previous section, we showed how standard PCA can be modified in order to be used with very high-dimensional vectors such as traces. This provides us with the projection matrix $\mathbf{W}$, which identifies successively the directions with maximal variance. Now, in order to build PSTA, we assume a Gaussian noise model after projection. So we need to estimate the projected means $\{\boldsymbol{\nu}_k\}_{k=1}^K$ and the covariance matrices of the projected traces along the (retained) principal directions $\{\boldsymbol{\Lambda}_k\}_{k=1}^K$. These parameters are respectively given by

$$\boldsymbol{\nu}_k = \mathbf{W}^{\mathrm{T}} \hat{\boldsymbol{\mu}}_k, \quad \boldsymbol{\Lambda}_k = \mathbf{W}^{\mathrm{T}} \hat{\boldsymbol{\Sigma}}_k \mathbf{W}. \tag{8}$$

As in standard TA, the noise model is here given by a multivariate Gaussian distribution. However, it is expected that the number of principal directions M is much smaller than N. Note that a direction can be considered as not being principal when the associated eigenvalue is small compared to the largest one. This will be further discussed in Section 4.

Next, in order to classify a new trace $\mathbf{t}_{\mathrm{new}}$, we apply Bayes' rule. This leads to the following classification rule (or attack):

$$\widehat{O}_k = \underset{O_k}{\operatorname{argmax}} \, \hat{p}(\mathbf{W}^{\mathrm{T}} \mathbf{t}_{\mathrm{new}} | O_k) P(O_k), \tag{9}$$

where the distribution in projection space is given by $\hat{p}(\mathbf{W}^{\mathrm{T}} \mathbf{t}_{\mathrm{new}} | O_k) = \mathcal{N}(\mathbf{W}^{\mathrm{T}} \mathbf{t}_{\mathrm{new}} | \boldsymbol{\nu}_k, \boldsymbol{\Lambda}_k)$.

4 Experimental Results

In the experiments, the recorded traces are power leakages. We validate PSTA both on stream ciphers (RC4) and block ciphers (AES Rijndael). Two examples of leakage traces for each encryption algorithm are shown in the Figures of Appendix B.

From a practical point of view, considering a very small number K of different operations/keys can lead to a degenerate solution as only very few principal directions can be identified. This in turn may lead to poorly performing attacks. Therefore, it is convenient to augment the number of mean traces artificially in this case. For example, one can compute for each operation a pre-defined number of mean traces by picking several traces at random in the training set. Another approach is to use resampling techniques from statistics (see for example [3]).

4.1   RC4

The first experiments were carried out on a PIC 16F877 8-bit RISC-based microprocessor [7]. The microchip was clocked at a frequency around 4 MHz. This microprocessor requires four clock cycles to process an instruction. Each instruction is divided into four steps: (i) fetch (update of the address bus), (ii) decode and operands fetch (driven by the bus), (iii) execute and (iv) write back. We monitored the power consumption of a device by inserting a small resistor at its ground pin or power pin. The resistor value is chosen such that it disrupts the voltage supply by at most 5% from its reference[2]. The 1-Ohm method[3] was used to attack the device at the ground pin and a differential probe in the case of targeting the power pin.

RC4 is a stream cipher working on a 256-byte state table denoted S hereafter. It generates a pseudo-random stream of bits which is mixed with the plaintext using a XOR function to yield a ciphertext. The state S is initialized with a variable key length (typically between 40 and 256 bytes) using the following key-scheduling algorithm:

```
for i from 0 to 255
   S[i] := i
j := 0
for i from 0 to 255
   j := (j + S[i] + key[i mod keylength]) mod 256
   swap(S[i],S[j])
```

The power consumption of the first iteration was monitored; the dependence on the first byte of the key is here obvious. The 256-byte state was placed in the data memory by allocating 64 bytes per bank. Therefore, it is expected to be easier to distinguish the keys located in different banks even if they have the same Hamming weight.

In the RC4 experiments, 10 keys that are believed to be "close" are considered. For each one, 500 traces are used to construct the models and 300 to validate them. In other words, 500 traces are used to estimate the parameters and 300 to assess the performance. For each trace, there are 300,000 time samples. Figure 1 shows the eigenvalues in decreasing order. Clearly, most of the variance is located in very few components. In practice, 7 components are sufficient to ensure an average rate of correct classification of 93.3% (see Figure 2), meaning that most of the test traces are correctly classified at once.

By contrast, in [2] 42 test samples were selected according to some heuristic. The noise model was chosen to be multivariate Gaussian as in (1). When considering a diagonal covariance matrix (i.e., the time samples are considered

---

[2] This is advised in IEC 61967-3: Integrated circuits - Measurement of electromagnetic emissions, 150kHz to 1GHz Part 3: Measurement of radiated emissions, surface scan method (10kHz to 3GHz), 47A/620/NP, New Work Item Proposal (July 2001).

[3] See IEC 61967-4: Integrated circuits - Measurement of electromagnetic emissions, 150 kHz to 1 GHz - Part 4: Measurement of conducted emissions 1Ω / 150Ω. Direct coupling method, 47A/636/FDIS, Final Draft International Standard, Distributed on 2002-01-18.

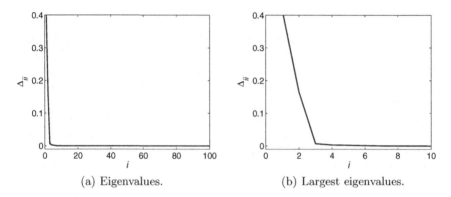

(a) Eigenvalues.   (b) Largest eigenvalues.

Fig. 1. Eigenvalues in descending order for RC4

independent) the classification errors reported by [2] were up to 35% for similar keys. Since the power of the attack strongly depends on the implementation and the measurement noise, we also reproduced the experiments for a fully multivariate Gaussian noise model (i.e., for full covariance matrices) for comparison purposes. The samples were selected as the ones where maximal variance occurred. The minimal distance between successive samples was chosen to be equal to the clock cycle. For 42 time samples , the average classification success was 91.8%, which is already considerable. However, note that this approach requires to choose a particular distance between the samples a priori, which affects the performances considerably. For example here, a distance of half the clock cycle leeds to an average classification error of only 80.5%. A similar loss of performance is observed when choosing to few samples to construct the multivariate noise model, but when too many samples are taken, the model reliability might be questionable. Indeed, when the dimension of the data space increases, the number of observations to reliability estimate the parameters needs to increase as well. In the case of standard TA with a 42 points of interest, estimating the mean and the covariance matrix of the multivariate Gaussian noise model requires to fit $M(M + 3)/2 = 945$ parameters. However, there is only a limited number of measurements (or traces), typically few hundreds. The number of constraints increases linearly with the dimension M. There are thus only very few measurements to estimate each model parameter.

An important advantage of PSTA over TA is that the number of relevant features can be inferred from the eigenvalues. Only the significant ones need to be retained; the remaining ones are thought of as being noise. Clearly, from Figure 1, it can be observed that only the first two components are important, and indeed, the average correct classification rate for two components is already 88.7% (see Figure 2). The next few components only slightly increase the power of the attack. Furthermore, in the 7-dimensional principal subspace of the traces only 70 parameters need to be estimated (as opposed to 945), while the number of data is the same. The model parameters are thus expected to be more reliably estimated. Note also that a minimal distance between the features needs not to be

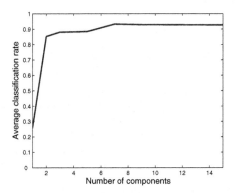

Fig. 2. Average correct classification rate for RC4 as a function of the number of components

chosen in the case of subspace TA. As a matter of fact, the principal components are a weighted sum of many time samples, the weights being determined as the ones minimizing the loss of variance in the data.

4.2 AES Rijndael

Template attacks are usually applied to stream ciphers, key scheduling algorithms and pseudo-random number generators. This is motivated by the fact that such primitives are difficult to target with standard side-channel attacks like the DPA, since the attacker can only observe a single use of the key. However, in general, one could apply template attacks to any kind of cryptographic primitive in order to take advantage of a more efficient information extraction from side-channel observations. For example, in this section we show that an adaptation of subspace based TA can be applied to FPGA implementations of block ciphers. Such a context is practically interesting since it allows to evaluate how the construction of templates may be affected by (large) amounts of algorithmic noise. It also yields particular constraints since the objective is to characterize only a part of the implemented design.

For illustration purposes, let us observe the simplified block cipher of Figure 3, where only one round is represented. In this picture, let us also assume that we want to build templates for the key bits entering the first (upper) substitution box s. Clearly, if we only want to identify the power consumption patterns of this s-box (more specifically, we want to identify the dark grey computations in the scheme, before the application of a diffusion layer), it is important to randomize all the other points in the implementation. They will then contribute to the overall leakage as random noise source. That is, all the inputs to the other s-boxes should be feed with a random number generator. Therefore, we will construct our templates according to the following procedure:

1. Select the target key bits in the implementation.
2. For each key candidate:

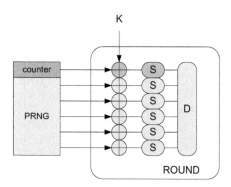

Fig. 3. Simplified view of one round in AES Rijndael. The counter feeds a particular sequence of messages to the device. PRNG is a pseudo-random generator producing arbitraty message sequences. K is the encryption key, S denotes an s-box and D is the diffusion layer of the round.

- Feed the s-box corresponding to these target key bits with a deterministic sequence of plaintexts (e.g., a counter).
- Feed the other s-boxes in the scheme with random inputs[4].
- Build the templates from the measurement of these computations.

An important feature of this process is that each key candidate will be characterized by a number of encryptions. This is because every value in the counter will give rise to a computation that identifies these candidates. As a matter of fact, this will allow us to evaluate the efficiency of our template attack, by checking the number of encryptions required to reach a successful classification and therefore to compare our results with previous attacks against similar implementations.

In practice, we targeted an FPGA implementation of the AES Rijndael [11]. Basically, we selected a loop architecture with only one round implemented in the circuit. The key scheduling was not implemented on-the-fly, but executed once, before the execution of our encryptions. However, note that the possible implementation of an on-the-fly key scheduling would not affect the construction of the templates as long as the key is fixed and therefore, once initialized, the key scheduling does not lead to any switching activity anymore.

In the experiments, 10 different keys were considered. For each one, 500 traces were used to estimate the model parameters and 500 to validate the resulting models. The number of samples per trace is equal to 500, 000. Figure 4 shows the eigenvalues for AES Rijndael. Again, it can be observed that most of the variance in the data can be summarized with relatively few components. For example, with 20 components and for 128 encrypted messages the average classification success is equal to 86.7% (see Figure 5). Compared to the results with

---

[4] Random inputs are used not only when constructing the templates, but also when evaluating the performance of the attack. Therefore, this set up mimics a device with unknown inputs for the other s-boxes as desired. Note that a convenient way to generate these random inputs is to use the feedback from the block cipher outputs.

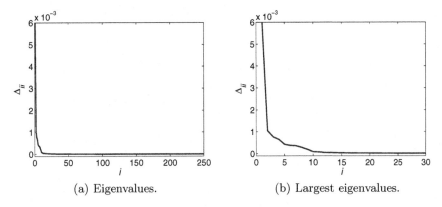

(a) Eigenvalues.   (b) Largest eigenvalues.

Fig. 4. Eigenvalues in descending order for AES Rijndael

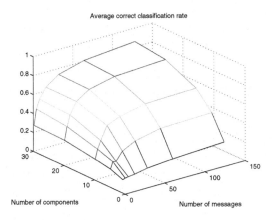

Fig. 5. Average correct classification rate for AES, as a function of the number of encrypted messages and the number of retained components

RC4, a higher number of components is necessary for a comparable classification accuracy. This result can be explained by the fact that the power traces are here much noisier (due to the parallel hardware implementation).

Although, there are relatively few significant components needed with respect to the number of encrypted messages, it is important to realize that it does not mean that the information in most of them is discarded. Indeed, in PSTA, the PCA-step seeks of the optimal projection in the feature space. Each component corresponds thus to a weighted sum of a possibly high number of time samples. Therefore, the information leakage due to a possibly high number of encrypted messages is summarized in a single component.

Figure 5 shows the average correct classification rate as a function of the number of retained components and the number of messages. As expected, when the number of encryptions decreases, the performances drops. This is due to the fact that there is less information leakage available. Similarly, when the number of

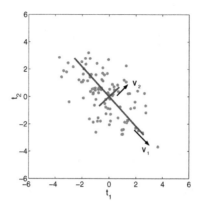

Fig. 6. Illustration of principal component analysis (PCA)

components is small, there is only a poor capacity to classify correctly, as too many relevant features have been discarded. However, when the number of messages and the number of components increases the average correct classification rate rapidly increases.

Compared to recent correlation-based power analysis attacks of AES Rijndael (also on FPGA), the number of message required to recover the correct key bytes is much smaller. The factor of proportionality ranges from 2 to 5 depending on the fact that the attack uses trace averaging [10] or not [9]. Note also that correlation attacks require in general to carefully preprocess the traces, for example using several filters. By contrast, PSTA is much more practical as it exploits the information in the raw data directly and does not require to adjust any tuning parameters, but the number of components to retain.

5   Conclusion

In this work, we introduced principal subspace template attacks and showed that they can be successfully applied to both stream and block ciphers. Preprocessing the leakage traces beforehand by PCA allows avoiding the practical issues of ordinary template attacks. Principal subspace template attacks are motivated by the fact that template attacks consider the time instants having a great variability as being important to discriminate. If this assumption is correct, then PCA is the optimal (linear) transformation to identify the most relevant features. Besides, the eigenvalues provide a systematic rule for determining how many and which features should be selected to mount a powerful attack. Finally, it is also important to realize that the main difference between both attacks resides in the way they extract information from traces. In template attacks M of the N samples are used to mount the noise model, the selection being based on heuristics, while in principal subspace template attacks M linear combinations (preserving maximal variance) of these N samples are used.

References

1. Eric Brier, Christophe Clavier, and Francis Olivier. Correlation power analysis with a leakage model. In Marc Joye and Jean-Jacques Quisquater, editors, *CHES*, volume 3156 of *Lecture Notes in Computer Science*, pages 16–29. Springer, 2004.
2. Suresh Chari, Josyula R. Rao, and Pankaj Rohatgi. Template attacks. In Burton S. Kaliski Jr., Çetin Kaya Koç, and Christof Paar, editors, *4th International Workshop on Cryptographic Hardware and Embedded Systems (CHES)*, volume 2523 of *Lecture Notes in Computer Science, 13–28. Springer, 2002.*
3. B. Efron and R.J. Tibshirani. *An introduction to the Bootstrap.* Chapman and Hall, London, 1993.
4. K. Fukunaga. *Introduction to Statistical Pattern Recognition.* Elsevier, New York, 1990.
5. I. T. Jolliffe. *Principal Component Analysis.* Springer-Verlag, New York, 1986.
6. Paul C. Kocher. Timing attacks on implementations of Diffie-Hellman, RSA, DSS, and other systems. In Neal Koblitz, editor, *16th Annual International Cryptology Conference (CRYPTO)*, volume 1109 of *Lecture Notes in Computer Science, 104–113. Springer, 1996.*
7. Microship. PIC16F877 datasheet. url: ww1.microchip.com/downloads/en/ Device-Doc/30292c.pdf, 2001.
8. Christian Rechberger and Elisabeth Oswald. Practical template attacks. In Chae Hoon Lim and Moti Yung, editors, *5th International Workshop on Information Security Applications (WISA)*, volume 3325 of *Lecture Notes in Computer Science, 440–456. Springer, 2004.*
9. F.-X. Standaert, S.B. Ors, and B. Preneel. Power analysis of an FPGA implementation of Rijndael: Is pipelining a DPA countermeasure? In Marc Joye and Jean-Jacques Quisquater, editors, *6th International Workshop Cryptographic Hardware and Embedded Systems (CHES)*, volume 3156 of *Lecture Notes in Computer Science, 30–44. Springer, 2004.*
10. F.-X. Standaert, E. Peeters, F. Macé, and J.-J. Quisquater. Updates on the security of FPGAs against power analysis attacks. In *proceedings of ARC 2006*, LNCS 3985, pp. 335-346, 2006.
11. F.-X. Standaert, G. Rouvroy, J.-J. Quisquater, and J.-D. Legat. Efficient implementation of Rijndael encryption in reconfigurable hardware: Improvements and design tradeoffs. In Colin D. Walter, Çetin Kaya Koç, and Christof Paar, editors, *5th International Workshop Cryptographic Hardware and Embedded Systems (CHES)*, volume 2779 of *Lecture Notes in Computer Science, 334–350. Springer, 2003.*
12. M. Turk and A.Pentland. Eigenfaces for recognition. *Journal of Cognitive Neuroscience*, 3(1):71–86, 1991.

A   Appendix

An illustration of PCA is shown Figure 6. The data is drawn from a 2-dimensional Gaussian distribution. The two principal directions v_1 and v_2 are shown by the solid lines. The length of the lines is proportional to the variance of the projected data onto the corresponding direction. If we remove the second dimension (after rotation) and describe the data only by the first one, then we will minimize the loss of information (i.e., loss of variance) due to this new representation.

B   Appendix

The examples of the recorded RC4 and AES Rijndael power traces are shown respectively in Figure 7 and 8.

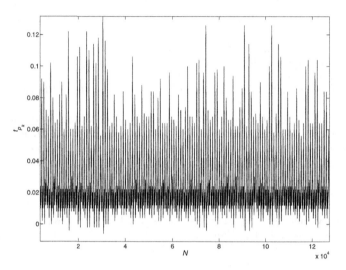

Fig. 7. Example of a RC4 power trace

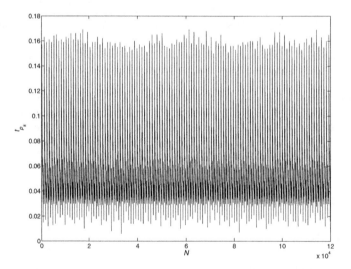

Fig. 8. Example of an AES Rijndael power trace

Templates vs. Stochastic Methods

A Performance Analysis for Side Channel Cryptanalysis

Benedikt Gierlichs[1,2,*], Kerstin Lemke-Rust[2,**], and Christof Paar[2]

[1] K.U. Leuven, ESAT/COSIC
Kasteelpark Arenberg 10
B-3001 Leuven-Heverlee, Belgium
benedikt.gierlichs@esat.kuleuven.be
[2] Horst Görtz Institute for IT Security
Ruhr University Bochum
44780 Bochum, Germany
{gierlichs, lemke, cpaar}@crypto.rub.de

Abstract. Template Attacks and the Stochastic Model provide advanced methods for side channel cryptanalysis that make use of 'a-priori' knowledge gained from a profiling step. For a systematic comparison of Template Attacks and the Stochastic Model, we use two sets of measurement data that originate from two different microcontrollers and setups. Our main contribution is to capture performance aspects against crucial parameters such as the number of measurements available during profiling and classification. Moreover, optimization techniques are evaluated for both methods under consideration. Especially for a low number of measurements and noisy samples, the use of a T-Test based algorithm for the choice of relevant instants can lead to significant performance gains. As a main result, T-Test based Templates are the method of choice if a high number of samples is available for profiling. However, in case of a low number of samples for profiling, stochastic methods are an alternative and can reach superior efficiency both in terms of profiling and classification.

Keywords: Template Attack, Stochastic Model, Performance Analysis, Side Channel Cryptanalysis, High-Order Attacks, Power Analysis.

1 Introduction

Side channel cryptanalysis makes use of physical leakage of a cryptographic implementation as an additional source of information for mathematical cryptanalysis. An adversary is successful, if side channel cryptanalysis yields a (sufficient) entropy loss of a secret key used in a cryptographic implementation.

The underlying working hypothesis for side channel cryptanalysis assumes that computations of a cryptographic device have an impact on instantaneous

---

* The research was done in cooperation with gemalto.
** Supported by the European Commission through the IST Contract IST-2002-507932 ECRYPT, the European Network of Excellence in Cryptology.

L. Goubin and M. Matsui (Eds.): CHES 2006, LNCS 4249, pp. 15–29, 2006.

physical observables in the (immediate) vicinity of the device, e.g., power consumption or electromagnetic radiation [6,5]. The dependency of the measurable observables on the internal state of a cryptographic algorithm is specific for each implementation and represents the *side channel*. This relationship can be predicted, e.g., by applying a (standard) power consumption model of the implementation such as the Hamming weight or Hamming distance model [2]. Alternatively, the probability density of the observables can be profiled in advance for every key dependent internal state of the implementation.

The methods under consideration are the Template Attack [3] and the Stochastic Model [7]. Both methods include a profiling step for the estimation of a key dependent multivariate probability density of the physical observable. Our work is driven by the demand for an objective and systematic performance comparison in identical physical conditions since the *quality* of side channel measurements is one of the most crucial factors in terms of attack efficiency. Both methods are applied to measurements from two setups using two different microcontrollers running an AES implementation in software. Moreover, we apply and evaluate optimization strategies, especially with respect to the selection of time instants for the multivariate density.

This work is organized as follows. In Section 2 we give an introduction to Template Attacks and the Stochastic Model, i.e., the two methods under consideration. Our testing framework used for performance analysis is presented in Section 3. Section 4 presents results that were obtained by using the known approach for both methods, whereas Section 5 evaluates optimizations. Our contribution is summarized in Section 6.

2   Side Channel Cryptanalysis

Methods used for side channel cryptanalysis can be distinguished into *one-stage* methods without any prior knowledge about the expected side channel leakage that are directly used for key extraction and *two-stage* methods that make use of a profiling step to obtain 'a priori' knowledge on the side channel leakage that can be used for extracting keys later on. Both, Templates and the Stochastic Model are two-stage attacks. For profiling, two-stage methods require a cryptographic device which is identical to the device used at key extraction. While in case of attacks against stream ciphers, a further requirement is that the profiling device must allow to load keys (cp. [3]), our attacks against AES do not require this, which weakens the assumptions on the adversary's power.

2.1   Template Attack

Templates were introduced as the strongest side channel attack possible from an information theoretic point of view [3]. For each (sub)key-dependency, a Template, i.e., a multivariate characterization of the noise in the instantaneous leakage signal, is produced during profiling. Let us assume K different (sub)key-dependent operations O_i with $1 \leq i \leq K$. During profiling, Templates T_i, one for each key dependency O_i, are generated from a large number N[1] of samples. The first part in a Template estimates the data-dependent portion of the side channel for each time instant, i.e., it is the average m_i[2] of all available samples representing the same key-dependency O_i. The second part in a Template estimates the probability density of the noise in the side channel. Before starting to characterize the noise, it is highly advisable to identify and select those time instants where the averages m_i differ significantly in order to reduce computational and storage efforts. Reference [3] proposes to compute the sum of pairwise differences between the averages, $\sum_{j,l=1}^{K} m_j - m_l$ for $l \geq j$, and to choose p points $(P_1, \ldots, P_p)$ along the peaks of the resulting difference curve. It is assumed that the noise in the side channel approximately has a multivariate normal distribution with respect to the selected instants. A p-dimensional noise vector $\boldsymbol{n_i}(L)$ is extracted from each sample L representing the Template's key dependency O_i as $\boldsymbol{n_i}(L) = (L[P_1] - m_i[P_1], \ldots, L[P_p] - m_i[P_p])$. One computes the $(p \times p)$ covariance matrix C_i from these noise vectors. The probability density of the noise occurring under key dependency O_i is then given by the p-dimensional multivariate normal distribution $\text{prob}_{C_i}(\cdot)$ where the probability of observing a noise vector $\boldsymbol{z}$ is

$$\text{prob}_{C_i}(\boldsymbol{z}) = \frac{1}{\sqrt{(2\pi)^p |C_i|}} \exp\left(-\frac{1}{2} \boldsymbol{z}^T C_i^{-1} \boldsymbol{z}\right), \quad \boldsymbol{z} \in \mathbb{R}^p, \tag{1}$$

$|C_i|$ denotes the determinant of C_i, and C_i^{-1} its inverse.

The strategy to classify a single sample S is a maximum likelihood hypothesis test. For each hypothetical key dependency O_i, one extracts the noise in S by subtracting the average m_i at the p selected instants yielding a noise vector $\boldsymbol{n_i}(S)$ and computes the probability $\text{prob}_{C_i}(\boldsymbol{n_i}(S))$ to observe such a noise vector using (1). The hypothesis O_i maximizing (1) is then the best candidate for the observed key dependency.

Use of Template Attacks against AES. In [3] an "expand and prune" strategy is described that is particularly useful when attacking stream ciphers. Applying this strategy, profiling and classification build a recurring cycle for sieving key candidates which means in particular that the vast effort of the profiling step cannot be precomputed. In contrast, if the attacked key is known to be sufficiently small or assailable in such blocks[3], profiling can be done independently before or after obtaining S from the device under attack. For example, to recover an 128-bit AES key one can precompute $2^8 \cdot 16$ instead of (infeasible) 2^{128} templates and - after obtaining S - immediately start the classification step which may take only a few seconds.

IMPROVEMENT 1 (concerning the selection of *interesting* instants): We discovered that the sum of pairwise differences of the average signals, i.e., $\sum_{j,l=1}^{K} m_j - m_l$

---

[1] In this contribution, N is the number of samples available for profiling. The number of samples per key dependency is about N/K in case of a uniform distribution.

[2] We denote that each sample and m_i is a vector of sampled points in time.

[3] This is true for many block ciphers.

for $l \geq j$ is not an appropriate basis for choosing the *interesting* points in time. This is due to the fact that positive and negative differences between the averages may zeroize, which is desirable to filter noise but hides as well valuable peaks that derive from significant signal differences with alternating algebraic sign. Therefore we implemented the sum of *squared* pairwise differences of the average signals $\sum_{j,l=1}^{K}(m_j - m_l)^2$ for $l \geq j$ (also referred to as *sosd* in this work) so that the hiding effect does not emerge anymore at the cost of a non-zero noise floor. Further, large differences get amplified.

IMPROVEMENT 2 (concerning the classification step): The original Template Attack only provides a sample classification strategy based on one available sample. While this may be a realistic scenario in the context of stream ciphers[4], the situation is probably less tight in the context of block ciphers. Moreover, in case of a low-leakage implementation, one sample may not be sufficient for a reliable classification. For these reasons, a classification strategy that processes one or several samples is applied.

2.2   Stochastic Model

The Stochastic Model [7] assumes that the physical observable $I_t(x, k)$ at time t is composed of two parts, a data-dependent part $h_t(x, k)$ as a function of known data x and subkey k and a noise term R_t with zero mean: $I_t(x, k) = h_t(x, k) + R_t$. $I_t(x, k)$ and R_t are seen as stochastic variables. For this paper, we use the maximum likelihood based approach of [7] and skip the minimum principle as it is already proven to be less efficient in [7]. Profiling processes $N = N_1 + N_2$ samples representing a known subkey k and known data $x_1, x_2, \ldots, x_N$ and consists of two parts. The first part yields an approximation of $h_t(\cdot, \cdot)$, denoted as $\widetilde{h}_t^*(\cdot, \cdot)$, i.e., the data-dependent part of the side channel leakage, in a suitable u-dimensional chosen vector subspace $\mathcal{F}_{u;t}$ for each instant t. The second part then computes a multivariate density of the noise at relevant instants. For the computation of $\widetilde{h}_t^*(\cdot, \cdot)$, an overdetermined system of linear equations has to be solved for each instant t. The $(N_1 \times u)$ design matrix is made up by the representation of the outcome of a selection function combining k and x_n ($1 \leq n \leq N_1$) in $\mathcal{F}_{u;t}$ and the corresponding N_1-dimensional vector includes the instantiations i_{t_n} of the observable. As preparation step for the computation of the multivariate density, p side channel relevant time instants have to be chosen based on $\widetilde{h}_t^*(\cdot, \cdot)$. The complementary subset of N_2 measurements is then used to compute the covariance matrix C. For this, p-dimensional noise vectors have to be extracted from all N_2 measurements at the p instants by subtracting the corresponding data-dependent part. Given the covariance matrix C, this leads to a Gaussian multivariate density $\widetilde{f}_0 \colon \mathbb{R}^p \to \mathbb{R}$.

Key extraction applies the maximum likelihood principle. Given N_3 measurements at key extraction, one decides for key hypothesis $k \in \{1, \ldots, K\}$ that maximizes

---

[4] Reference [9] presents an amplified attack against stream ciphers for the case of several available samples.

$$\alpha(x_1, \ldots, x_{N_3}; k) = \prod_{j=1}^{N_3} \widetilde{f_0}\left(\boldsymbol{i_t}(x_j, k^\circ) - \widetilde{\boldsymbol{h}}_t^*(x_j, k)\right). \tag{2}$$

Herein, k° is the unknown correct key value.

Use of Stochastic Methods Against AES. We chose the vector subspace $\mathcal{F}_9$, i.e., bitwise coefficients at the S-Box outcome as selection function as suggested by [7]. The base vectors $g_l(x \oplus k)$ $(0 \le l \le 8)$ are

$$g_l(x \oplus k) = \left\{ \begin{array}{ll} 1 & \text{if } l = 0 \\ l\text{-th bit of S-box}(x \oplus k) & \text{if } 1 \le l \le 8 \end{array} \right\}. \tag{3}$$

The choice of relevant time instants is based on sosd[5]. Other parameters are kept fixed, as e.g., we use $N_1 = \frac{N}{2}$ measurements for profiling the data-dependent part and $N_2 = \frac{N}{2}$ measurements for profiling the noise throughout this paper[6].

2.3   Compendium of Differences

Table 1 summarizes the fundamental differences in the approaches of both attacks. Following the notation in [7], Templates estimate the data-dependent part h_t itself, whereas the Stochastic model approximates the linear part of h_t in the chosen vector subspace (e.g., $\mathcal{F}_9$) and is not capable of including non-linear parts. Templates build a covariance matrix for each key dependency whereas the Stochastic Model generates only one covariance matrix, hereby neglecting possible multivariate key dependent noise terms. A further drawback may be that terms of the covariance matrix are distorted because of non-linear parts of h_t in $\mathcal{F}_9$.

Table 1. Fundamental differences between Templates and the Stochastic Model

Sample portion	Template Attack	Stochastic Model
signal	estimation of key dependent signal → 256 average signals	linear approximation of key dependent signal in $\mathcal{F}_9$ → 9 sub-signals
noise	key dependent, characterized → 256 cov matrices	non-key dependent , characterized → one cov matrix

3   Performance Evaluation

In this contribution, performance aspects for side channel cryptanalysis are elaborated for the Template Attack and the Stochastic Model. Our goal is to provide a systematic performance comparison with respect to resources[7] needed for a successful attack. An adversary is *successful* if the (unknown) key value is correctly identified at classification.

---

[5] The Euclidean norm proposed in [7] produces very similar results.

[6] One may argue that the choice of instants can be done using all N samples.

[7] We focus on the number of available samples (side channel quality) since computational complexity is of minor importance for the attacks under consideration.

3.1   Metrics, Parameters, and Factors to Study

Hence in determining performance of side channel based techniques we first have to answer four related questions: (i) which are the relevant parameters that have an impact on attack performance, (ii) which of these parameters can be controlled resp. their influence measured and hence should be in the scope of our experiments, (iii) on which values for the remaining parameters this case study should be based, and (iv) what metrics should we select in order to best capture performance aspects?

From the standpoint of resources needed for a successful attack, parameters that influence the success rate are manifold ranging from the measurement equipment and its environment, the knowledge about the attacked implementation, the configuration of the implementation during profiling, and the concrete methodical approach used for analysis to the number of measurements in the profiling and classification steps.

Among them, we evaluate (I) the methodical approach, (II) the number of curves for profiling, and (III) the number of curves in the classification step. The remaining parameters are chosen to be identical for both methods evaluated. Because of this, we are able to exclude any measurement or implementation dependent impact on our analysis results for each setup.

We evaluate two methodical approaches as these are the Template Attack and the Stochastic Model. Concrete parameter settings of both methods additionally include the number and composition of time instants chosen for the multivariate probability density. We implemented identical point selection algorithms operating on sosd (cp. Sections 2.1 and 2.2) selecting at most one point per clock cycle. The number of measurements, both during profiling and key extraction, is regarded as the relevant and measurable parameter. Let N be the number of measurements used in the profiling step and N_3 the number of measurements used at key extraction. For both, the Template Attack and the Stochastic Model, the concrete parameter values to study are given in Section 3.2.

Profiling efficiency is measured (1) as efficiency in estimating the data-dependent sample portion (refers only to N) and (2) as ability to determine the correct set of points of interests (refers to N and p). Both metrics relate to reference values obtained for maximal N (referred to as N_{max} below) used in the concrete setting.

Metric 1: The first efficiency metric for profiling evaluates the correlation coefficient ρ of the average vectors $m_i(N)$ obtained from N samples and the reference vectors $m_i(N_{max})$: $\frac{1}{K}\sum_{i=0}^{K}\rho(m_i(N), m_i(N_{max}))$. For the Stochastic Model, we approximate the $m_i(N)$ with $\widetilde{h}_t^*(\cdot,\cdot)$ and use the reference $m_i(N_{max})$ that we assume to be the best possible estimator of the data-dependent part h_t.

Metric 2: The second metric compares the set of selected points based on N samples to the reference set obtained using N_{max} samples and returns the percentage of points that are located in the correct clock cycle.

Metric 3: Classification efficiency (refers to N_3, N and p) is measured as success rate to obtain the correct key value. The success rate at key extraction is empirically determined by classifying N_3 randomly chosen measurements out of the key extraction measurement series. This random choice is repeated one thousand times and the success rate is then defined as the percentage of success in determining the correct key value.

In Section 5 optimizations for both methods are included in the performance analysis.

3.2   Experimental Design

The performance analysis is applied to two experimental units performing AES in software without any countermeasures. Our first experimental unit (device A) is an ATM163 microcontroller. A set of more than 230,000 power measurements was recorded for profiling purposes with a fixed AES key and randomly chosen plaintexts. For classification purposes, we recorded a second set comprising 3000 measurements with a different fixed AES key. The experimental design is full factorial. Our second experimental unit is another 8-bit microcontroller from a different manufacturer (device B). Furthermore, the power measurements of device B stem from a different, low-noise, measurement setup. We obtained a set of 50,000 power measurements for profiling purposes and a classification set of 100 power measurements, both with fixed but different AES keys. Table 2 shows all concrete parameter values we studied. However, Sections 4 and 5 only provide the most relevant results.

Table 2. Concrete parameter values to study

Device	Parameter	Parameter Values
A	N	231k, 50k, 40k, 30k, 25k, 20k, 10k, 5k, 2k[8], 1k[8], 200[8]
A	p	3, 6, 9, x[9]
A	N_3	1, 2, 5, 10
B	N	50k[10], 10k, 5k, 500[8], 100[8]
B	p	x[9]
B	N_3	1, 2, 5

4   Experimental Evaluation: Results for Original Attacks

4.1   Comparison of Profiling Efficiency

Profiling metrics 1 and 2 are summarized in Fig. 1 and Table 3. Metric 1 clearly yields enhanced results for Templates which is reasonable as the Stochastic Model uses only half of the measurements for the determination of the data-dependent part. Though less efficient in determining the data-dependent part,

---

[8] Stochastic Model only.

[9] x = maximum number identified after profiling.

[10] Template Attack only.

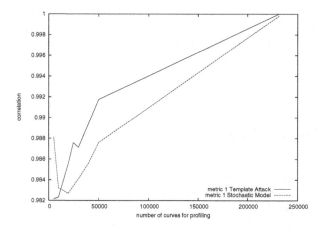

Fig. 1. Metric 1 for device A

Table 3. Metric 2 for device A as function of N

	231k	50k	40k	30k	25k	20k	10k	5k
Template Attack	1	0.89	0.89	0.78	0.67	0.56	0.23	0.23
Stochastic Model	1	1	1	1	1	1	0.67	0.78

Table 3 clearly indicates the superiority of the Stochastic Model in terms of selecting the right points in time.

4.2   Comparison of Classification Efficiency

We compare the success rates for variations of N, $N_3 \in \{1, 10\}$ and the optimal number of selected instants to maximize the success rates. Fig. 2 shows metric 3 plotted as function of these parameters. One can observe, that each pair of plots intersects at least once. Hence, a general statement on which attack yields better success rates is not feasible as this depends on the number of curves that are available in the profiling step. If a large number of samples is available (e.g., more than twenty thousand), the Template Attack yields higher success rates. If only a small number of samples is available (e.g., less than twenty thousand), stochastic methods are the better choice.

4.3   Weaknesses and Strengths

Template Attack The strength of the Template Attack is, that it extracts far more information from the samples than the Stochastic Model. Given sufficient samples in the profiling step, it is clearly superior to the Stochastic model in the classification step, due to the precise estimation of the average signal and the use of 256 covariance matrices. On the other hand, it requires much more

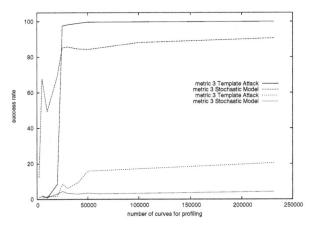

Fig. 2. Metric 3 for device A, $N_3 = 10$ for upper and $N_3 = 1$ for lower curves

samples than stochastic methods to reduce the noise in the side channel and to select correct instants (see Table 3).

Stochastic Model. The Stochastic Model's strength is the ability to "learn" quickly from a small number of samples. One weakness lies in the reduced precision due to the linear approximation in a vector subspace. A second weakness is the usage of only a single covariance matrix. If the approximation of the data-dependent part is not precise enough, errors in the approximation affect the remaining "noise".

5   Experimental Evaluation: Optimized Results

The maximum efficiency achievable at key extraction for each method is of high importance, so that we carried out optimizations for each method. Particularly, Section 4 reveals that the point selection algorithm is crucial for the key extraction efficiency. Both, for Templates and the Stochastic Model, we evaluate the statistical *t*-distribution as the basis of instant selection in this Section. For the Stochastic Model, the choice of the vector subspace (single intermediate result vs. two intermediate results) is studied additionally.

Template Attack with T-Test. The Template Attack's weakness is its poor ability to reduce the noise in the side channel samples if the adversary is bounded in the number of samples in the profiling step. For small N, the remaining noise distorts the sosd curve, which we used as the basis for the selection of interesting points so far.

The T-Test is a standard statistical tool to meet the challenge of distinguishing noisy signals. When computing the significant difference of two sets (i, j), it does not only consider the distance of their means m_i, m_j but as well their variability (σ_i^2, σ_j^2) in relation to the number of samples (n_i, n_j). We modified our implementation to compute the sum of squared pairwise t-differences (also referred to as *sost* in this work)

$$\sum_{i,j=1}^{K} \left(\frac{m_i - m_j}{\sqrt{\frac{\sigma_i^2}{n_i} + \frac{\sigma_j^2}{n_j}}} \right)^2 \text{ for } i \geq j$$

as basis for the point selection instead of sosd. Fig. 3 illustrates the striking difference between sosd and sost for $N = 50000$ and 10000 samples. The scale

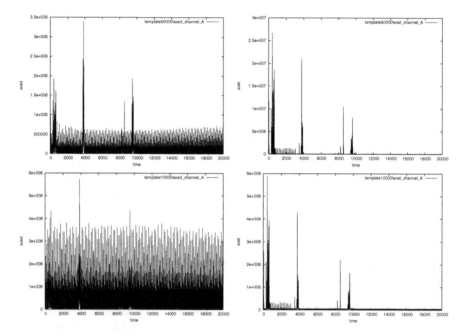

Fig. 3. sosd (left) and sost (right) as functions of time, $N = 50000$ (top) and 10000 (bottom)

of the vertical axis is not the same for all plots, but as one is not interested in comparing the absolute height of the peaks, this can be disregarded. What is important is the relative distance between the peaks and the noise floor in each curve. While the reduction of N by a factor 5 leads to a very distorted sosd signal, the significance of sost in terms of where to find interesting points does not change. Apart from the different scale, the peaks have a virtually identical shape.

High-Order Stochastic Model with F_{17} and T-Test. According to the improvements for Templates, we apply a slightly modified sost for the use with stochastic methods. Here, the data-dependent approximators $\widetilde{h}_t^*(\cdot, \cdot)$ and the empirical variance σ^2 derived from N_1 measurements are used in the computation. As for Templates, we observe a significant improvement of the point selection performance.

The weakness of the Stochastic Model with $\mathcal{F}_9$ is the limited precision due to the approximation of the data-dependent sample portion. An obvious solution to this problem is to increase the number of dimensions of the vector subspace in order to generate a more precise approximator at the cost of needing more samples in the profiling step (trade off problem). But as the authors of [7] already analyzed several high-dimensional vector subspaces and concluded that $\mathcal{F}_9$ seems to be most efficient, we decide to follow a different attempt.

Our approach arises from comparing the sosd curves of the Stochastic Model and the Template Attack. Due to the fact that the underlying samples represent only one fixed key, the Template Attack's sosd curve shows peaks for x, $x \oplus k$, and Sbox($x \oplus k$). Since the Stochastic Model only approximates the data-dependent sample portion at Sbox($x \oplus k$), it can not track bits "through" the Sbox and hence the point selection algorithm only finds instants for Sbox($x \oplus k$). Our approach aims at the fact that the Stochastic Model "overlooks" instants covering the Sbox lookup which yield the strongest peaks in the sosd curve of the Template Attack. We increase the number of dimensions of the vector subspace, but rather than increasing the level of detail at one intermediate result of the AES encryption, we add consideration of a second intermediate result. We (re-)define the selection functions g_l of the 17-dimensional vector subspace $\mathcal{F}_{17}$ as follows:

$$g_l(x \oplus k) = \begin{cases} 1 & \text{if } l = 0 \\ l\text{-th bit of S-box}(x \oplus k) & \text{if } 1 \leq l \leq 8 \\ (l-8)\text{-th bit of } x \oplus k & \text{if } 9 \leq l \leq 16 \end{cases}. \tag{4}$$

As desired, additional clear peaks during the Sbox lookup ($x \oplus k$) were found by the point selection algorithm.

5.1 Comparison Templates vs. T-Test Based Templates

When comparing the optimized Template Attack with the original attack, we evaluate the basis on which the point selection algorithm operates.

PROFILING EFFICIENCY
Table 4 shows the efficiency of both attacks in the profiling step using metric 2. The numbers clearly indicate the superiority of the improved version, the T-Test Template Attack, in terms of selecting the right instants and hence, in the profiling step. Considering Fig. 3 again, the improved profiling efficiency obviously derives from the enhanced ability to suppress noise in the side channel.
CLASSIFICATION EFFICIENCY
In the following, we compare the classification success rates of the attacks in Fig. 4. We restrict our attention to variations of N, $N_3 \in \{1, 10\}$ for the sake of clarity, and, each time, the optimal number of selected instants to maximize the

Table 4. Metric 2 for device A as function of N

	231k	50k	40k	30k	20k	10k	5k
Template Attack	1	0.89	0.89	0.78	0.56	0.23	0.23
T-Test Templates	1	1	1	1	1	1	1

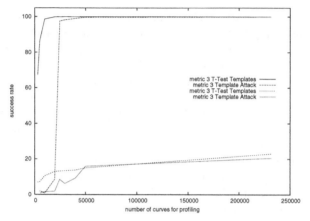

Fig. 4. Metric 3 for device A, $N_3 = 10$ for upper and $N_3 = 1$ for lower curves

success rates. For small N, e.g., N smaller than thirty thousand, the improved profiling of the optimized attack clearly leads to a higher success rate at classification.

5.2 Comparison First-Order Stochastic Model vs. T-Test Based High-Order Stochastic Model

When comparing the optimized Stochastic Model with the original attack, we evaluate the choice of the vector sub-space and the T-Test based point selection.

PROFILING EFFICIENCY
Table 5 shows the profiling efficiency of both attacks in metric 2. The numbers indicate the improved attack's advanced ability to select the right points, in particular when processing only a small number of profiling measurements.

Table 5. Metric 2 for device A as function of N

	231k	50k	40k	30k	25k	20k	10k	5k	2k	1k	200
Stochastic Model	1	1	1	1	1	1	0.67	0.78	0.67	-	-
T-Test based Stochastic Model	1	1	1	1	1	1	1	0.9	1	1	0.5

CLASSIFICATION EFFICIENCY
In the following, we compare the classification success rates of both attacks. We restrict our attention to variations of N, $N_3 \in \{1, 10\}$, and, each time, the

optimal number of selected instants to maximize the success rates. Fig. 5 shows metric 3 plotted as function of these parameters.

The benefit of generating eight additional base vectors with respect to the Sbox input and using sost instead of sosd is clearly visible. Following the profiling efficiency (cp. Table 5), the efficiency in the classification step is significantly increased. Particularly, for N larger than thirty thousand and $N_3 = 10$, the T-Test based high-order Stochastic Model clearly exceeds the 90% success rate "boundary" and finally reaches 100% success.

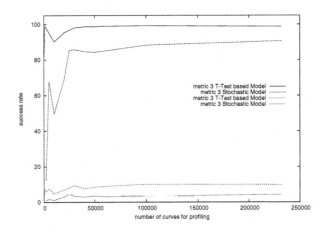

Fig. 5. Metric 3 for device A, $N_3 = 10$ for upper and $N_3 = 1$ for lower curves

5.3   Overall Comparison

In this Section we illustrate the efficiency of the improved methods in the classification step and give a short summary of the observations. We provide them to give an overall survey of our work. Fig. 6 contrasts the classification efficiency of the attacks using metric 3.

The T-Test Template Attack is the best possible choice in almost all parameter ranges. For small N (e.g., N less than five thousand), the T-Test based high-order Stochastic Model leads to better results. We would like to point out that the improved version of the Stochastic Model still operates successfully using extremely small N. For example, using $N = 200$ profiling measurements and $N_3 = 10$ curves for classification it still achieves a success rate of 81.7%.

To stress the impact of the factor "measurement quality" we present success rates of the improved attacks for measurements of device B that stem from the low-noise setup. Table 6 provides the attack efficiencies in metric 3 for variations of N, $N_3 \in \{1, 5\}$, and, each time, the optimal number of selected instants to maximize the success rates.

Besides the fact that the relation of N to success rate of both attacks is better by orders of magnitude when using low-noise measurements, we would like to point out, that the improved Stochastic Model still classifies keys successfully,

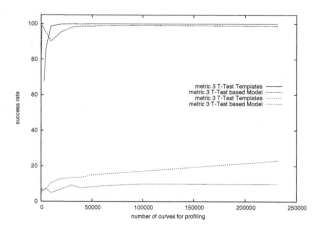

Fig. 6. Metric 3 for device A, $N_3 = 10$ for upper and $N_3 = 1$ for lower curves

Table 6. Metric 3 for device B as function of N

		50k	10k	5k	500	100
T-Test Templates	$N_3 = 1$	94.8	93.0	88.2	-	-
	$N_3 = 5$	100.0	100.0	100.0	-	-
T-Test based Stochastic Model	$N_3 = 1$	-	57.5	60.1	46.8	27.1
	$N_3 = 5$	-	100.0	99.9	100.0	96.5

even if the profiling has been done with as little as $N = 100$ curves, which is far less than the number of subkey hypotheses.

6   Conclusion

In this contribution, an experimental performance analysis is applied to the Template Attack and the Stochastic Model. We concentrate on measurable parameter settings such as the number of curves during profiling and classification. By using the originally proposed attacks, it was revealed that towards a low number of profiling measurements stochastic methods are more efficient whereas towards a high number of profiling samples Templates achieve superior performance results. For improvements, we introduce T-Test based Templates and give experimental results for the use of high-order stochastic methods in combination with a T-Test based choice of instants. It is shown that the improved variants are indeed practical, even at a low number of profiling measurements[11]. As a main result, T-Test based Templates are generally the method of choice. However, in

---

[11] This is of particular importance when applying these attacks to noisy EM samples. We experimentally proved that the T-Test based attacks yield far better results than the original attacks in such a setting.

case of a low number of samples for profiling, stochastic methods can still turn out to be more efficient.

References

1. D. Agrawal, J.R. Rao, P. Rohatgi: Multi-Channel Attacks. In: C.D. Walter, Ç.K. Koç, C. Paar (eds.): Cryptographic Hardware and Embedded Systems — CHES 2003, Springer, LNCS 2779, 2003, 2–16.
2. E. Brier, C. Clavier, F. Olivier: Correlation Power Analysis with a Leakage Model. In: M. Joye and J.-J. Quisquater (eds.): Cryptographic Hardware and Embedded Systems — CHES 2004, Springer, LNCS 3156, 2004, 16-29.
3. S. Chari, J.R. Rao, P. Rohatgi: Template Attacks. In: B.S. Kaliski Jr., Ç.K. Koç, C. Paar (eds.): Cryptographic Hardware and Embedded Systems — CHES 2002, Springer, LNCS 2523, 2003, 13–28.
4. P.N. Fahn, P.K. Pearson: IPA: A New Class of Power Attacks. In: Ç.K. Koç and C. Paar: Cryptographic Hardware and Embedded Systems — CHES 1999, Springer, LNCS 1717, 1999, 173–186.
5. K. Gandolfi, C. Mourtel, F. Olivier: Electromagnetic Analysis: Concrete Results. In: Ç Koç, D. Naccache, C. Paar (eds.): Cryptographic Hardware and Embedded Systems — CHES 2001, Springer, LNCS 2162, 2001, 251–261.
6. P.C. Kocher, J. Jaffe, B. Jun: Differential Power Analysis. In: M. Wiener (ed.): Advances in Cryptology — CRYPTO '99, Springer, LNCS 1666, 1999, 388–397.
7. W. Schindler, K. Lemke, C. Paar: A Stochastic Model for Differential Side Channel Cryptanalysis. In: J.R. Rao, B. Sunar (eds.): Cryptographic Hardware and Embedded Systems — CHES 2005, Springer, LNCS 3659, 2005, 30–46.
8. W.H. Press, S.A. Teukolsky, W.T. Vetterling, B.P. Flannery: Numerical Recipes in C — The Art of Scientific Computing. Second Edition, Cambridge University Press, 1992.
9. C. Rechberger, Side Channel Analysis of Stream Ciphers, Master Thesis, Technical University Graz, 2004
10. Trochim, William M., The Research Methods Knowledge Base, 2nd Edition, http://trochim.human.cornell.edu/kb/index.htm, January 16 2005

Towards Security Limits in Side-Channel Attacks
(With an Application to Block Ciphers)

F.-X. Standaert[*], E. Peeters, C. Archambeau, and J.-J. Quisquater

UCL Crypto Group, Place du Levant 3, B-1348 Louvain-la-Neuve, Belgium
{fstandae, peeters, archambeau, quisquater}@dice.ucl.ac.be

Abstract. In this paper, we consider a recently introduced framework that investigates physically observable implementations from a theoretical point of view. The model allows quantifying the effect of practically relevant leakage functions with a combination of security and information theoretic metrics. More specifically, we apply our evaluation methodology to an exemplary block cipher. We first consider a Hamming weight leakage function and evaluate the efficiency of two commonly investigated countermeasures, namely noise addition and masking. Then, we show that the proposed methodology allows capturing certain non-trivial intuitions, *e.g.* about the respective effectiveness of these countermeasures. Finally, we justify the need of combined metrics for the evaluation, comparison and understanding of side-channel attacks.

1 Introduction

In [14], a formal practice-oriented model for the analysis of cryptographic primitives against side-channel attacks was introduced as a specialization of Micali and Reyzin's "physically observable cryptography" paradigm [8]. The model is based on an theoretical framework in which the effect of practically relevant leakage functions is evaluated with a combination of security and information theoretic measurements. A central objective of the model was to provide a fair evaluation methodology for side-channel attacks. This objective is motivated by the fact that side-channel attacks may take advantage of different statistical tools (*e.g.* difference of means [5], correlation [2], Bayesian classification [1], stochastic models [13]) and are therefore not straightforward to compare. Additionally to the comparisons of side-channel attacks, a more theoretical goal was the understanding of the underlying mechanisms of physically observable cryptography.

Specifically, [14] suggests to combine the average success rate of a (well specified) adversary with some information theoretic metrics in order to capture the intuition summarized in Figure 1. Namely, an information theoretic metric should measure the average amount of information that is available in some physical observations while a security metric measures how efficiently an actual adversary can turn this information into a successful key recovery.

---

[*] François-Xavier Standaert is a post doctoral researcher funded by the FNRS (Funds for National Scientific Research, Belgium).

L. Goubin and M. Matsui (Eds.): CHES 2006, LNCS 4249, pp. 30–45, 2006.

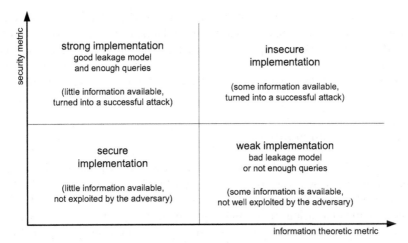

Fig. 1. Summary of side-channel evaluation criteria

In this paper, we consequently study the relevance of the suggested methodology, by the analysis of a practical case. For this purpose, we investigate an exemplary block cipher and consider a Hamming weight leakage function in different attack scenarios. First, we consider an unprotected implementation and evaluate the information leakages resulting from various number of Hamming weight queries. We discuss how actual block cipher components compare to random oracles with respect to side-channel leakages. Then, we evaluate the security of two commonly admitted countermeasures against side-channel attacks, *i.e.* noise addition and masking. Through these experiments, we show that the proposed evaluation criteria allows capturing certain non-trivial intuitions about the respective effectiveness of these countermeasures. Finally, we provide some experimental validations of our analysis and discuss the advantages of our combination of metrics with respect to other evaluation techniques.

Importantly, in our theoretical framework, side-channel analysis can be viewed as a classification problem. Our results consequently tend to estimate the security limits of side-channel adversaries with two respects. First, because of our information theoretic approach, we aim to evaluate precisely the average amount of information that is available in some physical observations. Second, because we consider (one of) the most efficient classification test(s), namely Bayesian classification, it is expected that the computed success rates also correspond to the best possible adversarial strategy. However, we mention that the best evaluation and comparison metrics to use in the context of side-channel attacks are still under discussion. Our results intend to show that both are useful, but other similar metrics should still be investigated and compared.

2   Model Specifications

In general, the model of computation we consider in this paper is the one initially presented in [8] with the specializations introduced in [14]. In this section, we first describe our target block cipher implementation. Then, we specify the leakage function, the adversarial context and adversarial strategy that we consider in this work. Finally, we provide the definitions of our security and information theoretic metrics for the evaluation of the attacks in the next sections. Both the adversarial classifications and the metrics were introduced and detailed in [14].

2.1   Target Implementation

Our target block cipher implementation is represented in Figure 2. For convenience, we only represent the combination of a bitwise key addition and a layer of substitution boxes. We make a distinction between a *single block* and a *multiple block* implementation. This difference refers to the way the key guess is performed by the adversary. In a single block implementation (*e.g.* typically, an 8-bit processor), the adversary is able to guess (and therefore exploit) all the bits in the implementation. In a multiple block implementation (*e.g.* typically, a hardware implementation with data processed in parallel), the adversary is only able to guess the bits at the output of one block of the target design. That is, the other blocks are producing what is frequently referred to as algorithmic noise.

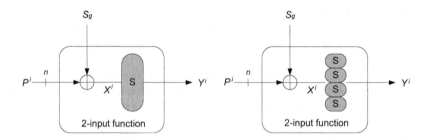

Fig. 2. Single block and multiple block cipher implementation

2.2   Leakage Function

Our results consider the example of a Hamming weight leakage function. Specifically, we assume a side-channel adversary that is provided with the (possibly noisy) Hamming weight leakages of the S-boxes outputs in Figure 2, *i.e.* $W_H(Y^i)$. With respect to the classification introduced in [14], perfect Hamming weights correspond to non-profiled leakage functions while noisy Hamming weights relate to the context of device profiled (stochastic) leakage functions. In the latter one, the leakage function includes a characterization of the noise in the target device. For this purpose, we assume a Gaussian noise distribution. We note also that our exemplary leakage functions are univariate since they only consider one leaking point in the implementations, namely the S-boxes outputs.

2.3   Adversarial Context

We consider a non-adaptive known plaintext adversary that can perform an arbitrary number of side-channel queries to the target implementation of Figure 2 but cannot choose its queries in function of the previously observed leakages.

2.4   Adversarial Strategy

We consider a side-channel key recovery adversary with the following (hard) strategy: *"given some physical observations and a resulting classification of key candidates, select the best classified key only"*.

2.5   Security Metric: Average Success Rate of the Adversary

The success rate of a side-channel key recovery attack can be written as follows. Let S and O be two random variables in the discrete domains $\mathcal{S}$ and $\mathcal{O}$, respectively denoting the target secret signals and the side-channel observations. Let $O_{S_g}^i$ be an observation generated by a secret signal S_g. Let finally $\mathbf{C}(\mathcal{L}(S), O_{S_g}^i)$ be the statistical tool used by the adversary to compare an actual observation of a device with its prediction according to a leakage function $\mathcal{L}^1$. This statistical tool could be a difference of mean test, a correlation test, a Bayesian classification, or any other tool, possibly inspired from classical cryptanalysis. For each observation $O_{S_g}^i$, we define the set of keys selected by the adversary as:

$$M_{S_g}^i = \{\hat{s} \mid \hat{s} = \underset{S}{argmax}\ \mathbf{C}[\mathcal{L}(S)|O_{S_g}^i]\}$$

Then, we define the result of the attack with the index matrix:

$$\mathrm{I}_{S_g,S}^i = \quad \frac{1}{|M_{S_g}^i|} \ \mathbf{if}\ S \in M_{S_g}^i, \qquad \mathbf{else}\ 0.$$

The success rate of the adversary for a secret signal S_g is estimated as:

$$\mathbf{S_R}(S_g) = \underset{O_{S_g}^i}{\mathbf{E}}\ \mathrm{I}_{S_g,S_g}, \tag{1}$$

and the average success rate of the adversary is defined as:

$$\overline{\mathbf{S_R}} = \underset{S_g}{\mathbf{E}}\ \underset{O_{S_g}^i}{\mathbf{E}}\ \mathrm{I}_{S_g,S_g} \tag{2}$$

In the following, we will *only* consider a Bayesian classifier, *i.e.* an adversary that selects the keys such that $\mathbf{P}[S|O_{S_g}^i]$ is maximum, since it corresponds to (one of) the most efficient way(s) to perform a side-channel key recovery.

Finally, it is interesting to remark that one can use the complete index matrix to build a confusion matrix $\mathrm{C}_{S_g,S} = \mathbf{E}_{O_{S_g}^i}\ \mathrm{I}_{S_g,S}$. The previously defined average success rate simply corresponds to the averaged diagonal of this matrix.

---

[1] In our following examples, $\mathcal{L}$ is the Hamming weight function.

2.6   Information Theoretic Metric: Conditional Entropy

In addition to the average success rate, [14] suggests the use of an information theoretic metric to evaluate the information contained in side-channel observations. We note (again) that different proposals could be used for such evaluation purposes and their comparison is a scope for further research. In the present paper, we selected the classical notion of Shannon conditional entropy and investigate how one can take advantage of the approach to understand and evaluate side-channel attacks. Let $\mathbf{P}[S|O_{S_g}^i]$ be the probability vector of the different key candidates S given an observation $O_{S_g}^i$ generated by a correct key S_g. Similarly to the confusion matrix of the previous section, we define a probability matrix: $P_{S_g,S} = \mathbf{E}_{O_{S_g}^i}\mathbf{P}[S|O_{S_g}^i]$ and an entropy matrix $H_{S_g,S} = \mathbf{E}_{O_{S_g}^i} - \log_2 \mathbf{P}[S|O_{S_g}^i]$. Then, we define the average probability of the correct key as:

$$\overline{\mathbf{P}[S_g|O_{S_g}]} = \mathop{\mathbf{E}}_{S_g} P_{S_g,S_g} \tag{3}$$

And the conditional entropy:

$$\mathbf{H}[S_g|O_{S_g}] = \mathop{\mathbf{E}}_{S_g} H_{S_g,S_g} \tag{4}$$

We note that this definition is equivalent to Shannon conditional entropy[2]. We simply used the previous notation because it is convenient to compute the probability (or entropy) matrices. For example, it allows to detect a good leakage function, i.e. a leakage function such that $\max_S H_{S_g,S} = H_{S_g,S_g}$. In the following, the leakages will be quantified as conditional entropy reductions that corresponds to the mutual information $\mathbf{I}[S_g; O_{S_g}] = \mathbf{H}[S_g] - \mathbf{H}[S_g|O_{S_g}]$.

It is important to observe that the average success rate fundamentally describes an adversary. In general, it has to be computed for different number of queries in order to evaluate how much observations are required to perform a successful attack. By contrast, the information theoretic measurement says nothing about the actual security of an implementation but characterizes the leakage function, independently of the number of queries.

3   Investigation of Single Leakages

In this section, we analyze a situation where an adversary is provided with the observation of one single Hamming weight leakage. First, we evaluate single block implementations. Then, we discuss multiple block implementations and key guesses. Finally, we evaluate the effect of noise addition in this context.

---

[2] Since: $\mathbf{H}[S_g|O] = \mathbf{E}_{O^i} \mathbf{E}_{S_g} \mathbf{H}[S_g|O^i]$
$$= \textstyle\sum_{O^i} \mathbf{P}[O^i] \sum_{S_g} \mathbf{P}[S_g|O^i] \cdot -\log_2(\mathbf{P}[S_g|O^i])$$
$$= \textstyle\sum_{O^i} \mathbf{P}[O^i] \sum_{S_g} \frac{\mathbf{P}[O^i|S_g] \cdot \mathbf{P}[S_g]}{\mathbf{P}[O^i]} \cdot -\log_2(\mathbf{P}[S_g|O^i])$$
$$= \textstyle\sum_{O^i} \sum_{S_g} \mathbf{P}[O^i|S_g] \cdot \mathbf{P}[S_g] \cdot -\log_2(\mathbf{P}[S_g|O^i])$$
$$= \textstyle\sum_{S_g} \sum_{O^i} \mathbf{P}[O^i|S_g] \cdot \mathbf{P}[S_g] \cdot -\log_2(\mathbf{P}[S_g|O^i])$$
$$= \textstyle\sum_{S_g} \mathbf{P}[S_g] \sum_{O^i} \mathbf{P}[O^i|S_g] \cdot -\log_2(\mathbf{P}[S_g|O^i]) = \mathbf{E}_{S_g} H_{S_g,S_g}$$

3.1 Single Block Implementations

Let us assume the following situation: we have an n-bit secret key S_g and an adversary is provided with the leakage corresponding to a computation $Y^i = f(S_g, P^i) = \mathrm{S}(P^i \oplus S_g)$. That is, it obtains an observation $O^i_{S_g} = W_H(Y^i)$ and we assume a single block implementation as the one in the left part of Figure 2. Therefore, the adversary can potentially observe the $n + 1$ Hamming weights of Y^i. Since the Hamming weights of a random value are distributed as binomials, one can easily evaluate the average success rate of the adversary as:

$$\overline{\mathrm{S_R}} = \mathop{\mathbf{E}}_{S_g} \mathop{\mathbf{E}}_{O^i_{S_g}} \mathrm{I}_{S_g, S_g} = \sum_{h=0}^{n} \frac{\binom{n}{h}}{2^n} \cdot \frac{1}{\binom{n}{h}} = \frac{n+1}{2^n} \tag{5}$$

This equation means that on average, obtaining the Hamming weight of a secret n-bit value increases the success rate of a key-recovery adversary from $\frac{1}{2^n}$ to $\frac{n+1}{2^n}$. Similar evaluations will be performed for the conditional entropy in Section 3.3.

3.2 Multiple Blocks and Key Guesses

Let us now assume a situation similar to the previous one, but the adversary tries to target a multiple block implementation. Therefore, it is provided with the Hamming weight of an n-bit secret value of which it can only guess b bits, typically corresponding to one block of the implementation. Such a key guess situation can be analyzed by considering the un-exploited bits as a source of algorithmic noise approximated with a Gaussian distribution. This will be done in the next section. The quality of this estimation will then be demonstrated in Section 5, by relaxing the Gaussian estimation.

3.3 Noise Addition

Noise is a central issue in side-channel attacks and more generally in any signal processing application. In our specific context, various types of noise are usually considered, including physical noise (*i.e.* produced by the environment), measurement noise (*i.e.* caused by the sampling process and tools), model matching noise (*i.e.* meaning that the leakage function used to attack does possibly not perfectly fit to real observations) or algorithmic noise (*i.e.* produced by the untargeted values in an implementation). All these disturbances similarly affect the efficiency of a side-channel attack and their consequence is that the information delivered by a single leakage point is reduced. For this reason, a usually accepted method to evaluate the effect of noise is to assume that *there is an additive effect between all the noise sources and their overall effect can be quantified by a Gaussian distribution*. We note that this assumption may not be perfectly verified in practice and that better noise models may allow to improve the efficiency of side-channel attacks. However, this assumption is reasonable in a number of contexts and particularly convenient for a first investigation.

In our experiments, we will consequently assume that the leakage function is affected by some Gaussian noise such that the physical observations are represented by a variable: $O^i_{S_g} = W_H(Y^i) + N(0, \sigma^2)$. It is then possible to estimate the average success rate of the adversary and the conditional entropy as follows:

$$\overline{\mathbf{S_R}} = \underset{S_g}{\mathbf{E}} \, \underset{O^i_{S_g}}{\mathbf{E}} \, \mathbf{I}_{S_g, S_g} = \sum_{h=0}^{n} \frac{\binom{n}{h}}{2^n} \cdot \int_{-\infty}^{+\infty} \mathbf{P}[O_{S_g}|h] \cdot \mathbf{I}_{S_g, S_g} \, do, \qquad (6)$$

$$\mathbf{H}[S_g|O_{S_g}] = \underset{S_g}{\mathbf{E}} \, \mathbf{H}_{S_g, S_g} = \sum_{h=0}^{n} \frac{\binom{n}{h}}{2^n} \cdot \int_{-\infty}^{+\infty} \mathbf{P}[O_{S_g}|h] \cdot -\log_2(\mathbf{P}[S_g|O_{S_g}]) \, do, \quad (7)$$

where $\mathbf{P}[O_{S_g} = o|W_H(Y^i) = h] = \frac{1}{\sigma\sqrt{2\pi}} \exp^{\frac{-(o-h)^2}{2\sigma^2}}$ and the a posteriori probability $\mathbf{P}[S_g|O_{S_g}]$ can be computed thanks to Bayes's formula: $\mathbf{P}[S_g|O_{S_g}] = \frac{\mathbf{P}[O_{S_g}|S_g] \cdot \mathbf{P}[S_g]}{\mathbf{P}[O_{S_g}]}$, with $\mathbf{P}[O_{s_g}] = \sum_S \mathbf{P}[O_{S_g}|S] \cdot \mathbf{P}[S]$. As an illustration, the average success rate and the mutual information are represented in Figure 3 for an 8-bit value, in function of the observation signal-to-noise ratio (SNR$=10 \cdot \log_{10}(\frac{\varepsilon^2}{\sigma^2})$), where ε and σ respectively denote the standard deviation of the signal and the noise emanated from the implementation).

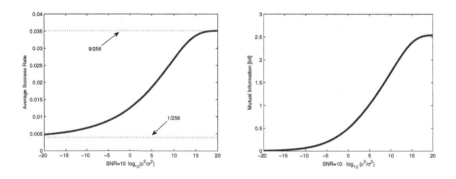

Fig. 3. Average success rate and mutual information in function of the SNR

Note that the average success rate starts at 9/256, $i.e.$ the noise-free value computed with Equation (5) and tends to 1/256 which basically means that very little information can be retrieved from the leakage. The figures also shows the correlation between the information available and the resulting success rate.

4   Investigation of Multiple Leakages

In the previous section, we analyzed a situation in which an adversary performs one single query to a leaking implementation and evaluated the resulting average success rate and mutual information. However, looking at Figure 3, it is clear that such a context involves limited success rates, even in case of high SNRs. As a matter of fact, actual adversaries would not only perform one single query to the target device but multiple ones, in order to increase their success rates. This section consequently studies the problem of multiple leakages.

For this purpose, let us consider the following situation: we have an n-bit secret key S_g and an adversary is provided with the leakages corresponding to two computations $Y^1 = f(S_g, P^1)$ and $Y^2 = f(S_g, P^2)$. That is, it obtains $W_H(Y^1)$ and $W_H(Y^2)$ and we would like to evaluate the average predictability of S_g. The consequence of such an experiment (illustrated in Figure 4) is that the key

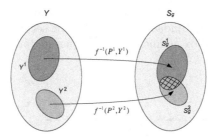

Fig. 4. Multiple point leakages

will be contained in the intersection of two sets of candidates obtained by inverting the 2-input functions $Y^1 = f(S_g, P_1)$ and $Y^2 = f(S_g, P_2)$. The aim of our analysis is therefore to determine how the keys within this intersection are distributed. Importantly, and contrary to the single query context, this analysis requires to characterize the cryptographic functions used in the target implementation, since they will determine how the intersection between the sets of candidates behaves. Therefore, we will consider two possible models for these functions.

4.1 Assuming Random S-Boxes

A first (approximated) solution is to consider the functions $f^{-1}(P^i, Y^i)$ to behave randomly. As a consequence, each observed Hamming weight leakage $h_i = W_H(Y^i)$ will give rise to a uniform list of candidates for the key S_g of size $n_i = \binom{n}{h_i}$, without any particular dependencies between these sets but the key. Let us denote the size of the set containing S_g after the observation of q leakages respectively giving rise to these uniform lists of n_i candidates by a random variable $I_q(n_1, n_2, \ldots, n_q)$. From the probability density function of I_q (given in appendix A), it is straightforward to extend the single leakage analysis of Section 3.1 to multiple leakages. The average success rate can be expressed as:

$$\overline{\mathbf{S_R}} = \sum_{h_1=0}^{n} \sum_{h_2=0}^{n} \cdots \sum_{h_q=0}^{n} \frac{\binom{n}{h_1}}{2^n} \cdot \frac{\binom{n}{h_2}}{2^n} \cdots \frac{\binom{n}{h_q}}{2^n} \cdot \sum_i \mathbf{P}[I_q = i] \cdot \frac{1}{i} \qquad (8)$$

4.2   Using Real Block Cipher Components

In order to validate the previous theoretical predictions of the average success rate, we performed the experiments illustrated in Figure 5. In the first (upper) experiment, we generated a number of plaintexts, observed the outputs of the function $f = \mathrm{S}(P^i \oplus S_g)$ through its Hamming weights $W_H(Y^i)$, derived lists of n_i candidates for Y^i corresponding to these Hamming weights and went through the inverted function $f^{-1}(P^i, Y^i)$ to obtain lists of key candidates. In the second (lower) experiment, a similar procedure is applied but the n_i key candidates were selected from random lists (including the correct key). As a matter of fact, the first experiment corresponds to a side-channel attack against a real block cipher (we used the AES Rijndael S-box) while the second experiment emulates the previous random S-box estimation. We generated a large number (namely

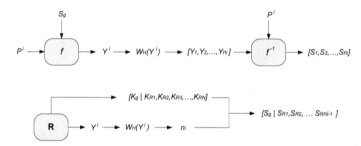

Fig. 5. Multiple leakages experiments: real S-boxes and random S-boxes simulation

100 000) of observations and, for these generated observations, derived the experimental average success rate in the two previous contexts. Additionally, we compared these experiments with the theoretical predictions of the previous section. The results of our analysis are pictured in Figure 6, where we can observe that the real S-box gives rise to lower success rates (*i.e.* to less information) than a random function. The reason of this phenomenon is that actual S-boxes

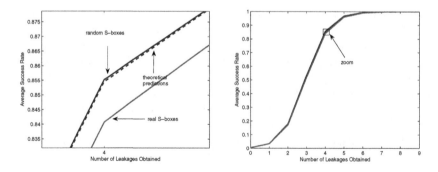

Fig. 6. Multiple leakages experimental results

give rise to correlated lists of key candidates and therefore to less independence between consecutive observations, as already suggested in [2, 11]. These experiments suggest that even if not perfectly correct, the assumption that block cipher components are reasonably approximated by random functions with respect to side-channel attacks is acceptable. We note that this assumption is better verified for large bit sizes since large S-boxes better approximate the behavior of a random function than small ones.

5   Investigation of Masked Implementations

The previous sections illustrated the evaluation of simple side-channel attacks based on a Hamming weight leakage function thanks to the average success rate and mutual information. However, due to the simplicity of the investigated contexts, these notions appeared to be closely correlated. Therefore it was not clear how one could need both criteria for our evaluation purposes. In this section, we consequently study a more complex case, namely masked implementations and higher-order side-channel attacks. This example is of particular interest since it allows us to emphasize the importance of a combination of security and information theoretic metrics for the physical security evaluation process of an implementation. As a result of our analysis, we provide (non-trivial) observations about the respective effectiveness of masking and algorithmic noise addition that can be easily turned into design criteria for actual countermeasures.

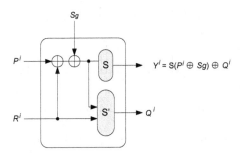

Fig. 7. 1st order boolean masking

The masking technique (*e.g.* [4]) is one of the most popular ways to prevent block cipher implementations from Differential Power Analysis. However, recent results suggested that it is not as secure as initially thought. Originally proposed by Messerges [7], second and higher-order power analysis attacks can be successfully implemented against various kinds of designs and may not require more hypotheses than a standard DPA [9]. In [12], an analysis of higher-order masking schemes is performed with respect to the correlation coefficient. In the following, we intend to extend this analysis to the (more powerful but less flexible) case of a Bayesian adversary, as introduced in [10].

For the purposes of our analysis, we will use the masked implementation illustrated in Figure 7 in which the plaintext P^i is initially XORed with a random mask R^i. We use two S-boxes S and S' such that: $S(P^i \oplus R^i \oplus S_g) = S(P^i \oplus S_g) \oplus Q^i$, with $Q^i = S'(P^i \oplus R^i \oplus S_g, R^i)$. According to the notations introduced in [10], it is particularly convenient to introduce the secret state of the implementation as $\Sigma_g = S(P^i \oplus S_g)$ and assume an adversary that obtains (possibly noisy) observations: $O^i_{\Sigma_g} = W_H[\Sigma_g \oplus Q^i] + W_H[Q^i] + N(0, \sigma^2)$. Similarly to a first-order side-channel attack, the objective of an adversary is then to determine the secret state Σ_g (it directly yields the secret key S_g). Because of the masking, Σ_g is not directly observable through side-channel measurements but its associated PDFs do, since these PDFs only depend on the Hamming weight of the secret state $W_H(\Sigma_g)$. As an illustration, we provide the different discrete PDFs (over the random mask values) for a 4-bit masked design in Figure 8, in function of the secret state Σ_g. We also depict the shapes of the discrete PDFs corresponding to an unmasked secret state affected by four bits of algorithmic noise (*i.e.* we add 4 random bits to the 4-bit target and the PDF is computed over these random bits). Similar distributions can be obtained for any bit size. In general, knowing the probability distributions of the secret state, the average success rate and conditional entropy can be straightforwardly derived:

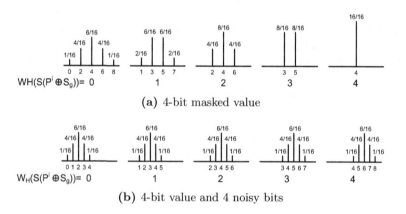

(a) 4-bit masked value

(b) 4-bit value and 4 noisy bits

Fig. 8. Exemplary discrete leakage PDFs

$$\overline{S_R} = \mathop{E}_{\Sigma_g} \mathop{E}_{O^i_{\Sigma_g}} I_{\Sigma_g, \Sigma_g} = \sum_{h=0}^{n} \frac{\binom{n}{h}}{2^n} \cdot \int_{-\infty}^{+\infty} \mathbf{P}[O_{\Sigma_g}|h] \cdot I_{\Sigma_g, \Sigma_g} \, do, \qquad (9)$$

$$\mathbf{H}[S_g|O_{S_g}] = \mathop{E}_{\Sigma_g} H_{\Sigma_g, \Sigma_g} = \sum_{h=0}^{n} \frac{\binom{n}{h}}{2^n} \cdot \int_{-\infty}^{+\infty} \mathbf{P}[O_{\Sigma_g}|h] \cdot - \log_2(\mathbf{P}[\Sigma_g|O_{\Sigma_g}]) \, do, \qquad (10)$$

where $\mathbf{P}[O_{\Sigma_g} = o|W_H(\Sigma_g) = h]$ can be computed as in Section 3.3, assuming that the O_{Σ_g} are distributed as a mixture of Gaussians. In the following, we illustrate these metrics in different contexts. First, we consider 2nd and 3rd order masking schemes for 8-bit S-boxes. Then, we consider unmasked implementations where 8 (*resp.* 16) random bits of algorithmic noise are added to the secret signal S_g, corresponding to the 2nd (*resp.* 3rd) order mask bits.

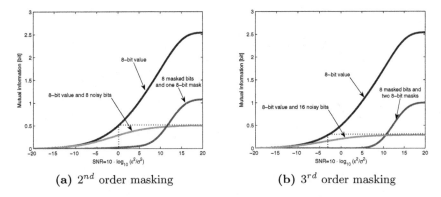

(a) 2nd order masking   **(b)** 3rd order masking

Fig. 9. Mutual information of 2nd, 3rd order masking and equivalent algorithmic noise

The first (and somewhat surprising) conclusion of our experiments appears in Figure 9. Namely, looking at the mutual information for high SNRs, the use of a n-bit mask is less resistant (*i.e.* leads to lower leakages) than the addition of n random bits to the implementation. Fortunately, beyond a certain amount of noise the masking appears to be a more efficient protection. The reason of this behavior appears clearly when observing the evolution of the PDFs associated to each secret state in function of the SNR, pictured in Appendix B, Figures 13 and 14. Clearly, the PDFs of the masked implementation are very different with small noise values (*e.g.* in Figure 13.a, the probability that an observation belong to both PDFs is very small) but becomes almost identical when the noise increases, since they are all identically centered (*e.g.* in Figure 13.b). Conversely, the means of each PDF in the unmasked implementations stay different whatever the noise level (*e.g.* in Figure 14.b). Therefore the Bayesian classification is easier than in the masked case when noise increases. These observations confirm the usually accepted fact that efficient protections against side-channel attacks require to combine different countermeasures. A practically important consequence of our results is the possibility to derive the exact design criteria (*e.g.* the required amount of noise) to obtain an efficient masking.

It is also interesting to observe that Figure 9 confirms that algorithmic noise is nicely modeled by Gaussians. Indeed, *e.g.* for the 2nd order case, the mutual information of an 8-bit value with 8 noisy bits for high SNRs exactly corresponds to the one of an unprotected 8-bit value with SRN=0.

The second interesting conclusion is that the average success rate after one query (pictured in Figure 10) does *not* follow an identical trend. Namely, the masked implementations and their equivalent noisy counterparts do *not* cross over at the same SRN. This situation typically corresponds to the intutive category of weak implementations in Figure 1. That is, some information is available but the number of queries is too low to turn it into a successful attack. If our information theoretic measurement is meaningful, higher number of queries should therefore confirm the intuition in Figure 9.

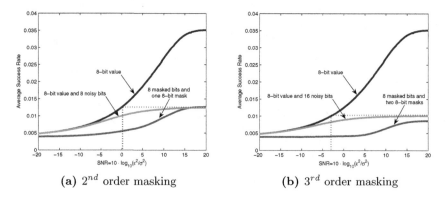

(a) 2nd order masking

(b) 3rd order masking

Fig. 10. Avg. success rate of 2nd, 3rd order masking and equivalent algorithmic noise

Success rates with higher number of queries for a 3rd order masking scheme (and noisy equivalent) were simulated in Figures 11, 12. In Figure 11, a very high SNR=20 is considered. As a consequence, we observe that the masks bring much less protection than their equivalent in random bits, although the initial value (for one single query) suggests the opposite. Figure 12 performs similar experiments for two SNRs that are just next to the crossing point. It illustrates the same intuition that the efficiency of the key recovery when increasing the number of queries is actually dependent on the information content in the observations.

Importantly, these experiments illustrate a typical context where the combination of security and information theoretic metrics is meaningful. While the average success rate is the only possible metric for the comparison of different side-channel attacks (since it could be evaluated for different statistical tools), the information theoretic metric allows to infer the behavior of an attack when increasing the number of queries. As an illustration, the correlation-based analysis performed in [12] only relates to one particular (sub-optimal) statistical tool and was not able to lead to the observations illustrated in Figure 9.

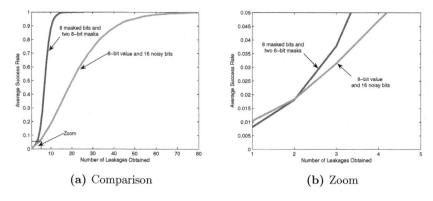

(a) Comparison

(b) Zoom

Fig. 11. Avg. success rate of an 8-bit 3rd order masking scheme with noisy counterpart

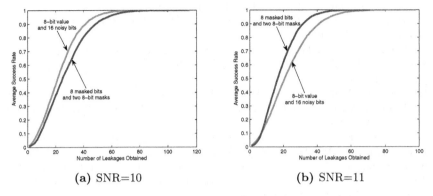

(a) SNR=10   (b) SNR=11

Fig. 12. Avg. success rate of an 8-bit 3rd order masking scheme with noisy counterpart

6   Concluding Remarks

This paper discusses the relevance of a recently introduced theoretical framework for the analysis of cryptographic implementations against side-channel attacks. By the investigation of a number of implementation contexts, we illustrate the interest of a combination of security and information theoretic metrics for the evaluation, comparison and understanding of side-channel attacks. Specifically, in a well defined adversarial context and strategy, the average success rate would allow the comparison of different usually considered side-channel attacks (*e.g.* DPA, correlation analysis, template attacks). By contrast, independently of the statistical tools used by the adversary, an information theoretic metric provides theoretical insights about the behavior and effects of a particular leakage function that can possibly be turned into practical design criteria.

References

1. S. Chari, J.R. Rao, P. Rohatgi, *Template Attacks*, CHES 2002, LNCS, vol. 1965, pp. 13–28.
2. E. Brier, C. Clavier, F. Olivier, *Correlation Power Analysis with a Leakage Model*, CHES 2004, LNCS, vol 3156, pp 16-29.
3. J.-S. Coron, P. Kocher, D. Naccache, *Statistics and Secret Leakage*, Financial Crypto 2000, LNCS, vol. 1972, pp. 157–173.
4. L. Goubin, J. Patarin, *DES and Differential Power Analysis*, CHES 1999, LNCS, vol. 1717, pp. 158-172.
5. P. Kocher, J. Jaffe, B. Jun, *Differential Power Analysis*, CRYPTO 1999, LNCS, vol. 1666, pp. 15–19.
6. S. Mangard, *Hardware Countermeasures against DPA - a Statistical Analysis of their Effectiveness*, CT-RSA 2004, LNCS, vol. 2964, pp. 222-235.
7. T.S. Messerges, *Using Second-Order Power Analysis to Attack DPA Resistant Software.*, CHES 2000, LNCS, vol. 2523, pp. 238–251.
8. S. Micali, L. Reyzin, *Physically Observable Cryptography (extended abstract).*, TCC 2004, LNCS, vol. 2951, pp. 278–296.

9. E. Oswald, S. Mangard, C. Herbst, S. Tillich, *Practical Second-Order DPA Attacks for Masked Smart Card Implementations of Block Ciphers.*, CT-RSA 2006, LNCS, vol. 3860, pp. 192–207.
10. E. Peeters, F.-X. Standaert, N. Donckers, J.-J. Quisquater, *Improved Higher-Order Side-Channel Attacks with FPGA Experiments*, CHES 2005, LNCS, vol. 3659, pp. 309–323.
11. E. Prouff, *DPA Attacks and S-Boxes*, FSE 2005, LNCS, vol. 3557, pp. 424-441.
12. K. Schramm, C. Paar, *Higher Order Masking of the AES*, CT-RSA 2006, LNCS, vol. 3860, 208-225.
13. W. Schindler, K. Lemke, C. Paar, *A Stochastic Model for Differential Side-Channel Cryptanalysis*, CHES 2005, LNCS, vol 3659, pp 30-46.
14. F.-X. Standaert, T.G. Malkin, M. Yung, *A Formal Practice-Oriented Model For The Analysis of Side-Channel Attacks*, Cryptology ePrint Archive, Report 2006/139, 2006, http://eprint.iacr.org/.

A   Probability Density Function of the Variable I_q

We take an iterative approach and first consider the intersection after two leakages. Assuming that the leakages respectively give rise to uniform lists of n_1 and n_2 candidates and the the key space has size $N = 2^n$, it yields $\mathbf{P}[I_2 = i | n_1, n_2] = \dfrac{\binom{n_1 - 1}{i - 1} \cdot \binom{N - n_1}{n_2 - i}}{\binom{N - 1}{n_2 - 1}}$, where the binomials are taken among sets of $N - 1$ possible elements since there is one fixed key that is not chosen uniformly. Then, assuming the knowledge of the distribution of $I_q(n_1, n_2, ..., n_q)$ and an additional leakage that gives rise to a uniform list of n_{new} candidates, we can derive the distribution of I_{q+1} as follows: $\mathbf{P}[I_{q+1} = j | I_q, n_{new}] = \sum_i \mathbf{P}[I_{q+1} = j | I_q = i, n_{new}] \cdot \mathbf{P}[I_q = i]$, with: $\mathbf{P}[I_{q+1} = j | I_q = i, n_{new}] = \dfrac{\binom{i - 1}{j - 1} \cdot \binom{N - i}{n_{new} - j}}{\binom{N - 1}{n_{new} - 1}}$.

B   Additional Figures

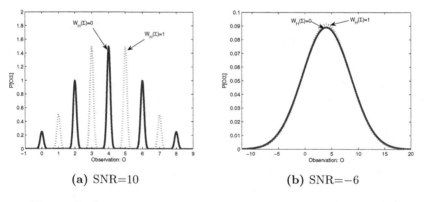

(a) SNR=10   (b) SNR=-6

Fig. 13. Leakages PDFs in function of the noise: masked implementation

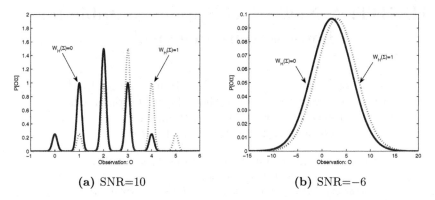

(a) SNR=10   (b) SNR=−6

Fig. 14. Leakages PDFs in function of the noise: unmasked implementation

HIGHT: A New Block Cipher Suitable for Low-Resource Device*

Deukjo Hong[1], Jaechul Sung[2], Seokhie Hong[1], Jongin Lim[1],
Sangjin Lee[1], Bon-Seok Koo[1], Changhoon Lee[1], Donghoon Chang[1],
Jesang Lee[1], Kitae Jeong[1], Hyun Kim[4],
Jongsung Kim[1], and Seongtaek Chee[3]

[1] Center for Information Security Technologies (CIST),
Korea University, Seoul, Korea
{hongdj, hsh, jilim, sangjin, bskoo, crypto77,
pointchang, jslee, kite, joshep}@cist.korea.ac.kr
[2] Department of Mathematics, University of Seoul, Seoul, Korea
jcsung@uos.ac.kr
[3] National Security Research Institute (NSRI),
161 Gajeong-dong, Yuseong-gu, Daejeon 305-350, Korea
chee@etri.re.kr
[4] Korea Information Security Agency (KISA),
78 Karak-dong, Songpa-gu, Seoul 138-160, Korea
hkim@kisa.or.kr

Abstract. In this paper, we propose a new block cipher HIGHT with
64-bit block length and 128-bit key length. It provides low-resource hardware implementation, which is proper to ubiquitous computing device
such as a sensor in USN or a RFID tag. HIGHT does not only consist
of simple operations to be ultra-light but also has enough security as
a good encryption algorithm. Our hardware implementation of HIGHT
requires 3048 gates on 0.25 μm technology.

Keywords: Block Cipher, Ubiquitous, Low-Resource Implementation.

1 Introduction

Cryptographic applications providing various security services such as confidentiality, integrity, protection of privacy, and so on, are admitted as core technologies
for advances in digital information society based on internet. Recently, ubiquitous
computing system is in a matter of concern and interest, and designing cryptographic algorithms and applications suitable for such environment is an interesting research issue. For example, radio frequency identification (RFID) systems are
useful for the automated electronic toll collection system, identifying and tracing
pets, the administration of physical distribution, and so on, while the radio frequency communication between a reader and a tag causes the problems about
confidentiality and privacy. Such problems have been considered as obstacles to

---

* This research was supported by the MIC(Ministry of Information and Communication), Korea, under the ITRC(Information Technology Research Center) support
program supervised by the IITA(Institute of Information Technology Assessment).

L. Goubin and M. Matsui (Eds.): CHES 2006, LNCS 4249, pp. 46–59, 2006.

the advancement of RFID technology. However, since such ubiquitous computing technology has low-cost low-power light-weight platform, existing cryptographic algorithms can be hardly implemented under such resource constraint.

Recently, research on cryptographic protocols based on AES (Advanced Encryption Standard) [1] for resource-constraint environment is receiving a lot of attention. Further essentially, a few low-resource ASIC implementations of AES are presented [11,12].

In this paper, we propose a new block cipher HIGHT (high security and light weight) with 64-bit block length and 128-bit key length, which is suitable for low-cost, low-power, and ultra-light implementation. HIGHT has a 32-round iterative structure which is a variant of generalized Feistel network. The prominent feature of HIGHT is that it consists of simple operations such as XOR, addition mod 2^8, and left bitwise rotation. So, it is hardware-oriented rather than software-oriented. We checked that HIGHT can be implemented with 3048 gates on 0.25 μm technology. Our circuit processes one round encryption per one clock cycle, thus its data throughput is about 150.6 Mbps at a 80 MHz clock rate.

Table 1. Comparison the hardware implementation of HIGHT with AES's

Algorithm	Technology (μm)	Area (GEs)	throughput (Mbps)	Max frequency (MHz)
AES [12]	0.35	3400	9.9	80
HIGHT	0.25	3048	150.6	80

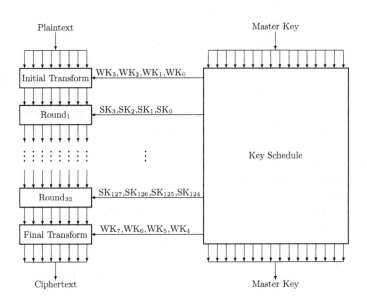

Fig. 1. Encryption process of HIGHT

This performance is much faster than those of recently proposed low-resource hardware implementations of AES [11,12].

The embedded CPU to sensor nodes in sensor networking system is 8-bit oriented. In case of 8-bit oriented software implementation, HIGHT is far faster than AES. The key schedule algorithm of HIGHT is designed to keep the original value of the master key after generating all whitening keys and all subkeys. Due to this property, the subkeys are generated on the fly in both encryption and decryption processes.

The paper is organized as follows. In Section 2, we present the specification and the design principle of HIGHT. Section 3 presents the design principles of HIGHT. In Section 4, we give the security analysis and statistical randomness tests of HIGHT against various existing attacks including differential and linear cryptanalysis. Section 5 treats the hardware implementation of HIGHT. In Section 6, we conclude this paper.

2   Specification

2.1   Notations

We use the following notations for the description of HIGHT. The 64-bit plaintext and ciphertext are considered as concatenations of 8 bytes and denoted by $P = P_7||\cdots P_1||P_0$ and $C = C_7||\cdots C_1||C_0$, respectively. The 64-bit intermediate values are analogously represented, $X_i = X_{i,7}||\cdots X_{i,1}||X_{i,0}$ for $i = 0,\cdots,32$. The 128-bit master key is considered as a concatenation of 16 bytes and denoted by $\mathrm{MK} = \mathrm{MK}_{15}||\cdots||\mathrm{MK}_0$. The followings are notations for mathematical operations:

$$\boxplus : \text{addition mod } 2^8$$
$$\boxminus : \text{subtraction mod } 2^8$$
$$\oplus : \text{XOR (eXclusive OR)}$$
$$A^{\lll s} : s\text{-bit left rotation of a 8-bit value } A$$

We focus on the encryption process in the description of the specification of HIGHT because the decryption process is explained in the similar to the encryption process. The encryption process of HIGHT HightEncryption consists of key schedule, initial transformation, round function, and final transformation. Its description is as follows.

```
HightEncryption(P, MK) {
    KeySchedule(MK,WK,SK);
    HightEncryption(P, WK, SK) {
        InitialTransfomation(P, X_0, WK_3, WK_2, WK_1, WK_0);
        For i = 0 to 31 {
            RoundFunction(X_i, X_{i+1}, SK_{4i+3}, SK_{4i+2}, SK_{4i+1}, SK_{4i});
        }
        FinalTransfomation(X_32, C, WK_7, WK_6,, WK_5, WK_4);
    }
}
```

WK and SK mean whitening keys and subkeys, respectively.

2.2   Key Schedule

The key schedule KeySchedule for HightEncryption consists of two algorithms, WhiteningKeyGeneration which generates 8 whitening key bytes $WK_0, \cdots, WK_7$, and SubkeyGeneration which generates 128 subkey bytes $SK_0, \cdots, SK_{127}$.

```
KeySchedule(MK, WK, SK)  {
    WhiteningKeyGeneration(MK, WK);
    SubkeyGeneration(MK, SK);
}
```

Whitening Key Generation. HIGHT uses 8 whitening key bytes $WK_0, \cdots, WK_7$ for the initial and final transformations. The algorithm WhiteningKeyGeneration generates them as follows.

```
WhiteningKeyGeneration  {
    For i = 0 to 7 {
        If 0 ≤ i ≤ 3, then WK_i ← MK_{i+12};
        Else, WK_i ← MK_{i-4};
    }
}
```

Subkey   Generation.   128   subkeys   are   used   for   1   computation   of HightEncryption, 4 subkeys per round. The algorithm SubkeyGeneration uses the subalgorithm ConstantGeneration to generate 128 7-bit constants $\delta_0, \cdots, \delta_{127}$, and then generates the subkeys $SK_0, \cdots SK_{127}$ with the constants.

δ_0 is fixed as 1011010_2. This is also the initial state $(s_6, \cdots, s_0)$ of 7-bit LFSR h. The connection polynomial of h is $x^7 + x^3 + 1 \in \mathbb{Z}_2[x]$. The algorithm ConstantGeneration uses the LFSR h to produce $\delta_1, \cdots, \delta_{127}$ from δ_0 as follows.

```
ConstantGeneration  {
    s_0 ← 0; s_1 ← 1; s_2 ← 0;      s_3 ← 1;
    s_4 ← 1; s_5 ← 0; s_6 ← 1;
    δ_0 ← s_6||s_5||s_4||s_3||s_2||s_1||s_0;
    For i = 1 to 127 {
        s_{i+6} ← s_{i+2} ⊕ s_{i-1};
        δ_i ← s_6||s_5||s_4||s_3||s_2||s_1||s_0;
    }
}
```

Since $x^7 + x^3 + 1$ is a primitive polynomial in $\mathbb{Z}_2[x]$, the period of h is $2^7 - 1 = 127$ and so $\delta_0 = \delta_{127}$.

The algorithm SubkeyGeneration generates the subkeys as follows.

```
SubkeyGeneration(MK, SK)  {
    Run ConstantGeneration
    For i = 0 to 7 {
        For j = 0 to 7 {
            SK_{16·i+j} ← MK_{j-i mod 8} ⊞ δ_{16·i+j};
        }
        For j = 0 to 7 {
            SK_{16·i+j+8} ← MK_{(j-i mod 8)+8} ⊞ δ_{16·i+j+8};
        }
    }
}
```

2.3   Initial Transformation

InitialTransformation transforms a plaintext P into the input of the first RoundFunction, $X_0 = X_{0,7}||X_{0,6}||\cdots||X_{0,0}$ by using the four whitening-key bytes, WK_0, WK_1, WK_2, and WK_3.

```
InitialTransfomation(P, X_0, WK_3, WK_2, WK_1, WK_0)  {
    X_{0,0} ← P_0 ⊞ WK_0; X_{0,1} ← P_1; X_{0,2} ← P_2 ⊕ WK_1; X_{0,3} ← P_3;
    X_{0,4} ← P_4 ⊞ WK_2; X_{0,5} ← P_5; X_{0,6} ← P_6 ⊕ WK_3; X_{0,7} ← P_7;
}
```

2.4   Round Function

RoundFunction uses two auxiliary functions F_0 and F_1:

$$F_0(x) = x^{\lll 1} \oplus x^{\lll 2} \oplus x^{\lll 7},$$
$$F_1(x) = x^{\lll 3} \oplus x^{\lll 4} \oplus x^{\lll 6}.$$

For $i = 0, \cdots, 31$, RoundFunction transforms $X_i = X_{i,7}||\cdots||X_{i,0}$ into $X_{i+1} = X_{i+1,7}||\cdots||X_{i+1,0}$ as follows.

```
RoundFunction(X_i, X_{i+1}, SK_{4i+3}, SK_{4i+2}, SK_{4i+1}, SK_{4i})  {
    X_{i+1,1} ← X_{i,0}; X_{i+1,3} ← X_{i,2}; X_{i+1,5} ← X_{i,4}; X_{i+1,7} ← X_{i,6};
    X_{i+1,0} = X_{i,7} ⊕ (F_0(X_{i,6}) ⊞ SK_{4i+3});
    X_{i+1,2} = X_{i,1} ⊞ (F_1(X_{i,0}) ⊕ SK_{4i+2});
    X_{i+1,4} = X_{i,3} ⊕ (F_0(X_{i,2}) ⊞ SK_{4i+1});
    X_{i+1,6} = X_{i,5} ⊞ (F_1(X_{i,4}) ⊕ SK_{4i});
}
```

2.5   Final Transformation

FinalTransformation untwists the swap of the last round function and transforms $X_{32} = X_{32,7}|| X_{32,6}||\cdots||X_{32,0}$ into the ciphertext C by using the four whitening-key bytes WK_4, WK_5, WK_6, and WK_7.

FinalTransfomation(X_{32}, C, WK$_7$, WK$_6$, WK$_5$, WK$_4$) {
    $C_0 \leftarrow X_{32,1} \boxplus \text{WK}_4$; $C_1 \leftarrow X_{32,2}$; $C_2 \leftarrow X_{32,3} \oplus \text{WK}_5$; $C_3 \leftarrow X_{32,4}$;
    $C_4 \leftarrow X_{32,5} \boxplus \text{WK}_6$; $C_5 \leftarrow X_{32,6}$; $C_6 \leftarrow X_{32,7} \oplus \text{WK}_7$; $C_7 \leftarrow X_{32,0}$;
}

2.6 Decryption Process

The decryption process HightDecryption is done in the canonical way to invert HightEncryption. Key schedule generates the subkeys in the reverse order. The round function in the decryption process has $\boxminus$ instead of $\boxplus$ and byte-swap with the opposite direction to that in the encryption process.

3 Design Principles

In this section we list brief description of design principles of HIGHT.

- The structure of HIGHT is generalized Feistel-like. This kind of structure reduces restriction of designing inner auxiliary functions. Compared to SP-like structure, the round function is light. Since encryption process is simply converted into decryption process, implementation of the circuit supporting both encryption and decryption processes does not require much more cost than the encryption-only circuit.
- Every operation in HIGHT is 8-bit-processor-oriented. CPUs embedded into the sensors in USN (Ubiquitous Sensor Network) are based on 8-bit processor. So, HIGHT has efficient performance in such environment. We checked that in 8-bit-oriented software implementation HIGHT is faster than AES-128.
- We intend to combine XOR and addition mod 2^8 alternatively. The combination of these quite different operations spread out the whole round of the algorithm. It plays an important role for resistance against existing attacks.
- The inner functions F_0 and F_1 of the round function provide bitwise diffusion. These functions can be viewed as linear transformations from $GF(2)^8$ to $GF(2)^8$. We selected two among linear transformations which have best diffusion.
- The 128-bit register used in the key schedule algorithm contains the master key value both before and after running the algorithm. So, only one 128-bit register is required for both encryption and decryption processes.
- The whitening keys are used in the first and the last rounds of HIGHT. If the whitening keys are not used, then the inputs to F_0 and F_1 in the first and the last rounds are directly revealed from plaintexts and ciphertexts.
- The sequence $\delta_0, \cdots, \delta_{127}$ generated by the linear feedback shift register h enhances randomness of subkey bytes. It also provides the resistance against slide attack.

4 Security Analysis

We analyze the security of HIGHT against various attacks. As a result, we claim that HIGHT is secure enough for cryptographic applications. In this subsection, we present not only brief description of our analysis but also the result of the statistical tests on HIGHT.

4.1 Differential Cryptanalysis

The resistance of a block cipher against differential cryptanalysis [6] depends on the maximum probability of differential characteristics, which are paths from the plaintext difference to the ciphertext difference. First of all, we have implemented a simulation for finding the maximum differential characteristics of a small version of HIGHT, Mini-HIGHT, which consists of four 8-bit input registers when 2^{32} of all possible input values are given. As a result, we found two 8-round maximum differential characteristics $\alpha \to \beta$ with a probability of 2^{-28} in which there always exist a difference pattern such that hamming weight is one at a particular round, where $(\alpha, \beta) \in \{(d0\ 00\ ed\ 86_x, 00\ 84\ 82\ 01_x), (04\ dc\ 20\ e2_x, 00\ 84\ 82\ 01_x)\}$.

Since it is impossible for us to find all of the corresponding differential characteristics of HIGHT for given 2^{64} possible input values, we considered the above difference pattern of Mini-HIGHT with a noticeable feature and then found several 11-round differential characteristics $\alpha \to \beta$ with probability 2^{-58} where $(\alpha, \beta) \in \{(11\ 89\ 25\ e2\ c8\ 01\ 00\ 00_x, 45\ 02\ 01\ 00\ 00\ 91\ 29\ 95_x), (c8\ 01\ 00\ 00\ 11\ 89\ 25\ e2_x, 00\ 91\ 29\ 95\ 45\ 02\ 01\ 00_x)\}$. Each of them are constructed by setting a difference of a particular intermediate variable to the starting point, and by prepending and appending good one-round differential characteristics to it. We expect that they have the best probability over all the 11-round differential characteristics and that for $r > 11$, no r-round differential characteristic is useful for differential cryptanalysis of HIGHT because we checked that there is no any efficient iterative differential characteristic. Differential attack on 13-round HIGHT without the final transformation recovers the subkeys of the 12th and 13th rounds with 2^{62} plaintexts.

4.2 Linear Cryptanalysis

Linear cryptanalysis [17,18] uses linear relations of the plaintext, ciphertext, and key which hold with a probability. We call them, linear approximations. Let $p = 1/2 + \varepsilon$ be the probability of a linear approximation. ε is called, bias. If ϵ^2 is relatively high, the linear approximation is very useful for linear cryptanalysis. We found several 10-round linear approximations with $\varepsilon^2 = 2^{-54}$. Similarly to differential cryptanalysis of HIGHT, they were constructed by putting a 1-bit position of an intermediate variable to the starting point, and by prepending and appending good one-round linear approximations to it. We expect that they have the best bias over all the 10-round approximations and that for $r > 10$, no r-round linear approximation has good bias because we checked that there is no any iterative linear approximation in HIGHT. Linear attack on 13-round

HIGHT without the final transformation recovers 36 bits of the subkeys of the 1st, 12th, and 13th rounds. It requires 2^{57} plaintexts with the success rate 96.7%.

4.3 Truncated Differential Cryptanalysis

Truncated differential characteristic [15] is a path from a partial difference of the input to a partial difference of the output. In order to find good truncated differential characteristics, we computed the probabilities of all differential characteristics with the following form:

$$00 \ \alpha_1 \ 00 \ \alpha_2 \ 00 \ \alpha_3 \ 00 \ \alpha_4 \rightarrow 00 \ \beta_1 \ 00 \ \beta_2 \ 00 \ \beta_3 \ 00 \ \beta_4 \qquad (1)$$

where all α_i, β_j are 1-byte values. The truncated differential characteristics with such form can be iterated, but their probabilities are terribly low. Even the sum of them is too low to be applied to the attack.

As the second approach, we considered several 10-round truncated differential characteristics with probability 1. For example, one among them has the following form: the input difference is 80 e9 00 00 00 00 00 00_x and the output difference is $\gamma \ \delta_1 \ \delta_2 \ \delta_3 \ \delta_4 \ \delta_5 \ \delta_6 \ \delta_7$ where γ is a nonzero 1-byte value and δ_i's are arbitrary 1-byte values. This truncated differential characteristic provides us with only one information about the output difference that the left-most byte of the output difference is nonzero. Since the probability of the characteristic is 1, we have information enough for the attack on HIGHT. We can use the truncated differential characteristic to recover 96 bits of the subkeys used from the 11th round to the 16th round in 16-round HIGHT. The attack requires $2^{14.1}$ plaintexts and $2^{108.69}$ encryptions of 16-round HIGHT.

4.4 Impossible Differential Cryptanalysis

We can construct a differential characteristic, which never occurs, by composing two short truncated differential characteristics with the probability 1 which do not meet in the middle. We call it an impossible differential characteristic [2]. Such differential characteristic can be used for attacks on block ciphers. Roughly speaking, since a key candidate satisfies an impossible differential characteristic is a wrong key, we can reduce the number of the key candidates by repeating such tests. We investigated all of the possible characteristics for all of the possible input differences and then found a 14-round impossible differential characteristic $\alpha \rightarrow \beta \neq \gamma \leftarrow \delta$ where $\alpha = (80 \ e9 \ 00 \ 00 \ 00 \ 00 \ 00 \ 00)_x$, $\beta = (\triangle, \ ?, \ ?, ..., \ ?)_x$ ($\triangle$: a nonzero), $\gamma = (00, \ 00, \ ?, \ ?, \ ?, \ ?, \ ?, \ ?)_x$, and $\delta = (00 \ ? \ ? \ ? \ 00 \ 00 \ 00 \ 00)_x$. We can use this 14-round impossible differential characteristic to attack 18-round HIGHT. This attack requires $2^{46.8}$ chosen-plaintexts and $2^{109.2}$ encryptions of 18-round HIGHT.

4.5 Saturation Attack

The saturation attack [10,16] uses a saturated multiset of plaintexts. The attacker needs the property that XOR sum of particular parts of the corresponding ciphertexts is zero. We call it a saturation characteristic. Saturation characteristics useful for the attack are often found in block ciphers in which small portions of the bits are interleaved by a strong nonlinear function while the main interleaving stage is linear. There exist 12-round saturation characteristics with the probability 1 in HIGHT, e.g., $\alpha = (S, C, C, C, C, C, C, C) \to \beta = (?, ?, ?, ?, B_0, ?, ?, ?)$ where S: a saturation set, C: a fixed constant, and B_0: a balanced set for the least significant bit. We can apply them to the attack on 16-round HIGHT. It requires 2^{42} plaintexts and 2^{51} encryptions of 16-round HIGHT.

4.6 Boomerang Attack

The main idea behind the boomerang attack [20] is to use two short differential characteristics with relatively high probabilities instead of one long differential with low probability. The boomerang attack has been improved to the amplified boomerang [14] and the rectangle [4,5] attacks. This kind of attacks treat the block cipher E as $E = E_1 \circ E_0$ a cascade of E_0 and E_1. We assume that for E_0 there exists a differential characteristic $\alpha \to \beta$ with probability p and that for E_1 there exists a differential characteristic $\gamma \to \delta$ with probability q. Then the boomerang characteristic which is constructed from two differential characteristics $\alpha \to \beta$ and $\gamma \to \delta$ has probability $p^2 q^2$. We applied the amplified boomerang attack to 13-round HIGHT without final transformation. We build a 11-round boomerang characteristic of HIGHT with probability 2^{-58} from two differential characteristics — one with probability 2^{-12} depicted in Table 2 and the other one with probability 2^{-17} depicted in Table 3. We use the 11-round boomerang characteristic to recover the subkeys of the 13th round with 2^{62} plaintexts.

Table 2. The 5 rounds differential characteristics (the 1st round $\sim$ the 5th round) with probability 2^{-12}

$\alpha \longrightarrow \beta$
82 01 00 00 00 00 00 00$_x$ $\longrightarrow$ 00 90 95 ca 01 00 00 00$_x$
00 00 00 00 82 01 00 00$_x$ $\longrightarrow$ 01 00 00 00 00 90 95 ca$_x$

Table 3. The 6 rounds differential characteristics (the 6th round $\sim$ the 11th round) with probability 2^{-17}

$\gamma \longrightarrow \delta$
42 82 01 00 00 00 00 00$_x$ $\longrightarrow$ 00 90 95 ca 01 00 00 00$_x$
00 00 00 00 42 82 01 00$_x$ $\longrightarrow$ 01 00 00 00 00 90 95 ca$_x$

4.7 Interpolation and Higher Order Differential Attack

Interpolation [13] and higher order differential [15] attacks are aimed against block ciphers which have low algebraic degree. Since the degree of a round function of HIGHT is 8, the full-round HIGHT has a high degree as a vector Boolean function. Furthermore, we believe that the result of higher order differential attack on HIGHT is less than the result of saturation attack on HIGHT because saturation attack can be viewed as a special and more effective case of higher order differential attack.

4.8   Algebraic Attack

In order to apply the algebraic attack [9] to block ciphers, we should derive an over-defined system of algebraic equations. Since a round function of HIGHT is the degree 8 as a vector Boolean function, it may be impossible to convert any equation system in HIGHT into an over-defined system.

4.9   Slide and Related-Key Attacks

Slide [7,8] and related-key [3] attacks use some weakness of key schedule. The subkey generation algorithm of HIGHT has a simplicity and a linearity but resistance enough to frustrate those attacks due to the use of the round function with strong non-linearity and avalanche effect. It is known that the iterated ciphers with identical round functions, that is, equal structures and equal subkeys in the round functions, are vulnerable to slide attacks. However, since HIGHT uses the different constant for each round, it is secure against slide attack.

We are also convinced that the key schedule and round function of HIGHT makes related-key attacks difficult although the relation between two master keys is known and the corresponding relations between the subkeys can be predetermined due to linearity of the key schedule. To find long related-key differential characteristics with high probability and mount a successful distinguishing attack, we must keep the number of additions small. This can be done by trying to cancel out differences in XORs and additions but this work is not easy. So, by trial and error, we constructed 18-round related-key boomerang distinguisher which is composed of two short related-key differential characteristics with relatively high probability; one is the first 8 rounds, $(2c\ 00\ 80\ 00\ 00\ 00\ 00\ 00)_x \rightarrow (00\ 00\ 00\ 00\ 43\ 80\ 00\ 00)_x$ under the related-key difference $(00\ 00\ 80\ 2c\ 00, ..., 00)$ with probability 2^{-6} and the other one is 10 rounds, $(08\ 9e\ 6f\ 80\ 2c\ 00\ 80\ 00)_x \rightarrow (2c\ 00\ 80\ 00\ 00\ 00\ 00\ 00)_x$ under the related-key difference $(80\ 2c\ 00\ 00, ..., 00)$ with probability 2^{-23}. This is useful to attack on 19 rounds HIGHT but can be used to attack on full-round HIGHT.

4.10   Weak Keys

Originally, a weak key is defined as a key under which the encryption function is involution [19]. We checked that there does not exists any equivalent or weak key in HIGHT. In a broad sense, a weak key can be defined as a key under which the resistance of the block cipher against any attacks falls off. We suppose that it is very difficult to find such kind of weak keys in HIGHT.

Table 4. Results of HIGHT

Statistical Test	Proportion	
	High Density	Low Density
Frequency	0.994(Pass)	0.986(Pass)
Block Frequency ($m = 100$)	0.993(Pass)	0.991(Pass)
Runs	0.990(Pass)	0.982(Pass)
Long Runs of Ones	0.990(Pass)	0.994(Pass)
Rank	0.988(Pass)	0.992(Pass)
Spectral DFT	1.00(Pass)	0.990(Pass)
Non-overlapping Templates ($m = 9$)	0.990(Pass)	0.990(Pass)
Overlapping Templates ($m = 9$)	0.978(Pass)	0.984(Pass)
Universal	0.992(Pass)	0.980(Pass)
Lempel-Ziv Complexity	0.986(Pass)	0.980(Pass)
Linear Complexity ($M = 500$)	0.984(Pass)	0.994(Pass)
Serial ($m = 5$)	0.992(Pass)	0.985(Pass)
Approximate Entropy ($m = 5$)	0.986(Pass)	0.990(Pass)
Cusum	0.992(Pass)	0.988(Pass)
Random Excursions	0.986(Pass)	0.990(Pass)
Random Excursions Variant	0.989(Pass)	0.987(Pass)

4.11 Random Test

We show the results of the NIST statistical test on HIGHT. We use 500 samples of about 10^6 bit sequences for each test. Consequently, 500 (sample) $\times$ 10^6 (sequence) bits are used for each test. The Table 4 shows results of HIGHT. Here input parameters used in these tests has been included in parenthesis beside the name of the statistical test. From the Table 4, it is clear that the statistical test results for HIGHT don't indicate a deviation from random behaviour.

5   Hardware Implementation

We designed a simple circuit of HIGHT in order to check the hardware complexity on $0.25\mu m$ CMOS technology. The circuit consists of three parts: Round-Function, KeySchedule, and Control Logic. RoundFunction processes whitening-key addition or round function with 64-bit input data and 4-byte round key, and KeySchdule generates 4-byte round key (four byte whiteningkeys or subkeys). Control Logic controls RoundFunction and KeySchedule to process HIGHT algorithm. The total size corresponds to 3048 NAND gates as you see in Table 5. Our circuit processes one round encryption per one clock cycle, thus its data throughput is about 150.6 Mbps at a 80 MHz clock rate. Note that our circuit is not area-optimized, and in order to reduce the gate count, we can simply modify it to process 1/2 or 1/4 of one round operation per a clock cycle. In the case of 1/4 round design, we estimate the minimized circuit would require much less than 3000 gates on $0.25\mu m$ technology and its data throughput would be about 37.6 Mbps at a 80 MHz clock rate. Meanwhile the last hardware implementation result of AES-128 [12] requires about 3400 gates and its data throughput is about 9.9 Mbps under the same clock rate.

Table 5. Gate count for hardware implementation of HIGHT

Component	Gate Count
RoundFunction	838
KeySchedule	1648
Control Logic	562
Total	3048

6   Conclusion

We proposed a block cipher HIGHT with 64-bit block length and 128-bit key length. HIGHT was designed to be proper to the implementation in the low-resource environment such as RFID tag or tiny ubiquitous devices. From security analysis, we are sure that HIGHT has enough security. Our implementation circuit processes one HIGHT encryption with 34 clock and requires 3048 gates. The data throughput of the circuit is about 150.6 Mbps under the operating frequency 80 MHz.

References

1. National Institute of Standards and Technology (NIST), FIPS-197: Advanced Encryption Standard, November 2001. http://www.itl.nist.gov/fipspubs/
2. E. Biham, A. Biryukov and A. Shamir, "Cryptanalysis of Skipjack reduced to 31 rounds using impossible differentials," *Advances in Cryptology - EUROCRYPT'99*, J. Stern, Ed., LNCS 1592, Springer-Verlag, pp. 12-23, 1999.
3. E. Biham, "New Types of Cryptanalytic Attack Using Related Keys," *Journal of Cryptology*, Volume 7, Number 4, pp. 156–171, 1994.
4. E. Biham, O. Dunkelman, N. Keller, "The Rectangle Attack – Rectangling the Serpent," *Advances in Cryptology – EUROCRYPT 2001*, LNCS 2045, Springer-Verlag, pp. 340–357, 2001.
5. E. Biham, O. Dunkelman, N. Keller, "New Results on Boomerang and Rectangle Attacks," *FSE 2002*, LNCS 2365, Springer-Verlag, pp. 1–16, 2002.
6. E. Biham, A. Shamir, "Differential Cryptanalysis of the Data Encryption Standard," Springer-Verlag, 1993.
7. A. Biryukov, D. Wagner, "Slide Attacks," *Advances in Cryptology – FSE'99*, LNCS 1687, Springer-Verlag, pp. 244-257, 1999.
8. A. Biryukov, D. Wagner, "Advanced Slide Attacks," *Advances in Cryptology – EUROCRYPT 2000*, LNCS 1807, Springer-Verlag, pp. 589–606, 2000.
9. N. Courtois, J. Pieprzyk, "Cryptanalysis of Block Ciphers with Overdefined Systems of Equations," *Advances in Cryptology – ASIACRYPT 2002*, LNCS 2501, Springer-Verlag, pp. 267–287, 2002.
10. J. Daemen, L. Knudsen and V. Rijmen, "The Block Cipher SQUARE," *FSE'97*, LNCS 1267, Springer-Verlag, pp. 137–151, 1997.

11. M. Feldhofer, S. Dominikus, and J. Wolkerstorfer, "Strong Authentication for RFID Systems Using the AES Algorithm," *CHES'04*, LNCS 3156, pp. 357–370, Springer-Verlag, 2004.
12. M. Feldhofer, J. Wolkerstorfer, and V. Rijmen, "AES Implementation on a Grain of Sand," *IEE Proceedings on Information Security*, Volume 152, Issue 1, pp. 13–20, 2005.
13. T. Jakoben and L. R. Knudsen, "The Interpolation Attack against Block Ciphers," *FSE'97*, LNCS 1267, Springer-Verlag, pp. 28–40, 1997.
14. J. Kelsey, T. Kohno, B. Schneier, "Amplified Boomerang Attacks Against Reduced-Round MARS and Serpent," *FSE 2000*, LNCS 1978, Springer-Verlag, pp. 75–93, 2001.
15. L. R. Knudsen, "Truncated and Higher Order Differential," *FSE 94*, LNCS 1008, Springer-Verlag, pp. 229–236, 1995.
16. S. Lucks, "The Saturation Attack – a Bait for Twofish," *FSE 2001*, LNCS 1039, Springer-Verlag, pp. 189-203, 2001.
17. M. Matsui, "Linear Cryptanalysis Method for DES Cipher," *Advances in Cryptology – EUROCRYPT'93*, T. Helleseth, Ed., LNCS 765, Springer-Verlag, pp. 386–397, 1994.
18. M. Matsui, "The First Experimental Cryptanalysis of DES," *Advances in Cryptology – CRYPTO'94*, LNCS 839, Springer-Verlag, pp. 1–11, 1994.
19. A. Menezes, P. van Oorschot, S. Vanstone, *Handbook of Applied Cryptography*, CRC Press, 1996.
20. D. Wagner, "The Boomerang Attack," *FSE'99*, LNCS 1636, Springer-Verlag, pp. 156–170, 1999.

A   Figure of Functions in HIGHT

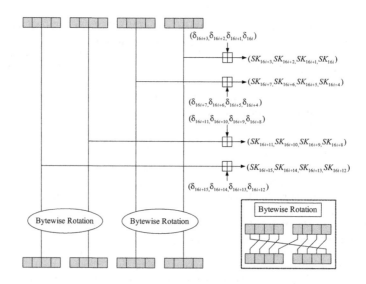

Fig. 2. Subkey generation of HIGHT key schedule

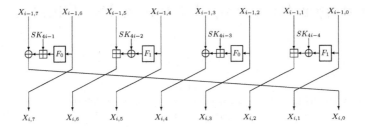

Fig. 3. The i-th RoundFunction of HIGHT for $i = 1, \cdots, 32$

Integer Factoring Utilizing PC Cluster

Kazumaro Aoki

NTT
1-1 Hikari-no-oka, Yokosuka-shi, Kanagawa-ken, 239-0847 Japan
maro@isl.ntt.co.jp

The integer factoring problem is one of the oldest and important problems and it is considered as hard, i.e., the problem cannot be solved in polynomial time for the worst case, because the security of RSA is heavily dependent on the difficulties of integer factoring. As is well known, hardware technology is progressing rapidly from year to year and it seems that the time is now ripe to factor 1024-bit integers. Recently, there have been many studies that have investigated the possibility of 1024-bit integer factoring.

Base on the progress in hardware, several studies claim that special purpose hardware for integer factoring can factor a 1024-bit integer in a year at a reasonable cost. However, there seems to be no published report that the world record for integer factoring was superseded by this kind of hardware. A supercomputer is a promising candidate for factoring large integers, but it is not cost effective. Considering a limited budget, a PC cluster seems to be the most cost effective hardware for factoring a large integer. Actually, recent world records were superseded using a PC cluster.

This presentation introduces the usage of a PC cluster for integer factoring. In particular, the experience of achieving the world record will be discussed. Our factoring team wrote several tens of thousands of lines of source code, and used hundreds of PCs. They spent several months to achieve the record. We did not expect any PC miscomputation, however, it is still of serious concern. It is hoped that this presentation provides a better understanding of what has been accomplished toward world-class integer factoring.

L. Goubin and M. Matsui (Eds.): CHES 2006, LNCS 4249, p. 60, 2006.

Optically Enhanced Position-Locked Power Analysis

Sergei Skorobogatov

University of Cambridge, Computer Laboratory,
15 JJ Thomson Avenue, Cambridge CB3 0FD, United Kingdom
sps32@cl.cam.ac.uk

Abstract. This paper introduces a refinement of the power-analysis attack on integrated circuits. By using a laser to illuminate a specific area on the chip surface, the current through an individual transistor can be made visible in the circuit's power trace. The photovoltaic effect converts light into a current that flows through a closed transistor. This way, the contribution of a single transistor to the overall supply current can be modulated by light. Compared to normal power-analysis attacks, the semi-invasive position-locking technique presented here gives attackers not only access to Hamming weights, but to individual bits of processed data. This technique is demonstrated on the SRAM array of a PIC16F84 microcontroller and reveals both which memory locations are being accessed, as well as their contents.

Keywords: side-channel attacks, power analysis, semi-invasive attacks, optical probing.

1 Introduction

Power analysis, especially in the form of differential power analysis (DPA), became a serious concern since it was first announced in 1999 by Kocher et al. [1]. Since then, it proved to be a useful technique to breach security in many devices, including smartcards [2]. During the last six years, many attempts were made to improve protection against power analysis. This involved both hardware and software countermeasures [3,4,5]. On one hand, such improvements reduced the success of known techniques, on the other, they only pushed away poorly funded or less knowledgeable attackers, thereby creating the impression of an already solved problem.

Power analysis attacks had a huge impact on the industry since their effectiveness in helping to break many cryptographic algorithms was demonstrated in the late nineties [2]. However, in spite of the relatively simple setup necessary for power analysis (resistor in the ground line, digitizing oscilloscope and a computer) it is still not reliably and straightforwardly applicable to each situation. This is due to a number of reasons. Firstly, the power analysis technique is usually applied to a whole chip rather than to a small area of interest. As a result, power transitions in areas that are not relevant to the data processing also affect

L. Goubin and M. Matsui (Eds.): CHES 2006, LNCS 4249, pp. 61–75, 2006.

the power trace. Secondly, as the power fluctuations are affected by a number of bits being set or reset, only a Hamming weight of data (number of bits set) can be guessed, rather than the actual value. Finally, in order to get a reliable result from a power analysis, often hundreds or even thousands of traces have to be acquired and averaged. This is because the signal from a single transition is too small compared to the inevitable noise from the resistor in the power line and the noise from the A/D converter of the oscilloscope. Also, the number of transitions happening at a time might be so high that the signal from a single bit of information would be too small to be distinguished with 8-bit resolution. The easiest way to increase the resolution is averaging the signal. However, this requires precise triggering or post processing of the acquired power traces.

Recently introduced electro-magnetic analysis (EMA) [6] can increase the level of a useful signal by placing an antenna close to the area of interest, for example, above the internal RAM, CPU or ALU. However, this is still not enough to distinguish between values of data with the same Hamming weights, because the minimum size of the antenna is significantly larger than the data buffer or the memory cell.

In our laboratory, we have for many years tried to improve the effectiveness of power analysis during security evaluations of microcontrollers and smartcards. One idea was to combine optical probing attacks [7] with a standard power analysis setup. As such analysis will require partial decapsulation of the chip without direct connection to its internal wires, it should be considered to be a semi-invasive attack. If we could influence the power consumption of a certain area on the chip surface by exposing it to ionizing radiation, we would be able to see if the signal in the power trace came from this area or not. Thus, by moving from one location to another, we should be able to recognise which areas on the chip contribute to the power trace. Vice versa, if we know the point of interest, for example, an address of the variable which holds the security flag, we could point to the corresponding location inside the SRAM and find out the exact time when this memory address is accessed.

Lasers have been used in failure analysis for testing states of on-chip transistors for many years and the ability of laser radiation to ionize silicon substrate was studied long ago [8]. One of these techniques, called light-induced voltage alteration (LIVA) [9], uses the photovoltaic effect to distinguish between open and closed transistors. However, this technique assumes that the chip is in a static condition and the result of scanning cannot be updated faster than a few frames per second. Another technique, published in 1992 [10], was designed specifically to detect electrical signals at internal nodes in silicon ICs and uses the phenomenon that charge density affects the refractive index of silicon within the device. However, the setup necessary for detecting this change of refractive index in a tiny area is very difficult and expensive to implement. Therefore, methods which are less expensive and easier to implement are desirable.

Successful position-locked power analysis would be highly useful for failure analysis and security testing of secure microcontrollers as it would offer a faster and less expensive solution. It would also help in partial reverse engineering of a chip operation and help with the analysis of signals inside a chip. Of course, failure analysis techniques such as using a focused-ion beam (FIB) machine followed by microprobing [11] will with high probability give the required result, but at the cost of many hours of preparation work and a large number of analysed points. Optical probing can give a result in a significantly shorter time (normally minutes) and does not require expensive sample preparation techniques, which often irreversibly modify the die of an analysed chip.

In spite of the seeming simplicity of the proposed idea, it took me a long time until I managed to get a useful and reliable result. The main problem to solve was to find a reliable way of influencing the power consumption from a particular CMOS inverter, flip-flop or memory cell, without interfering with its operation.

2   Background

Most digital circuits built today are based on CMOS technology, using complementary transistors as basic elements. When a CMOS gate changes its state, it charges/discharges a parasitic capacitive load and causes a dynamic short circuit of the gate [12]. The more gates change their state, the more power is dissipated. The current consumed by a circuit can be measured by placing a 10–50 Ω resistor in the power supply line, usually a ground pin, because an ordinary oscilloscope probe has a ground connection.

Drivers on the address and data bus consist of many parallel inverters per bit, each driving a large capacitive load. During transition they cause a significant power surge, in the order of 0.5–1 mA per bit, which is sufficient to estimate the number of bus bits changing at a time using a 12-bit A/D converter [13]. By averaging the measurements of many repeated identical operations, smaller transitions can be identified. Of particular interest for attacking cryptographic algorithms would be observing the state change of a carry bit. Each type of instruction executed by a CPU causes different levels of activity in the instruction decoder and arithmetic unit, therefore instructions can be often quite clearly distinguished such that parts of algorithms can be reconstructed.

Memory inside a microcontroller or a smartcard, especially SRAM, is of particular interest to an attacker, because it may store sensitive variables, encryption keys, passwords and intermediate results of cryptographic operations. When accessing an SRAM memory cell, not only data bits are contributing to the power trace, but also the address being accessed, because of the different number of bits set inside the address latches. An SRAM cell consists of six transistors (Figure 1), four of which create a flip-flop while the other two are used for accessing the cell inside the memory array. An SRAM write operation often generates the strongest signal, because the output of the flip-flop is connected to the output of the bit lines, causing a current surge. However, still only bits which are changed during the write operation will contribute to the power trace.

In order to apply optical attacks, the surface of the chip must be accessible. Originally, optical attacks were demonstrated with light from a photoflash [7]. In order to influence each memory cell independently, a better light source should

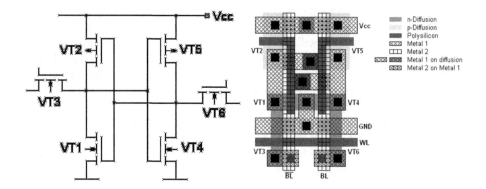

Fig. 1. The architecture and layout of an SRAM cell

be used, for example a laser beam [14]. As the target of my experiments was SRAM, we should look at the structure of such memory first. One example of the SRAM layout is shown in Figure 1. If it is possible to partially open one of the transistors forming the flip-flop, then the cell will behave differently when accessed, consuming more power, and this can be detected by comparing the acquired power trace with a reference trace. If the flip-flop switches, this will reduce the leakage current, because the leaking channel will be closed. However, if it were possible to influence both transistors of the flip-flop simultaneously, then any access to the cell will result in a change of the power consumption.

Laser radiation can ionize semiconductor regions in silicon chips if its photon energy exceeds the semiconductor band gap (> 1.1 eV or $\lambda < 1100$ nm). This results in free carriers (electrons and holes) being created that produce a photocurrent at p-n junctions and this can be detected, for example, by observing a voltage drop over a resistor inserted in the power supply line. The injected photocurrent can also influence the normal operation of the chip and this can be simulated [15]. From a practical point of view, it is more efficient to influence n-channel transistors, as they have higher doping concentrations and their carriers (electrons) have higher mobility. P-channel transistors can be influenced as well, but will require a higher level of ionizing radiation.

3   Experimental Method

For my experiments, I chose a common microcontroller, the Microchip PIC16F84 [16], which has 68 bytes of SRAM memory on chip. The allocation of data bits in the memory array and the mapping from the addresses to the corresponding physical location of each memory cell were already documented for this chip [7]. The microcontroller was decapsulated in a standard way [13] and placed in a computer-controlled test board with a ZIF socket under a special microscope for semi-invasive analysis (Figure 2).

As a light source, I chose a red laser, which can be easily focused down to a submicron point on a chip surface. The most difficult part was choosing the right equipment for my experiments. Firstly, precise control over the sample position with submicron precision was essential. Secondly, as any sort of fault injection was undesirable, precise control over the laser power was required. Finally, because the chip has a metal layer, the optical system must allow focusing the laser beam at any point within several micrometers distance from the focal plane of the microscope. Otherwise, most of the energy will be reflected or deflected by the metal wires. Optical fault injection equipment, such as industrial laser cutters [17], was unsuitable for my needs because they offer limited control over timing. I performed several tests and also found that the pulses emitted by such laser cutters have too much power variability and too short and uncontrollable duration.

Fig. 2. Test setup for semi-invasive analysis

After a long time of searching, I finally chose equipment from Semiconductors Research Ltd – a company specialising in security testing and evaluation of integrated circuits [18]. What I used in my experiments was a special semi-invasive diagnostic system that combines several laser sources with extended positioning control, mounted on a specialized optical microscope with long working distance high-magnification objectives and a CCD camera for imaging. The software control toolbox for this equipment allowed fully computerised control over all parameters of the laser sources in both manual and automatic modes (Figure 2). The last capability was very important as it allowed me to synchronize the supply of test signals with the photon sources. In addition, the system has a very useful high-resolution laser scanning capability, which helps to find active areas on the chip surface.

To acquire power traces with a sampling rate of 500 MHz, I used a Tektronix TDS7054 oscilloscope with a P6243 active probe (DC coupled) connected on the test board across a 10 Ω resistor. A metal-film resistor was used to minimize noise. The oscilloscope's built-in analogue 20 MHz low-pass filter was activated (anti-aliasing filter), along with the "Hi-Res" acquisition mode, in which a digital low-pass filter implemented in the oscilloscope further reduces noise and increases the effective A/D-converter resolution to slightly more than 8 bits per sample.

The images of the SRAM area and the image produced by a video camera during the experiment with a 100× objective are presented in Figure 3. The laser source (639 nm) was set to a safe reference mode (0.01 mW) in which the image can be taken with a camera and the laser can be directly observed without any danger to eyes.

Fig. 3. Optical image of the SRAM area in the PIC16F84 microcontroller and the laser beam focused with a 100× objective

Although the circuit diagrams of most SRAM cells are identical, their layouts can differ. The layout of the SRAM cell presented in Figure 4 is very similar to the one found in the PIC16F84.

In order to locate active areas inside the memory cell, a passive laser scanning operation was applied to the sample. In failure analysis, this technique is called optical beam induced current (OBIC) and the image produced as location-dependent induced current. The result of scanning the SRAM cell with the laser is presented in Figure 4. Having such a reference helps in focusing the laser beam on any of the MOS transistors forming the flip-flop. The right bright areas correspond to light-sensitive areas of p-channel transistors VT2 and VT5, where the left grey lines correspond to n-channel transistors VT1 and VT4. The left grey areas correspond to light-sensitive areas of the select transistors VT3 and VT6.

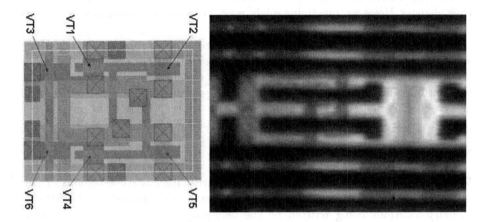

Fig. 4. Layout and laser scan of the SRAM cell

The PIC16F84 microcontroller was programmed with a simple test program which firstly initialised SRAM locations 0x10, 0x11, 0x20, 0x31 with value 0x00 and locations 0x21, 0x30, 0x40, 0x41 with 0xFF, and then executed the following code:

```
bsf PORTA,test ; generate pulse on PA0 for triggering
bcf PORTA,test
nop
movf 0x10, W   ; read location 0x10
nop
movwf 0x11     ; write to location 0x11
nop
movf 0x20, W   ; read location 0x20
nop
movwf 0x21     ; write to location 0x21
nop
movf 0x30, W   ; read location 0x30
nop
movwf 0x31     ; write to location 0x31
nop
movf 0x40, W   ; read location 0x40
nop
movwf 0x41     ; write to location 0x41
```

Finally, it outputs the contents of all memory locations to Port B.

I put NOP commands between each instruction to avoid the influence of instruction pipelining, so that the result from a previous instruction will not affect the next instruction. This was necessary only for the evaluation stage. In a power-analysis comparison, such an influence will be eliminated anyway, because we are not interested in the absolute values in the power traces, but in their changes. However, pipelining might pose problems for recognising particular instructions.

Previous experiments with power analysis of a similar microcontroller [19] showed that instructions can be distinguished, and that there is a correlation to the number of bits set or changed in the data during operations. My aim was to identify, which particular bits were set and which addresses in the memory array were accessed.

4   Results

Writing into an SRAM cell causes a significantly larger current response than a read operation, therefore my first experiment was performed on the SRAM memory locations being written by the test program. The aim was to check whether write operations performed on a particular memory location can be reliably identified.

In the test program, the write operation does not change the state of memory locations 0x11 and 0x41, which are 0x00 and 0xFF, respectively. Location 0x21 was changed from 0x00 to 0xFF and location 0x31 from 0xFF to 0x00. For each memory cell, I performed a series of tests with different focusing points and power settings for the laser. The optimum laser power I found to be between 1 mW and 3 mW. The laser was switched on in the beginning of the test program and switched off before sending the contents of the memory locations to Port B.

As predicted, the maximum response was received from areas close to n-channel transistors. I averaged the traces of 16 repeated program executions to reduce noise and the acquired waveform with the laser focused on transistor VT1 of memory location 0x31 is presented in Figure 5. The power trace is compared with a reference waveform acquired without laser light. The difference between the reference and the acquired waveforms is presented in enlarged scale. The trace difference is clearly noticeable, however, the signal is very close to the noise level. Any attempts to influence transistor VT1 at address 0x21 and transistor VT4 at 0x31 were unsuccessful. Also, for unchanged locations (0x11, 0x41), I was unable to see any noticeable change in the power consumption.

Any attempts to improve the signal-to-noise ratio by increasing the laser power caused the memory cell to change its state, resulting in noticeable changes in the power analysis traces (Figure 6). Similar waveforms, if the state of the memory cell was changed, were received for memory locations 0x11, 0x21 and 0x41. This was still a positive result, because it allowed detection of memory access events, however, from an attacker's point of view, it is always better to be unnoticeable.

Similar measurements were performed for memory locations which were read by the test program. Unfortunately, I received only a very small signal response, which was very hard to distinguish from noise. Again, increasing the laser power caused these memory locations to change their state and this was detectable in the power trace in a similar way as with the written locations.

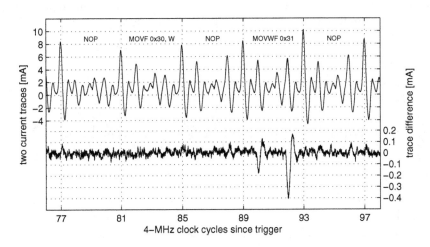

Fig. 5. Laser focused on VT1 of memory cell 0x31, write leaves state unchanged

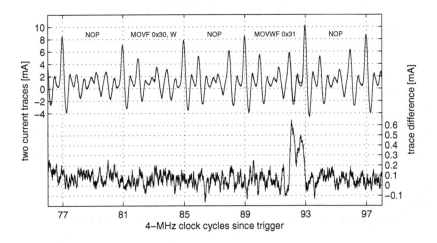

Fig. 6. Laser focused on VT1 of memory cell 0x31, write changes state

My next idea was to try focusing the laser at the area in between the two n-channel transistors, hoping that this will influence both CMOS inverters of the flip-flop and, therefore, might result in influencing the power consumption each time the memory cell was accessed (previously it was either VT1 or VT4 which influenced the signal). Again, I decided to start with the write operations as they always give a stronger signal in the power trace.

However, the result of the measurements surpassed my expectations. The difference signal had significantly increased, such that it became possible to see a clearly distinguishable difference between two traces, even without averaging the waveforms (Figure 7). Still, increasing the laser power resulted in the contents of the memory location to be changed (Figure 8). However, the difference in the waveforms is significantly easier to distinguish than before, when either VT1 or VT4 was influenced.

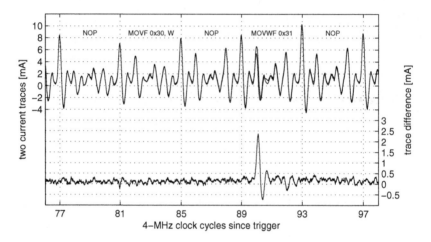

Fig. 7. Laser focused on VT1+VT4 of memory cell 0x31, write leaves state unchanged

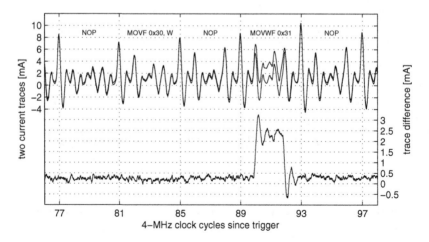

Fig. 8. Laser focused on VT1+VT4 of memory cell 0x31, write changes state

This is very likely an outcome of a short circuit created inside a memory cell if both n-channel transistors forming a flip-flop were opened for a short period of time. Such a situation happens because the ionizing radiation creates excessive carriers, which require additional time to recombine, keeping a transistor in the open state longer. I described the influence of laser radiation on microcontrollers in the form of laser pulses already in [20]. If the energy of the laser is too high, the memory cells become unstable and can spontaneously switch into the other state. This causes a surge in the power consumption.

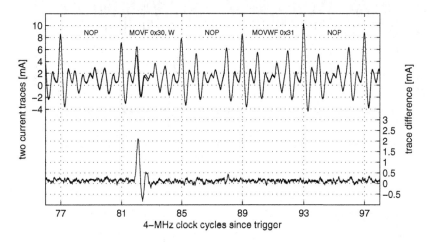

Fig. 9. Laser focused on VT1+VT4 of memory cell 0x30, read

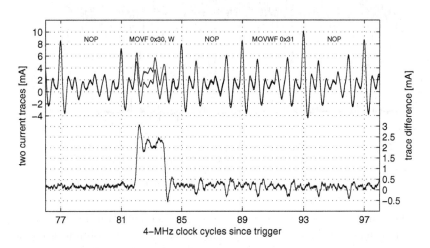

Fig. 10. Laser focused on VT1+VT4 of memory cell 0x30, read changes state

Applying the same approach to a memory addresses being read, the same level of current response was achieved when the state of a memory cell was not changed (Figure 9). However, higher laser power was destructive to the memory contents (Figure 10). Repeating the non-destructive operation of data analysis

for each bit of the memory with the same address revealed the actual value of
the byte.

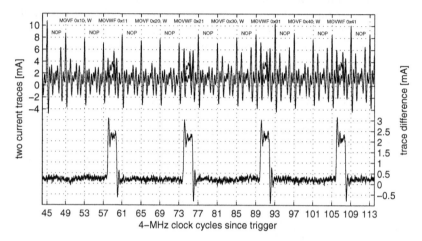

Fig. 11. Laser focused on VT3+VT6 of memory cell 0x31

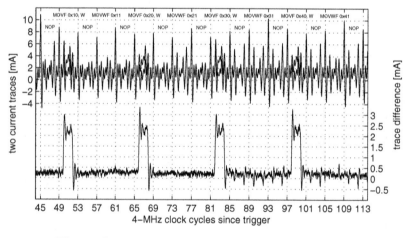

Fig. 12. Laser focused on VT3+VT6 of memory cell 0x30

Another surprise came at a point when a laser was focused on the area between
cell select transistors VT3 and VT6. In this case, the whole column of memory
cells was affected, independently of which cell in the row was influenced. In my
first experiment, the laser beam was pointed between VT3 and VT6 of memory cell
0x31, which caused all cells from this row (addresses 0x31, 0x41, 0x11 and 0x21) to
be detectable in the power trace (Figure 11). Similar, by pointing between VT3 and
VT6 of memory location 0x30, responses were received if any of the addresses 0x30,
0x40, 0x10 and 0x20 were accessed (Figure 12). However, in both experiments the
state of the selected memory locations always changed to zero.

5   Limitations and Further Improvements

My results were achieved on a relatively old microcontroller (PIC16F84) built with 0.9 μm technology. The majority of modern microcontrollers are built with 0.35 μm and 0.25 μm technology (three or four metal layers) and some high-end microcontrollers employ now 0.18 μm technology (up to six metal layers). This fact, in addition to interlayer polishing and gap filling techniques, significantly reduces the amount of laser radiation which can reach the underlying transistor gates.

One improvement could be to approach memory cells from the rear side of the chip. However, in this case, laser radiation with a longer wavelength must be used, which causes lower levels of ionization and also creates unnecessary carriers in the whole volume of the silicon substrate. In order to achieve similar results, it might be necessary to reduce the thickness of the substrate.

6   Conclusions

My experiments showed how combining optical probing techniques with power analysis methods can significantly improve the results. Using such techniques, partial reverse engineering to locate data bits and addresses being accessed in memory becomes easier and significantly faster compared to with other methods [20]. However, this technique has some limitations, especially for modern deep submicron technologies, where multiple metal layers and small transistor sizes prevent easy and precise analysis. Further improvements to these methods might involve approaching the die from its rear side, but this requires more expensive equipment.

Possible forms of protection against such attacks could involve using tamper sensors to prevent direct access to the chip surface, as well as implementing light sensors. Top metal protection might help, but is very likely to be overcome by approaching the sample from the rear side. Using modern deep submicron technologies will also eliminate most of these attacks.

Acknowledgements

I would like to thank Semiconductors Research Ltd for providing me with the special equipment necessary for optical analysis of semiconductors. I would also like to thank Markus Kuhn for his helpful discussions and Matlab programming.

References

1. Paul Kocher, Joshua Jaffe, Benjamin Jun: Differential Power Analysis. CRYPTO '99, LNCS, Vol. 1666, Springer-Verlag, 1999, pp. 388–397
2. Thomas Messerges, Ezzy Dabbish, Robert Sloan: Investigations of Power Analysis Attacks on Smartcards. USENIX Workshop on Smartcard Technology, Chicago, Illinois, USA, May 10–11, 1999

3. Jean-Sebastien Coron: Resistance against Differential Power Analysis for Elliptic Curve Cryptosystems. Cryptographic Hardware and Embedded Systems Workshop (CHES-1999), LNCS, Vol. 1717, Springer-Verlag, 1999, pp. 292–302

4. Simon Moore, Ross Anderson, Robert Mullins, George Taylor, Jacques Fournier: Balanced Self-Checking Asynchronous Logic for Smart Card Applications. Microprocessors and Microsystems Journal, Vol. 27, No. 9 (October 2003), pp 421–430

5. Thomas Popp, Stefan Mangard: Masked Dual-Rail Pre-charge Logic: DPA-Resistance Without Routing Constraints, Cryptographic Hardware and Embedded Systems Workshop (CHES-2005), LNCS, Vol. 3659, Springer-Verlag, 2005, pp. 172–186

6. Jean-Jacques Quisquater and David Samyde: ElectroMagnetic Analysis (EMA): Measures and Counter-Measures for Smard Cards. Smart Card Programming and Security (E-smart 2001), Cannes, France, LNCS Vol. 2140, Springer-Verlag, 2001, pp. 200–210

7. Sergei Skorobogatov, Ross Anderson: Optical Fault Induction Attacks, Cryptographic Hardware and Embedded Systems Workshop (CHES-2002), LNCS Vol. 2523, Springer-Verlag, 2002, pp. 2–12

8. D.H. Habing: Use of Laser to Simulate Radiation-induced Transients in Semiconductors and Circuits. IEEE Transactions on Nuclear Science, Vol. 12(6), December 1965, pp. 91–100

9. Cheryl Ajluni: Two New Imaging Techniques Promise to Improve IC Defect Identification. Electronic Design, Vol. 43(14), July 1995, pp. 37–38

10. H.K. Heinrich, N. Pakdaman, J.L. Prince, G. Jordy, M. Belaidi, R. Franch, D.C. Edelstein: Optical Detection of Multibit Logic Signals at Internal Nodes in a Flip-chip Mounted Silicon Static Random-Access Memory Integrated Circuit. Journal of Vacuum Science and Technology, Microelectronics and Nanometer Structures, Vol. 10(6), November 1992, pp. 3109–3111

11. Lawrence C. Wagner: Failure Analysis of Integrated Circuits: Tools and Techniques. Kluwer Academic Publishers, 1999

12. Manfred Aigner, Elisabeth Oswald: Power Analysis Tutorial http://www.iaik.tugraz.at/aboutus/people/oswald/papers/dpa_tutorial.pdf

13. Oliver Kömmerling, Markus G. Kuhn: Design Principles for Tamper-Resistant Smartcard Processors. USENIX Workshop on Smartcard Technology, Chicago, Illinois, USA, May 10–11, 1999

14. David Samyde, Sergei Skorobogatov, Ross Anderson, Jean-Jacques Quisquater: On a New Way to Read Data from Memory. SISW2002 First International IEEE Security in Storage Workshop, Greenbelt Marriott, Maryland, USA, December 11, 2002

15. Vladimir V. Belyakov, Alexander I. Chumakov, Alexander Y. Nikiforov, Vyacheslav S. Pershenkov, Peter K. Skorobogatov, A.V. Sogoyan: Prediction of Local and Global Ionization Effects on ICs: The Synergy between Numerical and Physical Simulation. Russian Microelectronics, Vol. 32(2), March 2003, pp. 105–118

16. Microchip PIC16F8X 18-pin Flash/EEPROM 8-Bit Microcontrollers http://ww1.microchip.com/downloads/en/DeviceDoc/30430c.pdf

17. Hagai Bar-El, Hamid Choukri, David Naccache, Michael Tunstall, and Claire Whelan: Workshop on Fault Detection and Tolerance in Cryptography, Florence, Italy, June 30, 2004

18. Semiconductors Research Ltd: Special equipment for semi-invasive hardware security analysis of semiconductors `http://www.semiresearch.com/inc/equipment_for_sale.html`
19. Rita Mayer-Sommer: Smartly Analyzing the Simplicity and the Power of Simple Power Analysis on Smart Cards. Cryptographic Hardware and Embedded Systems (CHES-2000), LNCS Vol. 1965, Springer-Verlag, 2000, pp. 78–92
20. Sergei Skorobogatov: Semi-invasive attacks – A new approach to hardware security analysis. Technical Report UCAM-CL-TR-630, University of Cambridge, Computer Laboratory, April 2005

Pinpointing the Side-Channel Leakage of Masked AES Hardware Implementations[*]

Stefan Mangard[1] and Kai Schramm[2]

[1] Institute for Applied Information Processing and Communciations (IAIK),
Graz University of Technology, Inffeldgasse 16a, 8010 Graz, Austria
[2] Horst Görtz Institute for IT Security (HGI),
Universitätsstr. 150, Ruhr University Bochum, 44780 Bochum, Germany
stefan.mangard@iaik.tugraz.at, schramm@crypto.ruhr-uni-bochum.de

Abstract. This article starts with a discussion of three different attacks on masked AES hardware implementations. This discussion leads to the conclusion that glitches in masked circuits pose the biggest threat to masked hardware implementations in practice. Motivated by this fact, we pinpointed which parts of masked AES S-boxes cause the glitches that lead to side-channel leakage. The analysis reveals that these glitches are caused by the switching characteristics of XOR gates in masked multipliers. Masked multipliers are basic building blocks of most recent proposals for masked AES S-boxes. We subsequently show that the side-channel leakage of the masked multipliers can be prevented by fulfilling timing constraints for $3 \cdot n$ XOR gates in each $GF(2^n)$ multiplier of an AES S-box. We also briefly present two approaches on how these timing constraints can be fulfilled in practice.

Keywords: AES, DPA, Glitches, Zero-Offset DPA, Zero-Input DPA, Masking, Delay Chains.

1 Introduction

The Advanced Encryption Standard (AES) [13] is the most commonly used block cipher in modern applications. This is why there has been a significant effort during the last years to design implementations of this algorithm that are resistant against power analysis attacks [7].

One approach to secure implementations of AES against power analysis attacks is to mask the intermediate values that occur during the execution of the algorithm. Masking schemes for AES have been presented in [2], [22], [5], [11], [3], and [15]. The first two of these schemes have turned out to be susceptible to so-called zero-value attacks [5] and the second one is even susceptible to standard DPA attacks [1]. The third scheme is quite complex to implement and there are no published implementations of this approach so far. The last three schemes are provably secure against DPA attacks and the schemes can also be efficiently

---

[*] The work described in this paper has been supported in part by the European Commission through the IST Programme under Contract IST-2002-507932 ECRYPT.

L. Goubin and M. Matsui (Eds.): CHES 2006, LNCS 4249, pp. 76–90, 2006.

implemented in hardware. This is why these schemes are the most commonly used schemes to secure implementations of AES in hardware.

However, in 2005 several publications have shown that even provably secure masking schemes can be broken in practice, if they are implemented in standard CMOS. The reason for this is that in CMOS circuits a lot of unintended switching activities occur. These unintended switching activities are usually referred to as dynamic hazards or glitches. The effect of glitches on the side-channel resistance of masked circuits has first been analyzed in [8]. A similar analysis has also been presented in [19]. A technique to model the effect of glitches on the side-channel resistance of circuits has been published in [20]. The fact that glitches can indeed make circuits susceptible to DPA attacks in practice was finally shown in [9].

After the publication of these articles it was clear that considering the effect of glitches is crucial when implementing masking schemes in hardware. However, one important question has remained unanswered so far. The existing articles only show that implementations of masking schemes leak side-channel information. They do not pinpoint the exact gates or parts of the masked circuits that account for the leakage. In [9] for example, it has been shown that a CMOS implementation of [15] can be attacked because of glitches. However, it is not clear which gates within the masked S-box implementation actually account for this fact.

The current article answers this question by performing a close analysis of masked multipliers which are the basis of masking schemes such as [11], [15], and [3]. In fact, we show that the switching characteristics of the XOR gates in these multipliers account for the side-channel leakage. This insight and the fact how this insight can be used to develop DPA-resistant implementations of masking schemes constitute the main contribution of this article.

However, before we start our analysis of the masked multipliers, Sect. 2 first briefly recapitulates the different DPA attacks on masked AES hardware implementations that have been published recently. In particular, this section compares the attack presented in [9] with the zero-offset DPA attack presented in [23]. Both attacks are performed on a masked AES hardware implementation according to [15]. The comparison turns out that the first attack is significantly more effective. In fact, we are even able to show that a much simpler power model of the masked S-box leads to successful attacks as well.

Motivated by this fact Sect. 3 analyzes which parts of the AES S-box actually cause the side-channel leakage. As already pointed out, this analysis leads to the conclusion that the XOR gates within the masked multipliers of the AES S-box account for the leakage. This insight is used in Sect. 4 to present new approaches in order to securely implement masking schemes. Sect. 5 summarizes the most important results of this article and provides some conclusions.

2   Attacks on Masked AES Hardware Implementations

This section discusses results of three DPA attacks against a masked AES hardware implementation. The device under attack was an AES ASIC that is based on the masking scheme that has been proposed in [15]. The chip uses a 32-bit architecture and hence the computation of one AES round takes four clock cycles, and a complete AES encryption takes 40 clock cycles. All of our DPA attacks are based on a set of 1,000,000 power traces which we collected from the masked AES chip. The traces have been measured at 1 GS/s using a differential probe.

The first attack we discuss is the zero-offset DPA (ZODPA) as proposed in [23]. This attack requires that masks and masked data of the attacked device leak simultaneously and it uses squaring as a preprocessing step. Subsequently, we discuss a DPA attack based on a toggle-count power model of a masked S-box of our chip. This attack has been performed in the same way as it has been proposed in [9]. Finally, we present a simplification of this attack, which we refer to as zero-input DPA. This attack is based on the fact that the power consumption of our masked AES S-box implementation has a significant minimum for the case that the mask and the masked input are equal.

2.1   Zero-Offset DPA

Zero-offset DPA was originally proposed by Waddle *et al.* in [23] and it represents a special case of second-order DPA [10,6,14,18]. This can be shown as follows. Let us assume the power consumption at time t_0 of the attacked device can be described as

$$P(t_0) = \epsilon \cdot (W(M) + W(Y)) + N \tag{1}$$

where $W(M)$ represents the Hamming weight of a random mask M, $W(Y)$ represents the Hamming weight of key-dependent data masked by M, ϵ is a constant of proportionality, and N represents additive Gaussian noise. When squaring this power signal, it can be observed that a zero-offset DPA is essentially equivalent to a second-order DPA. Both attacks rely on the term $W(M) \cdot W(Y)$.

$$P^2(t_0) = \epsilon^2 \cdot (W(M) + W(Y))^2 + 2 \cdot \epsilon \cdot (W(M) + W(Y)) \cdot N + N^2 \tag{2}$$
$$= \epsilon^2 \cdot \left(W^2(M) + 2 \cdot W(M) \cdot W(Y) + W^2(Y)\right)$$
$$+ 2 \cdot \epsilon \cdot (W(M) + W(Y)) \cdot N + N^2 \tag{3}$$

However, zero-offset DPA can only be used, if the mask and the masked data are processed simultaneously. While this scenario is unlikely to happen in masked software implementations, it commonly occurs in masked hardware implementations. In particular, it also occurs in our attacked AES ASIC and hence a zero-offset DPA should theoretically be possible. Consequently, we have squared our power traces and have computed the correlation coefficient between the squared traces and corresponding hypotheses. However, even with 1,000,000 measurements we have not been able to perform a successful zero-offset DPA.

2.2   Toggle-Count DPA

In conventional CMOS circuits, signal lines typically toggle several times during a clock cycle. In [8] it has been shown that the total number of signal toggles in

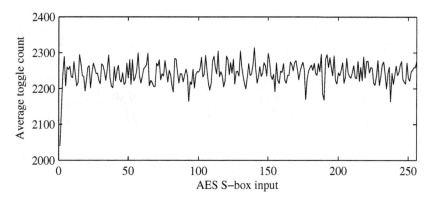

Fig. 1. Average number of toggles in our masked S-box circuit

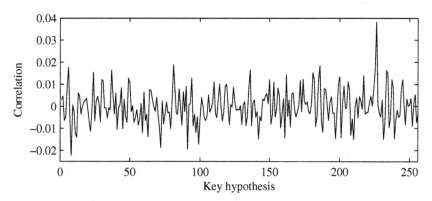

Fig. 2. Correlation coefficients of the toggle-count DPA against the masked AES ASIC with 15,000 measurements. The correct key hypothesis (225) is clearly distinguishable from all false key hypotheses.

masked non-linear gates, *e.g.* in masked AND or masked OR gates, is correlated to the unmasked input and output signals. This fact has been exploited in a simulated DPA attack.

A similar approach has been pursued in [9] to break masked AES hardware implementations in practice. A back-annotated netlist of the attacked device has been used in order to derive a toggle-count model of masked AES S-boxes. Subsequently, these models were used in DPA attacks to reveal the secret key of an AES chip[1].

In order to confirm these results, we have performed these attacks on our masked ASIC implementation again. We have first simulated our chip to determine the

---

[1] Note that the toggle-count model assumes that each signal toggle has an equal contribution to the power consumption. This condition is typically not met in real life. Nevertheless, the model is usually sufficient mount successful DPA attacks on masked implementations.

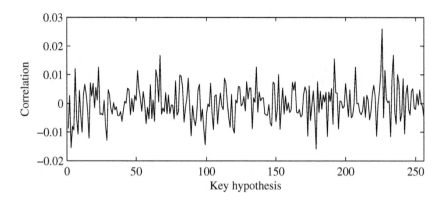

Fig. 3. Correlation coefficients of a zero-input DPA against the masked AES ASIC with 30,000 measurements. The correct key hypothesis (225) is clearly distinguishable from the false correlation coefficients.

average number of toggles that occur in our masked AES S-box for different data inputs. The power model of our S-box is shown in Fig. 1. In this figure, the number of toggles of our masked S-box are shown for all possible 256 S-box inputs. Please note that there occurs a distinct minimum for S-box input 0, $i.e.$ the case when mask and masked data are equal.

We have used the power model shown in Fig. 1 to mount a DPA attack on our masked AES chip. We have correlated the measured power traces of our masked AES implementation with hypotheses based on the power model. In this attack, we have obtained a correlation coefficient of $r = 0.04$ for the correct key hypothesis using $1,000,000$ measurements. Approximately $15,000$ measurements were necessary to distinguish this correlation coefficient from the false correlation coefficients. The correlation coefficients for an attack based on $15,000$ measurements are shown in Fig. 2.

2.3 Zero-Input DPA

As shown in Fig. 1, the simulated masked AES S-box has a significant power consumption minimum, if the S-box input $x = x_m \oplus m_x = 0$. This significant minimum suggests that it should also be possible to perform DPA attacks that just exploit this property. Hence, we have adapted our power model of the S-box to the following much simpler model $P(x)$.

$$
\begin{aligned}
P(x) &= 0 & if \quad x &= 0 \\
&= 1 & if \quad x &\neq 0
\end{aligned}
$$

Using this generic zero-input power model we have repeated our attack based on the same set of power traces. We have obtained a correlation coefficient of $r = 0.022$ for the correct key hypothesis. About $30,000$ measurements were necessary to clearly distinguish this correlation coefficient from the ones of false key hypotheses. Fig. 3 shows the result of an attack based on $30,000$ measurements.

The number of measurements that are needed for a zero-input DPA is greater compared to the attack based on the more precise power model. However, the attack is still feasible and it is much more effective than a zero-offset DPA attack. The biggest advantage of the zero-input DPA over the two other attacks we have discussed, is that the zero-input DPA does not require detailed knowledge about the attacked device and it is still very effective. It exploits the fact that the power consumption of the masked S-box implementation has a significant minimum for the input value zero. In the following section, we analyze why implementations of masked S-boxes actually leak side-channel information and we pinpoint where the side-channel leakage is caused.

3   Pinpointing the Side-Channel Leakage of Masked S-boxes

The masked AES S-box implementation we have attacked in the previous section is based on composite field arithmetic. In fact, most recent proposals for masked AES S-boxes (see [11], [15], and [3]) are based on this approach. Masked AES S-boxes of this kind essentially consist of an affine transformation, isomorphic mappings, adders and multipliers. All these elements except for the multipliers are linear and hence it is easy to mask them additively. An additive masking of a linear operation can be done by simply performing the operation separately for the masked data and the mask.

In hardware, masked linear operations are usually implemented by two completely separate circuits. One circuit performs the linear operation for the masked data and one circuit performs the linear operation for the corresponding mask. There is no shared signal line between these two circuits. Therefore, the power consumption P_1 of the first circuit exclusively depends on the masked data and the power consumption P_2 of the second circuit exclusively depends on the mask. According the definition of additive masking [2], the masked data and the mask are pairwise statistically independent from the corresponding unmasked data. Hence, P_1 and P_2 are also pairwise independent from the unmasked data.

In practice this means that an attacker who does not know the mask can not perform a successful first-order DPA attack on the power consumption of either of these two circuits. An attacker can only formulate hypotheses about unmasked intermediate values of the performed cryptographic algorithm. In this article, we denote the set of all unmasked intermediate values of the attacked algorithm as $\mathcal{H}$. Our previous argumentation hence formally means that $\rho(H, P_1)$ and $\rho(H, P_2)$ are both 0 for all $H \epsilon \mathcal{H}$. This also implies that the total power consumption is uncorrelated to all intermediate values, *i.e.* $\rho(H, P_1 + P_2) = 0 \ \forall H \epsilon \mathcal{H}$. Throughout this article, we use the common assumption that the total power consumption of a circuit is the sum of the power consumption of its components. Using this assumption, it is clear that the linear elements of a masked S-box do not account for the side-channel leakage we have observed in the toggle-count and zero-input DPA attacks presented in Sect. 2. As the power traces are not pre-processed in these attacks, the side-channel leakage can only be caused by the non-linear elements, *i.e.* the multipliers which combine masks and masked data.

In general, there exist several approaches to mask a multiplier. However, there is also one very common approach. Fig. 4 shows the architecture of a masked $GF(2^n)$ multiplier according this common approach. The multiplier takes two masked inputs a_m and b_m that are masked with m_a and m_b, respectively. The output q_m is the product of the corresponding unmasked values a and b masked with m_q.

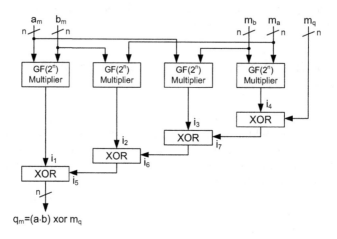

Fig. 4. Common architecture of a masked multiplier

The masked multiplier consists of four unmasked multipliers that calculate the intermediate values $i_1 \ldots i_4$. These intermediate values are then summed by $4 \cdot n$ XOR gates. A masked multiplier of this kind has been used as a masked AND gate ($n = 1$) in [21]. Furthermore, this architecture is also used in the masked S-boxes presented in [11], [3], and [15]. This is why we now analyze this architecture more closely. We start our analysis by first looking at a masked AND gate ($n = 1$). Subsequently, we look at multipliers in $GF(2^2)$ and $GF(2^4)$. Finally, we look at the side-channel leakage of masked S-boxes as a whole that contain several such masked multipliers.

3.1 Masked AND Gate

Masked AND gates that are based on the architecture shown in Fig. 4 have already previously been analyzed in [8] and [20]. These analyses have revealed that such gates indeed leak side-channel information. However, in neither of these publications the source of the leakage has been pinpointed exactly. Both publications essentially state that there occurs leakage due to timing properties.

Yet, these properties are not analyzed further. In the current article, we pinpoint the exact cause of the side-channel leakage.

For this purpose we have implemented a masked AND gate based on the architecture shown in Fig. 4. We have then simulated the back-annotated netlist of this gate for all possible input transitions. There are five input signals and hence there are 2^{10} possible input transitions[2]. For each of these 2^{10} cases we have counted the number of transitions that occur on each signal line in the design. We denote the these numbers of transitions with $T(a_m)$, $T(b_m)$, $T(m_a)$, $T(m_b)$, $T(m_q)$, $T(q_m)$, and $T(i_1) \ldots T(i_7)$.

In order to analyze which signal lines account for the side-channel leakage of the gate, we have calculated the correlation between these numbers on the one hand and the unmasked values a, b and q on the other hand. Due to the masking $T(a_m)$, $T(b_m)$, $T(m_a)$, $T(m_b)$, and $T(m_q)$ do not leak side-channel information. Furthermore, it turns out that also $\rho(T(i_j), a) = 0$, $\rho(T(i_j), b) = 0$ and $\rho(T(i_j), q) = 0$ for $j = 1 \ldots 4$. This result is actually not surprising. The four multipliers (the four AND gates in case of $n = 1$) never take a masked value and a corresponding mask as input. For example, there is no multiplier that takes a_m and m_a as input. Each pair of inputs of the multipliers is not only pairwise independent of a, b and q, but it is completely statistically independent of these values. Therefore, also the power consumption of the multipliers and their outputs are independent of a, b and q. The side-channel leakage can only be caused by the XOR gates.

At first sight this might seem counter-intuitive because the number of transitions that occur at the output of an XOR gate intuitively correspond to the sum of transitions that occur at the inputs of the gate. Each input transition should lead to one output transition. The number of input transitions does not leak side-channel information and hence also the number of output transitions should not. Unfortunately, this reasoning is wrong in practice.

It is true that an XOR gate usually switches its output each time an input signal switches. However, the gate does not switch its output, if both input signals switch simultaneously or within a short period of time. In this case, the input transitions are "absorbed" by the XOR gate and not propagated further. Exactly this effect accounts for the side-channel leakage of the masked AND gate. Our simulations have shown that the number of absorbed transitions is indeed correlated to a, b and q. This means that the arrival times of the input signals at the XOR gates depend on the unmasked values. It is the joint distribution of the arrival times of the signals $i_1 \ldots i_4$ that causes the side-channel leakage of the gate. The arrival times are different for different unmasked values and hence a different number of transitions is absorbed. This in turn leads to a different power consumption.

It is important to point out that it is exclusively this effect that accounts for the side-channel leakage of the masked AND gate. If each XOR gate would switch its output as often as its inputs switch, the gate would be secure. This is a consequence of the fact that $T(i_1) \ldots T(i_4)$ are uncorrelated to a, b and q.

---

[2] In our simulation all input signals are set at the same time.

3.2   Masked Multipliers for $GF(2^2)$ and $GF(2^4)$

In order to confirm the insights gained from the analysis of the masked AND gate, we have also implemented masked multipliers for $GF(2^2)$ and $GF(2^4)$. Multipliers of this kind are used in the masked AES S-boxes of [11], [3], and [15]. As in the case of the masked AND gates, we have performed different simulations based on back-annotated netlists of these multipliers.

First, we have confirmed that $T(i_1) \ldots T(i_4)$ are indeed independent of a, b and q. This analysis was actually just done for sake of completeness. From a theoretical point of view it is clear that the power consumption of the four multipliers shown in Fig. 4 is independent of the unmasked values. As already pointed out before, the inputs of each multiplier are completely statistically independent from the unmasked values. This fact is independent of the bit width of the multipliers.

In the second step, we have again analyzed the switching characteristics of the XOR gates. Our simulations have confirmed that the number of absorbed transitions depends on the unmasked values a, b and q—exactly as in the case of the masked AND gate. The side-channel leakage of all masked multipliers that are based on the architecture shown in Fig. 4 is obviously caused by the same effect.

However, unfortunately it is not possible to make a general statement on how much information such masked multipliers leak. The fact how many transitions are absorbed by the XOR gates depends on many implementation details. The arrival times of the signals at the XOR gates strongly depend on the placement and routing of the circuit. Of course also the used CMOS library has a strong impact. The library affects the timing of the input signals and it also determines how big the delay between two input transitions of an XOR gate has to be in order propagate.

Based on our experiments, we can make one general statement. We have implemented several masked multipliers and we have also placed and routed them several times. In all cases, we have observed side-channel leakage. In order to prevent that the XOR gates absorb transitions, it is therefore necessary to explicitly take care of this issue during the design process (see Sect. 4).

3.3   Masked AES S-boxes

Masked AES S-boxes as they are presented in [11], [15], [3] contain several masked multipliers. We now analyze two concrete implementations of masked AES S-boxes in order to check how the side-channel leakage of the multipliers affects the other components of the S-boxes. We first analyze an implementation of the AES S-box proposed in [15] and then we look at an implementation of [11].

Masked S-box of Oswald *et al.* The first step of our analysis was to generate a back-annotated netlist of the masked AES S-box described in [15]. Subsequently, we have simulated this netlist for $200,000$ randomly selected input transitions. During these simulations, we have counted the number of transitions that occur on each of the internal signal lines of the S-box. Based on these numbers it was possible to determine which signal lines cause the most side-channel leakage.

As expected, all the linear operations that are performed at the beginning of the S-box do not leak any information. The transitions that occur on the corresponding signal lines are independent of the unmasked S-box input. The first leakage within the S-box occurs in the first masked multiplier. The XOR gates of this multiplier absorb a different number of transitions for different data inputs. The number of transitions that occur on the output signal of the masked multiplier is therefore correlated to the unmasked version of the S-box input.

The fact that the switching activity of this signal is correlated to the unmasked S-box input has severe consequences for all components that use this signal as input. The switching activity of all these components typically also becomes correlated to the unmasked S-box input[3]. This holds true for linear and non-linear components. Therefore, the leakage that is caused by the first masked multiplier spreads out like an avalanche through the remaining S-box.

This leakage is additionally amplified by the leakage of all other masked multipliers in the S-box. In fact, the leakage continuously grows on its way through the S-box. In case of our S-box implementation of [15] this leads to the power consumption characteristic we have already shown in Fig. 1. A different amount of transitions occurs for every unmasked S-box input. A significant minimum for the number of transitions occurs for the case that the input value is 0. In this case, the masked S-box input and the corresponding mask are equal. The arrival times of the signals in the masked multipliers are more uniform in this case than in all other cases. Therefore, more transitions are absorbed by the XOR gates and also less transitions propagate through the components that are connected to the multipliers.

Masked S-box of Morioka and Akishita. We have also analyzed the masked AES S-box proposed by Morioka and Akishita in [11]. The architecture of this S-box is based on the unmasked S-box proposed by Satoh *et al.* in [17]. As in the case of the masked S-box by Oswald *et al.* [15] we have first generated a back-annotated netlist of the design. Subsequently, we have simulated 200,000 random input transitions and we have counted the number of transitions for each signal line. Again, we have noticed that the total number of transitions in the masked S-box circuit is clearly correlated to the unmasked S-box input. As a matter of fact, we were able to successfully mount a simulated zero-input attack on this masked S-box. The attack only required a few thousand simulated power traces, *i.e.* simulations of transition counts. This result also confirms our aforementioned claim that a precise power model of a masked S-box implemented in CMOS is not always necessary to successfully perform a DPA attack.

In order to investigate why the number of toggles has a minimum, if the mask and the masked input are equal, we have evaluated transition count data of

---

[3] There are of course also gates that do not propagate the leakage. For example, the output signal of a NAND gate that is connected to a leaking signal on input one and to 0 on input two does not leak any information. However, there are typically sufficient gates connected to a leaking signal that at least some of the gates propagate the leakage.

various S-box subcircuits. We have then performed zero-input attacks against these subcircuits. Exactly as in the case of the masked S-box by Oswald *et al.* we have found out that glitches are absorbed in XOR gates of a masked finite field multiplier. Our analysis has confirmed that the number of absorbed transitions is again correlated to the unmasked S-box input and that there is a significant power consumption minimum for input 0. The masked S-box of Morioka and Akishita is highly symmetric with regard to the signal paths of the mask and the masked input. This symmetry seems to be the main reason why transitions are absorbed by the XOR gates, if the mask and the masked input are equal.

In general, it is difficult to make a general statement on whether all masked S-boxes have a significant minimum of the power consumption for the case that the input is 0. Many implementation details influence the exact switching characteristic of an S-box. However, based on our observations we assume that most masked S-boxes are vulnerable to zero-input attacks.

4   Countermeasures

In the previous section, we have analyzed the side-channel leakage of masked multipliers that are based on the architecture shown in Fig. 4. It has turned out that the XOR gates summing the outputs of the four unmasked multipliers of this architecture, account for the side-channel leakage. These XOR gates absorb transitions and the number of absorbed transitions is correlated to the unmasked operands of the masked multiplier.

In Sect. 3, we have already pointed out that it is exclusively this absorbtion that causes the side-channel leakage. A masked multiplier is secure against DPA attacks, if no transitions are absorbed by the XOR gates. This means that the number of transitions at the output of an XOR gate needs to be equal to the total number of transitions occurring at the inputs. A masked multiplier that implements XOR gates in this way is secure. The transitions of the signal lines $i_1 \ldots i_4$ are uncorrelated to a, b and q. If the XOR gates propagate these transitions to the output q_m without any absorbtion, the whole multiplier is secure.

In a masked $GF(2^n)$ multiplier, there are $4 \cdot n$ XOR gates that sum the signals $i_1 \ldots i_4$ and m_q. When looking at Fig. 4, it is clear that the n XOR gates that sum i_4 and m_q, are actually not critical. The input signals of these gates depend on mask values only and hence the absorbed number of transitions of these gates cannot depend on a, b or q. As a consequence, there are actually only $3 \cdot n$ XOR gates in a masked multiplier that must not absorb any transitions. These are the gates summing i_1, i_2, i_3 and i_7. Preventing an absorbtion at these gates means that the inputs of these gates must not arrive simultaneously or within the propagation delay of the XOR gate. This is the timing constraint that needs to be fulfilled by the input signals.

In general, timing constraints are quite challenging to fulfill in practice. However, there exist two approaches that can be used to reach this goal. The first approach is to insert delay elements into the paths of the input signals of the XOR gate. A similar approach has actually already been used in [12] to reduce the power consumption of an unmasked AES S-box. In case of a masked multiplier, delay elements need be inserted into the lines i_1, i_2 and i_3 in such a way that the timing constraints for the XOR gates are fulfilled. We have successfully implemented a secure $GF(2)$ multiplier based on this approach. Simulations of this multiplier have confirmed that the transitions of all signal lines in the design are indeed independent of a, b and q.

However, it is important to point out that it is not always possible to efficiently fulfill the timing constraints of the XOR gates by inserting delay elements. For our masked multiplier we have assumed that all masked input signals arrive at the same time. However, the arrival times of the operands at a masked multiplier can vary significantly, if the multiplier is not connected to flip flops directly. If the multiplier is part of a long combinational path, the approach of inserting delay elements is usually not the best one to fulfill the timing constraints.

An alternative to inserting delay elements is to use enable signals in the circuit. The basic idea of this approach is to generate enable signals by a dedicated circuit that enable the inputs of the critical XOR gates just at the right time. Enable signals of this kind have for example also been used in [19] to control the switching activity of masked gates. Of course, the generation of enable signals requires a certain effort and it increases the design costs.

However, building secure masked circuits is always associated with costs. The proposal for secure masked gates presented in [4] is also associated with timing constraints that need to be fulfilled when building a masked circuit. One approach for secure masked circuits without timing constraints has been presented in [16]. However, this approach requires a pre-charging phase and hence the throughput of such implementations is halved compared to standard CMOS circuits.

5   Conclusions

In the first part of this article, we have presented results of three different DPA attacks on a masked AES ASIC implementation. One of these attacks was a simplification of the attack presented in [9]. Comparing this attack with zero-offset DPA has turned out that glitches are indeed the biggest problem of masked hardware implementations of AES. Motivated by this fact, we have pinpointed which parts of masked AES S-boxes cause glitches that lead to side-channel leakage. Our analysis has turned out that the glitches are caused by switching characteristics of XOR gates in masked multipliers.

We have subsequently shown that the side-channel leakage can be prevented by fulfilling timing constraints for $3 \cdot n$ XOR gates in each $GF(2^n)$ multiplier of an AES S-box. In practice, these timing constraints can essentially be fulfilled by two approaches: the insertion of delay elements and the usage of enable signals.

Acknowledgements

The authors would like to thank Elisabeth Oswald, Takashi Wanatabe, and Takashi Endo for the very helpful discussions.

References

1. Mehdi-Laurent Akkar, Régis Bevan, and Louis Goubin. Two Power Analysis Attacks against One-Mask Methods. In Bimal K. Roy and Willi Meier, editors, *Fast Software Encryption, 11th International Workshop, FSE 2004, Delhi, India, February 5-7, 2004, Revised Papers*, volume 3017 of *Lecture Notes in Computer Science*, pages 332–347. Springer, 2004.
2. Mehdi-Laurent Akkar and Christophe Giraud. An Implementation of DES and AES, Secure against Some Attacks. In Çetin Kaya Koç, David Naccache, and Christof Paar, editors, *Cryptographic Hardware and Embedded Systems – CHES 2001, Third International Workshop, Paris, France, May 14-16, 2001, Proceedings*, volume 2162 of *Lecture Notes in Computer Science*, pages 309–318. Springer, 2001.
3. Johannes Blömer, Jorge Guajardo, and Volker Krummel. Provably Secure Masking of AES. In Helena Handschuh and M. Anwar Hasan, editors, *Selected Areas in Cryptography, 11th International Workshop, SAC 2004, Waterloo, Canada, August 9-10, 2004, Revised Selected Papers*, volume 3357 of *Lecture Notes in Computer Science*, pages 69–83. Springer, 2005.
4. Wieland Fischer and Berndt M. Gammel. Masking at Gate Level in the Presence of Glitches. In Josyula R. Rao and Berk Sunar, editors, *Cryptographic Hardware and Embedded Systems – CHES 2005, 7th International Workshop, Edinburgh, Scotland, August 29 - September 1, 2005, Proceedings*, volume 3659 of *Lecture Notes in Computer Science*, pages 187–200. Springer, 2005.
5. Jovan D. Golić and Christophe Tymen. Multiplicative Masking and Power Analysis of AES. In Burton S. Kaliski Jr., Çetin Kaya Koç, and Christof Paar, editors, *Cryptographic Hardware and Embedded Systems – CHES 2002, 4th International Workshop, Redwood Shores, CA, USA, August 13-15, 2002, Revised Papers*, volume 2535 of *Lecture Notes in Computer Science*, pages 198–212. Springer, 2003.
6. Marc Joye, Pascal Paillier, and Berry Schoenmakers. On Second-Order Differential Power Analysis. In Josyula R. Rao and Berk Sunar, editors, *Cryptographic Hardware and Embedded Systems – CHES 2005, 7th International Workshop, Edinburgh, UK, August 29 - September 1, 2005, Proceedings*, volume 3659 of *Lecture Notes in Computer Science*, pages 293–308. Springer, 2005.
7. Paul C. Kocher, Joshua Jaffe, and Benjamin Jun. Differential Power Analysis. In Michael Wiener, editor, *Advances in Cryptology - CRYPTO '99, 19th Annual International Cryptology Conference, Santa Barbara, California, USA, August 15-19, 1999, Proceedings*, volume 1666 of *Lecture Notes in Computer Science*, pages 388–397. Springer, 1999.
8. Stefan Mangard, Thomas Popp, and Berndt M. Gammel. Side-Channel Leakage of Masked CMOS Gates. In Alfred Menezes, editor, *Topics in Cryptology - CT-RSA 2005, The Cryptographers' Track at the RSA Conference 2005, San Francisco, CA, USA, February 14-18, 2005, Proceedings*, volume 3376 of *Lecture Notes in Computer Science*, pages 351–365. Springer, 2005.
9. Stefan Mangard, Norbert Pramstaller, and Elisabeth Oswald. Successfully Attacking Masked AES Hardware Implementations. In Josyula R. Rao and Berk Sunar, editors, *Cryptographic Hardware and Embedded Systems – CHES 2005, 7th International Workshop, Edinburgh, Scotland, August 29 - September 1, 2005, Proceedings*, volume 3659 of *Lecture Notes in Computer Science*, pages 157–171. Springer, 2005.

10. Thomas S. Messerges. Using Second-Order Power Analysis to Attack DPA Resistant Software. In Çetin Kaya Koç and Christof Paar, editors, *Cryptographic Hardware and Embedded Systems – CHES 2000, Second International Workshop, Worcester, MA, USA, August 17-18, 2000, Proceedings*, volume 1965 of *Lecture Notes in Computer Science*, pages 238–251. Springer, 2000.

11. Sumio Morioka and Toru Akishita. A DPA-resistant Compact AES S-Box Circuit using Additive Mask. In *Computer Security Composium (CSS), October 16, 2004, Proceedings*, pages 679–684, September 2004. (in Japanese only).

12. Sumio Morioka and Akashi Satoh. An Optimized S-Box Circuit Architecture for Low Power AES Design. In Burton S. Kaliski Jr., Çetin Kaya Koç, and Christof Paar, editors, *Cryptographic Hardware and Embedded Systems – CHES 2002, 4th International Workshop, Redwood Shores, CA, USA, August 13-15, 2002, Revised Papers*, volume 2535 of *Lecture Notes in Computer Science*, pages 172–186. Springer, 2003.

13. National Institute of Standards and Technology (NIST). FIPS-197: Advanced Encryption Standard, November 2001. Available online at http://www.itl.nist.gov/fipspubs/.

14. Elisabeth Oswald, Stefan Mangard, Christoph Herbst, and Stefan Tillich. Practical Second-Order DPA Attacks for Masked Smart Card Implementations of Block Ciphers. In David Pointcheval, editor, *Topics in Cryptology - CT-RSA 2006, The Cryptographers' Track at the RSA Conference 2006, San Jose, CA, USA, February 13-17, 2006, Proceedings*, volume 3860 of *Lecture Notes in Computer Science*, pages 192–207. Springer, 2006.

15. Elisabeth Oswald, Stefan Mangard, Norbert Pramstaller, and Vincent Rijmen. A Side-Channel Analysis Resistant Description of the AES S-box. In Henri Gilbert and Helena Handschuh, editors, *Fast Software Encryption, 12th International Workshop, FSE 2005, Paris, France, February 21-23, 2005, Proceedings*, volume 3557 of *Lecture Notes in Computer Science*, pages 413–423. Springer, 2005.

16. Thomas Popp and Stefan Mangard. Masked Dual-Rail Pre-Charge Logic: DPA-Resistance without Routing Constraints. In Josyula R. Rao and Berk Sunar, editors, *Cryptographic Hardware and Embedded Systems – CHES 2005, 7th International Workshop, Edinburgh, Scotland, August 29 - September 1, 2005, Proceedings*, volume 3659 of *Lecture Notes in Computer Science*, pages 172–186. Springer, 2005.

17. Akashi Satoh, Sumio Morioka, Kohji Takano, and Seiji Munetoh. A Compact Rijndael Hardware Architecture with S-Box Optimization. In Colin Boyd, editor, *Advances in Cryptology - ASIACRYPT 2001, 7th International Conference on the Theory and Application of Cryptology and Information Security, Gold Coast, Australia, December 9-13, 2001, Proceedings*, volume 2248 of *Lecture Notes in Computer Science*, pages 239–254. Springer, 2001.

18. Kai Schramm and Christof Paar. Higher Order Masking of the AES. In David Pointcheval, editor, *Topics in Cryptology - CT-RSA 2006, The Cryptographers' Track at the RSA Conference 2006, San Jose, CA, USA, February 13-17, 2006, Proceedings*, volume 3860 of *Lecture Notes in Computer Science*, pages 208–225. Springer, 2006.

19. Daisuke Suzuki, Minoru Saeki, and Tetsuya Ichikawa. Random Switching Logic: A Countermeasure against DPA based on Transition Probability. Cryptology ePrint Archive (http://eprint.iacr.org/), Report 2004/346, 2004.

20. Daisuke Suzuki, Minoru Saeki, and Tetsuya Ichikawa. DPA Leakage Models for CMOS Logic Circuits. In Josyula R. Rao and Berk Sunar, editors, *Cryptographic Hardware and Embedded Systems – CHES 2005, 7th International Workshop, Edinburgh, UK, August 29 - September 1, 2005, Proceedings*, volume 3659 of *Lecture Notes in Computer Science*, pages 366–382. Springer, 2005.

21. Elena Trichina, Tymur Korkishko, and Kyung-Hee Lee. Small Size, Low Power, Side Channel-Immune AES Coprocessor: Design and Synthesis Results. In Hans Dobbertin, Vincent Rijmen, and Aleksandra Sowa, editors, *Advanced Encryption Standard - AES, 4th International Conference, AES 2004, Bonn, Germany, May 10-12, 2004, Revised Selected and Invited Papers*, volume 3373 of *Lecture Notes in Computer Science*, pages 113–127. Springer, 2005.

22. Elena Trichina, Domenico De Seta, and Lucia Germani. Simplified Adaptive Multiplicative Masking for AES. In Burton S. Kaliski Jr., Çetin Kaya Koç, and Christof Paar, editors, *Cryptographic Hardware and Embedded Systems – CHES 2002, 4th International Workshop, Redwood Shores, CA, USA, August 13-15, 2002, Revised Papers*, volume 2535 of *Lecture Notes in Computer Science*, pages 187–197. Springer, 2003.

23. Jason Waddle and David Wagner. Towards Efficient Second-Order Power Analysis. In Marc Joye and Jean-Jacques Quisquater, editors, *Cryptographic Hardware and Embedded Systems – CHES 2004, 6th International Workshop, Cambridge, MA, USA, August 11-13, 2004, Proceedings*, volume 3156 of *Lecture Notes in Computer Science*, pages 1–15. Springer, 2004.

A Generalized Method of Differential Fault Attack Against AES Cryptosystem

Amir Moradi[1], Mohammad T. Manzuri Shalmani[1],
and Mahmoud Salmasizadeh[2]

[1] Department of Computer Engineering, Sharif University of Technology,
Azadi St., Tehran, Iran
[2] Electronic Research Center, Sharif University of Technology,
Azadi St., Tehran, Iran
a_moradi@ce.sharif.edu, {manzuri, salmasi}@sharif.edu

Abstract. In this paper we describe two differential fault attack techniques against Advanced Encryption Standard (AES). We propose two models for fault occurrence; we could find all 128 bits of key using one of them and only 6 faulty ciphertexts. We need approximately 1500 faulty ciphertexts to discover the key with the other fault model. Union of these models covers all faults that can occur in the 9th round of encryption algorithm of AES-128 cryptosystem. One of main advantage of proposed fault models is that any fault in the AES encryption from start (*AddRoundKey* with the main key before the first round) to *MixColumns* function of 9th round can be modeled with one of our fault models. These models cover all states, so generated differences caused by diverse plaintexts or ciphertexts can be supposed as faults and modeled with our models. It establishes a novel technique to cryptanalysis AES without side channel information. The major difference between these methods and previous ones is on the assumption of fault models. Our proposed fault models use very common and general assumption for locations and values of occurred faults.

Keywords: AES, Fault Attacks, Smart Card, Side Channel Attacks, Cryptanalysis.

1 Introduction

At first, Boneh, Demillo and Lipton in 1997 indicated using computational errors occurred during execution of cryptographic algorithm can help to break it and find the secret key [1]. This idea was applicable only on public key cryptosystems and they presented successful results to discover the secret key of a RSA implementation. Subsequently, Biham and Shamir extended this idea for applying it on implementations of symmetric block ciphers such as DES [2] and introduced Differential Fault Attack (DFA) concept. DFAs are powerful and applicable against cryptographic hardwares specially on smart cards.

Many activities have been done on employing DFA to AES implementations by several researches and some methods were introduced [3,5,4,6]. All previous

L. Goubin and M. Matsui (Eds.): CHES 2006, LNCS 4249, pp. 91–100, 2006.

techniques assumed very specific models for fault location and value. Using these methods, such attacks in real world is applicable only with sophisticated equipments such as narrow Laser beam. The most of the results appeared in these papers are simulation based [3,4], however the second attack of [5] was put into practice. In this paper we present two general models for fault occurrence in AES cryptosystem which neither of them needs any sophisticated equipment. The first model covers 1.55% of all possible faults between the beginning of AES-128 and the input of *MixColumns* in round 9, and the reminder (98.45% of them) are covered with the second one. We should emphasize that these models do not cover faults induced during the Key Scheduling as well as safe-errors attacks described in [3]. But in previous methods coverage rate of fault models were tiny. For example, fault models in [4,5] cover approximately $2.4 \times 10^{-5}\%$ of all possible faults induced at input of *MixColumns* in round 9. Therefore, these attacks are applicable with special equipments for injecting certain faults in desired locations. However, our proposed methods could be implemented by power supply disturbance or glitch in clock pulse.

The rest of this paper organized as follows: we explain both of fault models and illustrate their coverage in section 2. The next section describes algorithm of the proposed attack using presented fault models. Section 4 presents simulation results of the proposed attack. In section 5 we show how we can use proposed methods for breaking AES cryptosystem without fault injection. We will show how the AES encryption will be broken only by changing assumptions. Finally section 6 concludes the paper.

2   Proposed Fault Models

In AES with 128-bit key, faults may occur in any function, i.e. *SubBytes*, *ShiftRows*, *MixColumns* and *AddRoundKey*, of each 10 rounds. Some previous works [4,5] assumed faults occur in the input of *MixColumns* of the 9th round. Figure 1 shows the last two rounds of AES encryption algorithm, for more information see [7]. We assumed any type of fault appears as a random data to be added to the original data.

Suppose that only one byte of column 1 of input of *MixColumns* is influenced by fault then, 4 bytes of its output will change. Let M stands for *MixColumns* and considering the fact that *MixColumns* operates on each column independently, then equations (1) to (4) could be summarized as equation (5).

$$M\left(A \oplus \begin{bmatrix} e\,0\,0\,0 \\ 0\,0\,0\,0 \\ 0\,0\,0\,0 \\ 0\,0\,0\,0 \end{bmatrix}\right) = M\left(A\right) \oplus \begin{bmatrix} 2 \bullet e\,0\,0\,0 \\ e\quad 0\,0\,0 \\ e\quad 0\,0\,0 \\ 3 \bullet e\,0\,0\,0 \end{bmatrix} \qquad (1)$$

$$M\left(A \oplus \begin{bmatrix} 0\,0\,0\,0 \\ e\,0\,0\,0 \\ 0\,0\,0\,0 \\ 0\,0\,0\,0 \end{bmatrix}\right) = M\left(A\right) \oplus \begin{bmatrix} 3 \bullet e\,0\,0\,0 \\ 2 \bullet e\,0\,0\,0 \\ e\quad 0\,0\,0 \\ e\quad 0\,0\,0 \end{bmatrix} \qquad (2)$$

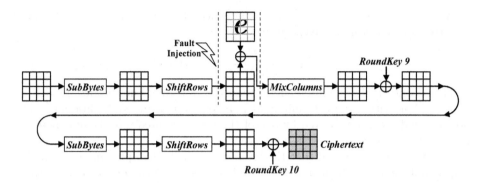

Fig. 1. Last two rounds of AES encryption function

$$M\left(A \oplus \begin{bmatrix} 0\,0\,0\,0 \\ 0\,0\,0\,0 \\ e\,0\,0\,0 \\ 0\,0\,0\,0 \end{bmatrix}\right) = M(A) \oplus \begin{bmatrix} e & 0\,0\,0 \\ 3 \bullet e\,0\,0\,0 \\ 2 \bullet e\,0\,0\,0 \\ e & 0\,0\,0 \end{bmatrix} \tag{3}$$

$$M\left(A \oplus \begin{bmatrix} 0\,0\,0\,0 \\ 0\,0\,0\,0 \\ 0\,0\,0\,0 \\ e\,0\,0\,0 \end{bmatrix}\right) = M(A) \oplus \begin{bmatrix} e & 0\,0\,0 \\ e & 0\,0\,0 \\ 3 \bullet e\,0\,0\,0 \\ 2 \bullet e\,0\,0\,0 \end{bmatrix} \tag{4}$$

$$M\left(A \oplus \begin{bmatrix} e_1\,0\,0\,0 \\ e_2\,0\,0\,0 \\ e_3\,0\,0\,0 \\ e_4\,0\,0\,0 \end{bmatrix}\right) = M(A) \oplus \begin{bmatrix} 2 \bullet e_1 \oplus 3 \bullet e_2 \oplus e_3 \oplus e_4 = e_1'\,0\,0\,0 \\ e_1 \oplus 2 \bullet e_2 \oplus 3 \bullet e_3 \oplus e_4 = e_2'\,0\,0\,0 \\ e_1 \oplus e_2 \oplus 2 \bullet e_3 \oplus 3 \bullet e_4 = e_3'\,0\,0\,0 \\ 3 \bullet e_1 \oplus e_2 \oplus e_3 \oplus 2 \bullet e_4 = e_4'\,0\,0\,0 \end{bmatrix} \tag{5}$$

In the first model we suppose that at least one of the bytes e_1 to e_4 is zero.

$$FM_1 = \{\varepsilon : (e_1,\ e_2,\ e_3,\ e_4) \mid \exists\, e_i = 0;\ (1 \leq i \leq 4)\} \tag{6}$$

In other words, at least one byte of *MixColumn* (in one column only) is fault free, but we don't know any other thing about occurred faults such as locations and values. In consequence, this model covers one byte, two bytes and three bytes fault(s) among four bytes of each column. The coverage rate of this model, *CR*, is defined as the proportion of the number of covered faults to the number of all possible faults. Equation (7) gives the *CR* of this model.

$$CR_1 = \frac{\binom{4}{1} \times 255 + \binom{4}{2} \times 255^2 + \binom{4}{3} \times 255^3}{256^4 - 1} = 0.0155 \tag{7}$$

The second model is the complement of the first one i.e., in the second model all four bytes of one column should be faulty.

$$FM_2 = \{\varepsilon : (e_1,\ e_2,\ e_3,\ e_4) \mid \forall\, e_i \neq 0;\ (1 \leq i \leq 4)\} \tag{8}$$

So, all four bytes of one column are influenced by the occurred fault. In this case the fault coverage is given by (9).

$$CR_2 = \frac{255^4}{256^4 - 1} = 0.9845 \qquad (9)$$

The second model is more general than the first one, but the first model is more similar with assumed fault models in previous attacks. Additionally, all possible faults can be covered by one of the two presented models and there is no fault that is not included in one of these two models.

It should be emphasized that the intersection of the two presented models is empty and the union of them is all possible faults which can occur in four bytes $(256^4 - 1)$. Consequently, any occurred fault in other units of the encryption algorithm from the beginning of the algorithm up to *MixColumns* of round 9 can be considered as another fault occurred in *MixColumns* input of the 9th round, then it's coverable with one of the illustrated models. None of previous fault models against AES had this capability.

According to the structure of AES, *ShiftRows* exchanges contents of the rows and *MixColumns* composes each column of exchanged rows. Thus, changes in one byte before *ShiftRows* will affect at most on four bytes after *MixColumns*. Figure 2 shows an example that two bytes of *ShiftRows* were induced by fault injection and finally two columns of *MixColumns* output were affected. Consequently, every fault which occurs in a round with high probability leads to big changes in the next round.

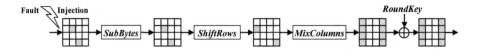

Fig. 2. Effects of faults that occur before *ShiftRows* on *MixColumns*

3   Attack Methods

In this section we show how the new proposed models can be used and then illustrate attack techniques. Consideration equation (5) we generated two set S_1 and S_2.

$$S_1 = \{\varepsilon' : (e'_1, e'_2, e'_3, e'_4) \mid \forall \, e'_i \neq 0; \ (1 \leq i \leq 4),$$
$$\exists \, \varepsilon : (e_1, e_2, e_3, e_4) \in FM_1; \ MixColumn\,(\varepsilon) = (\varepsilon')\} \qquad (10)$$

$$S_2 = \{\varepsilon' : (e'_1, e'_2, e'_3, e'_4) \mid \forall \, e'_i \neq 0; \ (1 \leq i \leq 4),$$
$$\exists \, \varepsilon : (e_1, e_2, e_3, e_4) \in FM_2; \ MixColumn\,(\varepsilon) = (\varepsilon')\} \qquad (11)$$

These two sets can be generated using function *MixColumns* independent of plaintext and key. The (12) and (13) show the number of elements of S_1 and S_2 respectively.

$$|S_1| = \binom{4}{1} \times 255 + \binom{4}{2} \times 255^2 \binom{4}{3} \times 255^3 = 66,716,670 \qquad (12)$$

$$|S_2| = 255^4 = 4,228,250,625 \qquad (13)$$

According to the figure 3, after *MixColumns* of round 9 each byte of its output affects on one byte of ciphertext independent of other bytes, because the *MixColumns* of round 10 is omitted. In fact this algorithmic weakness of AES causes the success of these attacks. As a result, we could consider each column of *MixColumns* output in round 9 independently. Gray cells in figure 3 show the effects of the first column of the input of *MixColumns* in round 9 on the other internal values. Therefore, errors on each byte of output of *MixColumns* can be traced independently. Equations (15) to (18) show it for the first column.

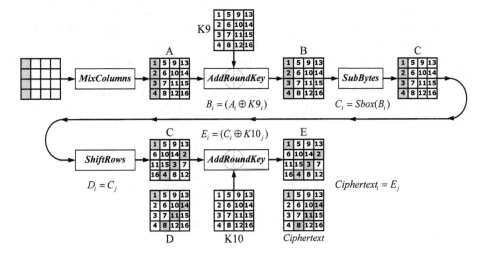

Fig. 3. The AES encryption scheme from *MixColumns* of round 9 to the end

$$Ciphertext = ShiftRows \left(SubBytes \left(A \oplus RoundKey_9 \right) \right) \oplus RoundKey_{10} \qquad (14)$$

A : output of *MixColumns* in round 9,   *AddRK* : *AddRoundKey*

$$AddRK \left(\begin{bmatrix} A_1 \oplus e_1' \\ A_2 \oplus e_2' \\ A_3 \oplus e_3' \\ A_4 \oplus e_4' \end{bmatrix}, \begin{bmatrix} K9_1 \\ K9_2 \\ K9_3 \\ K9_4 \end{bmatrix} \right) = AddRK \left(\begin{bmatrix} A_1 \\ A_2 \\ A_3 \\ A_4 \end{bmatrix}, \begin{bmatrix} K9_1 \\ K9_2 \\ K9_3 \\ K9_4 \end{bmatrix} \right) \oplus \begin{bmatrix} e_1' \\ e_2' \\ e_3' \\ e_4' \end{bmatrix} \qquad (15)$$

$$SubBytes \left(\begin{bmatrix} B_1 \oplus e_1' \\ B_2 \oplus e_2' \\ B_3 \oplus e_3' \\ B_4 \oplus e_4' \end{bmatrix} \right) = SubBytes \left(\begin{bmatrix} B_1 \\ B_2 \\ B_3 \\ B_4 \end{bmatrix} \right) \oplus \begin{bmatrix} e_1'' \\ e_2'' \\ e_3'' \\ e_4'' \end{bmatrix} \qquad (16)$$

$$ShiftRows : \begin{bmatrix} D_1 \\ D_{14} \\ D_{11} \\ D_8 \end{bmatrix} \oplus \begin{bmatrix} e_1'' \\ e_2'' \\ e_3'' \\ e_4'' \end{bmatrix} = \begin{bmatrix} C_1 \\ C_2 \\ C_3 \\ C_4 \end{bmatrix} \oplus \begin{bmatrix} e_1'' \\ e_2'' \\ e_3'' \\ e_4'' \end{bmatrix} \qquad (17)$$

$$AddRK\left(\begin{bmatrix} D_1 \oplus e_1'' \\ D_{14} \oplus e_2'' \\ D_{11} \oplus e_3'' \\ D_8 \oplus e_4'' \end{bmatrix}, \begin{bmatrix} K10_1 \\ K10_{14} \\ K10_{11} \\ K10_8 \end{bmatrix}\right) = AddRK\left(\begin{bmatrix} D_1 \\ D_{14} \\ D_{11} \\ D_8 \end{bmatrix}, \begin{bmatrix} K10_1 \\ K10_{14} \\ K10_{11} \\ K10_8 \end{bmatrix}\right) \oplus \begin{bmatrix} e_1'' \\ e_2'' \\ e_3'' \\ e_4'' \end{bmatrix} \quad (18)$$

AddRoundKey is a linear transformation so (e_1', e_2', e_3', e_4') (errors on output of *MixColumn* and input of *AddRoundKey*) are transferred to its output. But *SubBytes* uses *S-box* transformation and it's a non linear function. As a consequence, $(e_1'', e_2'', e_3'', e_4'')$ presented on output of *SubBytes* does not have any linear relation with (e_1', e_2', e_3', e_4') (errors on its input). But each e_i'' relates to only e_i' and the non linearity of this relation is very high. *ShiftRows* and *AddRoundKey* are linear functions, thus $(e_1'', e_2'', e_3'', e_4'')$ appears exactly on ciphertext but in (1, 14, 11, 8) locations respectively. At the first for presenting the attack, we suppose that all occurred fault are coverable by the first model and consider the first column of input of *MixColumns* in round 9 only. We have one fault free ciphertext (*FFC*) and another faulty ciphertext (*FC*) that occurred fault is covered by the first fault model. Consequently, $\varepsilon'' : (e_1'', e_2'', e_3'', e_4'')$ is given by equation (19).

$$\begin{bmatrix} e_1'' \\ e_2'' \\ e_3'' \\ e_4'' \end{bmatrix} = \begin{bmatrix} FFC_1 \\ FFC_{14} \\ FFC_{11} \\ FFC_8 \end{bmatrix} \oplus \begin{bmatrix} FC_1 \\ FC_{14} \\ FC_{11} \\ FC_8 \end{bmatrix} \quad (19)$$

We know that ε'' is the difference at the output of *SubBytes*. So, we generate set *EI*.

$$EI = \{\ (\varepsilon' : (e_1', e_2', e_3', e_4'), \ \iota : (I_1, I_2, I_3, I_4))\ |$$

$$SubBytes\left(\begin{bmatrix} I_1 \\ I_2 \\ I_3 \\ I_4 \end{bmatrix}\right) \oplus SubBytes\left(\begin{bmatrix} I_1 \oplus e_1' \\ I_2 \oplus e_2' \\ I_3 \oplus e_3' \\ I_4 \oplus e_4' \end{bmatrix}\right) = \begin{bmatrix} e_1'' \\ e_2'' \\ e_3'' \\ e_4'' \end{bmatrix} \} \quad (20)$$

But all values of ε' are not useful then we generate set *I*.

$$I = EI \cap S_1 = \{\iota : (I_1, I_2, I_3, I_4) \mid \exists\ \varepsilon';\ \varepsilon' \in S_1 \ \wedge \ (\varepsilon', \iota) \in EI\} \quad (21)$$

In other words, set *I* contains all possible values for the first column of *Sub-Bytes* input at the last round. Thus, we gather some faulty ciphertexts caused by same plaintext and different faults that are covered by the first model. Then we will decrease the size of set *I* by repeating the proposed method using collected faulty ciphertexts until set *I* has only one element. Now we know four bytes of *SubBytes* input at the last round. As a consequence, we know its output. On the other hand, we know ciphertext (*FFC*) and according to (23) we can calculate four bytes of the 10th *RoundKey* (*K10*).

$$SubBytes\left(\begin{bmatrix} I_1 \\ I_2 \\ I_3 \\ I_4 \end{bmatrix}\right) \oplus \begin{bmatrix} K10_1 \\ K10_{14} \\ K10_{11} \\ K10_8 \end{bmatrix} = \begin{bmatrix} FFC_1 \\ FFC_{14} \\ FFC_{11} \\ FFC_8 \end{bmatrix} \tag{22}$$

$$\begin{bmatrix} K10_1 \\ K10_{14} \\ K10_{11} \\ K10_8 \end{bmatrix} = SubBytes\left(\begin{bmatrix} I_1 \\ I_2 \\ I_3 \\ I_4 \end{bmatrix}\right) \oplus \begin{bmatrix} FFC_1 \\ FFC_{14} \\ FFC_{11} \\ FFC_8 \end{bmatrix} \tag{23}$$

Running this method for all other columns of *MixColumns* input of round 9, we will find all 16 bytes of 10th *RoundKey* (*K10*). As a result, we can find the secret key of attacked system by knowing one *RoundKey* completely [4]. The essential functions for discovering the main key from *RoundKey* are *Inverse S-box* and *Exclusive-OR* only.

One of the advantages of this attack is that finding every four bytes of 10th *Roundkey* can be processed separately and parallel. Also, we can employ four dedicated systems that each one tries to find four bytes of *K10*. (1, 14, 11, 8) locations of ciphertexts are examined by the first attacker, the second one employs (5, 2, 15, 12) locations, the third one used (9, 6, 3, 16) locations and the final attacker tries with (13, 10, 7, 4). Then, we will find all 128 bits of *K10*.

The other method to attack is completely similar to the presented one but we assume occurred faults can be covered by the second fault model and we use S_2 for limiting (e'_1, e'_2, e'_3, e'_4) in *EI*. All other specifications and advantages of the first method are true for the second method.

The main difference between the two attack methods is their fault model. The first model based attack uses any faulty ciphertext with probability of 0.0155 but this value is 0.9845 for the second model based attack.

In these two methods we supposed all faulty ciphertexts are coverable with the first model or by the second model. We can use combination of two models, in each round of attack if we know faulty ciphertext caused by a fault that is covered by the first model (the second model) we limit *EI* by S_1 (S_2). In this method we should know each occurred fault is coverable with which fault model. But knowing this characteristic of happened fault seems not applicable.

4   Experimental Results

According to the coverage rate of the used fault models, we predicated that we need more faulty ciphertexts in the second attack method than the first one. Because the second fault model has greater coverage rate and many faults are covered with this model. Additional experiments verified this idea.

At the first, we implemented the first method of attack. We started with the first column of *MixColumn* input in round 9 and we selected faulty ciphertexts that all four bytes in 1, 14, 11 and 8 locations are different with fault free ciphertext. In this situation, we ran the attack algorithm to 1000 encryption unit with different random generated keys. In average 6 faulty ciphertexts were

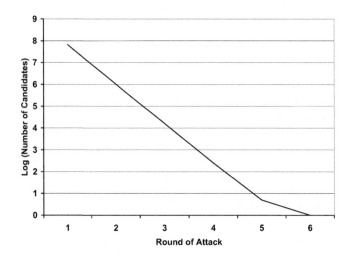

Fig. 4. Average number of candidates for *SubBytes* input in each round of the first attack method

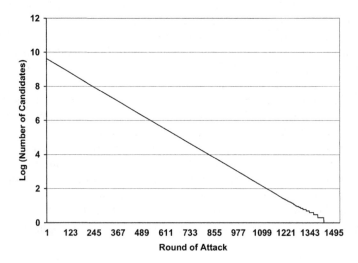

Fig. 5. Average number of candidates for *SubBytes* input in each round of the second attack method

needed to find all four bytes of 10th *RoundKey* and the needed time is not considerable (10 seconds). In the first round of attack we had 6.6×10^7 candidates for *SubBytes* input in average and this number of candidates decreased to 10^6 at the second round of attack. Figure 4 shows average number of candidates in each round of attack.

The explained results were for the the first column of *MixColumns* input and for finding four bytes of *RoundKey*, but those results are correct for other columns and other bytes of *RoundKey*. As we explained previously, the attack algorithm can be applied to each column synchronously.

But conditions for the second attack method were different because S_2 has more elements and calculating of intersection between S_2 and *EI* needs more time comparing to the first method. On the other hand, S_2 needs 15.5 GB memory. After improving, optimizing and using memory management techniques on the implementation of the attack, we succeeded to do it with 762.5 MB memory and in almost 2 hours. We should specify that the simulations have been done using Visual C++ on a 2GHz centrino with 1GB memory.

We applied this attack to AES with 100 random keys. Each attack needed 1495 faulty ciphertexts and 2 hours in average to find four bytes of *K10*. It's noticeable, these results are expected according to the previous results of coverage rates. Figure 5 presents the average number of candidates for *SubBytes* inputs on this method.

5   Using Fault Attack Assumption for Breaking AES

We used faulty ciphertexts to find secret key of attacked systems. In proposed methods we supposed faults occur only on internal values, but we assumed *RoundKeys* and *KeyExpansion* unit is completely fault free. As previously described, any fault that happen before the *MixColumns* of round 9 is coverable with one of our proposed fault models. We can suppose fault occurred on the beginning of the encryption algorithm means plaintext. Thus, changing in plaintext that leads to different ciphertexts can be assumed as a fault that occurred in the plaintext and is covered by one of our two models. Then that's enough to know that the caused difference in *MixColumns* input of round 9 is coverable with which of our fault models. We implemented this idea and we supposed that we can access to the input of *MixColumns* in round 9 and we can understand only which model can cover the caused changes in this location. The results of this attack were as successful as previous experimental results. Furthermore, finding a way to know the caused changes in *MixColumns* input of 9th round is coverable with which fault model, is enough to break the AES cryptosystem and finish its era.

Additionally, we don't need to know plaintexts and if we can find a method to distinguish and classify the different ciphertexts based on *MixColumns* input of round 9, we will have a successful *Ciphertext Only Attack* and it's not necessary to run *Known Plaintext Attack*.

6   Conclusion and Future Works

We presented two models for covering all possible faults on input of *MixColumns* in round 9 of the AES-128 encryption algorithm. Then we designed two methods to attack using new proposed fault models. The biggest advantage of these attack methods is high coverage rate of used fault models. One of them covers 1.55% and the other one covers 98.45% of all possible faults on each four bytes of

MixColumns input. None of previous DFAs to the AES had this coverage rate and none of them used general fault models. Additionally, we presented very successful results of proposed attacks implementation. With the first fault model we needed only 6 faulty ciphertexts in average for discovering the main key and 1495 faulty ciphertexts for the second one. Hence, we will succeed in attacking to the implementations of AES-128 with simple fault injection equipments such as power supply disturbance or glitch in clock signal. It's applicable for attacking to new smart cards that implemented AES cryptosystem.

At last we introduced a method for breaking AES without fault injection and with changing assumptions that different ciphertexts caused by different plaintexts not by fault occurrence or injection. In consequence, finding a method to know difference between two ciphertexts is coverable with the first fault model or the other one, is one of our future works. We are working on designing a method to generate some ciphertexts that we know which model covers the difference between each of them. Also, we are trying to construct a test method to know the difference between two ciphertexts at *MixColumns* input in round 9 is coverable with which fault models. Then, by finding any method or designing a rule, we will break AES with 128-bit key and its period will be finished.

Another work for future is trying to run these methods for attacking to the AES cryptosystem with 192 and 256 bits keys. It's noticeable that by illustrated methods we can find completely a *RoundKey* of AES-192 and AES-256. But we can not discover the main key of these systems. We should design other methods for finding the half of another *RoundKey* for AES-192 and whole of another *RoundKey* for AES-256 to reach the secret key.

References

1. D. Boneh, R. A. DeMillo, and R. J. Lipton. On the Importance of Eliminating Errors in Cryptographic Computations. In *Journal of Cryptology 14(2)*, pages 101-120, 2001.
2. E. Biham and A. Shamir. Differential Fault Analysis of Secret Key Cryptosystems. In B. Kaliski, editor, *Advances in Cryptology - CRYPTO 97*, volume 1294 of *Lecture Notes in Computer Science*, pages 513-525. Springer, 1997.
3. J. Blömer and J.-P. Seifert. Fault Based Cryptanalysis of the Advanced Encryption Standard (AES). In *Financial Cryptography 03*, LNCS. Springer, 2003. Also available at http://eprint.iacr.org/,2002/075.
4. P. Dusart, G. Letourneux, and O. Vivolo. Differential Fault Analysis on A.E.S. Available at http://eprint.iacr.org/, 2003/010.
5. C. Giraud. DFA on AES. In H. Dobbertin, V. Rijmen, and A. Sowa, editors, *Advanced Encryption Standard (AES): 4th International Conference, AES 2004*, volume 3373 of *Lecture Notes in Computer Science*, pages 27-41. Springer-Verlag, 2005.
6. G. Piret and J.J. Quisquater. A Differential Fault Attack Technique against SPN Structures, with Application to the AES and KHAZAD. In *Cryptographic Hardware and Embedded Systmes - CHES 2003*, volume 2779 of *Lecture Notes in Computer Science*. Springer, 2003.
7. National Institute of Standards and Technology, *Advanced Encryption Standard*, **NIST FIPS PUB 197**, 2001.

Breaking Ciphers with COPACOBANA – A Cost-Optimized Parallel Code Breaker

Sandeep Kumar[1], Christof Paar[1], Jan Pelzl[1],
Gerd Pfeiffer[2], and Manfred Schimmler[2]

[1] Horst Görtz Institute for IT Security, Ruhr University Bochum, Germany
{kumar, cpaar, pelzl}@crypto.rub.de
[2] Institute of Computer Science and Applied Mathematics, Faculty of Engineering,
Christian-Albrechts-University of Kiel, Germany
{gp, masch}@informatik.uni-kiel.de

Abstract. Cryptanalysis of symmetric and asymmetric ciphers is computationally extremely demanding. Since the security parameters (in particular the key length) of almost all practical crypto algorithms are chosen such that attacks with conventional computers are computationally infeasible, the only promising way to tackle existing ciphers (assuming no mathematical breakthrough) is to build special-purpose hardware. Dedicating those machines to the task of cryptanalysis holds the promise of a dramatically improved cost-performance ratio so that breaking of commercial ciphers comes within reach.

This contribution presents the design and realization of the COPACOBANA (Cost-Optimized Parallel Code Breaker) machine, which is optimized for running cryptanalytical algorithms and can be realized for less than US$ 10,000. It will be shown that, depending on the actual algorithm, the architecture can outperform conventional computers by several orders in magnitude. COPACOBANA hosts 120 low-cost FPGAs and is able to, e.g., perform an exhaustive key search of the Data Encryption Standard (DES) in less than nine days on average. As a real-world application, our architecture can be used to attack machine readable travel documents (ePass). COPACOBANA is intended, but not necessarily restricted to solving problems related to cryptanalysis.

The hardware architecture is suitable for computational problems which are parallelizable and have low communication requirements. The hardware can be used, e.g., to attack elliptic curve cryptosystems and to factor numbers. Even though breaking full-size RSA (1024 bit or more) or elliptic curves (ECC with 160 bit or more) is out of reach with COPACOBANA, it can be used to analyze cryptosystems with a (deliberately chosen) small bitlength to provide reliable security estimates of RSA and ECC by extrapolation[1].

1 Introduction

All modern practical ciphers, both symmetric and asymmetric ones, use security parameters (in particular the key-length) which makes them secure against

---

[1] The basic architecture of COPACOBANA was presented as a poster at a hardware workshop (not disclosed here in order to keep this submission anonymous).

L. Goubin and M. Matsui (Eds.): CHES 2006, LNCS 4249, pp. 101–118, 2006.

attacks with current computers. Depending on the security margin chosen in a given application, many ciphers are potentially vulnerable to attacks with special-purpose machines which have, say, a cost-performance ratio which is several orders of magnitude better than that of current PCs. This contribution describes a design and successful prototype realization of such a special-purpose cryptanalytical machine based on low-cost FPGAs.

Cryptanalysis of modern cryptographic algorithms requires massive computational effort, often between 2^{56} to 2^{80} operations. A characteristic of many (but not all) cryptanalytical algorithms is that they can run in a highly parallel fashion with very little interprocess communication. Such applications map naturally to a hardware based design, requiring repetitive mapping of the basic block, and can be easily extended by adding more chips as required. However, it should be stressed that the mere availability of computational resources is not the core problem, but providing massive computational resources *at affordable costs* is. The non recurring engineering costs for ASICs have put special-purpose hardware for cryptanalysis in almost all practical situations out of reach for commercial or research institutions, and have been considered only feasible by government agencies.

An alternative approach to distributed computing with loosely coupled processors is based on using the idle cycles of the huge number of computers connected via the Internet, for instance the SETI@home project [16]. The results of this approach has been quite successful for some applications (even though the confirmed detection of extraterrestrial life is still an open problem) and is used for selected problems which are not viable with the computing power within a single organization. Using distributed computing, however, has the disadvantage of, first, having to find individuals who would be interested in joining to solve a problem and, secondly, trusting the nodes from introducing errors. Finally, for many code-breaking application, shared computation is not a method of choice in many cases.

With the recent advent of low-cost FPGA families with much logic resources, field programmable gate arrays provide a very interesting alternative tool for the massive computational effort required for cryptanalytic applications. Reconfigurable computing has been emerged as a cost effective alternative for various applications which require the power of a custom hardware but require the flexibility provided by a software based design, e.g., in rapid prototyping. In addition, to the cost-performance advantage over PC-based machines, such a machine has the advantage over ASIC-based designs that it can be used to attack various different cryptosystems without the need to rebuilt a new machine each time. In cryptanalysis, certain algorithms are very well suited for special-purpose hardware. A prime example for this is an exhaustive key search of the Data Encryption Standard (DES) [10]. Such a brute-force attack is more than two orders of magnitude faster when implemented on FPGAs than in software on general purpose computers at equivalent costs[2].

---

[2] Based on our existing implementations, a single FPGA at a cost of US$ 50 (current market price) can test 400 million keys, a PC (Pentium4, 2GHz) for US$+ 200 approx. 2 million keys per second. Hence, 4 FPGAs can perform the same task approximately 800 times faster than a PC at the same cost.

This contribution describes the design, implementation, and applications of COPACOBANA, a massively parallel machine based on FPGAs. The hardware is suitable for computational problems which are parallelizable and have low communication requirements and can be used, e.g., to attack elliptic curve cryptosystems and to factor numbers. Even though breaking full-size RSA (1024 bit or more) or elliptic curves (ECC with 160 bit or more) is out of reach with CO-PACOBANA, it provides for the first time a tool for a reliable security estimation of RSA and ECC. Even more relevant is the fact that resource constrained applications, in particular mobile devices, sometimes settle with shorter parameters, such as the 112 bit and 128 bit ECC systems recommended by the SECG standard, which become vulnerable with our machine. Also, assuming Moore's law, we can predict the security margin of RSA and ECC in the years to come.

Another interesting application emerges in the area of machine readable travel documents (ePass): The International Civil Aviation Organization (ICAO) initiated biometric and RFID technologies for border and visa control. Current realizations of Basic Access Control deploy symmetric cryptography (Triple-DES) and generate the corresponding encryption and authentication keys from passport information. As pointed out by many experts however, the low entropy of the key allows for attacks of complexity of not more than single DES. Using our hardware architecture this kind of attack can be mounted in much shorter time, and even real-time, i.e., the time needed to pass the inspection system.

The outline of the paper is as follows: In the next Section, we identify a model for an optimized hardware architecture for breaking codes which we realized as a custom-designed computing machine. We will present the architectural concept and the prototype of COPACOBANA, consisting of a backplane, an FPGA DIMM module, and a controller card. In Section 3, cryptanalytical applications which are suited for running on low-cost FPGAs will be discussed: First, we show how cryptographically weak systems can be attacked with COPACOBANA. An implementation of the Data Encryption Standard (DES) on COPACOBANA impressively shows how DES can be broken with low effort in less than nine days, making many existing legacy implementations of DES vulnerable to attacks by nearly everyone. Furthermore, we show how the DES implementation at hand can be used for attacks on machine readable travel documents, which use Triple-DES with keys of low entropy. Secondly, we briefly sketch how an efficient hardware implementation of the elliptic curve method (ECM) on COPACOBANA can be used to factor composite integers in parallel. As another asymmtetric cryptanalytical example, a specially tweaked implementation of Pollard's rho algorithm, can be used for breaking elliptic curve cryptosystems (ECC).

2   Proposed Architecture for Cryptanalysis

As we will see in Section 3, many algorithms tackling the most important problems in cryptanalysis can be implemented on FPGAs. However, code breaking involves more effort than programming just a single FPGA with a particular algorithm. Due to the enormous dimensions of cryptanalytical problems, much more resources than a single FPGA are required. What is needed is a powerful massively parallel machine, tweaked to the needs of the targeted algorithms.

Most problems can be parallelized and are perfectly suited for a distributed architecture. In many cases, not much communication overhead is required. Conventional parallel computing architectures, such as provided by Cray, can in theory also be used for cryptanalytical applications. However, the cost-performance ratio is not optimized with this approach, resulting in prohibitively expensive attack machines. Similarly, many features of current high-end processors are not required for the targeted cryptanalytical problems. For instance, high-speed communication between CPUs, fast floating point operations, etc., cannot be used in our context. All of these features usually increase the cost of such a device, which is in particular annoying when they are superfluous. Even a simple grid of conventional PCs is not efficient, as can be seen from implementations of DES: An implementation on a single FPGA can be more than 100 times faster than an implementation on a conventional PC, while the FPGA is much cheaper than the PC. Therefore, a custom design is inevitable in order to obtain a low-cost architecture with the required performance.

Our metric to decide whether an architecture is "good" or not is a function of performance, flexibility, and monetary cost. A good performance metric for hardware implementations is the area-time (AT) complexity. Whenever we can minimize the AT-complexity, the design can be called efficient. ASIC implementations can be AT-minimal and are the best choice for high-volume applications. However, ASICs are not flexible since they can implement only a single architecture. FPGAs in contrast are reprogrammable and, thus, are flexible. Moreover, if only a relatively small number of chips ($< 10\,000$) is required, FPGAs are preferable since the production of ASICs is profitable only when targeting high volumes.

In the following, we describe an optimized architecture for cryptanalytical purposes and its implementation as custom-designed FPGA machine which hosts 120 FPGAs and can be produced for less than US$ 10,000, including material and manufacturing costs.

2.1   An Optimal Architecture to Break Ciphers

All targeted algorithms (see Section 3) have the following common characteristics: First, the computational expensive operations are parallelizable. Secondly, single parallel instances do not need to communicate with each other. Thirdly, the overall communication overhead is low, driven by the fact that the computation phase heavily outweighs the data input and output phases. In fact, computation time dominates compared to the time for data input or output. Ideally, communication is almost exclusively used for initialization and reporting of results. A central control instance for the communication can easily be accomplished by a conventional (low-cost) PC, connected to the instances by a simple interface. No high-speed communication interface is required. Forthly, all presented algorithms and their corresponding implementations call for very little memory. As a consequence, the available memory on contemporary low-cost FPGAs such as the Xilinx Spartan3 is sufficient.

2.2   Realization of COPACOBANA

Recapitulating, the Cost-Optimized Parallel Code Breaker (COPACOBANA) fitting our needs consists of many independent low-cost FPGAs, connected to a host-PC via a standard interface, e.g., USB or Ethernet. Furthermore, such a standard interface allows to easily extend a host-PC with more than one CO-PACOBANA device. The initialization of FPGAs, the control, and the accumulation of results is done by the host. Since the cryptanalytical applications

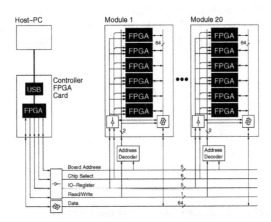

Fig. 1. Architecture of COPACOBANA

demand for plenty of computing power, the targeted platform aggregates up to 120 FPGAs (Spartan3-1000). Building a system of such a dimension with commercially available FPGA boards is certainly feasible, but comes with a cost penality. Hence we decided to design, layout, and build our own hardware. We considered several different design options. Our cost-performance optimized design became only feasible by strictly restricting all functionality to those directly necessary for code breaking, and to make several design choices based on readily available components and interfaces. The design of COPACOBANA is depicted in Figure 1 and consists of

- *FPGA modules* for the actual implementation of the presented hardware architectures,
- a *backplane*, connecting all FPGA modules to a common data bus, address bus, and power supply,
- and a *controller card*, connecting the data bus and address bus to a host-PC via USB.

FPGA Modules: We decided to pick a contemporary low-cost FPGA for the design, the Xilinx Spartan3-1000 FPGA (XC3S1000, speed grade -4, FT256 packaging). This comes with 1 million system gates, 17280 equivalent logic cells,

1920 Configurable Logic Blocks (CLBs) equivalent to 7680 slices, 120 Kbit Distributed RAM (DRAM), 432 Kbit Block RAM (BRAM), and 4 digital clock managers (DCMs) [20].The choice for this chip was derived by an evaluation of size and cost over several FPGA series and types.

A step towards an extendable and simple architecture has been accomplished by the design of small pluggable FPGA modules. We decided to settle with small modules in the standard DIMM format, comprising 6 Xilinx XC3S1000 FPGAs. Figure 4 (Appendix A) shows its realization as custom made 4-layer printed circuit board. The FPGAs are directly connected to a common 64-bit data bus on board of the FPGA module which is interfaced to the backplane data bus via transceivers with 3-state outputs. While disconnected from the bus, the FPGAs can communicate locally via the internal 64-bit bus on the DIMM module. The

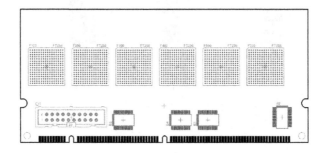

Fig. 2. FPGA module (DIMM)

DIMM format allows for a very compact component layout, which is important to closely connect the modules by a bus. Figure 2 depicts the chip arrangement. From the experience with current implementations on the same FPGA type, we dispense with active cooling of the FPGAs at these times. Depending on the heat dissipation of future applications, passive or active cooling might be an option for an upgrade.

Backplane: The backplane hosts all FPGA-modules and the controller card. All modules are connected by a 64-bit data bus and a 16-bit address bus. This single master bus is easy to control because no arbiter is required. Interrupt handling is totally avoided in order to keep the design as simple as possible. If the communication scheduling of an application is unknown in advance, the bus master will need to poll the FPGAs.

Moreover, the power supply is routed to every FPGA module and the controller interface. The backplane distributes two clock signals from the controller card to the slots. Every FPGA module is assigned a unique hardware address, which is accomplished by Generic Array Logic (GAL) attached to every DIMM socket. Hence, all FPGA cores can have the same configuration and all FPGA modules can have the same layout. They can easily be replaced in case of a defect. Figure 5 (Appendix A) shows the prototype of the backplane equipped with one FPGA module and the control interface card which will be described in the next subsection. The entire bus has been successfully tested by use of the prototype FPGA module with frequencies of up to 50 MHz. For the fully equipped board, the bus speed will be limited to 33 MHz due to power dissipation.

Control Interface: Data transfer from and to the FPGAs and to the host-PC is accomplished by the control interface. We decided to pick a small development board with an FPGA (CESYS USB2FPGA [3]) in favor of a flexible design. The development board comes with a Xilinx XC2S200 SPARTAN II FPGA (PQ208), an integrated USB controller (CYPRESS FX-2), and 1 MByte SRAM. Moreover, the board provides an easy-pluggable 96-pin connector which we use for the connection to the backplane. In later versions of the design, it is also possible to replace the FPGA development board by a small microcontroller with a standard USB or Ethernet interface.

The controller hardware has to handle the adaptation of different clock rates: The USB interface uses a clock rate of 24 MHz, the backplane is clocked with 33 MHz, and the controller itself is running at an internal clock of 133 MHz. The internal clock is generated by an external clock synthesizer, the system clock is derived from a digital clock manager (DCM) present on the FPGA.

The main state machine of the control interface is used to decode and execute host commands received via USB, program the FPGAs via the data bus in slave parallel mode, initialize (write to) FPGAs and start the computation, and regularly poll the FPGAs and check for new results.

Programming can be done for all FPGAs simultaneously, for a set of such, or for a particular one. Since the targeted cryptanalytic applications do not require different code on distinct FPGAs, a concurrent programming of all devices is very helpful.

Host-PC: The top level entity of COPACOBANA is a host-PC which is used to program and control all FPGA implementations. For this purpose, a software library has been written to issue commands to the USB connected controller card of COPACOBANA. All software routines are based on the closed source library provided by the board manufacturer (CESYS). With the low-level functions, FPGAs can be addressed and data can be stored and read to/ from a particular FPGA. Further functions include the detection of the hardware and some configuration routines such as, e.g., a backplane reset. Higher-level functions comprise commands at application level. E.g., for the DES Cracker, we can store a certain plaintext in the DES units, check its status, etc.

3   Cryptanalytic Motivation for COPACOBANA

In this section, we will point to possible applications in cryptanalysis. COPA-COBANA can be used to break cryptographically weak or outdated algorithms such as DES, A5, and SHA-1 which have an attack complexity of at most 2^{70} operations. But, clearly, COPACOBANA can not recover keys from actual strong cryptosystems such as AES, ECC, and RSA. However, the hardware approach allows to implement attacks on such systems with a deliberately chosen small bitlength and to extrapolate the results to finally obtain a much better estimate of the security of actual cryptosystems against attacks with special-purpose hardware.

We will investigate the complexity of following attacks:

- An exhaustive key search of DES (Subsection 3.1). DES still is used for compatibility reasons and/ or in legacy products. Out-dated DES-based cryptosystems such as Norton Diskreet (a very popular encryption tool in the 1990ies which was of the well-known Norton Utilities package) can be broken with COPACOBANA. Diskreet was used to encrypt single files as well as to create and manage encrypted virtual disks.
- Attacks on machine readable travel documents (ePass): With the DES implementation at hand, an intimidating real-world example of a weak cryptosystem, namely the recently introduced ePass by ICAO, can be attacked in certain ways which we will sketch in Subsection 3.2.
- Factoring composites with the elliptic curve factorization method (ECM) (Subsection 3.3). ECM can be used as a crucial step for factoring actual RSA moduli and a reliable estimate of its complexity is indispensable for the security evaluation of factorization-based cryptosystems such as RSA.
- Attacks against ECC with a parallel variant of Pollard's rho method (Subsection 3.4). The hardware implementation of an algorithm solving the discrete logarithm problem on elliptic curves gives rise to a more realistic estimate of the security of ECC against attacks with special-purpose hardware.

3.1   Exhaustive Key Search of DES

Ideally, the security of symmetric ciphers is dependent on the impracticability of an exhaustive key search. This requires examining through each key in the possible key space. The cost of the attack is calculated based on the available technology and expected future developments. Usually, the key size is chosen such that it allows for a fast and efficient implementation of the cryptosystem but making such brute force attacks impracticable.

The Data Encryption Standard (DES) with a 56-bit key size was chosen as the first commercial cryptographic standard by NIST in 1977 [10]. A key size of 56-bits was considered to be good choice considering the huge development costs for computing power in the late 70's, making a search over all the possible 2^{56} keys impractical. But DES has survived long beyond its recommended lifetime and still is being used in legacy systems or due to backward compatibility reasons. The advances in the hardware and decreasing costs have made DES vulnerable to brute force attacks.

Previous Work: There has been a lot of feasibility studies on the possible use of parallel hardware and distributed computing for breaking DES. The first estimates were proposed by Diffie and Hellman [5] for a brute force machine that could find the key within a day at US$ 20 million.

A first ever detailed hardware design description for a brute force attacker was presented by Michael Wiener at the rump session of CRYPTO'93 and is reprinted in [18]. The machine could be built for less than a million US$ with 57,000 DES chips that could recover a key every three and half hours. The estimates were updated in 1998 due to the advances in hardware for a million dollar machine to 35 minutes for each key recovery [19].

Ian Goldberg and David Wagner estimated the cost for building a DES brute force attacker using FPGAs at US$ 45,000 for a key recovery within a year [6]. In 1997, a detailed cost estimate for three different approaches for DES key search: distributed computing, FPGAs and custom ASIC designs, was compiled by a group of cryptographers [1].

The real practical attempts at breaking DES were encouraged by the RSA Secret Key challenge launched in 1997 [15]. The first challenge was solved by Rocke Verser, Matt Curtin, and Justin Dolske using the DESCHALL distributed network in 1997. The RSA DES Challenge II-1 was broken by *distributed.net* within 39 days in 1998. The RSA DES Challenge II-2 was won by the Electronic Frontier Foundation (EFF) DES hardware cracker called *Deep Crack* in 1998 within 56 hours [6]. The DES cracker consisted of 1,536 custom designed ASIC chips at a cost of material of around US$ 250,000 and could search 88 billion keys per second. The final blow to DES was given by the DES Challenge III which was solved in 22 hours 15 minutes using the combined effort of *Deep Crack* and *distributed.net*

A first low-cost approach in attacking a DES-based protocol was realized by [4]. The authors describe their experiences attacking the IBM 4758 CCA with an off-the-shelf FPGA development board.

Though this proved to be an end for DES for many applications, the huge cost involved to producing a machine like *Deep Crack* and access to foundries makes building such machines still impractical for smaller organizations. Therefore, we propose a more practical approach of an off-the-shelf-FPGA based hardware cracker.

DES on FPGAs: When DES was first proposed as a standard, its main application was seen in hardware based implementations. Hence DES is extremely efficient in terms of area and speed for hardware but unsuitable for a good software implementation due to the bit-level addressing in the design. Therefore an FPGA implementation of DES can be more than a 100 times faster than an implementation on a conventional PC at much lower costs. This allows a hardware based key search engine to be much faster and efficient compared to a software based approach.

The main aim of our key search engine is to check as many keys as possible in the least time to find the right key that could encrypt a known plaintext to its ciphertext that is made available. It is obvious that such a key search can be done in a highly parallelized fashion by partitioning the key space. This requires hardly any inter-process communication, as each of the DES engines can search for the right key within its allocated key subspace.

For the DES engine, we implemented a highly pipelined design of the Université Catholique de Louvain's Crypto Group [14]. The design can test one key per clock per engine and the pipelined architecture is adjusted such that the critical path is as small as possible, allowing for a fast implementation. For COPACOBANA, we can fit four such DES engines inside a single FPGA, and therefore allow for sharing of control circuitry and the key space as shown in Figure 3. It consists of a 64-bit *Plaintext* register and 64-bit *Ciphertext* register. The key space is allocated to each chip as the most-significant 15-bits of the key which is stored in the *Key* register. The *Counter* is used to run through the least significant 39 bits of the key. The remaining two bits of the 56-bit key for each of the DES engines is hardwired and is different for each of them. Thus, for every such FPGA, a task is assigned to search through all the keys with the 15 most-significant bits fixed, that is 2^{41} different keys. The partitioning of the key space

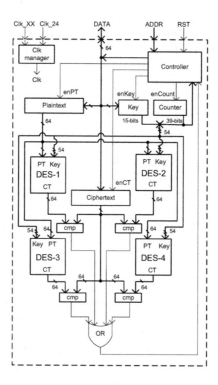

Fig. 3. Overview of an FPGA with four DES key search units

is done by the host-PC such way that each chip takes around 90 minutes (at 100 MHz) to check through its allocated key subspace, thus, avoiding huge communication requirements. This also allows the machine to restart the key search easily from a previous state if a power failure occurs. The generated cipher text (*CT*) is compared to that of the given *Ciphertext* stored in the register, using the comparator (*cmp*) block. The results of the four comparators are ORed and reported to the controller. If any of the DES engines provides a positive match, the controller reports the counter value to the host-PC. The host-PC keeps track of the key range that is assigned to each of the FPGAs and, hence, can match the right key from a given counter value. If no match is found until the counter overflows, the FPGA reports completion of the task and remains idle until a new key space is assigned. Since each FPGA can search through its key space totally independent of any other FPGA, only the host-PC needs to keep track of the number of FPGAs and the allocated key space. The estimated time to complete the key search using COPACOBANA is discussed in the following.

Exhaustive Key Search with COPACOBANA: We can operate each of the FPGAs at 100 MHz and, therefore, each FPGA can check four keys every 10 ns. Consequently, a partial key space of 2^{41} keys can completely be checked in $2^{39} \cdot 10$ ns by a single FPGA, which is approximately 92 minutes. Since COPACOBANA hosts 120 of these low-cost FPGAs, the key search machine can check $4 \cdot 120 = 480$ keys every 10 ns, i.e., 48 billion keys per second. To find the right key, COPACOBANA has to search through an average of 2^{55} different keys. Thus on average, COPACOBANA can find the right key after $(2^{55} \cdot 10)/480$ ns which is approximately 8.7 days. The time required for loading the plaintext, ciphertext and key space allocation are ignored as they are negligibly small compared to the overall running time.

3.2 ePass

One important application of our architecture concerns the current scheme for machine readable travel documents, also known as ePass, which is initiated by organizations[3] in United States and several other countries to deploy biometric and RFID technologies for border and visa control. The claimed goal is to enhance security, protect against forgery and manipulation of travel documents and ease identity checks. The initiative has been subject to many political and technical debates. Several researchers have pointed out the security and privacy weaknesses of the deployed schemes and proposed improvements (see, e.g. [8,9]). The cryptographic parts of the scheme shall consist of a Passive Authentication, Basic Access Control and an Active Authentication. Whereas Passive Authentication means that the data stored on an ePass are signed by the issuing nation, Basic Access Control should setup a secure (confidential) channel between the reader device (part of the inspection system) and the ePass chip and Active Authentication is deployed for anti-clonig purposes and requires an integer factorization based signature scheme implemented on the ePass chip. Note, that both Basic Access Control and Active Authentication are optional mechanisms. Basic Access Control is already implemented, e.g., in Germany and the Netherlands.

Current realizations of Basic Access Control deploy symmetric cryptography (Triple-DES) and generate the corresponding encryption and authentication keys

---

[3] More concretely, the International Civil Aviation Organization (ICAO).

from passport information that is visible in the physical document (e.g., serial number, date of birth and expiration date). More concretely, the key derivation scheme (e.g., implemented in reader devices) includes three computations of SHA-1, one to derive the chip individual key K_Seed, and two consecutive computations that derive encryption key K_Enc and authentication key K_MAC. One of the main concerns pointed out by many experts is the low entropy of this visible information being insecure for key generation. The scheme has been already successfully attacked using offline dictionary attacks[4].

Using our hardware architecture this kind of attack can be mounted in much shorter time, and even real-time, i.e., the time needed to pass the inspection system. Note that the dictionary attack can be accelerated by pre-computing possible encryption keys using SHA-1 in advance. Then our hardware only has to check for a matching of ciphertexts implementing Triple-DES only.

Moreover, we are currently working on a device that can continuously read and record RF based communication at public places with high ePass density like airports. After the real-time decryption with our DES cracker, the information can be injected into distributed databases. Having installed such devices on many different airports and other similar places one can trace any person similar to tracing packages sent using postal services such as UPS.

3.3 Factorization

Since the introduction of public-key cryptography, the problem of factoring large composites is of increased interest. These days, the by far most popular asymmetric cryptosystem is RSA which was developed by Ronald Rivest, Adi Shamir and Leonard Adleman in 1977 [13]. The security of the RSA cryptosystem relies on the difficulty of factoring large numbers. Hence, the development of a fast factorization method could allow for cryptanalysis of RSA messages and signatures. The best known method for factoring large integers is the General Number-Field Sieve (GNFS). One important step within the GNFS is the factorization of mid-size numbers for smoothness testing, an efficient algorithm for which is the Elliptic Curve Method (ECM). Since ECM is suitable for parallelization, it is promising to be implemented in hardware.

The algorithm itself is almost ideal for improving the area-time product through special purpose hardware. First, it performs a very high number of operations on a very small set of input data, and is, thus, not very I/O intensive. Secondly, it requires relatively little memory. Thirdly, the operands needed for supporting GNFS are well beyond the width of current computer buses, arithmetic units, and registers, so that special purpose hardware can provide a much better fit. This justifies the higher development costs compared to a solution with DSPs. Lastly, it should be noted that the nature of the application allows for a very high degree of parallelization.

---

[4] Experiments on the Netherlands' epass demonstrated that the encrypted information can be revealed in 2 hours after intercepting the communication, see http://www.riscure.com/news/passport.html. The issuing scheme in the Netherlands has about 35 bits of entropy.

The first reported implementation of ECM in hardware was used to factor numbers of up to 200 bit [11]. However, the monetary cost of the used System-on-Chip hardware is quite high. Practical applications demand for a cheap realization of such ECM units. Therefore, a hardware platform consisting of many low-cost FPGAs seems to be an appropriate choice. As a result of the simple control logic for the ECM algorithm, no complex microcontroller is required and most logic can easily be put into the FPGA.

We propose to extend the proof-of-concept implementation of [11] to a highly parallel design comprised of many (cheap) FPGAs which can be used to assist attacks on RSA cryptosystems with moduli of sizes up to 1024 bit. For larger moduli, such a design demands for large quantities of ECM engines such that an ASIC implementation is preferable.

All algorithms are chosen such that they allow for an implementation with a low area consumption and a relatively high speed. At the time of writing, a basic ECM unit has been realized with a very efficient ALU and first performance results are available in Table 1 (the values include overhead for memory access).

Table 1. ECM implementation (200 bit modulus) (Xilinx XC3S1000, 40MHz)

Operation	Time
modular addition/ subtraction	100 ns
modular multiplication/ squaring	5.13 μs
point addition	31.4 μs
point duplication	26.0 μs

A single unit can be clocked with 40 MHz and requires approximately 40% of the slices of the Spartan3 device. Most memory has been realized with internal dual-port RAM.

3.4   Solving Elliptic Curve Discrete Logarithms

Besides factorization, many public-key cryptosystems are based on the difficulty of solving discrete logarithms in cyclic groups, known as the Discrete Logarithm Problem (DLP). A popular choice of such is the Elliptic Curve Cryptosystem (ECC) [7].

Attacking ECC requires the same algorithmic primitives as the cryptosystem itself, namely point addition and point doubling. Similar to the case of ECM in the previous section, these primitives can be implemented very efficiently in hardware. A parallel Pollard's Rho (PR) algorithm is described in [17].

The PR algorithm essentially does a great many computations without the necessity of communication. Only particular results have to be reported to a central control unit, which can be realized by, e.g., a host-PC connected to the FPGA. The parameterization of the algorithm can be optimized for a low area-time product and a low communication overhead. Hence, the reports of the PR units to the host occur not very frequently. As with the ECM unit, a single PR unit is comprised of an ALU, some memory and a control logic. The ALU for PR comprises modular inversion as additional function. Opposed to ECM, every single PR unit requires an individual control flow. Hence, the logic overhead for the algorithmic state machine is slightly higher. For curves defined over prime fields of 160 bit, two independent PR units can be loaded onto a XC3S1000 device. In this case, the maximum clock frequency is approximately 40 MHz and the area usage is 6067 slices (79%). With 160 bit curves, a point addition requires 846 cycles (21.15 μs) and 47 280 point operations can be performed per second by one unit. Consequently, a single FPGA can compute approximately 94 500 point operations per second.

We can parallelize Pollard's rho for COPACOBANA with the method presented in [17]. All instances of the algorithm can run independently from each other. Solely certain values have to be collected by a host-PC. Unlike ECM, we need a separate control logic for every single PR unit, yielding a slight overhead in logic on the FPGA. All units can be addressed individually by the host-PC using a unique address.

The chosen parameterization of the algorithm allows for a moderate communication overhead. In principle, all units compute point additions until they hit a point of a certain structure (so-called *distinguished points*). In such a case, the distinguished point is loaded to an output buffer for transmission to the host-PC while the computation continues.

For successfully solving the discrete logarithm problem over curves defined over prime fields $\mathbb{F}_p$, we have to compute approximately $\sqrt{q}$ points, where q is the largest prime power of the order of the curve. Appendix B provides estimates for solving the Certicom ECC challenges in hardware and software.

4   Conclusion and Future Work

The work at hand presents the design and first prototype of a cost-efficient hardware for running cryptanalytical algorithms. COPACOBANA can be built for for less than US$ 10,000 and hosts 120 low-cost FPGAs which can be adopted to any suitable task which is parallelizable and has low communication requirements. For instance, we demonstrated how the Data Encryption Standard (DES) can be broken within 9 days with the hardware at hand at an average rate of 48 billion keys per second.

We described how the DES implementation at hand can be used to attack the recently introduced machine readable travel documents. Furthermore, we introduced to two cryptanalytical algorithms which can be used to attack asymmetric algorithms. We propose a massively parallel implementation of the elliptic curve method for factorization. Building an efficient ECM machine is believed to speed-up the factorization of current RSA moduli. Furthermore, we can analyze the security of elliptic curve cryptosystems by solving the ECDLP with a hardware architecture for the parallel Pollard's rho algorithm.

Even though breaking full-size RSA (1024 bit or more) or elliptic curves (ECC with 160 bit or more) is out of reach with COPACOBANA, our machine provides for the first time a tool for a reliable security estimation of RSA and ECC. Even more relevant is the fact that resource constrained applications, in particular mobile devices, sometimes settle with shorter parameters, such as the 80 bit and 112 bit ECC systems recommended by the SECG standard, which become vulnerable with our machine. Also, assuming Moore's law, we can predict the security margin of RSA and ECC in the years to come.

Recapitulating, COPACOBANA is the first and currently the only available cost-efficient design to solve cryptanalytical challenges. COPACOBANA was intended to, but is not necessarily restricted to solving problems related to cryptanalysis. Almost certainly there will exist more interesting problems apart from cryptology, which can be solved efficiently with the design at hand. In an ongoing project, we plan to apply the Smith-Waterman algorithm [21,12] for scanning sequences of DNA or RNA against databases.

Future work includes optimization of the parallel implementations of the presented cryptanalytical algorithms to guarantee the best possible throughput. Furthermore, it seems promising to mount a real-world attack on the ePass and on other cryptographically weak systems such as SHA-1 with help of COBACOBANA.

Acknowledgments. We like to thank the Xilinx Inc. for the generous donation of Spartan-3 FPGAs which formed the basis of our design. We are also indebted to Jean-Jacques Quisquater and François-Xavier Standaert of the Université Catholique de Louvain for making their high-speed DES design available. Furthermore, we would like to thank Kerstin Lemke and Ahmad-Reza Sadeghi for interesting discussions on the security of machine readable travel documents.

References

1. M. Blaze, W. Diffie, R. L. Rivest, B. Schneier, T. Shimomura, E. Thompson, and M. Wiener. Minimal Key Lengths for Symmetric Ciphers to Provide Adequate Commercial Security: A Report by an Ad Hoc Group of Cryptographers and Computer Scientists. Technical report, January 1996. Available at http://www.counterpane.com/keylength.html.
2. Certicom Corporation. Certicom ECC Challenges, 2005. http://www.certicom.com
3. CESYS GmbH. USB2FPGA Product Overview. http://www.cesys.com, January 2005.
4. R. Clayton and M. Bond. Experience Using a Low-Cost FPGA Design to Crack DES Keys. In B.S. Kaliski, C.K. Koc Cetin, and C. Paar, editors, *Cryptographic Hardware and Embedded Systems - CHES 2002, 4th International Workshop, Redwood Shores, CA, USA*, volume 2523 of *series*, pages 579 – 592. Springer-Verlag, August 2002.
5. W. Diffie and M. E. Hellman. Exhaustive cryptanalysis of the NBS Data Encryption Standard. *COMPUTER*, 10(6):74–84, June 1977.
6. Electronic Frontier Foundation. *Cracking DES: Secrets of Encryption Research, Wiretap Politics & Chip Design*. O'Reilly & Associates Inc., July 1998.
7. D. R. Hankerson, A. J. Menezes, and S. A. Vanstone. *Guide to Elliptic Curve Cryptography*. Springer Verlag, 2004.

8. A. Juels, D. Molnar, and D. Wagner. Security and privacy issues in e-passports. In *SecureComm 2005, First International Conference on Security and Privacy for Emerging Areas in Communication Networks, Athens, Greece*, September 2005.
9. G.S. Kc and P.A. Karger. Security and Privacy Issues in Machine Readable Travel Documents (MRTDs). RC 23575, IBM T. J. Watson Research Labs, April 2005.
10. NIST FIPS PUB 46-3. *Data Encryption Standard*. Federal Information Processing Standards, National Bureau of Standards, U.S. Department of Commerce, January 1977.
11. J. Pelzl, M. Šimka, T. Kleinjung, J. Franke, C. Priplata, C. Stahlke, M. Drutarovský, V. Fischer, and C. Paar. Area-Time Efficient Hardware Architecture for Factoring Integers with the Elliptic Curve Method. *IEE Proceedings Information Security*, 152(1):67–78, October 2005.
12. G. Pfeiffer, H. Kreft, and M. Schimmler. Hardware Enhanced Biosequence Alignment. In *International Conference on METMBS*, pages 11–17. CSREA Press, 2005.
13. R. L. Rivest, A. Shamir, and L. Adleman. A Method for Obtaining Digital Signatures and Public-Key Cryptosystems. *Communications of the ACM*, 21(2):120–126, February 1978.
14. G. Rouvroy, F.-X. Standaert, J.-J. Quisquater, and J.-D. Legat. Design Strategies and Modified Descriptions to Optimize Cipher FPGA Implementations: Fast and Compact Results for DES and Triple-DES. In *Field-Programmable Logic and Applications - FPL*, pages 181–193, 2003.
15. RSA Laboratories. Announcements: The RSA Data Security Secret-Key Challenge. *CRYPTOBYTES*, 2(3):16, 1997. Available at `ftp://ftp.rsa.com/pub/cryptobytes/crypto2n3.pdf`.
16. University of California, Berkeley. Seti@Home Website, 2005. `http://setiathome.berkeley.edu/`.
17. P.C. van Oorschot and M.J. Wiener. Parallel Collision Search with Cryptanalytic Applications. *Journal of Cryptology*, 12(1):1–28, 1999.
18. M. J. Wiener. Efficient DES Key Search. In William R. Stallings, editor, *Practical Cryptography for Data Internetworks*, pages 31–79. IEEE Computer Society Press, 1996.
19. M. J. Wiener. Efficient DES Key Search: An Update. *CRYPTOBYTES*, 3(2):6–8, Autumn 1997.
20. Xilinx. Spartan-3 FPGA Family: Complete Data Sheet, DS099. `http://www.xilinx.com`, January 2005.
21. C.W. Yu, K.H. Kwong, K.H. Lee, and P.H.W. Leong. A Smith-Waterman Systolic Cell. In *Proceedings of the 13th International Workshop on Field Programmable Logic and Applications — FPL 2003*, pages 375–384. Springer, 2003.

A   Realization of COPACOBANA

Figure 4 shows the realization of a single FPGA DIMM module as printed circuit. COPACOBANA with a 19 DIMM modules is depicted in Figure 5.

B   Certicom ECC Challenges

To show how secure ECC is (and, thus, how hard it is to solve the discrete logarithm problem on elliptic curves), the company certicom announced challenges

Fig. 4. FPGA module (4-layer printed circuit board)

Fig. 5. COPACOBANA backplane with FPGA modules

for different bit-sizes [2]. The latest challenge solved was for a curve defined over a prime field of size of 109 bit. The challenge was estimated to take approximately $9 \cdot 10^6$ machine days on a conventional PC. For $q \approx 109$ bit, we would need to compute approximately 2^{54} point additions. In this case we would send every

2^{30}th point to a host-PC for subsequent comparisons. With COPACOBANA, the discrete logarithm could be solved in approximately 10^6 days with a single FPGA. Since the targeted FPGA is low-cost (approx. US\$ 50 per piece at small quantities[5]), it is fair to assume that we can buy more than one FPGA for the price of a single PC. We assume that COPACOBANA can solve the challenge approximately 90 times faster than a PCs at equivalent costs.

Table 2 provides a comparison of the expected running time in days of a conventional PC versus the running time of COPACOBANA built of 120 FP-GAs[6]. Furthermore, we assume the presence of 3, 2, and 1 PR unit(s) on a single FPGA for the bit-length 79-97, 109-191, and 239, respectively. Furthermore, a fixed clock rate of 40 MHz is assumed. The estimates for the machine days are taken from [2].

Table 2. Expected runtime on different platforms and for different Certicom ECC challenges

Challenge	Pentium M@1.7GHz	COPACOBANA
ECCp-79	49.0 d	0.13 d
ECCp-89	4.64 y	4.90 d
ECCp-97	74.7 y	93.4 d
ECCp-109	5570 y	24.2 y
ECCp-131	$1.40 \cdot 10^7$ y	$6.17 \cdot 10^4$ y
ECCp-163	$1.09 \cdot 10^{12}$ y	$7.63 \cdot 10^9$ y
ECCp-191	$2.17 \cdot 10^{16}$ y	$1.58 \cdot 10^{14}$ y
ECCp-239	$4.44 \cdot 10^{23}$ y	$7.18 \cdot 10^{21}$ y

---

[5] Xilinx offers this particular FPGA for US\$ 12 at large quantities ($> 250,000$ pcs.).

[6] For simplicity, we neglect the central control instance and the required memory which is, in fact, the same for both the PC and the FPGA solution.

Implementing the Elliptic Curve Method of Factoring in Reconfigurable Hardware

Kris Gaj[1], Soonhak Kwon[2], Patrick Baier[1], Paul Kohlbrenner[1],
Hoang Le[1], Mohammed Khaleeluddin[1], and Ramakrishna Bachimanchi[1]

[1] Dept. of Electrical and Computer Engineering, George Mason University,
Fairfax, Virginia 22030, USA
{kgaj, pkohlbr1, hle7, mkhaleel, rbachima}@gmu.edu, districtline@gmx.net
[2] Inst. of Basic Science, Sungkyunkwan University,
Suwon 440-746, Korea
shkwon@skku.edu

Abstract. A novel portable hardware architecture for the Elliptic Curve Method of factoring, designed and optimized for application in the relation collection step of the Number Field Sieve, is described and analyzed. A comparison with an earlier proof-of-concept design by Pelzl, Šimka, et al. has been performed, and a substantial improvement has been demonstrated in terms of both the execution time and the area-time product. The ECM architecture has been ported across three different families of FPGA devices in order to select the family with the best performance to cost ratio. A timing comparison with a highly optimized software implementation, GMP-ECM, has been performed. Our results indicate that low-cost families of FPGAs, such as Xilinx Spartan 3, offer at least an order of magnitude improvement over the same generation of microprocessors in terms of the performance to cost ratio.

Keywords: Cipher-breaking, factoring, ECM, FPGA.

1 Introduction

The fastest known method for factoring large integers is the Number Field Sieve (NFS), invented by Pollard in 1991 [1,2]. It has since been improved substantially and developed from its initial "special" form (which was only used to factor numbers close to perfect powers, such as Fermat numbers) to a general purpose factoring algorithm. Using the Number Field Sieve, an RSA modulus of 663 bits was successfully factored by Bahr, Boehm, Franke and Kleinjung in May 2005 [3]. The cost of implementing the Number Field Sieve and the time it takes for such an implementation to factor a b-bit RSA modulus provide an upper bound on the security of b-bit RSA.

In order to factor a big integer N, such as an RSA modulus, NFS requires the factorization of a large number of moderately sized integers created at run time, perhaps of size 200 bits. Such numbers can be routinely factored in very little time. However, because an estimated 10^{10} such factorizations are necessary for NFS to succeed in factoring a 1024 bit RSA modulus, it is of crucial importance

L. Goubin and M. Matsui (Eds.): CHES 2006, LNCS 4249, pp. 119–133, 2006.

to perform these auxiliary factorizations as fast and efficiently as possible. Even tiny improvements, once multiplied by 10^{10} factorizations, would make a significant difference in how big an RSA modulus we can factor. The Elliptic Curve Method (ECM), which is the main subject of this paper, is a sub-exponential factoring algorithm, with expected run time of $O(\exp(c\sqrt{\log p \log \log p})\, M(N))$ where $c > 0$, p is a factor we aim to find, and $M(N)$ denotes the cost of multiplication (mod N). ECM is the best method to perform the kind of factorizations needed by NFS, for integers in the 200-bit range, with prime factors of up to about 40 bits [16,17].

The contribution of this paper is an implementation of the elliptic curve method in hardware (FPGAs). We describe in detail how to optimize the design and compare our work both to an existing software implementation (GMP-ECM)[4,5] and an earlier hardware implementation [6,7].

2   Elliptic Curve Method

2.1   ECM Algorithm

Let K be a field with characteristic different from $2, 3$. An elliptic curve can be represented by a homogeneous equation $Y^2 Z = X^3 + AXZ^2 + BZ^3$ with $X, Y, Z \in K$ not all zero, where A, B are in K with $4A^3 + 27B^2 \neq 0$, together with a special point $O = (0, 1, 0)$ called a "point at infinity". Points of the curve E together with the addition operation form an abelian group which is denoted by $E(K)$, where O is the identity element of the group [8].

The Elliptic Curve Method of factoring was originally proposed by Lenstra [9] and subsequently extended by Brent [10] and Montgomery [11,12]. The original part of the algorithm proposed by Lenstra is typically referred to as Phase 1 (or Stage 1), and the extension by Brent and Montgomery is called Phase 2 (or Stage 2). The pseudocode of both phases is given below as Algorithm 1.

Algorithm 1. ECM Algorithm

Require: N: composite number to be factored, E: elliptic curve, $P_0 = (x_0, y_0, z_0) \in E(\mathbb{Z}_N)$: initial point, B_1: smoothness bound for Phase 1, B_2: smoothness bound for Phase 2, $B_2 > B_1$.
Ensure: q: factor of N, $1 < q \leq N$, or FAIL.

Phase 1.

1: $k \leftarrow \prod_{p \leq B_1} p^{\lfloor \log_p B_1 \rfloor}$
2: $Q_0 \leftarrow kP_0$
   $\{Q_0 = (x_{Q_0}, y_{Q_0}, z_{Q_0})\}$
3: $q \leftarrow \gcd(z_{Q_0}, N)$
4: **if** $q > 1$ **then**
5:    return q
6: **else**
7:    go to Phase 2
8: **end if**

Phase 2.

9: $d \leftarrow 1$
10: **for** each prime $p = B_1$ to B_2 **do**
11:    $(x_{pQ_0}, y_{pQ_0}, z_{pQ_0}) \leftarrow pQ_0$.
12:    $d \leftarrow d \cdot z_{pQ_0} \pmod{N}$
13: **end for**
14: $q \leftarrow \gcd(d, N)$
15: **if** $q > 1$ **then**
16:    return q
17: **else**
18:    return FAIL
19: **end if**

2.2   Implementation Issues

An efficient algorithm for computing scalar multiplication was proposed by Montgomery [11] in 1987, and is known as the Montgomery ladder algorithm.

This algorithm is especially efficient when an elliptic curve is expressed in the Montgomery form, $E : by^2 = x^3 + ax^2 + x$. This form is obtained by a suitable change of variables [4] from the standard Weierstrass form. The corresponding expression in projective coordinates is

$$E : by^2 z = x^3 + ax^2 z + xz^2, \tag{1}$$

with $b(a^2 - 4) \neq 0$.

When one uses the Montgomery ladder algorithm with the Montgomery form of elliptic curve given in (1), all intermediate computations can be carried on using only x and z coordinates. As a result, we denote the starting point P_0 by $(x_0 : : z_0)$, intermediate points P, Q, by $(x_P : : z_P)$, $(x_Q : : z_Q)$, and the final point kP_0 by $(x_{kP_0} : : z_{kP_0})$. The pseudocode of the Montgomery ladder algorithm is shown below as Algorithm 2., and its basic step is defined in detail as Algorithm 3..

Algorithm 2. Montgomery Ladder Algorithm

Require: $P_0 = (x_0 : : z_0)$ on E with $x_0 \neq 0$, an s-bit positive integer $k = (k_{s-1} k_{s-2} \cdots k_1 k_0)_2$
    with $k_{s-1} = 1$
Ensure: $kP_0 = (x_{kP_0} : : z_{kP_0})$
1: $Q \leftarrow P_0$, $P \leftarrow 2P_0$
2: **for** $i = s - 2$ **downto** 0 **do**
3:    **if** $k_i = 1$ **then**
4:        $Q \leftarrow P + Q$, $P \leftarrow 2P$
5:    **else**
6:        $Q \leftarrow 2Q$, $P \leftarrow P + Q$
7:    **end if**
8: **end for**
9: **return** Q

Algorithm 3. Addition and Doubling using the Montgomery's Form of Elliptic Curve

---

Require: $P = (x_P : : z_P)$, $Q = (x_Q : : z_Q)$ with $x_P x_Q (x_P - x_Q) \neq 0$, $P_0 = (x_0 : : z_0) =$
    $(x_{P-Q} : : z_{P-Q}) = P - Q$, $a_{24} = \frac{a+2}{4}$, where a is a parameter of the curve E in (1)
Ensure: $P + Q = (x_{P+Q} : : z_{P+Q})$, $2P = (x_{2P} : : z_{2P})$
1: $x_{P+Q} \leftarrow z_{P-Q}[(x_P - z_P)(x_Q + z_Q) + (x_P + z_P)(x_Q - z_Q)]^2$
2: $z_{P+Q} \leftarrow x_{P-Q}[(x_P - z_P)(x_Q + z_Q) - (x_P + z_P)(x_Q - z_Q)]^2$
3: $4x_P z_P \leftarrow (x_P + z_P)^2 - (x_P - z_P)^2$
4: $x_{2P} \leftarrow (x_P + z_P)^2 (x_P - z_P)^2$
5: $z_{2P} \leftarrow (4x_P z_P)\left((x_P - z_P)^2 + a_{24} \cdot (4x_P z_P)\right)$

A careful analysis of formulas in Algorithm 3 indicates that point addition $P+Q$ requires 6 multiplications, and point doubling 5 multiplications. Therefore, a total of 11 multiplications are required in each step of the Montgomery ladder algorithm. In Phase 1 of ECM, the initial point, P_0, can be chosen arbitrarily. Choosing $z_0 = 1$ implies $z_{P-Q} = 1$ throughout the entire algorithm, and thus reduces the total number of multiplications from 11 to 10 per one step of the algorithm, independent of the i-th bit k_i of k. This optimization is not possible in Phase 2, where the initial point Q_0 is the result of computations in Phase 1, and thus cannot be chosen arbitrarily.

2.3   Implementation of Phase 2

Phase 1 computes one scalar multiplication kP_0, and the implementation issues are relatively easy compared with Phase 2. For Phase 2, we follow the basic idea of the standard continuation [11] and modify it appropriately for efficient FPGA implementation. Choose $2 < D < B_2$, and let every prime p, $B_1 < p \leq B_2$, be expressed in the form

$$p = mD \pm j \tag{2}$$

where m varies between $M_{MIN} = \lfloor (B_1 + \frac{D}{2})/D \rfloor$ and $M_{MAX} = \lceil (B_2 - \frac{D}{2})/D \rceil$, and j varies between 1 and $\lfloor \frac{D}{2} \rfloor$. The condition that p is prime implies that $\gcd(j, D) = 1$. Thus, possible values of j form a set $J_S = \{j : 1 \leq j \leq \lfloor \frac{D}{2} \rfloor, \gcd(j, D) = 1\}$, of the size of $\phi(D)/2$, and possible values of m form a set $M_T = \{m : M_{MIN} \leq m \leq M_{MAX}\}$, of the size $M_N = M_{MAX} - M_{MIN} + 1$, where M_N is approximately equal to $\frac{B_2 - B_1}{D}$. Then, the condition $pQ_0 = O$, implies $(mD \pm j)Q_0 = O$, and thus $mDQ_0 = \pm jQ_0$.

Writing $mDQ_0 = (x_{mDQ_0} : : z_{mDQ_0})$ and $jQ_0 = (x_{jQ_0} : : z_{jQ_0})$, the condition $mDQ_0 = \pm jQ_0 \in E(\mathbb{Z}_q)$ is satisfied if and only if $x_{mDQ_0} z_{jQ_0} - x_{jQ_0} z_{mDQ_0} \equiv 0 \pmod{q}$. Therefore existence of such pair m and j implies that one can find a factor of N by computing

$$\gcd(d, N) > 1, \quad \text{where } d = \prod_{m,j} (x_{mDQ_0} z_{jQ_0} - x_{jQ_0} z_{mDQ_0}) \tag{3}$$

In order to speed up these computations, one precomputes one of the sets $S = \{jQ_0 : j \in J_S\}$ or $T = \{mDQ_0 : m \in M_T\}$. Typically, the first of these sets, S, is smaller, and thus only this set is precomputed. One then computes the product d in the (3) for a current value of mDQ_0, and all precomputed points jQ_0, for which either $mD + j$ or $mD - j$ is prime. For each pair, (m, j), where $j \in J_S$ and $m \in M_T$, we can precompute a bit value: prime_table$[m, j] = 1$ *when $mD + j$ or $mD - j$ is prime*, and 0 *otherwise*. This table can be reused for multiple iterations of Phase 2 with the same values of B_1 and B_2, and is of the size of $M_N \cdot \phi(D)/2$ bits. Similarly, we can precompute a bit table: GCD_table$[j] = 1$ *when $j \in J_S$, and 0 otherwise*. This table will have $D/2$ bits for odd D and $D/4$ for even D (no need to reserve bits for even values of j). The exact pseudocode of the algorithm used in our implementation of Phase 2 is given in Algorithm 4.

The value B_1 is usually chosen as $B_1 \approx e^{\sqrt{\frac{1}{2} \log q \log \log q}}$ where q is unknown prime we want to find, and the value B_2 is between $50B_1$ and $100B_1$ depending on the computational resources for Phase 2. In our case, like Šimka et al. [6,7], we choose $B_1 = 960$ and $B_2 = 57000$ to find a 40-bit prime divisor of 200-bit integers. Note that one has $e^{\sqrt{\frac{1}{2} \log q \log \log q}} \approx 988$ by setting $q = 2^{41}$ which is close to 960, and the ratio B_2/B_1 is $57000/960 \approx 59$. In general, the larger values of B_1 and B_2 increase the probability of success in Phase 1 and Phase 2 respectively (and thus decrease the expected number of trials), but at the same time, increase the execution time of these phases. Values of $D = 30 = 2 \cdot 3 \cdot 5$ and $D = 210 = 2 \cdot 3 \cdot 5 \cdot 7$ are the two most natural choices for D as they minimize the size of sets J_S and S and as a result of the amount of memory storage and computations required for Phase 2. The larger D, the larger the amount of Precomputations in Algorithm 4., but the smaller M_N, and thus the smaller number of iterations of the outer loop during Main computations in Algorithm 4.. A theoretical analysis of the optimal parameter choices is given in [19], with a view towards software implementations. The techniques developed there - which use Dickman's function to estimate the probability of success of the Elliptic Curve Method - can be adapted to a hardware setting and make it possible to determine optimal parameter choices via numerical approximations to Dickman's function. While our choices are not strictly optimal, they are fairly good and allow for direct comparsion with Šimka et al. [6,7].

Algorithm 4. Standard Continuation Algorithm of Phase 2

Require: N: number to be factored, E: elliptic curve, $Q_0 = kP_0$: initial point for Phase 2 calculated as a result of Phase 1, B_1: smoothness bound for Phase 1, B_2: smoothness bound for Phase 2, $B_2 > B_1$, D: parameter determining a trade-off between the computation time and the amount of memory required; D is assumed even in this version of the algorithm.
Ensure: q: factor of N, $1 < q \leq N$ or FAIL

Precomputations:
1: $M_{MIN} \leftarrow \lfloor (B_1 + \frac{D}{2})/D \rfloor$
2: $M_{MAX} \leftarrow \lceil (B_2 - \frac{D}{2})/D \rceil$
3: clear GCD_table, clear J_S
4: **for each** $j = 1$ to $\frac{D}{2}$ step 2 **do**
5:     **if** $\gcd(j, D) = 1$ **then**
6:         GCD_table$[j] = 1$
7:         add j to J_S
8:     **end if**
9: **end for**
10: clear prime_table
11: **for each** $m = M_{MIN}$ to M_{MAX} **do**
12:     **for each** $j = 1$ to $\frac{D}{2}$ step 2 **do**
13:         **if** ($mD + j$ or $mD - j$ is prime) **then**
14:             prime_table$[m, j] = 1$
15:         **end if**
16:     **end for**
17: **end for**
18: $Q \leftarrow Q_0$
19: **for** $j = 1$ to $\frac{D}{2}$ step 2 **do**
20:     **if** GCD_table$[j] = 1$ **then**
21:         store Q in S
            $\{Q = jQ_0 = (x_{jQ_0} : : z_{jQ_0})\}$
22:     **end if**
23:     $Q \leftarrow Q + 2Q_0$
24: **end for**

Main computations:
25: $d \leftarrow 1$, $Q \leftarrow DQ_0$, $R \leftarrow M_{MIN}Q$
26: **for each** $m = M_{MIN}$ to M_{MAX} **do**
27:     **for each** $j \in J_S$ **do**
28:         **if** prime_table$[m, j] = 1$ **then**
29:             retrieve jQ_0 from table S
30:             $d \leftarrow d \cdot (x_R z_{jQ_0} - x_{jQ_0} z_R)$
                $\{R = (x_R : : z_R)\}$
31:         **end if**
32:     **end for**
33:     $R \leftarrow R + Q$
34: **end for**
35: $q \leftarrow \gcd(d, N)$
36: **if** $q > 1$ **then**
37:     return q
38: **else**
39:     return FAIL
40: **end if**

---

3   ECM Architecture

3.1   Top-Level View: ECM Units

Our ECM system consists of multiple ECM units working independently in parallel, as shown in Figure 1. Each unit performs the entire ECM algorithm for one number N, one curve E and one initial point P_0. All units share the same global control unit and the same global memory. All components of the system are located on the same integrated circuit, either an FPGA or an ASIC, depending on the choice of an implementation technology. The exact number of ECM units per integrated circuit depends on the amount of resources available in the given integrated circuit. Multiple integrated circuits may work independently in parallel, on factoring a single number, or factoring different numbers. All integrated circuits are connected to a central host computer, which distributes tasks among the individual ECM systems, and collects and interprets results.

The operation of the system starts by loading all parameters required for Phase 1 of ECM from the host computer to the global memory on the chip. These parameters include:

1. Number to be factored, N, coordinates of the starting point P_0, and the parameter a_{24} dependent on the coefficient a of the curve E - all of which can be separate for each ECM unit.
2. Integer k, used as an input in the ECM Phase 1 (see Algorithm 1.), its size k_N, and the parameter $n = \lfloor \log_2 N_{MAX} \rfloor + 2$, related to the size of the largest N, N_{MAX}, processed by the ECM units - all of which are common for all ECM units.

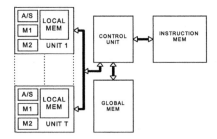

Fig. 1. Block diagram of the top-level unit. Notation: MEM-memory; $M1$, $M2$-multipliers 1 and 2; A/S adder/subtractor.

In the next step, N, the coordinates of P_0, and the parameters a_{24} and n are loaded to the local memories of the respective ECM units, and the operation of these units is started. All units operate synchronously, on different data sets, performing all intermediate calculations exactly at the same time.

The results of these calculations are the coordinates x_{Q_0} and z_{Q_0} of the ending point $Q_0 = kP_0$, separate for each ECM unit. These coordinates are downloaded to the host computer, which performs the final calculations of Phase 1, $q = \gcd(z_{Q_0}, N)$.

If no factor of N was found, the ECM system is ready for Phase 2. The values of N, the parameters a_{24} and n, and the coordinates of the points Q_0 obtained as a result of Phase 1 are already in the local memories of each ECM unit. The host computer calculates and downloads to the global memory of the ECM system the following parameters dependent on B_2 and D: M_{MIN}, M_N, GCD_table, and prime_table, defined in Section 2.3. The Phase 2 is then started simultaneously in all ECM units, and produces as final results, the accumulated product d (see (3)). These final results are then downloaded to the host computer, where the final calculations $q = \gcd(d, N)$ are performed.

Note that with this top level organization, there is no need to compute greatest common divisor or division in hardware. Additionally, the overhead associated with the transfer of data between the ECM system and the host computer, and the time of computations in software are both typically insignificant compared to the time used for ECM computations in hardware, even in the case of a relatively slow interface and/or a slow microprocessor.

3.2 Medium-Level View: Operations of the ECM Unit

Medium-Level Operations. The primary operation constituting Phase 1 of ECM is a scalar multiplication $Q_0 = kP_0$. As discussed in Section 2.2, this operation can be efficiently implemented in projective coordinates using Algorithm 2.

In Phase 1, one coordinate of P_0 can be chosen arbitrarily, and therefore the computations can be simplified by selecting $z_{P_0} = z_{P-Q} = 1$. The remaining computations necessary to simultaneously compute $P + Q$ and $2P$ can be interleaved, and assigned to three functional units working in parallel, as shown in Table 1. The entire step of a scalar multiplication, including both point addition and doubling can be calculated in the amount of time required for 2 modular additions/subtractions and 5 modular multiplications. Please note that because the time of an addition/subtraction is much shorter than the time of a multiplication, two *sequential* additions/subtractions can be calculated in parallel with two multiplications.

Table 1. One step of a scalar multiplication, including the concurrent operations $P+Q$ and $2P$, for the case of $z_{P-Q} = 1$. Notation: A: operations used for addition only, D: operations used for doubling only, A/D: operations used for addition and doubling.

Adder/Subtractor		Multiplier 1	Multiplier 2
A/D:	$a_1 = x_P + z_P$ $s_1 = x_P - z_P$		
A/D:	$a_2 = x_Q + z_Q$ $s_2 = x_Q - z_Q$	D: $m_1 = s_1^2$	D: $m_2 = a_1^2$
D:	$s_3 = m_2 - m_1$	A: $m_3 = s_1 \cdot a_2$	A: $m_4 = s_2 \cdot a_1$
A:	$a_3 = m_3 + m_4$ $s_4 = m_3 - m_4$	D: $x_{2P} = m_5 = m_1 \cdot m_2$	D: $m_6 = s_3 \cdot a_{24}$
D:	$a_4 = m_1 + m_6$	A: $x_{P+Q} = m_7 = a_3^2$	A: $m_8 = s_4^2$
		A: $z_{P+Q} = m_9 = m_8 \cdot x_{P-Q}$	D: $z_{2P} = m_{10} = s_3 \cdot a_4$

The storage used for temporary variables $a_1, \ldots, a_4, s_1, \ldots, s_4$, and $m_1, \ldots, m_{10}$ can be reused whenever any intermediate values are no longer needed. With the appropriate optimization, the amount of local memory required for Phase 1 has been reduced to 11 256-bit operands, i.e., 88 32-bit words. The remaining portion of this memory is used in Phase 2 of ECM.

In Phase 2, the initial computation

$$D \cdot Q_0 \quad \text{and} \quad M_{MIN} \cdot (D \cdot Q_0)$$

can be performed using an algorithm similar to the one used in Phase 1. The only difference is that now, $P - Q = Q_0$ cannot be chosen arbitrarily, and thus,

$z_{P-Q} = z_{Q_0} \neq 1$. As a result, the computations will take the amount of time required for 2 modular additions/subtractions and 6 modular multiplications.

The second type of operation required in Phase 2 is a simple point addition $P + Q$. This operation can be performed in the time of 6 additions/subtractions and 3 modular multiplications.

Finally, the last medium level operation required in Phase 2 is the accumulation of the product d, as defined in (3). We can rewrite the expression for d as

$$d \equiv \prod_{i,n} d_{in} \equiv \prod_{i,n} (x_n z_i - x_i z_n) \pmod{N} \tag{4}$$

where, $(x_i, z_i) \in \{(x, z): (x: : z) = jQ_0\}$, $(x_n, z_n) \in \{(x, z): (x: : z) = mDQ_0\}$ and GCD_table[j]=1 and prime_table[m, j]=1. In Table 2, we show how these operations can be distributed in an optimum way among three arithmetic units working in parallel. As shown in Table 2, after the initial delay of one multiplication, the time required to compute and accumulate any *two* subsequent values of a partial product $x_{mDQ_0} z_{jQ_0} - x_{jQ_0} z_{mDQ_0}$ is equal to the time of three multiplications.

Table 2. Accumulation of the partial results $\prod_{i,n}(x_n z_i - x_i z_n) \pmod{N}$ in Phase 2 (for fixed n and moving i)

Adder/Subtractor	Multiplier 1	Multiplier 2
	$m_1 = x_n \cdot z_0$	$m_2 = x_0 \cdot z_n$
$d_{0n} = m_1 - m_2$	$m_3 = x_n \cdot z_1$	$m_4 = x_1 \cdot z_n$
$d_{1n} = m_3 - m_4$	$d = d \cdot d_{0n}$	$m_1 = x_n \cdot z_2$
	$d = d \cdot d_{1n}$	$m_2 = x_2 \cdot z_n$
$d_{2n} = m_1 - m_2$	$m_3 = x_n \cdot z_3$	$m_4 = x_3 \cdot z_n$
$d_{3n} = m_3 - m_4$	$d = d \cdot d_{2n}$	$m_1 = x_n \cdot z_4$
	$d = d \cdot d_{3n}$	$m_2 = x_4 \cdot z_n$
$\cdots \cdots$	$\cdots \cdots$	$\cdots \cdots$

Instructions of the ECM Unit. Each ECM unit is composed of two modular multipliers, one adder/subtractor, and one local memory. The local memory size is 512 32-bit words, equivalent to 64 256-bit registers. In Phase 1, only 11 out of 64 256-bit registers are in use. In Phase 2, with $D = 210$, the entire memory is occupied.

Every ECM unit forms a simple processor with its own instruction set. Since all ECM units perform exactly the same instructions at the same time, the instructions are stored in the global instruction memory, and are interpreted using the global control unit, as shown in Figure 1. Three sequences of ECM instructions describe three kinds of medium-level operations:

1. One step of a scalar multiplication kP ($P = 2P$, $Q = P + Q$) in Phase 1, i.e., with $z_{P_0} = 1$ (see Table 1).
2. One step of a scalar multiplication kP ($P = 2P$, $Q = P + Q$) in Phase 2, i.e., with $z_{P_0} \neq 1$.
3. Addition $P + Q$ in Phase 2, i.e., with $z_{P_0} \neq 1$.

Since only 11 256-bit registers are necessary to perform each of the sequences of instructions given above, only 4 bits are required to encode each input/output address.

The operation performed by each instruction is determined based on the position of the instruction in the instruction sequence, and thus does not need to be encoded in the instruction body. In particular, a group of four instructions corresponds to one row of Table 1 and is stored in the order: Multiplication 2, Multiplication 1, Subtraction, and Addition. These four consecutive instructions are fetched serially, but executed in parallel. The processor progresses to the next group of four instructions only when all instructions of the previous group have been completed. If the given arithmetic unit should remain inactive in the given sequence of four instructions, this inactivity is described using the zero value of a special flag in the body of the respective instruction.

3.3 Low-Level View: Modular Multiplication and Addition/Subtraction

The three low level operations implemented by the ECM unit are Montgomery modular multiplication [13], modular addition, and modular subtraction. Modular addition and subtraction are very similar to each other, and as a result they are implemented using one functional unit, the adder/subtractor. For 256-bit operands, both addition and subtraction take 41 clock cycles.

In order to simplify our Montgomery multiplier, all operations are performed on inputs X, Y in the range $0 \leq X, Y < 2N$, and return an output S in the same range, $0 \leq S < 2N$. This is equivalent to computing all intermediate results modulo $2N$ instead of N, which increases the size of all intermediate values by one bit, but shortens the time of computations, and leads to exactly the same final results as operations mod N.

In our implementation we have adopted the Radix-2 Multiplier Algorithm with Carry Save Addition, reported earlier in [14]. With this algorithm applied, the total execution time of a single Montgomery multiplication is equal to $n + 16$ clock cycles. For a typical use within ECM, n is greater than 100, and thus one addition followed by one subtraction can easily execute in the amount of time smaller than the time of a single Montgomery multiplication.

4   Implementation Results

Our ECM system has been developed entirely in RTL-level VHDL, and written in a way that provides portability among multiple families of FPGA devices and standard-cell ASIC libraries. In the case of FPGAs, the code has been synthesized using Synplicity Synplify Pro v. 8.0, and implemented on FPGAs using Xilinx ISE v. 6.3, 7.1 and 8.1. Three different families of FPGA devices have been targeted, including high-performance families, Virtex E and Virtex II, as well as a low-cost family, Spartan 3. The design has been debugged and verified using a test program written in C, and using GMP-ECM [4,5].

Table 3. Execution time of Phase 1 and Phase 2 in the ECM hardware architecture for 198-bit numbers $N, B_1 = 960$ (which implies number of bits of $k, k_N = 1375$), $B_2 = 57000$, and $D = 30$ or $D = 210$

Operation	Notation	Formula	# clk cycles $D = 30$	# clk cycles $D = 210$
Elementary operations				
Modular addition	T_A		41	
Montgomery multiplication	T_M	$T_M = n + 16$	216	
Point addition and doubling (Phase 1)	T_{AD1}	$T_{AD1} = 5T_M + 2T_A + 50$	1212	
Point addition and doubling (Phase 2)	T_{AD2}	$T_{AD2} = 6T_M + 2T_A + 50$	1428	
Point addition (Phase 2) (Phase 2)	T_{ADD2}	$T_{ADD2} = 3T_M + 6T_A + 30$	924	
Phase 1				
Phase 1 (estimation)	$T_{P1\,est}$	$T_{P1} \approx k_N \cdot T_{AD1}$	1,666,500	
Phase 1 (simulation)	$T_{P1\,sim}$		1,713,576	
Phase 2				
Precalculating jQ_0	T_{jQ}	$T_{jQ} \approx 2T_{AD2}$ $+(\lfloor D/4 \rfloor - 2)T_{ADD2}$	7476 (0.19%)	49,056 (2.56%)
DQ_0	T_{DQ}	$T_{DQ} \approx \lceil log_2(D + 1) \rceil T_{AD2}$	7140 (0.18%)	11,424 (0.60%)
$M_{MIN}DQ_0$	$T_{M_{min}DQ}$	$T_{M_{min}DQ} \approx$ $\lceil log_2(M_{MIN} + 1) \rceil T_{AD2}$	8568 (0.22%)	4284 (0.22%)
Calculating mDQ_0 for $M_{MIN} < m \leq M_{MAX}$	T_{mDQ}	$T_{mDQ} \approx (M_N - 2)T_{ADD2}$	1,725,108 (44.29%)	244,860 (12.78%)
Number of ones in the prime_table	$n_{\text{prime\_table}}$		4531	4361
Calculating accumulated product d	T_d	$T_d \approx \lceil 1.5 \cdot n_{\text{prime\_table}} \rceil (T_M + 12)$ $+M_N(T_M + T_A)/2$	1,789,883 (45.95%)	1,525,886 (79.67%)
Phase 2 (estimation)	$T_{P2\,est}$	$T_{P2} \approx T_{jQ} + T_{DQ} + T_{M_{min}DQ}$ $+T_{mDQ} + T_d$	3,538,175 (90.84%)	1,835,510 (95.84%)
Phase 2 (simulation)	$T_{P2\,sim}$		3,895,013 (100%)	1,915,219 (100%)

The execution times of Phase 1 and Phase 2 in the ECM hardware architecture are shown in Table 3. The generic formulas for major component operations are provided, together with the estimated values of the execution times for the case of 198-bit numbers N, and the smoothness bounds $B_1 = 960$ and $B_2 = 57000$. The estimated values are compared with the accurate values obtained from simulation. The difference is less than 10%, and can be attributed to the time needed for control operations and data movements within local memories, and between global memory and local memories. Two values of the parameter D are considered for Phase 2, $D = 30$ and $D = 210$. The table proves that the choice of the parameter $D = 210$, reduces the execution time of Phase 2 in our architecture by a factor of two compared to the case of $D = 30$. As confirmed by exhaustive search, the choice of $D = 210$ results in the smallest possible execution time for Phase 2 for the given values of the smoothness bounds

$B_1 = 960$ and $B_2 = 57000$, assuming execution times of basic operations given in Table 3. For $D = 210$, the largest contribution to Phase 2, around 80%, comes from the calculation of the accumulated product d.

In order to estimate an overhead associated with the transfer of control and data between a microprocessor and an FPGA, the ECM system with 10 ECM units has been ported to a reconfigurable computer SRC 6 from SRC Computers [18], based on 2.8 GHZ Xeon microprocessors and Xilinx Virtex II XC2V6000-6 FPGAs running at a fixed clock frequency of 100 MHz. The data and control transfer overheads have been experimentally measured to be less than 4% of the end-to-end execution time for the combined Phase 1 and Phase 2 calculations.

In Table 4, we compare our ECM architecture to an earlier design by Pelzl, Šimka, et al., presented at SHARCS 2005, and described in subsequent publications [6,7]. Every possible effort was made to make this comparison as fair as possible. In particular, we use an identical FPGA device, Virtex 2000E-6. We also do not take into account any limitations imposed by an external microcontroller used in the Pelzl/Šimka architecture. Instead, we assume that the system could be redesigned to include an on-chip controller, and it would operate with the maximum possible speed reported by the authors for their ALUs [6,7], i.e., 38 MHz (clock period = 26.3 ns). We also ignore a substantial input/output overhead reported by the authors, and caused most likely by the use of an external microcontroller.

In spite of these equalizing measures, our design outperforms the design by Pelzl, Šimka, et al. by a factor of 9.3 in terms of the execution time for Phase 1, by a factor of 7.4 in terms of the execution time for Phase 2 with the same value of parameter D, and by a factor of 15.0 for Phase 2 with the increased value of $D = 210$, not reported by Pelzl/Šimka. The main improvements in Phase 1 come from the more efficient design for a Montgomery multiplier (a factor of 5 improvement) and from the use of two Montgomery multipliers working in parallel (a factor of 1.9 improvement). An additional smaller factor is the ability of an adder/subtractor to work in parallel with both multipliers, as well as, the higher clock frequency.

One might expect that such improvement in speed comes at the cost of substantial sacrifices in terms of the circuit area and cost. In fact, our architecture is bigger, but only by a factor of 2.7 in terms of the number of CLB slices. Additionally, the design reported in [6,7] has a number of ECM units per FPGA device limited not by the number of CLB slices, but by the number of internal on-chip block RAMs (BRAMs). If this constraint was not removed, our design would outperform the design by Pelzl/Šimka in terms of the amount of computations per Xilinx Virtex 2000E device by a factor of $9.3 \cdot 2.33 = 22$ for Phase 1 and 35 for Phase 2. If the memory constraint is removed, the product of time by area still improves compared to the design by Pelzl and Šimka by a factor of $9.3/2.7 = 3.4$ for Phase 1 and 5.6 for Phase 2.

In Table 5, we show the results of porting our design to three families of Xilinx FPGAs. For each family, a representative device is selected and used in our implementation. For each device we determine the exact amount of resources

Table 4. Comparison with the design by Pelzl, Šimka, et al., both implemented using Virtex 2000E-6

Part 1: Execution Time						
	Pelzl, Šimka, et al.		Our design		Ratio Pelzl, Šimka / ours	
	# clk cycles	Time	# clk cycles	Time	# clk cycles	Time
Clock period		26.3 ns		18.5 ns		
Modular addition	16	0.62 μs	41	0.78 μs	0.6	0.8
Modular subtraction	24	0.42 μs	41	0.78 μs	0.4	0.5
Montgomery multiplication	796	20.7 μs	216	4.1 μs	3.7	**5.0**
Point addition & doubling (Phase 1)	8200	213.2 μs	1212	23.0 μs	6.8	**9.3**
Phase 1	11,266,800	292.9 ms	1,713,576	31.7 ms	6.6	**9.3**
Point addition & doubling (Phase 2)	8998	233.9 μs	1428	27.1 μs	5.6	8.6
Point addition (Phase 2)	4920	127.9 μs	924	17.6 μs	4.8	**7.3**
Calculation and accumulation of two values of d_{in} (Phase 2)	4776	124.2 μs	648	12.3 μs	6.2	10.1
Phase 2 ($D = 30$)	20,276,060	527.2 ms	3,895,013	72.1 ms	5.2	**7.4**
Phase 2 ($D = 210$)	-	-	1,915,219	35.5 ms	10.6	15.0

Part 2: Resource usage per one ECM unit						
	Pelzl, Šimka, et al.		Our design ($D = 210$)		Ratio Ours / Pelzl, Šimka	
Number of	#	%	#	%		
CLB slices	N/A	6.0	3102	16	**2.7**	
LUTs	1754	4.5	4933	13	2.8	
FFs	506	1.25	3129	8	6.2	
BRAMs	44	27	2	1.25	0.045	
Maximum number of ECM units per chip	3 (limited by BRAMs)		7 (limited by CLB slices)		**2.33**	

needed per single ECM unit, the maximum number of ECM units per chip, the maximum clock frequency, and then the maximum amount of ECM computations (Phase 1 and Phase 2) per unit of time. Finally, we normalize the performance by dividing it by the cost of a respective FPGA device. From the last row in the table one can see that the low-cost FPGA devices from the Spartan 3 family outperform the high-performance Virtex II devices by a factor of 16, and thus are more suitable for cost effective code breaking computations.

In Table 6, we compare the execution time of Phase 1 and Phase 2 between the two representative FPGA devices and a highly optimized software implementation (GMP-ECM) running on Pentium 4 Xeon, 2.8 GHz. GMP-ECM is one of the most powerful software implementations of ECM and contains multiple optimization techniques for both Phase 1 and Phase 2 [4,5]. Additionally, we run our own test program in C that mimics almost exactly the behavior of

Table 5. Results of the FPGA implementations (resources and timing for one ECM unit per FPGA device, execution time of Phase 1 and Phase 2 for 198-bit numbers $N, B_1 = 960$, $B_2 = 57000$, $D = 210$)

Results	Virtex XCV2000E-6	Virtex II XC2V6000-6	Spartan 3 XC3S5000-5
Resources for one ECM unit			
- CLB slices	3102 (16%)	3197 (9%)	3322 (10%)
- LUTs	4933 (13%)	5025 (7%)	5134 (8%)
- FFs	3129 (8%)	3102 (5%)	3130 (5%)
- BRAMs	2/160	2/144	2/104
Maximum number of ECM units per FPGA device	7	10	10
Technology	0.15/0.12 μm	0.15/0.12 μm	90 nm
Cost of an FPGA device[a]	$1230	$2700	$130
Maximum clock frequency for one ECM unit	54 MHz	123 MHz	100 MHz
Time for Phase 1 and Phase 2	67.2 ms	29.5 ms	36.3 ms
# of ECM computations per second with the maximum number of ECM units	104	339	276
# of ECM computations per second per $100 with the maximum number of ECM units	8	13	212

[a] Approximate cost per unit for a batch of 10,000+ devices

Table 6. Comparison of the execution time between 2.8 GHz Xeon Pentium 4 (w/512KB cache) and two types of FPGA devices Virtex II XC2V6000-6 and Spartan 3 XC3S5000-5 (198-bit number $N, B_1 = 960$, $B_2 = 57000$, $D = 210$, maximum number of ECM units per FPGA device)

	Virtex II XC2V6000-6	Spartan 3 XC3S5000-5	Pentium 4 (testing program)	Pentium 4 (GMP-ECM)
Clock frequency	123 MHz	100 MHz	2.8 GHz	
No. of parallel ECM computations	10	10	1	
Time of Phase 1	13.9 ms	17.1 ms	18.3 ms	11.3 ms
Time of Phase 2	15.6 ms	19.2 ms	18.6 ms	13.5 ms
Time of Phase 1 & Phase 2	29.5 ms	36.3 ms	36.9 ms	24.8 ms
# of Phase 1 computations per second	718	584	55	89
# of Phase 2 computations per second	642	522	54	74
# of Phase 1 & 2 computations per second	339	276	27	40

hardware, except for using calls to the multiprecision GMP library for all low level operations, such as modular multiplication and addition. One can see that the algorithmic optimizations used in GMP-ECM matter, and reduce the overall execution time for Phase 1 from 18.3 ms to 11.3 ms (38%), and Phase 2 from 18.6 ms to 13.5 ms (27%).

Interestingly, the execution time for an ECM unit running on Virtex II, 6000E is only slightly greater than the execution time of GMP-ECM on a Pentium

4 Xeon. At the same time, since this FPGA device can hold up to 10 ECM units, its overall performance is about 8.5 times higher for combined Phase 1 and Phase 2 computations. However, the current generation of high-end FPGA devices cost about 10 times as much as comparable microprocessors. Therefore, the advantage of Virtex II over Pentium 4 disappears when cost is taken into account. In order to get an advantage in terms of the performance to cost ratio, one must use a low-cost FPGA family, such as Xilinx Spartan 3. In this case, the ratio of the amount of computations per chip is about 7 in favor of the biggest Spartan 3. Additionally this device is actually cheaper than the state-of-the-art microprocessor, so the overall improvement in terms of the performance to cost ratio exceeds a factor of 10.

5   Conclusions

A novel hardware architecture for the Elliptic Curve Method of factoring has been proposed. The main differences as compared to an earlier design by Pelzl, Šimka, et al. [6,7] include the use of an on-chip optimized controller for Phase 1 and Phase 2 (in place of an external controller based on an ARM processor), substantially smaller memory requirements, an optimized architecture for the Montgomery multiplier, the use of two (instead of one) multipliers, and the ability of all arithmetic units (two multipliers and one adder/subtractor) to work in parallel. When implemented on the same Virtex 2000E-6 device, our architecture has demonstrated a speed-up by a factor of 9.3 for ECM Phase 1 and 15.0 for ECM Phase 2, compared to the design by Pelzl/Šimka, et al. At the same time, memory requirements have been reduced by a factor of 22, and the requirements for CLB slices have increased by a factor of 2.7. If the same optimizations regarding the memory usage and the use of an internal controller were applied to the design by Pelzl/Šimka, our architecture would still retain an advantage in terms of the performance to cost ratio by a factor of 3.4 for Phase 1 and 5.6 for Phase 2.

Our architecture has been implemented targeting two additional families of FPGA devices, Virtex II and Spartan 3. Our analysis revealed that the low-cost Spartan 3 devices outperformed the high-performance Virtex II devices in terms of the performance to cost ratio by a factor of about 16.

We have also compared the performance of our hardware architecture implemented using Virtex II XC2V6000-6 and Spartan 3 XC3S5000-5 with the optimized software implementation running on Pentium 4 Xeon, with a 2.8 GHz clock. Our analysis shows that the high performance FPGA device outperforms the same generation microprocessor by a factor of about 8.5, but looses its advantage when the cost of both devices is taken into account. On the other hand, the low-cost FPGA device Spartan 3 achieves about an order of magnitude advantage over the same generation Pentium 4 processor in terms of both performance and performance to cost ratio. This feature makes low-cost FPGA devices an appropriate basic building block for cost-optimized hardware for breaking cryptographic systems, which is consistent with the conclusions of other research groups reported earlier in the literature [15].

References

1. J.M. Pollard, "Factoring with cubic integers", *Lecture Notes in Mathematics 1554*, pp. 4-10, Springer, 1993.
2. A.K. Lenstra and H.W. Lenstra, *The Development of the Number Field Sieve*, *Lecture Notes in Mathematics 1554*, Springer, 1993.
3. Factorization of RSA-200, F. Bahr, M. Boehm, J. Franke, T. Kleinjung, http: crypto-world.com/announcements/rsa200.txt.
4. P. Zimmermann, "20 years of ECM," *preprint*, 2005, http://www.loria.fr/~ zimmerma/papers/ecm-submitted.pdf.
5. J. Fougeron, L. Fousse, A. Kruppa, D. Newman, and P. Zimmermann, "GMP-ECM", http://www.komite.net/laurent/soft/ecm/ecm-6.0.1.html, 2005.
6. M. Šimka, J. Pelzl, T. Kleinjung, J. Franke, C. Priplata, C. Stahlke, M. Drutarovsky, V. Fischer, and C. Paar, "Hardware factorization based elliptic curve method", *IEEE Symposium on Field-Programmable Custom Computing Machines - FCCM'05*, Napa, CA, USA, 2005.
7. J. Pelzl, M. Šimka, T. Kleinjung, J. Franke, C. Priplata, C. Stahlke, M. Drutarovsky, V. Fischer, and C. Paar, "Area-time efficient hardware architecture for factoring integers with the elliptic curve method", *IEE Proceedings on Information Security,* vol . 152, no. 1, pp. 67-78, 2005.
8. D. Hankerson, A.J. Menezes, and S.A. Vanstone, *Guide to Elliptic Curve Cryptography*, Springer–Verlag, 2004.
9. H.W. Lenstra, "Factoring integers with elliptic curves", *Annals of Mathematics*, vol. 126, pp. 649–673, 1987.
10. R.P. Brent, "Some integer factorization algorithms using elliptic curves", *Australian Computer Science Communications*, vol. 8, pp. 149–163, 1986.
11. P.L. Montgomery, "Speeding the Pollard and elliptic curve methods of factorization", *Mathematics of Computation*, vol. 48, pp. 243–264, 1987.
12. P.L. Montgomery, "An FFT extension of the elliptic curve method of factorization", *Ph.D. Thesis*, UCLA, 1992.
13. P.L. Montgomery, "Modular multiplication without trivial division", *Mathematics of Computation*, vol. 44, pp. 519–521, 1985.
14. C. McIvor, M. McLoone, J. McCanny, A. Daly, and W. Marnane, "Fast Montgomery modular multiplication and RSA cryptographic processor architectures", *Proc. 37th IEEE Computer Society Asilomar Conference on Signals, Systems and Computers*, Monterey, USA, pp. 379-384, Nov. 2003.
15. S. Kumar, C. Paar, J. Pelzl, G. Pfeiffer, A. Rupp, M. Schimmler, "How to break DES for 8,980 Euro", *2nd Workshop on Special-purpose Hardware for Attacking Cryptographic Systems - SHARCS 2006*, Cologne, Germany, April 3-4, 2006.
16. J. Franke, T. Kleinjung, C. Paar, J. Pelzl, C. Priplata, and C. Stahlke, "SHARK : A realizable special hardware sieving device for factoring 1024-bit integers", *Cryptographic Hardware and Embedded Systems - CHES 05*, LNCS 3659, pp. 119–130, Springer-Verlag, 2005.
17. W. Geiselmann, F Januszewski, H Koepfer, J. Pelzl, and R. Steinwandt, "A simpler sieving device: Combining ECM and TWIRL", *Cryptology ePrint Archive*, http://eprint.iacr.org/2006/109.
18. SRC Computers, Inc., http://www.srccomp.com.
19. R.D. Silverman and S.S. Wagstaff,"A practical analysis of the elliptic curve factoring algorithm", *Mathematics of Computation,* vol. 61, no. 203, pp. 465-462, 1993.

Implementing Cryptographic Pairings on Smartcards

Michael Scott, Neil Costigan, and Wesam Abdulwahab

School of Computer Applications
Dublin City University
Ballymun, Dublin 9, Ireland
mike@computing.dcu.ie

Abstract. Pairings on elliptic curves are fast coming of age as cryptographic primitives for deployment in new security applications, particularly in the context of implementations of Identity-Based Encryption (IBE). In this paper we describe the implementation of various pairings on a contemporary 32-bit smart-card, the Philips HiPerSmart^{TM}, an instantiation of the MIPS-32 based SmartMIPS^{TM} architecture. Three types of pairing are considered, first the standard Tate pairing on a nonsupersingular curve $E(\mathbb{F}_p)$, second the Ate pairing, also on a nonsupersingular curve $E(\mathbb{F}_p)$, and finally the η_T pairing on a supersingular curve $E(\mathbb{F}_{2^m})$. We demonstrate that pairings can be calculated as efficiently as classic cryptographic primitives on this architecture, with a calculation time of as little as 0.15 seconds.

Keywords: Elliptic curves, pairing-based cryptosystems, fast implementations.

1 Introduction

The appreciation that the Weil and Tate pairings can be used for constructive cryptographic application has caused a minor revolution in cryptography. After a flurry of research results involving new protocols based on new but plausible security assumptions, it is time for the first commercial applications to start appearing. The final, and perhaps most demanding, niche for the implementation of many cryptographic protocols is in the smart-card, a constrained computing environment in which private keys can be adequately protected. It is the purpose of this paper to demonstrate that such implementations are perfectly feasible.

In the beginning it was original research by Menezes, Okamoto and Vanstone [27], and by Frey et al. [16], which pointed out that the Weil and Tate pairings could be used for cryptanalytic purposes, undermining the security of certain types of elliptic curves, some of which had been suggested as suitable vehicles for the implementation of Elliptic Curve Cryptography (ECC). However this was followed by a prolonged hiatus before Sakai, Ohgishi and Kasahara [33] and Joux [23] independently observed that these very same condemned elliptic curves had in fact useful cryptographic properties. Almost immediately Boneh

L. Goubin and M. Matsui (Eds.): CHES 2006, LNCS 4249, pp. 134–147, 2006.

and Franklin famously came up with a very simple solution to the problem of Identity-Based Encryption [10], an open problem in cryptography since the idea was first mooted by Shamir [37].

Since then there has been a veritable flood of ideas, of new protocols for identity-based encryption [10], [32], short signatures [11] and identity-based signcryption [26] to mention but a few. We do not attempt to provide a complete history here, but instead refer the interested reader to the pairing-based cryptolounge [2].

There have been two previously reported implementations of pairings on smartcards, the first in the form of an announcement by Gemplus [17], and the second in a paper by Bertoni et al. [8]. There have also been proposals for implementations, such as that by Granger et al. [18], which would require special supporting hardware. Bertoni et al. report a timing of 752 milliseconds on a 33MHz ST22 32-bit smartcard [8], for the same level of security as considered here.

2   Pairing-Friendly Elliptic Curves

When it comes to the selection of elliptic curves suitable for pairing-based cryptography, one is currently limited to either the supersingular curves or certain special non-supersingular curves of prime characteristic. A basic requirement is that the selected elliptic curve should have a small *embedding degree*, or *security multiplier*, denoted as k. In this paper it will be assumed that k is even.

So for cryptographic purposes a pairing-friendly elliptic curve over a finite field consists of the finite set of points (including a point at infinity) on a curve which can be described by one of

$$E(\mathbb{F}_{p^m}): \quad y^2 = x^3 + Ax + B$$
$$E(\mathbb{F}_{2^m}): \quad y^2 + y = x^3 + x + b$$
$$E(\mathbb{F}_{3^m}): \quad y^2 = x^3 - x + b$$

In the first case the curve can be either supersingular, with an embedding degree of $k = 2$, or nonsupersingular with $m = 1$ and any finite embedding degree [9]. In the second case the curve is supersingular and has a maximum embedding degree of $k = 4$, where $b = 0, 1$. In the third case the curve is also supersingular with a maximum embedding degree of $k = 6$, and where $b = \pm 1$.

As is common in elliptic curve cryptography over $E(\mathbb{F}_q)$, one wants to work with a group of points of prime order r, where $r \mid q + 1 - t$ the total number of points on the curve (denoted $\#E$), and where t is the trace of the Frobenius, with $|t| \leqslant 2\sqrt{q}$ (the Hasse condition) [27]. These points then form a prime order cyclic abelian group. This group size needs to be large enough to avoid various generic attacks on the elliptic curve discrete logarithm problem, and therefore at a minimum r should be 160-bits. The embedding degree k is related to this group of points on the elliptic curve by the condition that k is the smallest positive integer such that $r \mid (q^k - 1)$. A further security requirement for these elliptic curves is that $\mathbb{F}_{q^k}$, where $q = p, 2^m$ or 3^m, should be an extension field of sufficient size to prevent an index calculus attack on the discrete logarithm problem in that field. So at a minimum $k. \lg(q)$ should be 1024 bits.

So we have the interesting constraints that r can at most be about as big as q (due to the Hasse condition), with $\lg(r)$ a minimum of 160, and that $k. \lg(q)$ should then be at least 1024. One obvious feasible solution would be to choose $\lg(r) \approx 170$, $r = q + 1 - t$, and $k = 6$ so that $6. \lg(q) \approx 1024$. This explains the early popularity of curves of characteristic 3 with $k = 6$. This also has the advantage of keeping the size of the elliptic curve as small as those required for standard ECC while still attaining the minimum levels of index calculus security. However another valid and popular choice would be to use a supersingular [10] or non-supersingular curve [34] over $\mathbb{F}_p$, with $\lg(r) = 160$, $\lg(p) = 512$ and $k = 2$.

In the case of fields of low characteristic the security situation is rather unclear. As first pointed out by Coppersmith [14], the discrete logarithm problem in $\mathbb{F}_{2^m}$ is somewhat easier than it is over a prime characteristic field. According to the current record holder [38], who was able to calculate discrete logarithms for $m = 607$, it would require $m \approx 1200$ to obtain a greater level of security than 1024-bit RSA. Interpolating into the tables provided by Lenstra [24] would suggest that 1300 bits would be sufficient. Page, Smart and Vercauten [31] have observed that since the record for prime field discrete logarithms is 398 bits [25], $607/298 = 1.53$. So perhaps 50% more bits for characteristic 2 might be about right. We believe that our choice of $m = 379$ bits and hence $4m = 1516$ bits, is an appropriately conservative one.

A pairing is denoted as $e(P, Q)$, where P is taken as a point of order r, usually on $E(\mathbb{F}_q)$, and Q is a point on $E(\mathbb{F}_{q^k})$ linearly independent of P. The pairing evaluates naturally as an element of order r in $\mathbb{F}_{q^k}$. Its most important cryptographic property is its *bilinearity*

$$e(aP, bQ) = e(P, Q)^{ab}$$

If Q should be linearly dependent on P and $P \in E(\mathbb{F}_q)$, then the pairing is degenerate and $e(P, Q) = 1$, and so for example $e(P, P) = 1$. On a supersingular curve it is usual to exploit the existence of a distortion map $\psi(.)$, which maps a point from $E(\mathbb{F}_q)$ to a linearly independent point on $E(\mathbb{F}_{q^k})$. Now both P and Q can be linearly dependent points from the same group of order r on $E(\mathbb{F}_q)$, and the distorted pairing can be calculated as $\hat{e}(P, Q) = e(P, \psi(Q))$. This pairing has the additional and sometimes useful property that $\hat{e}(P, Q) = \hat{e}(Q, P)$, which is implied by the condition that $\hat{e}(P, P) \neq 1$. As our chosen smart-card has special support for multiprecision arithmetic over $\mathbb{F}_p$, and over $\mathbb{F}_{2^m}$, we will restrict our attention here to these two cases, although the field $\mathbb{F}_{3^m}$ has undoubted advantages (with its nice embedding degree $k = 6$) and has received considerable attention in the context of pairing based cryptography [18].

3   The SmartMIPS^{TM} Architecture

The SmartMIPS^{TM} specification is of an instruction-set enhanced version of the popular RISC MIPS32 architecture [1]. The enhancements are designed to improve the performance of popular cryptographic algorithms, and are largely those envisaged and described by Großschädl and Savas [19]. It is interesting to note that this new generation of 32-bit smartcards do not employ a classic cryptographic co-processor, with its restricted and specialised set of operations, but rather use carefully selected instruction set enhancements, which when combined with the improved overall performance of the 32-bit chip, permit standard cryptographic algorithms to be executed with sufficient speed. It is also fortunately flexible enough to efficiently support new algorithms that were not envisaged when the processor was being designed.

The main idea is that an extended ACX|HI|LO triple of registers can be used to accumulate the partial products that arise when employing the popular Comba/Montgomery technique for multi-precision multiplication [19]. This is supported by a modified MADDU instruction which carries out an unsigned integer multiplication and addition to the triple register. Another important addition to the instruction set is the inclusion of a MADDP instruction which supports binary polynomial multiplication, and which therefore supports field multiplication over $\mathbb{F}_{2^m}$. For many years algorithms over this field have been disadvantaged with respect to the field $\mathbb{F}_p$ by the absence of such an instruction in standard processors. The addition of this instruction finally "levels the playing field", and allows the full potential of fast arithmetic over the field $\mathbb{F}_{2^m}$ to be realised.

One disadvantage of the MIPS architecture for multi-precision integer arithmetic is the lack of a carry flag, and specifically an add-with-carry ADC instruction. In fact it takes 5 instructions just to process one digit in a multi-precision integer addition in order to handle the carry-in and carry-out correctly, not including memory loads and stores. Note however that this is not an issue in $\mathbb{F}_{2^m}$ as in this context addition is carry-free.

When considering the performance of any processor the CPU performance equation [20] is relevant

$$\texttt{CPU Time} = \frac{\texttt{Number of Instructions} \times \texttt{Average Clocks Per Instruction}}{\texttt{Clock Speed in cycles per second}}$$

As instantiated by the Philips HiPerSmart[TM] our targeted processor is characterised by

- A five stage pipeline
- Maximum clock speed of 36MHz
- 2k Instruction cache
- 256k Flash memory
- 16k RAM memory

One of the most significant attributes from a programming point of view is the small size of the 2-way associative instruction cache. The MIPS processor as described in [20] is very much designed as a classic RISC processor, which can benefit enormously from loop-unrolling as is indeed the default behaviour of

GCC -O3 compiler optimization. However this is entirely inappropriate with such a small instruction cache. Cache misses are very expensive, and are the main reason for increased CPI (Clocks-Per-Instruction), leading to poorer performance. Ruthless loop unrolling can dramatically decrease overall instruction count, but only at the cost of much poorer CPI.

While the majority of instructions can complete one pipeline stage per clock tick, certain combinations of instructions will cause a stall in the pipeline. Most of these stalls can be identified and avoided by instruction scheduling (re-ordering). A typical cause for such a stall might be the latency of a multiply instruction like MADDU. However as pointed out in [19] these potential performance hits can be avoided if we use the right algorithm. While such pipeline stalls increase CPI, they do so in a fashion which is independent of the clock speed. Cache capacity misses must happen given the small size of the cache, and furthermore conflict misses are inevitable give that the cache is only 2-way associative. These cache misses exact a cost in wasted cycles which can increase dramatically with clock speed, as the access time of main memory becomes much slower than the 1-cycle access time of a cache hit.

4   Calculating the Pairing

We consider the scenario in which a smart-card is required to carry out IBE decryption, using either the IBE method of Boneh and Franklin [10] or the method of Sakai and Kasahara as described in [12]. In both cases the critical calculation to recover the plaintext is of the pairing $e(A, B)$, where A is the recipient's private and constant key, and B is a public and variable value associated with the ciphertext. For provable chosen ciphertext security an additional point multiplication is required in both cases, but this is multiplication of a constant point and so fast methods can be used. We omit a formal description of either scheme and instead refer the interested reader to the referenced material.

Much effort has been made to optimize the Tate pairing. In this work we will describe an implementation of the pairing over a prime order finite field $\mathbb{F}_p$ using the BKLS algorithm [4], as described by Scott [34], an implementation of the recently discovered Ate pairing [21], and an implementation over the small characteristic field $\mathbb{F}_{2^m}$ using the η_T pairing approach described in [3]. In all cases we will exploit the setting in which the pairing is to be calculated to maximize performance.

4.1   The BKLS Pairing Algorithm

All algorithms for calculating a pairing are elaborations and improvements of the basic Miller algorithm [29]. This particular variation [4] has general applicability to pairing-friendly elliptic curves $E(\mathbb{F}_p)$, either supersingular or non-supersingular. In this case we choose to use an embedding degree of 2 with a non-supersingular curve, very much following the description given in [34]. We use the same non-supersingular curve as described there, where p is a 512-bit prime number and r is the low Hamming weight Solinas prime $2^{159}+2^{17}+1$. The point Q is handled as a point on the twisted curve $E'(\mathbb{F}_p)$. Since $p = 3 \bmod 4$, elements of the extension field $\mathbb{F}_{p^2}$ such as m can be described as $m_R + i m_I$, where i is the "imaginary" square root of the quadratic non-residue -1.

The helper function $g(.)$ calculates the line functions required by Miller's algorithm, and returns a value in $\mathbb{F}_{p^2}$. This function in turn requires a function $A.add(B)$ which adds the elliptic curve points $A = A + B$ using standard methods, and returns the slope of the line joining A and B.

Algorithm 1. Function $g(.)$

INPUT: A, B, Q
1: **let** $A = (x_i, y_i)$, $Q = (x_Q, y_Q)$
2: $\lambda_i = A.add(B)$
3: **return** $y_i - \lambda_i(x_Q + x_i) - i.y_Q$

Algorithm 2. Computation of the Tate pairing $e(P, Q)$ on $E(\mathbb{F}_p) : y^2 = x^3 + Ax + B$ where P is a point of prime order r on $E(\mathbb{F}_p)$ and Q is a point on the twisted curve $E'(\mathbb{F}_p)$

INPUT: P, Q
1: $m = 1$
2: $A = P$
3: $n = r - 1$
4: **for** $i \leftarrow \lfloor \lg(r) \rfloor - 1$ **downto** 0 **do**
5:     $m = m^2 \cdot g(A, A, Q)$
6:         **if** $n_i = 1$ **then** $m = m \cdot g(A, P, Q)$
7: **end for**
8: $m = \bar{m}/m$
9: **return** $V_{(p+1)/r}(m_R)$

After the Miller loop, the value of m needs to be subject to a final exponentiation to the power of $(p-1)(p+1)/r$. This is done in two parts – first we calculate m^{p-1} using a conjugation and a division, and then we use a Lucas sequence to raise this value to the power of $(p+1)/r$. The returned value is thus compressed to a single element in $\mathbb{F}_p$ [36].

Observe that the parameter P is in effect being multiplied by its group order r using a standard double-and-add method. The points generated as a result of this process (the x_i and y_i in the $g(.)$ function), and the associated line slopes λ_i, can be precalculated and stored if P is a constant, which it will be in the context under consideration here – in fact its the IBE private key of the card-holder.

Therefore we will precompute and store the points (x_i, y_i, λ_i) that arise in the multiplication of P by r. This results in a much simplified algorithm, where the expensive $A.add(B)$ function is no longer required and curve points can be represented using simple affine coordinates.

4.2   The Ate Pairing Algorithm

The Ate pairing [21] is calculated faster than the Tate pairing over non-supersingular curves $E(\mathbb{F}_p)$ if $\lg(t)/\lg(r)$ is less than one, as it uses a truncated Miller loop of length $\lg(t)$ instead of $\lg(r)$ as required above. It was once considered "natural" when implementing the Tate pairing on non-supersingular curves with embedding degree $k \geq 4$, that the first parameter P should be on the the curve defined over the base field $E(\mathbb{F}_p)$ and that the second parameter Q should be a point on a twist of the curve $E'(\mathbb{F}_{p^{k/d}})$, where d can always be 2 [6], but can be as high as 6 for certain curves, such as the BN curves [7]. The authors of [21] however observed that, rather counter-intuitively, the Ate pairing idea works best with P on $E'(\mathbb{F}_{p^{k/d}})$ and Q on $E(\mathbb{F}_p)$. In our application this swapping of roles is not an important issue, as P will be fixed and its multiples can be precalculated and stored as above. More important is the fact that we can get away with a possibly much shorter Miller loop, and still calculate a viable bilinear pairing.

To exploit the Ate pairing we first need a family of elliptic curves which have the required properties. Not only must they be pairing-friendly, but to get the full advantage we want $\lg(t) < \lg(r)$. The best that can be hoped for is that $\lg(t)/\lg(r) = 1/\deg(\Phi_k(x))$, where $\Phi_k(x)$ is the k-th cyclotomic polynomial [21]. So for a $k = 12$ curve such as that described in [5], the loop may be shortened to as little as one-quarter size. However for our targeted level of security, $k = 12$ is too big. Consider instead the family of elliptic curves defined by

$$x = (Dz^2 - 3)/4, \ t = x + 1, \ r = x^2 + 1$$
$$p = (x^3 + 13x^2 + 26x + 13)/25, \ \#E = ((x + 13)r)/25$$

It can easily be verified that these parameters define a family of pairing-friendly elliptic curve with embedding degree $k = 4$, and with complex multiplication by $-D$. Note that $r = \Phi_4(x)$, and that $\lg(t)/\lg(r) = 0.5$ which is optimal, and so we can leverage the maximum advantage from the Ate pairing idea with a half-length loop. The actual parameters of a curve in the form $y^2 = x^3 + Ax + B$ can then be found using the method of complex multiplication [22]. By choosing random z such that p is prime and 256 bits in length, then we can easily find a value for r which has a 160-bit prime divisor. In this way the conditions that $k.\lg(p) = 1024$ and $\lg(r) = 160$ can be satisfied. For our particular curve (Appendix A), $t - 1$ has a relatively low Hamming weight of 31, and the discriminant $D = 259$. The full algorithm can now be given

---

Algorithm 3. Function $g(.)$

INPUT: A, B, Q
  1: **let** $A = (x_i, y_i)$, $Q = (x_Q, y_Q)$
  2: $\lambda_i = A.add(B)$
  3: **return** $i^2 y_Q - i(i^2 y_i/2 + \lambda_i(i^2 x_i/2 + x_Q))$

Algorithm 4. Computation of the Ate pairing $a(P,Q)$ on $E(\mathbb{F}_p) : y^2 = x^3 + Ax + B$ where P is a point of prime order r on the twisted curve $E'(\mathbb{F}_{p^2})$ and Q is a point on the curve $E(\mathbb{F}_p)$

INPUT: P, Q
1: $m = 1$
2: $A = P$
3: $n = t - 1$
4: **for** $i \leftarrow \lfloor \lg(n) \rfloor - 1$ **downto** 0 **do**
5:     $m = m^2 \cdot g(A, A, Q)$
6:     **if** $n_i = 1$ **then** $m = m \cdot g(A, P, Q)$
7: **end for**
8: $m = \bar{m}/m$
9: **return** $V_{(p^2+1)/r}(m_R)$

In this case the function $g(.)$ returns a value in $\mathbb{F}_{p^4}$ and the Ate pairing returns a compressed value in $\mathbb{F}_{p^2}$. Since we choose $p = 5 \bmod 8$, -2 is a quadratic non-residue in $\mathbb{F}_p$ and $\sqrt{-2}$ is a quadratic non-residue in $\mathbb{F}_{p^2}$, elements in $\mathbb{F}_{p^4}$ can be represented as a pair of elements in $\mathbb{F}_{p^2}$, $m = m_R + im_I$ with $i = (-2)^{1/4}$ [30]. In the function $g(.)$, points on the twisted curve $E'(\mathbb{F}_{p^2})$ must first be converted to coordinates on $E(\mathbb{F}_{p^4})$, which explains the apparent complexity of this function. However given that these can all be precalculated, this is not an issue in practise.

4.3   The BGOhES Pairing Algorithm

On the supersingular curve

$$E(\mathbb{F}_{2^m}) : y^2 + y = x^3 + x + 1$$

where m is prime and $m = 3 \bmod 8$, the number of points is $2^m + 2^{(m+1)/2} + 1$ [3]. For our choice of $m = 379$, this value is a prime. A suitable irreducible polynomial for the field $\mathbb{F}_{2^{379}}$ is $x^{379} + x^{315} + x^{301} + x^{287} + 1$. This supersingular curve has an embedding degree of $k = 4$. To represent the quartic extension field $\mathbb{F}_{2^{4m}}$, we use the irreducible polynomial $X^4 + X + 1$.

Recall that in a characteristic 2 field with a polynomial basis, field squarings are of linear complexity. Furthermore on this supersingular curve, point doublings require only cheap field squarings (using affine coordinates). Therefore we can anticipate that calculations on this curve will be very efficient.

A distortion map for this particular supersingular curve is $\psi(x,y) = (x + s^2.y + sx + t)$, where $t = X$ and $s = X + X^2$ [27]. A major insight from [3] is that the Tate pairing can be calculated from the more primitive η_T pairing, which requires a half-length loop compared to the Duursma-Lee method [15], with considerable computational savings. The algorithm as described benefits from unrolling the loops times 2, in which case each iteration costs just seven base field multiplications. The final exponentiation looks a little complex, but in fact can be accomplished with only 4 extension field multiplications, $(m + 1)/2$ cheap extension field squarings and some nearly-free Frobenius operations.

Algorithm 5. Computation of $\hat{e}(P,Q)$ on $E(\mathbb{F}_{2^m}) : y^2 + y = x^3 + x + b : m \equiv 3$ (mod 8) case

---

INPUT: P, Q
OUTPUT: $\hat{e}(P,Q)$
  1: let $P = (x_P, y_P)$, $Q = (x_Q, y_Q)$
  2: $u \leftarrow x_P + 1$
  3: $f \leftarrow u \cdot (x_P + x_Q + 1) + y_P + y_Q + b + 1 + (u + x_Q)s + t$
  4: for $i \leftarrow 1$ to $(m+1)/2$ do
  5:     $u \leftarrow x_P,\ x_P \leftarrow \sqrt{x_P},\ y_P \leftarrow \sqrt{y_P}$
  6:     $g \leftarrow u \cdot (x_P + x_Q) + y_P + y_Q + x_P + (u + x_Q)s + t$
  7:     $f \leftarrow f \cdot g$
  8:     $x_Q \leftarrow x_Q^2,\ y_Q \leftarrow y_Q^2$
  9: end for
 10: return $f^{(2^{2m}-1)(2^m - 2^{(m+1)/2})+1)(2^{(m+1)/2}+1)}$

Since P will be fixed, all the square roots in this algorithm can be precalculated and stored with some savings. With this modification, our implementation is largely the same as that described in [3].

5   Implementation Issues

Our implementation makes use of the MIRACL multiprecision library [35]. The current version (5.01) of this library is fortunately friendly towards those attempting implementations in a constrained environment, like a smartcard. Typically a big number library forces allocation of memory for big variables from the heap. In a constrained environment however a heap is a luxury that often cannot be afforded. Therefore allocation from the stack is appropriate, and is supported. Header file definitions were used to cut down the amount of code required. This was supplemented with some manual pruning of unwanted functionality.

For optimal performance MIRACL includes a mechanism for generating unrolled Comba code for modular multiplication, squaring, and reduction with respect to a fixed modulus, including specific support for the SmartMIPS™ processor. However as pointed out above, fully unrolled code is inappropriate in an environment where the instruction cache is very small. Therefore we found it necessary to take the automatically generated (and correct) code, and to roll it up again into tight loops, much as described in [19]. Extra manually written inline assembly code was provided to support fast squaring in $\mathbb{F}_{2^m}$ using the MADDP instruction, and short unrolled assembly language code was provided for fast field addition in $\mathbb{F}_{2^m}$. With these exceptions, the rest of the code was written in standard C.

Precomputation was used to advantage in all cases. The amount of ROM required to store precomputed values was 31232, 25036 and 18432 bytes respectively, for the Tate, Ate and η_T pairing. The RAM requirement in all cases was comfortably with the 16K available, typically requiring only half of that. As stack memory is inherently re-usable, a simple restructuring of the programs could reduce this requirement still further.

6   Results

We present our results in a series of tables. As well as the timings for the pairings, we include timings for (non-fixed) point multiplications and pairing exponentiations, as these as often relevant to pairing based protocols. For each of the three implementations we assume projective coordinates are used for point multiplication, as field inversions which are required for affine point addition are very slow on the smartcard. The point multiplication is taken over the base field $E(\mathbb{F}_q)$ using a random 160-bit multiplier. Field exponentiation is of the pairing value to a random 160-bit exponent. For the $E(\mathbb{F}_p)$ cases we use Lucas exponentiation (also known as a "Montgomery powering ladder") of the compressed pairing, while for the $E(\mathbb{F}_{2^{379}})$ case we use standard windowed exponentiation, as we believe these to be the fastest methods in each case.

Our hardware emulator is only cycle accurate up to 20.57MHz, and so we estimate the timings for the maximum supported speed of 36MHz, using linear interpolation for CPI. For comparision purposes we include figures for 1024-bit RSA decryption (using the Chinese Remainder Theorem), and timings on a standard PC (note that these are faster than previously reported timings, due to their implementation in C rather than C++).

Table 1. Instructions required (% icache misses) - Philips HiPerSmart[TM]

	$E(\mathbb{F}_{2^{379}})$ η_T pairing	$E(\mathbb{F}_p)$ Tate pairing	$E(\mathbb{F}_p)$ Ate pairing
Pairing	3705344 (10.9%)	7753341 (7.3%)	8156645 (15.8%)
Point Mult.	2589569 (9.6%)	7418768 (6.1%)	2663217 (17.5%)
Field exp.	1551117 (11.4%)	1364124 (7.2%)	1614016 (15.7%)
RSA decryption	4372772 (3.4%)		

Table 2. Clock cycles required/CPI/time in seconds @ 9 MHz

	$E(\mathbb{F}_{2^{379}})$ η_T pairing	$E(\mathbb{F}_p)$ Tate pairing	$E(\mathbb{F}_p)$ Ate pairing
Pairing	4311454/1.16/0.48	9104450/1.17/1.01	10860479/1.33/1.21
Point Mult.	3118344/1.20/0.35	8529176/1.15/0.95	3739596/1.40/0.42
Field exp.	1924596/1.24/0.21	1593313/1.17/0.18	2122221/1.31/0.24
RSA decryption	4740271/1.08/0.53		

The most surprising and significant observation to be made is that the η_T pairing can be calculated just about as quickly as a standard RSA decryption, for approximately the same level of security. As expected CPI goes up as clock speed increases, as we are punished more heavily for cache misses. This has less impact on algorithms that spend more time in tight loops, and hence disadvantages the η_T and Ate pairings with their more elaborate structures and higher extension fields. Note that RSA, due to its simplicity, suffers least from increasing CPI.

Table 3. Clock cycles required/CPI/time in seconds @ 20.57 MHz

	$E(\mathbb{F}_{2^{379}})$ η_T pairing	$E(\mathbb{F}_p)$ Tate pairing	$E(\mathbb{F}_p)$ Ate pairing
Pairing	4590712/1.24/0.22	9755457/1.26/0.47	12207440/1.50/0.59
Point Mult.	3391127/1.31/0.16	9049457/1.22/0.44	4278858/1.61/0.21
Field exp.	2118707/1.37/0.10	1705365/1.25/0.08	2374885/1.47/0.12
RSA decryption	4880323/1.12/0.24		

Table 4. Clock cycles required/CPI/time in seconds @ 36MHz (estimated)

	$E(\mathbb{F}_{2^{379}})$ η_T pairing	$E(\mathbb{F}_p)$ Tate pairing	$E(\mathbb{F}_p)$ Ate pairing
Pairing	4891054/1.32/0.14	10467010/1.35/0.29	13621597/1.67/0.38
Point Mult.	3677188/1.42/0.10	9570210/1.29/0.27	4847055/1.82/0.13
Field exp.	2326675/1.50/0.06	1814285/1.33/0.05	2630846/1.63/0.07
RSA decryption	5072415/1.16/0.14		

Table 5. Timings in milliseconds on 3GHz Pentium IV

	$E(\mathbb{F}_{2^{379}})$ η_T pairing	$E(\mathbb{F}_p)$ Tate pairing	$E(\mathbb{F}_p)$ Ate pairing
Pairing	3.88	2.97	3.16
Point Mult.	1.82	3.08	1.17
Field exp.	1.14	0.54	0.62
RSA decryption	1.92		

7   Does Pairing Delegation Make Sense?

The idea of securely delegating the calculation of a pairing to the terminal was considered in [13]. This was motivated by the assumption that the pairing calculation might be too resource consuming to be carried out on a smartcard. Here we present a slightly modified version of the method described in Section 6.2 of [13]. In the context of IBE decryption the calculation of $e(A, B)$ involves a constant and private A (in fact the IBE private key), and a public B (in fact part of the ciphertext). It is assumed that the smartcard also has stored a random secret point Q and the value of $e(A, Q)$.

– The card generates random x, y, and z, and queries the following pairings to the terminal.

$$\alpha_1 = e(x^{-1}A, B), \quad \alpha_2 = e(yA, z(B + Q))$$

– The card computes

$$e_{AB} = \alpha_1^x$$

– The card checks that

$$\alpha_1^r = 1, \quad \alpha_1^{xyz \bmod r} = \alpha_2/e(A, Q)^{yz \bmod r}$$

If successful the protocol outputs $e(A, B) = e_{AB}$. Observe that two of the point multiplications are of the fixed point A. These may be calculated offline, or at the very least can benefit from fast methods for fixed-point multiplication. Also $e(A, Q)^{yz}$ can be precalculated, or calculated using fixed-base exponentiation [28]. So the major online cost will be of 3 exponentiations and one point multiplication. ¿From the tables above it is clear that the η_T pairing is so fast that delegation is unlikely to be beneficial. The standard Tate pairing ($k = 2$) implementation suffers badly as point multiplication is over a large 512-bit field. However in the case of our Ate pairing implementation, with its smaller 256-bit field size, it appears that delegation might be beneficial.

8   Conclusions

We have demonstrated for the first time that cryptographic pairings can be implemented just as quickly as classic public key cryptographic operations on a standard smartcard, hence clearing the way for their more widespread adoption. The issue of pairing delegation has been investigated, and it appears that despite the efficiency of our implementations, it may be advantageous in certain circumstances.

References

1. http://www.mips.com/content/Products/Architecture/SmartMIPSASE/
   ProductCatalog/P_SmartMIPSASE/productBrief.
2. P. S. L. M. Barreto. The pairing-based crypto lounge. http://paginas.terra.
   com.br/informatica/paulobarreto/pblounge.html.
3. P. S. L. M. Barreto, S. Galbraith, C. O'hEigeartaigh, and M. Scott. Efficient pairing computation on supersingular abelian varieties. Cryptology ePrint Archive, Report 2004/375, 2004. http://eprint.iacr.org/2004/375.
4. P. S. L. M. Barreto, H. Y. Kim, B. Lynn, and M. Scott. Efficient algorithms for pairing-based cryptosystems. In *Advances in Cryptology – Crypto'2002*, volume 2442 of *Lecture Notes in Computer Science*, pages 354–368. Springer-Verlag, 2002.
5. P. S. L. M. Barreto, B. Lynn, and M. Scott. Constructing elliptic curves with prescribed embedding degrees. In *Security in Communication Networks – SCN'2002*, volume 2576 of *Lecture Notes in Computer Science*, pages 263–273. Springer-Verlag, 2002.
6. Paulo S. L. M. Barreto, B. Lynn, and M. Scott. On the selection of pairing-friendly groups. In *Selected Areas in Cryptography – SAC'2003*, volume 3006 of *Lecture Notes in Computer Science*, pages 17–25, Ottawa, Canada, 2003. Springer-Verlag.
7. P.S.L.M. Barreto and M. Naehrig. Pairing-friendly elliptic curves of prime order. Cryptology ePrint Archive, Report 2005/133, 2005. http://eprint.iacr.org/2005/133.

8. G. M. Bertoni, L. Chen, P. Fragneto, K. A. Harrison, and G. Pelosi. Computing tate pairing on smartcards, 2005. http://www.st.com/stonline/products/families/smartcard/ches2005_v4.pdf.

9. I. F. Blake, G. Seroussi, and N. P. Smart, editors. *Advances in Elliptic Curve Cryptography, Volume 2*. Cambridge University Press, 2005.

10. D. Boneh and M. Franklin. Identity-based encryption from the Weil pairing. *SIAM Journal of Computing*, 32(3):586–615, 2003.

11. D. Boneh, B. Lynn, and H. Shacham. Short signatures from the Weil pairing. In *Advances in Cryptology – Asiacrypt'2001*, volume 2248 of *Lecture Notes in Computer Science*, pages 514–532. Springer-Verlag, 2002.

12. L. Chen and Zhaohui Cheng. Security proof of Sakai-Kasahara's identity-based encryption scheme, 2005. http://eprint.iacr.org/2005/226.

13. B. Chevallier-Mames, J-S. Coron, N. McCullagh, D. Naccache, and M. Scott. Secure delegation of elliptic-curve pairing, 2005. http://eprint.iacr.org/2005/150.

14. D. Coppersmith. Fast evaluation of logarithms in fields of characteristics two. In *IEEE Transactions on Information Theory*, volume 30, pages 587–594, 1984.

15. I. Duursma and H.-S. Lee. Tate pairing implementation for hyperelliptic curves $y^2 = x^p - x + d$. In *Advances in Cryptology – Asiacrypt'2003*, volume 2894 of *Lecture Notes in Computer Science*, pages 111–123. Springer-Verlag, 2003.

16. G. Frey, M. Müller, and H. Rück. The Tate pairing and the discrete logarithm applied to elliptic curve cryptosystems. *IEEE Transactions on Information Theory*, 45(5):1717–1719, 1999.

17. Gemplus. ID based Cryptography and Smartcards, 2005. http://www.gemplus.com/smart/rd/publications/pdf/Joy05iden.pdf.

18. R. Granger, D. Page, and M. Stam. Hardware and software normal basis arithmetic for pairing based cryptography in characteristic three. Cryptology ePrint Archive, Report 2004/157, 2004. http://eprint.iacr.org/2004/157.

19. Johann Großschädl and Erkay Savas. Instruction set extensions for fast arithmetic in finite fields GF(p) and GF(2^m). In *CHES*, pages 133–147, 2004.

20. J. Hennessy and D. Patterson. *Computer Architecture - a Qualitative Approach (third edition)*. Morgan Kaufmann, 2003.

21. F. Hess, N. Smart, and F. Vercauteren. The eta pairing revisited. Cryptology ePrint Archive, Report 2006/110, 2006. http://eprint.iacr.org/2006/110.

22. IEEE Computer Society, New York, USA. *IEEE Standard Specifications for Public-Key Cryptography – IEEE Std 1363:2000*, 2000.

23. A. Joux. A one-round protocol for tripartite Diffie-Hellman. In *Algorithm Number Theory Symposium – ANTS IV*, volume 1838 of *Lecture Notes in Computer Science*, pages 385–394. Springer-Verlag, 2000.

24. A. K. Lenstra. Unbelievable security. Matching AES security using public key systems. In *Advances in Cryptology – Asiacrypt 2001*, volume 2248, pages 67–86. Springer-Verlag, 2001.

25. R. Lercier. Discrete logarithms in GF(p). Posting to NMBRTHRY List, 2001.

26. N. McCullagh and P. S. .L. M. Barreto. Efficient and forward-secure identity-based signcryption. Cryptology ePrint Archive, Report 2004/117, 2004. http://eprint.iacr.org/2004/117

27. A. Menezes. *Elliptic Curve Public Key Cryptosystems*. Kluwer Academic Publishers, 1993.

28. Alfred J. Menezes, Paul C. van Oorschot, and Scott A. Vanstone. *Handbook of applied cryptography*. CRC Press, Boca Raton, Florida, 1996. URL: http://cacr.math.uwaterloo.ca/hac.

29. V. Miller. Short programs for functions on curves. unpublished manuscript, 1986. http://crypto.stanford.edu/miller/miller.pdf.
30. Y. Nogami and Y. Morikawa. A fast implementation of elliptic curve cryptosystem with prime order defined over f_{p^8}, 1998. http://www.trans.cne.okayama-u.ac.jp/nogami-group/papers/kiyou(2).pdf.
31. D. Page, N. P. Smart, and F. Vercauteren. A comparison of MNT curves and supersingular curves. Cryptology ePrint Archive, 2004. http://eprint.iacr.org/2004/165.
32. R. Sakai and M. Kasahara. ID based cryptosystems with pairing on elliptic curve. Cryptography ePrint Archive, Report 2003/054, 2003. http://eprint.iacr.org/2003/054 .
33. R. Sakai, K. Ohgishi, and M. Kasahara. Cryptosystems based on pairing. The 2000 Symposium on Cryptography and Information Security, Okinawa, Japan, 2000.
34. M. Scott. Computing the Tate pairing. In *CT-RSA*, volume 3376 of *Lecture Notes in Computer Science*, pages 293–304. Springer-Verlag, 2005.
35. M. Scott, 2006. http://ftp.computing.dcu.ie/pub/crypto/miracl.zip.
36. M. Scott and P. Barreto. Compressed pairings. In *Advances in Cryptology – Crypto' 2004*, volume 3152 of *Lecture Notes in Computer Science*, pages 140–156. Springer-Verlag, 2004. Also available from http://eprint.iacr.org/2004/032/.
37. A. Shamir. Identity-based cryptosystems and signature schemes. In *Proceedings of Crypto 1984*, volume 196 of *Lecture Notes in Computer Science*, pages 47–53. Springer-Verlag, 1984.
38. E. Thomé. Computation of discrete logarithms in $\mathbb{F}_{2^{607}}$. In *Advances in Cryptology – Asiacrypt'2001*, volume 2248 of *Lecture Notes in Computer Science*, pages 107–124. Springer-Verlag, 2001.

A   The Ate Pairing Non-supersingular $k = 4$ Curve

The curve over $\mathbb{F}_p$ is described in the Weierstrass form as

$$E : y^2 = x^3 - 3x + B$$

The curve has $p + 1 - t$ points on it, which is a number divisible by a large prime r. For our chosen curve

B = 4775710463765407644671976798373402339901846555779987963875848321193582773900

p = 73190453176371233031922874717260488242507261313747586254294463297030724930453

r = 7039968169563831716203361508047454068025613140101

t = 122310802304306476153797569

SPA-Resistant Scalar Multiplication on Hyperelliptic Curve Cryptosystems Combining Divisor Decomposition Technique and Joint Regular Form

Toru Akishita, Masanobu Katagi, and Izuru Kitamura

Information Technologies Laboratories, Sony Corporation,
6-7-35 Kitashinagawa, Shinagawa-ku, Tokyo, 141-0001 Japan
akishita@pal.arch.sony.co.jp,
{Masanobu.Katagi, Izuru.Kitamura}@jp.sony.com

Abstract. Hyperelliptic Curve Cryptosystems (HECC) are competitive to elliptic curve cryptosystems in performance and security. Recently efficient scalar multiplication techniques using a theta divisor have been proposed. Their application, however, is limited to the case when a theta divisor is used for the base point. In this paper we propose efficient and secure scalar multiplication of a general divisor for genus 2 HECC over $\mathbb{F}_{2^m}$. The proposed method is based on two novel techniques. One is divisor decomposition technique in which a general divisor is decomposed into two theta divisors. The other is joint regular form for a pair of integers that enables efficient and secure simultaneous scalar multiplication of two theta divisors. The marriage of the above two techniques achieves both about 19% improvement of efficiency compared to the standard method and resistance against simple power analysis without any dummy operation.

Keywords: hyperelliptic curve cryptosystems, scalar multiplication, theta divisor, signed binary representation, simple power analysis.

1 Introduction

Elliptic Curve Cryptosystems (ECC) have increased their importance in public key cryptosystems because of their higher efficiency than RSA cryptosystems. Hyperelliptic Curve Cryptosystems (HECC) are generalization of ECC: ECC just correspond to HECC of genus 1. The security of HECC whose genus is smaller than 4 is thought to match that of ECC of the same group size. On the other side, the performance of HECC was believed to be slower than that of ECC due to their complex group operations. However, since Harley proposed an efficient group addition and doubling algorithm, so-called Harley algorithm, for genus 2 curves of odd characteristics in 2000 [7], optimizations and generalizations of Harley algorithm have been carried out [2], and at present HECC are competitive to ECC also in performance.

L. Goubin and M. Matsui (Eds.): CHES 2006, LNCS 4249, pp. 148–159, 2006.

In recent years, a new class of attacks has been proposed to extract some secret information from a cryptographic device using its power consumption: so-called power analysis. This paper deals with only Simple Power Analysis (SPA), which utilizes a power consumption trace during a single execution. Differential Power Analysis (DPA) is the more sophisticated attack that requires many power consumption traces with statistical tools.

In regard to HECC, the countermeasure against SPA must be considered when an ephemeral and secret scalar is used for scalar multiplication. The standard countermeasure is the double-and-add-always method that *always* repeats a divisor class doubling and a divisor class addition per bit of the scalar [3]. Recently the useful countermeasure for ECC, Montgomery ladder, was applied to HECC [4], but underlying curves of the HECC version are limited.

On the contrary, efficient and SPA-resistant scalar multiplication techniques peculiar to HECC have been recently proposed, which use a *theta* divisor [9,8]. A theta divisor has weight smaller than the genus of the underlying curve. For a genus 2 hyperelliptic curve over $\mathbb{F}_q$, a theta divisor is represented as $D = (x + u_0, v_0)$, whereas a *general* divisor is represented as $D = (x^2 + u_1 x + u_0, v_1 x + v_0)$, where $u_i, v_i \in \mathbb{F}_q$. The cost of an addition of a theta divisor is smaller than that of a general divisor due to its simple representation, so that scalar multiplication of a theta divisor is faster than that of a general divisor. This efficiency, however, can be utilized in the limited case, when the base point is a theta divisor and scalar multiplication of the base point is carried out, for example, in HEC Diffie-Hellman phase 1 or HEC-DSA signature generation.

In this paper we enhance the efficient use of a theta divisor to scalar multiplication of a general divisor for a genus 2 curve over $\mathbb{F}_{2^m}$. The enhancement is based on the following two novel techniques. The first one is *Divisor Decomposition Technique* (DDT). A general divisor $D = (U(x), V(x))$ can be decomposed into two theta divisors D_1 and D_2 if $U(x)$ is reducible over $\mathbb{F}_{2^m}$. The second one is *Joint Regular Form* (JRF), which is a new signed binary representation of a pair of integers such that one is even and the other is odd. Any signed bits at the same position of JRF satisfy that one is 0 and the other is ± 1.

In order to utilize both DDT and JRF, we compute $dD_1 + (d + 1)D_2$ and then subtract D_2 as compensation instead of the scalar multiplication dD. The simultaneous scalar multiplication $dD_1 + (d+1)D_2$ with JRF of $(d, d+1)$ repeats a divisor class doubling and an addition of a theta divisor $\pm D_1$ or $\pm D_2$ per bit of d. Its cost is almost equal to the cost of the double-and-add-always method of a theta divisor, and is smaller than that of a general divisor. Moreover, SPA-resistance is guaranteed because of regularity without any dummy operation, which causes the possibility of fault-based attacks. Even if D is unable to be decomposed into D_1 and D_2, we update D by repeating a divisor class doubling of D until D can be decomposed into D_1 and D_2. Then, after computing $(dD_1 + (d+1)D_2) - D_2 = dD$, we repeat a divisor class halving [10] of dD the corresponding times. The proposed method is 18.7% faster than the double-and-add-always method of a general divisor.

The rest of paper is organized as follows. In next two sections, we briefly introduce HECC mainly focused to theta divisors and scalar multiplication. In Section 4 and 5, we present two novel techniques: Divisor Decomposition Technique (DDT) and Joint Regular Form (JRF). In Section 6, we show the efficient and secure scalar multiplication of a general divisor by combining DDT and JRF. Section 7 analyzes the computational efficiency of the proposed method. Finally, we draw our conclusion and discuss further work in Section 8.

2   Hyperelliptic Curve Cryptosystems

We give only a brief introduction of Hyperelliptic Curve Cryptosystems (HECC) because of space limitation. More details can be found, for example, in [1,2,11].

In this paper, we discuss genus 2 HECC over $\mathbb{F}_{2^m}$. A hyperelliptic curve over $\mathbb{F}_{2^m}$ is defined by $C : y^2 + h(x)y = f(x)$, where $h(x) = x^2 + h_1 x + h_0 \in \mathbb{F}_{2^m}[x]$ and $f(x) = x^5 + \sum_{i=0}^{3} f_i x^i \in \mathbb{F}_{2^m}[x]$. In contrast to ECC, points P on a hyperelliptic curve C do not form a group. The group law is defined over Jacobian variety $\mathcal{J}_C$. $\mathcal{J}_C$ is isomorphic to a divisor class group which forms an additive group, and each divisor class is uniquely represented as a reduced divisor. A reduced divisor $D = \sum m_i P_i - (\sum m_i)P_\infty$, where $P_i = (x_i, y_i)$ and P_∞ is a point at infinity, can be represented by two polynomials $(U(x), V(x))$ [16],

$$U(x) = \prod_i (x + x_i)^{m_i}, \quad V(x_i) = y_i,$$

$$\deg V < \deg U \le 2, \quad V^2 + hV + f \equiv 0 \bmod U.$$

The $\deg U$ of a reduced divisor is called weight. We denote the weight of a reduced divisor D by $w(D)$.

2.1   Theta Divisor and General Divisor

In the case of genus 2 hyperelliptic curves, a reduced divisor has weight smaller than or equal to 2. A divisor is called a *theta* divisor[1] if its weight is smaller than 2 [12]. On the other hand, we call a divisor of weight 2 a *general* divisor. A theta divisor is represented as $D = (x + u_0, v_0)$, whereas a general divisor is represented as $D = (x^2 + u_1 x + u_0, v_1 x + v_0)$.

Let $D_1 = (U_1, V_1)$, $D_2 = (U_2, V_2) \in \mathcal{J}_C(\mathbb{F}_{2^m})$ be reduced divisors. The computational cost of a divisor class doubling $D_3 = (U_3, V_3) = 2D_1$ and a divisor class addition $D_3 = D_1 + D_2$ depends on the conditions that D_1, D_2 and D_3 satisfy. We list some conditions as follows:

DBL $w(D_1) = 2$, $w(D_3) = 2$, $\gcd(h, U_1) = 1$,
ADD $w(D_1) = 2$, $w(D_2) = 2$, $w(D_3) = 2$, $\gcd(U_1, U_2) = 1$,
TDBL $w(D_1) = 1$, $w(D_3) = 2$, $\gcd(h, U_1) = 1$,
TADD $w(D_1) = 2$, $w(D_2) = 1$, $w(D_3) = 2$, $\gcd(U_1, U_2) = 1$.

---

[1] A theta divisor is called a degenerate divisor in [9].

DBL and ADD correspond to so-called *most frequent cases* of a divisor class doubling and an addition, respectively. TDBL denotes the doubling of a theta divisor. TADD denotes the addition of a general divisor and a theta divisor.

The computational cost of TDBL and TADD is smaller than that of DBL and ADD, respectively, because of simple representation of a theta divisor. We summarize their cost in Table 1. M, S, and I denote the required time of multiplication, squaring, and inversion, respectively.

Table 1. Cost of group operations (genus 2, $C/\mathbb{F}_{2^m}$)

Group operations	Cost
DBL [13]	$1I + 22M + 5S$
ADD [13]	$1I + 22M + 3S$
TDBL [8]	$1I + 5M + 2S$
TADD [13]	$1I + 10M + 1S$

3   Scalar Multiplication on HECC

3.1   Double-and-Add-Always Method

In order to construct HECC, it is necessary to compute scalar multiplication dD, where d is a non-negative integer and D is a reduced divisor. Let $d = (d_{n-1} \cdots d_0)_2$ be the binary representation of d, where $d_{n-1} = 1$. The most standard SPA-resistant method to compute dD is called the Double-and-Add-Always method (DAA), shown in Algorithm 1.

Algorithm 1. *Double-and-add-always Method* (DAA)

Input: a non-negative integer d, a reduced divisor $D \in \mathcal{J}_C(\mathbb{F}_{2^m})$
Output: dD

1. $Q[0] \leftarrow D$
2. For $i = n - 2$ downto 0 do:
   2.1 $Q[0] \leftarrow 2Q[0]$
   2.2 $Q[1] \leftarrow Q[0] + D$
   2.3 $Q[0] \leftarrow Q[d_i]$
3. return($Q[0]$)

In step 2.1 and step 2.2, a divisor class doubling and a divisor class addition are computed, respectively. If the input divisor D is a general divisor, a doubling in step 2.1 corresponds to DBL and an addition in step 2.2 corresponds to ADD with very high probability. On the other hand, if D is a theta divisor, ADD is replaced by TADD. From Table 1, we estimate the computational cost of scalar multiplication dD of both a general divisor and a theta divisor. DAA of a General Divisor, which we call DAA_GD, takes $(1I + 22M + 3S) + (1I + 22M + 5S) = 2I + 44M + 8S$ per bit of the scalar d. On the other hand, DAA of a Theta

Divisor, which we call DAA_TD, takes only $(1I+10M+1S)+(1I+22M+5S) = 2I+32M+6S$ per bit of d [8]. Therefore the idea choosing a theta divisor as the input divisor can achieve about 20% improvement of efficiency under $I = 8M$ and $S = 0.1M$. Its cryptographic application, however, is limited; even if we choose a theta divisor as the base point of HECC, we must often compute scalar multiplication of a general divisor.

DAA repeats the identical sequence of a doubling and an addition by inserting dummy additions for $d_i = 0$ in step 2.2. Thus, an SPA attacker cannot guess any bit information of d. The insertion of dummy operations, however, causes the possibility of fault-based attacks.

3.2   Simultaneous Scalar Multiplication

Let us consider the sum of scalar multiplication kD_1 and lD_2, where k, l are non-negative integers and D_1, D_2 are reduced divisors. It is necessary to compute the sum $kD_1 + lD_2$ in HEC-DSA signature verification. The efficient method to compute $kD_1 + lD_2$ is known as Shamir's method. This method computes $kD_1 + lD_2$ simultaneously instead of computing kD_1 and lD_2 independently, so that it is called *simultaneous scalar multiplication*.

Let $k = (k_{n-1} \cdots k_0)_2$ and $l = (l_{n-1} \cdots l_0)_2$ be the binary representations of k and l, respectively, where $k_{n-1} = 1$ or $l_{n-1} = 1$. The simultaneous scalar multiplication $kD_1 + lD_2$ is shown in Algorithm 2.

Algorithm 2. *Simultaneous Scalar Multiplication*

Input: non-negative integers k, l and reduced divisors D_1, D_2
Output: $kD_1 + lD_2$

---
1. (pre-computation) compute $D_1 + D_2$
2. $Q \leftarrow k_{n-1}D_1 + l_{n-1}D_2$
3. For $i = n - 2$ downto 0 do:
    3.1. $Q \leftarrow 2Q$
    3.2. if $(k_i, l_i) \neq (0, 0)$ then
            $T \leftarrow Q + (k_iD_1 + l_iD_2)$
4. return Q

Algorithm 2 can reduce the number of doublings to half compared to computing kD_1 and lD_2 separately. Furthermore we define the following terms in order to evaluate the number of additions.

Definition 1. *Let $\langle k_{n-1} \cdots k_0 \rangle$ and $\langle l_{n-1} \cdots l_0 \rangle$ be signed binary representations of non-negative integers k and l, respectively. The number of i ($0 \leq i \leq n-1$) satisfying $(k_i, l_i) \neq (0, 0)$ is called* Joint Hamming Weight *of (k, l).*

Definition 2. *Let $\langle k_{n-1} \cdots k_0 \rangle$ and $\langle l_{n-1} \cdots l_0 \rangle$ be signed binary representations of non-negative integers k and l, respectively. The ratio of Joint Hamming Weight of (k, l) to n is called* Joint Hamming Density.

The average Joint Hamming Density is $3/4$ for the binary representations of k and l. As a result, the number of additions required in Algorithm 2 is about $3n/4$ on average.

In order to speed up simultaneous scalar multiplication, Solinas gave the efficient signed binary representation of two non-negative integers [17]. The representation is called Joint Sparse Form (JSF), and any pair of non-negative integers has unique JSF. The average Joint Hamming Density of JSF is $1/2$, so that simultaneous scalar multiplication with JSF can reduce the number of additions to about $n/2$ on average.

4   Divisor Decomposition Technique

In this section we propose a novel technique called *Divisor Decomposition Technique* (DDT).

We now consider a general divisor $D = (x^2 + u_1 x + u_0, v_1 x + v_0)$, where $u_i, v_i \in \mathbb{F}_{2^m}$ for $i = 0, 1$. D can be decomposed into two theta divisors $D_1 = (x + x_1, y_1)$ and $D_2 = (x + x_2, y_2)$ if $x^2 + u_1 x + u_0$ is factored to $(x + x_1)(x + x_2)$ over $\mathbb{F}_{2^m}$. It depends on only the reducibility of $x^2 + u_1 x + u_0$ over $\mathbb{F}_{2^m}$ whether D can be decomposed or not. Consequently, $Tr(u_0/u_1^2) = 0$ is the only condition of divisor decomposition, where $Tr(c)$ is trace of $c \in \mathbb{F}_{2^m}$. We show the procedure of DDT in Algorithm 3, where $Hr(c)$ is half-trace of c. T and H denote the computational cost of trace and half-trace, respectively.

Algorithm 3. *Divisor Decomposition Technique* (DDT)

Input: a general divisor $D = (x^2 + u_1 x + u_0, v_1 x + v_0)$	
Output: theta divisors $D_1, D_2, s.t. D = D_1 + D_2$ or FAILURE	
Step Procedure	Cost
1. if $Tr(u_0/u_1^2) = 1$ return FAILURE	$1I + 1M + 1S + 1T$
2. $x_1 \leftarrow u_1 Hr(u_0/u_1^2)$, $x_2 \leftarrow x_1 + u_1$	$1M + 1H$
3. $y_1 \leftarrow v(x_1)$, $y_2 \leftarrow v(x_2)$	$2M$
4. $D_1 \leftarrow (x + x_1, y_1)$, $D_2 \leftarrow (x + x_2, y_2)$	
5. return D_1, D_2	

The question we have to ask here is whether DDT contributes to the efficiency of scalar multiplication dD. As we have seen, each scalar multiplication dD_1, dD_2 is faster than dD. The direct computation of $dD_1 + dD_2$, however, is slower than scalar multiplication dD because Table 1 shows that TADD is not twice as fast as ADD.

5   Joint Regular Form

In this section we propose the other novel technique called *Joint Regular Form* (JRF).

We define a signed binary representation for a pair of non-negative integers as follows.

Definition 3. *Let* $\langle k_{n-1} \cdots k_0 \rangle$ *and* $\langle l_{n-1} \cdots l_0 \rangle$ *be signed binary representations of* k *and* l, *respectively, satisfying* $k+l \equiv 1 \pmod 2$. $\langle k_{n-1} \cdots k_0 \rangle$ *and* $\langle l_{n-1} \cdots l_0 \rangle$ *is called* Joint Regular Form (JRF) *of* (k, l), *if* k_i *and* l_i *satisfy* $k_i + l_i = \pm 1$, *that is,* $(k_i, l_i) = (0, \pm 1)$ *or* $(\pm 1, 0)$ *for any* i.

Example 1. JRF of $(52, 39)$ is represented as follows, where $\bar{1}$ denotes -1.

$$52 = \langle\, 1\ 0\ \bar{1}\ 0\ 1\ 0\ 0\, \rangle$$
$$39 = \langle\, 0\ 1\ 0\ 1\ 0\ \bar{1}\ 1\, \rangle$$

The Joint Hamming Density of JRF is always 1. JRF has the following properties:

 - A pair of non-negative integers (k, l) satisfying $k+l \equiv 1 \pmod 2$ has a JRF.
 - JRF of a certain length is unique.

We first prove the uniqueness of JRF.

Theorem 1. *A pair* (k, l) *of non-negative integers has at most one Joint Regular Form of a certain length.*

Proof. Assume that there are two distinct JRFs of length n as

$$k = \langle k_{n-1} \cdots k_0 \rangle = \langle k'_{n-1} \cdots k'_0 \rangle$$
$$l = \langle l_{n-1} \cdots l_0 \rangle = \langle l'_{n-1} \cdots l'_0 \rangle.$$

Let j be the minimal value satisfying $k_i \neq k'_i$ or $l_i \neq l'_i$, and

$$s = \langle k_{n-1} \cdots k_j \rangle = \langle k'_{n-1} \cdots k'_j \rangle$$
$$t = \langle l_{n-1} \cdots l_j \rangle = \langle l'_{n-1} \cdots l'_j \rangle.$$

We may assume that $k_j \neq k'_j$ by exchanging k and l if necessary. It follows that k_j and k'_j have value 1 and -1. We assume that $k_j = 1$ and $k'_j = -1$ without loss of generality. By the definition of JRF, $l_j = 0$ and $l'_j = 0$. Suppose that $s \equiv 1 \pmod 4$. $k_{j+1} = 0$ and $k'_{j+1} = \pm 1$ since $k_j = 1$ and $k'_j = -1$. It follows that $l_{j+1} = \pm 1$ and $l'_{j+1} = 0$. The former indicates that $t \equiv 2 \pmod 4$ and the latter indicates that $t \equiv 0 \pmod 4$. This contradiction shows that the initial assumption must be wrong. Supposing $s \equiv 3 \pmod 4$, the similar contradiction occurs.   □

The most straightforward way to prove the existence of JRF for any pair of non-negative integers (k, l) satisfying $k + l \equiv 1 \pmod 2$ is to present an algorithm for constructing it. We explain how to construct JRF from the least significant bit. Let $(k_{n-1} \cdots k_0)_2$ and $(l_{n-1} \cdots l_0)_2$ be the binary representations of k and l, respectively. Firstly, $(k_0, l_0) = (0, 1)$ or $(1, 0)$ by $k + l \equiv 1 \pmod 2$.

Next, we notice (k_1, l_1). If $(k_1, l_1) = (0, 0)$, either of the following transformations is carried out according to (k_0, l_0).

$$
\begin{array}{cc}
k_1 & k_0 \\
0 & 1 \\
0 & 0 \\
l_1 & l_0
\end{array}
\Rightarrow
\begin{array}{cc}
k_1 & k_0 \\
1 & \bar{1} \\
0 & 0 \\
l_1 & l_0
\end{array}
\qquad
\begin{array}{cc}
k_1 & k_0 \\
0 & 0 \\
0 & 1 \\
l_1 & l_0
\end{array}
\Rightarrow
\begin{array}{cc}
k_1 & k_0 \\
0 & 0 \\
1 & \bar{1} \\
l_1 & l_0
\end{array}
$$

If $(k_1, l_1) = (1, 1)$, one performs either of the following transformations according to (k_0, l_0).

$$
\begin{array}{cc}
k_1 & k_0 \\
1 & 1 \\
1 & 0 \\
l_1 & l_0
\end{array}
\overset{+1}{\Rightarrow}
\begin{array}{cc}
k_1 & k_0 \\
0 & \bar{1} \\
1 & 0 \\
l_1 & l_0
\end{array}
\qquad
\begin{array}{cc}
k_1 & k_0 \\
1 & 0 \\
1 & 1 \\
l_1 & l_0
\end{array}
\Rightarrow
\overset{\quad}{\underset{+1}{}}
\begin{array}{cc}
k_1 & k_0 \\
1 & 0 \\
0 & \bar{1} \\
l_1 & l_0
\end{array}
$$

$+1$ means 1 is carried over to either $(k_{n-1} \cdots k_2)_2$ or $(l_{n-1} \cdots l_2)_2$. If $(k_1, l_1) = (0, 1)$ or $(1, 0)$, one needs no transformation. In all cases of (k_1, l_1), it is possible to satisfy the following conditions: $(k_0, l_0) = (0, \pm 1)$ or $(\pm 1, 0)$, and $(k_1, l_1) = (0, 1)$ or $(1, 0)$.

By applying this transformation from the least significant bit, we construct the signed binary representations $\langle k_{n-1} \cdots k_0 \rangle$ and $\langle l_{n-1} \cdots l_0 \rangle$ satisfying $(k_i, l_i) = (0, \pm 1)$ or $(\pm 1, 0)$ for any i. The detailed algorithm is shown in Algorithm 4.

Algorithm 4. *Joint Regular Form (JRF)*

Input: a pair of non-negative integers (k, l) s.t. $k + l \equiv 1 \pmod 2$
Output: JRF of (k, l): $\langle k_{n-1} \cdots k_0 \rangle$, $\langle l_{n-1} \cdots l_0 \rangle$

---

1. $i \leftarrow 0$, $s \leftarrow k$, $t \leftarrow l$,
2. while $s > 0$ or $t > 0$ do:
   2.1. $k_i = s \bmod 2$, $l_i = t \bmod 2$
   2.2. if $(k_i, l_i) = (0, 0)$ then
        $k_i \leftarrow k_{i-1}$, $k_{i-1} \leftarrow -k_{i-1}$, $l_i \leftarrow l_{i-1}$, $l_{i-1} \leftarrow -l_{i-1}$, $s \leftarrow s/2$, $t \leftarrow t/2$
        else if $(k_i, l_i) = (1, 1)$ then
        $k_i \leftarrow 1 - k_{i-1}$, $k_{i-1} \leftarrow -k_{i-1}$, $l_i \leftarrow 1 - l_{i-1}$, $l_{i-1} \leftarrow -l_{i-1}$,
        $s \leftarrow (s - 2k_i + 1)/2$, $t \leftarrow (t - 2l_i + 1)/2$
        else then
        $s \leftarrow (s - k_i)/2$, $t \leftarrow (t - l_i)/2$
   2.3. $i \leftarrow i + 1$
3. $n \leftarrow i$
4. return $\langle k_{n-1} \cdots k_0 \rangle$ and $\langle l_{n-1} \cdots l_0 \rangle$

If we apply JRF of (k, l) to the simultaneous scalar multiplication $kD_1 + lD_2$, we *always* compute a divisor class doubling and an addition of $\pm D_1$ or $\pm D_2$ per bit of (k, l). Consequently, we achieves the SPA-resistant simultaneous scalar multiplication without any dummy operation and pre-computation $D_1 \pm D_2$.

Remark 1. The advantages of simultaneous scalar multiplication with JRF are useful to not only HECC but also ECC. Lim-Lee method [14], GLV method [6], and BRIP [15] seem to be nice applications of JRF.

6   Combination of DDT and JRF

We show that the combination of DDT and JRF achieves efficient and secure scalar multiplication of a general divisor.

Suppose that a general divisor D can be decomposed into two theta divisors D_1 and D_2 as $D = D_1 + D_2$. We compute $(dD_1 + d'D_2) - D_2$ instead of the scalar multiplication dD, where $d' = d+1$. JRF of (d, d') is applied to the simultaneous scalar multiplication $dD_1 + d'D_2$. As we have discussed above, $dD_1 + d'D_2$ with JRF computes a divisor class doubling and an addition of a theta divisor $\pm D_1$ or $\pm D_2$ per bit of (d, d').

Indeed, JRF of (d, d'), $\langle d_n \cdots d_0 \rangle$ and $\langle d'_n \cdots d'_0 \rangle$, can be represented very easily without Algorithm 4 as follows:

1. Let $\langle d_{n-1} \cdots d_0 \rangle$ be the binary representation of d.
2. $d'_i = d_i - 1$ for $0 \leq i \leq n - 1$.
3. Append $d_n = 0$ and $d'_n = 1$.

The validity of this representation is clearly shown by $d = \sum_{i=0}^{n-1} d_i 2^i$ and $d' = d + 1 = 2^n + \sum_{i=0}^{n-1} (d_i - 1) 2^i$. For example, JRF of $(53, 54)$ is represented as $53 = \langle 0110101 \rangle$ and $54 = \langle 100\bar{1}0\bar{1}0 \rangle$.

We present the detailed algorithm for theta divisors D_1 and D_2 in Algorithm 5. Obviously Algorithm 5 *always* computes a divisor class doubling and an addition of a theta divisor whether $d_i = 0$ or 1. Therefore, an SPA-attacker cannot guess any bit information of d.

Algorithm 5. *Simultaneous Scalar Multiplication with JRF* (SimJRF)

Input: a non-negative integer d, theta divisors D_1, D_2 s.t. $D = D_1 + D_2$
Output: dD

---
1. $D[0] \leftarrow -D_2$, $D[1] \leftarrow D_1$
2. $Q \leftarrow \mathsf{TDBL}(D_2)$
3. $Q \leftarrow \mathsf{TADD}(Q, D_1)$
4. for $i = n - 2$ downto 0 do:
   4.1. $Q \leftarrow \mathsf{DBL}(Q)$
   4.2. $Q \leftarrow \mathsf{TADD}(Q, D[d_i])$
5. $Q \leftarrow \mathsf{TADD}(Q, D[0])$
6. return Q

As described in Section 4, a general divisor D cannot be always decomposed to two theta divisors; D can be decomposed only if $x^2 + u_1 x + u_0$ is reducible over $\mathbb{F}_{2^m}$, where $D = (x^2 + u_1 x + u_0, v_1 x + v_0)$. In order to apply DDT to any general divisor, we utilize a divisor class doubling (DBL) and its inverse operation, that is, a divisor class halving (HLV) [10]. If D cannot be decomposed, one repeats i times until $D' = 2^i D$ can be decomposed by $D' = D'_1 + D'_2$. After computing dD' using SimJRF, one then repeats a divisor class halving i times by $dD = 1/2^i (dD')$. We summarize our efficient and secure scalar multiplication algorithm for a general divisor in Algorithm 6.

Algorithm 6. DDT *and* SimJRF (DDT+SimJRF)

Input: a non-negative integer d, a general divisor D

Output: dD

1. $i \leftarrow 0$
2. while DDT(D) outputs "FAILURE" do:
   2.1. $D \leftarrow$ DBL(D), $i \leftarrow i+1$
3. $Q \leftarrow$ SimJRF(D_1, D_2, d)
4. while $i > 0$ do:
   4.1. $Q \leftarrow$ HLV(Q), $i \leftarrow i-1$
5. return Q

The iteration count i becomes 1 on average since DDT returns "FAILURE" in probability of about $1/2$. Accordingly, we require *two* DDT and *one* DBL in step 2, and *one* HLV in step 4.

Remark 2. In HEC ElGamal-type decryption, a receiver A needs to compute $s_A D$, where s_A is A's secret key and D is a random divisor. In the case, instead of the operations DBL and HLV, we can utilize an addition of the base point G and a subtraction of $s_A G$, where $s_A G$ is A's public key.

7   Computational Efficiency

We estimate the computational cost of DDT+SimJRF proposed in Algorithm 6 and compare it to that of the Double-and-Add-Always method of a General Divisor (DAA_GD) and the Double-and-Add-Always method of a Theta Divisor (DAA_TD). The cost of divisor doublings and additions is referred to Table 1. As we have mentioned in Section 3.1, the cost of DAA_GD and DAA_TD is $(n-1)(2I + 44M + 8S)$ and $(n-2)(2I + 32M + 6S) + 2I + 28M + 3S$, respectively, where n is the bit length of d.

In order to estimate the cost of DDT+SimJRF in Algorithm 6, we evaluate the cost required in **divisor decomposition step** (step 2), SimJRF (step 3), and **compensation step** (step 4) as following.

divisor decomposition step. According to our analysis in Section 6, we require *two* DDT, one of which returns "FAILURE", and *one* DBL on average. The estimated cost is $2(1I + 1M + 1S + 1T) + (3M + 1H) + (1I + 22M + 5S) = 3I + 27M + 7S + H + 2T$.

SimJRF. We estimate the cost of SimJRF through Algorithm 5. In step 1, the inverse of a theta divisor $D_2 = (x + x_2, y_2)$, $-D_2 = (x + x_2, y_2 + h(x_0))$, is computed, which corresponds to $1M$. Step 2 and 3 are the main procedures of SimJRF. We then require *one* TDBL, $(n-1)$ DBL, and n TADD, which correspond to $(1I + 5M + 2S) + (n-1)(1I + 22M + 5S) + n(1I + 10M + 1S) = (n-1)(2I + 32M + 6S) + 2I + 15M + 3S$. Step 4 requires $1I + 10M + 1S$. As a result, the total cost of SimJRF is estimated to be $(n-1)(2I + 32M + 6S) + 3I + 26M + 4S$.

compensation step. We require *one* HLV as we have shown in Section 6. According to [10], the cost of HLV is $1I + 19.5M + 2S + 2.5SR + 2H + 2T$, where SR denotes the cost of square root over $\mathbb{F}_{2^m}$.

Consequently, the cost of DDT+SimJRF is estimated to be $n(2I + 32M + 6S) + 5I + 40.5M + 7S + 2.5SR + 3H + 4T$ in total.

Suppose that the bit length of d is 160, that is, $n = 160$. According to [5,10], we may assume that the following ratios of field operations to multiplication are satisfied: $I = 8M$, $S = 0.1M$, $SR = 0.5M$, $H = 0.6M$, and $T = 0$.

Table 2 summarizes the comparison of DAA_GD, DAA_TD, and DDT+SimJRF. The column 'Divisor' indicates whether each method computes scalar multiplication of a general divisor or a theta divisor; the column 'Dummy' indicates whether each method uses any dummy operation or not. The proposed method DDT+SimJRF is 18.7% faster than DAA_GD and eliminates any dummy operation. DDT+SimJRF requires no more than 1.8% increase of computational cost compared to DAA_TD that can be used only in the limited case.

Table 2. Comparison of scalar multiplication (160bit)

Method	Divisor	Dummy	Cost
DAA_GD	general	use	$318I + 6996M + 1272S$ $\quad(9667.2M)$
DAA_TD	theta	use	$318I + 5084M + 951S$ $\quad(7723.1M)$
DDT+SimJRF	general	NOT use	$325I + 5160.5M + 967S$ $+2.5SR + 3H + 4T$ $(7860.3M)$

8   Conclusion and Further Work

In this paper, efficient and secure scalar multiplication of a general divisor for genus 2 HECC over $\mathbb{F}_{2^m}$ is proposed through Divisor Decomposition Technique (DDT) and Joint Regular Form (JRF). The proposed method achieves both about 19% improvement of efficiency compared to the double-and-add-always method and SPA resistance without any dummy operation.

It must be emphasized that the strategy of the proposed method is applicable to not only genus 2 HECC over $\mathbb{F}_{2^m}$. For genus 3 HECC, a general divisor whose weight is 3 might be decomposed into either three theta divisors of weight 1 or two theta divisors of weight 2. In the former case, we must generalize the concept of JRF to three non-negative integers. In the latter case, we need to develop efficient DDT in which a weight 3 divisor is decomposed into two weight 2 divisors.

References

1. D.G. Cantor, "Computing in the Jacobian of a Hyperelliptic Curve", *Mathematics of Computation*, 48, 177, pp.95-101, 1987.
2. H. Cohen, G. Frey, R. Avanzi, C. Doche, T. Lange, K. Nguyen, and F. Vercauteren, *Handbook of Elliptic Curve and Hyperelliptic Curve Cryptography*, Chapman & Hall, 2005.

3. J.-S. Coron, "Resistance against Differential Power Analysis for Elliptic Curve Cryptosystems", *Cryptographic Hardware and Embedded Systems - CHES '99*, LNCS 1717, pp.292-302, Springer-Verlag, 1999.
4. S. Duquesne, "Montgomery Scalar Multiplication for Genus 2 Curves", *Algorithmic Number Theory - ANTS VI*, LNCS 3076, pp.153-168, Springer-Verlag, 2004.
5. K. Fong, D. Hankerson, J. López and A. Menezes, "Field inversion and point halving revised," Technical Report CORR 2003-81, 2003. http://www.cacr.math.uwaterloo.ca/techreports/2003/corr2003-18.pdf
6. R.P. Gallant, R.J. Lambert, and S.A. Vanstone, "Faster Point Multiplication on Elliptic Curves with Efficient Endomorphisms", *Advances in Cryptology - CRYPTO 2001*, LNCS 2139, pp.190-200, Springer-Verlag, 2001.
7. R. Harley, "Adding.txt, Doubling.c", 2000. http://cristal.inria.fr/ harley/hyper/
8. M. Katagi, T. Akishita, I. Kitamura, and T. Takagi, "Efficient Hyperelliptic Curve Cryptosystems Using Theta Divisors", *IEICE Trans. Fundamentals*, vol.E89-A, no.1, pp.151-160, 2006.
9. M. Katagi, I. Kitamura, T. Akishita, and T. Takagi, "Novel Efficient Implementations of Hyperelliptic Curve Cryptosystems Using Degenerate Divisors", *Information Security Application s - WISA 2004*, LNCS 3325, pp.345-359, Springer-Verlag, 2004.
10. I. Kitamura, M. Katagi, and T. Takagi, "A Complete Divisor Class Halving Algorithm for Hyperelliptic Curve Cryptosystems of Genus Two", *Information Security and Privacy - ACISP 2005*, LNCS 3674, pp.146-157, Springer-Verlag, 2005.
11. N. Koblitz, "Hyperelliptic Cryptosystems", *Journal of Cryptology*, vol.1, pp. 139-150, Springer-Verlag, 1989.
12. S. Lang, "Abelian Varieties", Springer-Verlag, 1983.
13. T. Lange, "Formulae for Arithmetic on Genus 2 Hyperelliptic Curves", *Applicable Algebra in Engineering, Communication and Computing*, vol.15, pp.295-328, Springer-Verlag, 2005.
14. C.H. Lim and P.J. Lee, "More Flexible Exponentiation with Precomputation", *Advances in Cryptology - CRYPTO '94*, LNCS 839, pp.95-107, Springer-Verlag, 1994.
15. H. Mamiya, A. Miyaji, and H. Morimoto, "Efficient Countermeasure against RPA, DPA, and SPA", *Cryptographic Hardware and Embedded Systems - CHES 2004*, LNCS 3156, pp.343-356, Springer-Verlag, 2004.
16. D. Mumford, *Tata Lectures on Theta II*, Progress in Mathematics 43, Birkhäuser, 1984.
17. J.A. Solinas, "Low-Weight Binary Representations for Pairs of Integers", Technical Report CORR 2001-41, 2001. http://www.cacr.math.uwaterloo.ca/techreports/2001/corr2001-41.ps

Fast Generation of Prime Numbers on Portable Devices: An Update

Marc Joye[1,*] and Pascal Paillier[2]

[1] Thomson R&D France
Technology Group, Corporate Research, Security Laboratory
1 avenue Belle Fontaine, 35576 Cesson-Sévigné, France
marc.joye@thomson.net
[2] Gemalto, Security Labs
34 rue Guynemer, 92447 Issy-les-Moulineaux Cedex, France
pascal.paillier@gemalto.com

Abstract. The generation of prime numbers underlies the use of most public-key cryptosystems, essentially as a primitive needed for the creation of RSA key pairs. Surprisingly enough, despite decades of intense mathematical studies on primality testing and an observed progressive intensification of cryptography, prime number generation algorithms remain scarcely investigated and most real-life implementations are of dramatically poor performance.

We show simple techniques that substantially improve all algorithms previously suggested or extend their capabilities. We derive fast implementations on appropriately equipped portable devices like smart-cards embedding a cryptographic coprocessor. This allows onboard generation of RSA keys featuring a very attractive (average) processing time.

Our motivation here is to help transferring this task from terminals where this operation usually took place so far, to portable devices themselves in near future for more confidence, security, and compliance with network-scaled distributed protocols such as electronic cash or mobile commerce.

Keywords: Public-key cryptography, RSA, primality testing, prime number generation, embedded software, efficient implementations, cryptoprocessors, smart cards, PDAs.

1 Introduction

Undoubtedly, the lack of *efficient* prime number generators severely restricts the development of public-key cryptography in embedded environments. Several algorithms that generate prime numbers do exist, some of them being well-known and popular [5,6,8,17], but most of them are hardly adapted to the computational context of portable devices like smart cards or PDAs, where memory capabilities and processing power are somewhat limited. A noticeable exception is found in a recent heuristic algorithm by Joye, Paillier and Vaudenay [13].

---

* This work was done while the author was with Gemalto (formerly Gemplus).

L. Goubin and M. Matsui (Eds.): CHES 2006, LNCS 4249, pp. 160–173, 2006.

In this paper, we improve their algorithm in multiple directions. First, we give a more general description with extended parameter choices that fit any (crypto-)processor architecture. Second, we present new techniques that speed up the entire process and reduce the standard statistical deviation, especially in the generation of so-called units. Third, we consider the issue of length extendability, that is, algorithmic solutions for obtaining primes of arbitrary and dynamically chosen bitsize.

The way prime numbers are selected during (e.g., RSA) key generation is critical towards the security of generated key pairs. Therefore we investigate the mathematical properties fulfilled by our improved algorithms. Using an analogue of Gallagher's empiric law on the distribution of primes in arithmetic progressions [10,11], we accurately evaluate the output entropy of our generators. We also analyze the probability that two outputs are identical, i.e., that one gets the same prime number when running the generation twice with randomly selected independent inputs. It is shown that the output entropy is nearly optimal (the entropy loss is < 0.61 bits compared to uniform distribution) and that collisions remain extremely unlikely.

The prime number generation algorithms we consider here find their main application in the generation of RSA keys on embedded platforms. This context of use implies the additional condition on a prime q being generated, that $q - 1$ be coprime to a prescribed public RSA exponent e. We show how our algorithm may automatically fulfill this latter condition at negligible cost, at least for small or smooth values of e. Further, as an additional application of our techniques, we show how to efficiently generate a random safe (resp. quasi-safe) prime. This answers a problem left open in [13].

The rest of the paper is organized as follows. In the next section, we present our improved prime generation algorithms. We then provide a security analysis in Section 3. In Section 4, we apply our techniques to the generation of RSA keys and of safe primes. Finally, we conclude in Section 5.

2   Efficient Generation of Prime Numbers

This section describes efficient (trial-division free as opposed to [3,6,8,17]) algorithms for producing a prime q uniformly distributed in some given interval $[q_{min}, q_{max}]$ or a sub-interval thereof; q_{min} and q_{max} being two arbitrarily chosen integers and $q_{min} < q_{max}$. Our proposal actually consists of a pair of algorithms: the prime generation algorithm itself and an algorithm for generating invertible elements, also called *units* [13]. We assume that a random number generator is available, and that some fast (pseudo-)primality (resp. compositeness [2,4,14,20,22,25,19]) testing function T is provided as well.

Parameter setup. Let $0 < \varepsilon \leqslant 1$ denote a quality parameter (a typical value for ε is 10^{-3}). Let also ϕ denote Euler's totient function. Our setup phase requires to choose a product of primes, $\Pi = \prod_i p_i$, such that there exist integers t, v, w satisfying

(P1) $1 - \varepsilon < \dfrac{w\varPi - 1}{q_{\max} - q_{\min}} \leqslant 1$;

(P2) $v\varPi + t \geqslant q_{\min}$;

(P3) $(v + w)\varPi + t - 1 \leqslant q_{\max}$;

(P4) the ratio $\phi(\varPi)/\varPi$ is as small as possible .

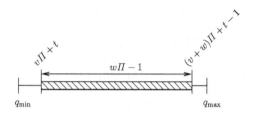

Fig. 1. ε-approximated output domain

The primes output by our algorithm lie, in fact, in the sub-interval $[v\varPi + t, (v + w)\varPi + t - 1] \subseteq [q_{\min}, q_{\max}]$ as illustrated on Fig. 1. The error in the approximation is captured by the value of ε meaning that a smaller value for ε gives better results (cf. Property (P1)). The minimality of the ratio $\phi(\varPi)/\varPi$ in Property (P4) ensures that $\varPi$ contains a maximum number of distinct primes and that these primes are as small as possible. Given any tuple $(q_{\min}, q_{\max}, \varepsilon)$, computing the tuple $(\varPi, v, w, t)$ that best matches Properties (P1)–(P4) is experimentally easy.

Prime number generation. We now proceed to describe our prime number generation algorithm in its most generic version, as depicted on Fig. 2.

The first step requires the random selection of an integer $k \in (\mathbb{Z}/m\mathbb{Z})^*$ (see Section 2.2) where $m = w\varPi$ is a smooth integer. At this stage, it is worthwhile noticing that since $a \in (\mathbb{Z}/m\mathbb{Z})^*$, k remains coprime to m and also to $\varPi$ throughout the algorithm —remember that $\varPi$ contains a large number of

---

```
Parameters:  t, v, w and a ∈ (ℤ/mℤ)* \ {1}
Output:      a random prime q ∈ [qmin, qmax]
```

```
1. Compute l ← vΠ and m ← wΠ
2. Randomly choose k ∈ (ℤ/mℤ)*
3. Set q ← [(k − t) mod m] + t + l
4. If (T(q) = false) then
     (a) Set k ← a · k (mod m)
     (b) Go to Step 3
5. Output q
```

Fig. 2. Generic prime generation algorithm for $q \in [q_{\min}, q_{\max}]$

prime factors by Property (P4). This, in turn, implies that q is coprime to Π as $q \equiv [(k - t) \bmod m] + t + l \equiv k \pmod{\Pi}$ and $k \in (\mathbb{Z}/\Pi\mathbb{Z})^*$. Hence, this technique ensures *built-in* coprimality of our prime candidate q with a large set of small prime numbers. Consequently, the probability under which q is prime at Step 3 is in fact quite high. When q is found to be composite, a new candidate is derived by "recycling" q in a way that preserves its coprimality to Π.

2.1 An Implementation Example

The previous algorithm is actually very general and can be adapted in numerous ways, depending on hardware capabilities of the targeted processor architecture. Public-key crypto-processors generally allow super-fast (modular) additions, subtractions and multiplications over large integers, and this renders other types of computations comparatively prohibitive, unless specific hardware is integrated to support these. We now give a possible implementation to illustrate this, in which we attempt to increase our algorithm's performance to its uppermost level while running on a general-purpose crypto-processor. Other choices of parameters may lead to better results on specific platforms.

A first improvement is to choose $w = 1$ and to let the value of t varying as a random multiple of Π, say $t = b\Pi$ for some integer b, instead of fixing it. This allows to compute modulo Π, resulting in faster arithmetic. Also, the constant a may be chosen such that performing a multiplication by a modulo m turns out to be a somewhat trivial operation. In the end, the best possible choice is $a = 2$, because multiplying by 2 then amounts to a single bit shift or addition, possibly followed by a subtraction. Unfortunately, 2 must belong to $(\mathbb{Z}/m\mathbb{Z})^*$ and owing to Property (P4), 2 is a factor of Π, a contradiction. A simple trick here consists in choosing m odd (so that $2 \in (\mathbb{Z}/m\mathbb{Z})^*$) and in slightly modifying the above framework in order to ensure that a prime candidate q is always odd. We require $\Pi = \prod_i p_i$ (with $p_i \neq 2$) and integers b_{min}, b_{max}, v satisfying:

(P1) $1 - \varepsilon < \dfrac{(b_{max} - b_{min} + 1)\Pi - 1}{q_{max} - q_{min}} \leqslant 1$;

(P2) $v\Pi + b_{min}\Pi \geqslant q_{min}$;

(P3) $(v + 1)\Pi + b_{max}\Pi - 1 \leqslant q_{max}$;

(P4) the ratio $\phi(\Pi)/\Pi$ is as small as possible .

Putting it all together, we obtain the algorithm shown on Fig. 3.[1] Note that if $k+t+l$ is even then $\Pi-k+t+l$ is odd since $\Pi-k+t+l \equiv \Pi+(k+t+l) \equiv \Pi \equiv 1 \pmod 2$. Hence, as before, any candidate q belonging to our search sequence is coprime to 2Π: we get $\gcd(q,2) = 1$ as q is odd. Also, $\gcd(q,\Pi) = 1$ as $q \equiv \pm k \pmod{\Pi}$ and $\pm k \in (\mathbb{Z}/\Pi\mathbb{Z})^*$.

---

[1] Stricly speaking, the algorithm of Fig. 3 is a particular case of the generic algorithm of Fig. 2 only if, at Step 6(b), we go to Step 3 (instead of Step 4).

Parameters: Π odd, $b_{\min}$, $b_{\max}$, v
Output: a random prime $q \in [q_{\min}, q_{\max}]$

---

1. Compute $l \leftarrow v\Pi$
2. Randomly choose $k \in (\mathbb{Z}/\Pi\mathbb{Z})^*$
3. Randomly choose $b \in \{b_{\min}, \ldots, b_{\max}\}$ and set $t \leftarrow b\Pi$
4. Set $q \leftarrow k + t + l$
5. If (q even) then $q \leftarrow \Pi - k + t + l$
6. If ($T(q) = \mathtt{false}$) then
    (a) Set $k \leftarrow 2k \pmod{\Pi}$
    (b) Go to Step 4
7. Output q

Fig. 3. Faster prime generation algorithm

2.2   Generation of Units

All prime generation algorithms presented in this paper require the random selection of some element $k \in (\mathbb{Z}/m\mathbb{Z})^*$ in the spirit of [13]. This section provides an algorithm that efficiently produces such an element with uniform output distribution. We base our design on the next two propositions, making use of Carmichael's function λ.

Proposition 1 (Carmichael [7]). *Let $m > 1$ and let k be any integer modulo m. Then $k \in (\mathbb{Z}/m\mathbb{Z})^*$ if and only if $k^{\lambda(m)} \equiv 1 \pmod{m}$.*   □

Proposition 2. *Let k, r be integers modulo m and assume $\gcd(r, k, m) = 1$. Then*

$$[k + r(1 - k^{\lambda(m)}) \bmod m] \in (\mathbb{Z}/m\mathbb{Z})^* \ .$$

Proof. Let $\prod_i p_i^{\delta_i}$ denote the prime factorization of m. Define $\omega(k, r) := [k + r(1 - k^{\lambda(m)}) \bmod m] \in \mathbb{Z}/m\mathbb{Z}$. Let p_i be a prime factor of m. Suppose that $p_i \mid k$ then $\omega(k, r) \equiv r \not\equiv 0 \pmod{p_i}$ since $\gcd(r, p_i)$ divides $\gcd(r, \gcd(k, m)) = \gcd(r, k, m) = 1$. Suppose now that $p_i \nmid k$ then $k^{\lambda(m)} \equiv 1 \pmod{p_i}$ and so $\omega(k, r) \equiv k \not\equiv 0 \pmod{p_i}$. Therefore for all primes $p_i \mid m$, we have $\omega(k, r) \not\equiv 0 \pmod{p_i}$ and thus $\omega(k, r) \not\equiv 0 \pmod{p_i^{\delta_i}}$, which, invoking Chinese remaindering, concludes the proof.   □

We benefit from these facts by devising the unit generation algorithm shown on Fig. 4.

This algorithm is self-correcting in the following sense: as soon as k is relatively prime to some factor of m, it remains coprime to this factor after the updating step $k \leftarrow k + rU$. This is due to Proposition 2. What happens in simple words is that, viewing k as the vector of its residues $k \bmod p_i^{\delta_i}$ for all $p_i^{\delta_i} \mid m$ (i.e., the RNS representation of k based on m, see [9]), non-invertible coordinates of k are continuously re-randomized until invertibility is reached for all of them.

```
Parameters:  m and λ(m)
Output:      a random unit k ∈ (Z/mZ)*
```

```
1. Randomly choose k ∈ [1, m[
2. Set U ← (1 − k^λ(m)) mod m
3. If (U ≠ 0) then
   (a) Choose a random r ∈ [1, m[
   (b) Set k ← k + rU (mod m)
   (c) Go to Step 2
4. Output k
```

Fig. 4. Our unit generation algorithm

This ensures that the output distribution is strictly uniform provided that the random number generator is uniformly distributed over $[1, m[$.

2.3 Efficiency

A complexity analysis for generating an n_0-bit prime q is easily driven from the work of [13]. The expected number of calls to T, i.e., the number of primality or compositeness tests required on average, heuristically amounts to

$$n_0 \cdot \ln 2 \cdot \frac{\phi(\Pi)}{\Pi} = O\left(\frac{n_0}{\ln n_0}\right) \, .$$

Naturally the exact, concrete efficiency of our implementation also depends on hardware-related features. In any case, in practice, a spectacular execution speed-up[2] is generally observed in comparison with usual, incremental and trial-division-based prime number generators. It can be shown that the unit generation requires about 2.15 modular exponentiations $x \mapsto x^{\lambda(m)} \bmod m$ where the bitsize of $\lambda(m)$ is much smaller than the bitsize of m, and experimentally never exceeds $|m|/3$. For instance, one has $|\lambda(m)| \simeq 160$ when $|m| = 512$. Note also that all computations fall into the range of operations easily and efficiently performed by any crypto-processor.

We note that many previous works such as [24,16,15] make use of trial-divisions up to a large bound to decrease the number of calls to T. This common technique is hardly adapted to cryptoprocessors where each and every modular reduction may impose a prior, time-prohibitive modulus-dependent initialization. Experience shows that practical smart-card implementations are found to impressively benefit from our above algorithm in comparison to these.

2.4 Length Extendability

So far, our implementation parameters are Π, a, the tuple (v, w, t) and $\lambda(m)$ with $m = w\Pi$. These values are chosen once and for all and heavily depend on $q_{min} =$

---

[2] Which usually amounts to one order of magnitude.

$\lceil 2^{n_0-1/2} \rceil$ and $q_{\max} = 2^{n_0}$, if n_0 denotes the bitsize of prime numbers being generated. Now, the feature we desire here (and this is motivated by code size limitations embedded platforms usually have to work with), consists in the ability to use the parameters sized for n_0 to generate primes numbers of bitsize $n \neq n_0$. A performance loss is acceptable compared to the situation when parameters are generated for both lengths.

We propose an implementation solving that problem for any $n \geqslant n_0$, provided that a was chosen odd and that arithmetic computations can still be carried out over n-bit numbers on the processor taken into consideration. It is an extended version of the algorithm depicted on Fig. 2. We exploit the somewhat obvious, following facts:

1. Letting $q_{\max}(x) = 2^x$ and $q_{\min}(x) = \lceil 2^{x-1/2} \rceil$, we have of course $q_{\max}(n) = q_{\min}(n_0)2^{n-n_0}$ and $q_{\min}(n) \approx q_{\min}(n_0)2^{n-n_0}$;
2. Given $\Pi(n_0)$ chosen as per Section 2, we take

$$\begin{cases} \Pi(n) = \Pi(n_0) \\ v(n) = v(n_0)2^{n-n_0} \\ w(n) = w(n_0)2^{n-n_0} \\ t(n) = t(n_0)2^{n-n_0} \end{cases},$$

hence $l(n) = l(n_0)2^{n-n_0}$ and $m(n) = m(n_0)2^{n-n_0}$;
3. $a(n) = a(n_0)$, hence $a(n) \in (\mathbb{Z}/m(n)\mathbb{Z})^*$ since $a(n_0)$ is taken odd;
4. Given $\lambda(n_0) = \lambda(m(n_0))$, it is easy to see that denoting $\lambda(n) = \lambda(n_0)2^{n-n_0}$, we have again $\lambda(n) = \lambda(m(n))$, or at least $\lambda(n) \propto \lambda(m(n))$ which is a sufficient condition for the unit generation algorithm to be effective.

These transformations happen to preserve Properties (P1), (P2) and (P3) we required earlier, with $\varepsilon(n) = \varepsilon(n_0)$. It is easy to see that all parameters for some bitsize n may, as a direct consequence, be replaced by the respective parameters computed for n_0 multiplied by 2^{n-n_0}, except for $\Pi(n) = \Pi(n_0)$. By performing this replacement, we just accept to live with sub-optimized performances because the ratio $\phi(\Pi(n))/\Pi(n)$ will not be chosen minimal. Still, our algorithm will output n-bit primes in a correct manner, for any dynamic choice of $n \geqslant n_0$, with a 1-bit granularity.

Our extended algorithm is depicted on Fig. 5. In **Step 1**, the random unit generation is carried out with parameters $m(n_0)2^{n-n_0}$ and $\lambda(n_0)2^{n-n_0}$ instead of $m(n_0)$ and $\lambda(n_0)$. This does not affect the algorithm whatsoever. Another observation is that the order of $a(n)$ modulo $m(n)$ is necessarily larger than (or equal to) the order of $a(n_0)$ modulo $m(n_0)$. It is therefore large enough for all our choices of n provided that $a(n_0)$ was correctly chosen in the first place.

3   Security Analysis

We outline in this section a mathematical analysis of our generic prime generation algorithm (Fig. 2). The results are easily transposable to the other prime

---

Parameters:	$l(n_0) = v(n_0)\Pi(n_0)$, $m(n_0) = w(n_0)\Pi(n_0)$,
	$t(n_0)$, $a(n_0) \in (\mathbb{Z}/m(n_0)\mathbb{Z})^* \setminus \{1\}$, n_0
Input:	bitsize $n \geqslant n_0$
Output:	a random prime $q \in [q_{min}(n), q_{max}(n)]$

---

1. Set $m \leftarrow m(n_0)2^{n-n_0}$, $t \leftarrow t(n_0)2^{n-n_0}$ and $l \leftarrow l(n_0)2^{n-n_0}$
2. Randomly choose $k \in (\mathbb{Z}/m\mathbb{Z})^*$
3. Set $q \leftarrow [(k - t) \bmod m] + t + l$
4. If $(\mathsf{T}(q) = \mathsf{false})$ then
   (a) Set $k \leftarrow a(n_0) k \pmod{m}$
   (b) Go to Step 3
5. Output q

Fig. 5. Our scalable prime generation algorithm

generation algorithms presented in this paper. We answer the following critical questions:

Question 1. Are output primes well distributed? How much entropy is there in the output distribution?

Question 2. What is the probability that the same prime is output for two independently selected input values?

3.1 Output Entropy

We accurately evaluate the entropy H of the output distribution which, following Brandt and Damgård's methodology [5], is considered as a quality measure of a prime number generator.

Theorem 1. *Let H_{max} be the maximal possible value of H. Then, under Hardy and Littlewoods' prime r-tuple conjecture [11] and Gallagher's heuristic [10], we have for any $n \geqslant 256$,*

$$H_{max} - H < \frac{1 - \gamma}{\ln 2} = 0.609949$$

where γ is the Euler-Mascheroni constant [22]. □

Theorem 1 shows that the entropy loss with respect to a perfectly uniform generator is less that 0.61 bit for any prime bitlength. Due to lack of space, we omit the proof here and refer the reader to the extended version of this work for more detail [12].

Table 1 represents the concrete values for H, H_{max} and $\rho = (H_{max} - H)/H_{max}$ for various bitlengths n. We see that the output entropy of our generator is similar to the one of random search, in which one sets candidate q to successive random numbers until q is prime. Our figures show that

Table 1. Output entropy H as a function of n

n	256	384	512	640	768	896	1024
$H_{\max}$	246.767	374.179	501.762	629.439	757.176	884.953	1012.76
H	246.194	373.596	501.173	628.847	756.581	884.356	1012.16
$H_{\max} - H$	0.572795	0.583093	0.588773	0.592377	0.594834	0.59669	0.598092
ρ (%)	0.23212	0.155833	0.117341	0.094111	0.078559	0.067426	0.0590557

- asymptotically, the output entropy gets arbitrarily close to its maximal possible value, and
- the gap is already negligibly small for concrete bitsizes of practical interest $256 \leqslant n \leqslant 1024$.

3.2   Collision Probability

Theorem 2. *We denote by ν the probability that the same prime number is output twice for two uniformly and independently distributed random inputs. Then*

$$\nu < \frac{\ln 2}{1 - \frac{1}{\sqrt{2}}} \cdot n \cdot 2^{-n+1} \ .$$

$\square$

Again, we refer to the extended version of this paper [12] for a detailed proof of Theorem 2 and related insights. Table 2 displays ν for common values of n.

Table 2. Collision probability

n	128	256	384	512	1024
$\nu \leqslant$	$1.91 \cdot 10^{-75}$	$3.30 \cdot 10^{-152}$	$4.28 \cdot 10^{-229}$	$4.93 \cdot 10^{-306}$	$5.49 \cdot 10^{-614}$

As a result, from Theorems 1 and 2, we conclude that our prime generation algorithms are *provably reliable*.

4   Concrete Cryptographic Applications

We apply the prime number generators above to the concrete generation of RSA primes, in which the public exponent e is fixed and set to a standard value. We also consider the case of safe primes as they underly many variants of RSA and other popular cryptosystems.

4.1   Generating RSA Primes

This section deals with the generation of an RSA prime q. Let $e = \prod_i e_i^{\nu_i}$ denote the prime factorization of a given public exponent e. Because the RSA primitive (see Appendix A) induces a permutation (i.e., $\gcd(e, \lambda(N)) = 1$), it turns out that q must be such that $\gcd(e_i, q - 1) = 1$ for each prime e_i dividing e.

First, let us assume that $e_i \mid \Pi$ for all i. This happens in the most popular scenario where e is some small prime (like 3 or 17) or when e is chosen smooth. Let α be an integer such that

$$\gcd(\alpha, m) = 1 \text{ and } \text{order}(\alpha \bmod e_i, e_i) = e_i - 1 \text{ for each } e_i \mid e . \tag{1}$$

In practice, the choice of a value for α may be done easily using Chinese remaindering. Note that for such an α, we get that $\text{order}(\alpha, e_i)$ is simultaneously even for all prime factors $\{e_i\}_i$. We define $e^+ = \gcd(e, \Pi) = \prod_i e_i$ and denote by k_0 the initial value for k that the unit generation algorithm of Fig. 4 gets by invoking the random number generator in Step 1. It is easily seen that if we force

$$k_0 \equiv \alpha \pmod{e^+} , \tag{2}$$

then the unit k eventually output by the algorithm will also verify that $k \equiv \alpha \pmod{e^+}$. This is due to the algorithm's self-correctness. We then adapt the generic prime generation algorithm by choosing $a = \alpha^2$. By doing so, every candidate q generated by the sequence will satisfy

$$q \equiv \alpha^{2j+1} \pmod{e^+} ,$$

for some integer j, because $e^+ \mid \Pi$. Hence we can never have $q \equiv 1 \pmod{e_i}$ since α is of even order modulo e_i and q is an odd power of α. Consequently, $q \not\equiv 1 \pmod{e_i}$ for all i, which implies $\gcd(q - 1, e) = 1$.

So our technique works when $e_i \mid \Pi$ for all i, that is, when e has only small prime factors. To deal with cases when $e_i \nmid \Pi$ for some $e_i \mid e$, we face the following options:

- either e is a prime number itself (like Fermat's fourth prime $2^{16} + 1$) and we add the verification step

$$q - 1 \stackrel{?}{\not\equiv} 0 \pmod{e}$$

  before or after the primality test T is applied; or
- e is not prime but its factorization is known. We already know that $q \not\equiv 1 \pmod{e_i}$ when $e_i \mid \Pi$, so we have to ensure that the same holds when $e_i \nmid \Pi$. To do this, we simply check that $q - 1 \not\equiv 0 \pmod{e_i}$ for all prime factors $e_i \nmid \Pi$, or equivalently (but preferably) invoke Proposition 1 and make sure that

$$(q - 1)^{\lambda(e^-)} \equiv 1 \pmod{e^-} ,$$

where $e^- = \prod_i e_i$ for all $e_i \nmid \Pi$.

In both cases, unfortunately, adding at least one additional test to the implementation cannot be avoided.

Finally, forcing $k_0 \equiv \alpha \pmod{e^+}$ in Eq. (2) is easily done by picking a random number r and setting $k_0 = \alpha + e\,r \pmod{m}$.

4.2   Generating Safe and Quasi-safe Primes

We now show how to apply our generic techniques to the specific case of generating safe primes or quasi-safe primes. A *safe prime* is a prime q such that $(q-1)/2$ is also a prime. More generally, a *d-quasi-safe prime* is a prime q such that $(q-1)/2^d$ is prime.

All the point here resides in the way the search sequence is carried out. It should ideally verify that each and every candidate q be such that both q and $(q-1)/2$ are always coprime to Π. It is somewhat easy to guarantee that for q by ensuring (like in previous sections) that

$$q \equiv ak \pmod{\Pi}$$

for some $a, k \in (\mathbb{Z}/m\mathbb{Z})^*$. However, the later constraint on $(q-1)/2$ is a bit more delicate. Our need here is to ensure that for each prime divisor p_i of Π, $p_i \neq 2$,

$$q \not\equiv 1 \pmod{p_i} .$$

Our idea is to make sure that $q \bmod p_i$ just cannot be an element of $\mathrm{QR}(p_i)$, the subgroup of quadratic residues modulo p_i. Doing so, we ensure that $q \not\equiv 1 \pmod{p_i}$. We proceed in the following way. First, the constant a is chosen in $\mathrm{QR}(m)$. Next, we choose once for all a parameter $u \in (\mathbb{Z}/m\mathbb{Z})^*$ such that

$$\forall(\text{odd})\ p_i \mid \Pi : \quad u \notin \mathrm{QR}(p_i) . \tag{3}$$

From there on, the initial unit k (to avoid confusion, we denote it by k_0) is chosen as $k_0 = u\chi^2 \bmod m$ for some random $\chi \in (\mathbb{Z}/m\mathbb{Z})^*$. Then, as before, we have at iteration j

$$q = [(a^j k_0 - t) \mod m] + t + l .$$

It is now easy to see that for each and every odd prime $p_i \mid \Pi$, $q \equiv a^j u\chi^2 \pmod{p_i}$ has a Legendre symbol different from 1, and consequently $q-1$ cannot be 0 modulo p_i, i.e., $q-1$ is coprime to Π.

When $2^\tau \mid m$ for some $\tau \geqslant 2$, we have to make sure, in addition to the above, that $q \equiv 3 \pmod 4$ meaning that the last two bits in the binary representation of q are forced to $\ldots 11_2$, thereby ensuring that $(q-1)/2$ is an odd number and consequently that $(q-1)/2 \in (\mathbb{Z}/\Pi\mathbb{Z})^*$. This is done by forcing $k \equiv 3 \pmod 4$ and $a \equiv 1 \pmod 4$.

The resulting algorithm is described on Fig. 6.

It is straightforward to extend our algorithm to the case of d-quasi-safe prime numbers whenever $d < \tau$. In this case, the constraint $q \equiv 3 \pmod 4$ has to be extended to $q \equiv 2^d + 1 \pmod{2^{d+1}}$.

A note on efficiency. Heuristically, about

$$\left(n_0 \cdot \ln 2 \cdot \frac{\phi(\Pi)}{\Pi} + 1\right)\left(n_0 \cdot \ln 2 \cdot \frac{\phi(\Pi)}{\Pi}\right)$$

primality tests are required for generating a n_0-bit safe prime q. This is ≈ 25 times faster than incremental search algorithms (where we iterate $q \leftarrow q+2$ until q and

---

Parameters: $l = v\Pi$, $m = w\Pi$, $m' = m/2^\tau$,
             t, $a \in \mathrm{QR}(m)$ and u as above
Output: a random prime $q \in [q_{min}, q_{max}]$ with $(q-1)/2$ prime

---

1. Randomly choose $\chi \in (\mathbb{Z}/m\mathbb{Z})^*$
2. Set $k \leftarrow 4u\chi^2 + 3m' \bmod m$
3. Set $q \leftarrow [(k - t) \bmod m] + t + l$
4. If $(\mathsf{T}(q) = \mathtt{false}$ or $\mathsf{T}((q - 1)/2) = \mathtt{false})$ then
   (a) Set $k \leftarrow ak \pmod m$
   (b) Go to Step 3
5. Output q

Fig. 6. Safe-prime generation algorithm for $q \in [q_{min}, q_{max}]$

$(q - 1)/2$ are simultaneously prime) for 512-bit numbers. Another obvious benefit of our technique resides in its simplicity when compared to classical algorithms.

5   Conclusion

We devised and analyzed simple computational techniques that improve the work of [13] in multiple ways. It is argued that our algorithms present much better performances than previous, classical methods.

We also would like to stress that our prime generation algorithm may support additional modifications *mutatis mutandis* in order to simultaneously reach other properties on q — for instance forcing the last bits of q to fit the Rabin-Williams cryptosystem with even public exponents. Independently, some applications require that the pair of primes satisfy specific properties such as being strong or compliant with ANSI X9.31 recommendations [1]. We refer the reader to [13] for a collection of mechanisms allowing to produce such primes. We point out that our improvements may coexist perfectly with these.

We also proposed a specific implementation for generating safe prime numbers which really boosts real-life execution performances. We emphasize that, implementing our techniques, a complete RSA key generation process can be executed on any given crypto-enhanced embedded processor in nearly all circumstances and with extremely attractive running times.

References

1. ANSI X9.31. Public-key cryptography using RSA for the financial services industry. American National Standard for Financial Services, draft, 1995.
2. A.O.L. Atkin and F. Morain. Elliptic curves and primality proving. *Mathematics of Computation*, vol. 61, pp. 29–68, 1993.

3. D. Boneh and M. Franklin. Efficient generation of shared RSA keys. In *Advances in Cryptology — CRYPTO '97*, vol. 1294 of Lecture Notes in Computer Science, pp. 425–439, Springer-Verlag, 1997.

4. W. Bosma and M.-P. van der Hulst. Faster primality testing. In *Advances in Cryptology — CRYPTO '89*, vol. 435 of Lecture Notes in Computer Science, pp. 652–656, Springer-Verlag, 1990.

5. J. Brandt and I. Damgård. On generation of probable primes by incremental search. In *Advances in Cryptology — CRYPTO '92*, vol. 740 of Lecture Notes in Computer Science, pp. 358–370, Springer-Verlag, 1993.

6. J. Brandt, I. Damgård, and P. Landrock. Speeding up prime number generation. In *Advances in Cryptology — ASIACRYPT '91*, vol. 739 of Lecture Notes in Computer Science, pp. 440–449, Springer-Verlag, 1991.

7. R.D. Carmichael. *Introduction to the Theory of Groups of Finite Order*, Dover, 1956.

8. C. Couvreur and J.-J. Quisquater. An introduction to fast generation of large prime numbers. *Philips Journal of Research*, vol. 37, pp. 231–264, 1982.

9. C. Ding, D. Pei, and A. Salomaa. *Chinese Remainder Theorem*, Word Scientific, 1996.

10. P.X. Gallagher. On the distribution of primes in short intervals. *Mathematica*, vol. 23, pp. 4–9, 1976.

11. G.H. Hardy and J.E. Littlewood. Some problems of 'Partitio Numerorum' III: On the expression of a number as a sum of primes. *Acta Mathematica*, vol. 44, pp. 1–70, 1922.

12. M. Joye and P. Paillier. Fast generation of prime numbers on portable devices: An update. *Extended version of this work*. Available on http://eprint.iacr.org.

13. M. Joye, P. Paillier, and S. Vaudenay. Efficient generation of prime numbers. In *Cryptographic Hardware and Embedded Systems — CHES 2000*, vol. 1965 of Lecture Notes in Computer Science, pp. 340–354, Springer-Verlag, 2000.

14. D.E. Knuth. *The Art of Computer Programming - Seminumerical Algorithms*, vol. 2, Addison-Wesley, 2nd ed., 1981.

15. C. Lu and A.L.M. Dos Santos. A note on efficient implementation of prime generation in small portable devices. *Computer Networks*, vol. 49, pp. 476–491, 2005.

16. C. Lu, A.L.M. Dos Santos, and F.R. Pimentel. Implementation of fast RSA key generation on smart cards. In *17th ACM Symposium on Applied Computing*, pp. 214–221, ACM Press, 2002.

17. U. Maurer. Fast generation of prime numbers and secure public-key cryptographic parameters. *Journal of Cryptology*, vol. 8, pp. 123–155, 1995.

18. A.J. Menezes, P.C. van Oorschot, and S.A. Vanstone. *Handbook of Applied Cryptography*, CRC Press, 1997.

19. L. Monier. Evaluation and comparison of two efficient probabilistic primality testing algorithms. *Theoretical Computer Science*, vol. 12, pp. 97–108, 1980.

20. H.C. Pocklington. The determination of the prime or composite nature of large numbers by Fermat's theorem. *Proc. of the Cambridge Philosophical Society*, vol. 18, pp. 29–30, 1914.

21. J.-J. Quisquater and C. Couvreur. Fast decipherment algorithm for RSA public-key cryptosystem. *Electronics Letters*, vol. 18, pp. 905–907, 1982.

22. H. Riesel. *Prime Numbers and Computer Methods for Factorization*, Birkhäuser, 1985.

23. R.L. Rivest, A. Shamir, and L.M. Adleman. A method for obtaining digital signatures and public-key cryptosystems. *Communications of the ACM*, vol. 21, pp. 120–126, 1978.
24. R.D. Silverman. Fast generation of random, strong RSA primes. *Cryptobytes*, vol. 3, pp. 9–13, 1997.
25. R. Solovay and V. Strassen. A fast Monte-Carlo test for primality. *SIAM Journal on Computing*, vol. 6, pp. 84–85, 1977.

A   The RSA Primitive

RSA is certainly the most widely used public-key cryptosystem today. We give hereafter a short description of the RSA primitive and refer the reader to the original paper [23] or any textbook in cryptography (e.g., [18]) for further details.

Let $N = pq$ be the product of two large primes. We let e and d denote a pair of public and private exponents, satisfying

$$ed \equiv 1 \pmod{\lambda(N)},$$

with $\gcd(e, \lambda(N)) = 1$ and λ being Carmichael's function. As $N = pq$, we have $\lambda(N) = \mathrm{lcm}(p - 1, q - 1)$. Given $x < N$, the public operation (e.g., message encryption or signature verification) consists in raising x to the e-th power modulo N, i.e., in computing $y = x^e \bmod N$. Then, given y, the corresponding private operation (e.g., decryption of a ciphertext or signature generation) consists in computing $y^d \bmod N$. From the definition of e and d, we obviously have that $y^d \equiv x \pmod{N}$. The private operation can be carried out at higher speed through Chinese remaindering (CRT mode [21,9]). Computations are independently performed modulo p and q and then recombined. In this case, private parameters are $\{p, q, d_p, d_q, i_q\}$ with

$$\begin{cases} d_p = d \bmod (p - 1), \\ d_q = d \bmod (q - 1), \text{ and} \\ i_q = q^{-1} \bmod p. \end{cases}$$

We then obtain $y^d \bmod N$ as

$$\mathrm{CRT}(x_p, x_q) = x_q + q\left[i_q(x_p - x_q) \bmod p\right],$$

where $x_p = y^{d_p} \bmod p$ and $x_q = y^{d_q} \bmod q$. We expect a theoretical speed-up factor close to 4 (see [21]), compared to the standard, non-CRT mode.

Thus, an *RSA modulus* $N = pq$ is the product of two large prime numbers p and q. If n denotes the bitsize of N then, for some $1 < n_0 < n$, p must lie in the range $\left[\lceil 2^{n-n_0-1/2}\rceil, 2^{n-n_0}\right]$ and q in the range $\left[\lceil 2^{n_0-1/2}\rceil, 2^{n_0}\right]$ so that $2^{n-1} < N = pq < 2^n$. For security reasons, so-called balanced moduli are generally preferred, which means $n = 2n_0$.

A Proposition for Correlation Power Analysis Enhancement

Thanh-Ha Le[1], Jessy Clédière[1], Cécile Canovas[1], Bruno Robisson[1],
Christine Servière[2], and Jean-Louis Lacoume[2]

[1] CEA-LETI
17 avenue des Martyrs, 38 054 Grenoble Cedex 9, France
{thanhha.le, jessy.clediere, cecile.canovas, bruno.robisson}@cea.fr
[2] Laboratoire des Images et des Signaux
961 rue de la Houille Blanche, 38 402 Saint Martin d'Hères Cedex
{christine.serviere, jean-louis.lacoume}@inpg.fr

Abstract. Cryptographic devices are vulnerable to the nowadays well
known side channel leakage analysis. Secret data can be revealed by
power analysis attacks such as Simple Power Analysis (SPA), Differential Power Analysis (DPA) and Correlation Power Analysis (CPA). First,
we give an overview of DPA in mono-bit and multi-bit cases. Next, the
existing multi-bit DPA methods are generalized into the proposed Partitioning Power Analysis (PPA) method. Finally, we focus on the CPA
technique, showing that this attack is a case of PPA with special coefficients and a normalization factor. We also propose a method that allows
us to improve the performance of CPA by restricting the normalization
factor.

Keywords: side channel, power analysis, DPA, multi-bit DPA, PPA,
CPA, correlation, DES, AES.

1 Introduction

Differential analysis on side channel signals were set up by Kocher et al. [10,11]
on DES algorithm. Power consumption signals of CMOS chips were used, giving
good results to retrieve key values by difference of mean curves selected on a defined criteria. Electromagnetic radiation signals, acquired by dedicated sensors,
were then successfully used by several authors [17,20,21]. Hereafter, the terms
DPA and CPA have been generalized for any side channel signal (i.e., power consumption and electromagnetic radiation signals). Since then, differential analysis
has been applied on various cryptographic algorithms, including DES and AES,
and several countermeasures have been proposed to secure those algorithms from
first and high order differential attacks [9,7,1,2]. Some authors [3,14,4,22] have
extended Kocher's et al. attack, introducing multi-bit DPA methods to improve
differential analysis. Currently, there are different multi-bit DPA concepts. We
propose in this paper the Partitioning Power Analysis (PPA) method to merge
these concepts in a single form.

L. Goubin and M. Matsui (Eds.): CHES 2006, LNCS 4249, pp. 174–186, 2006.

Lately, the power analysis technique based on the correlation has been widely studied [5,6,8,12]. We propose a reviewing of the correlation approach suggested by Brier et al., named Correlation Power Analysis [5], and the study of its normalization effect. We then propose a way to enhance the performance of CPA. The analytical results are finally confronted with the experimental ones.

The paper is organized as follows. Section 2 starts with an overview of power analysis including the original DPA method, the multi-bit PPA concept and the correlation based CPA method. In Sect. 3, a discussion about the CPA attack and its normalization factor is expressed. We also propose in this section a method to enhance CPA. Experimental results with electromagnetic radiation signals are shown in Sect. 4 and a brief conclusion is given in the last section.

2   Power Analysis Techniques

2.1   Differential Power Analysis

Differential Power Analysis was originally proposed by Kocher et al. [11]. This analysis is based on the fact that the power dissipation to manipulate one bit to 1 is different from the power dissipation to manipulate it to 0. To test different keys K_s, DPA uses N cipher messages (or plain messages) C_i ($i = 1 \ldots N$) and a selection function $D(C_i, b, K_s)$. This boolean function computes the value of an examined bit b, for example a bit of the S-box output. DPA computes a differential trace $\Delta_D(b)$ as the difference between the average of the traces for which $D(C_i, b, K_s)$ is 1 and the average of the traces for which $D(C_i, b, K_s)$ is 0. If we note $W(C_i)$ the power consumption or electromagnetic radiation signal corresponding to the message C_i, the differential trace $\Delta_D(b)$ is computed as follows:

$$\Delta_D(b) = \frac{\sum_{i=1}^{N} D(C_i, b, K_s) W(C_i)}{\sum_{i=1}^{N} D(C_i, b, K_s)} - \frac{\sum_{i=1}^{N} (1 - D(C_i, b, K_s)) W(C_i)}{\sum_{i=1}^{N} (1 - D(C_i, b, K_s))} \tag{1}$$

If the bits calculated during the cryptographic algorithm are statistically uniformly distributed and if the number of ciphering traces is sufficient, $\Delta_D(b)$ tends to 0 for wrong key hypothesis and $\Delta_D(b) \neq 0$ for the correct key K_s hypothesis at the instant τ where the bit b is handled, this is the DPA peak. However, in practice, the bit distribution is correlated to S-box output and so some peaks can be observed on wrong key differential traces. This is the ghost peak problem explained for example in [5,15]. For the correct key, peaks can also appear at instants other than τ due to the correlation between transient results during the cryptographic computation.

Note that there exist three main aspects to be considered for applying a power analysis method. The first one is how to choose **target bits** and **cipher messages**. For example, the bit b in DPA method is well chosen if the highest peak belongs to the differential trace of the correct hypothesis, which is not always true for any choice of b. The cipher messages can be random or chosen. By using chosen messages, attackers can reduce the algorithmic noise and also simplify the

Hamming distance to the Hamming weight for hardware implementation [14,15]. However a chosen message attack implies that the bits inside the algorithm are not independently distributed. So unexpected peaks related to the bits other than b can be observed.

The second aspect is how to determine different **classes**. In mono-bit DPA method, Kocher has proposed two classes:

$$G_0 = \{W(C_i), i = 1 \ldots N | D(C_i, b, K_s) = 0\}$$

$$G_1 = \{W(C_i), i = 1 \ldots N | D(C_i, b, K_s) = 1\}$$

These classes are computed with the Hamming weight, but can be extended with the Hamming distance considering a previous state for b.

The third aspect is related to the function that calculates differential traces in order to evaluate and detect efficiently the correct hypothesis. These traces can be called as the **decision signals**. In the mono-bit case, this decision signal is $\Delta_D(b)$. Different kinds of classes and decision signals will be discussed in further sections.

2.2   Partitioning Power Analysis

Multi-bit DPA: To enhance the original DPA, some authors have introduced d-bit DPA attacks which means that d bits are used instead of only one bit. The method proposed by Messerges et al [14] is still based on the idea of dividing power consumption signals into two classes. For a d-bit set $\mathcal{B} = b_1 b_2 \ldots b_d$, two classes of their multi-bit DPA are defined as follows:

$$G_0 = \left\{ W(C_i), i = 1 \ldots N | H(C_i, \mathcal{B}, K_s) < \frac{d}{2} \right\}$$

$$G_1 = \left\{ W(C_i), i = 1 \ldots N | H(C_i, \mathcal{B}, K_s) \geq \frac{d}{2} \right\}$$

where $H(C_i, \mathcal{B}, K_s)$ denotes the Hamming weight of $\mathcal{B}$ corresponding to K_s and C_i. Note that if we consider a previous state R of $\mathcal{B}$ as the reference state, $H(C_i, \mathcal{B}, K_s)$ can be used as the Hamming distance between R and the actual state of $\mathcal{B}$. [1]

The decision signal becomes:

$$\Delta_H(\mathcal{B}) = \frac{\sum_{G_1} W(C_i)}{N_1} - \frac{\sum_{G_0} W(C_i)}{N_0} \tag{2}$$

with $N_0 = card(G_0)$ and $N_1 = card(G_1)$.

---

[1] In the research of Brier et al.[5], the Hamming distance is used and defined as the number of flipping bits to switch from a reference state R to another state D, and is given by $H(R \oplus D)$. When the reference state R is 0, the Hamming distance $H(R \oplus D)$ becomes the Hamming weight of D.

In a 4-bit DPA case, Bevan et al. [4] suggested combining the $\Delta_D(b_i)$ computed independently for each bit b_i $(i = 1 \ldots 4)$ of $\mathcal{B}$:

$$\Sigma_D(\mathcal{B}) = \Delta_D(b_1) + \Delta_D(b_2) + \Delta_D(b_3) + \Delta_D(b_4) \qquad (3)$$

The notion of class in this case is the same as the one of mono-bit DPA but it is defined for each bit b_i $(i = 1 \ldots 4)$ of $\mathcal{B}$. The decision signal $\Sigma_D(\mathcal{B})$ is the sum of four other decision signals $\Delta_D(b_i)$ $(i = 1 \ldots 4)$. This method is efficient only if the values of the four bits influence the power consumption at the same time and in the same way. [2]

Partitioning Power Analysis: In order to generalize the multi-bit DPA methods, we propose here the Partitioning Power Analysis (PPA) method based on the Hamming distance. The multi-partition method has been suggested by Akkar et al.[3] with DiPA, but these authors did not formalize the concept.

We consider d-bit set $\mathcal{B} = b_1 b_2 \ldots b_d$ and divide N power consumption signals $W(C_i)$ $(i = 1 \ldots N)$ into $(d + 1)$ partitions (classes) $G_0, G_1, \ldots, G_d$.

$$G_j = \{W(C_i), i = 1 \ldots N | H(C_i, \mathcal{B}, K_s) = j\}$$

where $H(C_i, \mathcal{B}, K_s)$ denotes the Hamming distance between a previous state and the actual state of $\mathcal{B}$, corresponding to the message C_i and the key guess K_s. We note $N_j = card(G_j)$, so $\sum_{j=0}^{d} N_j = N$. The decision signal of PPA is given as follows, where a_j $(j = 1 \ldots N)$ are chosen weights.

$$\Sigma_H(\mathcal{B}) = \sum_{j=0}^{d} a_j \frac{\sum_{G_j} W(C_i)}{N_j} \qquad (4)$$

The choice of these weights can be determined with a known key algorithm or with a selection function based on known bits, for example input message bits.

Note: By the previous definition of PPA, the multi-bit DPA concepts proposed by Messerges and Bevan are two cases of PPA with special coefficients a_j. For the Messerges' method, $\Delta_H(\mathcal{B})$ derived from (2) can be formulated as (4), H being the Hamming distance and $a_j = -1$ for $0 \leq j < d/2$ and $a_j = 1$ for $d/2 \leq j \leq d$. Referring to Bevan's concept, in order to use the Hamming distance notion, we can choose the reference state of $\mathcal{B}$ as '0000'. After some algebraical manipulation, the $\Sigma_D(\mathcal{B})$ of (3) can be rewritten under a form of (4) as follows:

$$\Sigma_D(\mathcal{B}) = -\frac{1}{8} \sum_{G_0} W(C_i) - \frac{1}{4} \sum_{G_1} W(C_i) + \frac{1}{4} \sum_{G_3} W(C_i) + \frac{1}{8} \sum_{G_4} W(C_i) \qquad (5)$$

By the same way, if we consider the reference state of the target bit b is '0', the original DPA proposed by Kocher becomes the simplest PPA with a coefficient -1 for the group G_0 and a coefficient 1 for the group G_1.

---

[2] This point may be true for a hardware algorithm, but false for a software one.

2.3   Correlation Power Analysis

Correlation approaches are based on the dependence between the power consumption of the circuit and the Hamming weight [8,12] or the Hamming distance [5] of manipulated data. According to Brier's model, the relationship between the power consumption W and $H(R \oplus D)$ is linear ($W = aH + b$, a and b are constant). The correct key is the one which maximizes the correlation factor ρ_{WH}.

If we denote $H_{i,R} = H(R \oplus C_i)$ the Hamming distance between the actual state of the message C_i and the reference state R, the decision signal of the CPA method is the correlation factor $\hat{\rho}_{WH}$ [5]:

$$\hat{\rho}_{WH}(R) = \frac{N \sum W(C_i) H_{i,R} - \sum W(C_i) \sum H_{i,R}}{\sqrt{N \sum W(C_i)^2 - (\sum W(C_i))^2} \sqrt{N \sum H_{i,R}^2 - (\sum H_{i,R})^2}} \qquad (6)$$

According to this concept, the notion of class is not explicitly used, i.e., N power consumption signals $W(C_i)$ corresponding to N cipher messages C_i ($i = 1 \ldots N$) are not classified in to different classes. However, this notion can be introduced here by grouping the power consumption signals $W(C_i)$ where C_i has the same Hamming distance with a reference state R. Considering a d-bit set $\mathcal{B}$ of messages C_i and using the same notation described in the previous section, we divide N power consumption signals $W(C_i)$ ($i = 1 \ldots N$) into $(d+1)$ classes $G_0, G_1, \ldots, G_d$ with

$$G_j = \{W(C_i), i \in 1 \ldots N | H(C_i, \mathcal{B}, K_s) = j\}$$

We develop now the term $A = N \sum W(C_i) H_{i,R} - \sum W(C_i) \sum H_{i,R}$ by splitting N power consumption signals $W(C_i)$ into $(d + 1)$ partitions. The term A becomes:

$$A = N \sum_{j=0}^{d} \sum_{G_j} W(C_i).j - (\sum_{j=0}^{d} \sum_{G_j} W(C_i))(\sum_{k=0}^{d} \sum_{G_k} k)$$

$$= \sum_{j=0}^{d} N.j \sum_{G_j} W(C_i) - (\sum_{j=0}^{d} \sum_{G_j} W(C_i))(\sum_{k=0}^{d} N_k.k)$$

$$= \sum_{j=0}^{d} \left(N.j - \sum_{k=0}^{d} N_k.k \right) \sum_{G_j} W(C_i)$$

By denoting $\alpha_j = \frac{N_j}{N} \left(j - \sum_{k=0}^{d} \frac{N_k}{N}.k \right)$, the term A becomes:

$$A = N^2 \sum_{j=0}^{d} \left(\alpha_j \frac{\sum_{G_j} W(C_i)}{N_j} \right) \qquad (7)$$

Accordingly, from (6) and (7) the correlation between power consumption W and Hamming distance H is then rewritten as:

$$\hat{\rho}_{WH}(R) = \frac{\sum_{j=0}^{d}\left(\alpha_j \frac{\sum_{G_j} W(C_i)}{N_j}\right)}{\sigma_W \sigma_H} \tag{8}$$

Equation (8) shows that the differences between CPA and PPA are the coefficients α_j and the normalization factor $\sigma_W \sigma_H$. Note that while the coefficients α_j of CPA (see (8)) depend on the distribution of N_j, the a_j of PPA (see (4)) are flexibly chosen. If N is large and the bits of $\mathcal{B}$ are uniformly distributed, the coefficients α_j of CPA tend to constant values and can be calculated in function of d and j by the following formula:

$$\alpha_j = \frac{C_d^j}{2^d}\left(j - \sum_{k=0}^{d}\frac{C_d^k}{2^d}.k\right)$$

where $C_d^j = \frac{d!}{j!(d-j)!}$ is the number of combinations of d elements taken j at a time.

Some values of α_j when $d = 1\ldots4$ are given in the Table 1.

Table 1. Coefficients α_j for an uniform distribution of $\mathcal{B}$

d	α_0	α_1	α_2	α_3	α_4
1	-1/4	1/4	-	-	-
2	-1/4	0	1/4	-	-
3	-3/16	-3/16	3/16	-3/16	-
4	-1/8	-1/4	0	1/4	1/8

We can notice that the coefficients α_j ($i = 1\ldots4$) for $d = 4$ are identical to those of Bevan's method. This interesting remark shows the relation between the multi-bit DPA method of Bevan, a special case of PPA, and the correlation concept of Brier. The difference between these methods is the normalization by $\sigma_W \sigma_H$. This point is studied in the next section.

3   CPA and Normalization Effect

In this section, we discuss the normalization effects by $\sigma_W \sigma_H$ of CPA signals. For $d = 4$, we examine only 4 bits instead of all bits of messages C_i. If the bits of $\mathcal{B}$ are uniformly distributed and N is large enough, according to the Table 1, the correlation factor $\hat{\rho}_{WH}(R)$ given by the formula (8) becomes:

$$\hat{\rho}_{WH}(R) = \frac{-\frac{1}{8}\frac{\sum_{G_0} W(C_i)}{N_0} - \frac{1}{4}\frac{\sum_{G_1} W(C_i)}{N_1} + \frac{1}{4}\frac{\sum_{G_3} W(C_i)}{N_3} + \frac{1}{8}\frac{\sum_{G_4} W(C_i)}{N_4}}{\sigma_W \sigma_H} \tag{9}$$

Note that the numerator is equal to $\Sigma_H(\mathcal{B})$ given in (4) with $d = 4$, $a_0 = -\frac{1}{8}$, $a_1 = -\frac{1}{4}$, $a_2 = 0$, $a_3 = \frac{1}{4}$ and $a_4 = \frac{1}{8}$. With such choice of PPA weights $a_j = \alpha_j$, we can observe the effect of the normalization factor $\sigma_W \sigma_H$, which is the only difference between PPA and CPA in this case. Furthermore, if the messages are random, the number of messages N is large and if d bits are uniformly distributed, σ_H is independent to key hypothesis and equal to $\frac{d}{4}$. The normalization effect finally depends only on σ_W.

In order to have a better knowledge of σ_W, we use N power consumption signals to compute the standard deviation $\sigma_W(t)$ at every instant t. Because data are handled at clock edges, $\sigma_W(t)$ is larger at theses points of time than at other instants. Hence, $\Sigma_H(\mathcal{B})$ is divided by significant values at clock edges and by smaller values at other moments. Consequently, the noise level of the correlation factor $\hat{\rho}_{WH}(R)$ rises. It can be very high if $\sigma_W(t)$ tends toward zero.

A common numerical method [23] to reduce this normalization effect consists in adding to $\sigma_W(t)$ a positive constant ε. If the ε is correctly chosen, the noise should be reduced without modifying any principal result. We now obtain for the correlation factor:

$$\hat{\rho}_{WH}(R) = \frac{\Sigma_H(\mathcal{B})}{(\sigma_W + \varepsilon)\sigma_H} \qquad (10)$$

In our case, the choice of ε is delicate. If ε tends to zero, the CPA signals are always normalized by small values at the non-clock-edge moments. Thus, the noise level of CPA signal is still high. On the other hand, if ε is great in comparison with $\sigma_W(t)$ at clock edges, the correlation between H and W is not respected any more. The object of the following section is to explain the choice of ε that allows an improvement of the CPA detection capacity.

4   Experimental Confrontation

Experimental results from real measured signals shown in this section allow to compare the three techniques DPA, PPA, CPA and to valid our CPA enhancement proposition. Here we compare the PPA and CPA by observing 4 examined bits. The coefficients a_j of PPA and α_j of CPA are identically chosen for $j = 1 \ldots 4$. This choice of coefficients helps us to see the normalization effect. The results of original mono-bit DPA (i.e., $d = 1$) are also shown as a reference for comparison.

Signal acquisition: In our experiment, the electromagnetic radiation of a synthesized ASIC during a DES operation was measured. Up to 10000 messages randomly generated were used. The upper curve of Fig. 1 represents an experimental electromagnetic signal where the 16 peaks corresponding to 16 rounds of the DES can be observed. As the electromagnetic signal is used instead of the power consumption ones, the notation $W(C_i)$ represents here the voltage at the output of our electromagnetic sensor for the processing of the message C_i.

Variation of $\sigma_W(t)$: As mentioned in the previous section, we compute the standard deviation $\sigma_W(t)$ at each instant t to observe its variation. This one is

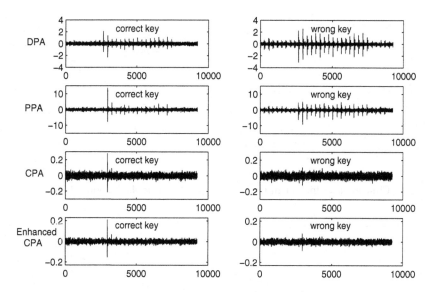

Fig. 2. Power analysis signals with 2000 messages. 1st line: DPA method, 2nd line: PPA method, 3rd line: CPA method and 4th line: Enhanced CPA method. Left column: correct key guess, Right column: wrong key guess resulting in the highest ghost peak. Horizontal axes: time sampling proportional to clock cycle, 1st line vertical axis: $\Delta_D(b)$, 2nd line vertical axis: $\Sigma_H(\mathcal{B})$, 3rd and 4th line vertical axes: $\hat{\rho}_{WH}(R)$.

curve and that of CPA is the dashdot curve. The solid curve corresponds to our proposed method to enhance the CPA. Figure 3 shows that the values i_1 of CPA are always greater than those of DPA/PPA. The better performance of CPA against DPA can easily be explained by the fact that the DPA method is based on the weighting with a single bit b and the CPA method is based on a weighting with 4 examined bits of the cipher messages. The result of CPA against PPA confirms the efficiency of the normalization factor of CPA. When comparing DPA and PPA, we observe that the index i_1 of PPA is always higher than DPA's index. Hence, the multi-bit attack PPA (4 bits in our case) performs better than the mono-bit attack DPA. This conclusion is also confirmed by Fig. 2 in which we observe that the PPA peak is much higher and clearer than the DPA one.

The **second index**, i_2, is the signal to noise ratio of the DPA/PPA/ CPA signal corresponding to the correct key. The DPA/PPA/CPA peak is considered as *signal* and the rest as *noise*. If i_2 is not large enough, the expected peak corresponding to the correct key does not appear and we can not confirm which key is correct. The limit is chosen equal to 3 through our experiment results. Figure 5 illustrates the variation of the second attack-efficient index i_2 as function of the number of curves C_i. We observe that the values i_2 of CPA are much lower than those of DPA/PPA. Accordingly, the noise in the CPA signal for correct key is more significant. By using our enhanced CPA method, we reduce this noise.

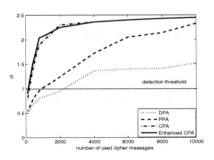

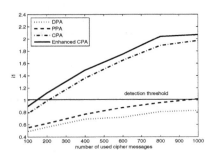

Fig. 3. First attack-efficient index

Fig. 4. A zoom of Fig. 3

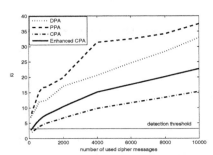

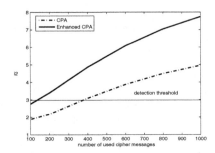

Fig. 5. Second attack-efficient index

Fig. 6. A zoom of Fig. 5

We choose $\varepsilon = 2$ which is about 10 % of $\sigma_W(\tau)$. This value is quite small compared to $\sigma_W(\tau)$ so that its influence on i_1 index, which is computed at instant τ, is negligible. This explains why the CPA and enhanced CPA curves in Fig. 3 are very close. On the other hand, the value $\varepsilon = 2$ is large enough to reduce the noise level observed in Fig. 2 (the rate of noise in the enhanced CPA signals is weaker than in the CPA signals) and Fig. 5 (the enhanced CPA curve is above the CPA curve) .

Number of cipher messages required for key detection: The key detection depends on both i_1 and i_2 indexes. The key detection is only feasible and reliable if the two following conditions are satisfied: $i_1 > 1$ and $i_2 > 3$. The first condition is trivial. The second condition is chosen through our experiment results.

Hence, if we take into account both indexes i_1 and i_2, according to Fig. 3 and Fig. 5, the DPA method needs about 2500 messages, the PPA needs about 1000 messages and the CPA needs about 400 messages to detect the correct key, i.e. both indexes are above the detection threshold. By using our proposed enhanced CPA method, only 200 messages are required to retrieve the coding key. Figure 7 confirms again our conclusion: with only 200 messages, **our enhanced CPA can detect the key but the original CPA can not.** The use of ε, that

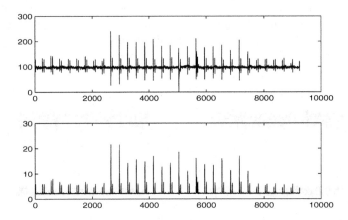

Fig. 1. The horizontal axes represent the time sampling proportional to clock cycles. The upper vertical axis represents the potential difference on the output of an electromagnetic sensor (mV) and the lower one represents its standard deviation.

depicted in the lower curve of Fig. 1. The figure validates our analytical results that the σ_W increases rapidly at each clock edge.

Signal observation: In the first experiment, we used 2000 cipher messages to test 64 key hypothesis with DPA, PPA, CPA and enhanced CPA methods. In Fig. 2, we present the DPA, PPA, CPA and enhanced CPA signals for the correct key (left column) and for a wrong key (right column) resulting in the highest ghost peak. From these figures, we realize that the unexpected peaks for the correct key and for the wrong key appear clearly in the DPA signals. We also see that the PPA method performs better than DPA in terms of the appearance of these unexpected peaks. This result shows the advantage of multi-bit concept compared to the mono-bit one. For the CPA method, the expected peak is clear and the signals coincide with our analysis in Sect. 3: the level of noise in the CPA signal is higher. We can also note that ghost peaks in CPA (see Fig. 2 for the wrong key) are overwhelmed in this described noise.

Evaluation and validation of the proposed method: In order to evaluate the success of an attack, we define two attack-efficient indexes which reflect the possibility of key detection. The ***first index***, i_1, is defined as the ratio between the DPA/PPA/CPA peak (expected peak) corresponding to the correct hypothesis at the moment τ where the bits are manipulated and the highest DPA/PPA/CPA peak among incorrect hypothesis at this instant. If this index is greater than 1, the expected peak is the highest one and the key detection is reliable. On the contrary, if this index is smaller than 1, there exists another peak higher than the expected peak, i.e the key detection is impossible.

The values of i_1 when the number of cipher messages varying from 100 to 10000 messages is illustrated in Fig. 3 and enlarged in Fig. 4. The attack-efficient index i_1 of DPA is represented by the dotted curve, that of PPA is the dashed

restricts the standard deviation used in CPA, allows us to considerably reduce the noise level (see Fig. 2),[3] and to retrieve the key with a lower number of curves (see Fig. 7). This restricted normalization can also be applied to PPA and DPA.

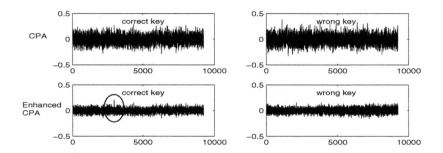

Fig. 7. Power analysis signals with 200 used messages, 1st line: CPA method, 2nd line: enhanced CPA method. Left column: correct key guess, Right column: wrong key guess resulting in the highest ghost peak. Horizontal axes: time sampling proportional to clock cycle, Vertical axes: $\hat{\rho}_{WH}$.

Let's also note that interesting clock cycles can be firstly investigated without normalization and then the restricted factor can be used to fully perform the differential analysis around the selected areas to find the correct keys.

5   Conclusions

First, we merged all existing multi-bit DPA methods into the PPA concept which consists of dividing power consumption signals into partitions. PPA could also be merged into existing cryptanalysis techniques such as partitioning attacks (see for example [18,19]).

We demonstrate that CPA is, in fact, a special form of PPA normalized by the standard deviation of power consumption signals. This normalization is efficient because it allows us to reduce significantly the number of messages required to break the cryptographic secrets. However, the normalization also increases the noise level of the CPA signal. This noise level can be reduced by using the proposed method with the restriction ε. Through the experiments, our enhanced CPA performs better than original CPA, DPA and four-bit PPA in terms of number of messages required for key detection. In future work, we would like to find the coefficients a_j that optimize the PPA efficiency. From this optimized PPA, we would expect to be able to propose a new power consumption model, taking into account for example the different bit contributions as suggested in [3,24,25].

---

[3] Note that the ghost peaks in CPA are hidden in the noise and are better revealed with the enhanced method proposed here.

References

1. M.L. Akkar, C. Giraud: An Implementation of DES and AES Secure Against Some Attacks. *In proceedings of CHES 2001*, LNCS 2162, pp. 309-318, Springer-Verlag, 2001.
2. M.L. Akkar, L. Goubin: A Generic Protection Against High-Order Differential Power Analysis. *In proceedings of FSE 2003*, LNCS 2887, pp. 192 - 205, Springer-Verlag, 2003.
3. M.L. Akkar, R. Bevan, P. Dischamp, D. Moyart: Power Analysis, What Is Now Possible... *In proceedings of ASIACRYPT 2000*, LNCS 1976, pp. 489 - 502, Springer-Verlag, 2000.
4. R. Bevan, E. Knudsen: Ways to Enhance DPA. *In proceedings of ICISC 2002*, LNCS 2587, pp.327-342, Springer-Verlag, 2003.
5. E. Brier, C. Clavier, F. Olivier: Correlation Power Analysis with a Leakage Model, *In proceedings of CHES 2004*, LNCS 3156, pp. 16-29, Springer-Verlag, 2004.
6. S. Chari, C.S. Jutla, J.R. Rao, P. Rohatgi: Towards Sound Approaches to Counteract Power Analysis Attacks. *In proceedings of CRYPTO 1999*, LNCS 1666, pp. 348-412, Springer-Verlag, 1999.
7. J.S. Coron, L. Goubin: On Boolean and Arithmetic Masking Against Differential Power Analysis. *In proceedings of CHES 2000*, LNCS 1965, pp. 231-237, Springer-Verlag, 2000.
8. J.S. Coron, P. Kocher, D. Naccache: Statistics and Secret Leakage. *In proceedings of Financial Cryptography*, LNCS 1972, pp. 157-173, Springer-Verlag, 2000.
9. L. Goubin, J. Patarin: DES and Differential Power Analysis: The Duplication Method. *In proceedings of CHES 1999*, LNCS 1717, pp. 158-172, Springer-Verlag, 1999.
10. P. Kocher, J. Jaffe, B. Jun: Introduction to Differential Power Analysis and related attacks. `http://www.cryptography.com`.
11. P. Kocher, J. Jaffe, B. Jun: Differential Power Analysis. *In proceedings of CRYPTO 1999*, LNCS 1666, pp. 388-397, Springer-Verlag, 1999.
12. R. Mayer-Sommer: Smartly Analysing the Simplicity and the Power of Simple Power Analysis on Smartcards. *In proceedings of CHES 2000*, LNCS 1965, pp. 78-92, Springer-Verlag, 2000.
13. T. S. Messerges, E. A. Dabbish, R. H. Sloan: Investigations of Power Analysis Attacks on Smartcards. *In proceedings of the USENIX Workshop on Smart Card Technology 1999*, `http://www.usenix.org/`, 1999.
14. T. S. Messerges, E. A. Dabbish, R. H. Sloan: Examining Smart-Card Security under the Threat of Power Analysis Attacks. *IEEE Transactions on Computers*, Vol. 51, N5, pp. 541-552, May 2002.
15. C. Canovas, J. Clédière: What do S-boxes Say in Differential Side Channel Attacks? *Cryptology ePrint Archive*, http://eprint.iacr.org/, Report 20085/311, 2005.
16. S. Guilley, P. Hoogvorst, R. Pacalet: Differential Power Analysis Model and some Results *In proceedings of CARDIS 2004*, Kluwer Academic Publishers, pp. 127-142, 2004.
17. K. Gandolfi, C.Mourtel, F.Olivier: Electromagnetic Attacks: Concrete Results. *In proceedings of CHES 2001*, LNCS 2162, pp. 252-261, Springer, 2001.
18. Carlo Harpes: Partitioning Cryptanalysis. Post-Diploma Thesis, Signal and Information Processing Lab., Swiss Federal Institute of Technology, Zurich, March 1995. http://www.isi.ee.ethz.ch/ harpes/pc.ps.

19. Thomas Jakobsen: Correlation Attacks on Block Ciphers, Master's Thesis, Dept. of Mathematics, Technical University of Denmark, January 1996.
20. J.J. Quisquater, D. Samyde: Electromagnetic Analysis (EMA): Measures and Countermeasures for Smart Cards. *In proceedings of e-Smart 2001,* LNCS 2140, pp. 200-201, Springer, 2001.
21. J.R. Rao, P. Rohatgi: EMpowering Side-Channel Attacks. *Cryptology ePrint Archive,* http://eprint.iacr.org/, Report 2001/037, 2001.
22. R. Bevan: Estimation statistique et sécurité des cartes à puces, évaluation d'attaques DPA évolués. OCS, rapport de thèse, 2004.
23. W.H. Press, S.A. Teukolsky, W.T. Vetterling, and B.P. Flannery: Numerical Recipes in C++. *Cambridge University Press,* Second Edition, 1002pp, New York, 2002.
24. J. R. Rao, P. Rohatgi, H. Scherzer, S. Tinguely : Partitioning Attacks : Or How to Rapidly Clone Some GSM Cards. *In proceedings of the 2002 IEEE Symposium on Security and Privacy,* pp. 31-41, IEEE Computer Society, 2002.
25. F.-X. Standaert, F. Mace, E. Peeters, J.-J. Quisquater: Updates on the Security of FPGAs Against Power Analysis Attacks. *In proceedings of ARC 2006,* LNCS 3985, pp. 335-346, Springer-Verlag, 2006.

High-Resolution Side-Channel Attack Using Phase-Based Waveform Matching

Naofumi Homma[1], Sei Nagashima[1], Yuichi Imai[1], Takafumi Aoki[1],
and Akashi Satoh[2]

[1] Graduate School of Information Sciences, Tohoku University
6-6-05, Aramaki Aza Aoba, Aoba-ku, Sendai-shi 980-8579, Japan
{homma, nagasima, imai}@aoki.ecei.tohoku.ac.jp, aoki@ecei.tohoku.ac.jp
[2] IBM Research, Tokyo Research Laboratory, IBM Japan, Ltd.
1623-14 Shimo-tsuruma, Yamato-shi, Kanagawa, 242-8502, Japan
akashi@jp.ibm.com

Abstract. This paper describes high-resolution waveform matching based on a Phase-Only Correlation (POC) technique and its application for a side-channel attack. Such attacks, such as Simple Power Analysis (SPA) and Differential Power Analysis (DPA), use a statistical analysis of signal waveforms (e.g., power traces) to reduce noise and to retrieve secret information. However, the waveform data often includes displacement errors in the measurements. The use of phase components in the discrete Fourier transforms of the waveforms makes it possible to estimate the displacements between the signal waveforms with higher resolution than the sampling resolution. The accuracy of a side-channel attack can be enhanced using this high-resolution matching method. In this paper, we demonstrate the advantages of the POC-based method in comparison with conventional approaches through experimental DPA and Differential ElectroMagnetic Analysis (DEMA) against a DES software implementation on a Z80 processor.

Keywords: side-channel attacks, DPA, DEMA, cryptographic module, waveform matching, phase-only correlation.

1 Introduction

Cryptanalysis based on side-channel information is of major concern for the evaluation of tamper-resistant devices. When a cryptographic module performs encryption or decryption, secret parameters correlated to the intermediate data being processed can be leaked via power dissipation [1], electromagnetic radiation [2], or operating times as side-channel information. These are now essential issues for designers of smartcards and other embedded cryptosystems.

In general, a side-channel attack requires a statistical analysis of waveforms (e.g., power traces) to reduce noise and to retrieve secret information. The important assumption here is that each waveform is captured by a digital measuring device at the exact moment as the corresponding cryptographic computation. However, it is almost impossible to time exactly when the data was captured for

L. Goubin and M. Matsui (Eds.): CHES 2006, LNCS 4249, pp. 187–200, 2006.

cryptographic modules in actual applications, because there is no trigger signal precisely synchronized with the cryptographic computation. For example, wireless devices and smartcards often have no internal clock generator, or devices using PLLs will not have any external clock synchronized with the internal clock. Even if a trigger signal is available, it often contains jitter-related deviations from the true timing of the encryption process. As a result, the measured waveforms always include displacement errors. The displacement errors are usually smaller than the sampling interval, but may cause significant loss of the secret information when the waveforms are averaged together, unless there is exact alignment during the statistical analysis.

Some approaches dealing with the displacements in waveforms were proposed [3], [4]. In a theoretical model, Differential Power Analysis (DPA) with the fast Fourier transform of the power waveforms is introduced to correct the displacement errors [3]. Reference [4], on the other hand, demonstrated a practical approach to analyze Rijndael and ECC on a Java-based wireless PDA. The reported methods were performed in the frequency domain, and thus it would be very difficult to use them in collaboration with other side-channel attacks in the time domain.

Addressing the displacement problem, we propose a high-resolution waveform matching method using a Phase-Only Correlation (POC) function. POC techniques have been successfully applied to high-accuracy image matching tasks [5]-[8]. The POC function employs phase components in the discrete Fourier transforms of waveforms, and makes it possible to determine displacement errors between signal waveforms with high noise tolerance by using the location of the correlation peak. By fitting the analytical model of the correlation peak to the actual numerical data, we can evaluate the displacement errors with a higher resolution than the sampling resolution. The waveform matching can be available directly for a wide variety of side-channel attacks in the time domain against real-world applications.

In this paper, we describe a high-resolution side-channel attack using POC-based waveform matching, and demonstrate its advantages in comparison with conventional methods through experimental analysis of DPA and Differential ElectroMagnetic Analysis (DEMA) against a DES software implementation on a Z80 processor. The essence of the proposed method is to use the POC-based waveform matching as a preprocessing step followed by standard analysis. In this experiment, the side-channel information is monitored with a digital oscilloscope for various sampling rates. The differential analysis with the POC-based matching shows better results in comparison with the conventional attacks for all of the sampling rates.

2   High-Resolution Waveform Matching Using Phase-Only Correlation

2.1   Phase-Based Waveform Matching

Consider two signal waveforms, $f(n)$ and $g(n)$, where we assume that the index range is $n = -M, \cdots, M$ for mathematical simplicity, and hence the length of waveforms $N = 2M + 1$. Let $F(k)$ and $G(k)$ denote the Discrete Fourier Transforms (DFTs) of the two waveforms. $F(k)$ and $G(k)$ are given by

$$F(k) = \sum_{n=-M}^{M} f(n)W_N^{kn} = A_F(k)e^{j\theta_F(k)}, \tag{1}$$

$$G(k) = \sum_{n=-M}^{M} g(n)W_N^{kn} = A_G(k)e^{j\theta_G(k)}, \tag{2}$$

where $W_N = e^{-j\frac{2\pi}{N}}$, $A_F(k)$ and $A_G(k)$ are amplitude components, and $e^{j\theta_F(k)}$ and $e^{j\theta_G(k)}$ are phase components.

The cross-phase spectrum (or normalized cross spectrum) $R_{FG}(k)$ is defined as

$$R_{FG}(k) = \frac{F(k)\overline{G(k)}}{\left|F(k)\overline{G(k)}\right|} = e^{j\theta_{FG}(k)}, \tag{3}$$

where $\overline{G(k)}$ denotes the complex conjugate of $G(k)$ and $\theta_{FG}(k) = \theta_F(k) - \theta_G(k)$. The POC function $r_{fg}(n)$ is the Inverse Discrete Fourier Transform (IDFT) of $R_{FG}(k)$ and is given by

$$r_{fg}(n) = \frac{1}{N} \sum_{k=-M}^{M} R_{FG}(k)W_N^{-kn}. \tag{4}$$

If there is a similarity between two waveforms, the POC function gives a distinct sharp peak. (When $f(n) = g(n)$, the POC function becomes the Kronecker delta function.) If not, the peak drops significantly. The height of the peak can be used as a good similarity measure for waveform matching, and the location of the peak shows the translational displacement between the two waveforms.

Now consider $f_c(t)$ as a waveform defined in continuous space with a real number index t. Let δ represents a displacement of $f_c(t)$. So, the displaced waveform can be represented as $f_c(t - \delta)$. Assume that $f(n)$ and $g(n)$ are spatially sampled waveforms of $f_c(t)$ and $f_c(t - \delta)$, and are defined as

$$f(n) = f_c(t)|_{t=nT}, \tag{5}$$
$$g(n) = f_c(t - \delta)|_{t=nT}, \tag{6}$$

where T is the sampling interval and the index range is given by $n = -M, \cdots, M$. For simplicity, we assume $T = 1$. The cross-phase spectrum $R_{FG}(k)$ and the POC function $r_{fg}(n)$ between $f(n)$ and $g(n)$ will be given by

$$R_{FG}(k) = \frac{F(k)\overline{G(k)}}{\left|F(k)\overline{G(k)}\right|} \simeq e^{j\frac{2\pi}{N}k\delta}, \tag{7}$$

$$r_{fg}(n) = \frac{1}{N} \sum_{k=-M}^{M} R_{FG}(k)W_N^{-kn}$$

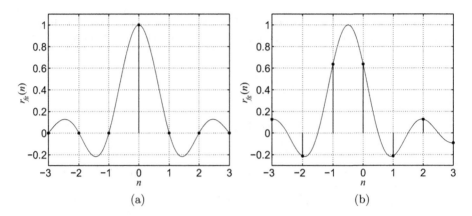

Fig. 1. POC functions: (a) for the case $\delta = 0$, (b) for the case $\delta = 0.5$

$$\simeq \frac{\alpha}{N} \frac{\sin\left\{\pi\left(n+\delta\right)\right\}}{\sin\left\{\frac{\pi}{N}\left(n+\delta\right)\right\}}, \tag{8}$$

where $\alpha = 1$. The above Eq. (8) represents the shape of the peak for the POC function between the same waveforms that are slightly displaced with each other. This equation gives a distinct sharp peak. The peak position δ of the POC function corresponds to the displacement between the two waveforms. We can prove that the peak value α decreases (without changing the shape of the function itself), when small noise components are added to the original waveforms. Hence, we assume $\alpha \leq 1$ in practice. For the waveform matching task, we evaluate the similarity between the two waveforms by the peak value α, and estimate the displacement by the peak position δ.

By calculating the POC function for two waveforms $f(n)$ and $g(n)$, we can obtain a numerical value of $r_{fg}(n)$ for each discrete index n, where $n = -M, \cdots, M$. Fig. 1 shows the POC functions around the correlation peaks when (a) $\delta = 0$ and (b) $\delta = 0.5$, where the black dots indicate the discrete data values from $r_{fg}(n)$. We use Eq. (8) (the closed-form peak model of the POC function) directly for estimating the peak position by function fitting. Fig. 1 also shows these examples, where the solid lines represent the estimated shapes of the POC functions. Thus, it is possible to find the location of the peak that may exist between sampling intervals by fitting the peak model to the calculated data around the correlation peak, where α and δ are fitting parameters. Note here that we can use other types of functions, such as a Gaussian function or a quadratic function, for the function fitting.

2.2   Preliminary Evaluation

Consider two waveforms $f(n)$ and $g(n)$, and an estimated displacement δ. The waveform matching finally calculates $g'(n)$ by shifting $g(n)$ by an amount corresponding to δ. For example, this waveform shifting is done by the phase rotation

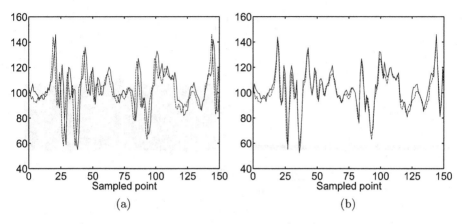

Fig. 2. Example of POC-based waveform matching: (a) input waveforms $f(n)$ and $g(n)$, (b) $f(n)$ and displacement-normalized waveform $g'(n)$

of the waveform in the frequency domain. Let $G'(k)$ denotes the DFT of $g'(n)$. $G'(k)$ will be given by

$$G'(k) \simeq G(k)e^{j\frac{2\pi}{N}k\delta}. \tag{9}$$

Therefore, $g'(n)$ is given by

$$g'(n) = \frac{1}{N}\sum_{k=-M}^{M} G'(k)W_N^{-kn}. \tag{10}$$

We can also implement the waveform shifting with various interpolation techniques, such as bicubic interpolation.

Fig. 2 shows an example of the POC-based waveform matching, where the two waveforms are power traces from a microprocessor captured by using a trigger signal at the times of the same computation. Due to the trigger jitter, there is a displacement error between these waveforms as shown in Fig. 2(a). Using the POC-based waveform matching, we can obtain the displacement $\delta = 1.5555$. Fig. 2(b) shows two waveforms after the waveform shifting. Thus, the proposed method can be used to match waveform positions with higher resolution than the sampling resolution.

Fig. 3 shows examples of the POC function and the ordinary correlation function, where we use the two waveforms shown in Fig. 2. We observe that the POC function provides a sharp peak in comparison to the ordinary function. The sharp peak typically exhibits good discrimination properties.

To evaluate the sharpness of a correlation peak, we consider the Peak-to-Sidelobe Ratio (PSR) between a central region around at the peak and the residual region (sidelobe region). PSR is determined as PSR = $(peak - mean)/std$, where $peak$ is the correlation peak value, and $mean$ and std are the mean and standard deviation in the sidelobe region [9]. In this example, the PSR values of

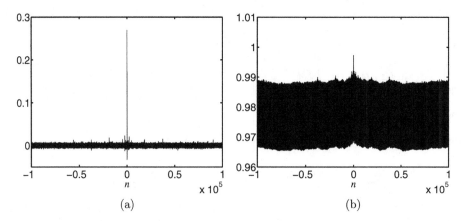

Fig. 3. Examples of the POC function and the ordinary correlation function between two similar waveforms: (a) POC function, (b) ordinary correlation function

the POC function and the ordinary function are 104.76 and 6.54, respectively. This suggests that the POC function exhibits much higher discrimination than the ordinary correlation function.

3   Side-Channel Attacks with POC-Based Waveform Matching

3.1   Basic Concept

The proposed waveform matching is used as a preprocessing step followed by standard analysis. Fig. 4 shows an overview of the proposed DPA with the POC-based waveform matching. We first collect power traces by sampling power consumption for a series of encryptions of different plaintexts. In the following experiment, a trigger signal is used as in the conventional DPAs for simplicity, and the measured waveforms are initially aligned at the trigger. However, the proposed method can get the same alignment of the waveforms without using a trigger signal. After gathering a number of power traces, we use the POC-based matching for the precise alignment of the waveforms. In the matching step, we select any one of the waveforms as a reference, and then evaluate the displacement errors between the other waveforms and the reference. The POC-based matching considered here includes the advanced techniques described in Appendix A. Finally, we resample each waveform according to the evaluated displacement.

After the waveform matching using POC, the standard analysis is performed. First, we divide the waveforms into two groups according to one bit output from a selection function calculated by guessing the secret key. If the guess is correct, a noticeable difference is found between the two averaged waveforms, but no significant difference appears for a wrong guess that gives no correlation between the selection function and the secret key.

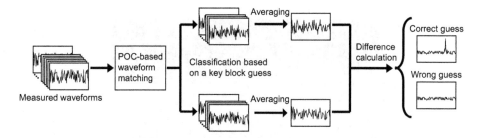

Fig. 4. Proposed differential analysis with POC-based waveform matching

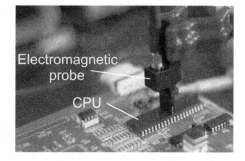

Fig. 5. Evaluation board (INSTAC-8)   **Fig. 6.** Electromagnetic probing

3.2   Experimental Conditions

We applied the POC-based matching technique to DPAs and to DEMAs against a DES software implementation on a Zilog Z80 processor (8 MHz). For the selection functions, we focus on the S-box computation in the 16-th (final) round. DES has eight 6-bit-input and 4-bit-output S-boxes, and thus $4 \times 8 = 32$ selection functions using the S-box output can be formed. For each selection function, we have $2^6 = 64$ key candidates derived from the 6-bit S-box input.

Fig. 5 shows the INSTAC-8 CPU board [10] designed for the side-channel attack experiment, and the measurement points on the board. The power consumption of the processor was monitored as the voltage drop caused by a resistor inserted between the Z80 ground pin and the ground plane of the board. The electromagnetic radiation was also monitored over the Z80 processor as illustrated in Fig. 6. We used a trigger signal synchronized with the beginning of round 15, and obtained four sets of waveforms at sampling rates of 100 MSa/s (millions of samples per second), 200 MSa/s, 400 MSa/s, and 1 GSa/s. Fig. 7 is the measured waveform at 400 MSa/s. The capture range of waveforms is from 4.22 ms to 4.24 ms after the trigger signal, which contains all of the operations of S-box 1 to S-box 8. Two sets of 1,000 waveforms (power and electromagnetic) were measured during encryption of 1,000 random plaintexts with a fixed key. The subkey values from S-box 1 to S-box 8 at the round 16 were fixed as 21, 16, 31, 35, 9, 51, 51, and 48 in decimal, respectively.

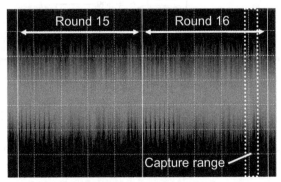

Vertical axis: 100 mV/div   Horizontal axis: 500 us/div
Sampling rate: 400 MSa/s

Fig. 7. Example of measured waveform

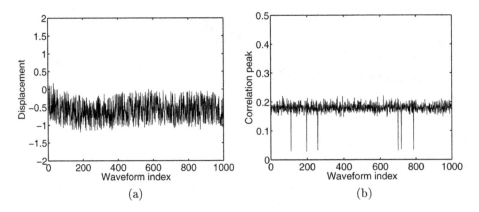

(a)

(b)

Fig. 8. Estimated displacements   **Fig. 9.** Correlation peak values

3.3   Experimental Results

Fig. 8 shows the evaluated displacements for the 1,000 waveforms sampled at 200 MHz (5 ns/point), where the horizontal and vertical axes indicate the waveform index and the displacement value, respectively. The waveforms contain relatively large displacement errors even though they were captured by using a trigger signal synchronized to the system clock, which was generated by the board. Fig. 9 shows the correlation peaks between each waveform and a reference. The peak between two waveforms was about 0.2 due to the different plaintexts and noise. (The peak between identical waveforms is 1.) However, we can identify the peak position clearly since the POC function gives a distinct sharp peak as shown in Fig. 10(a). Fig. 9 also shows that there are some small peaks among the waveforms. Fig. 10(b) shows one of the corresponding POC functions. We found that the waveforms at a low peak value were quite different in shape from the reference waveform. The proposed POC-based analysis can easily detect this kind

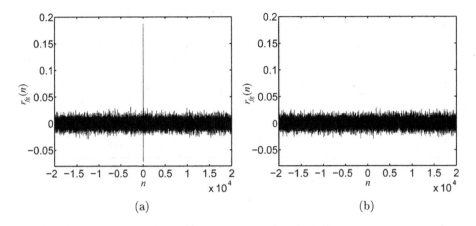

Fig. 10. POC functions: (a) for the case $\alpha \approx 0.2$, (b) for the case $\alpha \approx 0.02$

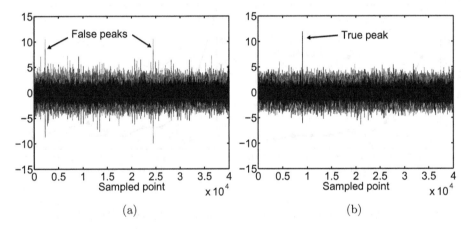

Fig. 11. Example of DPAs: (a) conventional DPA, (b) proposed DPA

of inaccurately measured waveform, and thus adverse effects on the statistical analysis can be prevented by removing them in an averaging process.

Fig. 11 illustrates the results of the conventional DPA and the proposed DPA, where both DPAs have used the same set of waveforms sampled at 200 MHz. These results were obtained by evaluating 64 possible keys with one out of the four selection functions of S-box 1. When the DPA succeeds, the highest peak appears in the averaged waveform indicating the correct key, but the conventional DPA in Fig. 11(a) gives many high false peaks for incorrect keys. In contrast, the proposed DPA clearly indicates the true peak with the correct key as shown in Fig. 11(b). In this experiment, we confirmed that the proposed DPA consistently increased the peak signal and reduced the noise at all four of the sampling rates, 100 MSa/s, 200 MSa/s, 400 MSa/s, and 1 GSa/s.

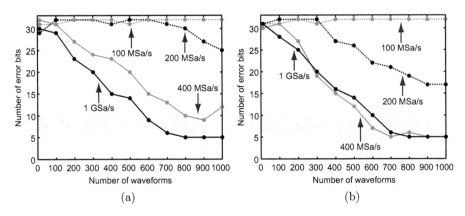

Fig. 12. Error rates for various sampling rates: (a) conventional DPA, (b) proposed DPA

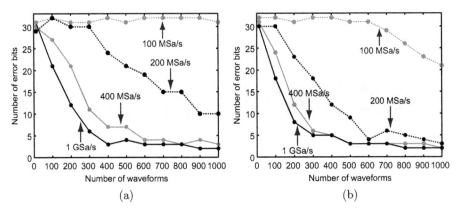

Fig. 13. Error rates for various sampling rates: (a) conventional DEMA, (b) proposed DEMA

Fig. 12 compares the error rates of the conventional DPA and those of the proposed DPA for different numbers of waveforms, where the vertical axis indicates the number of error bits. In other words, Fig. 12 shows the number of selection functions that could not distinguish a correct key from the incorrect keys by investigating the highest peak. If no secret key bit was obtained, the number of errors is 32 bits. The error rate comparisons between the conventional and proposed DEMA are also shown in Fig. 13. The sampling rate of 1 GSa/s is high enough to attack the slow 8-MHz processor by using conventional DPA and DEMA, but the proposed method has clear computational advantages at the sampling rates of 200 MSa/s and 400 MSa/s as shown in Figs. 12 and 13. For example, the proposed DEMA at 200 MSa/s requires less than half the number of waveforms to achieve the 50 % error rate in comparison with the conventional DEMA.

Tables 1 and 2 show the DPA results using 1,000 waveforms at 200 MSa/s and 400 MSa/s, respectively. The 4-bit output from each S-box S_i was used for four

Table 1. Estimation results of DPAs at 200 MSa/s

Conventional DPA								Proposed DPA							
S_1	S_2	S_3	S_4	S_5	S_6	S_7	S_8	S_1	S_2	S_3	S_4	S_5	S_6	S_7	S_8
21	16	31	35	5	51	51	48	21	16	31	35	9	51	51	48
51	5	44	33	27	54	32	11	38	16	31	21	12	49	51	48
15	22	43	58	33	13	26	60	11	25	53	58	2	26	8	7
8	45	54	14	11	11	60	20	10	16	31	14	50	51	19	20

Table 2. Estimation results of DPAs at 400 MSa/s

Conventional DPA								Proposed DPA							
S_1	S_2	S_3	S_4	S_5	S_6	S_7	S_8	S_1	S_2	S_3	S_4	S_5	S_6	S_7	S_8
21	16	31	35	9	51	51	48	21	16	31	35	9	51	51	48
21	16	31	53	47	51	51	39	21	16	31	35	47	51	51	48
11	25	31	35	9	26	8	51	21	25	31	35	9	26	8	48
55	16	31	14	9	32	51	36	21	16	31	14	9	51	51	48

selection functions, and thus four estimations were made for each 6-bit subkey that was XORed to 6 bits of S-box input data. Therefore, four 6-bit possible keys were obtained for each S-box in the tables, and the shaded boxes indicate the correctly guessed keys. If two or more of the values in an S-box column are the same, then there is a very high probability that we can obtain the correct subkey by majority vote. As shown in Table 1, the proposed DPA found five out of eight subkeys at 200 MSa/s while the conventional approach found none. In the 400 MSa/s measurements, the proposed DPA determined all of the subkeys, as shown in Table 2. It is important to note that both DPAs used exactly the same waveform data, and the POC pre-process is simply applied to the captured waveforms before statistical analysis. Therefore, our method can be applied to many varieties of side-channel attacks, such as SPA, SEMA, DPA, and DEMA, to improve the precision of the key estimations.

4   Conclusions

In this paper we proposed a high-resolution waveform matching method based on the POC technique and described its application to side-channel attacks. The POC-based matching method makes it possible to evaluate the displacement between signal waveforms with higher resolution than the sampling resolution. In addition to the waveform alignment, we can remove inaccurately measured waveforms by detecting significant drops of correlation peaks, eliminating their adverse effects on the statistical analysis.

The advantage of proposed method over the conventional methods was demonstrated by experimental DPAs and DEMAs against a DES software implementation. The results showed that the proposed method improved the accuracy of the differential analysis. A high success rate of finding correct subkeys was obtained even at a low sampling rate where the conventional attacks failed. At higher sampling rates, the proposed analysis requires fewer plaintexts to obtain the same error rate as the conventional analysis. As a result, we confirmed that the POC-based waveform matching can be used efficiently for both DPA and DEMA on software implementations without any drawbacks. Applications to other side-channel attacks and on other platforms such as FPGAs and ASICs remain for future study.

The important feature of the proposed method is its capability to enhance any side-channel analysis independently of the cryptographic algorithms, implementations (software or hardware), and kind (power or electromagnetic) of side-channel information. In experiments with a Z80 board, we used a trigger signal synchronized with the cryptographic operations for simplicity, but the POC-based matching does not require this for aligning a number of power traces. Therefore, our approach is very efficient for attacking cryptographic modules in actual applications, even where no trigger signal or no internal clock can be observed.

In addition, the proposed method can defeat some countermeasures creating distorted waveforms with random delays, dummy cycles, or unstable clocking. In this paper, the proposed waveform matching was used for relatively long waveforms, in which the number of sample points is from 20,000 to 200,000. Even when the waveforms have small numbers of sample points, the POC-based technique exhibits good discrimination properties. For example, high-accuracy block matching of small images (e.g., 33×33 pixels) have been implemented using the POC-based techniques [11]. The block matching technique can also be effective for waveforms. Thus, POC-based block matching would easily cancel out distortion components in waveforms. We are now conducting research to develop advanced waveform matching techniques and to investigate their utility in attacks against the waveform-distortion countermeasures.

Acknowledgments. We would like to thank Prof. M. Yamaguchi of Tohoku University for his important advice about electromagnetic measurements. We would also like to thank K. Degawa for his generous support.

References

1. P. Kocher, J. Jaffe, and B. Jun, "Differential power analysis," *CRYPTO 1999, Lecture Notes in Computer Science*, vol. 1666, pp. 388 – 397, Aug. 1999.
2. K. Gandolfi, C. Mourtel, and F. Olivier, "Electromagnetic analysis: Concrete results," *CHES 2001, Lecture Notes in Computer Science*, vol. 2162, pp. 251 – 261, May 2001.
3. J. Waddle and D. Wagner, "Towards efficient second-order power analysis," *CHES 2004, Lecture Notes in Computer Science*, vol. 3156, pp. 1 – 15, Aug. 2004.
4. H. C. Gebotys, S. Ho, and C. C. Tiu, "EM analysis of Rijndael and ECC on a wireless Java-based PDA," *CHES 2005, Lecture Notes in Computer Science*, vol. 3659, pp. 250 – 264, Aug. 2005.

5. Q. Chen, M. Defrise, and F. Deconinck, "Symmetric phase-only matched filtering of Fourier-Mellin transforms for image registration and recognition," *IEEE Transactions Pattern Analysis & Machine Intelligence*, vol. 16, pp. 1156 – 1168, Dec. 1994.

6. K. Takita, T. Aoki, Y. Sasaki, T. Higuchi, and K. Kobayashi, "High-accuracy sub-pixel image registration based on phase-only correlation," *IEICE Transactions on Fundamentals of Electronics, Communicati ons and Computer Sciences*, vol. E86-A, pp. 1925 – 1934, Aug. 2003.

7. K. Ito, H. Nakajima, K. Kobayashi, T. Aoki, and T. Higuchi, "A fingerprint matching algorithm using phase-only correlation," *IEICE Transactions on Fundamentals of Electronics, Communicati ons and Computer Sciences*, vol. E87-A, pp. 682 – 691, Mar. 2004.

8. K. Takita, A. M. Muquit, T. Aoki, and T. Higuchi, "A sub-pixel correspondence search technique for computer vision applications," *IEICE Transactions on Fundamentals of Electronics, Communicati ons and Computer Sciences*, vol. E87-A, pp. 1913 – 1923, Aug. 2004.

9. B. V. Kumar, *Correlation Pattern Recognition*. Cambridge University Press, 2005.

10. T. Matsumoto, S. Kawamura, K. Fujisaki, N. Torii, S. Ishida, Y. Tsunoo, M. Saeki, and A. Yamagishi, "Tamper-resistance standardization research committee report," *The 2006 Symposium on Cryptography and Information Security*, pp. 1 – 6, Jan. 2006.

11. A. M. Muquit, T. Shibahara, and T. Aoki, "A high-accuracy passive 3D measurement system using phase-based image matching," *IEICE Transactions on Fundamentals of Electronics, Communications and Computer Sciences*, vol. E89-A, pp. 686 – 697, Mar. 2006.

A   Advanced Techniques for High-Resolution Waveform Matching

Listed below are important considerations for high-resolution waveform matching.

A.1   Windowing to Reduce Boundary Effects

Due to the DFT's periodicity, a waveform can be considered to "wrap around" at an edge, and therefore discontinuities, which are not supposed to exist in real world, occur at every edge in DFT computations. We reduce the effect of a discontinuity at a waveform border by applying a window function to the input waveforms $f(n)$ and $g(n)$. For example, we can employ a Hanning window defined as

$$w(n) = \frac{1 + \cos(\frac{\pi n}{M})}{2}. \tag{11}$$

The use of window functions is especially useful when the length of waveforms is short.

A.2   Spectral Weighting Technique to Reduce Aliasing and Noise Effects

For natural waveforms, typically the high frequency components may have less reliability (low S/N ratio) compared with the low frequency components. We could improve the estimation accuracy by applying a low-pass-type weighting function $H(k)$ to $R_{FG}(k)$ in frequency domain and eliminating the high frequency components having low reliability. The simplest weighting function $H(k)$ is defined as

$$H(k) = \begin{cases} 1 & |k| \leq U \\ 0 & \text{otherwise} \end{cases}, \tag{12}$$

where U is an integer satisfying $0 \leq U \leq M$. The cross-phase spectrum $R_{FG}(k)$ is multiplied by the weighting function $H(k)$ when calculating the IDFT. Then the modified $r_{fg}(n)$ will be given by

$$r_{fg}(n) = \frac{1}{N} \sum_{k=-M}^{M} R_{FG}(k)H(k)W_N^{-kn}$$
$$\simeq \frac{\alpha}{N} \frac{\sin\left\{\frac{V}{N}\pi\left(n+\delta\right)\right\}}{\sin\left\{\frac{\pi}{N}\left(n+\delta\right)\right\}}, \tag{13}$$

where $V = 2U + 1$. When using the spectral weighting technique, Eq. (13) should be used for function fitting instead of Eq. (8). The main lobe of the POC function is extended by the spectral weighting technique.

Note that we can use any other weighting functions according to the reliability of the frequency components. If we use a weighting function, we need to change the peak model for function fitting correspondingly. The peak model can be calculated by the IDFT of the product of the weighting function and the cross-phase spectrum in Eq. (7).

A.3   Band-Limited POC Function

Another important technique for eliminating the high frequency components of waveforms is to use a band-limited POC function [7].

Assume that the range of the inherent frequency band is given by $k = -K, \cdots, K$, where $0 \leq K \leq M$. (The parameter K may be automatically detected by waveform processing.) The band-limited POC function is defined as

$$r_{fg}^K(n) = \frac{1}{L} \sum_{k=-K}^{K} R_{FG}(k)W_L^{-kn}$$
$$\simeq \frac{\alpha}{L} \frac{\sin\left\{\pi\left(n+\delta'\right)\right\}}{\sin\left\{\frac{\pi}{L}\left(n+\delta'\right)\right\}}, \tag{14}$$

where $L = 2K + 1$, $n = -K, \cdots, K$ and $\delta' = \frac{L}{N}\delta$. Therefore, the displacement is given by $\delta = \frac{N}{L}\delta'$. The maximum value of the correlation peak of the band-limited POC function is always normalized to 1 and is not dependent on the frequency band size L. In practice, we can combine the band-limited POC function with the above spectral weighting technique.

Cache-Collision Timing Attacks Against AES

Joseph Bonneau[1] and Ilya Mironov[2]

[1] Computer Science Department, Stanford University
jbonneau@stanford.edu
[2] Microsoft Research, Silicon Valley Campus
mironov@microsoft.com

Abstract. This paper describes several novel timing attacks against the common table-driven software implementation of the AES cipher. We define a general attack strategy using a simplified model of the cache to predict timing variation due to cache-collisions in the sequence of lookups performed by the encryption. The attacks presented should be applicable to most high-speed software AES implementations and computing platforms, we have implemented them against OpenSSL v. 0.9.8.(a) running on Pentium III, Pentium IV Xeon, and UltraSPARC III+ machines. The most powerful attack has been shown under optimal conditions to reliably recover a full 128-bit AES key with 2^{13} timing samples, an improvement of almost four orders of magnitude over the best previously published attacks of this type [Ber05]. While the task of defending AES against all timing attacks is challenging, a small patch can significantly reduce the vulnerability to these specific attacks with no performance penalty.

Keywords: AES, cryptanalysis, side-channel attack, timing attack, cache.

1 Introduction

Side-channel attacks have been demonstrated experimentally against a variety of cryptographic systems. Side-channel attacks utilize the fact that in reality, a cipher is not a pure mathematical function $E_K[P] \rightarrow C$, but a function $E_K[P] \rightarrow (C, t)$, where t is any additional information produced by the physical implementation. The attacks presented in this paper use timing data.

In 1997, Rijmen and Daemen proposed the Rijndael cipher to the National Institute of Standards and Technology (NIST) as a candidate to become the Advanced Encryption Standard (AES). After four years of competition, Rijndael was chosen by NIST in October 2000 and officially became AES in 2001 with US FIPS 197. The cipher is now widely deployed and is expected to be the world's predominant block cipher over the next 25 years. In its final evaluation of Rijndael [NBB+00], NIST stated that table lookup operations are "not vulnerable to timing attacks" and regarded Rijndael as the easiest among the finalists to defend against side-channel attacks.

In contrast to NIST's predictions, a number of side channel attacks have already been demonstrated against AES, including timing attacks by Bernstein

L. Goubin and M. Matsui (Eds.): CHES 2006, LNCS 4249, pp. 201–215, 2006.

[Ber05] and Tsunoo et al. [TSS+03]. This paper considers a model for attacking AES by using the timing effects of cache-collisions to gather noisy information about the likelihood of relations between key bytes. This leads to a multivariate optimization problem, where the unknown key is an optimal value of a certain objective function. We solve for the key using a variety of AI methods, including belief propagation and iterated local search, as discussed in Appendix D. We also deviate from previous work in attacking the final round of encryption instead of the first round. Table 1 demonstrates the improvements of the attacks in this paper over several previous attacks (see also [CLS06, NSW06, NS06]).

Table 1. Overview of timing attacks against AES

Attack	Samples needed	Sample type	Goal
Bernstein [Ber05]	$2^{27.5}$	Plaintext/timing	Full key recovery
Tsunoo et al. [TSS+03]	2^{26}	Plaintext/timing	Full key recovery
First round attack	$2^{14.58}$	Plaintext/timing	60 key bits recovered
Final round attack	2^{15}	Ciphertext/timing	Full key recovery
Expanded Final round attack	2^{13}	Ciphertext/timing	Full key recovery

2 Overview of the AES Cipher

A full description of the Rijndael cipher is provided in [DR02], but below is a brief description of the cipher's properties that were utilized in this study. This paper will focus exclusively on AES with a 128 bit key. 192 and 256 bit versions use a different key expansion algorithm and more rounds. AES is an iterated cipher: Each round i takes a 16-byte block of input X^i and a 16-byte block of key material K^i, producing a 16-byte block of output X^{i+1}. Each round is carried out by performing the algebraic operations SubBytes, ShiftRows, and MixColumns on X^i, then taking the exclusive-or with the round key K^i. Performance-oriented software implementations of AES combine all three operations and pre-compute the values. The values are stored in large lookup tables, T_0, T_1, T_2, T_3, each mapping one byte of input to four bytes of output. Each round is carried out by splitting up X^i into 16 bytes $x_0^i, x_1^i, \ldots, x_{15}^i$, and K^i into 16 bytes $k_0^i, k_1^i, \ldots, k_{15}^i$. The encryption round is then carried out as:

$$X^{i+1} = \{T_0[x_0^i] \oplus T_1[x_5^i] \oplus T_2[x_{10}^i] \oplus T_3[x_{15}^i] \oplus \{k_0^i, k_1^i, k_2^i, k_3^i\},$$
$$T_0[x_4^i] \oplus T_1[x_9^i] \oplus T_2[x_{14}^i] \oplus T_3[x_3^i] \oplus \{k_4^i, k_5^i, k_6^i, k_7^i\},$$
$$T_0[x_8^i] \oplus T_1[x_{13}^i] \oplus T_2[x_2^i] \oplus T_3[x_7^i] \oplus \{k_8^i, k_9^i, k_{10}^i, k_{11}^i\}, \quad (1)$$
$$T_0[x_{12}^i] \oplus T_1[x_1^i] \oplus T_2[x_6^i] \oplus T_3[x_{11}^i] \oplus \{k_{12}^i, k_{13}^i, k_{14}^i, k_{15}^i\}\}.$$

The round calculation can be performed very efficiently in software this way, using just 16 table lookups and 16 word-length x-or's. A complete encryption consists of an x-or with the first 16 bytes of key material, referred to as "input whitening," followed by 9 normal encryption rounds, plus a simplified final round. The final round performs no `MixColumns` operation as it might trivially be inverted by an attacker and would ostensibly slow down hardware implementations. This omission will prove crucial, as it causes software implementations to use a new table T_4 in the last round, which is just the AES S-Box.

A total of 10 rounds are used in 128-bit AES, but 11 16-byte blocks of key material are needed because of the input-whitening. These 176 bytes of key material are generated by taking the raw 16-bytes of the key and repeatedly carrying out a non-linear transformation which produces the next 16-byte block based on the previous 16-byte block until all 176 bytes are created. This key expansion structure was explicitly chosen [DR02] to be invertible given any 16 consecutive bytes of the expanded key. This is useful to an attacker in that recovery of the final 16 bytes of the expanded key (or any other 16 bytes) is equivalent to recovery of the original key.

This formulation was a part of the original Rijndael proposal [DR02]. The attacks in this paper are widely applicable as many AES implementations have made no significant changes to the original optimized Rijndael code In addition to OpenSSL v. 0.9.8.(a), which was used in our experiments, the AES implementations of Crypto++ 5.2.1 and LibTomCrypt 1.09 use the original Rijndael C implementation with very few changes and are highly vulnerable. The AES implementations in libgcrypt v. 1.2.2 and Botan v. 1.4.2 are also vulnerable, but use a smaller byte-wide final table which lessens the effectiveness of the attacks.

3   Related Work

Side-channel attacks have been demonstrated against implementations of many cryptosystems, utilizing timing [Ber05, TSS+03, Koc96, BB05], power consumption [ABDM00, KJJ99], electromagnetic radiation [GMO01], etc. Public key algorithms have proved the most vulnerable to timing attacks because they typically perform lengthy mathematical operations, the running time of which depends directly on the data due to branch statements. Kocher demonstrated timing attacks against a variety of software public-key systems in 1996 [Koc96]. Brumley and Boneh demonstrated more advanced timing attacks against RSA in 2003 which were effective even against a remote SSL server [BB05], these attacks were improved by another order of magnitude in 2005 [ASK05].

A similar timing attack was demonstrated against the reference AES implementation which uses branch statements to perform multiplication in the field $GF(2^8)$ [KQ99]. However, as noted above, performance AES implementations pre-compute this calculation, obviating this attack. During the AES selection process, it was believed that timing attacks were only applicable to software with a data-dependent execution path (i.e., branch statements, data-dependent shifts), although Kocher did suggest that timing attacks could be constructed against symmetric ciphers by studying "cache hit ratio" [Koc96], a conclusion also reached by Kelsey et al. [KSWH00]. Nevertheless, in an analysis of AES finalists done by Daemen and Rijmen, Rijndael was deemed a "favorable" candidate to secure against timing attacks, since it did not use branch instructions or data-dependent rotations [DR99]. Even by the final NIST evaluation [NBB$^+$00], it was not recognized that table lookups could lead to timing attacks due to the effects of cached memory and AES was considered to be safe.

The use of table lookups into cached memory has recently been recognized as an exploitable cryptographic side-channel [Pag02]. Recent attacks due to Osvik, Shamir, and Tromer demonstrate how specific information about what values in cached memory the encryption algorithm has accessed can quickly leak enough information to reconstruct an AES key [OST06]. For example, if the attacker can determine that, whenever $p_0 = z$, the data in $T_0[z']$ is accessed during encryption, then it must be the case that $x_0^0 = z'$. Since it holds that $p_0 \oplus k_0 = x_0^0$, the attacker can conclude that $k_0 = z \oplus z'$. These attacks are different from timing attacks because they require that the attacker gain direct knowledge about cache access patterns,[1] thus they are directly using cache accesses as a cryptographic side-channel instead of timing.

Another class of cache attacks focuses on the use of power consumption to detect whether lookups performed during AES encryption resulted in hits or misses. This technique was first demonstrated in [BBM$^+$06]. An attack using power analysis of the first round was also described by Lauradoux [Lau05]. Acıiçmez and Koç [AK06] extended this approach by considering the first two rounds of AES. Their attack requires a very low (~ 50) number of encryptions, but require physical access to a machine's power supply.

Cache access patterns also cause timing variation, which can be used to construct a timing attack against AES software without direct observation of the cache accesses. This principle was first demonstrated by Tsunoo et al. [TTMM02, TSS$^+$03] who demonstrated timing attacks against DES and MISTY. Tsunoo et al, assuming that cache hit ratio should be correlated with encryption time, collect a number of plaintexts with unusually long encryption times. These plaintexts are then used to infer information about key bytes by inferring that the correct key should be one that leads to the lowest cache-hit ratio when used with the set of "slow" plaintexts. While the authors focus on attacking DES, the possibility of an attack on AES is briefly mentioned in [TSS$^+$03]. Unfortunately, insufficient detail is provided to reproduce the attack, although a figure of 2^{18} plaintexts with long encryption times is presented for the attack. Assuming consistency with the attacks on DES, this means a total of 2^{24} plaintexts are needed.

Our approach is similar to that of Tsunoo et al. in utilizing the correlation between cache hits and encryption time. However, our attacks focus on individual cache-collisions during encryption, instead of overall hit ratio. Furthermore, we use the entire data set, instead of simply plaintexts resulting in long encryption, and we consider conditions which lead to a shorter encryption time, instead of a longer one. Our methods is similar to that used in recent attacks independently described by Acıiçmez [Acıi05] and Neve et al. [NSW06, NS06], although our attacks differ in focusing on the final round of encryption as opposed to the first round.

---

[1] As implemented in [OST06], knowledge of cache accesses is gained by running attack code on the target computer before and after the encryption operation.

Bernstein demonstrated a different type of timing attack against AES in 2005 [Ber05] which can be thought of as a *statistical* timing attack. Bernstein observed that since the input bytes to the first round of encryption are simply the bytes $x_i^0 = p_i \oplus k_i$, and these bytes are immediately used as indices into the lookup tables, the entire encryption time t can be affected by each of the values x_i^0. To carry out Bernstein's attack, first a large volume of timing data is collected for each value of an input byte x_i^0 using a reference machine, this data is then correlated with data from the target machine to recover the key.

Bernstein's attack is a generic attack because it does not utilize any specific knowledge of why the value of a specific x_i^0 affects the encryption time, only the empirical observation that certain values do cause time variation. This approach is widely applicable because, as Bernstein details, it is extremely difficult to achieve fast constant-time software, and any timing variation could potentially be exploitable. The statistical attack method can even be extended [CLS06] to exploit timing variation of individual bits of the key instead of whole bytes.

The first downside of the statistical approach is that it requires a large number of samples, approximately $2^{27.5}$ in Bernstein's experiments. More critically, the attack is very fragile because relies on subtle machine-specific cache effects, requiring that the attacker recreate the target platform exactly. In our own experiments with Bernstein's attack code, we found even small changes to the mix of background processes from the target machine to the reference machine were enough to make the attack fail, raising serious doubts on the practicality of the attack. Similar difficulty in reproducing the attacks was reported in [OST06] and [OT05]. A recent analysis by Neve et al. [NSW06] discusses the reasons the attack succeeds in some cases and why it is probably not practical.

In contrast, this paper focuses exclusively on white-box timing attacks, which use expected timing effects due to the structure of the cipher. This approach requires no specific information about the target platform, and is likely to require far fewer samples if encryption software lends itself to simple and predictable timing effects, as AES does.

4   Attack Model and Strategy

The attacks in this paper assume the computer performing the encryption operation uses cached memory which can be described using a simple model of the cache. A cache is a small, fast storage area situated between the CPU and main memory. When values are looked up in main memory, they are stored in the cache, evicting older values in the cache. Subsequent lookups to the same memory address can then retrieve the data from the cache, which is faster than main memory, this is called a "cache hit."

Complicating matters is the fact that modern caches do not store individual bytes, but groups of bytes from consecutive "lines" of main memory. Line size varies between 32 bytes for a Pentium III and 64 or 128 bytes on more recent Pentium IV or AMD Athlon processors. Since the usual size of AES table entries is 4 bytes, groups of 8 consecutive table entries share a line in the cache on a

Pentium III (this value is defined as δ in [OST06]). So, for any bytes l, l' which are equal ignoring the lower $\log_2 \delta$ bits (notated as $\langle l \rangle = \langle l' \rangle$ in [OST06]), looking up address l will cause an ensuing access to l' to hit in cache.

We view an AES encryption as a sequence of 160 table lookups to indices $l_1, l_2, ..., l_{160}$. A "cache collision" occurs if two separate lookups l_i, l_j satisfy $\langle l_i \rangle = \langle l_j \rangle$. In this situation, l_j should always hit in the cache.[2] If it were the case that $\langle l_i \rangle \neq \langle l_j \rangle$, then the access to l_j may result in a cache miss if $T[l_j]$ was out of memory prior to the encryption and no previous access fetched it. This should, on the average, take more time as it will require a second cache lookup with non-zero probability. We formalize this assumption:

Cache-Collision Assumption. *For any pair of lookups i, j, given a large number of random AES encryptions with the same key, the average time when $\langle l_i \rangle = \langle l_j \rangle$ will be less than the average time when $\langle l_i \rangle \neq \langle l_j \rangle$.*

This assumption rests on the approximation that the individual table lookups in the sequence are effectively independent for random plaintexts, which seems to hold in practice.[3] This assumption greatly oversimplifies many the intricacies of modern caches, as discussed in Appendix B and Appendix C, but is well supported by experimental data as shown in Figure 1. Notice that there is a clear correlation, especially for ≤ 10 collisions, which is where 90% of the data lies. We fit the experimental data with a linear model where the unknowns are defined as bonuses due to collisions between table lookups in the final round, a total of 120 variables. Depending on the mix of the processes running in the background the model explains between 13% and 28% of the variance in the timing data (the results are supported by five-fold cross-validation).

The notion of using collisions in the cache is by no means unique to this paper. Because caches are specifically designed to behave differently in the presence of a collision a non-collision, they are a natural side channel for attacking AES. This general notion has been used in several other attacks on AES [TTMM02, Pag02, TSS+03, Lau05, OST06], we seek to explicitly define the utility of cache collisions as they apply to timing attacks (similar to [Aci05, NSW06, NS06]).

5   First Round Attack

A natural approach to attacking AES is to analyze table lookups performed in the first round, because they use the indices $x_i^0 = p_i \oplus k_i$, each of which depends on only one key byte and one plaintext byte. In equation (1), we can see that in the first round of encryption, the bytes $x_0^0, x_4^0, x_8^0, x_{12}^0$ are each used as an index into table T_0; they make up a "family" of four bytes in that they are all used

---

[2] We are assuming that the AES encryption itself does not evict any table entries after loading them, a reasonable assumption given the large size of modern caches compared to the AES tables.

[3] This will not hold for the first round if plaintexts are not random. This should hold for the final round regardless of plaintext, since the output ciphertext should be statistically random in any secure cipher.

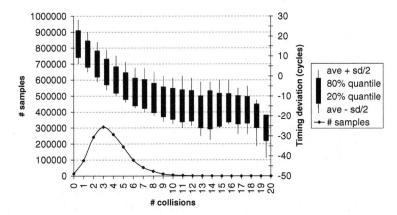

Fig. 1. Time deviation vs number of final round cache-collisions, Pentium III

to access the same table. There are three other families of bytes which share the tables T_1, T_2, and T_3 in round one. A cache collision occurs whenever two bytes x_i^0, x_j^0 in the same family satisfy $\langle x_i^0 \rangle = \langle x_j^0 \rangle$. This should occur when $\langle p_i \rangle \oplus \langle k_i \rangle = \langle p_j \rangle \oplus \langle k_j \rangle$, or after rearranging, $\langle p_i \rangle \oplus \langle p_j \rangle = \langle k_i \rangle \oplus \langle k_j \rangle$.

Plaintexts satisfying $\langle p_i \rangle \oplus \langle p_j \rangle = \langle k_i \rangle \oplus \langle k_j \rangle$ for a pair of bytes i, j should have a lower average encryption time due to the collision. The first round attack algorithm compiles timing data into a table $t[i, j, \langle p_i \rangle \oplus \langle p_j \rangle]$ of average encryption times for all i, j in the same table family. If a low average time occurs at $t[i, j, \Delta]$, the algorithm estimates that $\langle k_i \rangle \oplus \langle k_j \rangle = \Delta$. A t-test is used to identify values which are lower than the mean to a statistically significant degree. For each table family, the attacker will eventually have a redundant set of six equations, such as $\langle k_0 \rangle \oplus \langle k_4 \rangle = \Delta_1$, $\langle k_0 \rangle \oplus \langle k_8 \rangle = \Delta_2$, $\langle k_0 \rangle \oplus \langle k_{12} \rangle = \Delta_3$, $\langle k_4 \rangle \oplus \langle k_8 \rangle = \Delta_4$, $\langle k_4 \rangle \oplus \langle k_8 \rangle = \Delta_5$, $\langle k_8 \rangle \oplus \langle k_{12} \rangle = \Delta_6$ for table T_0.

The four sets of equations for key bytes within the same family are the only information gained by this attack; there is no way to gain exact key information without looking at other rounds (see Section 8).Furthermore, there is no way to learn the lower $\log_2 \delta$ bits of each key byte. The attacker must still guess a value for one complete byte in each table family, plus the low-order $\log_2 \delta$ bits of the other bytes, or a total of $4 \times (8 + 3 \cdot \log_2 \delta) = 68$ bits (for $\delta = 8$), which is impractical to search for almost any real attacker.The attack does provides a significant speedup over previous attacks, in experiments with 50 random keys on a Pentium III the attack succeeded with an average of $2^{14.6}$ timing samples.

6   Final Round Attack

To design a fast attack which can recover the full key, we consider the final round of encryption. As noted previously, the final round of AES omits the `MixColumns` operation, reducing equation (1) to simply:

$$C = \{T_4[x_0^{10}] \oplus k_0^{10}, T_4[x_5^{10}] \oplus k_1^{10}, T_4[x_{10}^{10}] \oplus k_2^{10}, T_4[x_{15}^{10}] \oplus k_3^{10},$$
$$T_4[x_4^{10}] \oplus k_4^{10}, T_4[x_9^{10}] \oplus k_5^{10}, T_4[x_{14}^{10}] \oplus k_6^{10}, T_4[x_3^{10}] \oplus k_7^{10}, \qquad (2)$$
$$T_4[x_8^{10}] \oplus k_8^{10}, T_4[x_{13}^{10}] \oplus k_9^{10}, T_4[x_2^{10}] \oplus k_{10}^{10}, T_4[x_7^{10}] \oplus k_{11}^{10},$$
$$T_4[x_{12}^{10}] \oplus k_{12}^{10}, T_4[x_1^{10}] \oplus k_{13}^{10}, T_4[x_6^{10}] \oplus k_{14}^{10}, T_4[x_{11}^{10}] \oplus k_{15}^{10}\}.$$

In this equation, C is the 16-byte output ciphertext, and T_4 is the AES S-box. The details of the S-box are inconsequential to this attack, the only important fact is that the S-box is a non-linear permutation over all 256 possible byte values. For any two ciphertext bytes c_i, c_j, it holds that $c_i = k_i^{10} \oplus T_4[x_u^{10}]$ for some u and $c_j = k_j^{10} \oplus T_4[x_w^{10}]$ for some w. Regardless of the actual values of u and w, whenever $x_u^{10} = x_w^{10}$, a cache collision occurs on T_4. Suppose $x_u^{10} = x_w^{10}$, and $T_4[x_u^{10}] = T_4[x_w^{10}] = \alpha$. Then it will hold that $c_i = k_i^{10} \oplus \alpha$ and $c_j = k_j^{10} \oplus \alpha$.

If, on the other hand, $c_i \oplus c_j \neq k_i^{10} \oplus k_j^{10}$, two different values α, β must have resulted from the table lookups. It would be true that $\alpha \oplus \beta = \gamma = c_i \oplus c_j \oplus k_i^{10} \oplus k_j^{10}$ with γ a constant for a fixed value of $c_i \oplus c_j$. Since α and β are the direct results of S-box lookups, though, a fixed differential γ does not guarantee a fixed offset of the lookup indexes used to produce them. Ironically, the non-linearity which is the raison d'être of the S-box also enables this attack to succeed. For the purposes of this attack, given values of α and β satisfying $\alpha \oplus \beta = \gamma \neq 0$, the indexes which were looked up in the S-box to produce α and β are essentially random. So, if $c_i \oplus c_j = k_i^{10} \oplus k_j^{10}$, then a cache collision occurs in T_4, otherwise, the lookups will be from two essentially random locations in T_4.

The goal of the attack is to record timing data for random ciphertexts at each value of $\Delta = c_i \oplus c_j$. For each ciphertext/time pair observed, the encryption time is used to update a table of average times $t[i, j, \Delta]$ for all values i, j. The goal to find one value $\Delta'_{i,j}$ for each i, j such that $t[i, j, \Delta'_{i,j}] < \bar{t}$ where $\bar{t}$ is the average encryption time over all ciphertexts. Eventually, the values of $\Delta'_{i,j}$ will become accurate guesses for the true values $\Delta_{i,j} = k_i^{10} \oplus k_j^{10}$, which should be the only values which cause significantly low encryption times.

These values can be used by an attacker to construct a guess at the final 16 bytes of the expanded key in the presence of noise, as described in Appendix D. The authors of Rijndael made it a specific design goal to enable recovery of the entire key given any 16 consecutive bytes of the expanded key [DR02]. Thus, it is simple to revert the key expansion algorithm to recover the raw key K given the final 16 bytes $k_0^{10}, k_1^{10}, \ldots, k_{15}^{10}$ of the expanded key. For each guess at the final key bytes, the attack program reverts the key and checks it against one known plaintext/ciphertext pair. Table 2 presents statistical data for the number of (C, t) pairs seen before the attack recovers a full 128-bit AES key, from attacks against 50 random keys.

7   Expanded Final Round Attack

One problem with the simple final round attack is that it considers only cache collisions due to lookups on the same table index. When the number of table entries per cache line δ is 8 or 16, however, the majority of cache collisions will not be on the same index but on two different indices of the same cache line. To take advantage of all cache collisions, we consider all conditions for which there will be a cache collision in the final round on two bytes i, j. Recall that $c_i = k_i^{10} \oplus S[x_u^{10}]$ and $c_j = k_j^{10} \oplus S[x_v^{10}]$ for some u, v. A collision will occur whenever $\langle x_u^{10} \rangle = \langle x_v^{10} \rangle$, or equivalently:

$$\langle S^{-1}[c_i \oplus k_i] \rangle = \langle S^{-1}[c_j \oplus k_j] \rangle. \tag{3}$$

An attacker can utilize this relationship by guessing exact values (k_i', k_j') for each i, j, instead of guessing only a differential. For each guess, an average time is computed for all timing samples which satisfy equation (3) under the guessed key bytes. The correct value will eventually have a lower average time due to the cache collision. The memory and time requirements for analyzing timing data are higher in this attack because there are $256 \cdot 256 = 65,536$ possible guesses for each pair of bytes. However, the data processing can be done off-line by the attacker after the data is collected. In practice, an attacker will want to reduce the amount of samples needed at the expense of increasing off-line processing time. Appendix D describes details of the attack algorithm.

This greatly speeds up the attack because the data collection rate is effectively increased by δ, since all cache-line collisions over any two bytes i, j are detected instead of exact byte collisions. That is, the proportion of random samples which satisfy equation (3) is $\frac{\delta}{256}$, instead of $\frac{1}{256}$ for the simpler version of the attack. Additionally, the data is more precise in that a guess can be made about the probability of the exact value of a pair of key bytes, instead of simply a differential. These factors combine to give the following performance numbers over 50 random keys:

Table 2. Median samples required, Final round Attacks

CPU	Attack Type			
	Final Round		Expanded Final Round	
	Cache Eviction Policy			
	L1	L2	L1	L2
Pentium III 1.0 GHz	2^{16}	2^{15}	2^{14}	2^{13}
Pentium IV Xeon 3.2 GHz	$2^{19.9}$	2^{16}	$2^{18.6}$	$2^{13.6}$
UltraSPARC-III+ 0.9 GHz	$2^{18.7}$	2^{15}	$2^{17.3}$	$2^{14.3}$

8   Attack Variants

The final round attacks are effective against decryption with only minor modifications, require known plaintext instead of known ciphertext. They are actually slightly simpler in that they recover information about the raw key, instead of the final bytes of the expanded key, so key reversion is not necessary.

A key area for further research is adaptive chosen plaintext/ciphertext attacks. In many real world, an attacker may be able to get encryption times for chosen plaintext and/or chosen ciphertext, this ability could likely be used to greatly decrease the number of samples required for an attack to succeed.

Another promising avenue is extending the first round attack shown here to two rounds. The problem of the first round attack only recovering partial key information is a common problem in cache-based attacks due to the use of cache lines on modern processors, considering the second round of cache accesses is a common solution [Acıi05, AK06, OST06, NSW06]. In the online version of the paper we discuss an approach to extending our first round attack to a two rounds attack, which could potentially recover the key with 2^{16} samples, but requires a very high offline search by the attacker.

9   Countermeasures and Conclusions

General countermeasures against cache-based side channel attacks on AES have been widely discussed in the literature. Suggested approaches vary from modifying hardware to limit the amount of data leaked by the cache [Pag02, Pag05, Ber05, OST06], to constant-time software [Ber05], to careful obfuscation of cache access patterns by the AES software [BGNS06]. Unfortunately, all of these approaches have performance implications. We add to the discussion the specific suggestion of scrapping the special final round lookup table T_4, whose function can be replaced by the other four tables. This small modification led to our attacks requiring as many as 1,000 times more samples, and has no performance cost. Details are presented in the online version of the paper. In lieu of stronger protections, this "free" defense should be considered.

Side-channel attacks were not given adequate treatment in the AES selection process. Rijndael, in optimized form, makes heavier use of lookup tables than any of the other four AES finalists, which exposes it to multiple side-channel attacks, including timing. By comparison, Serpent [BAK98], the AES runner-up, uses only tiny 4-bit by 4-bit S-boxes, which are in fact implemented only by logical operations, making Serpent invulnerable to cache-based side-channel attacks. At the time this was not recognized as an advantage, but it should be clear now that table lookups should be avoided or used with extreme caution in future cryptographic software.

The attacks described in this paper represent a significant step towards developing realistic *remote* timing attacks against AES, which are to make use of less accurate data than the processor cycle counts available in the simulated environment used in this study. There are a number of environments where such an attack could potentially be employed where direct observation of the pattern of cache accesses is not possible:

- On an encrypted network file system, an attacker which could time encryptions of single disk blocks and attempt to recover the encryption key.
- In a virtual machine environment, the virtual machine monitor could force cache flushes between context switches. An attacker could attempt to time another virtual machine performing encryptions.

- As recently proposed by Page [Pag05], a computer could partition cache between separate processes. User-level processes could not access the cache used by a root-level daemon process doing encryptions, but could time encryptions being done by that process.
- An SSL server (or client) could be a source of timing data to an attacker listening on the network. It is possible that both encryption and decryption could be observed in this setting.

In principle, the attacks in this paper could be employed in such scenarios, since they only require timing data and known plaintext or ciphertext. It remains to be seen if the timing data which could be obtained is accurate enough to attack, and there are additional complications as discussed in Appendix A. Nevertheless, the timing attacks in this paper should make clear the need for software AES implementations to protect against timing variation due to cached memory. While AES has resisted conventional cryptanalysis so far, it will be rendered useless if practical timing attacks are developed.

Acknowledgements

We are grateful to Dan Boneh for his encouragement of this research as well as many helpful comments, as well as Andrew Morrison and anonymous CHES 2006 reviewers for comments on drafts of this paper.

References

[ABDM00] Mehdi-Laurent Akkar, Régis Bevan, Paul Dischamp, and Didier Moyart. Power analysis, what is now possible.... In *Advances in Cryptology—ASIACRYPT 2000*, pages 489–502, 2000.

[AK06]   Onur Acıiçmez and Çetin Kaya Koç. Trace driven cache attack on AES. IACR Cryptology ePrint Archive, Report 2006/138, April 2006.

[Acıi05] Onur Acıiçmez. "Remote Timing Attacks". Given at Intel Corporation, Oregon, USA, December 2005. Available at: http://web.engr.oregonstate.edu/~aciicmez/osutass/

[ASK05]   Onur Acıiçmez, Werner Schindler, and Çetin Kaya Koç. Improving Brumley and Boneh timing attack on unprotected SSL implementations. ACM Conference on Computer and Communications Security, 2005.

[BAK98]   Eli Biham, Ross J. Anderson, and Lars R. Knudsen. Serpent: A new block cipher proposal. In *Fast Software Encryption '98*, pages 222–238, 1998.

[BGNS06] Ernie Brickell and Gary Graunke and Michael Neve and Jean-Pierre Seifert. Software mitigations to hedge AES against cache-based software side channel vulnerabilities. IACR ePrint Archive, Report 2006/052, Feb 2006.

[BB05]   David Brumley and Dan Boneh. Remote timing attacks are practical. *Computer Networks*, 48(5):701–716, 2005.

[BBM+06] Guido Bertoni, Luca Breveglieri, Matteo Monchiero, Gianluca Palermo, and Vittorio Zaccaria. AES power attack based on induced cache miss and countermeasure. ITCC(1), 2005.

[Ber05]   Daniel J. Bernstein. Cache-timing attacks on AES. April 2005. http://cr.yp.to/antiforgery/cachetiming-20050414.pdf.

[CLS06]   Anne Canteaut, Cedric Lauradoux, and Andre Seznec. Understanding cache attacks. Technical Report, April 2006. Available at: ftp://ftp.inria.fr/INRIA/publication/publi-pdf/RR/RR-5881.pdf

[DR99]   Joan Daemen and Vincent Rijmen. Resistance against implementation attacks: A comparative study of the AES proposals. *Second AES Candidate Conference*, February 1999.

[DR02]   Joan Daemen and Vincent Rijmen. *The design of Rijndael: AES—the advanced encryption standard.* Springer-Verlag, 2002.

[GMO01]   Karine Gandolfi, Christophe Mourtel, and Francis Olivier. Electromagnetic analysis: Concrete results. In *Cryptographic Hardware and Embedded Systems—CHES 2001*, pages 251–261, 2001.

[KJJ99]   Paul C. Kocher, Joshua Jaffe, and Benjamin Jun. Differential power analysis. In *Advances in Cryptology—CRYPTO '99*, pages 388–397, 1999.

[Koc96]   Paul C. Kocher. Timing attacks on implementations of Diffie-Hellman, RSA, DSS, and other systems. In *Advances in Cryptology—CRYPTO '96*, pages 104–113, 1996.

[KQ99]   F. Koeune and J.-J. Quisquater. A timing attack against Rijndael. Technical Report CG-1999/1, June 1999.

[KSWH00]   John Kelsey, Bruce Schneier, David Wagner, and Chris Hall. Side channel cryptanalysis of product ciphers. *J. of Computer Security*, 8(2/3), 2000.

[Lau05]   Cedric Laradoux. Collision attacks on processors with cache and countermeasures. Western European Workshop on Research in Cryptology—WEWoRC'05, C. Wolf, S. Lucks, and P.-W. Yau (editors), pp. 76–85, 2005.

[LMV04]   H. Ledig, F. Muller, and F. Valette. Enhancing collision attacks. In *Cryptographic Hardware and Embedded Systems—CHES 2004*, pp. 176–190, 2004.

[NBB+00]   J. Nechvatal, E. Barker, L. Bassham, W. Burr, M. Dworkin, J. Foti, and E. Roback. Report on the development of the Advanced Encryption Standard (AES). October 2000. http://csrc.nist.gov/CryptoToolkit/aes/round2/r2report.pdf.

[NSW06]   Michael Neve, Jean-Pierre Seifert, and Zhenghong Wang. A refined look at Bernstein's AES side-channel analysis. *ASIACCS*, p. 369, 2006.

[NS06]   Michael Neve and Jean-Pierre Seifert. Advances on access-driven cache attacks on AES. In *SAC'06*, to appear.

[OT05]   Mairead O'Hanlan and Anthony Tonge. Investigation of cache timing attacks on AES. School of Computing, Dublin City University, 2005.

[OST06]   Dag Arne Osvik, Adi Shamir, and Eran Tromer. Cache attacks and countermeasures: the case of AES. In *CT-RSA*, pages 1–20, 2006.

[Pag02]   Daniel Page. Theoretical use of cache memory as a cryptanalytic sidechannel. Technical Report CSTR-02-003, University of Bristol, April 2002.

[Pag03]   Daniel Page. Defending against cache based side channel attacks. Technical Report. Department of Computer Science, University of Bristol, 2003.

[Pag05]   Daniel Page. Partitioned cache as a side-channel defense mechanism. IACR Cryptology ePrint Archive, Report 2005/280, August 2005.

[Per05]   Colin Percival. Cache missing for fun and profit. Presented at BSDCan '05, 2005. http://www.daemonology.net/hyperthreading-considered-harmful/.

[SLFP04]   Kai Schramm, Gregor Leander, Patrick Felke, Christof Paar. A collision-attack on AES: Combining side channel- and differential-attack. In *Cryptographic Hardware and Embedded Systems—CHES 2004*, pp. 163–175, 2004.

[SWP03]   Kai Schramm, Thomas J. Wollinger and Christof Paar. A new class of collision attacks and its application to DES. In *Fast Software Encryption—FSE'03*, pages 206–222, 2003.

[TSS+03]   Y. Tsunoo, T. Saito, T. Suzaki, M. Shigeri, and H. Miyauchi. Cryptanalysis of DES implemented on computers with cache. In *Cryptographic Hardware and Embedded Systems—CHES 2003*, pp. 62–76, 2003.

[TTMM02]   Yukiyasu Tsunoo, Etsuko Tsujihara, Kazuhiko Minematsu, and Hiroshi Miyauchi. Cryptanalysis of block ciphers implemented on computers with cache. In *International Symposium on Information Theory and Applications 2002*, pages 803–806, 2002.

[TTS+06]   Yukiyasu Tsunoo, Etsuko Tsujihara, Maki Shigeri, Hiroya Kubo, and Kazuhiko Minematsu. Improving cache attacks by considering cipher structure. In *International Journal of Information Security 2006*.

A   Implementation Notes

All of the attacks described in this paper have been implemented as a UNIX command line program aes_attack, the source code of which is available at the author's website. The program can be recompiled to use any of the attack algorithms described, as well as options for decryption attacks and different cache eviction routines. The program first generates a large number of timing samples by repeatedly triggering one encryption for a random plaintext using an OpenSSL library call and recording the resulting ciphertext along with a processor cycle count. Each timing/ciphertext pair is added to a large buffer after being recorded, this allows a minimum of activity in between encryptions. An explicit cache eviction routine is called before each encryption, as described in Appendix B, no other work is done between encryptions. After each encryption, each byte of the resulting ciphertext is touched, this must be done to ensure the encryption has finished before recording the ending time on platforms such as the Pentium IV which support out-of-order instruction execution while waiting for cache misses.

After generating a large number of samples, the attack algorithm is called with a small set of the data. It is incrementally given more of the data until it succeeds in recovering the key. Samples are not used if their time is more than twice the lowest time seen, this eliminates noise due to page faults and context switches. These ignored samples are still counted when reporting the number of samples necessary for the attack to succeed.

B   Cache Eviction

All of the attacks described in this paper require the AES lookup tables to be (at least partially) out of the cache prior to an encryption operation. If all tables are cached, which would occur during a long run of consecutive encryptions, then cache collisions will not reduce timing. In a real attack scenario, an attacker must have some ability to remove the tables from cache before an encryption. The most likely approach would be simply waiting. If the target machine is doing other work, the tables will probably be quickly evicted from memory as other processes load their own data. Also, it is assumed that the target program only performs key expansion once, then stores the expanded key in memory and uses it for subsequent encryptions. Otherwise, key expansion before each encryption would have the side effect of loading some of the AES tables into memory, since they are used in key expansion.

For the purposes of this study, we consider two cases, if the AES tables are fully evicted from Level 1 cache, and if the AES tables are fully evicted from Level 2 cache. It is also easy to verify that if only some random fraction of the table entries are out of cache, the attack will still succeed with additional samples. To simulate the eviction of tables from L2 cache, we sequentially accesses a continuous block of memory the size of the cache, which will evict all previous contents. To save time in experiments on Pentium IV, we use the `clflush` instruction. Eviction from L1 cache is similar, although we must be careful not to evict tables from L2 cache. To do this, we read in a small amount of data to evict only L1 cache, but not the AES tables in L2 cache.

C   Pentium IV Complications

The model discussed in Section 4 appears to be a very good approximation for the cache behavior of the Pentium III and UltraSPARC processors. From our experiments, we have seen that it does not fully capture the complexity of the Pentium IV's cache structure. The first complication is that Pentium IV "usually" loads cache lines in pairs, making the cache lines 128 bytes. In some experiments two indices being in neighboring cache lines produced a bigger time drop than a traditional collision. Second, Pentium IV has a hardware pre-fetch mechanism. If it notices "several" straight cache misses, it will begin pre-fetching data in the direction the accesses are going, assuming it is a large serial data read. The Intel documentation uses the word several, which it says could be "as few as 2." So, certain cache collisions may trigger the hardware pre-fetcher, while others may not. Finally, Pentium IV supports out-of-order instruction execution while waiting for cache misses. This means that in certain situations, cache misses may have little effect on the overall encryption if there are enough instructions to be executed which do not depend on the fetched value. The net result of these Pentium IV features is somewhat chaotic behavior when a simple model is assumed, this was also observed in [OST06].

D   Final Round Optimizations

The final round attack looks at the average time for each possible value $\Delta_{i,j} = k_i^{10} \oplus k_j^{10}$ for all i, j, where the true value for each $\Delta_{i,j}$ should be lower than the average. The raw data is converted into a cost function, $c(i, j, \Delta)$, which should be low for values of Δ which represented low times. Eventually, the true values of each $\Delta_{i,j}$ should be the lowest values. However, in the presence of noise, the algorithm seeks to produce some guess K' at the key which minimizes the total cost function $C[K] = \sum_{i,j}[c(i, j, K_i \oplus K_j)]$. The guess K' will not be a guess of actual key bytes, but a set of offsets $\Delta_{0,i} = k_0^{10} \oplus k_i^{10}$ for all $1 \leq i \leq 15$. Two adapted AI algorithms can be used to attempt to minimize this function.

The first is a variant of local optimization search. The cost function used by this algorithm is simply $c(i, j, \Delta) = (\Delta - \Delta^*)^2$, where Δ^* is the lowest value observed for that particular i, j. After an initial guess K_0 is made at the key offsets, the total cost function is calculated for every key guess K_0' which can be obtained by changing one byte of K_0. The lowest cost K_0' then becomes the new key guess K_1. This process is repeated either until a local minimum is reached, or a preset maximum number of iterations is reached. Each guess K_i leads to 256 possible values for the actual key. These are obtained by guessing all values for k_0^{10}, the final 15 bytes of the key are then determined by the offsets $\Delta_{0,i}$. Finally, the guess at the final 16 bytes of expanded key is reverted to a guess at the original key, which can be checked against a known plaintext value.

The second approximation algorithm used is belief propagation. For this approach, a probability approximation $\varphi(i, j, \Delta)$ can be made based on the observed data by mapping it to a normal distribution, since the average and standard deviation are known. This is used in place of a cost function. Next, an initial set of probabilities are guessed for each key offset $p_0(i, \Delta) = \Pr[k_0^{10} \oplus k_i^{10} = \Delta]$. These probability guesses $p_0(i, \Delta)$ are updated as follows: For each $j \neq i$, the maximum value of $p_0(j, \Delta') \cdot \varphi(i, j, \Delta \oplus \Delta')$ over all Δ' is added to p_1. The guesses p_1 are then normalized. This process is repeated, and the probabilities $p(i, \Delta)$ should eventually be higher for the correct values. After each iteration, the probabilities are used to construct a best guess for the key, as before. In this study, both algorithms were used, since we found experimentally that each was successful before the other for certain data sets.

The expanded final round attack provides slightly different raw data than the simple final round attack, namely, a set of average times $t(i, j, \alpha, \beta)$, low times should occur at the values $k_i^{10} = \alpha$ and $k_j^{10} = \beta$. Instead of using a cost function, each pair is given a weight w. A threshold τ is chosen, times $t(i, j, \alpha, \beta)$ which are not among the τ lowest times for i, j are given weight 0. The lowest time is given weight $\tau - 1$, the next lowest time $\tau - 2$, and so on. The goal of the approximation algorithm is to produce a key guess which has the highest sum of weights $W[K] = \sum_{i,j}[w(i, j, K_i, K_j)]$. After making an initial guess, the algorithm proceeds to perform a series of local optimizations, changing one byte in each round which raises the total weight of the key as much as possible. Heuristically, this approach performed better than belief propagation for this attack. For this study, the algorithm was used with $\tau = 16$.

Provably Secure S-Box Implementation Based on Fourier Transform

Emmanuel Prouff[1], Christophe Giraud[2], and Sébastien Aumônier[1]

[1] Oberthur Card Systems,
71-73, rue des Hautes Pâtures, 92 726, Nanterre, France
{e.prouff, s.aumonier}@oberthurcs.com
[2] Oberthur Card Systems,
4, allée du doyen Georges Brus, 33 600, Pessac, France
c.giraud@oberthurcs.com

Abstract. Cryptographic algorithms implemented in embedded devices must withstand Side Channel Attacks such as the Differential Power Analysis (DPA). A common method of protecting symmetric cryptographic implementations against DPA is to use masking techniques. However, clever masking of non-linear parts such as S-Boxes is difficult and has been the flaw of many countermeasures. In this article, we take advantage of some remarkable properties of the Fourier Transform to propose a new method to thwart DPA on the implementation of every S-Box. After introducing criteria so that an implementation is qualified as DPA-resistant, we prove the security of our scheme. Finally, we apply the method to FOX and AES S-Boxes and we show in the latter case that the resulting implementation is one of the most efficient.

Keywords: Differential Power Analysis, Provably Secure Countermeasure, Fourier Transform, Symmetric Cryptosystems, S-Box, AES, FOX.

1   Introduction

In 1996, Kocher introduced the concept of *Side Channel Analysis* which utilizes side channel leakage of embedded devices such as timing execution to obtain Information about sensitive data [18]. This concept was pushed one step further in [17]. In this paper, Kocher *et al.* use power consumption measurements of the device during the execution of sensitive operations, allowing two kinds of Power Attacks: the *Simple Power Analysis* (SPA) and the *Differential Power Analysis* (DPA). The first attack consists in directly interpreting power consumption measurements and the second attack also involves statistical tests. From then on, many papers describing either countermeasures or attack improvements have been published (see [1,4,6,21] for example).

In the case of symmetric cryptosystems such as DES [11] and AES [10], the most critical part when securing implementations against DPA is to protect

L. Goubin and M. Matsui (Eds.): CHES 2006, LNCS 4249, pp. 216–230, 2006.

their non-linear operations (*i.e.* the calls to the *S-Boxes*). Indeed, all the other operations are more or less linear and can be protected in a straightforward manner (see [1] for instance). To protect the calculus of the output of an S-Box against DPA, three main kinds of methods have been proposed in the literature. The first one, called the *duplication method* [6,13], consists in randomly splitting every piece of sensitive data in a constant number of blocks. Then, the computation can be securely carried out by performing calculations with these random blocks. The second method, called the *re-computation method* [1,2,29], involves a re-computation of the lookup tables corresponding to the S-Box with one or several random value(s) which must be changed each time the algorithm is executed. The third generic method, that we call here *S-Box secure calculation*, has been essentially applied to protect AES implementations [5,15,28,32] due to the strong algebraic structure of the AES S-Box. In this case, S-Box outputs are not directly obtained by accessing a lookup table but are computed by using a mathematical representation of the S-Box. All the logical operations involved during this calculation are resistant to DPA.

In this paper, we present a new, secure and generic S-Box calculation method based on the discrete Fourier transform. In Section 2, we formalize DPA attacks on S-Boxes and we introduce a model allowing us to measure the efficiency of such attacks. We also exhibit criteria so that an implementation is qualified as DPA-resistant. In Section 3, we briefly present the Fourier transform and we use its properties to introduce a new S-Box secure calculation. We then prove that our method is DPA-resistant in accordance with the criteria established in Section 2. In Section 4, we apply our method to AES and FOX and we compare its efficiency with other existing countermeasures.

2   On the Notion of DPA-Resistant Implementation of S-Boxes

S-Boxes aim to ensure confusion of Information in many symmetric cryptosystems. Since they manipulate sensitive data, their implementation in embedded devices must withstand side-channel cryptanalysis such as DPA. During the last decade, several ways of securely implementing S-Boxes have been proposed. For some of them, no proof of resistance to DPA has been established and sometimes Information about the secret is recovered. In such cases, there is a need to quantify the relevance of the leaked Information from the attacker's point of view. In the following, we introduce a new notion called *Advantage* which allows us to measure how much DPA on the S-Box implementation impacts the security of the whole embedded cryptosystem. Even if we focus on block cipher algorithms, our study is valid for every symmetric cryptosystem involving S-Boxes.

A block cipher is the iteration of several *rounds*, each round involving S-Boxes. The rounds are parameterized by *round-keys* which are derived from a secret parameter usually called *master key*. A round-key *RK* can be viewed as an uplet of small vectors, called *sub-keys*, which are used separately by the

S-Boxes. In the following, we denote by n the bit-length of the sub-keys and by N the bit-length of the round-keys.

In a well-designed block cipher algorithm, recovering a sub-key K must be as difficult as recovering the whole round-key RK by brute force attack. An implementation of such an algorithm is said to be *secure* if this fundamental property is not only satisfied by the algorithm but also by its implementation.

When an S-Box implementation thwarts DPA, recovering the sub-key by attacking the S-Box calculus is as difficult as recovering the round-key itself (and thus requires around 2^N suppositions). In this case, the security of the cryptosystem is not impacted by DPA on the S-Boxes implementations.

On the contrary, when the S-Box implementation has some drawbacks from a DPA point of view, some Information about the sub-key is obtained. In this case, the efficiency of the attack depends on the amount of Information on K which has leaked:

- in the best case, the attack allows the attacker to get K completely.
- in less favorable situations, the attacker does not recover the sub-key directly, but some useful Information on it is obtained (for instance the Hamming weight of the sub-key or a linear relation which must be satisfied by some of its bit-coordinates [19]).

Let RK denote the round-key an attacker tries to recover by DPA. By performing a DPA for every S-Box which manipulates a sub-key extracted from RK, the attacker succeeds in isolating the round key in a proper subset of the *key-space*. Therefore, the attacker does not need to test all the N-bit round-keys but only a subset of them to recover RK. Depending on the efficiencies of the localized DPAs, the cardinality ε of this subset ranges from 1 (the best case from the attacker viewpoint) to 2^N (when all the attacks failed).

To compare the efficiency of different countermeasures against DPA, we introduce the notion of *Advantage* which aims to evaluate the attacker's capacity to recover a secret round-key RK manipulated partially by one or several S-Box(es), each of them being implemented through a method $\mathcal{M}$.

Definition 1. *Let RK be a N-bit secret value. The* Advantage *of an adversary in recovering the secret RK by DPA is the value* Adv *defined by:*

$$\text{Adv}(\mathcal{M}) = 2^N - \varepsilon ,\tag{1}$$

where ε denotes the cardinality of the subset of $\mathbb{F}_2^N$ containing all the candidate round-keys isolated by DPA.

When DPA allows the attacker to unambiguously recover all the sub-keys, the whole round-key is straightforwardly deduced and ε equals 1. On the contrary, when power consumption measurements give no Information on K, then ε equals 2^N. We deduce $0 \leq Adv(\mathcal{M}) \leq 2^N - 1$.

Proposition 1. *An S-Box implementation $\mathcal{M}$ is such that $\text{Adv}(\mathcal{M}) = 0$ if and only if $\mathcal{M}$ thwarts DPA. Such an implementation is said to be* DPA-resistant.

A first step in securing an S-Box implementation against DPA consists in *masking* the sensitive data manipulated at input and at output of the S-Box calculation. This is usually performed by securely adding random values to these data [6]. Then, while the S-Box computation is performed with the masked input, other operations must be involved (in parallel or as pre-computations) allowing the so-called *mask-correction* and the introduction of a new mask for the output. Let op denote either the bitwise-addition or a modular addition and let F denote the S-Box, an S-Box secure calculation $\mathcal{M}$ can be viewed as a process allowing to get the pair $(F(X) \text{ op } R_2, R_2)$ from the input pair $(X \text{ op } R_1, R_1)$. So, a generic solution to securely perform an S-Box calculation can be depicted by the following generic procedure:

Procedure 1. S-Box calculation

INPUTS: A random value R_1, a masked value $\widetilde{X} = X \text{ op } R_1$ (with X a sensitive data), a function F representing the S-Box, a method $\mathcal{M}$
OUTPUT: The pair $(F(X) \text{ op } R_2, R_2)$ with R_2 a random value

---

1 Generate a random value R_2
2 Compute $result \leftarrow \mathcal{M}(\widetilde{X}, R_1, R_2, F)$ $[result = F(X) \text{ op } R_2]$
3 **Return** $(result, R_2)$

Remark 1. We assume throughout this paper that the distribution of the generated random values is uniform which is a prerequisite for security.

The cost of the mask-correction is usually not negligible compared to the one of the entire block-cipher algorithm. Indeed, as it can be seen in [25] or [31] for instance, it induces a very high (timing and/or memory) overhead, especially because one must always ensure that the sensitive data are securely manipulated and that the mask-correction algorithm itself thwarts DPA.

For an S-Box calculation as depicted in Procedure 1., the method $\mathcal{M}$ is DPA-resistant if the computation of $F(X) \text{ op } R_2$ from $X \text{ op } R_1$, R_1 and R_2 is performed without revealing any useful Information for DPA. In order to design such a method, random values independent of the input X are usually involved when manipulating sensitive data during the calculation of the output stored in *result*.

By using and adapting ideas of [3], we decompose $\mathcal{M}$ into d steps at the *unit level*[1]. The intermediate results of the d steps are denoted by $I_1(X, Z_1), \cdots, I_d(X, Z_d)$, where X is the sensitive input of the S-Box and where Z_i denotes an uplet of random variables involved to securely manipulate the i-th intermediate data.

Let us assume that a method $\mathcal{M}$ is such that every intermediate value $I_i(X, Z_i)$ is independent of the sensitive input X. Then, the power consumption resulting from the manipulation of the values $I_i(X, Z_i)$ gives no Information on X. Based on this remark, we introduce a proposition characterizing the methods $\mathcal{M}$ for which $Adv(\mathcal{M}) = 0$:

---

[1] In hardware terms, this level is based on the contents of registers.

Proposition 2. *Let d denote the number of steps at the unit level of an S-Box implementation $\mathcal{M}$. Then, $\mathrm{Adv}(\mathcal{M})$ is null if and only if for every $i = 1, \cdots, d$, the random variables X and $I_i(X, Z_i)$ are independent.*

Remark 2. The *Mutual Information* can be used to formalize the notion of independency between two variables (see [22] for instance).

In the particular case of the AES algorithm, some S-Box implementations have been proved to be DPA-resistant [3,23]. Nevertheless, as they rely on the algebraic structure of the AES S-Box, they are not generic. In the next section, we present a new DPA-resistant method which can be applied to every S-Box.

3   A New Method to Protect S-Boxes Access from DPA

In this section we firstly recall some basics about the Fourier transform. Then, we exhibit an interesting property of this function from which a new S-Box secure calculation method is deduced. Finally, we prove that the corresponding implementation is DPA-resistant, *i.e.* the Advantage of an adversary over this implementation is equal to zero.

3.1   Fourier Transform

Let us recall the definition of the Fourier transform of a function defined from an abelian group G into $\mathbb{C}$.

Definition 2. *Let G be an abelian group and let $\widehat{G}$ denote the dual space of G. Let $\mathbb{C}[G]$ denote the set of applications from G into $\mathbb{C}$. Then, the Fourier transform on $\mathbb{C}[G]$, denoted by $\mathcal{F}$, is defined by:*

$$
\mathcal{F} : \mathbb{C}[G] \to \mathbb{C}[\widehat{G}] \\
F \mapsto \widehat{F} \qquad , \tag{2}
$$

where $\widehat{F}$ is defined by:

$$
\forall \chi \in \widehat{G}, \ \widehat{F}(\chi) = \sum_{X \in G} F(X) \chi(X) \ . \tag{3}
$$

In this paper, we use the Fourier transform in the particular case $G = \mathbb{F}_2^n$. When G is a n-dimensional vector space over $\mathbb{F}_2$, its dual group $\widehat{G}$ is the set of characters $\chi_A : X \mapsto (-1)^{A \cdot X}$, where $\cdot$ denotes the scalar product defined by $A \cdot X = \sum_{i \in \{0,\ldots,n-1\}} A_i \cdot X_i \mod 2$. So, if $G = \mathbb{F}_2^n$ then Relation (3) is equivalent to:

$$
\forall \chi_A \in \widehat{G}, \ \widehat{F}(\chi_A) = \sum_{X \in G} F(X)(-1)^{A \cdot X} \ . \tag{4}
$$

The Fourier transform of a function F defined on $\mathbb{F}_2^n$ satisfies $F = \frac{1}{2^n} \widehat{\widehat{F}}$, that is:

$$
\forall X \in \mathbb{F}_2^n, \ F(X) = \frac{1}{2^n} \sum_{\chi_A \in \widehat{G}} \widehat{F}(\chi_A)(-1)^{A \cdot X} \ . \tag{5}
$$

For simplicity reasons, the value $\widehat{F}(\chi_A)$ is denoted by $\widehat{F}(A)$ and the summation in Relation (5) is computed for $A \in G$.

3.2   DPA-Resistant Implementation of S-Boxes Access

The New Method. Relation (5) is the starting point of our study about how to find a new solution to protect S-Box access from DPA. From this relation and the involutive property of the Fourier transform, we observe that the image of a message X through a function F can be computed from a masked message $\widetilde{X}$ and the corresponding mask.

Let X, R_1 and A be three elements of $\mathbb{F}_2^n$ and let $\widetilde{X}$ denote the vector $X \oplus R_1$. As $A \cdot X \oplus \widetilde{X} \cdot R_1$ equals $A \cdot \widetilde{X} \oplus R_1 \cdot (\widetilde{X} \oplus A)$, one can re-write Relation (5) as follows:

$$(-1)^{\widetilde{X} \cdot R_1} F(X) = \frac{1}{2^n} \sum_{A \in \mathbb{F}_2^n} \widehat{F}(A)(-1)^{A \cdot \widetilde{X} \oplus R_1 \cdot (\widetilde{X} \oplus A)} \ . \tag{6}$$

The relation above is the core of our solution. When F denotes an S-Box, it provides a way to compute $\pm F(X)$ from a boolean masked input $\widetilde{X}$. The most remarkable fact in Relation (6) is that the mask-correction is performed *on-the-fly* during the computation of $F(X)$. The induced overhead is negligible compared to the whole calculus and the simplicity of the mask-correction operations makes it easy to evaluate the DPA-resistance of the method with the model introduced in Section 2. However, a direct implementation of this relation is not secure since the output and some intermediate results are unmasked. In particular, as $R_1 \cdot \widetilde{X}$ equals $R_1 \cdot \overline{X}$ (where $\overline{X}$ denotes the two-complement of X), the scalar multiplication $R_1 \cdot \widetilde{X}$ has a flaw when X equals the all-one vector (see [12] for the description of an attack exploiting such a flaw). To circumvent this default, the variable $\widetilde{X}$ must be masked by a random value R_2 independent of R_1.

In the following, we present a modified version of Relation (6) whose straightforward implementation is DPA-resistant (as proved in Section 3.3):

$$(-1)^{(\widetilde{X} \oplus R_2) \cdot R_1} F(X) + R_3 =$$
$$\left\lfloor \frac{1}{2^n} \left(R' + \sum_{A \in \mathbb{F}_2^n} \widehat{F}(A)(-1)^{A \cdot \widetilde{X} \oplus R_1 \cdot (\widetilde{X} \oplus A \oplus R_2)} \right) \right\rfloor \ , \tag{7}$$

where $R' = 2^n R_3 + R_4$ with $R_3, R_4 \in \mathbb{F}_2^n$. The $2n$-bit vector R' is used to mask the intermediate results of the summation.

Implementation Aspects. In the following, we denote by SP a function which computes $(-1)^{X \cdot Y}$ from a couple (X, Y) and by $AM2BM$ a procedure which transforms an arithmetic masking into a boolean masking:

$$AM2BM : (sign, sign \times X + R, R) \mapsto X \oplus R \ , \tag{8}$$

where $sign = \pm 1$.

From Relation (7), we deduce the following algorithm which computes the boolean masked output of an S-Box from a boolean masked input:

Algorithm 1. Computation of a boolean masked S-Box output from a boolean masked input

---

INPUTS: A masked input $\tilde{X} = X \oplus R_1$, the input mask R_1 and a lookup table $\widehat{F}$
OUTPUT: The couple $(F(X) \oplus R_3, R_3)$

---

1 Pick up three n-bit random R_2, R_3 and R_4
2 $result \leftarrow 2^n R_3 + R_4$
3 **for** A **from** 0 **to** $2^n - 1$ **do**
4 $\quad T_1 \leftarrow \text{SP}(A, \tilde{X})$ $\qquad\qquad\qquad\qquad\qquad\qquad\qquad [T_1 = (-1)^{A \cdot \tilde{X}}]$
5 $\quad T_2 \leftarrow \tilde{X} \oplus A$ $\qquad\qquad\qquad\qquad\qquad\qquad\qquad\quad [T_2 = \tilde{X} \oplus A]$
6 $\quad T_2 \leftarrow T_2 \oplus R_2$ $\qquad\qquad\qquad\qquad\qquad\qquad\quad [T_2 = \tilde{X} \oplus A \oplus R_2]$
7 $\quad T_2 \leftarrow \text{SP}(R_1, T_2)$ $\qquad\qquad\qquad\qquad\qquad [T_2 = (-1)^{R_1 \cdot (\tilde{X} \oplus A \oplus R_2)}]$
8 $\quad T_2 \leftarrow T_1 \times T_2$ $\qquad\qquad\qquad\qquad [T_2 = (-1)^{A \cdot \tilde{X} \oplus R_1 \cdot (\tilde{X} \oplus A \oplus R_2)}]$
9 $\quad T_2 \leftarrow T_2 \times \widehat{F}(A)$ $\qquad\qquad\quad [T_2 = \widehat{F}(A)(-1)^{A \cdot \tilde{X} \oplus R_1 \cdot (\tilde{X} \oplus A \oplus R_2)}]$
10 $\quad result \leftarrow result + T_2$ $\quad [result = 2^n R_3 + R_4 + \sum\limits_{i \in \{0, A\}} \widehat{F}(i)(-1)^{i \cdot \tilde{X} \oplus R_1 \cdot (\tilde{X} \oplus i \oplus R_2)}]$

11 $result \leftarrow result >> n$ $\qquad\qquad\qquad [result = (-1)^{(\tilde{X} \oplus R_2) \cdot R_1} F(X) + R_3]$
12 $T_1 \leftarrow \tilde{X} \oplus R_2$ $\qquad\qquad\qquad\qquad\qquad\qquad\qquad [T_1 = \tilde{X} \oplus R_2]$
13 $T_1 \leftarrow \text{SP}(T_1, R_1)$ $\qquad\qquad\qquad\qquad\qquad [T_1 = (-1)^{(\tilde{X} \oplus R_2) \cdot R_1}]$
14 $result \leftarrow \text{AM2BM}(T_1, result, R_3)$ $\qquad\qquad\qquad [result = F(X) \oplus R_3]$
15 **Return** $(result, R_3)$

In Algorithm 1, the lookup table $\widehat{F}$ is always accessed 2^n times in a way which is independent of the input X. The values X and R_1 only impact the combination of the values $\widehat{F}(A)$.

Random values R_3 and R_4 aim at masking the content of the buffer *result*. Before the right-shift operation of Step 11, the least significant half part of *result* contains the value R_4. After Step 11, the content of *result* equals the value $(-1)^{(\tilde{X} \oplus R_2) \cdot R_1} F(X) + R_3$ left-padded with zeros.

Computation performed in Step 14 (*cf.* Relation (8)) is essentially a transformation of an arithmetic masking into a boolean masking. Goubin [14] and Coron *et al.* [7] proposed DPA-resistant implementations of such a computation. To implement AM2BM we use a slightly modified version of Goubin's method which outputs $(X \oplus R, R)$ from $(X - R, R)$. To take into account the *sign* parameter, we use Goubin's algorithm with $(sign \times (sign \times X + R), -sign \times R)$ as input.

Efficiency of Algorithm 1 is strongly related to the dimension n of the S-Box since the lookup table $\widehat{F}$ contains 2^n signed integers belonging to $[-2^{2n}; 2^{2n}]$ and is accessed 2^n times. For $n = 8$, $\widehat{F}$ requires at most 544 bytes of ROM (which is reduced to 512 bytes if all the values $\widehat{F}(A)$ are even, which is often the case for cryptographic functions F) and it is accessed 256 times for each execution of Algorithm 1. The overhead becomes significantly smaller when $n = 4$: in this case only 16 access to the 18-byte lookup table $\widehat{F}$ are required (if all the values $\widehat{F}(A)$ are even, $\widehat{F}$ can be stored over 16 bytes).

3.3   Security Analysis

In this section we analyse the security of Algorithm 1. From Proposition 2, Algorithm 1 is DPA-resistant if and only if all the intermediate values $I_i(X, Z_i)$ are independent of the input X.

We do not focus on Step 14 since Goubin shows in [14, §4.3] that all the intermediate values that appear during the execution of his algorithm are independent of the input.

In Table 1, we list the different sensitive intermediate results $I_i(X, Z_i)$ which appear during the execution of Algorithm 1. The values which only depend on the loop counter or on a random value are obviously omitted:

Table 1. The different sensitive values manipulated during Algorithm 1

Step i	Instruction	Intermediate results $I_i(X, Z_i)$	Z_i
4.1	$reg \leftarrow \widetilde{X}$	$\widetilde{X}$	R_1
4.2	$T_1 \leftarrow \mathrm{SP}(A, \widetilde{X})$	$(\ 1)^{A \cdot \widetilde{X}}$	R_1
5	$T_2 \leftarrow \widetilde{X} \oplus A$	$\widetilde{X} \oplus A$	R_1
6	$T_2 \leftarrow T_2 \oplus R_2$	$\widetilde{X} \oplus A \oplus R_2$	(R_1, R_2)
7	$T_2 \leftarrow \mathrm{SP}(R_1, T_2)$	$(-1)^{R_1 \cdot (\widetilde{X} \oplus A \oplus R_2)}$	(R_1, R_2)
8	$T_2 \leftarrow T_1 \times T_2$	$(-1)^{A \cdot \widetilde{X} \oplus R_1 \cdot (\widetilde{X} \oplus A \oplus R_2)}$	(R_1, R_2)
9	$T_2 \leftarrow T_2 \times \widehat{F}(A)$	$\widehat{F}(A)(-1)^{A \cdot \widetilde{X} \oplus R_1 \cdot (\widetilde{X} \oplus A \oplus R_2)}$	(R_1, R_2)
10	$result \leftarrow result + T_2$	$2^n R_3 + R_4$ $+ \sum_i \widehat{F}(i)(-1)^{i \cdot \widetilde{X} \oplus R_1 \cdot (\widetilde{X} \oplus i \oplus R_2)}$	(R_1, R_2, R_3, R_4)
11	$result \leftarrow result >> n$	$(-1)^{(\widetilde{X} \oplus R_2) \cdot R_1} F(X) + R_3$	(R_1, R_2, R_3)
12	$T_1 \leftarrow \widetilde{X} \oplus R_2$	$\widetilde{X} \oplus R_2$	(R_1, R_2)
13	$T_1 \leftarrow \mathrm{SP}(T_1, R_1)$	$(-1)^{(\widetilde{X} \oplus R_2) \cdot R_1}$	(R_1, R_2)

To establish the independency of these intermediate values $I_i(X, Z_i)$ with X, we use the following lemma:

Lemma 1. *Let* $\alpha \in \mathbb{F}_2^n$ *be arbitrary and let* β *be uniformly distributed over* $\mathbb{F}_2^n$ *and independent of* α. *The variable* $\alpha \oplus \beta$ *is uniformly distributed and independent of* α. *The same holds for* $(-1)^{\alpha \oplus \beta}$ *if* $n = 1$.

The proof of this lemma is straightforward and therefore omitted.

The sensitive values $I_i(X, Z_i)$ can be divided into two groups:

1. the ones which are masked by adding or by XORing a random value: $\widetilde{X}$, $\widetilde{X} \oplus A$, $\widetilde{X} \oplus A \oplus R_2$, $\widetilde{X} \oplus R_2$ and $result$ in Steps 10 and 11,

2. the other values: $(-1)^{A \cdot \tilde{X}}$, $(-1)^{(\tilde{X} \oplus R_2) \cdot R_1}$, $(-1)^{R_1 \cdot (\tilde{X} \oplus A \oplus R_2)}$,
   $(-1)^{A \cdot \tilde{X} \oplus R_1 \cdot (\tilde{X} \oplus A \oplus R_2)}$ and $(-1)^{A \cdot \tilde{X} \oplus R_1 \cdot (\tilde{X} \oplus A \oplus R_2)} \widehat{F}(A)$.

The values belonging to the first group have a boolean or an arithmetic mask which is chosen uniformly at random, so it is obvious that they are independent of the input.

Now, let us analyse the values belonging to the second group:

- In the case $A = 0$, the variable $(-1)^{A \cdot \tilde{X}} = (-1)^{A \cdot (X \oplus R_1)}$ is always equal to 1 and so it is independent of X. When $A \neq 0$, the independency of the variables $(-1)^{A \cdot X \oplus A \cdot R_1}$ and $A \cdot X$ is established by applying Lemma 1 to $\alpha = A \cdot X$ and $\beta = A \cdot R_1$. Since the variable X only appears in the term $A \cdot X$, one deduces that $(-1)^{A \cdot X \oplus A \cdot R_1}$ is independent of X.

- By noticing that $(\tilde{X} \oplus R_2) \cdot R_1 = \overline{X} \cdot R_1 \oplus R_2 \cdot R_1$, one deduces in a similar way from Lemma 1 that variables $(-1)^{(\tilde{X} \oplus R_2) \cdot R_1}$ and $(-1)^{R_1 \cdot (\tilde{X} \oplus A \oplus R_2)}$ are independent of X.

- As $A \cdot \tilde{X} + R_1 \cdot (\tilde{X} \oplus A \oplus R_2)$ equals $A \cdot X \oplus \overline{X} \cdot R_1 \oplus R_2 \cdot R_1$, Lemma 1 implies that the variables $(-1)^{A \cdot \tilde{X} + R_1 \cdot (\tilde{X} \oplus A \oplus R_2)}$ and X are independent. The same conclusion holds for $(-1)^{A \cdot \tilde{X} + R_1 \cdot (\tilde{X} \oplus A \oplus R_2)} \widehat{F}(A)$.

We proved above that all the values $I_i(X, Z_i)$ manipulated during the execution of Algorithm 1 are independent of the input X. From Proposition 2, we thus deduce that our method is DPA-resistant, *i.e.* that its Advantage is null.

In the next section, we apply our method to protect S-Boxes access of AES and FOX. In the first case, we compare its performances with the ones of two other well-known countermeasures.

4   Applications

4.1   DPA-Resistant AES Implementation

Before the final choice for the Advanced Encryption Standard (AES) [10], several papers had investigated the security of the AES candidates against side-channel attacks, especially DPA [5,9,20]. Since 2000, many countermeasures have been proposed to counteract DPA on AES[2].

To counteract DPA, Kocher proposed in [18] a very simple and generic solution which can be applied to protect an AES implementation. It consists in using the lookup table F^* defined by $X \mapsto F[X \oplus R_1] \oplus R_2$, where R_1 and R_2 are two random values generated for each new execution of the algorithm. The main drawback of this solution is the large amount of RAM required to store F^*. Indeed, this kind of memory is very limited on embedded devices.

Another method called *Transformed Masking Method* (TMM) has been presented in [1]. However, it has a weakness when computing the AES S-Box

---

[2] A survey of the proposed countermeasures is done in [8].

(*cf.* [12]). In order to fix this flaw, several papers have been published (*cf.* [12,23] for example).

In the two methods above, the AES S-Box, which performs an inversion in $\mathbb{F}_{2^8}$ with 0 being mapped to 0, is implemented through a lookup table. Rijmen presented in [27] an alternative idea which essentially consists in using efficient combinational logic. In this approach, each element a of $\mathbb{F}_{2^8}$ is represented as a linear polynomial $a_h x + a_l$ over $\mathbb{F}_{2^4}$. The inversion of such a polynomial can be computed as follows when it is different from zero: $(a_h x + a_l)^{-1} = a_h' x + a_l'$ where $a_h' = a_h \times d^{-1}$ and $a_l' = (a_h + a_l) \times d^{-1}$ with $d = (a_h^2 \times \{e\}) + (a_h \times a_l) + a_l^2$ and with $\{e\}$ denoting the hexadecimal value 0x0E (*cf.* [26, §3.3]).

Rijmen's remark has been used in [24,23,32,30] to fix the flaw of TMM when accessing S-Box: the so-called *Tower Field Methods* perform the inversion in $\mathbb{F}_{2^8}$ by using masked multiplications and masked inversions in $\mathbb{F}_{2^4}$ or $\mathbb{F}_{2^2}$.

In the following algorithm, we present a new way to implement the AES S-Box based on the method presented in Section 3. As this method is much faster in $\mathbb{F}_{2^{n/2}}$ than in $\mathbb{F}_{2^n}$, we use Rijmen's remark to perform the computations in $\mathbb{F}_{2^4}$ instead of $\mathbb{F}_{2^8}$. We denote by $\widehat{Inv}_{\mathbb{F}_{2^4}}$ the Fourier transform of the inverse over $\mathbb{F}_{2^4}$ where the element 0 is mapped to itself, and by *map* the isomorphism defined in [26] which takes an element a of $\mathbb{F}_{2^8}$ as input and outputs the coefficients of the corresponding linear polynomial $a_h x + a_l$ over $\mathbb{F}_{2^4}$.

Algorithm 2. Inversion of a masked element $\widetilde{a} = a \oplus m_a$ in $\mathbb{F}_{2^8}$

INPUTS: $(\widetilde{a} = a \oplus m_a, m_a) \in \mathbb{F}_{2^8}{}^2$
OUTPUT: $(\widetilde{a^{-1}} = a^{-1} \oplus m_a', m_a')$

1 Pick up three 4-bit random m_d, m_h' and m_l'
2 $(m_h, m_l) \in \mathbb{F}_{2^4}^2 \leftarrow map(m_a)$
3 $(\widetilde{a_h}, \widetilde{a_l}) \in \mathbb{F}_{2^4}^2 \leftarrow map(\widetilde{a})$ $\qquad$ $[(\widetilde{a_h}, \widetilde{a_l}) = (a_h \oplus m_h, a_l \oplus m_l)]$
4 $\widetilde{d} \leftarrow \widetilde{a_h}^2 \otimes \{e\} \oplus \widetilde{a_h} \otimes \widetilde{a_l} \oplus \widetilde{a_l}^2 \oplus m_d \oplus \widetilde{a_h} \otimes m_l$ $\qquad$ $[\widetilde{d} = d \oplus m_d]$
$\qquad \oplus \widetilde{a_l} \otimes m_h \oplus m_h^2 \otimes \{e\} \oplus m_l^2 \oplus m_h \otimes m_l$
5 $(\widetilde{d^{-1}}, m_{d-1}) \leftarrow$ Algorithm 1$(\widetilde{d}, m_d, \widehat{Inv}_{\mathbb{F}_{2^4}})$ $\qquad$ $[\widetilde{d^{-1}} = d^{-1} \oplus m_{d-1}]$
6 $\widetilde{a_h'} \leftarrow \widetilde{a_h} \otimes \widetilde{d^{-1}} \oplus m_h' \oplus m_h \otimes \widetilde{d^{-1}} \oplus m_{d-1} \otimes \widetilde{a_h} \oplus m_{d-1} \otimes m_h$ $\qquad$ $[\widetilde{a_h'} = a_h' \oplus m_h']$
7 $\widetilde{a_l'} \leftarrow \widetilde{a_l} \otimes \widetilde{d^{-1}} \oplus m_l' \oplus \widetilde{a_h'} \oplus \widetilde{d^{-1}} \otimes m_l \oplus \widetilde{a_l} \otimes m_{d-1} \oplus m_h' \oplus m_l \otimes m_{d-1}$ $\qquad$ $[\widetilde{a_l'} = a_l' \oplus m_l']$
8 $m_a' \leftarrow map^{-1}(m_h', m_l')$
9 $\widetilde{a^{-1}} \leftarrow map^{-1}(\widetilde{a_h'}, \widetilde{a_l'})$ $\qquad$ $[\widetilde{a^{-1}} = a^{-1} \oplus m_a']$
10 **Return** $(\widetilde{a^{-1}}, m_a')$

Steps 1 to 4 and Steps 6 to 9 have been proved to be DPA-resistant in [23].

In the following table, we compare our method applied to AES with two other countermeasures. The three implementations use boolean masking of the intermediate results except when accessing S-Boxes where we use:
 – Algorithm 2,
 – Oswald *et al.*'s method [23,24]. It only differs from Algorithm 2 in its approach to compute the inversion of $\widetilde{d} \in \mathbb{F}_{16}$. In [23,24], the inversion is

performed by going down to $\mathbb{F}_4$ and its complexity approximatively equals the one of Algorithm 2 excluding the 5th Step which is replaced by a square operation (since the inversion operation in $\mathbb{F}_4$ is equivalent to squaring),
– Trichina *et al.*'s method [31] which uses log- and alog-tables.[3]

The timings were obtained with a CPU running at 8 MHz.

Table 2. Comparison of several methods to protect AES against DPA

Method	Timings (ms)	RAM (bytes)	ROM (bytes)
Straightforward implementation	5	32	1150
This paper (Algo. 2)	32	39	3100
Oswald *et al.* [23,24]	26	42	3400
Trichina *et al.* [31]	21	291	3050

To test the DPA-resistance of our method in practice, we mount a DPA attack on the implementation described above. The results are given in Appendix A.

4.2 DPA-Resistant FOX Implementation

In [16], Junod and Vaudenay introduce a new family of block ciphers called FOX. The non-linear part of a FOX-algorithm is ensured by an S-Box S. It consists in a Laï-Massey scheme with three rounds taking three different small S-Boxes as round functions; these functions, denoted by S_1, S_2 and S_3, operate on 4-bit words.

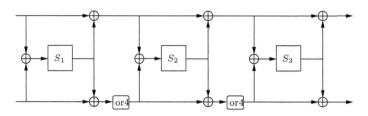

Fig. 1. Structure of the S-Box of FOX

In Figure 1, the `or4` operation consists in a single round of a 4-bit Feistel scheme with the identity function as round function: for every $X = (x_0, x_1, x_2, x_3) \in \mathbb{F}_2^4$, we have $\mathsf{or4}(X) = (x_2, x_3, x_0 \oplus x_2, x_1 \oplus x_3)$.

For every n-bit vector X, let us denote by X^l and X^r the two $\frac{n}{2}$-bit vectors such that $X = X^l || X^r$. To thwart DPA attack during the S-Box calculations, we perform the following algorithm which inherits the security of Algorithm 1:

---

[3] Trichina *et al.*'s method seems to have a flaw with regard to the Zero Value Attack (*cf.* [25]). Thus, its DPA-resistance is not well-established yet.

Algorithm 3. Secure computation of FOX S-Box

INPUTS: $\widetilde{X} = X \oplus R_1$ and R_1 in $\mathbb{F}_2^8$

OUTPUT: $S(X) \oplus R_2$ and R_2, where R_2 is a random vector

1 $T_1 \leftarrow \widetilde{X}^l$; $T_2 \leftarrow \widetilde{X}^r$; $T_3 \leftarrow R_1^l$; $T_4 \leftarrow R_1^r$

2 **for** i **from** 1 **to** 3 **do**

3     $(\widetilde{\text{result}}, \text{mask}) \leftarrow$ **Algorithm 1**$(T_1 \oplus T_2, T_3 \oplus T_4, \widehat{S_i})$

4     $T_2 \leftarrow \widetilde{\text{result}} \oplus T_2$

5     $T_4 \leftarrow \text{mask} \oplus T_4$

6   **if** $i \neq 3$ **then**

7         $T_1 \leftarrow \mathbf{or4}(\widetilde{\text{result}} \oplus T_1)$; $T_3 \leftarrow \mathbf{or4}(\text{mask} \oplus T_3)$

8   **else**

9         $T_1 \leftarrow \widetilde{\text{result}} \oplus T_1$; $T_3 \leftarrow \text{mask} \oplus T_3$

10 $\widetilde{\text{result}} \leftarrow (T_1 << 4) \oplus T_2$; $\text{mask} \leftarrow (T_3 << 4) \oplus T_4$

11 **Return** $(\widetilde{\text{result}}, \text{mask})$

Because the S-Boxes S_i of FOX operate on 4-bit vectors, computing their outputs by use of Algorithm 1 only implies 16 lookup table's access for each S_i. It is possible to check that this overhead is much smaller than the overhead induced by previous S-Box secure calculation methods.

5 Conclusion and Perspectives

In this paper, we describe a new and generic method based on the Fourier transform to obtain DPA-resistant S-Box implementations. After introducing a security model to resist DPA, we prove the resistance of our proposal. Since our method does not rely on specific S-Box properties, it can be applied to any symmetric cryptosystem. It is very efficient when the S-Box is applied to small fields such as FOX's or when the computations can be performed in vector spaces of small dimensions. In particular, we apply our method to AES and we evaluate in practice the efficiency and the resistance of the corresponding implementation.

This work raises two interesting open problems. The first one is to upgrade our security model and our method to take into account high-order DPA attacks. The second one is to find other transformations or operators which allow us to compute a masked output of an S-Box from a masked input, without revealing information on the sensitive data.

References

1. M.-L. Akkar and C. Giraud. An Implementation of DES and AES, Secure against Some Attacks. In *CHES 2001*, vol. 2162 of *LNCS*, pages 309–318. Springer, 2001.
2. M.-L. Akkar and L. Goubin. A Generic Protection against High-Order Differential Power Analysis. In *FSE 2003*, vol. 2887 of *LNCS*, pages 192–205. Springer, 2003.

3. J. Blömer, J. G. Merchan, and V. Krummel. Provably Secure Masking of AES. In *SAC 2004*, vol. 3357 of *LNCS*, pages 69–83. Springer, 2004.
4. E. Brier, C. Clavier, and F. Olivier. Correlation Power Analysis with a Leakage Model. In *CHES 2004*, vol. 3156 of *LNCS*, pages 16–29. Springer, 2004.
5. S. Chari, C. Jutla, J. Rao, and P. Rohatgi. A Cautionary Note Regarding Evaluation of AES Candidates on Smart-Cards. In *AES 2*, March 1999.
6. S. Chari, C. Jutla, J. Rao, and P. Rohatgi. Towards Sound Approaches to Counteract Power-Analysis Attacks. In *CRYPTO '99*, vol. 1666 of *LNCS*, pages 398–412. Springer, 1999.
7. J.-S. Coron and A. Tchulkine. A New Algorithm for Switching from Arithmetic to Boolean Masking. In *CHES 2003*, vol. 2779 of *LNCS*, pages 89–97. Springer, 2003.
8. N. Courtois and L. Goubin. An Algebraic Masking Method to Protect Against Power Attacks. In *ICISC 2005*, vol. 3935 of *LNCS*. Springer, 2006.
9. J. Daemen and V. Rijmen. Resistance Against Implementation Attacks: A Comparative Study of the AES Proposals. In *AES 2*, March 1999.
10. FIPS PUB 197. *Advanced Encryption Standard*. National Institute of Standards and Technology, 2001.
11. FIPS PUB 46. *The Data Encryption Standard*. National Bureau of Standards, January 1977.
12. J. Golić and C. Tymen. Multiplicative Masking and Power Analysis of AES. In *CHES 2002*, vol. 2523 of *LNCS*, pages 198–212. Springer, 2002.
13. L. Goubin and J. Patarin. DES and Differential Power Analysis – The Duplication Method. In *CHES '99*, vol. 1717 of *LNCS*, pages 158–172. Springer, 1999.
14. L. Goubin. A Sound Method for Switching between Boolean and Arithmetic Masking. In *CHES 2001*, vol. 2162 of *LNCS*, pages 3–15. Springer, 2001.
15. S. Gueron, O. Parzanchevsky, and O. Zuk. Masked Inversion in $GF(2^n)$ Using Mixed Field Representations and its Efficient Implementation for AES. In *Embedded Cryptographic Hardware: Methodologies and Architectures*, pages 213–228. Nova Science Publishers, 2004.
16. P. Junod and S. Vaudenay. FOX: a new family of block ciphers. In *SAC 2004*, vol. 3357 of *LNCS*, pages 114–129. Springer, 2004.
17. P. Kocher, J. Jaffe, and B. Jun. Differential Power Analysis. In *CRYPTO '99*, vol. 1666 of *LNCS*, pages 388–397. Springer, 1999.
18. P. Kocher. Timing Attacks on Implementations of Diffie-Hellman, RSA, DSS, and Other Systems. In *CRYPTO '96*, vol. 1109 of *LNCS*, pages 104–113. Springer, 1996.
19. S. Kunz-Jacques, F. Muller, and F. Valette. The Davies-Murphy Power Attack. In *ASIACRYPT 2004*, vol. 3329 of *LNCS*, pages 451–467. Springer, 2004.
20. T. Messerges. Securing the AES Finalists Against Power Analysis Attacks. In *FSE 2000*, vol. 1978 of *LNCS*, pages 150–164. Springer, 2000.
21. T. Messerges. Using Second-Order Power Analysis to Attack DPA Resistant software. In *CHES 2000*, vol. 1965 of *LNCS*, pages 238–251. Springer, 2000.
22. R. Oppligern. *Contemporary Cryptography*. ARTECH House, 2005.
23. E. Oswald, S. Mangard, N. Pramstaller, and V. Rijmen. A Side-Channel Analysis Resistant Description of the AES S-box. In *FSE 2005*, vol. 3557 of *LNCS*, pages 413–423. Springer, 2005.
24. E. Oswald, S. Mangard, and N. Pramstaller. Secure and Efficient Masking of AES – A Mission Impossible ? Cryptology ePrint Archive, Report 2004/134, 2004. http://eprint.iacr.org/.
25. E. Oswald and K. Schramm. An Efficient Masking Scheme for AES Software Implementations. In *WISA 2005*, vol. 3786 of *LNCS*, pages 292–305. Springer, 2006.

26. C. Paar. *VLSI Architectures for Bit Parallel Computations in Galois Fields*. PhD thesis, Universität Essen, 1994.
27. V. Rijmen. Efficient Implementation of the Rijndael S-box, 2000. Available at http://www.esat.kuleuwen.ac.be/~rijmen/rijndael/sbox.pdf.
28. A. Rudra, P. K. Bubey, C. S. Jutla, V. Kumar, J. Rao, and P. Rohatgi. Efficient Rijndael Encryption Implementation with Composite Field Arithmetic. In *CHES 2001*, vol. 2162 of *LNCS*, pages 171–184. Springer, 2001.
29. E. Trichina, D. DeSeta, and L. Germani. Simplified Adaptive Multiplicative Masking for AES. In *CHES 2002*, vol. 2523 of *LNCS*, pages 187–197. Springer, 2002.
30. E. Trichina, L. Korkishko, and K. H. Lee. Small Size, Low Power, Side Channel-Immune AES Coprocessor, Design and Synthesis Results. In *AES 4*, vol. 3373 of *LNCS*, pages 113–127. Springer, 2005.
31. E. Trichina and L. Korkishko. Secure and Efficient AES Software Implementation for Smart Cards. In *WISA 2004*, vol. 3325 of *LNCS*, pages 425–439. Springer, 2004.
32. E. Trichina. Combinatorial Logic Design for AES SubByte Transformation on Masked Data. Cryptology ePrint Archive, Report 2003/236, 2003. http://eprint.iacr.org/.

A   Practical Evaluation of Our Method Applied to AES

In this section we present the results of a practical evaluation of our method applied to AES (*cf.* Section 4.1). The implementation was done on a 8-bit smart card on which we do not activate the different hardware countermeasures. Concerning the statistical treatment, we use an improvement of traditional DPA called *Correlation Power Analysis* (CPA) (*cf.* [4]).

Firstly, we attack a straightforward implementation of the AES when accessing the first S-Box during the first round. By using the selection function equal to the Hamming weight of the output of the S-Box, we obtain the result depicted in Figure 2 after 100 executions of the algorithm. The value of the sub-key used by the S-Box is recovered with only 30 executions of the algorithm.

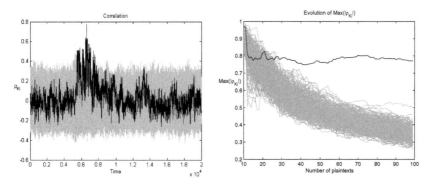

Fig. 2. CPA on non-masked AES S-Box implementation using 100 random plaintexts

Secondly, we perform the same attack against our DPA-resistant method (*cf.* Algorithm 2) by using 20 000 executions of the algorithm. As shown in Figure 3, the attack fails. We also apply CPA by using several other selection functions such as the Hamming weight of the input of the S-Box. All these attacks fail in the same way.

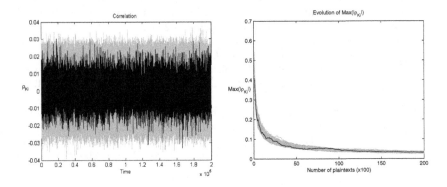

Fig. 3. CPA on Algorithm 2 using 20 000 random plaintexts

The Outer Limits of RFID Security

Ari Juels

RSA Laboratories
Bedford, MA 01730, USA
ajuels@rsasecurity.com

It is tempting to regard RFID security and privacy primarily as questions of cryptographic protocol design. We would like RFID tags to authenticate themselves in a trustworthy manner. We would also like them to protect the identities and personal data of their bearers. We might imagine that our aims should be to squeeze cryptographic primitives down to the constrained environments of RFID tags and to craft protocols that scale up to populations of millions or billions of devices. By adapting existing tools, it might seem that we can readily fulfill the majority of our needs with some more circuitry in tags, a greater abundance of cycles and memory on application servers, and a bit of clever economizing.

Ultimately, however, the issues of RFID security and privacy extend well beyond the confines of this neat, conventional picture. At the outer limits of research on RFID security today is a great variety of topics, including:

- *Side channels:* The best logical-layer protocols are in vain if RFID tags are insecure at other layers. For example, as a surprising challenge to RFID privacy, recent research has shown that "dead" tags may be detectable and even classifiable based on their RF signatures. What is the impact (negative and positive) of such information channels?
- *Covert channels:* RFID tags may be viewed loosely as sensors. They will increasingly act as such, gathering and transmitting data about their ambient environment. What can we say about the risk that they are covertly transmitting more?
- *Human-implantable RFID:* Surgically implantable RFID tags for medical identification and access control are commercially available today. What are the security and privacy implications of such "prosthetic biometrics?"
- *Ramping up security:* Moore's Law—or pressing security needs—may someday democratize cryptography among RFID devices. This is likely to happen when there exists a legacy RFID infrastructure with limited support for security. How can we accommodate growing RFID-security needs more gracefully than we have for the Internet?
- *Cooperative architectures:* A spectrum of devices with varying capabilities will operate in the RFID domain. How can high-resource devices assist low-resource ones through simulation and audit?

It is evident that RFID devices are not mere propagators of information, but devices whose physical characteristics and operating environments give rise to rich medley of security challenges and tools.

L. Goubin and M. Matsui (Eds.): CHES 2006, LNCS 4249, p. 231, 2006.

Three-Phase Dual-Rail Pre-charge Logic

Marco Bucci[1], Luca Giancane[2],
Raimondo Luzzi[1], and Alessandro Trifiletti[2]

[1] Infineon Technologies AG
[2] University of Rome "La Sapienza"
{marco.bucci, raimondo.luzzi}@infineon.com
{giancane, trifiletti}@die.mail.uniroma1.it

Abstract. This paper investigates the design of a dual-rail pre-charge logic family whose power consumption is insensitive to unbalanced load conditions thus allowing adopting a semi-custom design flow (automatic place & route) without any constraint on the routing of the complementary wires. The proposed logic is based on a three phase operation where, in order to obtain a constant energy consumption over the operating cycle, an additional discharge phase is performed after pre-charge and evaluation. In this work, the proposed concept has been implemented as an enhancement of the SABL logic with a limited increase in circuit complexity. Implementation details and simulation results are reported which show a power consumption independent of the sequence of processed data and load capacitances. An improvement in the energy consumption balancing up to 100 times with respect to SABL has been obtained.

Keywords: DPA, dual-rail logic, SABL, security.

1 Introduction

Side channel attacks can reveal confidential data (i.e. cryptographic keys and user PIN's) exploiting the information leaked by the hardware implementation of cryptographic algorithms. In particular, power analysis attacks, simple and differential, are based on the fact that logic operations feature a power consumption profile dependent on the processed data: with simple statistical analyses of a sufficient number of power traces, the correlation between the circuit switching activity and the key material can be revealed [1,2,3,4].

In the recent years, a wide spectrum of countermeasures against differential power analysis (DPA) have been proposed in the technical literature. In a classification which takes into account the involved abstraction level during the design flow, three classes can be defined: system-level, gate-level and transistor-level countermeasures.

System-level techniques include adding noise to the device power consumption [5], duplicating logics with complementary operations [6], active supply current filtering with power consumption compensation [7], passive filtering, battery on chip and detachable power supply [8]. Notice that some of the mentioned countermeasures have a pure theoretical interest since, with the current

L. Goubin and M. Matsui (Eds.): CHES 2006, LNCS 4249, pp. 232–241, 2006.

state of the art, their employment to design tamper resistant cryptographic devices (e.g. chipcard microcontrollers) is limited by technological and cost constraints.

As gate-level countermeasures, techniques that can be implemented using logic gates available in a standard-cell library are intended, e.g. random masking [9], random pre-charging [10], state transitions and Hamming weight balancing, random delay insertion [11]. Random masking is the most studied but, as it has been recently proved [12,13], implementations in an automatic synthesis flow starting from a HDL description, can be still attacked exploiting glitches generated in the combinatorial networks when the random masks are applied.

Finally, the transistor-level approach is based on the adoption of a logic style whose power consumption is constant or independent of the processed data. In a dual-rail pre-charge (DRP) logic style (e.g. SABL [14], WDDL [15], Dual-Spacer DRP[16]), signals are encoded as two complementary wires and power consumption is constant under the hypothesis that the differential outputs of each gate drive the same capacitive load. Dual-rail pre-charge logics are not affected by glitches but building two balanced wires requires a full-custom approach thus increasing design and maintenance costs.

Recently, semi-custom design flows with support differential logic families have been proposed in the technical literature. An approach based on a technique for the automatic routing of balanced complementary lines is reported in [17]. Even if an automatic place and route could sensibly reduce design time and increase the portability, the proposed balanced routing technique does not take into account the dependence of the capacitive load on a line on the logic state of the adjacent wires and, furthermore, introduces additional constraints for the routing tool thus limiting its efficiency and, likely, causing an area overhead especially if only few metal layers are available for the inter-cell routing (as it is the case in a chipcard where the top layers are reserved for shielding). Moreover, in a modern deep sub-micron technology, intra-chip process gradients cannot be neglected and they are the limiting factor for the load matching accuracy.

A second approach proposed in [18] is based on a masked dual-rail pre-charge logic style (MDPL) where, due to the random masking at the gate level, power consumption is randomized. Moreover, since MDPL is a dual-rail pre-charge logic, glitches are avoided but, at the same time, the complementary wires do not need to be balanced thus removing the main drawback of the dual-rail circuits. On the other hand, the authors report in [19] a significant penalty in terms of area and, above all, power consumption with respect to a CMOS implementation.

This paper proposes a further approach to the design of a dual-rail pre-charge logic family which is insensitive to unbalanced load conditions thus allowing adopting a semi-custom design flow (automatic place & route) without additional constraints on the routing of the complementary wires.

The proposed concept is based on a three phase operation where an additional discharge phase is performed after the pre-charge/evaluation steps typical of any dynamic logic style. Although the concept is general, it can be implemented as an improvement of the SABL logic with a limited increase in circuit complexity.

Implementation details and simulation results on a basic set of logic gates are reported in Section 2. A more complex case study is discussed in Section 3 and an extensive comparison with the corresponding SABL implementation is carried out.

2   The Proposed Logic Style

This paper proposes a three-phase dual-rail pre-charge logic (TDPL) where, during the first phase (pre-charge), the output lines of a generic logic gate are both charged to V_{DD}, then (second phase - evaluation) the proper line is discharged to V_{SS} according to the input data, thus generating a new output data. Finally, during the last phase (discharge), the other line is discharged too. As a consequence, since both wires are pre-charged to V_{DD} and discharged to V_{SS}, a TDPL logic gate shows a constant energy consumption over its operating cycle (independent of the input data), even if unbalanced capacitive loads to V_{DD} and/or V_{SS} are taken into account.

The proposed approach can be implemented as an enhancement of the SABL logic style with a minimum increase in the required area. Therefore, throughout this paper, SABL cells are assumed as the benchmark for the equivalent TDPL cells. An inverter is shown in Figure 1, where two additional pull-down NMOS transistors (N_1, N_4) and a PMOS switch (P_1) have been added to the SABL inverter in order to implement the discharge phase.

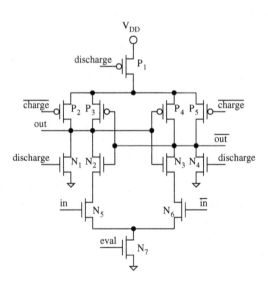

Fig. 1. TDPL inverter

With reference to the timing diagram shown in Figure 2, the circuit operation is the following:

1. charge: at the beginning of each cycle, signal *discharge* goes low, thus closing P1. Signal $\overline{charge}$ goes low too and both output lines are pre-charged to V_{DD}.
2. evaluation: during the charge phase new input data $(in, \overline{in})$ are presented to the circuit. On the raising edge of signal *eval*, N_7 is closed thus discharging one of the output lines according to the input data.
3. discharge: at the end of each operating cycle, input *discharge* is activated in order to pull down (through the additional pull-down transistors N_1, N_4) the output line which has not been discharged during the evaluation phase.

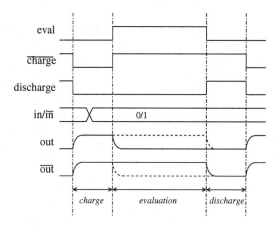

Fig. 2. Timing diagram of the TDPL inverter

More complex gates are obtained changing the pull-down logic. As an example, a 2-input NAND/AND and a XOR/NXOR are depicted in Figure 3.

This basic set of cells has been designed in a $0.12\mu m$ CMOS process from Infineon Technologies. A $1.5V$ supply voltage and a $200MHz$ operating frequency are adopted. Each transistor is designed with a width $W = 0.68\mu m$ and the minimum gate length $L = 0.12\mu m$ is assumed. Simulations are done in Spectre, using BSIM3v3 transistor models.

Table 1. Capacitive loads

	to V_{DD}	to V_{SS}
from *out*	$C_{out}^{VDD} = 8fF$	$C_{out}^{VSS} = 4fF$
from $\overline{out}$	$C_{\overline{out}}^{VDD} = 1fF$	$C_{\overline{out}}^{VSS} = 3fF$

In order to simulate the cells in a real operating condition, the testbench shown in Figure 4 has been defined where, each input to the gate under analysis is driven by a TDPL inverter and unbalanced load capacitances to V_{DD} (C_{out}^{VDD}, $C_{\overline{out}}^{VDD}$) and V_{SS} (C_{out}^{VSS}, $C_{\overline{out}}^{VSS}$) are assumed on the output lines (out, $\overline{out}$).

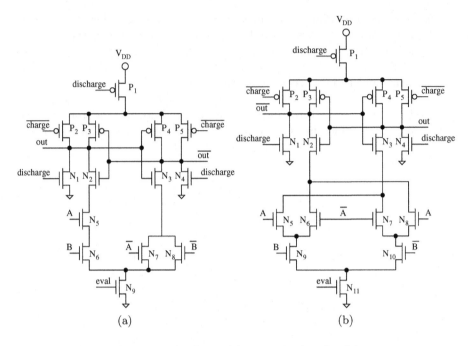

Fig. 3. NAND/AND (a) and XOR/NXOR (b)

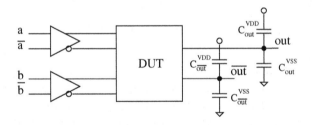

Fig. 4. Simulation testbench

Typical values for the parasitic interconnection capacitances in a standard-cell semi-custom layout are used (Table 1). The same testbench, with SABL inverters on the inputs, has been used to simulate the corresponding SABL cells. In both cases, only the current consumption of the gate under analysis is taken into account and every input data transition is simulated.

For the NAND/AND gate, a superimposition of the power supply current traces $I_{DD}(t)$ for the 16 input transitions is depicted in Figure 5. Both in the SABL and the TDPL cell, each operation phase can be clearly identified in the supply current profile. Notice that, in unbalanced load conditions, SABL cells show a data dependent current consumption during both pre-charge and evaluation. In the TDPL cells, the pre-charge current pulse is constant while a data dependency is visible in the evaluation and discharge phases.

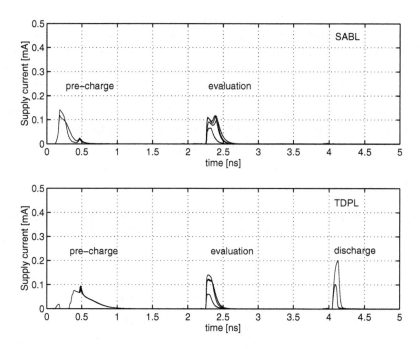

Fig. 5. NAND/AND - superimposition of the power supply current traces: SABL (above) vs. TDPL (bottom)

As in [14], the energy per cycle $E = V_{DD} \cdot \int_0^T I_{DD}(t)dt$ is adopted as figure of merit to measure the resistance against power analysis attacks. The obtained results for the three analyzed gates are summarized in Table 2, where the normalized energy deviation (NED) is defined as $(\max(E) - \min(E))/\max(E)$ and NSD is the normalized standard deviation $\sigma_E/\overline{E}$. As expected, SABL gates are sensible to unbalanced load conditions (NED> 30%, NSD> 15%) thus confirming that a balanced routing must be necessary employed to obtain a constant energy consumption. Vice versa, TDPL cells show an extremely balanced energy consumption (NED< 3%, NSD< 1%) in spite of unbalanced load capacitances.

Table 2. Simulation results for the three basic gates

	INV		NAND/AND		XOR/NXOR	
	SABL[14]	This work	SABL[14]	This work	SABL[14]	This work
$\max(E)$[fJ]	52.3	65.6	56.3	68.3	58.4	69.5
$\min(E)$[fJ]	31.1	65.3	35.2	66.4	39.4	68.0
NED	40.4%	0.4%	37.5%	2.7%	32.6%	2.1%
$\overline{E}$[fJ]	41.7	65.5	50.5	67.3	48.9	68.7
σ_E[fJ]	10.9	0.1	8.0	0.6	8.5	0.4
NSD	26.1%	0.2%	15.9%	0.9%	17.4%	0.6%

From Table 2, it follows that, as expected, an increase in the mean energy per cycle must be taken into account since both output lines are discharged in each cycle. On the contrary, the penalty in terms of silicon area is minimal (16% for the NAND/AND in Figure 3), especially if compared with what is reported for MDPL [19]. With respect to SABL, TDPL requires the routing of an additional signal (*discharge*). However, if at least four metal layers are available for signal routing, an increase in silicon area is not expected, especially in regular structures such as data-paths. Notice that MDPL is affected by a similar drawback due to the routing of the random data for masking.

3   A Case Study

In order to confirm the results discussed in the previous section, a TDPL full adder designed as depicted in Figure 6 has been tested and compared with the

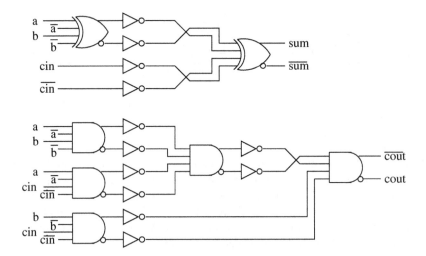

Fig. 6. TDPL full adder

Table 3. Simulation results for the FULLADDER

	FULLADDER	
	SABL[14]	This work
max(E)[fJ]	447.0	609.6
min(E)[fJ]	360.1	604.1
NED	19.4%	0.9%
$\overline{E}$[fJ]	405.6	606.8
σ_E[fJ]	22.1	1.3
NSD	5.4%	0.2%

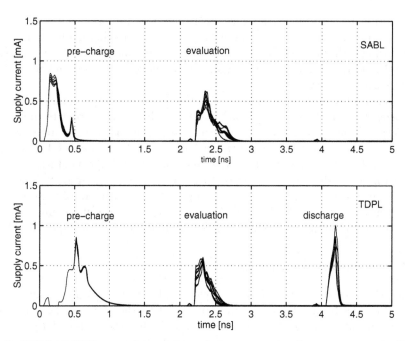

Fig. 7. FULLADDER- superimposition of the power supply current traces: SABL (above) vs. TDPL (bottom)

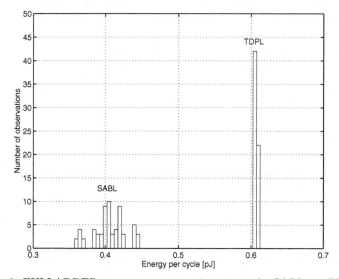

Fig. 8. FULLADDER - energy consumption per cycle: SABL vs. TDPL

equivalent SABL design. An implementation based on XOR/NXOR and NAND/ AND gates is employed and cascaded gates are connected using a Domino logic. The static inverters between two gates do not cause an unbalanced energy consumption because, in each cycle, both inverters on each couple of output wires switch two times (1-0 commutation during the pre-charge phase and a 0-1 event during either the evaluation or the discharge phase). On the contrary, in the SABL approach balanced interconnections between inverter and the following gate are necessary.

As done for the simulation of a single gate, unbalanced capacitances (Table 1) have been used on the output of each SABL/TDPL gate in order to model the routing parasitic capacitances. A superimposition of the power supply current traces $I_{DD}(t)$ for the 64 possible transitions of the 3-bit input $\{A, B, C_{in}\}$ is depicted in Figure 7 for both the SABL and the TDPL implementation.

A histogram of the observed energies per cycle reported in Figure 8 shows that TDPL guarantees a balanced energy consumption, independent of the processed data, even in presence of unbalanced interconnections. Results summarized in Table 3 confirm the improvement which has been obtained with respect to SABL.

4   Conclusions and Future Work

A novel DPA-resistant dual-rail logic style suitable to be used in a semi-custom design flow has been introduced and compared to the state of the art in the technical literature. Experimental results confirm that the proposed logic family shows a constant energy consumption even in presence of asymmetric interconnections. The simulated energy consumption per cycle is up to 100 times more balanced than in the corresponding SABL gates without requiring any constraint on the geometry of the complementary wires. At the same time, the penalty in terms of mean power consumption and silicon area is smaller than in the MDPL style thus representing a valid alternative approach in all the cases where the design and characterization of a new digital library can be afforded.

Further work on a TDPL storage element is planned. Actually, even if TDPL is compatible with SABL flip-flops, a memory element which supports the three phase operation allows to fully exploit the advantages of TDPL.

References

1. P. Kocher, J. Jaffe and B. Jun, *Differential power analysis*, Proc. Advances in Cryptology (CRYPTO '99), Lecture Notes in Computer Science, vol. 1666, Springer-Verlag, pp. 388-397, 1999.
2. T. S. Messerges, E. A. Dabbish and R. H. Sloan, *Examining Smart-Card Security under the Threat of Power Analysis Attacks*, IEEE Trans. Computers, vol. 51, no. 5, pp. 541-552, May 2002.
3. J. Coron, *Resistance Against Differential Power Analysis for Elliptic Curve Cryptosystems*, Proc. Workshop on Cryptographic Hardware and Embedded Systems (CHES '99), Lecture Notes in Computer Science, vol. 1717, Springer-Verlag, pp. 292-302, 1999.
4. C. Clavier, J. Coron and N. Dabbous, *Differential Power Analysis in the Presence of Hardware Countermeasures*, Proc. Workshop on Cryptographic Hardware and Embedded Systems (CHES '00), Lecture Notes in Computer Science, vol. 1965, Springer-Verlag, pp. 252-263, 2000.

5. L. Benini, E. Omerbegovic, A. Macii, M. Poncino, E. Macii, F. Pro, *Energy-aware design techniques for differential power analysis protection*, Proc. Design Automation Conf. (DAT '03), pp. 36-41, 2003.

6. H. Saputra, N. Vijaykrishnan, M. Kandemir, M. J. Irwin, R. Brooks, S. Kim, and W. Zhang, *Masking the energy behavior of DES encryption*, Proc. Design, Automation and Test in Europe Conf. (DAT '03), pp. 84-89, 2003.

7. G. B. Ratanpal, R. D. Williams and T. N. Blalock, *An On-Chip Suppression Countermeasure to Power Analysis Attacks*, IEEE Trans. Dependable and Secure Computing, vol. 1, no. 3, pp. 179-189, July-Sept. 2004.

8. A. Shamir, *Protecting Smart Cards from Passive Power Analysis with Detached Power Supplies*, Proc. Workshop on Cryptographic Hardware and Embedded Systems (CHES '00), Lecture Notes in Computer Science, vol. 1965, Springer-Verlag, pp. 71-77, 2000.

9. J. Dj. Golic and R. Menicocci, *Universal Masking on Logic Gate Level*, Electronics Lett., vol. 40, no. 9, April 2004.

10. M. Bucci, M. Guglielmo, R. Luzzi and A. Trifiletti, *A Power Consumption Randomization Countermeasure for DPA-Resistant Cryptographic Processors*, Proc. Int.l Workshop on Power and Timing Modeling, Optimization and Simulation (PATMOS '04), Lecture Notes in Computer Science, vol. 3254, Springer-Verlag, pp. 481-490, 2004.

11. M. Bucci, M. Guglielmo, R. Luzzi and A. Trifiletti, *A Countermeasure against Differential Power Analysis based on Random Delay Insertion*, Proc. IEEE Int.l Symp. Circuits and Systems (ISCAS '05), pp. 3547-3550, 2005.

12. S. Mangard, T. Popp and B. M. Gammel, *Side-Channel Leakage of Masked CMOS Gates*, Proc. Cryptographers' Track at the RSA Conference (CT-RSA '05), Lecture Note in Computer Science, vol. 3376, Springer-Verlag, pp. 351-365, 2005.

13. S. Mangard, N. Pramstaller and E. Oswald, *Successfully Attacking Masked AES Hardware Implementations*, Proc. Workshop on Cryptographic Hardware and Embedded Systems (CHES '05), Lecture Notes in Computer Science, vol. 3659, Springer-Verlag, pp. 157-171, 2005.

14. K. Tiri, M. Akmal and I. Verbauwhede, *A Dynamic and Differential CMOS Logic with Signal Independent Power Consumption to Withstand Differential Power Analysis on Smart Cards*, Proc. IEEE 28th European Solid-State Circuit Conf. (ESSCIRC '02), 2002.

15. K. Tiri and I. Verbauwhede, *A Logic Design Methodology for a Secure DPA Resistant ASIC or FPGA Implementation*, Proc. Design, Automation and Test in Europe Conference and Exposition (DATE '04), pp. 246-251, 2004.

16. D. Sokolov, J. Murphy, A. Bystrov and A. Yakovlev, *Improving the Security of Dual-Rail Circuits*, Proc. Workshop on Cryptographic Hardware and Embedded Systems (CHES '04), Lecture Notes in Computer Science, vol. 3156, Springer-Verlag, pp. 282-297, 2004.

17. K. Tiri and I. Verbauwhede, *Place and route for secure standard cell design*, Proc. Smart Card Research and Advanced Application IFIP Conf. (CARDIS '04), 2004.

18. T. Popp and S. Mangard, *Masked Dual-Rail Pre-Charge Logic: DPA-Resistance without Routing Constraints*, Proc. Workshop on Cryptographic Hardware and Embedded Systems (CHES '05), Lecture Notes in Computer Science, vol. 3659, Springer-Verlag, pp. 172-186, 2005.

19. T. Popp and S. Mangard, *Implementation Aspects of the DPA-Resistant Logic Style MDPL*, to appear in Proc. IEEE Int.l Symp. Circuits and Systems (ISCAS '06).

Dual-Rail Random Switching Logic: A Countermeasure to Reduce Side Channel Leakage*

Zhimin Chen and Yujie Zhou

Shanghai Jiao Tong University, China
chenzhimin@sjtu.edu.cn, zhou863@vip.sina.com.cn

Abstract. Recent research has shown that cryptographers with glitches are vulnerable in front of Side Channel Attacks (SCA). Since then, several methods, such as Wave Dynamic Differential Logic (WDDL) and Masked Dual-Rail Pre-charge Logic (MDPL), have been presented to make circuits clean. In this paper, we propose a more accurate power model based on logic gates' output transitions and divide it into pieces according to input signals' transformations. Based on our model, we demonstrate that 1-bit masked logic gates with asynchronous inputs always leak side-channel information from their output transitions. Therefore, even those gates designed without glitches are still susceptible to be attacked. To solve this problem, Dual-Rail Random Switching Logic (DRSL) is presented. By introducing a local pre-charge signal, DRSL gates have their inputs synchronized. Experimental results indicate that DRSL eliminates most of the leakage.

Keywords: Side Channel Attacks, DPA, Gate Level Masking, DRSL, Dual-Rail, Pre-charge.

1 Introduction

Until Paul Kocher *et al.* [1] proposed practical Side Channel Attacks (SCA) on chips, especially powerful Differential Power Analysis (DPA), people generally thought that cryptographic algorithms implemented in hardware chips were secure, therefore, they put more attention on security of protocols and mathematic algorithms. But since then, people began to pay more attention on implementations, and lots of countermeasures have been proposed in the last few years.

The earliest ways to act against DPA were called "Ad-hoc Approaches" [2], such as adding noises, randomizing execution sequence and so on. The drawback of this kind of countermeasures is that they do not prevent attacks completely: attacks can still be successful by taking more samples and signal processing.

For the purpose of preventing DPA completely, methods to protect cryptographers on the algorithm level were presented. Louis Goubin *et al.* [3] proposed

---

* This work has been supported by National Science Fund for Creative Research Groups (60521002) and Shanghai AM Fund (0425).

L. Goubin and M. Matsui (Eds.): CHES 2006, LNCS 4249, pp. 242–254, 2006.

a way called duplication (or masking). Subsequently, masking method has been improved by many researchers [12, 13, 16, 17, 18].

On the other hand, more generic countermeasures are also under discussion. These countermeasures are on circuit level. We call them more generic in that they are not constrained to a certain cryptographic algorithm. Once a practical method is found, designers need not to care about the security of implementations for a specific algorithm. This makes possible the automatic design. These measures fall into two categories: complementary circuits and gate level mask circuits.

Kris Tiri and Ingrid Verbauwhede [7] proposed a complementary logic called "Sense Amplifier Based Logic" (SABL), in which "Dual-rail" and "Pre-charge" are employed. Considering SABL requires a new core cell library, "Simple Dynamic Differential Logic" (SDDL) and its refinement "Wave Dynamic Differential Logic" (WDDL) came into being afterward also under efforts of Kris Tiri [8]. Compared with SABL, WDDL only makes use of common cells.

Besides complementary circuits, masking on gate level is analyzed in [9], and implementation of masked gate circuits has been presented by Trichina and Korkishko in [10, 11].

Though the above methods, in both algorithm level and circuit level, aim at preventing DPA completely, they still leak side channel information. For masking methods, outputs' transitions of logic gates are dependent on the input signals when glitches exist [4]. What's more, in [5], Stefan Mangard *et al.* did a successful attack on masked AES hardware implementations with glitches. For complementary circuits, loading capacitance is hard to control for deep submicron process technologies where the transistor sizes and wiring widths continuously shrink [6].

To overcome the disadvantages of both masked and complementary circuits, Thomas Popp and Stefan Mangard in [6] bound masked and complementary circuits together and showed us "Masked Dual-Rail Pre-charge Logic" (MDPL). By absorbing "pre-charge protocol" and "Dual-Rail encoding", no glitches appears in MDPL circuits; by masking intermediate value with random bit, designers do not have to consider routing constrains.

However, we find that predictable energy dissipation still appears whenever inputs of a logic gate arrive at different moments, no matter glitches exist or not. This means that the previous methods are still susceptible to be attacked, including WDDL and MDPL. We did attack simulation with Hspice and the results demonstrate that our opinion is reasonable.

What should be mentioned is that Daisuke Suzuki *et al.* [15] also presented a kind of masked logic gate called "Random Switching Logic" (RSL). RSL belongs to Single-Rail circuits. All inputs to a RSL gate are synchronized by a pre-charge signal (called "enable signal" in [15]), but how to generate such a pre-charge signal was not mentioned yet. We think it is hard to generate such a pre-charge signal for each gate respectively in Single-Rail circuits.

In this article, we propose a power dissipation model according to a gate's output transitions, and divide it into pieces according to the input transitions. Based on our model, we demonstrate that 1-bit masked logic gates still leak side channel information. As an effective countermeasure, Dual-Rail Random Switching Logic (DRSL) is presented, in which inputs are synchronized for each gate respectively. Our experimental results show that DRSL reduces most of the side channel leakage. Therefore, DRSL is more robust than other logics.

This article is organized as follows. In Section 2, a mathematical model of power consumption and theoretical analysis of gate leakage are proposed. Our logic DRSL is presented in Section 3. Experimental results are given in Section 4.

2   Mathematical Models and Analysis

2.1   Gate Model

A logic gate in a cryptographer performs a Boolean algebra function. Factors that influence a gate's output values can be categorized into two groups: one is those determinable factors that can be decided by internal keys and outside input (or output) data; the other is the independent factors, such as the internal generated random numbers. For simplicity, we, here, only consider gates with only one output. What's more, for the practical consideration, each logic gate discussed in this article has only one independent factor. Then our model can be described in Equation 1.

$$q = f(a_0, a_1, \cdots, a_{n-1}, m) \tag{1}$$

where q is the output value; $a_0, a_1, \cdots, a_{n-1}$ are n factors related to key and outside data while m is the internal independent factor, f is the Boolean function that the gate performs. Hereafter, we also represent $a_0, a_1, \cdots, a_{n-1}$ as A for simplicity.

In a gate level masked circuit, 'm' is a mask signal, 'a_i' is the unmasked value of a masked input and 'q' is a masked output. A common digital circuit can be considered as a special subset of masked circuits, in which 'm' equals to a constant '0' or '1'.

2.2   Power Model

Power consumed by a CMOS gate is determined by many factors, such as output transition, load capacitance, self capacitance, clock frequency, supply voltage, and switch voltage [14]. In this article, we mainly focus on output transitions. We define the output transition as (q_{i-1}, q_i). Correspondingly, energy consumed can be defined as $E(q_{i-1}, q_i)$.

In a combinational circuit, input signals to a gate always arrive at different moments. The result following this is that outputs would probably switch several times during a clock cycle before they reach stable values. This is what we usually call "glitches". Suppose inputs arrive at k different moments, then power consumption can be represented as shown in Equation 2.

$$E = (E_0, E_1, \cdots, E_i, \cdots, E_{k-1}, E_k) \tag{2}$$

where E_i is the gate's power consumption during the input arriving intervals between moment i and moment $i+1$. When voltage of the output at moment i (v_i) and $i+1$ (v_{i+1}) are both stable values (for example, 0v or 1.8v in 0.18μm technology), energy can be written as $E(0,0)$, $E(0,1)$, $E(1,0)$, or $E(1,1)$. Otherwise, if at least one of them is not stable, energy consumed can be represented as $tE(0,1)$ or $tE(1,0)$ by employing a coefficient 't' $(0 < t < 1)$. Here, t is determined by v_i and v_{i+1}. From another point of view, t is mainly determined by the length of the interval, and is independent on the value of A.

2.3 Analysis

When attacking cryptographers using DPA, attackers aim to discover whether their key guesses are correct. Explaining this with our model, a correct key guess brings us a correct prediction of internal predictable factors, while incorrect key guesses lead to wrong predictions. If some statistical characteristic of the energy dissipated depends on the predictable factors, then attackers can make use of the power consumption as side-channel information to judge whether their key guesses are valid. Hence, secure cryptographers should have their power dissipation statistically independent on those predictable factors.

DPA can target on a circuit element (CE), which is a (group of) gate(s). Output values of a CE are statistically independent of others, so independence between the power consumption and the internal predictable factors lays on no correlation between E and A of a CE. What's more, we hold the opinion that independence between E and A at every time can be satisfied only if every element E_i of E is statistically independent on A, otherwise, the cryptographers would probably suffer from DPA.

In pre-charge circuits, at the beginning of evaluation phase, every signal has an initialized value: 0. (In some logics, signals are pre-charged to 1, but there is no essential difference.) As mentioned before, coefficient 't' is independent on A, hence, independence of E_i and A stands on independence between q_{i+1} and A ($q_i = 0$). This is the main topic of the following discussion.

Single-Rail Circuits. In a Single-Rail circuit, each CE has only one output. The independence between q and A can be described in an equation as follows.

$$P(q = 0/A_i) = P(q = 0/A_j) \tag{3}$$

where P is the conditional probability, A_i and A_j are arbitrary sets of $(a_0, a_1, \cdots, a_{n-1})$. What's more, q must not be a constant and is related to every input.

Until now, the problem becomes to designing a logic gate that satisfies Equation 3 in all the k time intervals during a clock cycle. First, we consider the scenario that all inputs have arrived at this gate.

Lemma 1. *Let f be a logic gate's Boolean algebra function, q be its output and* $a_0, a_1, \cdots, a_{n-1}$, *and m be its n+1 independent variables:* $q = f(a_0, a_1, \cdots, a_{n-1}, m)$. *When q does not equal to constant 0 or 1, and is correlated to every input,* *then the necessary and sufficient condition for the statistical independence between q and $a_0, a_1, \cdots, a_{n-1}$ is*

$$q = f(a_0, a_1, \cdots, a_{n-1}, m) = g(a_0, a_1, \cdots, a_{n-1}) \oplus m \qquad (4)$$

and

$$P(m = 0) = P(m = 1) = 1/2$$

where g is a Boolean algebra function; P is the probability. (Since lemmas in this article are easy to prove, we do not list their proof here.)

As we can see, to make circuits designed resistant to DPA, signals propagating inside should be masked as $a \oplus m$ or $\bar{a} \oplus m$.

When considering other cases, we take the kth interval as an example. In this interval, only one input has not arrived at the gate, which means either one of the masked signals $(a_i \oplus m)$ or the masking signal (m) remains pre-charged.

If the last one is $a_i \oplus m$, we define the delayed signal as a_{im}. Since a_{im} is pre-charged to 0, we can assume that a_i equals to m in this interval. Then Equation 4 can be rewritten as follows.

$$q = f(a_0, a_1, \cdots, a_{n-1}, m) = g(a_0, a_1, \cdots, a_{i-1}, m, a_{i+1}, \cdots, a_{n-1}) \oplus m \qquad (5)$$

Is q in this case still independent on the remaining predictable factors $(a_0, a_1, \cdots, a_{i-1}, a_{i+1}, \cdots, a_{n-1})$? According to Lemma 1, we should make sure whether there exists a Boolean algebra function h satisfying the following equation.

$$q = f(a_0, a_1, \cdots, a_{n-1}, m) = h(a_0, a_1, \cdots, a_{i-1}, a_{i+1}, \cdots, a_{n-1}) \oplus m \qquad (6)$$

Lemma 2. *When a Boolean function f can be written as Equation 5, it cannot be rewritten into Equation 6.*

If the last one is signal m, we can represent output q with the same equation as before while replacing a_i with $a_i \oplus m$, and m with 0 (m is still pre-charged). So Equation 4 can be rewritten as follows.

$$q = g(a_0 \oplus m, a_1 \oplus m, \cdots, a_{n-1} \oplus m) \oplus 0 \qquad (7)$$

Still, we should make sure whether there is a function h which satisfies Equation 8.

$$q = h(a_0, a_1, \cdots, a_{n-1}) \oplus m \qquad (8)$$

Lemma 3. *when a gate's logic function can be described as Equation 7 and Equation 8, then n must be an odd number and*

$$h(a_0, a_1, \cdots, a_{n-1}) = f_a(a_0) \oplus a_1 \oplus \cdots \oplus a_{n-1} \qquad (9)$$

According to Lemma 3, gates, such as masked AND and OR, do not satisfy Equations 7 and 8 simultaneously. Therefore, when m arrives last, output q is dependent on predictable factors A. Since AND and OR gates are the main components of cryptographers, so we can say that delay of the mask signal also has side channel leakage.

Based on Lemma 1 to Lemma 3, we can make a conclusion:

Conclusion 1. *In Single-Rail Circuits with all signals masked by the same random bit, when inputs arrive at logic gates at different moments, predictable factors dependent power dissipation appears no matter glitches occur or not. What's more, if inputs to a gate are pre-charged asynchronously, leakage would also occur.*

Dual-Rail Circuits. As for the Dual-Rail Circuits, the independent circuit element is a pair of complementary signals. Therefore, Equation 4 should be rewritten as follows.

$$(Q_1, Q_0) = q + \bar{q} = f(A, m) + \overline{f(A, m)}$$
$$= g(a_0, a_1, \cdots, a_{n-1}) \oplus m + g(a_0, a_1, \cdots, a_{n-1}) \oplus \bar{m} \qquad (10)$$

where '+' represents common addition; q and $\bar{q}$ are a pair of complementary signals. $\bar{q}$ equals to the inversion of q in evaluation phase, while equals to q in pre-charge phase. Therefore,

$$Q_0 = q \oplus \bar{q}, Q_1 = q\bar{q}$$

For a Dual-Rail Circuit resistant to DPA, both Q_0 and Q_1 should be statistical independent on A.

Using the same proof methods employed in last section, we can demonstrate that when inputs to a gate arrive asynchronously, side-channel leakage occurs as well. Therefore, we can get Conclusion 2 as follows.

Conclusion 2. *In Dual-Rail Circuits with all signals masked by the same random bit, when inputs arrive at logic gates at different moments, predictable factors dependent power dissipation appears, no matter glitches occur or not. What's more, if inputs to a gate are pre-charged asynchronously, leakage would also occur.*

3   Dual-Rail Random Switching Logic

3.1   Basic Cells

Section 2 tells us that besides "free of glitches" and "no routing constrains", every internal gate in a DPA resistant cryptographer should have its inputs synchronized. DRSL is devised under such a guideline. To suppress glitches, "pre-charge" protocol is used; to remove routing constrains, random mask is introduced; to synchronize input signals, a local pre-charge signal is generated. The main idea of DRSL is derived from RSL and MDPL. But compared with MDPL, the advantage of DRSL is that it avoids side channel leakage caused by asynchronous inputs. As for RSL, DRSL makes use of Dual-Rail method to make practical the generation of the local pre-charge signal (called "enable" signal in RSL) for every gate.

The schematic of a two-input DRSL AND gate is shown in Fig. 1. Fig. 1(a) presents a single rail element; Fig. 1(b) describes a DRSL AND gate with a logic part (two Single-Rail elements) and a pre-charge generation circuit in it.

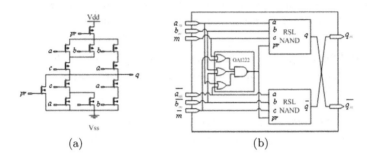

(a)   (b)

Fig. 1. (a). RSL NAND schematic, (b). DRSL AND schematic

In DRSL circuits, there are two work phases alternating with each other: one is pre-charge phase, the other is evaluation phase. In the pre-charge phase, all signals, including mask signal m, are pre-charged to 0; while in the evaluation phase, pre-charge signal turns to be invalid after all inputs are evaluated values. Pre-charge of the whole circuit is done in a way of waveform: starting from registers, propagating through combinational logic gates and finally running back to registers. A global pre-charge signal is not suitable in that, between logic gates, their inputs arrive at different moments. This is similar to WDDL and MDPL, however, the difference is that each DRSL gate has its own pre-charge circuit. A DRSL gate is pre-charged at the time when one of the inputs turns to be pre-charged value, and enabled after all its inputs are evaluated values. Thus, DRSL gates do not suffer from asynchronous inputs.

In a Single-Rail circuit, pre-charged values and evaluated values can both be 0, so it is hard to judge when all inputs are evaluated values. On the other hand, pre-charged and evaluated values in Dual-Rail circuit do not have intersection: the former can only be (0, 0), and the latter belong to (1, 0) and (0, 1). This makes it possible to identify the time when all evaluated inputs have arrived. Based on the above consideration, Dual-Rail circuits are preferable in our logic. Once the pre-charge signal is generated, input signals are synchronized. This property of DRSL allows converting all kinds of logic gates to DRSL. For example, XOR, which is not a monotonic gate, is not used in MDPL and WDDL. But in DRSL, XOR is accepted. What's more, since DRSL is Dual-Rail, an inverter can be implemented by just swapping its two complementary inputs. The same as mentioned in [15], odd-number-input XOR and XNOR function does not need a random signal input in DRSL.

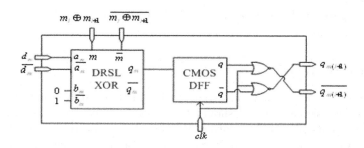

Fig. 2. DRSL D-flip-flop schematic

Since random mask changes every clock cycle, value stored in registers should be masked by the random signal for the following clock period. We incorporate the idea of MDPL D-flip-flop, in which a D-flip-flop consists of a RSL XOR gate, a common CMOS D-flip-flop and two CMOS NOR gates. Random signals for the XOR gate are $m_i \oplus m_{i+1}$ and $\overline{m_i \oplus m_{i+1}}$, where m_i is the random value for the current cycle and m_{i+1} is the one for the next. DRSL D-flip-flop schematic is presented in Fig. 2.

Table 1 compares DRSL cells in 0.18μm technology with the corresponding cells from TSMC 0.18μm standard cell library in area complexity.

Table 1. DRSL cells area complexity

DRSL Cell	Implementation	Area (gate equivalents)		Ratio
		DRSL	Standard	DRSL/std.
Inverter	Wire swapping	0	0.67	0
Buffer	2×Buffer	2.66	1.33	2
AND, OR(2-in)	2×RSL NAND, OAI	7.21	1.33	5.42
NAND, NOR(2-in)	2×RSL NAND, OAI	7.21	1	7.21
XOR, XNOR	2×RSL XOR, OAI	8.22	2.67	3.30
D-flip-flop	DRSL XOR, CMOS D-FF, 2×NOR	14.49	5.67	2.56

As can be seen from Table 1, DRSL AND, OR, NAND, and NOR gates cost much more area than standard gates. This is mainly caused by the local pre-charge circuit and the dual-rail circuit. However, as the gate becomes more complex, pre-charge circuit takes less proportion. Area ratio of DRSL XOR, XNOR, and D-flip-flop is smaller than DRSL AND and OR gates.

Compared with MDPL gates, DRSL AND (OR) gates cost more area than MDPL AND (OR) gates. But for XOR and DFF gates, DRSL costs less. Considering DRSL is compatible with MDPL, when designing DRSL circuits, a DRSL

AND (OR) gate can be replaced by a MDPL AND (OR) gate if inputs to it are already synchronized.

3.2   Security Analysis

For every DRSL gate, outputs only change after all inputs arrive, energy elements before the last signal's arrival should be $2E(0,0)$, assume signals arrive at k different moments and the final output is q, then the last energy piece is $E(0,0)+E(0,q)$. Power consumption of a DRSL gate can be represented as follows.

$$E = (2E_0(0,0), 2E_1(0,0), \cdots, 2E_i(0,0), \cdots, 2E_{k-1}(0,0), E_k(0,0) + E_k(0,q))$$

Since output q is masked by a random signal, the above equation is not influenced by those predictable factors. So we can see the logic part of DRSL is free of leakage caused by asynchronous inputs.

Similarly, for the pre-charge circuit in DRSL, its power consumption can be described as follows.

$$E = (E_0(0,0), E_1(0,0), \cdots, E_i(0,0), \cdots, E_{k-1}(0,0), E_k(0,1))$$

Again, the equation is not related to those predictable factors, which means the pre-charge circuit is secure as well.

4   Experimental Results

We have performed DPA attacks simulation with Hspice on four 2-input AND gates implemented by common Single-Rail masked logic, WDDL, MDPL, and DRSL. All these gates are in $0.18\mu m$ technology. The layout parasitics have been neglected. Test circuits are illustrated in Fig. 3. In Fig 3(a), a_m arrives last; in Fig. 3(b), the random mask signal m arrives last.

For the Single-Rail masked AND gate, when a_m arrives later than b_m and m, then in the time interval, output q can be shown as follows.

$$q = ((a_m \oplus m)(b_m \oplus m)) \oplus m = ((0 \oplus m)(b_m \oplus m)) \oplus m = \bar{b}m$$

For WDDL and MDPL, we can also get the following results ($m=0$ for WDDL):

$$\bar{q} = ((\bar{a}_m \oplus \bar{m})(\bar{b}_m \oplus \bar{m})) \oplus \bar{m} = ((0 \oplus \bar{m})(\bar{b}_m \oplus \bar{m})) \oplus \bar{m} = \bar{b}\bar{m}$$

$$q_0 = q \oplus \bar{q} = \bar{b}, q_1 = q\bar{q} = 0$$

We simulate all the 8 possible combinations of input transitions on each of the AND gate. Current I(Vd)from circuits to power Vdd is the probed signal. Waveforms are divided into two groups, one with $b = b_m \oplus m = 1$, while the other with $b = 0$. Finally, we subtract the average of group 2 ($b = 0$) by the means of group 1 ($b = 1$) to get the difference. In the time interval when b_m and m have arrived and a_m is still pre-charged, only group 2 is possible to change output to

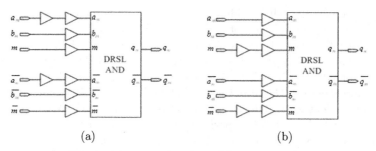

Fig. 3. (a). a_m arrives last, (b). m arrives last

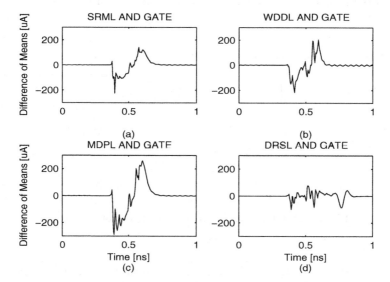

Fig. 4. Difference of means

be '1'; after a_m arrives, raise of output only occurs in group 1. So it is expected to get a figure with a valley followed by a peak in SRML, WDDL, and MDPL circuits. Results can be seen in Fig. 4.

When m arrives last, for Single-Rail masked AND gate:

$$q = ((a_m \oplus 0)(b_m \oplus 0)) \oplus 0 = (\bar{a}\bar{b}m) \vee (ab\bar{m})$$

For MDPL, we can also get the following results:

$$\bar{q} = ((\bar{a}_m \oplus 0)(\bar{b}_m \oplus 0)) \oplus 0 = (\bar{a}\bar{b}\bar{m}) \vee (abm)$$

$$q_0 = q \oplus \bar{q} = a \otimes b, q_1 = q\bar{q} = 0$$

In this case we divide waveforms of I(Vd) into two groups, one with $a = b$, while the other with $a \neq b$. Since this division happens to be the same as the former, their figures are similar (slight differences are caused by different self capacitance related to each input). We do not list the plots of this case here.

¿From Fig. 4 we can clearly notice the advantage of the DRSL AND Gate. The first three plots apparently have a valley followed by a peak, while the fluctuation of DRSL AND Gate is much smaller. Peak-to-peak values of each plot are approximately 418(SRML), 363(WDDL), 550(MDPL), and 117(DRSL) μA. Therefore, leakage of DRSL is reduced by at least 68%. When comparing the total power leakage, DRSL's performance is even better.

We also did an experiment in which every input reaches the gate at the same time. We divide the waveforms and get the difference of means in the same way as before. Result can be seen in Fig. 5(a). What's more, two immediate current I(Vd) plots ($a_m b_m m = 000$ and $a_m b_m m = 100$) are shown in Fig. 5(b).

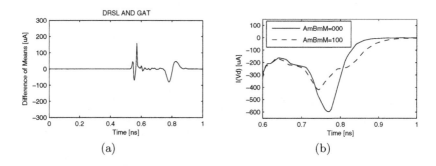

(a)   (b)

Fig. 5. (a). Inputs synchronized, (b). Immediate Current

By comparing Fig. 4(d) and Fig. 5(a), we notice that the two plots are identical around 0.75ns, which means this part of leakage occurs even if inputs arrive at the same time. Accordingly, we divide the plot in Fig. 4(d) into two parts: the high-frequency fluctuation around 0.5ns and the comparatively low-frequency part near 0.75ns. We think the former be related to self capacitance. Leakage in this part is hard to identify. As for the latter, it is caused by different charging speeds. If $a_m = b_m = m$, all P transistors in the transiting RSL AND gate are open. This brings larger current and quicker change than other cases. In Fig. 5(b), charging current (-I(Vd)) belonging to $a_m b_m m = 000$ (real line) is larger than that of $a_m b_m m = 100$ (dotted line) at the beginning of transition. Since the stored charge is limited, the former also ends earlier than the latter. According to the above categorization, all traces belonging to $a_m = b_m = m$ were grouped into the second group ($b = 0$), so when subtracting the means of the two groups, a small valley followed by a peak appears. This kind of leakage is not considered in our model, as it does not come from the total power difference but the immediate power trace disagreement. Unfortunately, DRSL cannot avoid this kind of leakage. To minimize such kind of leakage is our job in the future.

5   Conclusion

We presented a power model where the power consumption of a logic gate depends on the value of the gate's output transition. Based on the model, we establish conditions for statistical independence between output transitions and the input values. Theoretical analysis shows that 1-bit masked gates with asynchronous inputs always leak side channel information. After that, we propose a kind of logic called Dual-Rail Switching Logic, which employs a local pre-charge circuit in each gate. Experimental results show that DRSL can eliminate most of the side channel leakage and therefore is more secure.

References

[1] Paul Kocher, Joshus Jaffe, and Benjamin Jun. *Differential Power Analysis.* In proceeding of Advances in Cryptology - CRYPTO '99, pp. 388-397, Springer, 1999.

[2] Suresh Chari, Charanjit S. Jutla, Josyula R. Rao, and Pankaj Rohatgi. *Towards Sound Approaches to Counteract Power-Analysis Attacks.* In proceeding of Advances in Cryptology - CRYPTO '99, pp. 398-412, Springer, 1999.

[3] Louis Goubin and Jacques Patarin. *DES and Differential Power Analysis - The "Duplication" Method.* In proceeding of Cryptographic Hardware and Embedded Systems - CHES '99, pp. 158-172, Springer, 1999.

[4] Stefan Mangard, Thomas Popp, and Berndt M. Gammel. *Side-Channel Leakage of Masked CMOS Gates.* In Topics in Cryptology - CT-RSA 2005, pp. 351-365, Springer, 2005.

[5] Stefan Mangard, Norbert Pramstaller, and Elisabeth Oswald. *Successfully Attacking Masked AES Hardware Implementations.* In proceeding of Cryptographic Hardware and Embedded Systems - CHES 2005, pp. 157-171, Springer, 2005.

[6] Thomas Popp and Stefan Mangard. *Masked Dual-Rail Pre-charge Logic: DPA-Resistance Without Routing Constraints.* In proceeding of Cryptographic Hardware and Embedded Systems - CHES 2005, pp. 172-186, Springer, 2005.

[7] Kris Tiri and Ingrid Verbauwhede. *Securing Encryption Algorithms against DPA at the Logic Level Next Generation Smart Card Technology.* In proceeding of Cryptographic Hardware and Embedded Systems - CHES 2003, pp. 137-151, Springer, 2003.

[8] Kris Tiri and Ingrid Verbauwhede. *A Logic Level Design Methodology for a Secure DPA Resistant ASIC or FPGA Implementation.* In Design, Automatin and Test in Europe Conference and Exposition (DATE 2004), IEEE Computer Society, pp. 246-251, 2004.

[9] Yuval Ishai, Amit Sahai, and David Wagner. *Private Circuits: Securing Hardware against Probing Attacks.* In proceeding of Advances in Cryptology - CRYPTO 2003, pp. 463-481, Springer, 2003.

[10] Elena Trichina. *Combinational Logic Design for AES SubByte Transformation on Masked Data.* Cryptology ePrint Archive (http://eprint.iacr.org/) , Report 2003/236, 2003.

[11] Elena Trichina and Tymur Korkishko. *Small Size, Low Power, Side Channel-Immune AES Comprocessor: Design and Synthesis Results.* In proceeding of the Fourth Conference on the Advanced Encryption Standard (AES), 2004.

[12] Elena Trichina and Tymur Korkishko. *Secure AES Hardware Module for Resource Constrained Devices*. In proceeding of Security in Ad-hoc and Sensor Networks: First European Workshop, ESAS 2004, pp. 215-229, Springer 2005.

[13] Elena Trichina and Lesya Korkishko. *Secure and Efficient AES Software Implementation for Smart Cards*. In proceeding of Information Security Applications: 5th International Workshop, WISA 2004, pp. 425-439, Springer 2004.

[14] A.P. Chandrakasan, S. Shen and R.W.Brodersen. *Low Power Digital CMOS Design*. In IEEE Journal of Solid State Circuits, Vol.27, N0.4. pp. 473-484, 1992.

[15] Daisuke Suzuki, Minoru Saeki, and Tetsuya Ichikawa. *Random Switching Logic: A Countermeasure against DPA based on Transition Probability*. Cryptology ePrint Archive (http://eprint.iacr.org/), Report 2004/346, 2004.

[16] Mehdi-Laurent Akkar and Christophe Giraud. *An Implementation of DES and AES, Secure against Some Attacks*. In proceeding of Cryptographic Hardware and Embedded Systems: CHES 2001, pp. 309-318, Springer 2001.

[17] Johannes Blomer, Jorge Guajardo, and Volker Krummel. *Provably Secure Masking of AES*. In proceeding of Selected Areas in Cryptography: 11th International Workshop, SAC 2004, pp. 69-83, Springer 2005.

[18] Elisabeth Oswald, Stefan Mangard, Norbert Pramstaller, and Vincent Rijmen. *A Side-Channel Analysis Resistant Description of the AES S-Box*. In proceeding of Fast Software Encryption: 12th International Workshop, FSE 2005, pp. 413-423, Springer 2005.

Security Evaluation of DPA Countermeasures Using Dual-Rail Pre-charge Logic Style

Daisuke Suzuki and Minoru Saeki

Mitsubishi Electric Corporation, Information Technology R&D Center,
5-1-1 Ofuna Kamakura, Kanagawa, 247-8501, Japan
{Suzuki.Daisuke@bx, Saeki.Minoru@db}.MitsubishiElectric.co.jp

Abstract. In recent years, some countermeasures against Differential Power Analysis (DPA) at the logic level have been proposed. At CHES 2005 conference, Popp and Mangard proposed a new countermeasure named Masked Dual-Rail Pre-Charge Logic (MDPL) which combine dual-rail circuits with random masking to improve Wave Dynamic Differential Logic (WDDL). The proposers of MDPL claim that it can implement secure circuits using a standard CMOS cell library without special constraints for the place-and-route because the difference of loading capacitance between all pairs of complementary logic gates in MDPL can be covered up by the random masking. In this paper, we especially focus the signal transition of the MDPL gate and evaluate the DPA-resistance of MDPL in detail. Our evaluation results show that the leakage occurs in the MDPL gates as well as WDDL gates when input signals have difference of delay time even if MDPL has an effectiveness on reducing the leakage caused by the difference of loading capacitance. Furthermore, we demonstrate the problem with different input signal delays by measurements of an FPGA and show the validity of our evaluation.

1 Introduction

In recent years, some countermeasures against Differential Power Analysis (DPA) [1] at the logic level have been proposed. Since the logic level countermeasure is applied to the basic components of hardware and aims to cut off DPA leakage at its source, it indicates that we can take the versatile countermeasure independent of the algorithm.

Some problems of security and implementation are pointed out to the countermeasures at the logic level that have been already proposed. For example, Mangard pointed out that the countermeasure to implement random masking by combinational circuit [2] should leak out the secret information from the power consumption caused due to glitches [3] and actually, they found DPA leakage on the real ASIC [4]. Random Switching Logic (RSL) [5] proposed by Suzuki et al. can suppress the occurrence of glitch and make uniform the power consumption at each gate in the statistical analysis using the random number. However, RSL requires the special CMOS gates to perform effective implementing process and the special constraints of timing to assure the security. Wave Dynamic Differential Logic (WDDL) [6], which applies the dual-rail synchronous

L. Goubin and M. Matsui (Eds.): CHES 2006, LNCS 4249, pp. 255–269, 2006.

circuit, must adopt the specialized place-and-route method to adjust the loading capacitance for implementing of the secure circuit [7]. In addition, Suzuki et al. present the fact that DPA leakage occurs when there are differences in the delay time between the input signals at the WDDL gates [5,8].

As one of the recent research, Masked Dual-Rail Pre-Charge Logic (MDPL) [9] that improved WDDL was proposed at CHES 2005 conference. The proposers of MDPL claim that it can implement secure circuits using a standard CMOS cell library without special constraints for the place-and-route because the difference of loading capacitance between all pairs of complementary logic gates in MDPL can be covered up by the random masking.

In this paper, we especially focus the signal transition of the MDPL gate and evaluate the DPA-resistance of MDPL in detail. Our evaluation results show that the leakage occurs in the MDPL gates as well as WDDL gates when input signals have difference of delay time even if MDPL has an effectiveness on reducing the leakage caused by the difference of loading capacitance. Furthermore, we demonstrate the problem with different input signal delays by measurements of an FPGA and show the validity of our evaluation.

2   DPA Countermeasures Using Dual-Rail Circuits

2.1   Wave Dynamic Differential Logic [6]

Tiri et al. proposed WDDL applying DCVSL (Differential Cascode Voltage Switch Logic) as a countermeasure against DPA [6]. Figure 1 shows the basic components of WDDL. The WDDL circuits have the following features:

(1) WDDL gates have complementary outputs $(q, \bar{q})$.
(2) The pre-charge signal controls the pre-charge phase to transmit $(0, 0)$ and the evaluation phase to transmit $(0, 1)$ or $(1, 0)$.
(3) The pre-charge operation is performed at the first step in combinational circuit and, the components to be used are limited to AND, OR, and NOT (re-wiring) operations.
(4) The number of transitions in all circuits generated during an operation cycle is constant without depending on the values of input signals.

The power consumption in the CMOS circuits is generally proportional to the number of transitions at the gates. Therefore, the WDDL circuits are effective as a countermeasure against DPA since the power consumption may become constant without depending on the values of input signals as described in the feature above.

2.2   Masked Dual-Rail Pre-charge Logic [9]

Popp et al. proposed Masked Dual-Rail Pre-charge Logic (MDPL) that the random data masking is introduced into WDDL gates [9]. Figure 2 and Figure 3 show the basic components of MDPL. In addition, Table 1 shows the truth table

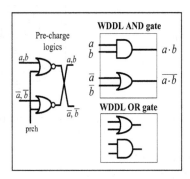

Fig. 1. Components of WDDL

of an MDPL AND gate. The logic AND function and OR function in the WDDL gate apply a pair of standard two-input AND gate and OR gate and on the other hand, those in the MDPL gate apply a pair of majority logic (MAJ) gates.

The architecture of cryptographic circuits using MDPL is shown in Figure 4. The signals $(a_m, b_m, \bar{a}_m, \bar{b}_m)$ masked with the random data m and $\bar{m}$ and those random data are entered into the MAJ gates in the combinational circuit shown in Figure 4. Hereupon, at the MAJ gates with the three input ports (x, y, r) shown in Figure 3, the signals $(a_m, \bar{a}_m)$ and $(b_m, \bar{b}_m)$ are entered into the input ports x and y, respectively and then, the signals $(m, \bar{m})$ are entered into the input port r.

When examining the security against DPA, we assume that an attacker can predict the architecture of the combinational circuit shown in Figure 4 and the pre-masking signals $(a, b, \bar{a}, \bar{b})$ corresponding to the signals $(a_m, b_m, \bar{a}_m, \bar{b}_m)$. And the random numbers m and $\bar{m}$ generated in the VLSI can be predicted only with a probability of $1/2$.

The relations between the signals are described below. In the beginning, there are following relations between the input signals.

$$a_m = a \oplus m, b_m = b \oplus m, \bar{a}_m = a \oplus \bar{m}, \bar{b}_m = b \oplus \bar{m}.$$

The output signals q_m and $\bar{q}_m$ of the MDPL AND gate are as follows:

$$q_m = MAJ(a_m, b_m, m) = a \cdot b \oplus m,$$
$$\bar{q}_m = MAJ(\bar{a}_m, \bar{b}_m, \bar{m}) = a \cdot b \oplus \bar{m}.$$

As realized from Figure 3 and the above formulas of q_m and $\bar{q}_m$, the MDPL gates have the following feature, including those of WDDL gates described in Section 2.1.

- Even if the correct signal values a, b $(\bar{a}, \bar{b})$ are predictable, the random transition occurs at the MAJ gate according to the value of random data m $(\bar{m})$.

For this reason, the power consumption is made uniform even if there is a difference of the loading capacitance between each complementary logic gate. Thus,

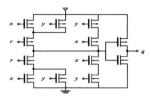

Fig. 2. MAJ gate

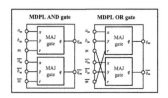

Fig. 3. Components of MDPL

Table 1. Truth table of
an MDPL AND gate

a b	a_m	b_m	m	q_m	$\bar{a}_m$	$\bar{b}_m$	$\bar{m}$	$\bar{q}_m$
0 0	0	0	0	0	1	1	1	1
0 0	1	1	1	1	0	0	0	0
0 1	0	1	0	0	1	0	1	1
0 1	1	0	1	1	0	1	0	0
1 0	1	0	0	0	0	1	1	1
1 0	0	1	1	1	1	0	0	0
1 1	1	1	0	1	0	0	1	0
1 1	0	0	1	0	1	1	0	1

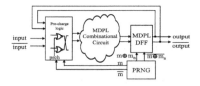

Fig. 4. Architecture of
MDPL circuit

the proposers of MDPL claim that MDPL does not need the constraints on the place-and-route to adjust the loading capacitance and can improve security and implementability.

3   Security Problems of WDDL

This section states the main factor of leakage in WDDL gate based on the contents that have been already discussed on the security of WDDL.

3.1   Main Factors of the Leakage in WDDL

As the main factors of the DPA leakage in WDDL, the following two contents have been pointed out [7,8]:

F1: Leakage caused by the difference of loading capacitance between two complementary logic gates in WDDL gate
F2: Leakage caused by the difference of delay time between the input signals of WDDL gates

We here describe the factor of the above-mentioned leakage in detail. At first, we explain the main factor of leakage in F1. The power consumption at the CMOS gate can be generally evaluated in the following formula [10]:

$$P_{\text{total}} = p_t \cdot C_L \cdot V_{\text{dd}}^2 \cdot f_{\text{clk}} + p_t \cdot I_{\text{sc}} \cdot V_{\text{dd}} \cdot f_{\text{clk}} + I_{\text{leakage}} \cdot V_{\text{dd}}, \qquad (1)$$

where C_L is the loading capacitance, f_{clk} is the clock frequency, V_{dd} is the supply voltage, p_t is the transition probability of the signal, I_{sc} is the direct-path short circuit current, and $I_{leakage}$ is the leakage current. As realized from the formula (1), the power consumption at the first term is different between the gates if there is a difference of the loading capacitance between each complementary logic gate. Since the existence of transition at each complementary logic gate is determined by the values of input signals, the total power consumption differ in dependence of the signal values even if the total number of transitions is equal between the gates. For this reason, the difference of power consumption occurs in dependence of the DPA selection function.

Next, we explain the main factor of leakage in F2. As described in Section 2.1, the transition probability during an operation cycle at the WDDL gates is assured $p_t = 1$ without depending on the input signals. However, the operation timing of each complementary logic gate are generally different due to the conditions of values or delay time of input signals during an operation cycle. In other words, this means that the timing of starting the power consumption varies in dependence of the signal values during an operation cycle. Therefore, since the average power traces specified by the predictable signal values have different phases, the spike can be detected after the DPA operation.

3.2 Countermeasures Against Main Factors of Leakage in WDDL

We here consider the above-mentioned two factors of the leakage from the viewpoint of implementing the logic circuit. First, we examine the leakage caused by the difference of loading capacitance in F1. The difference of loading capacitance generally arises between the gates in dependence of the number and type of gates connected to each other and the result of place-and-route. Complementary logic gates of WDDL are different in the point of logical expression (positive/negative), but their attribute (such as order and the number of connected gate) are designed to be equal. Thus, the number of gates connected to complementary logic gates of WDDL is equal basically. Therefore, the difference of loading capacitance in the WDDL circuit arises due to the difference of capacitance at the AND/OR gates themselves and the difference of place-and-route. Furthermore, when we consider the whole cryptographic circuit, a signal propagating path with transition is determined in probability depending on the values of input related signals. In a word, the leakage in F1 is a difference of power consumption that depends on the difference between the propagation probability and the loading capacitance of the signal in each path. We predict that the difference of the capacitance that depends on the place-and-route is more predominant as the factor of the leakage in F1 than the difference of capacitance at each gate such as AND/OR gate. Hereafter, we refer the leakage that depends on the place-and-route and does not depend on the logical formula as *incidental leakage*.

Next, we examine the leakage caused by the difference of delay time in F2. Suzuki et al. analyzed the existence of leakage on assumption that there is different delay time between a and b (or between $\bar{a}$ and $\bar{b}$) among four input signals

Table 2. Factors of the leakage caused by the difference of delay time

factor	classification	difference to cause the leakage
diff($a,\bar{a}$)	incidental	place-and-route
diff($b,\bar{b}$)	incidental	place-and-route
diff(a,b)	inevitable (+ incidental)	logic steps (+ place-and-route)
diff($\bar{a},b$)	inevitable (+ incidental)	logic steps (+ place-and-route)

of WDDL AND gate of Figure 1 [8]. We explain the propriety of this assumption below. Since the basic cryptographic components including the S-box as a representative generally have their randomness, the logical formula consists of various terms. Unless the special design is made as described in Ref. [12], the input signals at the gates have the different number of logic steps and are easy to cause differences in the delay time. On the contrary, since the number of gates connected to each complementary output of WDDL is equal as described above, the difference of place-and-route is predominant over a difference in the delay time between a and $\bar{a}$ (or b and $\bar{b}$). In fact, it is appropriate to realize that a difference in the delay time between a and b (or $\bar{a}$ and $\bar{b}$) occurs necessarily on the normal design of logic circuit. From the consideration above, it can be said that the leakage caused by the difference of delay time includes the *inevitable leakage* that occurs depending on the difference of the logical formula together with the *incidental leakage* that occurs depending on the place-and-route. Table 2 summarizes the relation of the leakage factors that correspond to the difference of delay time between each input signal (diff(): indicates difference of delay time between each argument signal).

A main factor of *incidental leakage* is the automatization of the place-and-route that is generally carried out in the VLSI design at present. Therefore, *incidental leakage* can be likely to improve with the place-and-route in the manual operation or the semi-automatic operation using the special constraints. Actually, Tiri et al. and Guilley et al. proposed "Fat Wire" [7] and "Backend Duplication" [11], respectively as a countermeasure in the place-and-route to improve the DPA-resistance.

On the other hand, there is no study of a countermeasure against the *inevitable leakage* in the dual-rail circuit so far as the authors know. The S-box design method for low power consumption proposed by Morioka et al. is recommended as one technique to reduce *inevitable leakage* [12]. In the circuit design, it generally needs high effort to adjust the delay time between the input signals at each gate.

4 Security Evaluation of MDPL

As for the main factors of leakage described in Section 3.1, we here evaluate the effectiveness of MDPL. As stated in Section 2.2, MDPL can improve in principle the leakage caused by the difference of loading capacitance in F1 of Section 3.1. Therefore, we focus the leakage caused by the difference of delay time in F2 of Section 3.1.

When examining the difference of delay time, it is first necessary to inquire the conditions of delay time between the input signals. As described in Section 3.2, differences of delay time between independent signals (e.g. a_m and b_m) are more likely to occur than those between complementary signals (e.g. a_m and $\bar{a}_m$) in the design of dual-rail circuit. In the case of the MDPL gate, we supposed that there are differences in the delay time between the signals a_m, b_m and m (or $\bar{a}_m$, $\bar{b}_m$ and $\bar{m}$). From the above matters, when assuming the single input change model and if $delay(a_m) < delay(b_m)$ ($delay()$: indicates the delay of the signal in parentheses) is satisfied, the following three delay condition (C1 - C3) cover the whole timing relations of inputs signals in the MDPL gate.

C1: $delay(a_m) < delay(b_m) < delay(m)$
C2: $delay(a_m) < delay(m) < delay(b_m)$
C3: $delay(m) < delay(a_m) < delay(b_m)$

In the case of $delay(a_m) > delay(b_m)$, the equivalent conditions C1 - C3 can be obtained by changing the DPA selection function, so that it is not necessary to distinguish the delay conditions between the data signals (a_m and b_m).

Table 3 shows the delay conditions and the timing of transition on evaluation and pre-charge phase in the MDPL AND gate. In addition, Table 3 indicates the

Table 3. Timing of transition in an MDPL AND gate

Delay condition: C1
$\Delta a_m \to \Delta b_m \to \Delta m$
$(\Delta \bar{a}_m \to \Delta \bar{b}_m \to \Delta \bar{m})$

phase	evaluation phase				pre-charge phase			
a b m	Δq_m	timing	$\Delta \bar{q}_m$	timing	Δq_m	timing	$\Delta \bar{q}_m$	timing
0 0 0	0	-	1	Δb_m	0	-	1	Δb_m
0 0 1	1	Δb_m	0	-	1	Δb_m	0	-
0 1 0	0	-	1	$\Delta \bar{m}$	0	-	1	$\Delta \bar{a}_m$
0 1 1	1	Δm	0	-	1	Δa_m	0	-
1 0 0	0	-	1	$\Delta \bar{m}$	0	-	1	$\Delta \bar{b}_m$
1 0 1	1	Δm	0	-	1	Δb_m	0	-
1 1 0	1	Δb_m	0	-	1	Δa_m	0	-
1 1 1	0	-	1	$\Delta \bar{b}_m$	0	-	1	$\Delta \bar{a}_m$

Delay condition: C2
$\Delta a_m \to \Delta m \to \Delta b_m$
$(\Delta \bar{a}_m \to \Delta \bar{m} \to \Delta \bar{b}_m)$

phase	evaluation phase				pre-charge phase			
a b m	Δq_m	timing	$\Delta \bar{q}_m$	timing	Δq_m	timing	$\Delta \bar{q}_m$	timing
0 0 0	0	-	1	$\Delta \bar{m}$	0	-	1	$\Delta \bar{m}$
0 0 1	1	Δm	0	-	1	Δm	0	-
0 1 0	0	-	1	$\Delta \bar{m}$	0	-	1	$\Delta \bar{a}_m$
0 1 1	1	Δm	0	-	1	Δa_m	0	-
1 0 0	0	-	1	$\Delta \bar{b}_m$	0	-	1	$\Delta \bar{m}$
1 0 1	1	Δb_m	0	-	1	Δm	0	-
1 1 0	1	Δb_m	0	-	1	Δa_m	0	-
1 1 1	0	-	1	$\Delta \bar{b}_m$	0	-	1	$\Delta \bar{a}_m$

Delay condition: C3
$\Delta m \to \Delta a_m \to \Delta b_m$
$(\Delta \bar{m} \to \Delta \bar{a}_m \to \Delta \bar{b}_m)$

phase	evaluation phase				pre-charge phase			
a b m	Δq_m	timing	$\Delta \bar{q}_m$	timing	Δq_m	timing	$\Delta \bar{q}_m$	timing
0 0 0	0	-	1	$\Delta \bar{a}_m$	0	-	1	$\Delta \bar{a}_m$
0 0 1	1	Δa_m	0	-	1	Δa_m	0	-
0 1 0	0	-	1	$\Delta \bar{a}_m$	0	-	1	$\Delta \bar{m}$
0 1 1	1	Δa_m	0	-	1	Δm	0	-
1 0 0	0	-	1	$\Delta \bar{b}_m$	0	-	1	$\Delta \bar{m}$
1 0 1	1	Δb_m	0	-	1	Δm	0	-
1 1 0	1	Δb_m	0	-	1	Δa_m	0	-
1 1 1	0	-	1	$\Delta \bar{b}_m$	0	-	1	$\Delta \bar{a}_m$

values (a, b, m) that bring Δq_m $(\Delta \bar{q}_m) = 1$ under each delay condition and the transition of the input signal which brings the output transition. For example, when the values (a, b, m) is set $(0, 0, 1)$ on evaluation phase under the delay condition C1, the transition of the output signal q_m (that is, Δq_m) occurs at a time when the transition of the input signal b_m (that is, Δb_m) occurs.

Next, we evaluate the DPA-resistance of the MDPL AND gate from Table 3. Here, the DPA selection function is a or b. The differential waveform (T_{1-0}) that the average power waveform (T_0) with the selection function "0" is subtracted from the average power waveform (T_1) with the selection function "1" is regarded as the DPA trace. Table 4 shows the evaluation result of the DPA-resistance of the MDPL AND gate. And also, Table 4 indicates the existence of leakage according to delay conditions and the spike polarity on the DPA trace T_{1-0}. As an example, we explain DPA-resistance on the evaluation phase under the delay condition C2. First, it is found that the transition Δq_m $(\Delta \bar{q}_m)$ occurs together with the transitions Δm $(\Delta \bar{m})$ and Δb_m $(\Delta \bar{b}_m)$ on the evaluation phase under the delay condition C2 in Table 3. Here, when the DPA selection function is a, the output transition with $a = 1$ is sure to occur with the transition Δb_m $(\Delta \bar{b}_m)$, but the output transition with $a = 0$ occurs with the transitions Δm $(\Delta \bar{m})$. Note that the transition Δm $(\Delta \bar{m})$ is performed prior to Δb_m $(\Delta \bar{b}_m)$ according to the delay conditions. Therefore, it is predictable that the average power waveform T_0 will show the peak value of power consumption prior to T_1. We here consider that detectable power waveform in an actual measurement shows the power consumption that some capacitance influence, and does not show pure power consumption at each gate. More detailed consideration is presented in Appendix A. From the abovementioned contents, the valley-type spike appears on the differential waveform T_{1-0}.

As shown in Table 4, it should be noted that the leakage occurs under any delay conditions. In short, there is no secure delay condition in MDPL on the single input change model. Therefore, in order to implement the secure logic circuits using MDPL gates, it is required to adjust differences in the delay time between the input signals.

5   Experimental Results

In this section, we show experimental results of evaluating DPA-resistance of the basic components of WDDL and MDPL implemented on FPGA. The measurement of the power consumption is done by measuring the potential difference between both ends of a 10 ohm resistance which is inserted between the power source and a power supply pin of the FPGA. Table 5 shows the evaluation environment applied this time. This evaluation aims to inspect the effectiveness of MDPL for the leakage caused by the difference of loading capacitance (see F1 in Section 3.1) and leakage caused by the difference of delay time described in Section 4.

Table 4. DPA-resistance of an MDPL AND gate

Delay condition	Phase	Selection function	Leakage	Spike polarity
C1	evaluation	a	No	-
		b	No	-
	pre-charge	a	No	-
		b	Yes	↑
C2	evaluation	a	Yes	↓
		b	No	-
	pre-charge	a	No	-
		b	Yes	↑
C3	evaluation	a	Yes	↓
		b	No	-
	pre-charge	a	No	-
		b	No	-

5.1 Implementation of Model Circuits for Evaluation

Figure 5 shows the architecture of a model circuit used for evaluation. In the circuits shown in Figure 5, we implement 32 AND operations by using each countermeasure and supply the same input signals[1]. In order to evaluate only the power consumption of each countermeasure, the model circuit is designed so that other circuit parts should not operate while the countermeasure (MDPL/WDDL) part operates. In addition, a pair of positive logic and negative logic (combinational circuits for pre-charge, WDDL AND gates, MDPL AND gates and input/output FF (Flip-Flop) circuits) in the countermeasures is integrated into two LUTs (Look-Up Tables) and FFs in the Slice that are the basic components of Xilinx FPGA. And, the random number for masking is generated by M-Sequence of degree 89, which is created by the shift register installed in the FPGA. By using above mentioned simple circuits, we experimented following two evaluations (E1 and E2):

E1: We use a variety of constraints in the place-and-route to the circuits of WDDL and MDPL respectively and compare each DPA-resistance.

E2: To satisfy each delay conditions (C1 - C3), we insert the proper delay element constructed of 4 LUTs connection in series after the pre-charge logic of MDPL and compare the obtained DPA traces with evaluation results shown as Table 4 in Section 4.

The evaluation E1 is to compare WDDL with MDPL in relation to the main factor of leakage described in F1 of Section 3.1. The evaluation E2 is to inspect the leakage caused by the difference of delay time in MDPL circuits shown in Table 4.

---

[1] This is to ease the measuring. In the case that only one AND operation is implemented, the amount of the leakage becomes 1/32 and the number of samples to obtain the same Signal-Noise ratio should become the square of 32 times.

Table 5. Evaluation environment

Design environment	
Language	Verilog-HDL
Simulator	NC-Verilog LDV5.1 QSR2
Logic synthesis	Synplify Pro 8.1
Place and Route	ISE 6.3.03i, IP update4

Measurement environment	
Target FPGA	XCV1000-6-BG560C
Oscilloscope	Tektronix TDS 7104

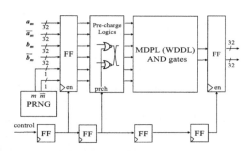

Fig. 5. Architecture of model circuit for evaluation

5.2   DPA Traces of Model Circuits

First, we explain the result for the evaluation E1. Figure 6 shows the DPA trace of the WDDL AND gates. The difference of constraints is location of LUTs and Slices used for the complementary logic for the WDDL and MDPL AND gates [2]. As realized from Figure 6, the polarity and height of spike change in dependence of the constraints. Figure 8 shows the DPA traces when the same constraints in the place-and-route are used for the MDPL AND gates. It is found that the spikes are difficult to recognize in Figure 8 by comparison with Figure 6. In other words, this indicates that MDPL has effectiveness on reducing leakage caused in dependence of the place-and-route.

Here, we consider each trace under the Constraint 1 in Figure 6 and Figure 8, respectively. Figure 7 and Figure 9 show magnified views of DPA traces under the Constraint 1. From Figure 6, Constraint 1 makes the complementary gates balance more than other constraints. Nevertheless, we can confirm slight leakages from the magnified views. Since these spikes have only narrow width, we guess that these leakages occur due to slight differences of delay time.

From the abovementioned matters, in order to make cryptographic circuits secure by using MDPL, we have to adopt the implementation method with attention on the number of logic steps of every signal and differences in the delay time between the signals, or the implementation method to adjust differences in

---

[2]   Each location is concretely specified by LOC and BEL command [13,14].

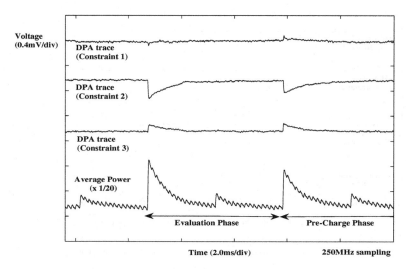

Fig. 6. DPA traces of WDDL AND gates (Evaluation E1, 200,000 samples)

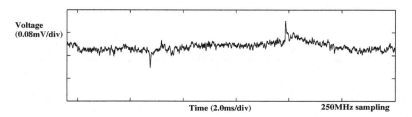

Fig. 7. Magnified view of the DPA trace with Consraint 1 in Fig.6

the delay time between the input signals by use of the delay elements. Moreover, if the slight leakages caused in Figure 8 become a problem, we also have to pay attention to constraints of the place-and-route.

Next, we explain the result of evaluation E2. Figure 10 shows the DPA trace of the MDPL AND gates corresponding to Table 4. From the content shown in Figure 10, it is found that the existence and polarity of spikes to be caused in the delay conditions are in good agreement with the content of Table 4. From this fact, we can confirm the leakage caused by the difference of delay time on the FPGA.

Here, we compare the height of spikes in Figure 8 and Figure 10. Since the delay elements are not entered intentionally into the input signals on the implementation for the evaluation E1, differences in the delay time between the input signals mainly depends on the place-and-route. Therefore, there are slight differences in the delay time between the input signals by comparison with the implementation for the evaluation E2. In short, because there is only a slight phase difference between the average power traces T_0 and T_1, the height of spikes (leakage) is also slight in Figure 8. On the contrary, as shown in Figure 10, it

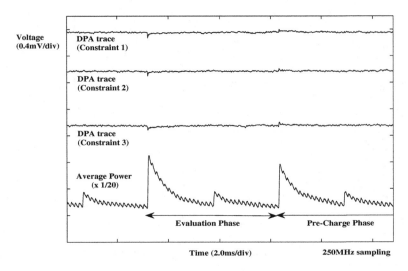

Fig. 8. DPA traces of the MDPL AND gates (Evaluation E1, 200,000 samples)

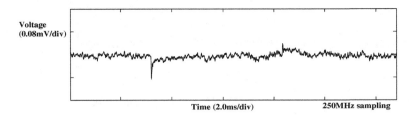

Fig. 9. Magnified view of the DPA trace with Consraint 1 in Fig.8

is found that the easily visible leakage occurs on the implementation for the evaluation E2 because there are large differences in the delay time between the input signals.

6   Conclusion

In this paper, we classified the main factors of leakage in DPA countermeasures using dual-rail circuit and especially evaluated the security of MDPL. As a result, it was found that MDPL has effectiveness on reducing the leakage caused by the difference of loading capacitance, but it makes the leakage occur as well as the WDDL when there are differences in the delay time between the input signals. In addition, experimental results using the FPGA showed that the more differences in the delay time between the input signals increases, the more leakage volume increases. Therefore, we expect that the DPA trace from the simulation has two spikes with different polarity, respectively. On the other hand, we run the DPA by measuring the voltage at both ends of the resistance connected outside of FPGA in our experiment.

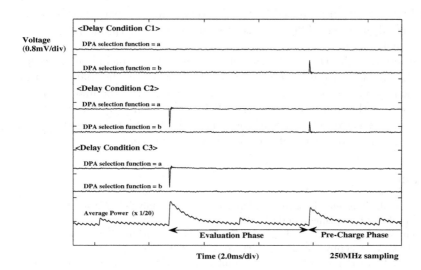

Fig. 10. DPA traces of the MDPL AND gates (Evaluation E2, 200,000 samples)

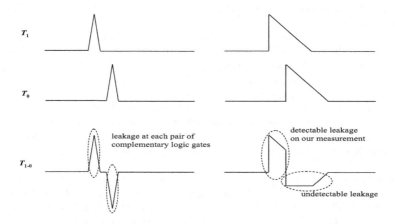

Fig. 11. Hypothesis concerning detectable leakage : from a simulation (left); and from our experiment (right)

The complicated logic circuits such as the cryptographic circuit generally cause differences in the delay time between the input signals. For this reason, the designer has to adjust the delay of signals with attention when designing the combinational circuit in order to structure the secure circuit using WDDL or MDPL. On the contrary, it needs some high-advanced complicated design at the logic level to adjust such differences in the delay time between the input signals. Moreover, if we assume an attacker who has high ability and can detect small spikes in Figure 8 which is caused by the differences in the delay time between the input signal, it is very difficult to keep security of the cryptographic circuit from the attacker.

When evaluating the DPA-resistance of the whole device including the cryptographic circuit, the visibility of leakage mostly depends on the characteristics of VLSI such as noise level, the evaluation environment, and the undetermined elements such as the ability of attackers. One of the future subjects is the research about how large differences in the delay time between the input signals are to be allowed (or to be a problem) on the whole device.

References

1. P. Kocher, J. Jaffe and B. Jun, "Differential Power Analysis," *Crypto'99*, LNCS 1666, pp. 388-397, Springer-Verlag, 1999.
2. E. Trichina, "Combinational Logic Design for AES SubByte Transformation on Masked Data," Cryptology ePrint Archive, 2003/236, 2003.
3. S. Mangard, T. Popp, and B. M. Gammel, "Side-Channel Leakage of Masked CMOS Gates," *CT-RSA 2005*, LNCS 3376, pp. 361-365, Springer-Verlag, 2005
4. S. Mangard, N. Pramstaller and E. Oswald, "Successfully Attacking Mased AES Hardware Implementation," *CHES 2005*, LNCS 3659, pp. 157-171, Springer-Verlag, 2005.
5. D. Suzuki, M. Saeki and T. Ichikawa, "Random Switching Logic: A Countermeasure against DPA based on Transition Probability," Cryptology ePrint Archive, Report 2004/346, 2004.
6. K. Tiri and I. Verbauwhede, "A Logic Level Design Methodology for a Secure DPA Resistant ASIC or FPGA Implementation," In Proc. of Design Automation and Test in Europe Conference, pp. 246-251, 2004.
7. K. Tiri and I. Verbauwhede, "Place and Route for Secure Stabdard Cell Design," *CARDIS'04*, pp.143-158, 2004.
8. D. Suzuki, M. Saeki, and T. Ichikawa, "DPA Lekage Models for CMOS Logic Circuits," *CHES 2005*, LNCS 3659, pp. 366-382, Springer-Verlag, 2005.
9. T. Popp and S. Mangard, "Masked Dual-Rail Pre-charge Logic : DPA-Resistance Without Routing Constraints," *CHES 2005*, LNCS 3659, pp. 172-186, Springer-Verlag, 2005.
10. A. P. Chandrakasan, S. Sheng, and R. W. Brodersen, "Low Power Digital CMOS Design," IEEE Journal of Solid State Circuits, Vol.27, N0.4. pp. 473-484,1992.
11. S. Guilley, P. Hoogvorst, Y. Mathieu, and R. Pacalet, "The "Backend Duplication" Method," *CHES 2005*, LNCS 3659, pp. 383-397, Springer-Verlag, 2005.
12. S. Morioka and A. Satoh, "An Optimized S-box Circuit Architecture for Low Power AES Design," *CHES 2002*, LNCS 2523, pp. 172-186, Springer-Verlag, 2002.
13. Xilinx, Inc., Data sheet "Virtex^{TM} 2.5 V Field Programmable Gate Arrays," http://direct.xilinx.com/bvdocs/publications/ds003.pdf
14. Xilinx, Inc., Software Manuals "Constraints Guide," http://www.xilinx.com/support/sw_manuals/xilinx6/download/cgd.zip

A   Detectable Leakage in an Actual Measurement

In this paper, we discussed the leakage due to the difference of delay time between the input signals of the complementary gates. We consider the difference between the leakage that occurs essentially and the leakage that can be observed in our experiment.

Figure 11 shows our qualitative hypothesis of the mechanism that the leakage occurs due to the difference of delay time. Current at each complementary gate that we can observe from the simulation (such as SPICE etc.) will show the sharp trace that the current change completes in the short time as shown in the left of Figure 11.

On the other hand, we run the DPA by measuring the voltage at both ends of the resistance connected outside of FPGA in our experiment. In this case, each trace shown in this paper has the feature shown in the right of Figure 11. First, the current incereases rapidly in the vicinity of the clock edge. Afterwards, the current decreases slowly until the next clock edges. Therefore, we can expect that only the first spike sharpens, and the next spike smoothes. As a result, we can recognize only the first spike from the DPA trace. One of the causes of different results from simulation and actual measurement is various capacitance of FPGA and measuring instruments.

Instruction Set Extensions for Efficient AES Implementation on 32-bit Processors

Stefan Tillich and Johann Großschädl

Graz University of Technology,
Institute for Applied Information Processing and Communications,
Inffeldgasse 16a, A–8010 Graz, Austria
{Stefan.Tillich, Johann.Groszschaedl}@iaik.tugraz.at

Abstract. Secure communication over public networks like the Internet requires the use of cryptographic algorithms as basic building blocks. Most cryptographic workloads pose a considerable burden on devices like PDAs, cell phones, and sensor nodes, which are limited in processing power, memory and energy. In this paper we present an approach to increase the efficiency of 32-bit processors for handling symmetric cryptographic algorithms with the help of instruction set extensions. We propose a number of custom instructions to support the Advanced Encryption Standard (AES). Using the SPARC V8-compatible Leon2 embedded processor, we evaluate the effects of the extensions on performance and code size of AES, as well as on silicon area. With a moderate increase in silicon area, AES performance can be improved by a factor of nearly 10, while code size is reduced significantly and implementation flexibility is retained. We also show that our approach is very beneficial for implementation in superscalar processors and that it can compete with the performance of previously proposed cryptographic processors and instruction set extensions.

Keywords: Advanced Encryption Standard, instruction set extensions, embedded RISC processor, SPARC V8 architecture, efficient implementation.

1 Introduction

The increasing need for secure communication and data handling requires more and more embedded systems to execute cryptographic algorithms. However, this task can impose a heavy burden on constrained devices like PDAs, cell phones, and sensor nodes due to their limited resources in terms of computing power, memory, and energy. The traditional approach to alleviate the computational cost of cryptographic primitives is to offload this workload from the host processor to a dedicated cryptographic coprocessor. Optimized hardware implementations of cryptographic primitives can be several orders of magnitude faster than software implementations on general-purpose processors. On the other hand, hardware solutions have drawbacks as well: For instance, coprocessors often lack the flexibility to support different key sizes, modes of operation, and other parameters of a cryptographic algorithm. Moreover, the integration of a coprocessor can entail a considerable increase in silicon area, which in turn raises production cost.

An alternative to coprocessors is the integration of custom instructions into general-purpose processors with the goal to better support cryptographic computations. The

L. Goubin and M. Matsui (Eds.): CHES 2006, LNCS 4249, pp. 270–284, 2006.

concept of *instruction set extensions* has been employed very successfully in the domain of multimedia and digital signal processing. Recent research has also shown the benefits of instruction set extensions for public-key cryptography. In this paper we examine support for symmetric cryptography and present our research on instruction set extensions for one of the most important symmetric cryptographic algorithms—the Advanced Encryption Standard (AES) [13].

From a system's perspective, the main aspect to consider is how much faster an application completes execution, but not the "raw" performance figures of a hardware accelerator. Recent work which examined the addition of an AES coprocessor to a SPARC V8 embedded processor has shown that the benefits of a hardware accelerator can be significantly mitigated through communication overhead, i.e. the transfer of data to and from the coprocessor [8,16]. For instance, the AES coprocessor used in [8] is able to encrypt a 128-bit block of data in 11 clock cycles, but loading the data and key into the coprocessor, performing the AES encryption itself, and returning the result back to the software routine takes 704 cycles altogether. In light of this result we argue that tightly-coupled custom instructions can deliver superior performance at lower hardware cost and with increased implementation flexibility. In any case, we demonstrate in this paper that instruction set extensions for symmetric cryptography can be an attractive design option for embedded systems which have a need for security.

The rest of the paper is organized as follows. In Section 2 we discuss some approaches for the efficient implementation of cryptographic primitives on a general-purpose processor with emphasis on AES. Section 3 lists previous publications which deal with architectural support for AES. In Section 4 we describe our approach in general and give details for each custom instruction. Impact on silicon area of the extensions is estimated in Section 5. In Section 6 we give a detailed analysis of performance and code size of our AES implementations using different sets of custom instructions and compare our results to related work. Conclusions are drawn in Section 7.

2 Efficient Implementation of Cryptography on General-Purpose Processors

Software implementations of cryptographic primitives generally offer the highest degree of flexibility, but may yield poor performance in embedded systems which are limited in terms of processing power, memory, or available energy. The straightforward way to overcome the inefficiencies of software solutions is the integration of a coprocessor to relieve the main processor from the cryptographic workload. Cryptographic hardware is typically much faster and more energy efficient than software running on an embedded processor. Depending on the application, a coprocessor may also help to reduce the memory footprint of a cryptographic algorithm. A third implementation option is the addition of custom instructions to the processor. Instruction set extensions for cryptography can lead to a considerable reduction of processing time, which in turn saves energy. Memory requirements may also be reduced with custom instructions.

Support for secret-key algorithms on programmable processors has mainly been investigated in the context of application-specific processors (ASIPs) for cryptographic workloads. The extension of general-purpose processors to better support secret-key algorithms has received relatively little attention. This paper is solely focussed at the AES algorithm and we will discuss previous work dealing with AES in Section 3.

AES software implementations on 32-bit processors always require memory lookup tables of a certain size. T-lookup implementations require up to three tables, where each size can be either 1 KB or 4 KB. The T-lookup approach circumvents the costly calculation of the MixColumns or InvMixColumns transformation within a normal AES round with the first table. The second table can be used for the last round, which does not include the MixColumns and InvMixColumns transformation. The third table is useful for speeding up the key expansion for AES decryption. The T-lookup approach increases code size and its performance highly depends on the size and organization of the cache subsystem. The alternative to T-lookup is to calculate all AES round transformations on the processor. The substitution using the S-box remains the only operation too inefficient to calculate and which requires a 256-byte lookup table for encryption and decryption, respectively. Such AES implementations—which we will denote as *calculating implementations* in the rest of this paper—can pack either one State column or one State row into a 32-bit register. The latter approach, which has been proposed by Bertoni et al. [1], allows for a more efficient realization of the MixColumns and especially of the InvMixColumns transformation at the cost of additional transpositions of the AES State and a slightly more complex key expansion function. In the following, implementations according to the approach of Bertoni et al. will be denoted as *row-oriented*, while conventional calculating implementations will be referred to as *column-oriented*.

3   Previous Work on Extensions for AES

This section outlines previous work on the support of AES in application-specific and general-purpose processors. A comparison of the respective performance figures with those of our approach is given in Table 4 in Section 6.1.

Burke et al. have developed custom instructions for several AES candidates [3]. They have proposed a 16-bit modular multiplication, bit-permutation support, several rotate instructions, and an instruction to facilitate address generation for memory table lookups. In a follow-up work, Wu et al. have designed CryptoManiac, a cryptographic coprocessor. CryptoManiac is a *Very Long Instruction Word (VLIW)* processor able to execute up to four instruction per cycle [20]. Additionally, short latency instructions (e.g. bitwise logical and arithmetic instructions) can be combined to be executed in a single cycle. To support this feature, instructions have up to three source operands.

The Cryptonite crypto-processor is a VLIW architecture with two 64-bit datapaths [14]. It features support for AES through a set of special instructions for performing byte-permutation, rotation and xor operations. The main part of AES is done with help of parallel table lookup from dedicated memories.

Fiskiran and Lee have investigated the inclusion of hardware lookup tables as a measure to accelerate different symmetric ciphers including AES [5]. They propose inclusion of on-chip scratchpad memory to support parallel table lookup. Examined are datapath widths of 32, 64 and 128 bit with 4, 8 and 16 tables, respectively, whereby each table contains 256 32-bit entries (i.e. is 1 KB in size).

Extensions for PLX—a general-purpose RISC architecture—have been proposed by Irwin and Page [9]. In their work they also examined the usage of the multimedia extensions of a PLX processor with a 128-bit datapath in order to implement AES with a minimal number of memory accesses. However, the presented concepts can hardly be adapted to 32-bit architectures.

Automatic generation of instruction set extensions for cryptographic algorithms (including AES) has been investigated by Ravi et al. using the 32-bit Xtensa processor from Tensilica [15]. Nadehara et al. proposed a single custom instruction which calculates most of the AES round transformations for a single State byte [12]. Their approach maps the round lookup (T lookup) of fast AES software implementations on 32-bit platforms into a dedicated functional unit. Bertoni et al. have proposed several instructions for AES and have recently published implementation details and estimated performance figures for an Intel StrongARM processor [2].

Schaumont et al. [16] and Hodjat et al. [8] have investigated the addition of an AES coprocessor to the 32-bit Leon2 embedded processor. Performance for a memory-mapped approach and a connection through a dedicated coprocessor interface (CPI) has been reported. An AES operation was one to two orders of magnitude slower in relation to the mere time required by the coprocessor.

In our previous work we have investigated the use of instruction set extensions for public-key cryptography for accelerating AES implementations [17]. We have also focussed on minimizing the memory requirements of AES software implementations with a single low-cost custom instruction [18]. The work presented in this paper deals with different custom instructions for AES which can be implemented independently or in combination, thereby enabling different trade-offs between performance and silicon area. For example, the focus can be set on low cost (for a moderate speed-up) or high performance (which is, of course, more costly in terms of area).

4   Proposed Instruction Set Extensions for AES

We designed several custom instructions to increase the performance of AES software implementations. These instructions have been developed for 32-bit processors with a RISC-like instruction format with two input operands and one output operand. All important 32-bit RISC architectures, such as SPARC, MIPS and ARM, adhere to this three-operand format. Our instructions do not require special architectural features like dedicated look-up tables or non-standard register files, which makes their integration into general-purpose RISC architectures relatively easy. An integration into extensible processors like Tensilica's Xtensa or the ARC 600/700 family of cores should also be straightforward. Furthermore, all of our instructions have been designed with the goal to keep the critical path of a concrete hardware implementation as short as possible.

The custom instructions can be categorized as byte-oriented or word-oriented, depending on whether a single byte or four bytes are processed at a time. All instructions calculate parts of AES round transformations, yielding either one or four transformed bytes as result. The targeted AES round transformations are SubBytes, ShiftRows, and MixColumns, as well as their respective inverses. Moreover, the custom instructions also support the SubWord-RotWord operation of the key expansion.

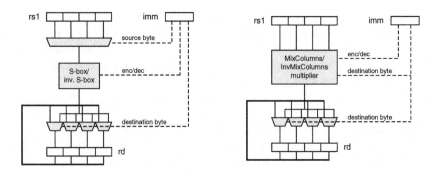

Fig. 1. Functionality of the sbox instruction   **Fig. 2.** Functionality of the mixcol instruction

4.1 Byte-Oriented AES Extensions (`sbox, mixcol`)

The byte-oriented instructions have fixed types of source operands. The first source operand is a register, while the second source operand is always an immediate value. This immediate value is used to configure the operation of the instruction. The single-byte result is written to a byte of the destination register, while the other three bytes retain their previous value. As the second source operand is an immediate value, the second read port of the register file is not occupied and can be used to load the value of the destination register. In this way, the old value from the destination register can be combined with the single-byte result, producing the complete 32-bit result of the instruction, which is written back to the register file.

The sbox instruction has been proposed in [17] to reduce the memory requirements of AES implementations. Its functionality is depicted in Figure 1. The sbox instruction transforms one byte of the source register (rs1) with the AES S-box or inverse S-box and writes the resulting byte into the destination register (rd). The immediate value (imm) is used to select the source byte from the source register, the transformation (S-box or inverse S-box) and the destination byte. With this instruction, both the SubBytes and the ShiftRows transformation can be implemented very efficiently. The sbox instruction also accelerates the SubWord-RotWord operation in the AES key expansion.

The mixcol instruction performs a part of the MixColumns or InvMixColumns transformation. Figure 2 shows the functionality of this instruction. The mixcol instruction takes the value in the source register (rs1) as input column and produces a single byte of the resulting column after the MixColumns operation. In this case, the immediate value sets the operation (MixColumns or InvMixColumns) as well as the destination byte. The complete resulting column can, therefore, be acquired with four executions of the mixcol instruction. As MixColumns and especially InvMixColumns are relatively costly in software, this instruction can lead to considerable speedups.

4.2 Plain Word-Oriented AES Extensions (`mixcol4, sbox4`)

The word-oriented instructions always produce a 32-bit result which is stored in the destination register. The trivial approach is to quadruple the functionality of the byte-oriented extensions. As our performance evaluation in Section 6 shows, this approach

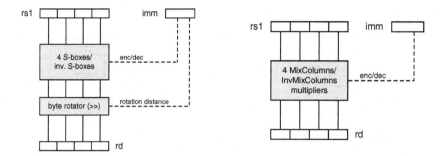

Fig. 3. Functionality of the sbox4 instruction   **Fig. 4.** Functionality of the mixcol4 instruction

yields sub-optimal results. However, a slight modification introduced in Section 4.3 can deliver very satisfactory support for AES.

The sbox4 instruction simply substitutes all four bytes of the first source register and places them into the destination register. A byte-wise rotation can optionally be performed on the result. The immediate value selects whether S-box or inverse S-box are used for substitution and sets the rotation distance for the result. The optional rotation is useful for row-oriented AES implementations, where ShiftRows can be performed with no additional cost. Moreover, the SubWord-RotWord operation of the key expansion is supported with the sbox4 instruction. The operation of sbox4 is shown in Figure 3.

The mixcol4 instruction calculates all four result bytes of the MixColumns or Inv-MixColumns operations. As illustrated in Figure 4, the input column is taken from the first source register while the immediate value as second operand just selects the operation (encryption or decryption).

4.3   Advanced Word-Oriented AES Extensions with Implicit ShiftRows (sbox4s/isbox4s/sbox4r, mixcol4s/imixcol4s)

The major drawback of the sbox4 and mixcol4 instructions is that they cannot be combined in a manner to allow an efficient AES implementation. The problem lies with the ShiftRows transformation, which has now become the performance bottleneck.

In a column-oriented implementation, SubBytes and MixColumns would be done with the respective custom instruction, while ShiftRows must be done separately. As the State columns are packed into registers, ShiftRows requires a number of shift and logical operations (about 44 instructions). Another option would be to hold the State rows in registers to perform SubBytes and ShiftRows with the sbox4 instruction, to map the State columns into registers prior to MixColumns with mixcol4 and to map then back to the State rows. However, each mapping would require similar effort as performing ShiftRows. With two mappings required per round, this approach would be even more inefficient than the column-oriented implementation with separate ShiftRows.

Luckily, the solution to this problem is quite simple. Assuming a column-oriented implementation, ShiftRows can be done implicitly with slightly modified sbox4 and mixcol4 instructions. In order to achieve this, the modified versions have two source register operands. From each source register, two bytes are extracted and assembled to

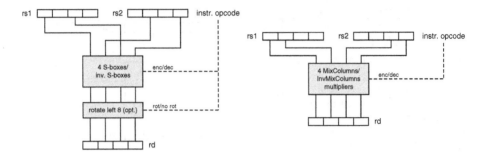

Fig. 5. Functionality of the `sbox4s`, `isbox4s` and `sbox4r` instructions

Fig. 6. Functionality of the `mixcol4s` and `imixcol4s` instructions

a new intermediate State column. The respective AES transformation is performed on this intermediate column and the result is stored in the destination register. By selecting the registers with the appropriate State columns as first and second source operands it is possible to perform the ShiftRows transformation implicitly. The same is true for InvShiftRows in decryption when the inverse equivalent cipher structure is used, i.e. InvSubBytes, InvShiftRows, and InvMixColumns are subsequent transformations.

As the second operand must now be a register, no intermediate value is available to configure the operation of the instruction. Therefore, separate instructions are used for S-box and inverse S-box substitution as well as MixColumns and InvMixColumns. The modified instructions are denoted with an "s" appended to the original mnemonic (`sbox4s`, `mixcol4s`). To indicate the mnemonic for the respective inverse operation, an "i" is prepended (`isbox4s`, `imixcol4s`).

Figure 5 shows the functionality of the `sbox4s` and `isbox4s` instructions. The first (i.e. most significant) and third byte of the first source register and the second and fourth (i.e. least significant) byte from the second source register are substituted using the AES S-box or inverse S-box. The optional rotation to the left by one byte is not used for these two instructions. The four S-boxes are used to realize a third instruction `sbox4r`, which performs S-box substitution followed by rotation to the left by 8 bits. This instruction implements the SubWord-RotWord operation of the AES key expansion. The byte rotation by a selectable distance of the `sbox4` instruction is not implemented as this functionality is not useful for column-oriented AES implementations.

The two instructions `mixcol4s` and `imixcol4s` perform MixColumns and InvMix-Columns, respectively. The functionality of these instructions is depicted in Figure 6. The input column is assembled from the two most significant bytes of the first source register and the two least significant bytes of the second source registers. Note that an AES State column contained in a single register can be transformed by indicating the register as both first and second source operand.

The selection of bytes from the two source registers of the `sbox4s`/`isbox4s` and `mixcol4s`/`imixcol4s` instructions allows to perform the ShiftRows and InvShiftRows transformation implicitly in the sequence of SubBytes, ShiftRows, and MixColumns in AES encryption and InvSubBytes, InvShiftRows, and InvMixColumns in AES decryption (using the equivalent inverse cipher structure).

Table 1. Area and delay of functional units for the proposed extensions as well as of the extended integer unit

Functional unit/Component	Area			Delay
	μ^2	Gate equiv.	Norm.	ns
S-box (Canright) [4]	3,362.69	650	0.05	2.21
S-box (HW LUT)	15,709.25	3,033	0.23	0.64
MixColumns multiplier [19]	2,248.13	435	0.03	0.51
IU without extensions	69,144.19	13,349	1.00	3.93
IU with sbox	73,417.54	14,174	1.06	4.00
IU with sbox4	77,849.86	15,029	1.13	4.00
IU with mixcol	71,865.79	13,874	1.04	3.90
IU with mixcol4	72,372.10	13,972	1.05	3.98
IU with sbox & mixcol	71,753.47	13,853	1.04	4.00
IU with sbox & mixcol4	75,536.06	14,583	1.09	4.00
IU with sbox4s & mixcol4s	84,794.69	16,370	1.23	4.00

5 Hardware Cost

We have integrated the instructions proposed in Section 4 into the SPARC V8-compatible Leon2 processor, which is freely available from Gaisler Research [6]. To estimate the cost for the additional hardware, we synthesized the new functional units and the complete Leon2 integer unit (IU)—i.e. the 5-stage processor pipeline—with the AES extensions using a UMC 0.13 μm standard-cell library. We used all viable combinations of custom instructions and have evaluated their performance in Section 6.

For the S-box extensions we have synthesized a single hardware S-box using two different approaches: The design of Canright, which calculates the S-box in hardware [4] and a hardware lookup table synthesized as an array of logic. The MixColumns multiplier follows the approach by Wolkerstorfer [19] and produces a single byte of the resulting column. For synthesis of the integer unit we have chosen a target delay for the critical path of 4 ns, which conforms to a maximal clock frequency of 250 MHz. These synthesis results include the complete area overhead of the extensions, e.g. new functional units, decoding of additional opcodes. The results are given in Table 1. Note that sbox4s indicates the three instructions sbox4s, isbox4s and sbox4r and that mixcol4s stands for the instructions mixcol4s and imixcol4s.

The S-box of Canright is about one fifth the size of the synthesized lookup table, but is also considerably slower. The MixColumns multiplier requires little area and has a shorter critical path than the S-boxes. The results in Table 1 for the integer unit use the approach of Canright [4] for S-box extensions. Area overhead is calculated in relation to an integer unit without extensions and ranges between a factor of 1.04 and 1.23.

We used the minimal configuration (no hardware multiplier and divider, no FPU, no Ethernet MAC, no PCI controller, no SDRAM controller, no Debug Support Unit), where the IU accounts for less than half of the area of the Leon2 processor (excluding register file and cache memories). The size of the register file and caches is configurable and depends heavily on the particular RAM implementation. For the largest extensions (sbox4s & mixcol4s), the area overhead will therefore be maximally half of the IU overhead (which is a factor of about 1.12), without taking register file or cache memory into consideration. In practice, these units will require a large portion of the total area, so that the overall overhead factor for the area will be much lower.

6   Performance and Code Size

We have implemented AES using different combinations of the proposed custom instructions on the modified Leon2. In total, we examined seven different sets of AES extensions, where one of these sets (just the sbox instruction) has already been investigated in [18]. For comparison, the performance of AES implementations using T lookup has also been determined on the same platform. Bitsliced implementations of AES are not expected to be faster than T lookup [10] and have therefore not been considered in this evaluation. Both AES encryption and decryption with precomputed key schedule as well as with on-the-fly key expansion have been examined. A pure-software AES implementation has been used as baseline implementation. It uses no extensions and calculates all AES round transformations except SubBytes. For all implementations the number of clock cycles per block encryption/decryption and code size are given. Moreover, the speedup as well as relative change of code size in comparison to the baseline implementation are cited. For AES implementations with precomputed key schedule, the performance of the key expansion is also given.

The Leon2 has been implemented on a GR-PCI-XC2V FPGA board with a cache size of 16 KB for both instruction and data cache. The number of cycles has been obtained with the help of a built-in cycle counter of the modified Leon2. For the timing measurements we have used the code from Gladman's AES implementation [7], which times the execution of 9 subsequent operations and of a single AES operation. The time for one operation is determined as the difference of these measurements divided by 8. The code size encompasses all functions and memory constants required to perform the respective AES operation. This includes the encryption/decryption function, the key expansion function (if required), and necessary lookup tables. The used custom instructions are indicated in the first column of each table. As before, sbox4s stands for sbox4s, isbox4s and sbox4r; mixcol4s stands for mixcol4s and imixcol4s.

When a set of extensions is useable for both column-oriented and row-oriented AES implementations, both of these options have been examined and the faster option cited in the tables. Most AES implementations are written in C and use inline assembly to make use of the custom instructions. Implementations marked with *ASM* are completely written in assembly. For the implementation which uses the sbox4s and mixcol4s instructions, an assembly-optimized version with unrolled loops has also been tested (marked with *unrolled*). For each T-lookup implementation, the size of the tables is indicated. The first number indicates the table size for the round lookup, the second number (if present) is the table size for the last round. For AES decryption, the third number (if present) indicates the size of the table used for the key expansion function.

Table 2 summarizes the performance and code size for AES-128 encryption with a precomputed key schedule. Table 5 in Appendix A gives the respective figures for

Table 2. AES-128 encryption, precomputed key schedule: Performance and code size

Implementation	Key exp.	Encr. perf.		Code size	
	Cycles	Cycles	Speedup	Bytes	Rel. change
No extensions (pure SW)	739	1,637	1.00	2,168	0.0%
sbox	647	1,140	1.44	1,464	-32.5%
sbox4 (C)	739	1,020	1.60	1,656	-23.6%
sbox4 (ASM)	739	718	2.28	1,520	-29.9%
mixcol	498	1,047	1.56	1,262	-41.8%
mixcol4	498	939	1.74	1,224	-43.5%
sbox & mixcol	346	566	2.89	612	-71.8%
sbox & mixcol4 (C)	346	458	3.57	564	-74.0%
sbox & mixcol4 (ASM)	346	337	4.86	480	-77.9%
sbox4s & mixcol4s (C)	316	458	3.57	568	-73.8%
sbox4s & mixcol4s (ASM)	316	219	7.47	412	-81.0%
sbox4s & mixcol4s, unrolled	316	196	8.35	896	-58.7%
T lookup (Gladman), 1 KB	436	1,585	1.03	9,956	+359.2%
T lookup (Gladman), 4 KB	436	1,097	1.49	10,900	+402.8%

decryption. For the proposed extensions, speedups of up to 8.35 for encryption and 9.97 for decryption are achieved. With the fastest extensions, AES-128 encryption and decryption of a single block can be done in 196 clock cycles. The code size of these implementations is always reduced, whereby the savings are more significant for the MixColumns extensions than for the S-box extensions. The T-lookup implementations from Brian Gladman have been used for comparison [7]. There the speedup is up to 1.5 for encryption and 1.78 for decryption at the cost of quite significant increases in code size.

The results for AES-128 encryption with on-the-fly key expansion are given in Table 3. For the respective figures for decryption refer to Table 6 in Appendix A. All decryption implementations are supplied with the last round key. For encryption, speedups up to 9.91 are achieved while the highest decryption speedup is 9.29. The fastest extensions allow for encryption in 226 cycles and decryption in 262 cycles. Note that decryption is slightly slower as it uses the inverse equivalent cipher structure, which requires a more complex key expansion with additional InvMixColumns transformations. Some extensions allow quite significant reductions of code size. Implementations which make use of S-box extensions require no data memory accesses except for the loading of the input block and key and the storing of the output block. T-lookup implementations for encryption have speedups up to 1.5. Decryption functions with T lookup are highly inefficient due to the more complex key expansion.

In order to get an idea of the worst-case execution time (WCET), we have also measured a single AES-128 encryption (rolled loops) with flushed data and instruction caches. Under these unfavorable conditions, encryption requires 565 cycles for a pre-computed key schedule and 420 cycles for on-the-fly key expansion. Any subsequent encryption requires only little more than the number of cycles given in Tables 2 and 3. For unrolled loops, the first encryption naturally gets more costly with 761 cycles (precomputed) and 595 cycles (on-the-fly).

Table 3. AES-128 encryption, on-the-fly key expansion: Performance and code size

Implementation	Encr. perf.		Code size	
	Cycles	Speedup	Bytes	Rel. change
No extensions (pure SW)	2,239	1.00	1,636	0.0%
sbox	1,595	1.40	952	-41.8%
sbox4	1,618	1.38	1,696	-3.7%
mixcol	1,294	1.73	1,260	-23.0%
mixcol4	1,186	1.89	1,212	-25.9%
sbox & mixcol (C)	747	3.00	580	-64.6%
sbox & mixcol (ASM)	505	4.43	396	-75.8%
sbox & mixcol4 (C)	639	3.50	532	-67.5%
sbox & mixcol4 (ASM)	397	5.64	348	-78.7%
sbox4s & mixcol4s (C)	616	3.63	528	-67.7%
sbox4s & mixcol4s (ASM)	255	8.78	260	-84.1%
sbox4s & mixcol4s, unrolled	226	9.91	852	-47.9%
T lookup, 1 KB	2,066	1.08	2,572	+57.2%
T lookup, 4 KB	1,497	1.50	5,420	+231.3%

6.1 Comparison with Related Work

Table 4 cites performance figures for most of the related work listed in Section 3. Note that it is difficult to compare the different approaches in a concise manner as some architectures have quite unique features. We categorized the different platforms by the width of their datapath (*DPW*), the number of instructions which can be executed per cycle (issue width, *IW*), and the number of data memory read ports (*DMRP*). Most architectures include dedicated lookup tables which allow parallel lookup. We have stated the number of lookup tables (*LUTs*), i.e. the number of possible parallel lookups, as well as the size of one table in bytes. The last two columns of Table 4 give the number of cycles required for encryption and decryption of an 128-bit block with AES-128.

The fastest implementation with our proposed extensions is contained in the table with an indicated issue width of 1. However, all of the proposed extensions are also beneficial for processors with larger issue width. For high-speed implementations we have examined the S-box and MixColumns extensions with implicit ShiftRows for their benefits on processors with an issue width of 4. This allows us to compare our extensions to existing architectures with superscalar processing and/or a datapath width above 32. Note that we have not implemented such a 4-way processor and that our performance figures are estimations based on pseudocode. Our code includes loading of input block and cipher key from memory, as well as storing of the output block back to memory. For our estimations we have assumed cache hits (one cycle latency) for all loaded values. This is an overhead of about 10% compared to AES encryption or decryption without loading of the input block and storing of the output block.

Except for [15], [2] and our work, all architectures have either a datapath width greater than 32, an issue width greater than 1 and/or include dedicated parallel lookup tables. Our single-issue approach is nearly an order of magnitude faster than [15] and it has about the same performance of the approach in [12], which uses a superscalar

Table 4. AES-128 performance comparison with related work

Platform	Reference	DPW	IW/DMRP	LUTs/Size	Encr.	Decr.
RISC-like	Fiskiran [5]	128	1/1	16/1,024	32	32
PLX-128	Irwin [9]	128	1/1	0/0	609	n/a
Alpha (8W+)	Burke [3]	64	8/4	4/1,024	99	n/a
Alpha (4W+)	Burke [3]	64	4/2	4/1,024	164	n/a
Cryptonite	Oliva [14]	64	2/1	16/256	71	83
RISC-like	Fiskiran [5]	64	1/1	8/1,024	126	126
CryptoManiac	Wu [20]	32	4/1	4/1,024	90	n/a
Leon2 + ISE	**This work**	**32**	**4/1**	**0/0**	**51**	**51**
RISC-like	Nadehara [12]	32	2/1	0/0	200	200
RISC-like	Fiskiran [5]	32	1/1	4/1,024	315	315
Xtensa + ISE	Ravi [15]	32	1/1	0/0	1,400	1,400
StrongARM	Bertoni [2]	32	1/1	0/0	311	n/a
Leon2 + ISE	**This work**	**32**	**1/1**	**0/0**	**196**	**196**
Leon2 + COP (CPI)	Hodjat [8]	32	1/1	0/0	704	n/a
Leon2 + COP (MM)	Hodjat [8]	32	1/1	0/0	1,228	n/a
Leon2 + COP (MM)	Schaumont [16][a]	32	1/1	0/0	1,494	n/a
Athlon 64	Matsui [10]	64	3/2	0/0	170	n/a
Pentium 4	Matsui [11]	32	3/1	0/0	251	n/a

[a] Performance calculated from time for encryption at 50 MHz.

processor with issue width 2. Despite the worse cited performance figures, the approach of [2] should be faster than our approach, but at the cost of a severe increase of the critical path and the need for non-standard parallel access to four processor registers. The CryptoManiac [20] with an issue width of 4 and four dedicated lookup tables of 1 KB each has only half of the cycle count of our single-issue approach, and is slower than our 4-way issue approach . Only the architecture of [5] with a 128-bit datapath and 16 dedicated lookup tables of 1 KB each and with a subsequent dedicated XOR-tree is faster than our 4-way issue approach by a factor of about 1.6.

Table 4 also includes the results of a Leon2 with attached AES coprocessor (COP) [8,16]. Both works have investigated a memory-mapped (MM) solution and Hodjat et al. have also examined an approach with a dedicated coprocessor interface (CPI) [8]. These works demonstrate impressively that the mere speed of an accelerator is not the important point to consider from a system's perspective. Hodjat et al. state in [8] that *the AES encryption itself takes only 11 cycles, but the complete program with loading the data and key, AES encryption, and returning the result back to the software routine takes a total of 704 cycles.* Our worst-case execution times with flushed caches for precomputed key schedule (565 cycles with rolled loops, 761 cycles with unrolled loops) and on-the-fly key expansion (420 cycles with rolled loops, 595 cycles with unrolled loops) compare very well to the coprocessor performance from [8,16].

For comparison we have also specified the performance of the currently fastest AES implementations for the Pentium 4 (Northwood core) [11] and the Athlon 64 processor [10]. A single-issue Leon2 processor with our extensions has an area of about 50k gates altogether and requires less cycles than the Pentium 4 (about 13.5M gates) and can nearly reach the cycle count of the Athlon 64 (about 17M gates).

6.2   A Note on Side-Channel Attacks

The investigation of side-channel attacks has not been in the main focus of the present work. The extensions for the S-box remove the need for memory accesses for table lookups and, therefore, completely prevent cache-based side-channel attacks. As data is manipulated similarly as on a processor without extensions, susceptibility to other side-channel attacks should not become higher when using the proposed extensions.

Possible side-channel countermeasures encompass all traditional options for microprocessors, e.g. use of secure logic styles, randomization, software masking. AES implementations which employ additive masking can also make use of the proposed extensions. Additive software masking can be directly used with all MixColumns extensions, as MixColumns is a linear transformation. The custom instructions for S-box substitution cannot be used in a masked SubBytes transformation, but they can be used to compute masked S-box tables for conventional memory-based S-box table lookup.

7   Conclusions

In this paper we have presented instruction set extensions for 32-bit processors for the Advanced Encryption Standard. We have proposed byte-oriented and word-oriented custom instructions which can be combined in a number of different ways and which provide support for the most time-consuming transformations of AES. Our extensions are very flexible and can be used for encryption and decryption as well as with precomputed key schedule and on-the-fly key expansion. With hardware costs of about 3k gates, AES-128 encryption and decryption is possible in 196 clock cycles. In relation to an AES implementation using only SPARC V8 instructions, speedups of up to 9.91 for encryption and 9.97 for decryption are achieved, while code size is reduced significantly. Furthermore, we have shown that our extensions can be implemented in a superscalar processor where they can compete very successfully with dedicated cryptographic processors and previously proposed instructions set extensions.

Acknowledgements. The research described in this paper has been supported by the Austrian Science Fund (FWF) under grant number P16952-NO4 and, in part, by the European Commission through the IST Programme under contract IST-2002-507932 ECRYPT. The information in this document reflects only the authors' views, is provided as is and no guarantee or warranty is given that the information is fit for any particular purpose. The user thereof uses the information at its sole risk and liability.

References

1. G. Bertoni, L. Breveglieri, P. Fragneto, M. Macchetti, and S. Marchesin. Efficient Software Implementation of AES on 32-Bit Platforms. In *Cryptographic Hardware and Embedded Systems — CHES 2002*, LNCS 2523, pp. 159–171. Springer Verlag, 2003.
2. G. Bertoni, L. Breveglieri, R. Farina, and F. Regazzoni. Speeding Up AES By Extending a 32-Bit Processor Instruction Set. In *Proceedings of the 17th IEEE International Conference on Application-Specific Systems, Architectures and Processors (ASAP 2006)*. IEEE CS Press, Sept. 2006. To be published.

3. J. Burke, J. McDonald, and T. Austin. Architectural support for fast symmetric-key cryptography. In Proceedings of the 9th Int. Conference on Architectural Support for Programming Languages and Operating Systems (ASPLOS 2000), pp. 178–189. ACM Press, 2000.

4. D. Canright. A very compact S-Box for AES. In *Cryptographic Hardware and Embedded Systems — CHES 2005*, LNCS 3659, pp. 441–455. Springer Verlag, 2005.

5. A. M. Fiskiran and R. B. Lee. On-Chip Lookup Tables for Fast Symmetric-Key Encryption. In *Proceedings of the 16th IEEE International Conference on Application-Specific Systems, Architectures and Processors (ASAP 2005)*, pp. 356–363. IEEE CS Press, 2005.

6. J. Gaisler. The LEON-2 Processor User's Manual (Version 1.0.30). Available for download at http://www.gaisler.com/doc/leon2-1.0.30-xst.pdf, March 2006.

7. B. Gladman. Implementations of AES (Rijndael) in C/C++ and assembler. Available at http://fp.gladman.plus.com/cryptography_technology/rijndael/index.htm.

8. A. Hodjat and I. Verbauwhede. Interfacing a high speed crypto accelerator to an embedded CPU. In *Proceedings of the 38th Asilomar Conference on Signals, Systems, and Computers*, vol. 1, pp. 488–492. IEEE Press, 2004.

9. J. Irwin and D. Page. Using Media Processors for Low-Memory AES Implementation. In *Proceedings of the 14th IEEE International Conference on Application-specific Systems, Architectures and Processors (ASAP 2003)*, pp. 144–154. IEEE CS Press, 2003.

10. M. Matsui. How far can we go on the x64 processors? In *Fast Software Encryption — FSE 2006, Pre-Proceedings*, pp. 488–492, March 2006.

11. M. Matsui and S. Fukuda. How to Maximize Software Performance of Symmetric Primitives on Pentium III and 4 Processors. In *Fast Software Encryption — FSE 2005*, LNCS 3557, pp. 398–412. Springer Verlag, 2005.

12. K. Nadehara, M. Ikekawa, and I. Kuroda. Extended Instructions for the AES Cryptography and their Efficient Implementation. In *Proceedings of the 18th IEEE Workshop on Signal Processing Systems (SIPS 2004)*, pp. 152–157. IEEE Press, 2004

13. National Institute of Standards and Technology (NIST). FIPS-197: Advanced Encryption Standard, November 2001. Available online at http://www.itl.nist.gov/fipspubs/.

14. D. Oliva, R. Buchty, and N. Heintze. AES and the Cryptonite Crypto Processor. In *Proceedings of the 2003 International Conference on Compilers, Architecture and Synthesis for Embedded Systems (CASES 2003)*, pp. 198–209. ACM Press, 2003.

15. S. Ravi, A. Raghunathan, N. Potlapally, and M. Sankaradass. System design methodologies for a wireless security processing platform. In *Proceedings of the 39th Design Automation Conference (DAC 2003)*, pp. 777–782. ACM Press, 2003.

16. P. Schaumont, K. Sakiyama, A. Hodjat, and I. Verbauwhede. Embedded Software Integration for Coarse-Grain Reconfigurable Systems. In *Proceedings of the 18th International Parallel and Distributed Processing Symposium (IPDPS 2004)*, pp. 137–142, IEEE CS Press, 2004.

17. S. Tillich and J. Großschädl. Accelerating AES Using Instruction Set Extensions for Elliptic Curve Cryptography. In *International Workshop on Information Security & Hiding (ISH 05), in conjunction with International Conference on Computational Science & Its Applications (ICCSA 2005)*, LNCS 3481, pp. 665–675. Springer, 2005.

18. S. Tillich, J. Großschädl, and A. Szekely. An Instruction Set Extension for Fast and Memory-Efficient AES Implementation. In *Communications and Multimedia Security — CMS 2005*, LNCS 3677, pp. 11–21. Springer Verlag, 2005.

19. J. Wolkerstorfer. An ASIC Implementation of the AES-MixColumn operation. In *Proceedings of Austrochip 2001*, pp. 129–132, 2001. ISBN 3-9501517-0-2.

20. L. Wu, C. Weaver, and T. Austin. Cryptomaniac: A fast flexible architecture for secure communication. In *Proceedings of the 28th Annual International Symposium on Computer Architecture (ISCA 2001)*, pp. 110–119. ACM Press, 2001.

A   Performance Figures for AES Decryption

Table 5. AES-128 decryption, precomputed key schedule: Performance and code size

	Key exp.	Decr. perf.		Code size	
Implementation	Cycles	Cycles	Speedup	Bytes	Rel. change
No extensions (pure SW)	739	1,955	1.00	2,520	0.0%
sbox	647	1,555	1.26	1,592	-36.8%
sbox4 (C)	739	1,435	1.36	1,784	-29.1%
sbox4 (ASM)	739	1,061	1.84	1,676	-33.5%
mixcol	498	1,078	1.81	1,548	-38.6%
mixcol4	498	970	2.02	1,244	-50.6%
sbox & mixcol	346	566	3.45	608	-75.9%
sbox & mixcol4 (C)	346	458	4.27	560	-77.8%
sbox & mixcol4 (ASM)	346	330	5.92	484	-80.8%
sbox4s & mixcol4s (C)	316	459	4.26	564	-77.6%
sbox4s & mixcol4s (ASM)	393	218	8.97	456	-81.9%
sbox4s & mixcol4s, unrolled	393	196	9.97	944	-62.5%
T lookup (Gladman), 1 KB	1,517	1,292	1.51	12,816	+408.6%
T lookup (Gladman), 4 KB	1,828	1,262	1.55	14,640	+481.0%
T lookup (Gladman), 4+4+1 KB	1,085	1,099	1.78	18,512	+634.6%
T lookup (Gladman), 4+4+4 KB	885	1,122	1.74	20,500	+713.5%

Table 6. AES-128 decryption, on-the-fly key expansion: Performance and code size

	Decr. perf.		Code size	
Implementation	Cycles	Speedup	Bytes	Rel. change
No extensions (pure SW)	2,434	1.00	2,504	0.0%
sbox	1,867	1.30	1,564	-37.5%
sbox4	1,715	1.42	1,748	-30.2%
mixcol	1,605	1.52	1,648	-34.2%
mixcol4	1,497	1.63	1,600	-36.1%
sbox & mixcol (C)	698	3.49	580	-76.8%
sbox & mixcol (ASM)	523	4.65	404	-83.9%
sbox & mixcol4 (C)	590	4.13	532	-78.8%
sbox & mixcol4 (ASM)	415	5.87	356	-85.8%
sbox4s & mixcol4s (C)	557	4.37	520	-79.2%
sbox4s & mixcol4s (ASM)	300	8.11	284	-88.7%
sbox4s & mixcol4s, unrolled	262	9.29	996	-60.2%
T lookup, 1 KB	6,528	0.37	4,504	+79.9%
T lookup, 4 KB	5,939	0.41	7,352	+193.6%
T lookup, 4+4+1 KB	3,257	0.75	11,272	+350.2%
T lookup, 4+4+4 KB	4,113	0.59	14,492	+478.8%

NanoCMOS-Molecular Realization of Rijndael

Massoud Masoumi, Farshid Raissi, and Mahmoud Ahmadian

ECE Dept., K. N. Toosi University of Technology, Tehran, Iran
m_masoumi@eetd.kntu.ac.ir, raissi@kntu.ac.ir,
mahmoud@kntu.ac.ir

Abstract. This paper describes the implementation of the Advanced Encryption Standard Algorithm, Rijndael, in a new nanoscale technology, called CMOL. This technology consists of an array of conventional CMOS gates and a wiring network, which consists of a high density mesh of nanowires. The basic Modules of Rijndael were implemented using CMOL architecture. It is observed that the implementation in such a technology has considerable advantages compared to a conventional CMOS approach as regards to defect tolerance, speed, area and power consumption.

Keywords: Rijndael, VLSI realization, CMOL.

1 Introduction

In our days, the need for secure transparent protocols seems to be one of the most important issues in the communication standards and new reliable and flexible algorithms specially designed to face the demand for secure but simple and flexible cryptosystems. This demand has been accelerated by the emergence of large-scale, high speed communication networks. Therefore, VLSI design and realization of cryptosystems has been a motivational and challenging subject. The inherent advantages of using VLSI chips for encryption are speed and more physical security. Software encryption has other features like portability and flexibility but is slow and suffers from insecurity in several aspects of key management and program manipulation. In 1997, NIST decided that a new standard algorithm is needed because attacks like exhaustive key search exploiting the short key length of DES had been demonstrated. Through three Advanced Encryption Standard (AES) conferences, Rijndael [1] was selected as AES in October 2000. After adoption of Rijndael, its VLSI realization was taken into consideration and nowadays it is integrated in many various embedded applications like Web Servers, ATMs, Fiber Distributed Data Interfaces (FDDIs), smart cards, cellular phones... Since 2000, several architectures for efficient VLSI realization of AES algorithm have been proposed and their performance evaluated using ASIC libraries and FPGAs [2], [3], [4], [5], [6], [7]. Further integration or speed-up of such circuits will not be easily possible in conventional manners. The ongoing feature size reduction of silicon based CMOS technology which has been basis of the development of the semiconductor industry for the last three decades will run into severe physical and economic problems. The scaling of MOSFETs is entering the deep-nanosized regime in which fundamental limits of CMOS and technological challenges with regard the

L. Goubin and M. Matsui (Eds.): CHES 2006, LNCS 4249, pp. 285–297, 2006.

scaling of CMOS are encountered [8], [9]. While traditional silicon based microelectronics is gradually approaching the end of its scaling [10], novel nanoelectronic solutions will be needed to surmount the physical and economic barriers of current semiconductor technology. A feasible scenario is the integration of silicon with nanoelectronic, i.e. a mixed CMOS/nano system [11]. This approach would allow a smooth transition and permit leveraging the beneficial aspects of both technologies. One potential alternative to supplement to or replace the CMOS microelectronics is the recently proposed semiconductor-nanowire-molecular architecture known as CMOL [12]. The basic idea for such circuits is to combine the advantages of current CMOS technology including flexibility and high fabrication yield with nanometer scale molecular devices, self assembled on a pre-fabricated nanowire fabric, enabling very high function density at modest fabrication cost. The implementation of such a structure via cross wire networks has been fully examined in literature [12], [13]. It seems at best at this point that CMOL circuits are suitable for embedded and stand-alone terabit memories and would be able to accomplish some tasks which are implemented by neural networks such as image processing, pattern recognition and classification [14], [15]. It is to this end that we are proposing that Rijndael can be implemented by CMOL technology and such implementation can bypass VLSI performance bottlenecks of this algorithm. Circuit density, speed and power consumption are three criteria which are of utmost importance in encryption VLSI realization and CMOL is by far the best scheme regarding these criteria. Moreover CMOL circuits have another advantage in comparison with regular CMOS circuits and are inherently defect tolerant [12], [13]. We have recently shown that basic modules of Rijndael can be implemented by CMOL technology with very interesting results [16]. The results we have obtained demonstrate that longer keys can be easily realized by CMOL, making unauthorized deciphering almost impossible. We had not obtained an estimate of power consumption of Rijndael's basic modules on CMOL platform but the new results show that the power consumption of theses modules are reduced with a factor of 1000-2000 in comparison with CMOS implementation. In this paper we focus on nanotechnology as a new solution for removing VLSI cryptosystem realization bottlenecks. We describe how basic modules of Rijndael can be implemented in CMOL technology and present the new results obtained. The organization of the paper is as follows. Section 2 explains AES algorithm briefly. Section 3 introduces CMOL technology and CMOL FPGA as the most promising structure for CMOL circuits. In section 4 we describe how the basic building modules of Rijndael are realized in CMOL technology and give the results of implementation. Finally, in the conclusion we briefly summarize the results of our discussion.

2 Rijndael Algorithm

Rijndael has been developed and published by Daemen and Rijmen [1], [17]. This algorithm is a byte-oriented symmetric block cipher, composed of a sequence of four primitive functions, SubBytes, ShiftRows, MixColumns, and AddRoundKey, executed round by round. Rijndael supports any key length and block length between 128 bits and 256 bits that is a multiple of 32 bits independently. The number of algorithm rounds denoted by Nr, depends on the message or key length. Prior to each round

AddRoundKey which combines the input with the cipher key is executed. The Key Expansion algorithm generates a key schedule for different rounds from the cipher key. In a 128-bit operation mode, at the start of the encryption, the message is divided to the blocks of length 128-bit and is copied to a 16 byte rectangular array called State. AddRoundKey is only a simple bit-wise XOR operation in which the elements of the State are XORed with RoundKey bit-by-bit. SubBytes is a non-linear bit-wise substitution of all bytes in the State. In SubBytes, each byte in the State is replaced by its corresponding byte in another table called S-Box. S-Box contains multiplicative inverse of all possible bytes over $GF(2^8)$ followed by an affine transformation. Each

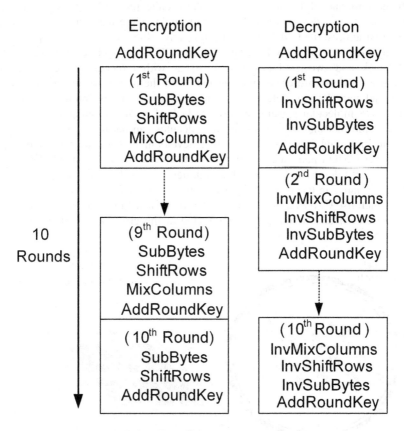

Fig. 1. Standard implementation of the AES algorithm

byte is an element of Galois field $GF(2^8)$ with irreducible polynomial $m(X) = X^8 + X^4 + X^3 + X + 1$. In the ShiftRows transformation, each row of the state is considered separately and the bytes in that row are cyclically shifted to the left based upon the key-size of the algorithm. For the 128-bit key, the first row is unchanged. However, the second, third and fourth rows are shifted one, two, and three bytes respectively. The MixColumns transformation is a bricklayer permutation operating on each column of the State. In MixColumns, columns of the State are considered as a four-term polynomial over GF(2^8), then are multiplied with a fixed polynomial c(X) = {03}X^3 + {01}X^2 + {01}X + {02}. Multiplications are performed modulo (x^4+1). The algorithm for the decryption has the same structure but uses mathematical inverses of the encryption steps, i.e. InvSubBytes, InvShiftRows, and InvMixColumns. The round keys are the same as those in encryption but are used in reverse order. Figure 1 shows the standard implementation of the AES.

3 CMOL-FPGA Architecture

CMOL is semiconductor–nanowire–molecular architecture [12]. Such architectures allow for significant design versatility. For example, while nano portion is restricted to regular structures, the CMOS portion can be any arbitrary circuit. Perhaps the most promising structure for CMOL circuits is an FPGA-like architecture combining a CMOS stack and two-level nanowire crossbar with molecular-scale nanodevices formed at each nanowire crosspoint together with the ability to reconfigure the circuits around nanodevices defects. Such reconfiguration is essential for any future mixed CMOS-molecular system because the lack of enough alignment accuracy and also due to the fact that self-assembly of molecules can hardly provide 100% yield. This is an important issue for the product development since an insufficient yield might render CMOS-nano technology unusable. It has been shown that CMOL circuits are defect tolerant and even with a high degree of defect rate can provide much better performance in terms of area-power consumption and speed when compared to circuits which use CMOS alone. CMOL circuits work with two-terminal nanodevices whose are electrically activated or deactivated at the cross-points of the mesh and

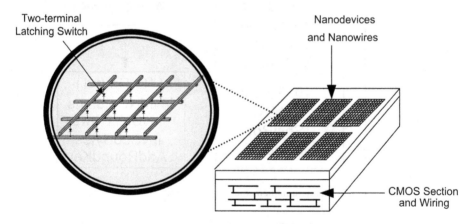

Fig. 2. A simplified diagram of a mixed CMOS/nano system

their fabrication is substantially less challenging than their three-terminal counterparts. Of course the limited functionality of two terminal devices is compensated by transistors of the CMOS subsystem. Two-terminal nanodevices provide us with high degree of integrability while CMOS devices provide us with other necessary functions such as voltage gain, address decoding and output signal sensing enabling digital performance with much speed and low power consumption. Novel ideas on the type of molecules and their connection scheme have been proposed and current estimate suggest that within 10-15 years such crossbar implementation of two-terminal devices becomes quite possible [12], [13]. A simplified diagram of a mixed CMOS/nano system and the hybrid complementary metal oxide semiconductor/molecular circuit structure are shown in figures 2 and 3 respectively.

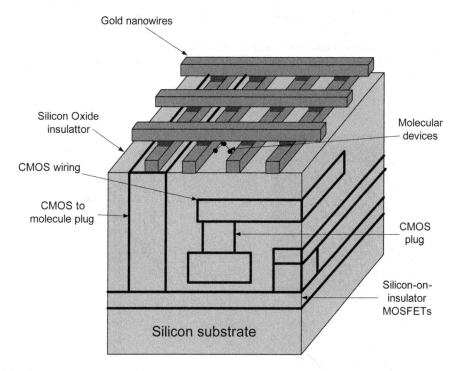

Fig. 3. The hybrid complementary metal oxide semiconductor/molecular circuit contains a molecule that may function as a latching switch activated by two input signals

The general configuration of a CMOL FPGA and a CMOL cell, as proposed in [13] is provided in Figures 4(a) and 4(b) respectively. Cross type nanowires (cross-net) are placed over a regularly placed matrix of CMOS cells. Nanomolecular two terminal devices are to be self assembled between the wires at each cross point. These molecules either work as latching switches or similar to diodes with a rectifying characteristic. The interesting proposed alignment of nanowires with respect to underlying CMOS cells, which is rotated by a certain angle, makes it possible to address each and every molecule. This is accomplished by CMOS cells which are accessible through column and row lines. The configuration of unit cell which is made of a CMOS NOT gate is shown in Figure 4(c) with its associated row and column lines. So called connection pins are placed on each cell to create connections to the bottom and top wire meshes. For example, the inputs are connected to the bottom nanowire and output to the top nanowire. In this manner several molecules are connected to each cell. To provide for a universal FPGA architecture, there are small breaks in nanowires in a periodic fashion. A square shaped connectivity domain can be defined for each cell. Connectivity domain is a region around the initial cell containing $2r(r-1)-1$ other cells, in which input or output of the original cell can be connected to any cell in this region. r is a positive integer number called connectivity radius. In the Figure 4(a) the connectivity radius is 3. This corresponds to the square shaped area in Figure 4(a). If all the molecules were conducting current, all the inputs and outputs of all the cells would be connected and circuits won't work. Molecules, however, are considered to act as latching switches. We can choose to make the appropriate ones to conduct their corresponding address lines. For example, the molecule connecting the output of each cell to its input must always be off or open. The same is true for all other molecules

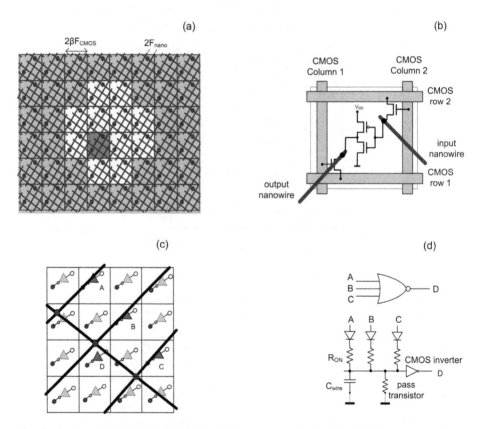

Fig. 4. The topology of a CMOL FPGA., (a) Each rectangular cell is a NOT gate whose input and output are shown by black dots. Input and outputs makes contact to separate layers of nanowires. (b) The CMOS transistor which makes each inverter cell with its associated address lines and so called "pass" transistors. (c) The molecules which have been turned ON and are shown by dark gray at the crosspoint of the wire meshes. Other connections whose molecules are not turned ON are not shown, (d) Circuit representation of the three input NOR gate which is equivalent to a diode-resistor connected NOR gate.

that connect the output to its connectivity domain. Now, each cell with its associated molecular devices can be considered as a NOR gate as given in Figure 4(d). Having NOT and NOR is sufficient to implement any Boolean function.

Due to the uniformity of the nanowiring/nanodevices levels of CMOL, they do not need to be precisely aligned with each other and the underlying CMOS stack. In addition, CMOL circuits are inherently defect-tolerant, since there are $M = 2r(r-1) -1$ nanodevices in each cell. In some cases, even a 75% loss of molecular devices due to misalignment results in acceptable functionality. After initial mapping on CMOL fabric and configuration stage, each cell whose associated molecules are not properly functioning may be swapped with another adjacent cell in its connectivity domain and the circuit would operate properly. Such gate swapping is not provided by physical relocation of gates but by using a new routing. This is shown in Figure 5 and the reader is encouraged to refer to references [13] for detail. It has been reported that, from the software point of view, a CMOL tile can be treated in the same way as that of the island-type CMOS FPGA. Indeed, we first map the original pre-optimized logic circuit onto a network of NOR gates (with a certain maximum fan-in) and latches (if any), to produce a netlist. Next, we fix a certain number (N) of CMOS cells inside each tile to perform logic operations, while the rest T−N CMOS cells are committed to routing [18].

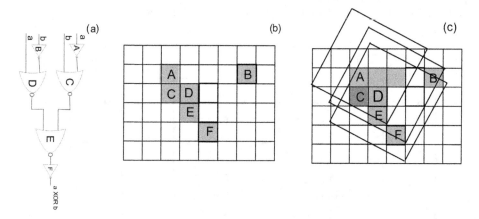

Fig. 5. Example of a circuit reconfiguration, (a) NOR-NOT equivalent circuit of an XOR gate, (b) mapping the circuit on a 6*8 CMOL rectangular block. At least one of the molecules of gate C is faulty and therefore this gate to be relocated. (c) The intersect of repair regions of input and output cells of gate C, i.e. gates A and E houses gate D, hence the repair region of this gate is calculated again. Since gate C lies in the repair region of gate D these gates can be swapped, connection quality permitting. Here r = 3 and there are 11 other cells in the connectivity region of each cell.

4 Implementation of Rijndael's Basic Transformations Using CMOL Scheme

In this section we discuss issues related to the implementation of Rijndael's basic building blocks, i.e. MixColumns and SubBytes. Several architectural and algorithmic optimization techniques have been proposed for efficient implementation of the AES algorithm. The aim of these optimization techniques is to reduce the critical path, chip area and power consumption of AES chips and are developed to suit the different demand of applications. We demonstrate that if these proposed architectures are implemented in CMOL performance of AES chips would be much improved. No optimization can be performed on the hardware structure of ShiftRows and AddRoundKey, since no logic gates are needed for the former transformation and only one step of XOR is needed for the latter. We present the new results obtained from realization and performance estimation of MixColumns and SubBytes on a typical CMOL fabric and compare them with their purely CMOS counterparts. While much of the analysis in this paper is applicable to several other cryptographic algorithms, we focus on Rijndael as a very good typical example.

4.1 Implementation of MixColumns

Over the years many implementations, with different levels of optimizations have been presented and there are several architectures for efficient implementation for MixColumns. A good possible implementation in the terms of speed and resource sharing as proposed in [7] is shown in the figure 6. In this figure, 'XTime' block implements the constant multiplication by $\{02\}$ in $GF(2^8)$. 'XTime' block consists of 3 XOR gates and its critical path includes only one XOR gate [6].

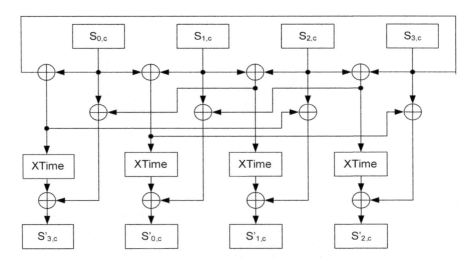

Fig. 6. Efficient implementation of MixColumns transformation

We represented this transformation to the fan-in two NOR gates and inverters, the only available logic primitives on a standard CMOL FPGA, as shown in Figure 8. In order to compare the performance of the implementation on CMOL with its CMOS counterpart and to evaluate the effectiveness of our approach, first we simulated it using VHDL codes with structural logic description and synthesized it on Spartan 3, the fastest commercially available FPGA from Xilinx family which is fabricated with 90-nm CMOS technology. The basic unit of such an FPGA is a slice consisting of two 4-input LUTs. Xilinx ISE 6.2i was used to synthesize the design and provide post-placement timing results. The results of synthesis showed that it consumes 60 logic cells and the total logic delay is about 0.62 ns. With the cell (tile) area approximated as 2100 um^2 [13], it means that the circuit will occupy about 126000 um^2 on the chip. Then, we mapped it manually on a 32*40 CMOL FPGA fabric with connectivity radius r = 12 and CMOL parameters as F_{COMS} = 32 nm, F_{nano} = 8 nm. The way to estimate density, speed, and power consumption of CMOL circuits has been described in [13]. If we estimate the cell area A_{cell} as $64(F_{CMOS})^2$ [12], [13] with logic depth equal to 28, the same implementation on CMOL FPGA with will result the total gate delay equal to 0.15 ns, the total area equal to 84 μm^2 and the area-delay product equal to 12.6 μm^2 ns. A computer program was written for finding a pseudo-optimum yield-optimized gate placement. Then we performed Mont Carlo simulation for reconfigu-ration algorithm. The circuit yield was about %98.5 for defect rate of molecular de-vices up to 25%. However, reconfigurable circuits are not yet frequently embedded into portable applications and our interest for power consumption was driven by an-other reason. Indeed, for the implementation of cryptographic algorithms, not only the speed and the size of the circuit are important, but also their security against imple-mentation attacks. For example, in Differential Power Analysis, it is assumed that the power consumption of a device is correlated with the data handled. The power dissi-pation of the two implementation approaches could be estimated and compared. Ig-noring the leakage current of molecular devices, the average total power consumption of a CMOL gate may be estimated as a sum of two constituents, the static power P_{ON} due to currents I_{ON}, and dynamic power P_{dyn} due to the recharging of nanowire capaci-tances. Considering the subject that the total power consumed per unit circuit area for CMOL FPGAs are limited at the level P/A = 200 W cm^{-2} [12], [13] we can estimate the total power dissipated at each CMOL cell by using a rule of thumb. With F_{CMOS} = 32 nm, A_{Cell} will be equal to $6.5536*10^{-11}$ cm^2 which means that there are about $1.52*10^{10}$ CMOL cell cm^{-2}, each cell dissipating about 0.13 nW. Hence, the MixCol-umns module will dissipate about 0.16 mW. The power consumption of this transfor-mation on Spartan-3 was estimated using ISE power analyzer and it was about 335 mW, about 2000 times larger than CMOL implementation. This estimate is close to the one given by Likharev. Recently he has implemented a 32-bit Kogge-stone adder on a CMOL FPGA fabric and has reported that power consumption of the circuit is 0.33 mW [12]. It is easy to justify this great difference between the power consumption of the CMOL and CMOS approaches. Most current CMOS FPGAs are SRAM-programmable, meaning that SRAM bits are connected to the configuration points in the FPGA, and programming these SRAM cells configures the device. These compo-nents are based on the static CMOS memory technology. Please notice that a 3-input NOR gate is implemented in CMOL technology by using only an inverter and four molecules, i.e. only one NMOS and one PMOS transistor, while it needs 3 PMOSs and 3 NMOSs to be implemented in a typical static CMOS technology. While major part of the power consumed in a CMOS FPGA is dissipated in its routing, intercon-nects, logic and clocking resources [19], CMOL FPGA has a completely different structure in which information is stored in molecules which consume very smaller energy in comparison with CMOS transistors. Also, the nanowiring section of CMOL

FPGA has a very smaller effective capacitance in comparison of wiring and routing section of CMOS FPGAs [12], [13], [19]. It is obvious from comparing the results obtained from these two different implementation approaches that the performance will be much improved by replacing CMOS with CMOL.

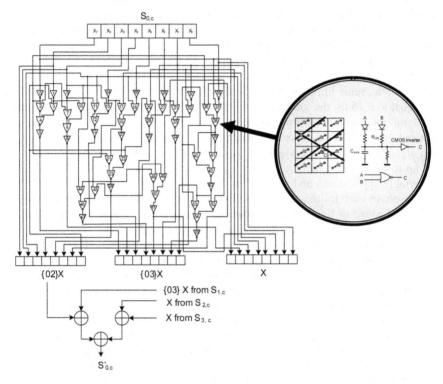

Fig. 7. Implementation of one column of the MixColumns transformation using NOT and 2-input NOR gates

4.1 Implementation of SubBytes

The area required by Rijndael is adversely affected by limited resource sharing between encryptor and decryptor, as well as by the use of large S-Boxes. The Rijndael S-Box is formed based on the mapping X to X^{-1}, where X^{-1} denotes the multiplicative inverse of X in $GF(2^8)$ followed by an affine transformation over $GF(2)$ [17]. The multiplicative inversion involved in SubBytes is a gate consuming and hardware demanding operation. There are various approaches for efficient designing of Rijndael S-Box. Most of them are based on two different methods: performing lower cost multiplicative inverse calculation on subfields of $GF(2^8)$ or constructing a circuit whose input-output relation is the same as S-Box. Vincent Rijmen during the second round of the AES process proposed an efficient architecture for implementation of the Rijndael S-Box using composite field arithmetic over $GF((2^4)^2)$ [20]. Using composite field mapping, hardware usage will be reduced and the total number of gates consumed to implement this transformation will be 99 XOR and 36 AND gates with 20

XOR gates and 4 AND gates in the critical path [7]. It is worth noting that although gate counts and area required for implementing SubBytes transformation is reduced by using composite field arithmetic, studies of Morioka and Satoh [21] shows that glitches and dynamic hazards caused by differences in signal arrival times at each time and probability of signal transitions, cause that about %75 of power consumed in a 128-bit, AES chip to be dissipated during SubBytes transformation. They have developed a multi-stage PPRM (Positive Polarity Reed-Muller) low power architecture for SubBytes based on $GF(((2^2)^2)^2)$ isomorphic mapping, shown in figure 8, which consumes 212 XOR and 189 AND gates for implementing S-Box and 200 XOR and 204 AND gates for implementing S^{-1}Box.

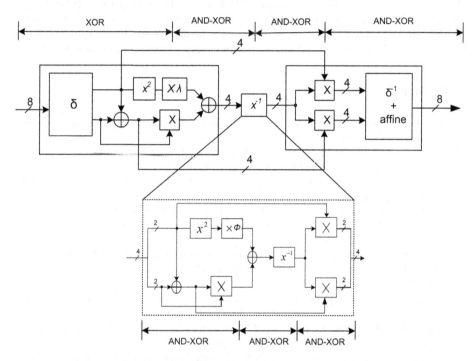

Fig. 8. Implementation of SubBytes based on the so called 3 stage PPRM architecture

We synthesized the 3-stage PPRM architecture for SubBytes transformation using Spartan 3. The total gate delay was about 6.2 ns and the FPGA cell usage was equal to 74. The area occupation on chip was about 155400 μm^2 and the area-delay product was equal to 963480 μm^2 ns. Then we mapped it on a 32*64 CMOL rectangular block, the area and the area-delay product are: 134 μm^2 and 255 μm^2 ns. While it dissipates approximately about 389 mW on Spartan 3 (estimation was obtained using Xilinx ISE 6.2i power analyzer) it consumes about 0.26 mW on a 32*64 CMOL fabric, about 1500 times less than its CMOS counterpart. Again we found a pseudo-optimum yield-optimized gate placement and performed Mont Carlo simulation for reconfiguration algorithm. The circuit yield was about %98.5 for defect rate of molecular devices up to 20%. It is observed that the basic block transformations of

Rijndael can be implemented by CMOL with much improvement in speed, power consumption, and chip area.

5   Conclusions

In this paper we presented a new methodology based on mixed CMOS/nano circuits for future VLSI realization of Rijndael algorithm and showed the suitability of the implementation of Rijndael in CMOL. High speed, very small required area, very low power consumption and defect tolerance of CMOL circuits along with the possibility of designing long key encryption make CMOL as an optimum possible platform for encryption VLSI realization in the future. Nanoelectronic and mixed CMOS/nano systems are steel quite young and will require new design and fabrication paradigm but can lead to higher levels of computation and many other beneficial aspects.

References

1. Daemen, J, and Rijmen, V.: AES Proposal Rijndael, National Institute of Standards and Technology, July 2001
2. Fischer, V, and Drutarovsky, M.: Two Methods of Rijndael Implementation in Reconfigurable Hardware Proc. CHES, Paris, France (2001) 77-92
3. Sklavos, N, and Koufopavlou, O.: Architectures and VLSI Implementation of the AES-Proposal Rijndael IEEE Trans Computers, 51, 12 (2002) 1454-59
4. Lu, C, C, and Tseng Y, S.: Integrated Design of AES (Advanced Encryption Standard) Encryptor and Decryptor, in Proc. IEEE Int. Conf. Application Specific Systems, Architectures Processors (2002) 277-285
5. Satoh, A, Morioka, S, Takano, K, and Munetoh, S.: A Compact Rijndael Hardware Architecture S-BOX Optimization, in Proc. ASIACRYPT 2001, Gold Coast, Australia (2000) 239-254
6. Zhang, X, and Parhi, K, K.: Implementation Approaches for the Advanced Encryption Standard Algorithm, IEEE Circuits Mag., 2, 4 (2002) 24-46
7. Zhang, X, and Parhi, K, K.: High-Speed VLSI Architectures for the AES Algorithm, IEEE Trans. Very Large Scale Integration (VLSI) Systems, 12, 9 (2004) 957-967
8. Fortes, J.: Future challenges in VLSI System Design, Proceedings IEEE Computer Society Annual Symposium on VLSI (ISVLSI'03) (2003) 5-7
9. Likharev K, K, and Strukov, D, B.: Electronics Below 10 nm, Nano and Giga Challenges in Microelectronics, (Amsterdam: Elsevier) (2003) 27-68
10. International Technology Roadmap for Semiconductors (ITRS), 2004, Update, available online at http://public. itrs. net/
11. Ziegler, M, M, and Stan, M, R.: CMOS/nano Co-Design for Crossbar-Based Molecular Electronic Systems, IEEE Trans. Nanotechnology, 2 (4) (2003) 217–230
12. Likharev K, K, and Strukov, D, B.: CMOL: Devices, Circuits, and Architectures, avail-able online at http://www-mcg.uni-regensburg.de/pages/admol/book/chapter_16.html/book/chapter_16.html
13. Strukov, D, B, and Likharev, K, K.: CMOL FPGA: a Reconfigurable Architecture for Hybrid Digital Circuits with Two-Terminal Nanodevices, Nanotechnology, 16 (2005) 888-900

14. Likharev, K, K, Türel, Ö, Lee, J, H, and Ma, X.: Architectures for Nanoelectronic Implementation of Artificial Neural Networks: New Results, Neurocomputing, 64, 1 (2005) 271-283

15. Strukov, D, and Likharev, K, Prospects for Terabit-Scale Nanoelectronic Memories, Nanotechnology, 16 (2005) 137-38

16. Masoumi, M, Raissi, F, Ahmadian, M, and Keshavarzi, P.: Design and Evaluation of Basic Standard Encryption Algorithm Modules using Nanosized CMOS-Molecular Circuits, Nanotechnology, 17 (2006) 89-99

17. Daemen, J, and Rijmen, V.: The Design of Rijndael, Springer (2002)

18. Strukov, D, B, and Likharev, K, K.: A Reconfigurable Architecture for Hybrid CMOS/Nanodevice Circuits, available online at: http://portal.acm.org/affiliated/citation. cfm?id=1117221&coll=ACM&dl=guide

19. Standaert, F, X.: Secure and Efficient Use of Reconfigurable Hardware Devices in Symmetric Cryptography, Ph. D. Thesis, University of Catholique de Louvain, Belgium, 2004.

20. Rijmen, V, Efficient Implementation of Rijndael S-Box, available online at: www.iaik. tugraz.at/research/ krypto/AES/old/~rijmen/rijndael/sbox.pdf

21. Morioka, S, and Satoh, A, An Optimized S-Box Circuit Architecture for Low Power AES Design, in Proc. of Cryptographic Hardware and Embedded Systems (CHES) 2002, San Francisco, USA (2002) 172-186

Improving SHA-2 Hardware Implementations

Ricardo Chaves[1,2], Georgi Kuzmanov[2],
Leonel Sousa[1], and Stamatis Vassiliadis[2]

[1] Instituto Superior Técnico/INESC-ID. Rua Alves Redol 9,
1000-029 Lisbon, Portugal
http://sips.inesc-id.pt/
[2] Computer Engineering Lab, TUDelft. Postbus 5031, 2600 GA Delft,
The Netherlands
http://ce.et.tudelft.nl/

Abstract. This paper proposes a set of new techniques to improve the
implementation of the SHA-2 hashing algorithm. These techniques consist mostly in operation rescheduling and hardware reutilization, allowing
a significant reduction of the critical path while the required area also decreases. Both SHA256 and SHA512 hash functions have been implemented
and tested in the VIRTEX II Pro prototyping technology. Experimental
results suggest improvements to related SHA256 art above 50% when compared with commercial cores and 100% to academia art, and above 70%
for the SHA512 hash function. The resulting cores are capable of achieving the same throughput as the fastest unrolled architectures with 25%
less area occupation than the smallest proposed architectures. The proposed cores achieve a throughput of 1.4 Gbit/s and 1.8 Gbit/s with a slice
requirement of 755 and 1667 for SHA256 and SHA512 respectively, on a
XC2VP30-7 FPGA.

Keywords: Cryptography, Hash functions, SHA-2 (256, 512), FPGA.

1 Introduction

Cryptography is becoming an essential part of most electronic equipments that
require data storing or manipulation. However, the algorithms used to enforce
this security are too demanding to be implemented in software for the current
required processing speeds. To achieve the require processing capability hardware
components have to be used. These hardware cores are usually implemented
either in dedicated ASIC cores [1–3] or in reconfigurable devices [4–7]. In this
paper we propose a new hardware implementation of the SHA-2 algorithm, used
in authentication systems and in the validity check of data. Several techniques
have been proposed to improve the implementation of the SHA-2 algorithm. The
most relevant are:

- the usage of parallel counters or well balanced Carry save Adders (CSA), in
  order to improve the partial additions. In technologies, like reconfigurable
  devices that have dedicated data paths for improving addition, this technique
  is not always beneficial;

L. Goubin and M. Matsui (Eds.): CHES 2006, LNCS 4249, pp. 298–310, 2006.

- unrolling techniques that optimize the data dependency. This technique allows for an improvement in the throughput, however, it usually significantly increases the required circuit area [2, 8, 6];
- delay balancing and the usage of improved addition units, since in this algorithm this is the critical operation;
- the usage of embedded memories to store the required constant values (K_t);
- use of pipelining techniques, to achieve higher working frequencies. Due to highly dependent data computation the resulting throughput is usually not improved and more complex control logic is required [2, 9].

However, the performance of the SHA-2 algorithm can be further improved with other techniques. To achieve this goal, this paper proposes operation rescheduling, that allows for an efficient use of a pipelined structure without an increase in area, and hardware reutilization techniques that allow for resource saving.

Both implementations of the SHA256 and SHA512 hash functions suggest:

- throughput per Slice efficiency metric improvement of 53% compared to commercial SHA256 cores, and more than 100% to current SHA256 academia art, and 77% for SHA512 implementations;
- a throughput of 1.4 Gbit/s for SHA256 and 1.8 Gbit/s for SHA512, with 755 and 1667 slices, on a XC2VP30-7 FPGA, respectively;
- 150 times speedup with respect to the software implementation.

The paper is organized as follows, Section 2 presents the SHA-2 algorithms. Section 3 describes the proposed design. The characteristics of FPGA implementations are presented in section 4. Section 5 presents the obtained results and compares them to related art. Section 6, concludes the paper with some final remarks.

2 SHA-2 Hash Algorithm

In 1993 the Secure Hash Standard (SHA) was first published by the NIST. In 1995 this algorithm was reviewed in order to eliminate some of the initial weakness, and in 2001 new Hashing algorithms were proposed. This new family of hashing algorithms known as SHA-2, use larger digest messages, making them more resistent to possible attacks and allowing them to be used with larger blocks of data, up to 2^{128} bits, e.g. in the case of SHA512. The SHA-2 hashing algorithm is the same for the SHA256, SHA224, SHA384, and SHA512 hashing functions, differing only in the size of the operands, the initialization vectors, and the size of the final digest message.

The following describes the SHA-2 algorithm applied to the SHA256 hash function, followed by the description of the SHA512 hash function, which differs mostly in the size of the operands, using 64-bit words instead of 32-bit. Note that SHA224 and SHA384 are computed as SHA256 and SHA512, respectively, with the final hash value truncated to the corresponding size, the Initialization Vector also differs.

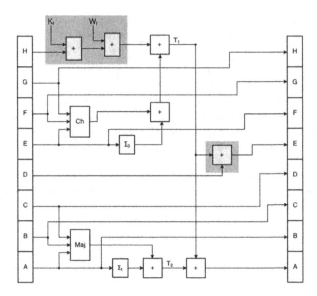

Fig. 1. SHA-2 round calculation

SHA256 Hash Function: The SHA256 Hash function produces a final digest message of 256 bits, that is dependent of the input message, composed by multiple blocks of 512 bits each. This input block is expanded and fed to the 64 cycles of the SHA256 function in words of 32 bits each (denoted by W_t). In each cycle or round of the SHA-2 algorithm the introduced data is mixed with the current state. This data scrambling is preformed by additions and logical operations, such as bitwise logical operations and bitwise rotations. The computational structure of each round of this algorithm is depicted in Figure 1. The several functions presented in this figure are described in Appendix I. The value W_t is the 32-bit data word, for the t round, and the K_t value represents the 32-bit constant that also depends on the round.

The 32-bit values of the A to H variables are updated in each round and the new values are used in the following round. The initial values of these variables is given by the 256-bit constant value specified in [10], this value is only set for the first data block. The consecutive data blocks use the intermediate hash value, computed for the previous data block. Each 512 data block is processed for 64 rounds, after which the values of the variables A to H are added to the previous digest message, in order to obtain partial digest message. To better illustrate this algorithm a pseudo code representation is depicted in Figure 2. The final Digest Message (DM) for a given data stream, is given by the result of the last data block.

In some higher level applications like the efficient implementation of the keyed-Hash Message Authentication Code (HMAC) [11] or when a message is fragmented, the initial hash value (IV) may differ from the constant specified in [10]. In these cases, the variables A to H are initialized by a variable Initialization Vector (IV).

```
for each data_block i do

    W = expand(data_block)
    A = DM₀ ; B = DM₁ ; C = DM₂ ; D = DM₃
    E = DM₄ ; F = DM₅ ; G = DM₆ ; H = DM₇

    for t= 0, t≤ 63 {79}, t=t+1 do
        T₁ = H + Σ₁(E) + Ch(E,F,G) + Kₜ + Wₜ
        T₂ = Σ₀(A) + Maj(A,B,C)
        H = G ; G = F ; F = E ;
        E = D + T₁
        D = C ; C = B ; B = A
        A = T₁ + T₂
    end for

    DM₀ = A + DM₀ ; DM₁ = B + DM₁
    DM₂ = C + DM₂ ; DM₃ = D + DM₃
    DM₄ = E + DM₄ ; DM₅ = C + DM₅
    DM₆ = D + DM₆ ; DM₇ = E + DM₇
end for
```

Fig. 2. Pseudo Code for SHA-2 algorithm

SHA512 Hash function: The SHA512 hash function computation is identical to that of the SHA256 hash function, differing in the size of the operands, that are of 64 bits and not 32 bits as for the SHA256, the size of the Digest Message, that has twice the size being composed by 512 bits, and in the Σ functions described in Appendix I. This Appendix also describes the functions σ used in the message schedule. The value W_t and K_t are of 64 bits and the each data block is composed by 16 64-bit words, having in total 1024 bits.

Message schedule: In the SHA-2 algorithm the computation described in Figure 1 is performed for 64 rounds for the SHA256 (80 rounds for the SHA512), in each round a 32-bit word (or 64-bit for SHA512) obtained from the intermidiate hash value is used. However each data block only has 16 32-bits words for SHA256 or 16 64-bit words for SHA512, resulting in the need to expand the initial data block to obtain the remaining words. This expansion is performed by the computation described in (1), where $M_t^{(i)}$ denotes the first 16 words of the i-th data block.

$$W_t = \begin{cases} M_t^{(i)} & , \ 0 \leq t \leq 15 \\ \sigma_1(W_{t-2}) + W_{t-7} + \sigma_0(W_{t-15}) + W_{t-16}, & 16 \leq t \leq 63 \ \{or \ 79\} \end{cases} \quad (1)$$

Message padding: In order to assure that the input message in a multiple of 512 bits, as required by the SHA256 hash function, or 1024 for the SHA512 hash function, it is necessary to pad the original message. This message padding also comprises the inclusion of the original message dimension to the padded message. This operation can be efficiently implemented in software with a minimal cost.

3   Proposed Design

In the SHA-2 algorithm, the operations that have to be performed are simple, however the data dependency of this algorithm does not allow for much parallelization. Each round of the algorithm can only be computed after the values A to H of the previous round have been calculated (see figure 2), imposing a sequentiality to the computation. It should be noticed that in each round the computation is only required to calculate the values of A and E, since the remaining values are obtained directly from the values of the previous round, as depicted in the pseudo code of Figure 2.

In this paper, we propose a new operation rescheduling technique, a new form to initialize the algorithm, and a more efficient hardware reutilization scheme.

Operation rescheduling: In our proposal, we identified the part of the computation of a given round t that can be computed ahead in the previous round $t-1$. Only the values that do not depend on the values computed in the previous round can be computed ahead. Unlike the rescheduling technique proposed in [12] for the SHA1 algorithm, where the inter round data dependency is low, in the SHA-2 algorithm the data dependency is more complex, as depicted in Figure 1. While the variables B, C, D, F, G, and H are obtained directly from the values of the round, not requiring any computation, the values of A and E require computation and depend on all the values. In other words, the values A and E for round t can not be computed until the values for the same variables have been computed in the previous round have, as shown in (2).

$$E_{t+1}=D_t+\Sigma_1(E_t)+ Ch(E_t, F_t, G_t)+ H_t+ K_t+ W_t \qquad (2)$$
$$A_{t+1}=\Sigma_0(A_t)+ Maj(B_t, C_t, D_t)+\Sigma_1(E_t)+ Ch(E_t, F_t, G_t)+ H_t+ K_t+ W_t$$

Taking into account that the value H_{t+1} is given directly by G_t which in its turn is given by F_{t-1}, the precalculation of H can thus be given by $H_{t+1} = F_{t-1}$. Since the value of K_t and W_t can be precalculated and are simply used in each round, (2) can be rewritten as:

$$\delta_t =H_t + K_t + W_t = G_{t-1} + K_t + W_t;$$
$$E_{t+1} =D_t + \Sigma_1(E_t) + Ch(E_t, F_t, G_t) + \delta_t; \qquad (3)$$
$$A_{t+1} =\Sigma_0(A_t) + Maj(B_t, C_t, D_t) + \Sigma_1(E_t) + Ch(E_t, F_t, G_t) + \delta_t,$$

where the value δ_t is calculated in the previous round. The value δ_{t+1} can be the result of a full addition or the Carry and the Save vectors from a Carry Save Addition. With this computational separation the calculation of the SHA-2 algorithm can be divided into two parts, allowing the calculation of δ to be rescheduled to the previous clock cycle, depicted by the grey area in Figure 3. Thus the critical path of the resulting hardware implementation can be reduced. Since the computation is now divided by a pipeline stage, the calculation of the SHA-2 requires an additional clock cycle, to perform all the rounds. In the case of the SHA256 hash function 65 clock cycles are necessary to calculate the 64 rounds. As specified in the SHA-2 algorithm and depicted in Figure 2, after all rounds have been computed, the internal variables (A to H) have to be added to the previous Digest Message.

Hash value addition and initialization: As mentioned after the computation of a given data block, the internal variables have to be added to the intermediate hash value. If this addition were to be implemented in a straightforward manner, 8 adders would be required, one for each internal variable, of 32 or 64 bits depending if SHA256 or SHA512 is being implemented. However, some hardware reuse can be achieved. By analyzing the data dependency and the fact that most of the internal variables do not require any computation, since their value is given directly by the previous values of the other variables, taking into account that:

$$H_t = G_{t-1} = F_{t-2} = E_{t-3}; \qquad (4)$$
$$D_t = C_{t-1} = B_{t-2} = A_{t-3}, \qquad (5)$$

the computation of the Digest Message for the data block i can be calculated from the internal variables A and E, as:

$$
\begin{aligned}
DM7_i &= E_{t-3} + DM7_{i-1} &;& \quad DM3_i = A_{t-3} + DM3_{i-1}; \\
DM6_i &= E_{t-2} + DM6_{i-1} &;& \quad DM2_i = A_{t-2} + DM2_{i-1}; \\
DM5_i &= E_{t-1} + DM5_{i-1} &;& \quad DM1_i = A_{t-1} + DM1_{i-1}.
\end{aligned}
\qquad (6)
$$

Thus the calculation can be performed by only 2 addition units, as:

$$
\begin{aligned}
DM(j+4)_i &= E_{t-3+j} + DM(j+4)_{i-1} &; \quad 1 \le j \le 3 \\
DM(j)_i &= A_{t-3+j} + DM(j)_{i-1} &; \quad 1 \le j \le 3.
\end{aligned}
\qquad (7)
$$

The selection of the corresponding part of the Digest Message (DMj), could be performed by a multiplexer. However, taking into account the sequentiality in which the values of DMj are used, a shifting buffer can be used, as depicted in the right most part of Figure 3. Since the values A_t and E_t require computation and the final value is only calculated in the last clock cycle, the calculation of the values $DM0_i$ and $DM4_i$ is performed in a different manner. Instead of using one full adder, after the calculation of the final value of A and E, the Digest Message (DM) is added during the calculation of their final values, by a Carry Save Adder (CSA). Since the value of the previous Digest Message is known, the value can be added during the first stage of the pipeline, not being on the critical path, located in the second stage of the pipeline, where the full adders are used. In the last round the value of A and E is not calculated, being directly calculated the value of the Digest Message. During the normal round calculation only the values A_t and E_t can be computed, in these cases the input of the used CSA is put to zero, as depicted in Figure 3.

After each data block has been computed, the internal values A to H have to be re-initialized with the newly calculated Digest Message. This is performed by a multiplexer that selects either the new value of the variable of the Digest Message, as depicted in the left most side of Figure 3. Once more the values A and E are the exception. Since the final value computed for these two variables

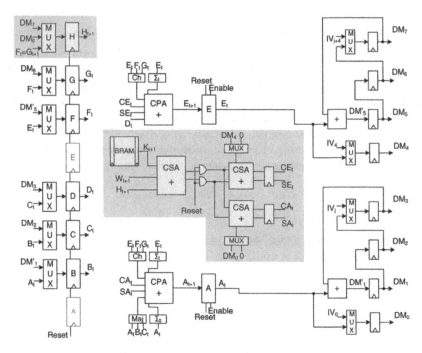

Fig. 3. SHA-2 round architecture

is already the Digest Message, the values are already loaded in the registers. An enable signal is used in the A and E registers, in order to maintain these values during the re-initialization of the other values.

In the first round the values of A to H also have to be initialized. All variables, except A and E, are simply loaded with the values in the DM registers, depicted in the leftmost part of Figure 3. For the A and E variables the value is fed through the round logic. In this case the, all the variables are set to zero (Reset) except the DM_0 and DM_4 inputs. Thus the resulting value for the A and E registers will be the initialization values of the DM registers.

In the standard for the SHA-2 algorithm the initial value of the Digest Message (loaded to the A to H variables) is a constant value, that can be loaded by using set/reset signals in the registers. If the SHA-2 algorithm is to be used in a wider set of applications and in the computation of fragmented messages, the initial Digest Message is no longer a constant value. In these cases the initial value is given by the IV that has to be loaded. This loading can be performed by multiplexers at the input of the Digest Message registers. In order to optimized the architecture the calculation structure for the Digest Message can be used to load the IV, not being directly loaded into all the registers. The value of the $A1$ and $E1$ registers is set to zero during this loading, thus the existing structure acts as a circular buffer, where the value is only loaded into one of the registers, and shifted to the others.

This circular buffer can also be used to more efficiently read the final Digest Message, in a structure with an interface with smaller output ports, since the values are simply shifted and less multiplexes are required.

4   SHA-2 FPGA Implementation

In order to evaluate the proposed design, the resulting SHA256 and SHA512 hash functions cores have been implemented in a Xilinx VIRTEX II Pro (XC2VP30-7) FPGA using the Xilinx ISE (6.3) and SimplifyPro (8.4) tools. All the values presented for our cores were obtained after Place and Route. A Custom Computing Unit (CCU) using these SHA-2 cores, has also been designed for the Molen polymorphic computational model [13], in order to fully test the cores.

In order to fully exploit the capabilities of the reconfigurable device, some design adaptation can be made. The main one lays in the use of fast carry chains for Carry Propagate Adders (CPA) instead of CSA in both the first and in the second pipeline stage, since they are able to achieve the same performance in FPGA, with less area resources. For ASIC technologies, the structure depicted in Figure 3 is more suitable. When implementing the SHA256 hash function, a single BRAM can be used, since the 64 32-bits fit in a single 32-bit port embedded memory. However, in the SHA512 hash function the operands have 64 bits, including the constant K_t. Since the existing BRAMs do not have 64-bit ports, more than one would be required. However, they have a dual output ports of 32 bits each. Thus the 80 64-bit constants can be mapped as two 32-bit words: one port addresses the low part of the memory, with the lower 32 bits of the constant and the other the high part of the memory with the higher 32 bits of the same constant. With this, only one BRAM is used to generate the 64 bit constant.

For the message schedule in the FPGA technology considered, CPA are also used instead of CSA. The structure of the data expansion component is represented in Figure 4.

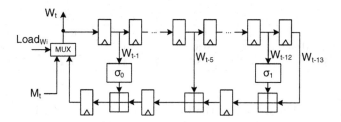

Fig. 4. SHA-2 data expansion module

These cores have also been integrated as a CCU for the MOLEN processor [13]. The MOLEN computational paradigm enables the SHA-2 core to be embedded in a reconfigurable co-processor, tightly coupled with the core General Purpose Processor (GPP). This, allows for a fast integration in existing software at a small cost in terms of additional area. This polymorphic architecture uses the FPGAs embedded PowerPC running at 300 MHz as a core GPP, with a main data memory running at 100 MHz. The implementation is identical to the one described in [12].

5   Performance Analysis and Related Work

Even though the SHA-2 cores have been developed with a VIRTEX II Pro FPGA (XC2P30-7) as the target technology, they have also been implemented on a VIRTEX (XCV400-6) and a VIRTEX II (XC2V2000-6), in order to compare with the related art.

SHA 256 hash function core: The proposed SHA256 hash function core has been compared with the most recent and most efficient related art, for both the cores proposed in the academia and the best commercial core currently available,as far as it is known by the authors. The obtained comparison figures are presented in Table 1. When compared with the most recent academic work [14, 8] the results show higher throughputs, from 17% up to 98%, while achieving a reduction in area above 25% and up to 42%. These results suggest a significant improvement to the Throughput per Slice (TP/Slice) metric in the range of 100% to 170%. When compared with the commercial SHA256 core from Helion [15], the proposed core suggests an identical area value (less 7%) while achieving a 40% gain to the throughput, resulting in an improvement of 53% to the Throughput per Slice metric. Note that from the analyzed cores, ours is

Table 1. SHA256 core performance comparison

Architecture	Sklav[14]	Our	McEv.[8]	Our	Helion[15]	Our
Device	XCV	XCV	XC2V	XC2V	XC2PV-7	XC2PV-7
IV	cst	yes	cst	yes	cst	yes
Slices	1060	764	1373	797	815	755
BRAMS	≥ 1	1	≥ 1	1	1	1
Freq. (MHz)	83	82	133	150	126	174
Cycles	n.a.	65	68	65	n.a.	65
ThrPut (Mbit/s)	326	646	1009	1184	977	1370
TP/Slice	**0.31**	**0.84**	**0.74**	**1.49**	**1.2**	**1.83**

the only one capable of loading the Initialization Vector (*IV*). In the proposed FPGA implementation the logic required for the *IV* loading is located between registers as depicted in Figure 3. If the *IV* loading mechanism were not present the reconfigurable logic located in the CLB of the final register would be unused. Thus one can say that the *IV* loading mechanism is implemented at zero cost. Since this loading is performed with only an additional multiplexer located between registers, it does not influence the critical path of the circuit, as confirmed by the implementation results. The structure proposed by McEvoy [8] also has message padding hardware. This message padding is performed once to the end of the message, and has no significant cost when implemented in software. Thus the majority of the proposed cores and commercial core do not include the hardware for this operation. McEvoy does not give figures for the individual cost of this extra hardware. All the SHA256 cores have the data expansion hardware.

SHA 512 hash function core: Table 2 presents the implementation results for our core and the most significant related art. The figures presented also suggest a significant reduction to the required reconfigurable area, from 25% up to 60%, while achieving a speedup to the hashing function. When compared with [14], the core that requires less area from those compared, the proposed core requires 25% less reconfigurable logic while a throughput increase of 85% is achieved, resulting in a Throughput per Slice metric improvement of 165%. From the known proposed SHA512 cores, the unrolled core proposed by Lien in [16] is the only one capable of achieving a higher throughput. However, this throughput is only 4% higher, while requiring twice as much area (100% more) as the one proposed in this paper. It should also be noticed that the results presented by Lien in [16], do not include the data expansion module, that would most likely influence the final throughput rate, not to mention the required area. Even in this case the proposed core indicates a Throughput per Slice metric 77% higher. All other analyzed cores have even lower values for this efficiency metric. Table 2 also presents the values for the VIRTEX II Pro implementation, for which the core was originally developed.

Table 2. SHA512 core performance comparison

Architecture	Sklav[14]	Lien [16]	Lien [16]	Our	McEv.[8]	Our	Our
Device	XCV	XCV	XCV	XCV	XC2V	XC2V	XC2VP
Expansion	yes	no	no	yes	yes	yes	yes
IV	cst	cst	cst	yes	cst	yes	yes
Slices	2237	2384[1]	3521[1]	1680	2726	1666	1667
BRAMS	n.a.	n.a.	n.a.	2	≥ 1	1	1
Freq. (MHz)	75	56	67	70	109	121	141
Cycles	n.a.	n.a.	n.a.	81	84	81	81
ThrPut (Mbit/s)	480	717	929	889	1329	1534	1780
TP/Slice	**0.21**	**0.3[1]**	**0.26[1]**	**0.53**	**0.49**	**0.92**	**1.01**

Polymorphic implementation of the SHA-2 cores: In order to integrate the proposed core in the existing software applications and to easily test the cores, they were integrated into the MOLEN polymorphic processor [13]. In this processor the cores are integrated has a CCU, that can directly access the main memory and communicates with the GPP via a set of exchange registers. The core is evoked as the equivalent software function call. In order to use the proposed cores as CCU units for the MOLEN processor, some additional logic

---

[1] These values do not include the expansion data block, that in our architecture has a cost of 224 slices.

is required. The CCU for the SHA256 core requires 994 Slices using in total 7% of the available resources of the XC2VP30 FPGA. The CCU for the SHA512 core requires 1806 Slices using in total 13% of the available resources. In this functional test, the CCU is running with same clock frequency as the main data memory, operating at 100MHz. Table 3 presents the speedup achieved with the use of this hardware core, when compared with the pure software algorithm. The values presented are for the SHA256 kernel function. The values suggest a

Table 3. SHA256 polymorphic performances

	Hardware		Software		
Bits	Cycles	(Mbps) ThrPut	Cycles	(Mbps) ThrPut	Kernel SpeedUp
512	354	434	30402	5.05	85
1024	552	556	60546	5.07	109
128k	50088	785	7718646	5.09	153

speedup up to 153 times for the SHA256 hash function, which is achieved when the total size of the data is sufficiently large to compensate the initialization of the core, achieving a throughput of 785 Mbit/s. When only one data block is hashed the initialization time is still relevant, reducing the speedup to 85 times. When at least two data block are sent, the initialization becomes less significant, allowing already a speedup of 109%. The SHA512 CCU is capable of achieving a maximum throughput of 1.2 Gbit/s.

6   Conclusions

The proposed hardware rescheduling and reutilization schemes for the SHA-2 algorithm implementations, allow for an improvement of both performance and area resources. With the operation rescheduling, we were able to reduce the critical path in a similar manner as in the loop unrolling, without duplicating the required hardware neither using more complex data expansion schemes. This rescheduling also allows the usage of a well balanced pipeline structure that does not need additional control logic, and where both stages are always being used. The required reconfigurable resources are also significantly reduced due to the way the Digest Message is added to the intermediate values, requiring less multiplexers and adders. By adding and loading the variables A and E through the round hardware, area can also be saved and one less computational cycle is required to add the Digest Message. Experimental results shown a significant gain compared to the existing commercial cores and related academia art. For the SHA256 hash function, the proposed core is capable of achieving a 17% higher throughput with an area reduction of 42%. When compared with the Helion commercial core a 40% higher throughput is achieved while reducing the required area by 7%. As an efficiency measure, the Throughput per Slice metric has been improved by 53% for the considered commercial core and more than 100% when compared with the related academic art. The SHA512 hash function implementation suggest identical results, requiring 25% less reconfigurable resources than the smallest related art while achieving a 85% higher throughput. Even when compared with the unrolled architectures, the proposed core is capable of achieving identical throughputs, only 4% slower than the fastest proposal, which uses loop unrolling, for a 50% area reduction. These values indicate an improvement to the Throughput per Slice metric of at least 77% and up to 165%. On a VIRTEX II Pro FPGA, the proposed cores are capable of a throughput of 1.37 Gbit/s for the SHA256 and 1.78 Gbit/s for the SHA512, with only 755 and 1667 slices usage, respectively.

References

1. Dadda, L., Macchetti, M., Owen, J.: The Design of a High Speed ASIC Unit for the Hash Function SHA-256 (384, 512). In: DATE, IEEE Computer Society (2004) 70–75
2. Macchetti, M., Dadda, L.: Quasi-pipelined hash circuits. In: IEEE Symposium on Computer Arithmetic, IEEE Computer Society (2005) 222–229
3. Dadda, L., Macchetti, M., Owen, J.: An ASIC design for a high speed implementation of the hash function SHA-256 (384, 512). In Garrett, D., Lach, J., Zukowski, C.A., eds.: ACM Great Lakes Symposium on VLSI, ACM (2004) 421–425
4. Grembowski, T., Lien, R., Gaj, K., Nguyen, N., Bellows, P., Flidr, J., Lehman, T., Schott, B.: Comparative analysis of the hardware implementations of hash functions SHA-1 and SHA-512. In Chan, A.H., Gligor, V.D., eds.: ISC. Volume 2433 of Lecture Notes in Computer Science., Springer (2002) 75–89
5. McLoone, M., McCanny, J.V.: Efficient single-chip implementation of SHA-384 & SHA-512. proc. of IEEE International Conference on Field-Programmable Technology (2002) 311–314
6. Sklavos, N., Koufopavlou, O.: Implementation of the SHA-2 hash family standard using FPGAs. The Journal of Supercomputing **31** (2005) 227248
7. Ting, K.K., Yuen, S.C.L., Lee, K.H., Leong, P.H.W.: An FPGA Based SHA-256 Processor. In Glesner, M., Zipf, P., Renovell, M., eds.: FPL. Volume 2438 of Lecture Notes in Computer Science., Springer (2002) 577–585
8. McEvoy, R.P., Crowe, F.M., Murphy, C.C., Marnane, W.P.: Optimisation of the SHA-2 family of hash functions on FPGAs. IEEE Computer Society Annual Symposium on Emerging VLSI Technologies and Architectures (ISVLSI'06) (2006) 317–322
9. Michail, H.E., Kakarountas, A.P., Selimis, G.N., Goutis, C.E.: Optimizing SHA-1 hash function for high throughput with a partial unrolling study. In Paliouras, V., Vounckx, J., Verkest, D., eds.: PATMOS. Volume 3728 of Lecture Notes in Computer Science., Springer (2005) 591–600
10. NIST: Announcing the standard for secure hash standard, FIPS 180-1. Technical report, National Institute of Standards and Technology (1995)
11. NIST: The keyed-hash message authentication code (HMAC), FIPS 198. Technical report, National Institute of Standards and Technology (2002)
12. (Omitted due to the blind review submission)

13. Vassiliadis, S., Wong, S., Gaydadjiev, G.N., Bertels, K., Kuzmanov, G., Panainte, E.M.: The Molen polymorphic processor. IEEE Transactions on Computers (2004) 1363– 1375
14. Sklavos, N., Koufopavlou, O.: On the hardware implementation of the SHA-2 (256,384,512) hash functions. proc. of IEEE International symposium on Circuits and systems (ISCAS 2003) (2003) 25–28
15. HELION: Fast SHA-2 (256) hash core for xilinx FPGA. http://www.heliontech. com/ (2005)
16. Lien, R., Grembowski, T., Gaj, K.: A 1 Gbit/s partially unrolled architecture of hash functions SHA-1 and SHA-512. In: CT-RSA. (2004) 324–338

Appendix I - SHA-2 Operations

In this appendix the several operations for the SHA2 algorithm are described. In Table 4 the logical operations Ch, Maj, Σ_i, and σ_i are presented, where $\oplus$ represents the bitwise XOR operation, $\wedge$ the bitwise AND operation, $ROTR^n(x)$ the right rotation operation by n bits, and $SHR^n(x)$ the right shift operation by n bits.

Table 4. SHA256 and SHA512 functions

Designation	Function
Maj(x,y,z)	$(x \wedge y) \oplus (x \wedge z) \oplus (y \wedge z)$
Ch(x,y,z)	$(x \wedge y) \oplus (\overline{x} \wedge z)$
$\Sigma_0^{\{256\}}(x)$	$ROTR^2(x) \oplus ROTR^{13}(x) \oplus ROTR^{22}(x)$
$\Sigma_1^{\{256\}}(x)$	$ROTR^{14}(x) \oplus ROTR^{18}(x) \oplus ROTR^{41}(x)$
$\sigma_0^{\{256\}}(x)$	$ROTR^7(x) \oplus ROTR^{18}(x) \oplus SHR^3(x)$
$\sigma_1^{\{256\}}(x)$	$ROTR^{17}(x) \oplus ROTR^{19}(x) \oplus SHR^{10}(x)$
$\Sigma_0^{\{512\}}(x)$	$ROTR^{28}(x) \oplus ROTR^{34}(x) \oplus ROTR^{39}(x)$
$\Sigma_1^{\{512\}}(x)$	$ROTR^{14}(x) \oplus ROTR^{18}(x) \oplus ROTR^{41}(x)$
$\sigma_0^{\{512\}}(x)$	$ROTR^1(x) \oplus ROTR^8(x) \oplus SHR^7(x)$
$\sigma_1^{\{512\}}(x)$	$ROTR^{19}(x) \oplus ROTR^{61}(x) \oplus SHR^6(x)$

Offline Hardware/Software Authentication for Reconfigurable Platforms

Eric Simpson and Patrick Schaumont

Virginia Tech, Blacksburg VA 24060, USA
{esimpson, schaum}@vt.edu

Abstract. Many Field-Programmable Gate Array (FPGA) based systems utilize third-party intellectual property (IP) in their development. When they are deployed in non-networked environments, the question raises how this IP can be protected against non-authorized use. We describe an offline authentication scheme for IP modules. The scheme implements mutual authentication of the IP modules and the hardware platform, and enables us to provide authentication and integrity assurances to both the system developer and IP provider. Compared to the Trusted Computing Platform's approach to hardware, software authentication, our solution is more lightweight and tightly integrates with existing FPGA security features. We are able to demonstrate an implementation of the authentication scheme that requires a symmetric cipher and a Physically Unclonable Function (PUF). In addition to the low hardware requirements, our implementation does not require any on-chip, non-volatile storage.

1 Introduction

The latest generation of Field Programmable Gate Arrays (FPGAs) can accommodate complex systems containing embedded hardware and software. While they are often used in a constrained, non-networked environment, their configuration presents a valuable piece of intellectual property that merits protection. Our contribution is an offline mutual authentication scheme for both the hardware and software configuration of a reconfigurable platform. The mutual authentication involves the FPGA chip manufacturers, who provide a standard security module in each of their FPGAs, and the IP providers, who commit to an identity for each release of their software. An FPGA system developer combines chips and IP components in their product. Using the hardware identity provided by the chip manufacturers and software identity committed to by the IP providers, they are able to construct a product where hardware and software components can authenticate each other.

In this section, we briefly review the roles that the chip manufacturers, IP providers, and system developers play in the authentication scheme, along with what it means to have a software or hardware identity. Also discussed is the meaning of software in an FPGA and the role it plays in modern FPGA design.

L. Goubin and M. Matsui (Eds.): CHES 2006, LNCS 4249, pp. 311–323, 2006.
© International Association for Cryptologic Research 2006

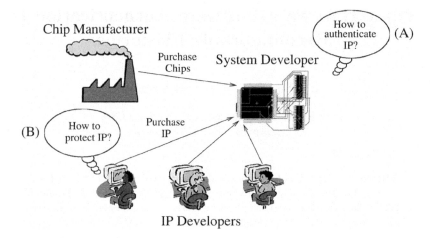

Fig. 1. Parties involved in modern FPGA design

1.1   Securing Intellectual Property in Modern FPGA Design

The rapidly increasing design capacity of FPGAs enables more complex and bigger designs than ever before. Many current models of FPGAs not only support traditional hardware design, but also have the ability to run embedded software. The software in an FPGA executes in either an embedded hardcore processor like the PowerPC, or in a softcore [1] that is synthesized with the rest of the hardware design. These software modules are often developed and distributed by third-party IP Providers. While design protection in FPGAs has been available for some time in the form of configuration encryption [2], this technique is ineffective at protecting third-party intellectual property and software modules. We point out two key issues.

The first issue is that IP-methodologies require additional authentication. As shown in Fig. 1, system developers design their product with a plug-and-play methodology in which they adopt third-party intellectual-property components (IP) for integration onto a chip. This IP can possibly come from multiple vendors in the case of so-called System-on-Chip design (SoC). The result is an intriguing multi-level authentication problem. At one level, system developers would like to authenticate the IP they are running (Fig. 1, A), and at another level the IP providers would like to authenticate the system into which they are integrated (Fig. 1, B). In this paper, we will specifically consider the integration of software IPs onto an FPGA platform, but it is understood that the need for authentication in IP-methodologies is generic.

The second issue is that current FPGA security mechanisms have a limited scope, focused on the hardware configuration. Bitstream encryption [3] for example will enforce bitstream privacy and integrity, but it will not protect the software running on the processors configured in the FPGA. In the case of third-party IP, and specifically in the case of software IPs, additional protection mechanisms are required.

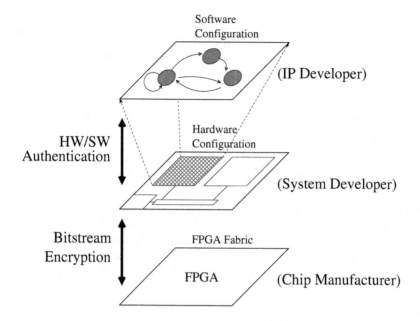

Fig. 2. Levels of Authentication

We present a solution to the above to problems, in the form of a protocol and an architectural extension for FPGA-based design. We also demonstrate a sample implementation and report on the complexity and performance of this implementation.

The system setup that we are considering for our protocol development is shown in Fig. 2. A hardware platform, designed by a System Developer, will be configured into an FPGA. The System Developer will also use third-party software IPs that execute on top of the platform. The System Developer can apply bitstream encryption to protect the hardware configuration in the FPGA, but an additional hardware-software authentication mechanism is needed to protect the software IPs.

The outline of this paper is as follows. In Section 2 we describe the protocol for enrolling the hardware and software identities in the authentication scheme. Then, in Section 3 we discuss the protocol for distributing mutually authenticated IP to system developers. After discussing the authentication protocol in Sections 2 and 3, we analyze the security properties in Section 4. Finally, a low-cost implementation of the offline, hardware, software authentication scheme is presented in Section 5.

2   Enrollment Protocol

The enrollment phase involves three parties: the chip manufacturers, IP providers and a trusted third-party that is used to store and communicate identity

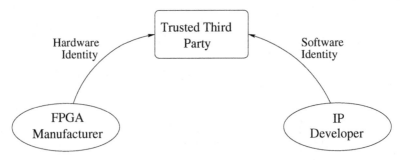

Fig. 3. Enrollment Phase

information among the participants. As shown in Fig. 3, the enrollment phase is composed of two communication channels. One channel is used by the chip manufacturer to communicate hardware identities to the trusted third-party, and the other channel is used by the IP provider to communicate software identities. The definition of hardware and software identities is given in the following sections.

2.1 Hardware Enrollment

In this phase, the manufacturer would like to distribute FPGAs that have the ability to securely run third-party IP. To enable their customers to securely run third-party IP, the FPGA manufacturers implement a standard security module in each chip. This security module contains two distinct hardware blocks:

1. PUF - Used for hardware authentication and key generation
2. Block Cipher - Used for symmetric encryption and software authentication

The PUF is a device that maps inputs (challenges) to outputs (responses). The mapping from a challenge to a response is determined by the physical properties of the chip it is implemented in. Therefore, an identical PUF circuit implemented on two different chips will result in different responses for the same challenge. Several implementations for PUFs have been reported in literature [4,5].

After building their FPGAs, the manufacturer enrolls them in the authentication scheme by sending each chip's identification information to the trusted third-party. The identity is composed of two data items:

$HW\#$: Public, unique 128-bit value that identifies the chip

$\overrightarrow{CRP}$: Private list of challenge, response pairs produced by the chip

To communicate the identity for each chip, the manufacturer opens an authenticated and secure link to the trusted third-party (over SSL, SSH, etc.). Over the authenticated and secure link, the manufacturer sends:

$Manufacturer \longrightarrow TTP : HW\#, \overrightarrow{CRP}$

2.2   Software/IP Enrollment

The enrollment of IP providers in the authentication scheme allows system developers to verify the integrity and authenticity of the software they are running. The identification information the IP provider sends to the trusted third-party is composed of two data items:

$$IP\# : \text{Public, unique 128-bit value that identifies the name}$$
$$\text{and version of the intellectual property}$$
$$Hash(SW, IP\#) : \text{Public hash of the } IP\# \text{ and software that the IP is}$$
$$\text{composed of}$$

Like the chip manufacturer, the IP provider opens a secure and authenticated link to the trusted third-party. For each version or release of their software, the IP provider sends:

$$IPP \longrightarrow TTP : IP\# , Hash(SW, IP\#)$$

Since the IP Provider only has to commit to a hash of their IP, they don't have to trust the third-party with the actual software. Also, the IP provider doesn't have to make any changes to their development process to enroll in the authentication scheme. They simply commit to a version and hash for each software release. There is no need to embed watermarks [6], or any other identification information in their software.

3   Authenticated IP Request and Distribution

Once the system developer has purchased FPGAs that have been enrolled in the authentication scheme, the developer can request authenticated IP from the trusted third-party. The request and distribution of an authenticated hardware-software configuration requires four messages per IP module. The first three messages, involving the trusted third-party, form the online phase of the protocol. The fourth message does not require the trusted third-party and forms the offline phase of the protocol.

The messages of the online phase are exchanged over a standard secure, and authenticated link.

First, some definitions of the symbols used in the protocol:

$$Nonce : \text{Number used once, a unique token used to ensure the freshness}$$
$$\text{of a message}$$
$$C_{ttp}, R_{ttp}: \text{Challenge, response pair used by the trusted third-party to}$$
$$\text{communicate the IP authentication and integrity data to the}$$
$$\text{system developer}$$
$$R_{ip} : \text{Response used by the IP provider to encrypt and package their}$$
$$\text{software for the target hardware platform}$$
$$C_{ip} : \text{Challenge that the target hardware can use to generate the } R_{ip}$$
$$\text{used to encrypt the software.}$$

3.1 Request and Distribution Messages

$(1) \quad SYS \longrightarrow TTP : IP\#, HW\#, Nonce$
$(2) \quad TTP \longrightarrow SYS \ : IP\#, HW\#, C_{ttp}, \{IP\#, Hash\,(SW, IP\#)\,, C_{ip}, Nonce\}_{R_{ttp}}$
$(3) \quad TTP \longrightarrow IPP \ : IP\#, HW\#, Nonce, R_{ip}$
$(4) \quad IPP \ \longrightarrow SYS \ : IP\#, HW\#, \{length, Nonce, SW\}_{R_{ip}}$

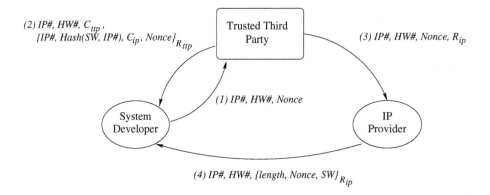

Fig. 4. Distribution Phase

3.2 Messages Explained

As shown in Fig. 4, the request and distribution of an authenticated hardware-software configuration requires four messages between the system developer, trusted third-party and the IP provider.

1. Message #1 is the system developer IP request to the trusted third-party.

2. Message #2 is sent by the trusted third-party to the system developer. The message is encrypted using a CRP that the security module can generate and use to decrypt the message. The message contains the requested IP's identity and integrity information. Also contained in this message is the challenge that can be used by the security module to generate the response used by the IP provider to encrypt their software.

3. Message #3 is the trusted third-party forwarding the system developer's request for IP to the IP provider. This message contains the response that the IP provider will use as the key to encrypt their software.
   After message #3, the trusted third-party is no longer involved in the mutual authentication, and the protocol becomes off-line. At this point, the IP provider can now securely package their software for a unique hardware identity. While this package could be sent over the network, it could also be in the form of a ROM chip that is given to the system developer.

4. Once the system developer has received message #4 from the IP provider, this data can be merged with authentication information contained in message #2. At this point, the system developer has the following information:

   (a) $C_{ttp}, \{IP\#, Hash\,(SW, IP\#)\,, C_{ip}, Nonce\}_{R_{ttp}}$
   (b) $\{length, Nonce, SW\}_{R_{ip}}$

   Part (a) of the message contains the necessary information to validate the authenticity and integrity of the software, and the software is assured that only the target hardware can decrypt the IP contained in part (b). Since the security module is the only one that can generate the required responses to decrypt the data, the merged message can then be saved to insecure storage by the system developer. This IP containing message can then be validated, loaded, and run by the offline FPGA indefinitely.

While the initial request and distribution of the messages involve active communication, the last stage of verification is able to be performed in an offline context. It is important that the last authentication stage can be performed offline because many systems are deployed in non-networked environments. This is an important distinction from protocols that require interactive zero-knowledge proofs [7,8], or active dialogue to perform authentication [9].

4   Analysis

The protocol is secure against cheating attempts by either the system developer, or IP provider.

4.1   Tampering with Data from the TTP

Since the response from the TTP in message #2 is encrypted with a random response, only the developer who possesses the target hardware with a valid security module, will be able to decrypt the message. Also, in order to create a fake encrypted portion of the message, the attacker needs to know the mapping from C_{ttp} to R_{ttp}, which is infeasible due to the properties of the PUF. Invalid messages in this step can be detected when the plaintext $IP\#$ doesn't match the $IP\#$ contained in the encrypted portion of the message.

4.2   Tampering with Data from the IP Provider

There are two hurdles an attacker must overcome to tamper with the software received by the system developer in Message #4. The first hurdle is that the attacker must not only know the C_{ip} the TTP sent in Message #2, but also the mapping from C_{ip} to R_{ip}. In addition, any modifications to the data will be detected when the $Hash(SW, IP\#)$ doesn't match the expected data, or the $Nonces$ don't agree.

4.3   Collusion Scenarios

Using an example from today's marketplace, it is interesting to look at the possible sources of cheating and fraud between the various parties. The parties are defined as follows:

System Developer: Customer designing a product or prototype

TTP: Fabless company that designs the actual FPGAs

IP Developer: Value-added seller that produces IP for a specific company's FPGAs

Chip Manufacturer: Third-party company that manufacturers the TTP designed chips

The company that designs the actual FPGAs is the trusted third-party in this scenario, because they have an incentive to be trustful to both the system developers that purchase their chips, and the IP providers that develop for their FPGAs. Since the FPGA designer is in the business of selling chips, it is desirable to have a a complete design portfolio of IP components available for their FPGAs. By designing the security module into their chips, they can assure IP providers that their chips provide a secure environment from IP piracy. Therefore, if the FPGA designing company wants to stay in business, they must stay trustworthy to both their chip purchasing customers and IP providers. For example, if they distributed a CRP that enabled a system developer to pirate an IP module, the FPGA designer would lose all trust and likely see an exodus of IP providers from their platform.

By having the trusted third-party directly generate the list of CRPs, the authentication system also protects the FPGA designer from a chip manufacturer who overbuilds and directly sells the FPGA designer's product. Since the overbuilt chips will not be in the TTP database, these chips will not be authorized to run authenticated, third-party IP. In addition, when a system developer uses a counterfeit chip, the FPGA designer will directly notice the counterfeits.

4.4   Implementation Practicality

One system issue is the ability of the TTP to store the authentication data. As an example, for each chip the TTP must store the hardware ID along with a CRP list. Making a rough estimate of 1,000 CRPs for each chip, this results in a storage requirement of 250KB per chip. Therefore, a TTP would be able to store the authentication data for a 1,000,000 chips on a single 250GB disk. Given that many of today's workstations have 250GB worth of storage, this is certainly a reasonable storage requirement.

Also, implementing IP authentication into the development process is a reasonable consideration as well. Given the fact that FPGA designers already distribute development software to system developers, implementing IP authentication into these tools would be of similar complexity. Therefore, integrating an authenticated IP distribution scheme into the development process does not appear to be an unreasonable task.

5 Results

The security module for the reconfigurable platform was developed on a Xilinx Spartan-3 FPGA. The security module block diagram is presented in Fig. 5. The authenticated IP is stored in an off-chip memory module and loaded into the FPGA on power-up. The security module's Protocol Controller is responsible for detecting the presence of authenticated IP on the input lines and coordinating the load of authenticated IP. The transfer from the external store into the security module is done over an 8-bit bus, with full-handshaking. Once the data is inside the security module, all data is passed over a shared 128-bit bus between the Protocol Controller, AES module and the PUF. All processing is done in a fully parallel manner, such that the AES block, PUF and IO can overlap execution. Therefore, after one IP block has completed authentication and is being loaded into FPGA for execution, another can be undergoing authentication, while the next IP block is simultaneously being loaded into the security module.

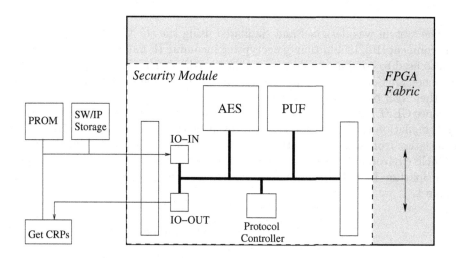

Fig. 5. Security Module block diagram

Whether the security module is loading authenticated IP or generating CRPs is determined by a leading opcode. Currently the opcode is one byte, with two predefined opcodes. One opcode is used to instruct the security module to generate a CRP, while the other causes IP to be loaded through the security module. Therefore, authenticated IP is stored in the following three-part format:

1. $Opcode_{load}$
2. $C_{ttp}, \{IP\#, Hash\,(SW, IP\#)\,, C_{ip}, Nonce\}_{R_{ttp}}$
3. $\{length, Nonce, SW\}_{R_{ip}}$

An important note is that the authentication scheme is not limited to loading a single authenticated IP module. The FPGA can load an arbitrary number of IP components through the security module. Even while running, the system can be configured to load new IP modules, or to swap old ones out of the system.

Generating a $\overrightarrow{CRP}$ requires the following message:

1. $Opcode_{CRP}, seed, \#$ of pairs to generate

Where the *seed* is a random number used to seed the PUF, and the number of pairs to generate is a 64-bit integer. The CRP list is generated by the following:

$$C_0 = PUF\,(PUF\,(seed)) \tag{1}$$
$$R_0 = PUF(C_0) \tag{2}$$
$$\text{For } i = 1 \text{ to } \# \text{ of pairs to generate}$$
$$C_i = R_{i-1} \tag{3}$$
$$R_i = PUF(C_i) \tag{4}$$

The system was designed and simulated using the the GEZEL language and environment [10]. In addition to decrypting incoming IP modules, the AES cipher is also used to compute hashes as in Cohen's AES-hash NIST proposal [11]. We have not yet built a PUF implementation, but have simulated its behavior using another AES block with a fixed key.

Since GEZEL is a cycle-based hardware description language, most of the work and simulation was completed before translating the GEZEL code to VHDL. The translation from GEZEL to VHDL was done by the `fdlvhd` tool provided by the GEZEL environment. After translation, the VHDL was synthesized and mapped to a Spartan-3 FPGA using Xilinx's toolchain. The results are summarized in Table 1.

Table 1. Security Module Synthesis

Component	HW	Slices	Speed
Protocol Controller (Input)	Spartan-3	169	202 MHz
Protocol Controller (Output)	Spartan-3	142	187 MHz
AES	Spartan-3	2046	124 MHz
Simulated PUF	Spartan-3	2025	124 MHz

As expected, the hardware requirements are dominated by the AES and simulated PUF. The important note though, is the low complexity and requirements of the Protocol Controller. Couple this protocol model with some of literature's low cost symmetric cipher and PUF implementations and this offline mutual authentication scheme not only fills a needed security gap in modern FPGA design, but is also low cost.

5.1   Related Work

While AES was chosen as the symmetric cipher, and a simulated PUF was used, it's important to note that our offline hardware, software authentication scheme only requires a single symmetric cipher, and a single PUF. This is in contrast to the Trusted Computing Group's (TCG) authentication scheme that requires the following components be implemented in their trusted platform module (TPM) [12,13]:

Non-volatile storage for storing various keys and authorization data

True random-bit generator for key and nonce generation

SHA-1 Engine for computing signatures

RSA Key Generation for at least a 2048-bit modulus

RSA Engine for digital signatures and encryption/decryption

Compared to the recommended components for the TPM, our security module is more practical to implement as a standard module in FPGAs. Also, the TPM requirement for secure on-chip non-volatile storage isn't likely to be met by current reconfigurable platforms.

In [14] the authors present a solution to the shortcomings of the TCG specifications with regards to sealed data. Our work is orthogonal to [14] because their focus is primarily on data that has been sealed to a particular TPM. This results in a different problem domain because the data we are protecting is not unique. While the data that an individual produces can be unique and irreplaceable, the protected software delivered to our security module is neither unique, nor irreplaceable. Instead, the software is able to duplicated by the IP provider on demand. Therefore, when switching to a new FPGA, the system developer can simply make a request to the TTP for another copy of the IP. The previously distributed software doesn't have to be exported in a secure way because it can be duplicated by the IP provider. If our authentication scheme was to be extended to protecting not only hardware and software, but also unique data, the ideas from [14] would be good addition for managing the secure data.

Other relevant work was done in [15] where the authors implemented a secure and cost-optimized verson of a TPM for hand-held devices. The work describes an architecture to cleanly implement the Trusted Computing Group specifications [12] in a hand-held context. By focusing on the ability to implement the TCG specifications though, this implementation has the same requirements as a standard TPM. A notable exception to the standard TPM implementation is that the authors discuss the possibility of using a PUF based system to avoid the need for onchip non-volatile memory to store secrets. Other relevant work that our security module could benefit from is in the [15] authors work on secure debugging interfaces and methods.

6   Conclusions

The use of intellectual-property components in FPGA-based design leads to new and particular security requirements. The protection of the configuration bitstream itself is insufficient to cope with multiple IP originators, and moreover it does not offer adequate guarantees with respect to IP protection. Our results show that a protocol can be designed that offers the required protection while meeting the constraints of a small embedded and offline implementation. We also don't require a major modification of the design process. In fact, our protocol can be made backward compatible with existing approaches for downloading FPGA bitstreams.

We believe that our scheme is applicable to situations outside of FPGA design, and are presently investigating its use in the context of other implementation technologies, as well as in the context of different forms of IP, including data and hardware IP blocks.

References

1. Moyer, B.: Using softcore-based FPGAs to balance hardware/software needs in a multicore design. Embedded System Design Magazine (2006)
2. Feng, J.: FPGA design security. ECN Magazine (2006) 23–24
3. Inc., X.: Using bitstream encryption. Handbook of the Virtex II Platform (2003)
4. Gassend, B.: Physical Random Functions. Master's thesis, Massachusetts Institute of Technology (2003)
5. Suh, G.E., O'Donnell, C.W., Sachdev, I., Devadas, S.: Design and Implementation of the AEGIS Single-Chip Secure Processor Using Physical Random Functions. SIGARCH Comput. Archit. News **33** (2005) 25–36
6. Kahng, A.B., Lach, J., Mangione-Smith, W.H., Mantik, S., Markov, I.L., Potkonjak, M., Tucker, P., Wang, H., Wolfe, G.: Watermarking techniques for intellectual property protection. In: Design Automation Conference. (1998) 776–781
7. Feige, U., Fiat, A., Shamir, A.: Zero-knowledge proofs of identity. J. Cryptol. **1** (1988) 77–94
8. Bellare, M., Palacio, A.: Gq and schnorr identification schemes: Proofs of security against impersonation under active and concurrent attacks. In: CRYPTO. (2002) 162–177
9. Otway, D., Rees, O.: Efficient and timely mutual authentication. Operating Systems Review **21** (1987) 8–10
10. Schaumont, P., Ching, D.: GEZEL homepage. http://rijndael.ece.vt.edu/gezel2 (2006)
11. Cohen, B., Laurie, B.: AES-Hash. NIST: Modes of Operation for Symmetric Key Block Ciphers (2001)
12. Group, T.C.: TCG Specification Architecture Overview. (2004)

13. DoCoMo, N., IBM, Corporation, I.: Trusted Mobile Platform Hardware Architecture Description. (2004)
14. Kuhn, U., Kursawe, K., Lucks, S., Sadeghi, A.R., Stuble, C.: Secure Data Management in Trusted Computing. In: Cryptographic Hardware for Embedded Systems (CHES 2005). (2005)
15. Khan, M., Seifert, J., Wheeler, D.M., Brizek, J.P.: A platform-level trust-architecture for hand-held devices. In: Cryptographic Advances in Secure Hardware (CRASH 2005). (2005)

Why One Should Also Secure RSA Public Key Elements

Eric Brier[1], Benoît Chevallier-Mames[1,2],
Mathieu Ciet[1], and Christophe Clavier[1]

[1] Gemalto, Security Labs,
La Vigie, Avenue du Jujubier, ZI Athélia IV,
F-13705 La Ciotat Cedex, France
`firstname.familyname@gemalto.com`
[2] École Normale Supérieure, Département d'Informatique,
45 rue d'Ulm,
F-75230 Paris 05, France

Abstract. It is well known that a malicious adversary can try to retrieve secret information by inducing a fault during cryptographic operations. Following the work of Seifert on fault inductions during RSA signature verification, we consider in this paper the signature counterpart.

Our article introduces the first fault attack applied on RSA in standard mode. By only corrupting one public key element, one can recover the private exponent. Indeed, similarly to Seifert's attack, our attack is done by modifying the modulus.

One of the strong points of our attack is that the assumptions on the induced faults' effects are relaxed. In one mode, *absolutely no knowledge* of the fault's behavior is needed to achieve the full recovery of the private exponent. In another mode, based on a fault model defining what is called *dictionary*, the attack's efficiency is improved and the number of faults is dramatically reduced. All our attacks are very practical.

Note that those attacks do work even against implementations with deterministic (*e.g.,* RSA-FDH) or random (*e.g.,* RSA-PFDH) paddings, except for cases where we have signatures with randomness recovery (such as RSA-PSS).

The results finally presented on this paper lead us to conclude that it is also mandatory to protect RSA's public parameters against fault attacks.

Keywords: RSA, Standard Mode, Fault Cryptanalysis, Seifert's Attack.

1 Introduction

1.1 Basics

RSA [16] is today the most widely used public key cryptosystem. Let $n = pq$ be the product of two large primes typically of 512 to 1024 bits. Let e be the public exponent, coprime with $\varphi(n) = (p-1)(q-1)$, where $\varphi(\cdot)$ is the Euler totient function. The public exponent e is linked to the so-called private exponent d by equation $ed \equiv 1 \pmod{\varphi(n)}$.

L. Goubin and M. Matsui (Eds.): CHES 2006, LNCS 4249, pp. 324–338, 2006.

Basically, in RSA cryptosystem [3, 4, 14], public operations (*i.e.,* signature verification or encryption) are done by computing an e-th power, while private operations (*i.e.,* signature generation or decryption) are done by computing a d-th power. To speed up private operations, an efficient technique based on the Chinese Reminder Theorem was proposed [15]: this is referred to the CRT mode, by opposition to the standard mode.

RSA and Physical Attacks. The security of the RSA public key cryptosystem is linked to the hardness of the factorization. In addition, when implementing cryptosystems, one needs to be very careful about information leakage, which else would allow so-called *side-channel analysis* [11].

In 1996, another type of attacks, called *fault attacks*, has been introduced against the RSA CRT implementation [6]. This attack is known as the *Bellcore attack*: only one fault induction on one half of the computation suffices to recover the modulus factorization from one correct and one faulty signature, by just computing a greatest common divisor. However, in case of the use of random padding, the Bellcore attack cannot be applied.

Nowadays, in case of the standard RSA, there is only one known fault induction attack in order to recover the private exponent. This attack is based on flipping bits of the private exponent one per one.[1]

Type of Faulted Parameters. All the previous methods are based on fault induction against private parameters.[2] An exception is presented in a recently published article by Seifert [17], where he proposes for the first time to attack the public part of RSA signature scheme, *i.e.,* signature verification. The RSA scheme itself is not endangered, *i.e.,* the attacker is not able to forge new valid signatures, but Seifert's attack allows the attacker to pass — with a certain probability — the signature verification step, for a message of her choice, by corrupting the public modulus: all in all, the attacker's goal is fulfilled, but the attack is "one shot", in the sense that it needs to be launched again to produce another wrong acceptance.

1.2   Our Contribution

In this paper, we propose the first fault attack that can be used against RSA in standard mode, to recover the private exponent by corrupting only *public key elements*. This point is very critical, as other existing attacks already target the private exponent, which should in essence be protected against faults. On the contrary, prior to our paper, it was unclear whether it was necessary or not to protect public elements: our paper clarifies this point by concluding that *RSA public key elements also have to be protected against fault attacks.*

Our attack has the same starting point as Seifert's one: it consists in corrupting the public modulus. However, Seifert's attack allows the attacker to pass

---

[1] This attack can also be generalized to modify small sets of bits, typically bytes.
[2] Inducing fault against public method has also been considered in the case of elliptic curves [5, 8].

a signature verification (with a certain probability), while our attack allows a *full key recovery*. Once the key is recovered, the adversary gets all power, while Seifert's attack allows just a single false acceptance.

An additional key property of our attack is that, in one of its mode, the attacker needs *absolutely no knowledge* of the fault effect. No matter what the fault's effect is, she might recover the private exponent. This clearly improves upon Seifert's attack (where the attacker must *guess* the faulty modulus), or upon flipping bit attack (where the fault attack must be unrealistically precise).

In another mode, our attack can be improved. With the help of a *fault model*, we are able to dramatically reduce the number of faults needed to fully recover the private key. As explained later, the attacker is not assumed to be so powerful, as her knowledge of the fault she produced may be probabilistic or unprecise: some of the off-line phases of the attack are proposed to deal with uncertainty.

The new fault attacks presented in this article apply to standard RSA and not to the CRT mode. Moreover, fixed paddings (*e.g.,* RSA-FDH [3]) or random paddings with joint randomness (*e.g.,* RSA-PFDH [9]) do not influence the attack. The only limitation is in case of the signature with randomness recovery (*e.g.,* RSA-PSS [4]) where the problem remains open.

1.3   Organization of the Paper

This article is organized as follows. In Section 2, we remind the background regarding fault attacks and the novelty introduced by Seifert. The core of our paper begins at Section 3 where we define the general framework of our attack. Then, in Section 4, we introduce the first mode of our attack, where the adversary needs no particular knowledge about the fault induced on the device. Later, in Section 5, we refine our attack to the case where a model of the fault attack is accessible to the adversary. Finally, we conclude in Section 6.

2   Preliminaries

In the paper, the notation $DL(\mu, s, n)$ is used to express the discrete logarithm of s with respect to the basis μ modulo n, which either is an integer defined modulo the multiplicative order of $\mu \bmod n$ or does not exist mean that s is not a power of $\mu \bmod n$. Clearly, it can be generalized to any prime power p^a dividing n, and any integer r dividing the multiplicative order of $\mu \bmod p^a$ as $DL(\mu, s, p^a) \bmod r$ (denoted $DL(\mu, s, p^a, r)$ in the sequel), which is an integer defined modulo r or does not exist.

We remind that for relatively small value of r — say from 15 to 20 digits —, the discrete logarithm $DL(\mu, s, n, r)$ can be computed efficiently by square root methods such as *baby-step giant-step* or *Pollard's rho* [12].

2.1   Fault Models

Fault based attacks can be realized in practice by various ways. In the past, it was possible on certain components to induce faults using VCC glitches [1]. Nowadays, chips are designed to resist such fault induction means.

The best tools today to inject fault is certainly using a laser [2]. The effects of the fault may vary according to the component, to the type of laser used, to the various smart mechanisms implemented by the hardware designers *etc.* Various fault models are commonly considered according to the "hypothetical" capabilities of the attacker, in terms of location and timing precision of her faults.

From a practical point of view, the fault effect is highly dependent on the component. The most simple fault to induce is to change a word (whose size depends on the architecture) in an undetermined way. This can simply be obtained by inducing a fault on address decoders for example, when parameters stored in EEPROM or in Flash are transferred to RAM. If this transfer includes a random ordering, then the location, in terms of word index is also unknown.

For some component the effect of the fault can be known, eventually with some probability. In the literature, single bit flip models are sometimes considered. However, this is not so easy to make in practice whereas faulty word models are very realistic. Moreover, a distinction is also done between permanent (sticky bits) and transient faults: in the following we mainly consider values changed from the beginning to the end of their use in a processus.

In this paper, we make less assumptions on the attacker's injection capabilities and stick a more realistic model

2.2 About the Attack of Seifert and Muir

Before going further, let us first give a brief description of the Seifert's paper that motivated this article [17] and its generalization by Muir [13]. For the sake of simplicity, the attack is called *Seifert's attack* in the rest of this article. We refer the interested reader to the original papers for further details.

The basic principle of Seifert's attack is the following: the attacker tries to find (off-line) a faulty modulus n' such that the public exponent e and $\varphi(n')$ are coprime, and such that n' is a *possible* or even *plausible* faulty value of modulus n. To this aim, the adversary should use a fault model.

Furthermore, the attacker needs to compute efficiently the inverse of e mod $\varphi(n')$. This is possible when the factorization of n' is known. Once d', the inverse of e mod $\varphi(n')$ is computed, the attacker constructs a signature $s' = \mu^{d'}$ mod n'.

This first operation, that consists in trying to find a n' satisfying an useful property and constructing an associated "faulty" signature, is done before the attack. Then, an *on-line* procedure is carried out: the attacker executes the signature verification algorithm with (s', μ) as input, and tries to inject a fault during this procedure in order to proceed computations modulo targeted n' instead of modulo n. Clearly, the probability of success, and so the average required number of faults, is dependent on the accuracy of the fault model and the capability for an attacker to produce an enough precise fault to be able to obtain the faulty modulus n' with non negligible probability.

3   Framework of Our Extensions to Seifert's Attack

Seifert's attack succeeds in forging a signature that is accepted as valid, but does not reveal any information about the private key elements. Some unauthorized access can be granted but the RSA key itself is not broken.

In the sequel, extensions of Seifert's attack are presented. They let an attacker recover the private exponent d from several faulty computations when the modulus is altered before a standard RSA exponentiation.

3.1   General Description and Constraints of Our Attack

General Methodology. Similarly to [17,13], our fault attack consists in modifying the modulus before an RSA exponentiation. The operation $s = \mu^d \bmod n$ is targeted, and several faults are induced to collect faulty signatures from which the attacker learns the private exponent d.

Definition 1 (Fault campaign, Fault couples). *It is said that an attacker processes the* fault attack campaign *if she executes the exponentiation* $s = \mu^d \bmod n$ I *times, and corrupts these executions by changing the modulus* n *into unknown moduli* n'_i, *to obtain* fault couples $(\mu_i, s_i)_{1 \leq i \leq I}$.

Paddings. A general constraint comes from the use of RSA in real life: it is folklore knowledge that one needs to use functions (called *paddings*, and denoted Λ) that reduces the malleability of the RSA prior to the exponentiation. Some of the paddings are *deterministic* — *i.e.*, $\mu = \Lambda(m)$—, others are *probabilistic* — *i.e.*, $\mu = \Lambda(m, r)$.[3] In the probabilistic case, the randomness can be either joint or self-recovered.

Because of redundancy checks of the paddings, after the decryption phase (*e.g.*, in RSA-OAEP), exploitation of fault attacks during decryption is generally not possible, and so decryption is out of scope of this paper. For signatures, fault attacks might be possible if μ_i are known to the attacker. It is the case when the padding is deterministic (*e.g.*, RSA-FDH) or if the randomness is joint with the signature (*e.g.*, RSA-PFDH). On the contrary, if the randomness is self-recovered from the signature (*e.g.*, RSA-PSS), then the faulty result does not allow recovering μ_i and our attack cannot be done.

From now, we suppose the attacker can compute bases μ_i used during the faulty exponentiations.

3.2   Dictionary of Moduli

The literature is plenty of fault models (*cf.* Section 2.1) that would allow the adversary to guess how she could have modified the modulus n into n'_i during the faulty exponentiations. Once such a choice is made, the adversary is then able to construct a dictionary.

---

[3] The notations here are obvious: m is the message, and r is the randomness.

Definition 2 (Dictionary). *Depending on a fault model that the attacker might have experimented, the attacker may be able to establish* a priori *a list of possible values for the faulty moduli n_i'. Such a list is called a* dictionary *(of moduli).*

Whether a dictionary is available to the attacker governs which methods she may use to recover the private exponent d. As shown below, if an attacker has access to a dictionary, then the main part of her work is to learn which of the possible moduli of the dictionary was used for a given fault.

A dictionary is not necessarily mandatory and a first general method where no dictionary is needed is presented in the next section. This particularly implies that *no fault model* is required.

4   Recovering the Private Exponent Without Dictionary

This section describes a method to recover the private exponent d when the attacker has no clue about what value a faulty modulus may take. This corresponds to an attacker who is unable to predict or identify any fault model from the experimental setting of the attack. Note also that in the case where the attacker has actually identified a fault model and that the induced dictionary is too large to be practically handled (typically 2^{32} entries) the attacker may ignore this "useless" dictionary and place herself in the context of no dictionary as well.

For the sake of clarity, in the description of the different attacks, we denote by p's the (possible) divisors of n_i', and by q's the (possible) divisors of the orders of considered subgroups. Of course, these integers are not to be confused with the unknown factorization of targeted modulus n.

4.1   General Description of the Attack

Once the fault campaign is performed, the attacker knows some fault couples $(\mu_i, s_i)_{1 \leq i \leq I}$, corresponding to unknown moduli $n_i' \neq n$, related by $s_i = \mu_i^d \bmod n_i'$. Input μ_i and output s_i are known to the attacker while n_i' is unknown and modeled as uniformly distributed over the integers less than 2^{ℓ_n}, where ℓ_n is the modulus bitsize.

From the data of the fault campaign, the private exponent d is retrieved offline, by progressively determining $d \bmod r_k$, for some small prime powers r_k. When the product $R = \prod_k r_k$ exceeds the modulus n (and so unknown $\varphi(n)$), d can be recovered by means of the Chinese Remainder Theorem.

Improving the Fraction of Bits of d to Know. If e is small (typically $e = 3$ or $e = 2^{16} + 1$), then the equation relating public and private RSA exponents

$$ed = 1 + k\varphi(n) = 1 + k(n + 1 - \alpha)$$

can be used in order to reduce the fraction of d's bits the attacker has to find to recover d. Here α is an unknown value, and k verifies $0 < k < e$. If k is known, or guessed by exhaustive search when e is small, we have

$$d = \frac{1 + k(n + 1)}{e} - \frac{k\alpha}{e}$$

where the unknown part $k\alpha/e$ verifies (assuming balanced factorization of n):

$$\frac{k\alpha}{e} < \alpha < 2^{\lceil \frac{\ell_n}{2}+1 \rceil} \quad .$$

Denoting $u = \lfloor \frac{\ell_n}{2} - 1 \rfloor$, d may be expressed as $d = \bar{d}2^u + \underline{d}$, where $\bar{d}$ is known, and $0 < \underline{d} < 2^u$ is unknown. Knowledge of $d \bmod R$ implies knowledge about $\underline{d} \bmod R$, so that d may be retrieved as soon as R is $\lceil \frac{\ell_n}{2} + 1 \rceil$ bits long. Hence, in the following, for each attack, the two cases e small or e relatively large are considered. It is thus possible to see how much it reduces the number of faults required.

4.2   A Useful Proposition

Before detailing the off-line part, we state the following heuristics used hereafter.

Proposition 1. *Let (μ_i, s_i) be a fault couple corresponding to modulus n_i', and p^a a prime power such that $p \nmid \mu_i$ and $p \nmid s_i$. Let also δ be the multiplicative order of μ_i modulo p^a. Then, for any r dividing δ we have:*

$$d \equiv DL(\mu_i, s_i, p^a) \pmod{r} \tag{1}$$

with probability 1 if $p^a \mid n_i'$, and probability close to $\frac{1}{r}$ otherwise.

Proof. By definition, $s_i = \mu_i^d \bmod n_i'$. Hence, when $p^a \mid n_i'$, we have:

$$s_i \equiv \mu_i^{d \bmod \varphi(p^a)} \pmod{p^a}$$
$$\equiv \mu_i^{d \bmod \delta} \pmod{p^a}$$

so that $d \equiv DL(\mu_i, s_i, p^a) \pmod{\delta}$, from which Equation (1) follows.

On the contrary, when $p^a \nmid n_i'$, we admit that uniform distribution of n_i' over the integers implies quasi uniform distribution of $DL(\mu_i, s_i, p^a)$ over residue classes modulo r, hence the proposition.   □

Of course, without knowing n_i', it is impossible to decide which p^a can be used to determine $d \bmod r$ with certainty, for some divisors r of $\varphi(p^a)$. Nevertheless, Proposition 1 suggests that, even if n_i' is unknown (and so its factorization), one can mount an attack based upon a bias in favor of the true value d_r of the residue class of d modulo r.

4.3   The Off-Line Phase

The basic idea is that determining d_r for some integer r, may be achieved by considering some p^a for which $r \mid \varphi(p^a)$, and by taking the discrete logarithm of s_i in base μ_i modulo p^a. From Proposition 1, and provided that r also divides the multiplicative order of μ_i modulo p^a, the probability distribution of $DL(\mu_i, s_i, p^a, r)$ is:

$$\Pr\left((DL(\mu_i, s_i, p^a, r)) = x\right) = \begin{cases} \frac{1}{p^a} + \frac{p^a - 1}{r \cdot p^a} & \text{if } x = d_r \\ \frac{p^a - 1}{r \cdot p^a} & \text{if } x \neq d_r \end{cases}$$

By computing the value $DL(\mu_i, s_i, p^a, r)$ for all the fault couples of the fault campaign, and counting how many times each residue class is suggested, we expect that the correct value d_r emerges from the noise, and is suggested more often than others.

Note that the value of the bias

$$\varepsilon = \frac{\frac{1}{p^a} + \frac{p^a - 1}{r \cdot p^a}}{\frac{p^a - 1}{r \cdot p^a}} - 1 = \frac{r}{p^a - 1}$$

vanishes proportionally to $p^a - 1$. This means that given r, the smaller p^a, the larger the bias, and the smaller the number of faults needed to determine d_r. This suggests Algorithm 1. which, given r as input, tries to find the residue class d_r. Among all possible values of p^a such that $r \mid \varphi(p^a)$, this algorithm only considers the smallest prime p such that $r \mid p - 1$ as this choice gives the largest possible bias with high probability.

Algorithm 1.   Predicting $d \bmod r$ by counting method

INPUT: $r = q^f$, a small power of a small prime
OUTPUT: A prediction for $d_r = d \bmod r$

Initialize an array $\mathsf{count}[0, \ldots, r - 1]$ to zero.

Phase 1: Search for the least prime p so that $r \mid p - 1$

$p \leftarrow 2r + 1$
while p is not prime
$\quad p \leftarrow p + r$

Phase 2: Compute $d_r = d \bmod r$ via the bias

for each fault couple (μ_i, s_i)
$\quad$**if** $p \nmid \mu_i$ and $p \nmid s_i$
$\quad\quad$**if** $r \mid$ **order of** μ_i **modulo** p **and if** $DL(\mu_i, s_i, p, r)$ **exists**
$\quad\quad\quad\mathsf{count}[DL(\mu_i, s_i, p, r)]{++}$
return d_r such that $\mathsf{count}[d_r] = \max_i \mathsf{count}[i]$

Algorithm 1. leads to the knowledge of d_r for individual prime powers $r = q^f$. The attacker may integrate this building block into a higher level procedure which determines d_r for as much r values as needed so that $R = \prod_k r_k$ is large enough to fully recover d (or $\underline{d}$ when e is small).

4.4   Results

This counting method have been implemented. 512 bits of residue class information about d are easily recovered within 25 000 faults, which is enough for a 1024-bit key with small public exponent. About 60 000 faults allow to recover 1024 bits of information, which is enough for either a 1024-bit key in the general case, or a 2048-bit key with small public exponent.

5   Recovering the Private Exponent with a Dictionary

As already mentioned, no dictionary is needed for applying the method of Section 4. Nevertheless, when a dictionary S is available to the attacker, it is then possible to improve upon this counting method.

5.1   General Methodology

The core observation is that, with a dictionary S, it becomes possible to relate a particular modulus $\nu_j \in S$ to some fault couple (μ_i, s_i). Let us thus introduce the following definition.

Definition 3 (Hit). *For any $\nu_j \in S$, we say that an attacker found a hit for ν_j if she was able to identify some fault couple (μ_i, s_i) for which $n'_i = \nu_j$.*

Given a hit in hand, a certain amount of information about d may be collected. Indeed, it is then possible to extract information related to each known p^a dividing ν_j as in Equation (1). One may then retrieve $d \bmod q^f$ for each q^f which divides the multiplicative order of μ_i modulo p^a.

We stress that the full factorization of ν_j is not needed since only some known factors of ν_j may be considered and exploited. The attack thus consists in identifying hits for a few moduli, and gathering information relative to known factors for each of them. This raises the question: how many hits provide enough information to recover the private exponent?

Table 1 shows some simulation results where the number of bits of information retrieved about d is given as a function of the number of hits exploited. These hit moduli were factorized by elliptic curve method up to 20–25 digits factors, and information was retrieved with respect to all q^f less than a given limit which took values 10^5, 10^7 and 10^9 respectively. Simulations have been conducted several times, and average over 200 experiments are presented below.

When the discrete logarithm computation limit is taken to 10^9, then 28 hits are enough to recover a 1024-bit RSA key (13 in the case of small public exponent), and 59 hits allow to recover the private exponent of a 2048-bit RSA key (28 in the case of small public exponent).

Beside knowing how many hits are needed, we now present in the next subsections, two methods aiming at identifying them.

5.2   Finding Hits by the Collision Method

Let r be an integer dividing the multiplicative order of μ_i modulo p^a. Proposition 1 implies that computing $DL(\mu_i, s_i, p^a, r)$ for different couples (μ_i, s_i) always gives the correct value of d_r, as soon as p^a divides n'_i. Otherwise, results are uniformly distributed between 0 and $r - 1$.

This suggests a method which detects collisions like:

$$DL(\mu_{i_1}, s_{i_1}, p^a, r) = DL(\mu_{i_2}, s_{i_2}, p^a, r) .$$

Table 1. Amount of information (in bits) deduced from exploitation of hits

DL limit	Number of hits									
	1	2	3	4	5	6	7	8	9	10
10^5	33	62	87	111	136	159	182	206	227	248
10^7	41	75	113	150	184	219	251	285	315	346
10^9	47	93	135	177	214	255	296	334	374	412
	11	12	13	14	15	16	17	18	19	20
10^5	267	289	312	331	352	373	396	416	436	455
10^7	374	406	436	465	493	**522**	553	580	609	639
10^9	452	490	**526**	561	599	638	673	709	744	780
	21	22	23	24	25	26	27	28	29	30
10^5	477	496	**516**	537	533	570	587	602	618	635
10^7	667	695	723	751	778	807	833	861	890	916
10^9	815	849	881	917	953	988	1018	**1055**	1088	1124

For suitably chosen p^a and r values, with high probability, such a collision reveals, not only that p^a divides both n'_{i_1} and n'_{i_2}, but also that $n'_{i_1} = n'_{i_2} = \nu_j$ (see Remark 1 below). This is particularly useful to identify one hit for this common modulus.

Definition 4 (Marker). *For a given modulus $\nu \in S$, a couple (p, q) is called a marker for ν, if p is a known prime factor of ν, and q is a not too small[4] prime dividing $p - 1$.*

Preparation Phase. For as many moduli $\nu \in S$ as possible, we try to find a specific marker. The set of moduli for which a marker has been identified is denoted S^*.

Collision Search Phase. For each $\nu_j \in S^*$ with marker (p_j, q_j), we maintain a list $\mathcal{D}_{\nu_j}$ of all $DL(\mu_i, s_i, p_j, q_j)$ for all fault couples exploited so far. As soon as two fault couples have the same modulus value $\nu_j = n'_{i_1} = n'_{i_2}$, a collision is found in $\mathcal{D}_{\nu_j}$. By disregarding possible false positive, we can identify a hit for ν_j.

Complexity. In the ideal case where a marker has been found for all moduli in S (*i.e.*, $S^* = S$), the number of faults required to obtain such a collision is $\mathcal{O}(\sqrt{|S|})$. For small t, obtaining t hits requires $\mathcal{O}(\sqrt{t|S|})$ faults.

In the more practical case where only a fraction $\alpha = |S^*|/|S|$ of all possible moduli are affiliated with a marker, the number of faults required for obtaining t hits is $\mathcal{O}(\sqrt{\frac{t}{\alpha}|S|})$.

Remark 1 (False positives). For a given ν_j, a true collision appears in $\mathcal{D}_{\nu_j}$ after $2|S|$ faults on average, while a false collision appears after $\mathcal{O}(\sqrt{q_j})$ faults. Therefore, false positive occurrence problem may be neglected as soon as $\min_j \sqrt{q_j} \gg |S|$. This inequality explains the notion of *not too small* introduced in Definition 4.

---

[4] The fact that q should be *not too small* is required to avoid false positive in the collision search (*cf.* Remark 1).

Application. Concretely, assume an attacker targeting the transfer of the modulus from EEPROM to RAM, able to randomly modify any individual byte of the modulus, but unable to control which particular byte she is modifying. This fault model is very realistic when, as a counter-measure, the modulus bytes are transferred in random order. The corresponding dictionary contains $2^8 \cdot \frac{1024}{8} = 2^{15}$ (resp. 2^{16}) moduli for a 1024-bit (resp. 2048-bit) RSA key. Furthermore, assume that a marker has been found for 80% of the moduli. Referring to Table 1, retrieving a key in the general case requires about $1\,100$ faults (resp. about $2\,200$ faults for 2048-bit). When a small public exponent is used, only about 750 faults are needed for 1024-bit (resp. about $1\,500$ faults for 2048-bit). This demonstrates that even when applied to such a pretty large dictionary, this *square root* method allows to dramatically reduce the number of required faults compared to the case where no fault model is identified.

5.3 Finding Hits by Optimally Exploiting Faults

The objective of this method is to guess vectors of hits by optimally exploiting the information brought by fault couples.

We incrementally build lists Σ_t containing information provided by the faults (μ_i, s_i) for $1 \leq i \leq t$. Σ_{t+1} is built by combining previous Σ_t with next fault (μ_{t+1}, s_{t+1}), and by removing elements that are incompatible. In other words, for a given t, this method considers t faults $(\mu_i, s_i)_{1 \leq i \leq t}$ acquired during the fault campaign, and exhibits the set Σ_t of data that are compatible with the given t faults.

More precisely, Σ_t is a list of triples $(\boldsymbol{\nu}, \boldsymbol{\rho}, \boldsymbol{\sigma})$, where :

- The t-uple $\boldsymbol{\nu} = (\nu_{j_1}, \ldots, \nu_{j_t})$ represents possible values taken by the faulty moduli corresponding to the considered t faults;
- The residue knowledge about d, $\boldsymbol{\rho}$, is a collection of triples (q, f, α_{q^f}), each meaning that $d \equiv \alpha_{q^f} \pmod{q^f}$, provided that $\boldsymbol{\nu}$ is the correct guess for the vector $(n'_1, \ldots, n'_t)$, i.e., each ν_{j_i} is the correct modulus corresponding to i-th fault;
- The selectivity $\boldsymbol{\sigma}$ associated to $\boldsymbol{\nu}$ and $\boldsymbol{\rho}$ is a scalar allowing to quantify the relative likelihood of this particular $\boldsymbol{\nu}$.

Below, we detail this method.

Initial Phase. Given (μ, s), not all $\nu \in S$ are compatible with this fault. Indeed, ν must simultaneously verify several conditions:

1. The signature s must be smaller than the modulus candidate ν.
2. For each p dividing ν, either $(p \mid \mu$ and $p \mid s)$ or $(p \nmid \mu$ and $p \nmid s)$
3. For each p^a dividing ν, denoting $\delta(\mu)$ and $\delta(s)$ the multiplicative orders modulo p^a of μ and s respectively, we must have $\delta(s) \mid \delta(\mu)$.
4. If $q^f \mid \varphi(p^a)$ and $q^f \mid \varphi(p'^{a'})$, where both p^a and $p'^{a'}$ divide ν, then if $DL(\mu, s, p^a, q^f)$ and $DL(\mu, s, p'^{a'}, q^f)$ both exist, their respective values must be equal.

This first phase hence consists, for every fault, in reducing, from S to $S_{(\mu,s)} \subseteq S$, the set of all moduli in the dictionary which are compatible with that fault. Note that this reduction is quite selective as — on average in our simulations — only a mere 3% of the moduli verify all four conditions.

In the list $S_{(\mu,s)}$, we associate to each modulus ν, the set ρ of all triples (q, f, α_{q^f}) with $\alpha_{q^f} = DL(\mu, s, p^a, q^f)$, for q of reasonable size, where $p^a \mid \nu$. Such a α_{q^f} value is always uniquely determined since all incompatible moduli (w.r.t. condition 4) have been removed from $S_{(\mu,s)}$. Furthermore, for each modulus, we also compute a selectivity parameter $\sigma = \tilde{\nu}/\delta(\mu)$, where $\tilde{\nu}$ is the factored part of ν, and $\delta(\mu)$ is the multiplicative order of μ modulo $\tilde{\nu}$ (i.e., the product of all q^f used in the DL computations). Doing this for all faults allows to compute I different potential initial sets Σ_1. We then choose one of them for initiating our process.

Combining Faults. Once we have extracted as much information as possible from each individual fault, we start a phase of combining these pieces of information. We use an iterative approach where we combine information from the list Σ_t with information brought by the $(t+1)$-th fault to update the data structure into a new Σ_{t+1}.

For this purpose, we exhaust all $(\boldsymbol{\nu}, \boldsymbol{\rho}, \boldsymbol{\sigma})$ of Σ_t, and all (ν, ρ, σ) where moduli ν belong to $S_{(\mu,s)}$. We consider combinations of each $(\boldsymbol{\nu}, \boldsymbol{\rho}, \boldsymbol{\sigma})$ with each (ν, ρ, σ). Each such combination results in a new triple $(f(\boldsymbol{\nu}, \nu), g(\boldsymbol{\rho}, \rho), h(\boldsymbol{\sigma}, \sigma))$, which will be kept and added to Σ_{t+1} only if evaluation of $g(\boldsymbol{\rho}, \rho)$ does not lead to any inconsistency (see below).

The new guess of moduli, $f(\boldsymbol{\nu}, \nu)$ trivially consists in appending ν to $\boldsymbol{\nu}$. That is, $f(\boldsymbol{\nu}, \nu) = (\nu_{j_1}, \ldots, \nu_{j_t}, \nu_{j_{t+1}})$ where $\nu_{j_{t+1}} = \nu$.

The new residue knowledge on d, $g(\boldsymbol{\rho}, \rho)$, consists in the union of $\boldsymbol{\rho}$ with ρ. If two triples $(q, f, d_{q^f}) \in \boldsymbol{\rho}$ and $(q, f', d_{q^{f'}}) \in \rho$ share the same prime q, then only the one with the largest exponent $\max(f, f')$ is kept. Moreover, in this case, the compatibility between both constraints modulo q must be checked. That is (assuming w.l.o.g. that $\max(f, f') = f$), $d_{q^f} \bmod q^{f'}$ must be equal to $d_{q^{f'}}$. If this consistency is not verified, then that particular combination of $(\boldsymbol{\nu}, \boldsymbol{\rho}, \boldsymbol{\sigma})$ with (ν, ρ, σ) is not kept.

The new selectivity $h(\boldsymbol{\sigma}, \sigma)$ takes the value $\boldsymbol{\sigma} \cdot \sigma \cdot \kappa$, where the multiplication by σ accounts for the selectivity of ν, and multiplication by κ accounts for a cross-selectivity between $\boldsymbol{\nu}$ and ν. This cross-selectivity factor is the product of moduli in the intersection of $\boldsymbol{\rho}$ and ρ, that is $\kappa = \prod_q q^{\min(f,f')}$. Of course, in this formula, if q is not in $\boldsymbol{\rho}$ (resp. in ρ), we set the corresponding exponent f (resp. f') to 0.

Final Phase. Now that we have combined information from a set of faults, we get a (possibly large) list of modular information about the private exponent d, each associated to a likelihood/selectivity parameter $\boldsymbol{\sigma}$. We can sort that list according to this last parameter, and, for each entry, check the value of d recovered by applying the Chinese Remainder Theorem on $\boldsymbol{\rho}$, until we get the correct one. Note that if the residue knowledge $\boldsymbol{\rho}$ corresponding to some entry does not allow to unambiguously determine d, then one or several more faults must be exploited again, and combined with Σ. As the correct guess ν about $(n'_1, \ldots, n'_t)$ necessarily belongs to Σ_t, this algorithm must eventually succeed in recovering d for some value t.

Remark 2. According to the size of the dictionary, handling these lists may become intractable. In this case, one can choose to keep only track of a fraction of the list, eliminating triples (ν, ρ, σ) with the lowest selectivity. The parameter σ is in strong connection with an *a posteriori* probability of the guess ν about faulty moduli. Practical implementation and tests we performed show undoubtedly that a strategy based on σ is efficient.

Of course, a drawback of this idea is that one might remove the correct combination of moduli from the list, and so this could lead to an unsuccessful end of the algorithm. This may be the price to pay for shortening the list to a manageable size.

Results. This method aims at determining the list of moduli vectors ν compatible with a given set of faults. Necessarily, it always succeeds in proposing the correct guess for ν,[5] leading to the identification of t hits with only t faults, which is obviously *optimal in terms of required number of faults*. Of course, the important question is whether the correct vector appears near the top of the sorted list. If so, d is retrieved within only a few trials. Otherwise, the exhaustive search for the correct guess on $(n'_1, \ldots, n'_t)$ may be out of reach, or this vector may have been dropped if the decimation process suggested by Remark 2 was implemented.

With a pretty well factorized dictionary of 1 000 moduli, we experimented that this method allows to recover d with little computational effort in most cases, with as few faults as required according to Table 1. We expect that similar results may be obtained with moderate effort in the case of a dictionary of 10 000 moduli.

6   Conclusion

In this paper, we have proposed the first fault attack that can be realized against RSA in standard mode, to recover the private exponent by corrupting only *public key elements*. Our contribution can, in this sense, be viewed as a generalization of Seifert's and Muir's recent articles on obtaining a false signature acceptance by corrupting the modulus. However, this latter kind of attack only allows to pass a signature verification, while ours allows a *full key recovery*.

Our attack is divided into two modes. In the first one, the attacker needs *absolutely no knowledge* of the fault's behavior to recover the private exponent. This attack is also very attractive from a practical point of view, and represents, to our knowledge, the only known fault attack on RSA in standard mode requiring no fault model. The second mode, based on a fault model, has been proved to be particularly efficient. It dramatically reduces the number of faults needed to

---

[5] If the trick discussed in Remark 2 is not used.

fully recover the private key. For this technique to work, the attacker does not need to be particularly powerful in the sense that she does not have to master the fault's exact effect. The fault she produces may be probabilistic or unprecise. Two variants have been proposed, with separate pros and cons and use cases.

There still are so open issues like whether our attacks can be adapted in the case of randomized exponent, or whether one could tackle with a probabilistic padding scheme with randomness recovery such as RSA-PSS.

Nevertheless, this paper teaches us that, as in the case of elliptic curves [5,8], *one should also protect RSA public key elements* against fault attacks.

Acknowledgements

The authors would like to thank the anonymous referees for their useful remarks and Marc Joye and Jacques Fournier for their careful reading of this paper.

The work described in this document has been financially supported by the European Commission through the IST Program under Contract IST-2002-507932 ECRYPT.

References

1. C. Aumüller, P. Bier, W. Fischer, P. Hofreiter, J.-P. Seifert. Fault attacks on RSA with CRT: Concrete results and practical countermeasures. In *CHES 2002*, volume 2523 of *LNCS*, pages 260-275
2. H. Bar-El, H. Choukri, D. Naccache, M. Tunstall, and C. Whelan. The sorcerer's apprentice guide to fault attacks. In *Workshop on Fault Detection and Tolerance in Cryptography*, 2004
3. M. Bellare and P. Rogaway. Random oracles are practical: A paradigm for designing efficient protocols. In *1st ACM Conference on Computer and Communications Security*, pages 62–73. ACM Press, 1993.
4. M. Bellare and P. Rogaway. The exact security of digital signatures - How to sign with RSA and Rabin. In *Advances in Cryptology – EUROCRYPT '96*, volume 1070 of *LNCS*, pages 399–416. Springer, 1996.
5. I. Biehl, B. Meyer, and V. Müller. Differential fault analysis on elliptic curve cryptosystems. In *Advances in Cryptology – CRYPTO 2000*, vol. 1880 of *LNCS*, pages 131–146. Springer, 2000.
6. D. Boneh, R.A. DeMillo, and R.J. Lipton. On the importance of checking cryptographic protocols for faults. In W. Fumy, editor, *Advances in Cryptology – EUROCRYPT '97*, volume 1233 of *Lecture Notes in Computer Science*, pages 37–51. Springer-Verlag, 1997.
7. D. Boneh, R.A. DeMillo, and R.J. Lipton. On the importance of eliminating errors in cryptographic computations. *Journal of Cryptology* 14(2):101–119, 2001. An earlier version appears in [6].
8. M. Ciet and M. Joye. Elliptic curve cryptosystem in presence of permanent and transient faults. *Designs Codes and Cryptography* 36(1), 2005.
9. J.-S. Coron. Optimal security proofs for PSS and other signature schemes. In *Advances in Cryptology – EUROCRYPT '02*, volume 2332 of *LNCS*, pages 272–287. Springer, 2002.

10. M. Joye, A.K. Lenstra, and J.-J. Quisquater. Chinese remaindering based cryptosystems in the presence of faults. *Journal of Cryptology* **12**(4):241–245, 1999.

11. P.C. Kocher, J. Jaffe, and B. Jun. Differential power analysis. In M. Wiener, editor, *Advances in Cryptology − CRYPTO '99*, volume 1666 of *Lecture Notes in Computer Science*, pages 388–397. Springer-Verlag, 1999.

12. A.J. Menezes, P.C. van Oorschot, and S.A. Vanstone. Handbook of applied cryptography. CRC Press, 1997.

13. J.A. Muir. Seiferts RSA fault attack: Simplified analysis and generalizations. IACR Eprint archive 2005.

14. PKCS #1 v 1.5: RSA Cryptography Standard.

15. J.-J. Quisquater and C. Couvreur. Fast decipherment algorithm for RSA public-key cryptosystem. *Electronics Letters* **18**(21):905–907, 1982.

16. R.L. Rivest, A. Shamir, and L.M. Adleman. A method for obtaining digital signatures and public-key cryptosystems. *Communications of the ACM* **21**(2):120–126, 1978.

17. J.-P. Seifert. On authenticated computing and RSA-based authentication. *ACM Conference on Computer and Communications Security 2005*: pages 122–127, 2005.

Power Attack on Small RSA Public Exponent

Pierre-Alain Fouque[1], Sébastien Kunz-Jacques[1,2], Gwenaëlle Martinet[2],
Frédéric Muller[3], and Frédéric Valette[4]

[1] École normale supérieure, 45 rue d'Ulm, 75005 Paris, France
`Pierre-Alain.Fouque@ens.fr`
[2] DCSSI Crypto Lab, 51 boulevard de La Tour-Maubourg
F-75700 Paris 07 SP, France
{`Gwenaelle.Martinet, Sebastien.Kunz-Jacques`}`@sgdn.pm.gouv.fr`
[3] HSBC, France
`Frederic.Muller@m4x.org`
[4] CELAR, 35 Bruz, France
`Frederic.Valette@dga.defense.gouv.fr`

Abstract. In this paper, we present a new attack on RSA when the public exponent is short, for instance 3 or $2^{16}+1$, and when the classical exponent randomization is used. This attack works even if blinding is used on the messages.

From a Simple Power Analysis (SPA) we study the problem of recovering the RSA private key when non consecutive bits of it leak from the implementation. We also show that such information can be gained from sliding window implementations not protected against SPA.

Keywords: RSA cryptosystem, sliding window methods, exponent randomization, Simple Power Analysis.

1 Introduction

Simple Power Analysis and Differential Power Analysis attacks are among the most efficient and devastating attacks on some RSA-based products. Many countermeasures have been proposed that prevent these attacks by securing the exponentiation algorithm which is usually targeted. This is the basis of a number of academic papers whose results are widely used in practice. However, such countermeasures often lead to a slower implementation and thus another area of research is the speedup of the exponentiation process. As we will show in this article, unfortunate interactions between side-channel countermeasures and optimized exponentiation algorithms may lead to insecure implementations.

The aim of this paper is to present a new attack on RSA in the special case where both a short public exponent and a randomization of the private exponent are used. In such a case, free information on the private exponent can be obtained from the public key and can be used to efficiently recover the whole private key. The attack studies the problem when non-consecutive bits of the private key can be found. It works on sliding window implementations not protected against SPA attack.

L. Goubin and M. Matsui (Eds.): CHES 2006, LNCS 4249, pp. 339–353, 2006.

Known Results on Partially Known Information. Partial information on the RSA private key allows it to be recovered in some cases. This kind of attacks has experienced a revival since 1998 with the work of Boneh, Durfee and Frankel [1]. In their article, they give some results about the security of RSA schemes when some bits of the private key are exposed. However, the lattice technique used in such cases cannot be applied for non-consecutive bits. None of the previous papers have considered this particular case. Boneh *et al.* have even considered in [1] that *"[the authors] view attacks that require non-consecutive bits of d as artificial"*, showing the lack of interest for this topic at that time.

However, some practical attacks are now very efficient and allow the attacker to recover some bits of the private key, not necessarily consecutive. This is mainly due to the combination of very specialized attacks, based on side channel analysis, and of the various countermeasures based on algorithmic remarks.

Main Idea of the Attack. Here, we do not solve the open problem of recovering the whole private key from non-consecutive partial information on it. However, we focus on the special case where several non-consecutive bits of randomized versions of the private key are known.

Efficient countermeasures against SPA attack are often not perfect. It is classical that some information about the secret exponent leaks. For example, sliding window implementations can leak when consecutive bits are equal to zero. By randomly generating bitstring and applying the parsing exponent algorithm of the sliding window algorithm, either Constant Length Non-zero Window (CLNW) or Variable Length Non-zero Window (VLNW), one can observe that the information gained is 40% of the bits. This is not sufficient to recover the entire secret by using previous results such as those of [1].

The first part of the attack is to record some power curves C_i which correspond to the exponentiation of a message with the unknown private key $d_i = d + \lambda_i \times \varphi(N)$ associated to an unknown short value λ_i. Then, using the fact that the public exponent is small, we can consider that the most significant bits of the secret exponent d are known. With this information, we can try all the possible values of λ and check if the most significant bits of the value $\tilde{d} + \lambda \cdot N$, where $\tilde{d}$ equals d on the half bits of high order, are compatible with the partial information that can be recovered from the power curve by SPA. If we have enough information, we can associate a single λ_i to the curve C_i.

The second part of the attack is now to recover the least significant bits of d. Once we have enough curves with the known random value λ_i we can then use partial information on the least significant bits of the randomized exponent on all the curves to retrieve the least significant bits of the secret exponent. The principle is to guess the least significant bits of $\varphi(N)$ and so of d and of the secret exponent d_i. Then, we check if the guess is compatible with the partial information on the curve C_i. If we have enough curves, only one guess will be compatible. We can then guess the next bits and continue until we know enough bits of d.

Our Results. We recall in section 2 how to get non-consecutive bits of the RSA secret exponent by using side channel attacks. Such leakage depends on the exponentiation algorithm used and on the various countermeasures implemented against side channel attacks.

Then, in section 3 we formally show how to recover the whole RSA secret key from such information in the case of the public exponent is 3. We extend this attack for $e = 2^{16} + 1$ in section 4, and we give practical results in section 5.

Related Works. A lot of work has already been done on the particular topic of attacks when countermeasures are implemented. Indeed, a countermeasure may allow or simplify a side channel attack.

Previous works have also been done to study the security of fast exponentiation algorithm. Walter, in [9], describes the Big Mac attack which works on sliding and m-ary window algorithms. He assumes that he can distinguish *squares and multiplies* and *operand of the multiplies*. Here, we only assume that we can distinguish *squares and multiplies* but we do not need to distinguish the different operands of the multiplications.

Walter has also see in [10] that *"in the classical m-ary and sliding windows exponentiation algorithms, the most significant half of the public modulus yields information which can be used to halve the number of key digits which need to be guessed."* Having reduce the key digit by half or a quarter is not sufficient for an 1024-bit value since 256 are missing.

The problem of computing the RSA private exponent from partial information on it has known only a little attention in the literature. In [8], Stinson presents two algorithms to compute discrete logarithms in a prime field, when the Hamming weight of the discrete log is small. As we want to recover d such that $s = f(H(m))^d \bmod N$, where f is the padding function, and we know s and $f(H(m))$, d can be viewed as the discrete log of s in basis $f(H(m))$ in $\mathbb{Z}_N^*$. In appendix A, we show that this algorithm can be used to recover d from non-consecutive bits of it if the number of missing bits is relatively small, 128 for instance. However the memory and time complexity of this algorithm is high compared to our algorithm and cannot recover a large number of bits.

2   Modular Exponentiation and Side Channel Attacks

2.1   Classical Countermeasures Against Side Channel Attacks

To defeat DPA attacks, many protections methods have been suggested in the literature. The most secure and widely used is the exponent randomization [6] as it is very easy to implement and it comes at a reasonable computational cost. The idea of this countermeasure is to use a classical SPA-protected implementation of the exponentiation and to randomize the private exponent at each computation. This randomization is based on the fact that the private exponent d is defined modulo $\varphi(N)$ since for all $M \in \mathbb{Z}_N^*$ and all $\lambda \in \mathbb{Z}$, $M^{\lambda \times \varphi(N)} = 1 \bmod N$. Figure 1 describes this randomized exponentiation algorithm.

The success of this countermeasure lies in its very good efficiency and the security it offers. Indeed, without randomization an attacker is able to guess the exponent bit per bit and his check would be confirmed with a DPA attack [7].

> - **Inputs:** a message M, an exponent d, a modulus N
>   and $\varphi(N)$
> - **Output:** $M^d \bmod N$
>
> 1. Pick at random $\lambda \in \{0, \ldots, 2^\ell - 1\}$
> 2. Compute $d' = d + \lambda \cdot \varphi(N)$
> 3. Return SPA protected exponentiation $M^{d'} \bmod N$

Fig. 1. The exponent randomization algorithm

With the randomization, such a guess cannot be made anymore on the value d' since the attacker does not know the random value used.

2.2   Optimized Exponentiation Algorithms

Timing attacks or SPA attacks are known to be very efficient on RSA-based cryptosystems. In [6], Kocher has shown how to recover the whole private key from the power consumption of a single RSA signature or decryption. If the square-and-multiply algorithm is used for the exponentiation without any countermeasure, various side channel attacks may be used to compromise the private key.

More efficient exponentiation algorithms may be used. Some of them use a parsing of the private exponent into windows of constant or variable length. In that case, side channel attacks cannot recover the whole private exponent anymore. Only some bits of it leak from the implementation, whose distribution depends on technical details of the exact algorithm used. The m-ary or the sliding window techniques are such methods.

The sliding window methods. Such methods have been developed to speed up the exponentiation algorithm by searching in the exponent large windows of bits equal to zero. Contrary to the m-ary algorithm, sliding window methods relax the splitting of the exponent into *sliding windows*. There are two variants known as the Constant Length Non-zero Window (CLNW) technique due to Knuth [3] and the Variable Length Non-zero Window (VLNW) technique due to Bos and Coster in [2]. Both of these techniques try to minimize the number of multiplications in the square-and-multiply algorithm by performing some precomputations. These techniques have been described and analyzed by Koç in [4,5] and allow 5 to 8% of the multiplications to be avoided compared to the binary exponentiation algorithm.

The CLNW method consists in splitting the exponent as follows: a non-zero window will always be of length m, for a given parameter m, often equal to 4 in practice, and the zero windows are of variable length. For the exponentiation, precomputations have to be done for all the 2^{m-1} values of the m non-zero windows (with a bit 1 in low order since the parsing is done from the least significant bit to the most significant one).

The Variable Length version is an optimization of it and is more tricky to detail. The rule is to split the exponent into zero windows of length at least a given value and non-zero windows of length at most another given parameter. We can show that the number of leaking bits during a SPA attack will be the same for both techniques and so we only focus on the CLNW variant.

Figure 2 details the sliding window exponentiation algorithm. Such a method assumes that the exponent is split into windows. This splitting may be done either with the m-ary, CLNW or VLNW method, depending on the splitting criteria used. The exponentiation just uses squarings and multiplications with precomputed values.

- **Inputs:** x, e, N, m
- **Output:** $y = x^e \bmod N$

1. Compute and store x^w for all **odd** integer $w \in \{1, \ldots, 2^m - 1\}$
2. Parse e into zero and non-zero windows F_i of length $L(F_i)$ at most m for the non-zero windows and for $i = 0, 1, \ldots k - 1$. The parsing algorithm may be CLNW or VLNW.
3. $y \leftarrow x^{F_{k-1}} \bmod N$ (which is a precomputed value)
4. for $i = k - 2$ downto 0
   - $y \leftarrow y^{2^{L(F_i)}} \bmod N$
   - if $F_i \neq 0$, then $y \leftarrow y \cdot x^{F_i} \bmod N$
5. **return** y

Fig. 2. The Sliding Window Algorithm

2.3 SPA Information Leakage

To mount the attack described in section 3, the underlying assumption will be that the attacker knows partial information on the exponent used during the RSA signature or decryption. To this end, we will assume that we can distinguish squares from multiplies.

The optimized exponentiation algorithms such as m-ary, CLNW or VLNW leak some information about the exponent. For example, the CLNW algorithm, as described in section 2.2, consists in splitting the exponent into non-zero windows of fixed length. For all these windows, some precomputations are made to reduce the total cost of the exponentiation. If no protection against SPA attacks is used, an attacker may be able to distinguish the squaring operations from the multiplications. Each time the number of squarings is greater than the length of the window, the attacker can deduce that there are some 0 bits in the exponent. The position is deduced from the total number of previous multiplications and squarings. When a multiplication is detected, the attacker knows that there is a non-zero window of exactly m bits. In this window, the lowest order bit is 1 and the other ones are unknown. Thus, in the worst case, when there are are only non-zero windows, the attacker learns one bit of the exponent over m. These bits are the least significant ones (equal to 1) of the non-zero windows.

Thus, if $m = 4$, the attacker learns 25% of the bits of the exponent in the worst case. In practice, we obtain 40% of the bits of each randomized exponent. For $m = 3$, we obtain 50% of these bits.

For the attack to be successful in the case $e = 2^{16} + 1$, the attacker has to obtain a given number of windows of two bits. Note that if the attacker learns 3 consecutive bits, the two overlapping windows of two bits can be used in the attack. Simulations show that for a 1024-bit modulus, the CLNW methods for parameter $m = 4$ may leak 200 such windows if squarings and multiplies are distinguishable. For 2048-bit modulus, 400 windows are obtained. For $m = 3$, we obtain 250 2-bit windows for 1024-bit modulus and 500 for 2048 ones.

3   Recovering a Private RSA Exponent from Partial Information on Randomized Versions of it

We focus in this section on the special case $e = 3$. In this context, additional and free information can be deduced from the public key. This gives the attacker the knowledge of some bits on the private key "for free". Although this does not allow an adversary to break RSA cryptosystems in general, such information is very useful when combined with a side channel attack on some particular implementation of the exponentiation.

3.1   Free Information

Let N be an RSA modulus, e the public exponent and d the private one.

The first remark is that the modulus N is a good approximation of $\varphi(N) = (p-1) \times (q-1) = N - p - q + 1$ on essentially the $n/2$ most significant bits. Since the number of these bits depends on a carry propagation, with high probability, the $n/2 - 10$ bits of high order of $\varphi(N)$ are those of N. To simplify, we consider that the $n/2$ bits of high order of $\varphi(N)$ are known and equal to those of N.

Secondly, when $e = 3$, the $n/2$ most significant bits of d are also known. Indeed, d satisfies the relation

$$ed = 1 + k\varphi(N) \tag{1}$$

for some positive integer k. Let us choose a representative of d in $[0, \varphi(N) - 1]$. Since $k \times \varphi(N) = ed - 1 < ed$, then $k < e$: if $e = 3$, then $k = 1$ or $k = 2$. In fact, 3 divides neither p nor q and since 3 is invertible $\mod \varphi(N)$, 3 also divides neither $p - 1$ nor $q - 1$. Thus, $p \neq 0 \mod 3$, $p - 1 \neq 0 \mod 3$ (resp. for q), and finally, $p = 2 \mod 3$ and $q = 2 \mod 3$. Consequently, $\varphi(N) = 1 \mod 3$. Finally, since $k = -1/\varphi(N) \mod 3$, then $k = 2 \mod 3$, and finally $k = 2$. Therefore,

$$3d - 2\varphi(N) = 1 \tag{2}$$

and

$$\tilde{d} = \left\lfloor \frac{1 + kN}{e} \right\rfloor = \left\lfloor \frac{1 + 2N}{3} \right\rfloor$$

is a good approximation of d on the half bits of high order. Equation (2) will be extensively used in the cryptanalysis described above.

3.2   Recovering the RSA Private Key

We consider the countermeasure consisting in randomizing the private exponent d. Thus for each exponentiation, an equivalent exponent d_i is first computed as $d_i = d + \lambda_i \times \varphi(N)$, for a random value λ_i of ℓ bits. Typically, $\ell = 20$ or $\ell = 32$. Furthermore, an optimized exponentiation algorithm, such as the CLNW or the VLNW method, is supposed to be used. In this context, as described in section 2.3, we suppose that the attacker knows a fraction $1/r$ of the bits of the private exponents used, randomly distributed amongst the $n + \ell$ bits of each exponent. We also suppose that these bits are available for ω different exponents d_i. The position of the known bits differ from one exponent to another. These bits are obtained by signing or decrypting ω messages whose value does not matter for the attack. This is a model for the side channel attack.

In the rest of this paper, the following notations will be used:

- for an integer x of n bits, the i-th bit of x is denoted by $x[i]$. The integer x can then be written as an n-bit string $x = x[n-1]x[n-2]\ldots x[0]$;
- for a randomized exponent d_i of n bits, $[d_i]$ is a vector of length n such that for all $j \in \{0, \ldots, n-1\}$:

$$[d_i][j] = d_i[j] \text{ if the bit } d_i[j] \text{ is known}$$
$$= 2 \text{ otherwise}$$

- for a vector $[d_i]$ of length n and integers a and b such that $0 \le a \le b \le n-1$, $[d_i]_{a,b}$ is the extracted vector for the positions a to b;
- for integers x and d_i of n bits, we write $[d_i] \doteq x$ if d_i and x matches on all the known bits of d_i. That is, for all $0 \le j \le n-1$ such that $[d_i][j] \ne 2$, we have $d_i[j] = x[j]$.

For example, for an 8-bit value $x = 01010101 = x[7]x[6]\ldots x[1]x[0]$ for which the bits known are in positions 1, 4, 5 and 7, $[x] = [0, 2, 0, 1, 2, 2, 0, 2]$ and $[x]_{3,6} = [2, 0, 1, 2]$.

We first show how partial knowledge of the randomized exponents d_i allows the attacker to recover the λ_i values used to generate them from d. We then show in a second step how to recover the entire private exponent d from the partial leakage on the randomized exponent and from the known bits of d.

Step 1: Recovering the λ_i. The strategy to recover the random values λ_i used to mask the private exponent d is to use the known approximation of d and $\varphi(N)$ to compute all the possible values

$$\tilde{d}_j = \tilde{d} + j \times N$$

for all $j \in [0, 2^\ell - 1]$. On the $n/2$ high order bits, $\tilde{d}_j$ is equal to $d_j = d + j \times \varphi(N)$. Indeed, $d_j = \tilde{d}_j + j(p + q - 1)$ and since $j(p + q - 1)$ is a number of at most $(n/2 + \ell)$ bits, the two $(n + \ell)$-bit values have near half of the most significant bits in common with high probability. Only if a carry propagates, some bits will not be equal. However, if two random bitstrings are added, a carry will be absorbed with probability $1/4$ at a step. Consequently, with probability $1-(3/4)^{10} \approx 0.94$, the carry coming from the least significant half bits will not propagate after the $(n/2 + \ell + 10)$-th bit.

Given these 2^ℓ values and the known bits of the ω randomized exponents d_i, the attacker is now able to recover the corresponding λ_i values. For each value d_i, he knows a ratio $1/r$ of the bits. In particular this applies for the $n/2$ high order ones. He then looks for a matching value from the computed $\tilde{d}_j$ on these bits. When he finds j such that d_i equals $\tilde{d}_j$ on the known bits, he deduces that $\lambda_i = j$. The detailed algorithm is given in figure 3.

- Inputs: $[d_i]_{n/2+\ell,n+\ell}$ the known bits of high order of d_i for all $i \in \{1, \ldots, \omega\}$
- Outputs: the value λ_i such that $d_i = d + \lambda_i \times \varphi(N)$, for all $i \in \{1, \ldots, \omega\}$

1. For $j = 0$ to $2^\ell - 1$, $\tilde{d}_j \leftarrow \tilde{d} + j \times N$
2. For $i = 1$ to ω,
   $\quad j \leftarrow 0$
   $\quad$ While $(j < 2^\ell)$
   $\quad\quad$ If $[d_i]_{n/2+\ell+10,n+\ell} \doteq \tilde{d}_{j\,n/2+\ell+10,n+\ell}$ then $\lambda_i \leftarrow j$, break;
   $\quad\quad$ else $j \leftarrow j + 1$;
3. Return λ_i for all $i \in \{1, \ldots, \omega\}$.

Fig. 3. The attacker strategy to recover the λ_i corresponding to each d_i

Some optimizations may be implemented depending on the value ℓ, and the best time-memory trade-off for the attacker. However, as long as the random values λ are relatively small, for example of at most 20 bits, the exhaustive search of figure 3 is clearly practical.

At the end of this step, the attacker has thus recovered each random value used to randomize the private exponent for ω RSA executions.

Let us now present some analysis of the success probability of the first step. For each given d_i, we compare it with the 2^ℓ values of $\tilde{d}_j$. Let us denote by Bad_i the event "a bad value λ is associated with d_i". If we assume that the bitstrings d_i and $\tilde{d}_j$ are uniformly distributed, we match a false j to λ_i with probability less than $(1/2)^{(n/2-\alpha)/r}$ where α depends on the carry propagation during the computation of $\tilde{d}_j$. As seen above, α may be upper bounded by 10 with high probability.

As we have 2^ℓ comparisons corresponding to all the $\tilde{d}_j$, the probability of Bad_i is upper bounded by $2^\ell/2^{(n/2-\alpha)/r}$. Therefore, we get

$$\Pr[\exists i\ 1 \le i \le \omega : \mathsf{Bad}_i] \le \frac{2^\ell \omega}{2^{(n/2-\alpha)/r}}$$

For $n = 1024$, $r = 5$, $\ell = 32$, $\alpha = 10$ and $\omega \approx 64$, we get a probability of a good association for each d_i of $1 - 1/2^{63}$. Such an estimation does not take into account imperfect input data.

Step 2: Recovering $\varphi(N)$ and d. The attacker's goal is now to recover the entire private key. To this end, he makes an exhaustive search, 8 bits per step, on the bits of $\varphi(N)$. He will now use the known *least significant bits* of d_i to recover d.

First, the attacker recovers the 8 least significant bits of $\varphi(N)$. This is performed by guessing $\varphi(N) \bmod 2^8$. From this guess, he computes the corresponding guess for $d \bmod 2^8$ from the equation 2:

$$d \bmod 2^8 = \frac{1 + 2\varphi(N)}{3} \bmod 2^8$$

Then with high probability there exists i s.t. some of the 8 least significant bits of d_i are known from the side channel attack. For this value d_i, the corresponding λ_i gives us some constraints on the low order bits of the value $d + \lambda_i \times \varphi(N) \bmod 2^8$. If the constraints on the corresponding d_i value cannot be met, another guess for $\varphi(N) \bmod 2^8$ is made. Otherwise, if for all $i \in \{1, \dots, \omega\}$, no incompatibility has been discovered, the guess is the good one with high probability. The attack can then be extended with a guess for $\varphi(N) \bmod 2^{16}$ and so on. Figure 4 details the algorithm to recover $\varphi(N) \bmod 2^{8k}$ from $\varphi(N) \bmod 2^{8(k-1)}$.

Note that in practice the attacker should deal with imperfect input data since these data are collected in a side channels context. Thus, candidates that match a sufficiently high fraction of these data should be accepted: this may be done by implementing a more complex version of the Boolean function OK.

We need to estimate the average number of false candidates at each step. We have 2^8 values for each $\bar{d}$ and we have $8/r$ bits on each 8-bit window for each $\bar{d}_i$

- **Inputs:**
    - $\{([d_i], \lambda_i)\}_{1 \leq i \leq \omega}$ the list of the known bits for each d_i and the corresponding λ_i value
    - a candidate for $\varphi(N) \bmod 2^{8(k-1)}$
- **Output:** a list of candidates for $\varphi(N) \bmod 2^{8k}$

1. For $j = 0$ to $2^8 - 1$,
    (a) $y_j \leftarrow \varphi(N) \bmod 2^{8(k-1)} + j \cdot 2^{8(k-1)}$;
    /* y_j is a candidate value for $\varphi(N) \bmod 2^{8k}$ */
    (b) $\bar{d} \leftarrow \frac{1+2y_j}{3} \bmod 2^{8k}$;
    /* $\bar{d}$ is the corresponding candidate for $d \bmod 2^{8k}$ */
    (c) $OK \leftarrow$ **true**;
    (d) $i \leftarrow 1$;
    (e) While $(OK = $ **true**$)$ and $(i \leq \omega)$
       $\bar{d}_i \leftarrow \bar{d} + \lambda_i \times y_j \bmod 2^{8k}$;
       if $[d_j]_{0,8k-1} \doteq \bar{d}_i$ then $i \leftarrow i + 1$;
       else $OK \leftarrow$ **false**;
    (f) if $OK = $ **true**, add y_j to the list of candidates for $\varphi(N) \bmod 2^{8k}$;
2. Return the list of candidates for $\varphi(N) \bmod 2^{8k}$

Fig. 4. The attacker strategy to recover $\varphi(N) \bmod 2^{8k}$ from $\varphi(N) \bmod 2^{8(k-1)}$

where $1/r$ is the ratio of known bits deduced from the side channel attack. As the correct value for $\bar{d}$ allows ω correct values $\bar{d}_i$ for all i to be computed, then on average the number of false candidates is $\left(1/2^{8/r}\right)^{\omega} \times 2^8$ if all the experiments are independent and the bitstrings uniformly distributed. Thus, the average number of candidates tends to 1 as the number of false candidates tends to 0 and the correct candidate matches the input data, or eventually almost fit the input data.

4   Extension for $e = 2^{16} + 1$

In case $e = 3$, one knows that $k = 2$. For each measure using a random value λ, as shown in previous section, some bits in the upper half of

$$\left\lfloor \frac{1 + kN}{e} \right\rfloor + \lambda N \tag{3}$$

are known: this allows us to retrieve λ with an exhaustive search. For other values of e, this approach cannot work directly as k is not known anymore. In this section, we show how to extract k *and* λ from only **one** measure yielding some bits of the randomized exponent, when e is not too large, the typical case being $e = 2^{16} + 1$. Once k is found, the attack can proceed exactly as described in Step 2 of the attack of section 3.

4.1   Finding k and λ by Exhaustive Search

The value (3) can be used to perform a direct exhaustive search of k and λ from one exponentiation measure. One has $0 < k < e$ and $0 \leq \lambda < 2^{\ell}$: if e is u-bit long, there are $2^{u+\ell}$ candidates to try, and the exhaustive search yields only the correct values with good probability if the number of known bits in equation (3) is above $u + \ell$. For the typical values of $u = 16$ and $\ell = 20$, this approach requires to perform 2^{36} additions of large integers, assuming the values of λN for $0 \leq \lambda < 2^{\ell}$ and $\frac{kN}{e}$ for $0 < k < e$ are precomputed. The aim is to recover k more efficiently.

4.2   Finding Matching Pairs of Values of k and λ

From now on, we consider a unique measure of an RSA signature or decryption with randomized exponent. Let δ denote the randomized exponent used during the exponentiation considered. One has:

$$\delta = d + \lambda \times \varphi(N)$$

As before, the most significant half $U(d)$ of the private exponent d is equal to $U\left(\left\lfloor \frac{1+kN}{e} \right\rfloor\right)$ except maybe on a few least significant bits. $U(\delta)$ can likewise be approximated by $U\left(\left\lfloor \frac{1+kN}{e} \right\rfloor\right) + U(\lambda N)$. Our goal is to recover k and λ.

If $U(\delta)$ were completely known, the exhaustive search on both k and λ could be transformed it into a list matching problem: indeed, correct values of k and λ correspond to matching elements in the lists

$$L_1 = \left\{ U(\delta) - U\left(\left\lfloor \frac{1 + kN}{e} \right\rfloor \right) \,\middle|\, 0 < k < e \right\} \text{ and } L_2 = \left\{ U(\lambda N) \mid 0 \le \lambda < 2^\ell \right\}$$

However, since only *some* bits of δ are known, some further work is required to find matching elements. In the next paragraphs, we show how to associate with each candidate value of k a partially known value for $\delta - \left\lfloor \frac{1+kN}{e} \right\rfloor$, and then how to find matches between the list of these partially known values and L_2.

Step 1a: Compute Partial Values for $\delta - \left\lfloor \frac{1+kN}{e} \right\rfloor$. In the following, $b(k)$ denotes $\left\lfloor \frac{1+kN}{e} \right\rfloor$.

For each candidate value of k, some bits of $\delta - b(k)$ can be computed. Indeed, assume that two consecutive bits δ_i, δ_{i+1} of δ are known as a result a side-channel attack like the one of paragraph 2.3. Let b_i and b_{i+1} the corresponding bits of $b(k)$, and c_i, c_{i+1} the corresponding carry bits in $\delta - b(k)$. The bits δ_i, δ_{i+1}, b_i, b_{i+1} are known while the carries are unknown. The subtraction looks as follows :

$$\begin{array}{ccc} \delta_{i+1} & & \delta_i \\ - \; b_{i+1} & \overset{c_{i+1}}{\leftarrow} & b_i \overset{c_i}{\leftarrow} \\ \cdots & & \cdots \end{array}$$

Assume that $b_i = 1 \oplus \delta_i$. Then one has:

$$\begin{array}{cccc} \delta_{i+1} & & 0 \\ \hline - & \overset{}{\leftarrow} b_{i+1} & \overset{1}{\leftarrow} 1 \overset{c_i}{\leftarrow} \\ \hline 1 \oplus \delta_{i+1} \oplus b_{i+1} & & 1 \oplus c_i \end{array} \quad \text{or} \quad \begin{array}{cccc} \delta_{i+1} & & 1 \\ \hline - & \overset{}{\leftarrow} b_{i+1} & \overset{0}{\leftarrow} 0 \overset{c_i}{\leftarrow} \\ \hline \delta_{i+1} \oplus b_{i+1} & & 1 \oplus c_i \end{array}$$

Therefore **whenever $b_i = 1 \oplus \delta_i$, the $(i+1)$-th bit of $\delta - b$ is equal to** $b_i \oplus \delta_{i+1} \oplus b_{i+1}$ **which is a known value.**

To compute partial values for $\delta - b(k)$, first mark the (possibly overlapping) windows of two consecutive known bits in the upper half of δ. Assume there are v such windows.

For each value of k in $[1, e-1]$, compute the value $b(k) = \left\lfloor \frac{1+kN}{e} \right\rfloor$. Depending on the bits of $b(k)$ aligned with the marked windows in δ, some bits of $\delta - b(k)$ can be computed according to the rules above : in each 2-bit window, the most significant bit of $\delta - b(k)$ can be computed with probability $1/2$, according to $b_i = 1 \oplus \delta_i$. A sequence (s_k) of v known or unknown bits in $\delta - b(k)$ is therefore obtained.

Step 1b: Find Matches for Partial Values. Associate to each value of λ the sequence t_λ of the values of the most significant bits of λN in the targeted 2-bit windows of δ (remember that there are v such windows). The correct value for k and λ yields a match between t_λ and the known bits in s_k. If there are sufficiently many windows, only the correct values gives a match.

For each value of k, let $L(k)$ denote the set of all λ such that t_λ matches s_k. Assuming $L(k)$ can be built efficiently, the exhaustive search for (k, λ) proposed in subsection 4.1 can be improved by adding an early elimination step where pairs (k, λ) s.t. $\lambda \notin L(k)$ are discarded. If $L(k)$ is small enough, this reduces the complexity of the exhaustive search. We therefore focus on efficiently computing the set $L(k)$.

A direct approach to the construction of $L(k)$ consists in considering every possible value of the unknown bits of s_k. For each of them, the set of the matching t_λ can be computed. Since each of the v bits in s_k is known with probability $1/2$, the number of possible values for the unknown bits in s_k is the product of v independent random variables that are equal to 2 with probability $1/2$ and to 1 with probability $1/2$. This number is therefore equal on average to $(3/2)^v$.

For $u = 16$, $v = 40$, there are about $2^{16} \times (3/2)^{40} \approx 2^{39.4}$ completions of the s_k, for all values of k, $0 < k < e$. Therefore, whatever the method used to find the corresponding t_λ for each of these completions, at least $2^{39.4}$ operations are required to build all lists $L(k)$ this way.

This approach can however be refined by splitting s_k into subpieces before exploring the possible values of the unknown bits. From now on, we assume that $v = 2\ell$; the attack is even faster for higher values v which correspond to cases where more information is available.

First, precompute the lists $L_l(\alpha) = \{\lambda \mid \text{the left half of } t_\lambda \text{ is equal to } \alpha\}$ for $0 \le \alpha \le 2^\ell$ and the lists $L_r(\beta) = \{\lambda \mid \text{the right half of } t_\lambda \text{ is equal to } \beta\}$ for $0 \le \beta \le 2^\ell$. This requires $2 \times 2^\ell$ operations on large integers.

Then for a candidate k, if $\alpha_1, \ldots, \alpha_n$ (resp. $\beta_1, \ldots, \beta_m$) are the values of the left (resp. right) half of s_k obtained by filling the unknown bits with any possible value,

$$L(k) = \left[\bigcup_{i=1}^{n} L_l(\alpha_i) \right] \cap \left[\bigcup_{i=1}^{m} L_r(\beta_i) \right]$$

On average, $n \approx m \approx (3/2)^{v/2}$, and for any i, $\#L_l(\alpha_i) \approx \#L_r(\beta_i) \approx 2^{\ell - v/2} = 1$. Using suitable data structure (of size $2^{v/2}$) to be able to compute an intersection in constant time, the formula above can therefore be evaluated using $2 \times (3/2)^{v/2}$ constant-size operations. This means that all the lists $L(k)$ can be built using only $2^u \times 2 \times (3/2)^{v/2}$ operations.

For $u = 16$, $\ell = 20$, $v = 2\ell = 40$, the total complexity is $2^{28.7}$ operations. One can show that cutting s_k in two halves is optimal when $v = 2\ell$.

Assuming that the t_λ and the completions of the s_k are random, the birthday paradox shows that the average number of elements in $L(k)$ is $\frac{(3/2)^v \times 2^\ell}{2^v}$. With $\ell = 20$, $v = 2\ell$, $\#L(k) \approx 2^{3.4}$. Therefore after the above early elimination step, $2^{19.4}$ pairs (k, λ) must be considered if $u = 16$, compared to 2^{36} pairs before the elimination step.

Overall, this improved attack retrieves k using $2^{28.7}$ constant-size operations and around 2^{20} operations on large integers. We implemented the attack; it runs in about one minute on an average PC.

In practice, as shown in section 2.3, the number of windows available is far above what is needed: with a 1024-bit exponent and the exponentiation algorithm of figure 2 with windows of size 4, one has approximately $v = 100$ windows of two known consecutive bits in the upper half of δ. This extra information can be taken into account to eliminate more pairs (k, λ). With v large enough, this filters out all the wrong pairs, thereby eliminating the need for an exhaustive search phase. On the other side, the complexity of the pair elimination phase is linear in v.

5   Practical Results

There are two limits for this attack: the first one is to have enough information on one curve to be able to recover only one λ for each curve, the second one is to have enough information on all the curves to recover only one possibility for the least significant bits. The following tables will give some examples where the attack is feasible or not. We can note that the attack is more efficient on larger modulus size. Table 5 gives the results in the case $e = 3$. In that case, only a ratio of bits has to be known in each randomized exponent. In practice, if side channel attack is possible on a CLNW or VLNW splitting method, we may obtain a better ratio than detailed in the table.

Modulus size	ℓ, size of random	$1/r$, ratio of partially known information	attack success
512	20	1/16	no
1024	20	1/16	yes
	32	1/16	no
2048	20	1/32	yes
	32	1/64	yes

Fig. 5. Practical results for $e = 3$

Modulus size	ℓ, size of random	number of 2-bit windows	$1/r$, ratio of partially known information	attack success
512	20	40	1/16	no
1024	20	40	1/16	yes
	32	64	1/16	yes
2048	32	64	1/32	yes

Fig. 6. Practical results for $e = 2^{16} + 1$

Table 6 gives the results for $e = 2^{16} + 1$. In that case, as explained in section 4, the attack has better complexity if 2-bit windows are obtained for one randomized exponent. Such information may be obtained with the CLNW or VLNW splitting algorithms. For the optimized method to be more efficient than exhaustive search, the number of 2-bit windows should be twice the length of the random value λ used to randomized the private exponent.

The fifth column is computed by using the formula $n/(2r) \gg \ell$. For each parameter, 50 curves are sufficient in practice, without considering imperfect input data.

In conclusion we can see that for classical size and reasonable information leaking, the attack is feasible and of low complexity.

Acknowledgments

The authors would like to thank the anonymous referees for many useful comments on the first version of this paper.

References

1. D. Boneh, G. Durfee, and Y. Frankel. An attack on RSA given a fraction of the private key bits. In K. Ohta and D. Pei, editors, *Advances in Cryptology – Asiacrypt'98*, volume 1514 of *LNCS*, pages 25 – 34. Springer-Verlag, 1998.
2. J. Bos and M. Coster. Addition Chain Heuristics. In G. Brassard, editor, *Advances in Cryptology – Crypto 1989*, volume 435 of *LNCS*, pages 400 – 407. Springer Verlag, 1989.
3. D. E. Knuth. *The Art of Computer Programming, Vol 2: Semi Numerical Algorithms*. Addison Wesley, 1969.
4. C. K. Koç. High Speed RSA Implementation. Technical report, Tech Rep. 201, RSA Laboratories, 1994.
5. C. K. Koç. Analysis of Sliding Window Technique for Exponentiation. *Computers and Mathematics with Applications*, 10(30):17 – 24, 1995.
6. P. C. Kocher. Timing Attacks on Implementations of Diffie-Hellman, RSA, DSS, and Others Systems. In N. Koblitz, editor, *Advances in Cryptology – Crypto '96*, volume 1109 of *LNCS*, pages 104 – 113. Springer-Verlag, 1996.
7. T. S. Messerges, E. A. Dabbish, and R. H. Sloan. Power Analysis Attacks of Modular Exponentiation in Smartcard. In Ç. K. Koç and C. Paar, editors, *Cryptographic Hardware and Embedded Systems – CHES 2000*, volume 1717 of *LNCS*, pages 144 – 157. Springer-Verlag, 1999.
8. D. R. Stinson. Some Baby-Step Giant-Step Algorithms for the Low Hamming Weight Discrete Logarithm Problem. *Mathematics of Computation*, 71:379 – 391, 2002.
9. C. D. Walter. Sliding Windows Succumbs to Big Mac Attack. In Ç. K. Koç and C. Paar, editors, *Cryptographic Hardware and Embedded Systems – CHES 2001*, volume 2162 of *LNCS*, pages 286 – 299. Springer-Verlag, 2001.
10. C. D. Walter. Seeing through MIST Given a Small Fraction of an RSA Private Key. In M. Joye, editor, *CT-RSA 2003*, volume 2612 of *LNCS*, pages 391 – 402. Springer-Verlag, 2003.

A   When Few Bits Are Missing

In this appendix, we show that when the number of missing bits is small, we can recover missing bits of d by using a discrete log based algorithm. Stinson describes and analyzes several algorithms due to Heiman and Odlyzko and Coppersmith in [8]. Let m be the number of missing bits of $x = \log_\alpha \beta$ and t is the Hamming weight of x. Heiman and Odlyzko describe a meet-in-the-middle attack. We search Y_1 and $Y_2 \subseteq \mathbb{Z}_m$ such that $\alpha^{\mathsf{val}(Y_1)} = \beta(\alpha^{\mathsf{val}(Y_2)})^{-1} \bmod N$ where $\mathsf{val}(Y_i) = \sum_{j \in Y_i} 2^j$ by ranging through all Y_1 and Y_2 such that $|Y_1| = |Y_2| = t/2$. As there are $\binom{m}{t/2}$ such sets Y_1 and Y_2, the space and time complexity of the attack is of order $O(\binom{m}{t/2})$. Moreover, if we have only an upper bound t' on t, we have to run through all $t = 1$ to $t = t'$ and the time complexity becomes $O(\sum_{t=1}^{t'} \binom{m}{t/2}) = O(t' \binom{m}{t'/2})$.

Coppersmith's algorithm, described in [8], allows one to lower the time complexity to $O(m \binom{m/2}{t/2})$ and the space complexity to $O(\binom{m/2}{t/2})$. The idea is to use an (m, t)-splitting system for $\mathbb{Z}_m$. Such combinatorial structure is a pair $(X, \mathcal{B})$ with the following properties:

1. $|X| = m$, and $\mathcal{B}$ is a set of subsets of size $m/2$ of X, called *blocks*
2. for every $Y \subseteq X$ s.t. $|Y| = t$, there exists a block $B \in \mathcal{B}$ s.t. $|B \cap Y| = t/2$

Coppersmith shows that there exists an (m, t)-splitting system of size $m/2$. Therefore by picking $Y_1 \subseteq B_i$ for all $B_i \in \mathcal{B}$ and $Y_2 \in \mathbb{Z}_m \setminus B_i$ for any t-set Y_2 in $\mathbb{Z}_m \setminus B_i$ the same algorithm finds the matching in time $O(\binom{m/2}{t/2})$.

The last algorithm can be adapted to work   mod N where N is a RSA modulus and when the missing bits are not consecutive. The memory complexity is $O(m \binom{m/2}{t/2})$ where t is the number of 1 bits among m bits.

Consequently, if we assume that in the m missing bits, one of two are a one, then $t = m/2$. Therefore, the complexity is $O(m^2 \binom{m/2}{m/4})$. Since, $\binom{N}{N/2} \approx \sqrt{2/\pi} \cdot 2^N$, then the complexity becomes $O(m^2 \cdot 2^{m/2})$, and in practice, we can only deal with $m \approx 128$.

Unified Point Addition Formulæ and Side-Channel Attacks

Douglas Stebila[1],[*] and Nicolas Thériault[2]

[1] Institute for Quantum Computing,
University of Waterloo, Waterloo, ON, Canada
dstebila@iqc.ca
[2] Department of Combinatorics and Optimization,
University of Waterloo, Waterloo, ON, Canada
ntheriau@math.uwaterloo.ca

Abstract. The successful application to elliptic curve cryptography of side-channel attacks, in which information about the secret key can be recovered from the observation of side channels like power consumption, timing, or electromagnetic emissions, has motivated the recent development of unified formulæ for elliptic curve point operations. In this paper, we show how an attack introduced by Walter can be improved and used against the unified formulæ of Brier, Déchène and Joye when it relies on a standard field arithmetic implementation, both in affine and projective coordinates. We also describe how the field arithmetic might be implemented to obtain more uniform operations that avoid this type of attack.

Keywords: elliptic-curve cryptography, side-channel attacks, unified point addition formulæ, projective coordinates.

1 Introduction

The study of elliptic curves in cryptography [1,2] has been ongoing for a number of years. Elliptic curve cryptography offers higher security per key bit compared to other public key cryptosystems and the smaller key size is more suitable for implementation on small devices such as smart cards. In recent years, a new class of attacks has been developed, called *side-channel* attacks [3], which use information observed during the execution of the algorithm to help to determine the secret key. There are two classes of side-channel attacks: *simple* side-channel attacks, which analyze the trace of a single execution of a cryptographic protocol, and *differential* side-channel attacks, which compare the traces of multiple executions of a protocol. The attack in this paper is only considered in a *simple* side channel context.

The central operation in an elliptic curve cryptosystem is the *point multiplication* operation, in which a point is multiplied by a scalar. The basic method for implementing point multiplication is the *double-and-add* technique, which uses

---

[*] Supported by NSERC, Sun Microsystems, CIAR, MITACS, CFI, and ORDCF.

L. Goubin and M. Matsui (Eds.): CHES 2006, LNCS 4249, pp. 354–368, 2006.

a binary representation of the scalar and performs a sequence of point additions and point doublings depending on the bits of the scalar. In double-and-add point multiplication, a point doubling is done for every bit of the key k, but a point addition is done only when a bit of the key is 1. If, in a side-channel analysis, a point addition is distinguishable from a point doubling, then the bits of the secret key can be determined; this has been demonstrated experimentally using timing [3], power analysis [4], and electromagnetic emissions [5]. Techniques for counteracting this problem include: performing dummy operations, such as forcing a point addition at each iteration [6]; using alternate point multiplication algorithms, such as Montgomery point multiplication [7]; using alternate curve parameterizations, such as the Jacobi or Hessian forms; and unifying the algorithms for point addition and point doubling so that they use the same sequence of field operations and hence are indistinguishable. It is this last technique that we address in this paper.

A *unified formula* for point addition and point doubling for elliptic curves in Weierstraß form, in which point addition and point doubling use the same sequence of field operations, was first given by Brier and Joye [8] in affine and projective form. Walter [9] demonstrated a theoretical side-channel attack on an implementation of the formula of Brier and Joye that, instead of exploiting any irregularity in the sequence of field operations performed, exploits an irregularity in the implementation of the field operations themselves in the context of the unified point addition formula. A subsequent paper of Brier, Déchène, and Joye [11] offers an infinite family of unified point addition formulæ in affine form.

In this paper, we give a projective version of the unified point addition formulæ of Brier, Déchène, and Joye. Whereas Walter's attack used the occurrence of the *conditional subtraction* in a Montgomery field multiplication, we note that a conditional addition is often an integral step of field subtraction. A typical algorithm for computing prime field subtraction is given in Fig. 1; the conditional addition is step 2.[1]

Input:	Integers c, d, q such that $0 \leq c, d \leq q - 1$.
Output:	Integer e such that $e = c - d \mod q$ and $0 \leq e \leq q - 1$.

1.	$e \leftarrow c - d$
2.	if $e < 0$ then $e \leftarrow e + q$

Fig. 1. Field subtraction algorithm

We find that the ability to detect the occurrence of the conditional addition in field subtractions in both the affine and projective form decreases the amount of work necessary to recover the key. In the projective case in Montgomery representation, the effect is substantial when combined with Walter's original

---

[1] Similarly, a field addition contains a conditional subtraction, however our techniques of Sec. 5 do not make use of this conditional subtraction.

attack. This observation reinforces the fact that a secure implementation requires constant-runtime field operations, not just unified point arithmetic. In fact, security against side-channel attacks needs to be addressed at three levels: the hardware level, the software level, and the algorithmic level.

We also provide some performance results for the various unified formulæ and discuss the applicability of timing attacks. We find in timing experiments that the runtime of a field subtraction with the conditional addition takes substantially longer than without (520 ns versus 330 ns) and thus seems exploitable.

This paper is organized as follows: Section 2 provides a short introduction to elliptic curve cryptography. In Sec. 3, we describe the unified formula of Brier and Joye and describe an attack by Walter. In Sec. 4, we describe the family of unified formulæ in affine coordinates given by Brier, Déchène, and Joye and give our derivation of the formulæ for projective coordinates. In Sec. 5, we present an extension of Walter's attack, analyze its effect on the implementation of the formulæ, and discuss countermeasures. Section 6 contains performance results and discusses the possibility of timing attacks on double-and-add projective unified point multiplication.

The attacks we discuss in this paper only apply to elliptic curves over prime fields and do not apply to curves over binary fields. The countermeasures we present are not intended to be secure against differential side channel attacks; standard countermeasures for that context should still be applied.

2   Background

For fields $\mathbb{K}$ of prime characteristic other than 2 or 3, the Weierstaß form of an elliptic curve is given by the equation $y^2 = x^3 + ax + b$, where $a, b \in \mathbb{K}$. The set of points in $\mathbb{K} \times \mathbb{K}$ on the curve, joined with the *point at infinity* $\mathcal{O}$, forms an abelian group, denoted $E(\mathbb{K})$. Two points $P = (x_1, y_1)$ and $Q = (x_2, y_2)$, $P \neq -Q$, can be added to obtain a third point $P + Q = (x_3, y_3)$, where $x_3 = \lambda^2 - x_1 - x_2$, $y_3 = \lambda(x_1 - x_3) - y_1$, and

$$\lambda = \begin{cases} \frac{y_2 - y_1}{x_2 - x_1}, & \text{if } P \neq Q \text{ (addition)} \\ \frac{3x_1^2 + a}{2y_1}, & \text{if } P = Q \text{ (doubling)} \end{cases} . \tag{1}$$

Because λ is defined differently depending on whether or not $P = Q$, the formula for point addition differs from the formula for point doubling.

The formula given above uses *affine coordinates*. The formula for λ requires an inversion, which can be computationally expensive in practice. This has motivated the development of formulæ using *projective coordinates*. In the ordinary projective case, a point is represented by three coordinates, $P = (X, Y, Z)$, with $x = X/Z$ and $y = Y/Z$. Denominators are used for all of the point additions and point doublings comprising a point multiplication, and only at the end is the inversion Z^{-1} computed to return the final result to affine coordinates.

3   Unified Formula of Brier and Joye

The formula for λ in (1) when $P \neq Q$ cannot be used for point doubling because $x_1 = x_2$ in that case and the denominator is 0. Starting with the point addition form of λ, Brier and Joye [8] use a series of algebraic manipulations to obtain a form of λ that is defined for both point addition and point doubling:

$$\lambda = \frac{(x_1 + x_2)^2 - x_1 x_2 + a}{y_1 + y_2}, \quad \text{if } y_1 + y_2 \neq 0 \ . \tag{2}$$

However, this formula for λ is not defined when $y_1 + y_2 = 0$ (see Section 4.1). Brier and Joye subsequently derive a projective formula for point addition using this unified value of λ, with $x_i = X_i/Z_i, y_i = Y_i/Z_i$:

$$X_3 = 2FW \ , \quad Y_3 = R(G - 2W) - L^2 \ , \quad Z_3 = 2F^3 \ , \tag{3}$$

where $U_1 = X_1 Z_2, U_2 = X_2 Z_1, S_1 = Y_1 Z_2, S_2 = Y_2 Z_1, Z = Z_1 Z_2, T = U_1 + U_2, M = S_1 + S_2, F = ZM, L = MF, G = TL, R = T^2 - U_1 U_2 + aZ^2$, and $W = R^2 - G$. This formula requires 13 field multiplications and 5 field squarings.

3.1   Walter's Side-Channel Attack

Walter's side-channel attack [9] is an attack that assumes the occurrence of a conditional subtraction in a Montgomery modular multiplication operation can be detected. This attack should be considered successful if a non-negligible proportion of the keys can be computed significantly faster than they would with an attack on the whole keyspace. We will see that in some cases, the attack becomes practical as a (relatively) high proportion of keys can be found with (relatively) few computations.

Walter considers the effect of being able to detect a conditional subtraction in Montgomery modular reductions in a point multiplication using the unified formula of Brier and Joye. For a point doubling using the projective formula of (3), the computations of U_1 and U_2 are identical, as are the computations of S_1 and S_2. The occurrence of a conditional subtraction in the Montgomery multiplication for U_1 must be the same as that for U_2, for a point doubling. Thus, if a conditional subtraction is observed in the computation of one of U_1 or U_2 but not the other, then a point doubling could not have occurred and the operation must be a point addition. (The same argument allows the computations of S_1 and S_2 to distinguish a point addition.) The probability that a conditional subtraction occurs in the computation of one of U_1, U_2 but not the other (and similarly for S_1 and S_2) is

$$p_{\text{diff}} = 2p_{\text{sub}}(1 - p_{\text{sub}}) \approx \frac{3}{8} \ . \tag{4}$$

where p_{sub} is the probability of a conditional subtraction occurring; for Montgomery modular reduction in practice, usually $p_{\text{sub}} \approx 1/4$. Hence, the probability that the occurrence of conditional subtractions in the computations of U_1, U_2, S_1, and S_2 can be used to distinguish a point addition from a point doubling is

$$p_{\text{dist}} = 1 - (1 - p_{\text{diff}})^2 \approx \frac{39}{64} \approx 0.61 \ . \tag{5}$$

In the sequence of operations in a double-and-add point multiplication algorithm, the position of a point addition determines the point doublings on either side of it. Let n be the size in bits of the prime field. Given p_{dist}, the expected total number of determined operations is:

$$\frac{3}{2}(n-1)p_{\text{dist}} - (n-2)\left(\frac{1}{2}p_{\text{dist}}\right)^2 \ . \tag{6}$$

The probabilistic analysis given above does not give the best estimate of the number of determined operations. In experiments, Walter found that, with a set of 512 samples, it is most efficient to just pick the sample that has the greatest number of distinguished point additions. This approach, combined with additional substring restrictions, can give effective keyspaces for a 192-bit prime curve of size just $2^{17.6}$, which can be easily searched. The analysis in Sec. 5 gives a probabilistic argument that generalizes Walter's experimental sampling.

4   Unified Formulæ of Brier, Déchène, and Joye

4.1   Affine Coordinates

The unified point addition formula of Brier and Joye from the previous section is defined when $y_1 + y_2 \neq 0$, which always holds in the case of point doubling, but it is not applicable to all possible point additions. Izu and Tagaki [10] showed that in some settings these special cases of the point addition could be used to reveal the key. Brier, Déchène, and Joye [11] developed an infinite family of unified point addition formulæ which are defined for all points. We are most concerned with the most efficient formula of the family, which has

$$\lambda = \frac{(x_1 + x_2)^2 - x_1 x_2 + a + (-1)^\delta (y_1 - y_2)}{y_1 + y_2 + (-1)^\delta (x_1 - x_2)}, \quad y_1 + y_2 + (-1)^\delta (x_1 - x_2) \neq 0 \ , \tag{7}$$

where $\delta = 0$ when $y_1 + y_2 + x_1 - x_2 \neq 0$ and $\delta = 1$ otherwise (or a randomized choice of δ when both choices give nonzero values). Unified point addition using this λ requires 2 field multiplications, 2 field squarings, and 1 field inversion. Although Brier, Déchène, and Joye give an infinite family of unified point addition formulæ, which would allow a different λ value to be randomly chosen at each point addition, we assume that the most efficient member, given in (7), is used for each operation. If any fixed λ is used, then it may be that the attack in Sec. 5 can still be applied.

4.2   Projective Coordinates

To mitigate the high cost of field inversion compared to the cost of field multiplication, points can be expressed in projective coordinates so that field inversion need only be done once per point multiplication rather than at each intermediate point addition or point doubling.

We now describe an ordinary projective form of the unified point addition formula given by λ as defined in (7). We begin by noting that since $P+Q = Q+P$, the value for y_3 in point addition is symmetric and hence $2y_3 = \lambda(x_1 + x_2 - 2x_3) - (y_1 + y_2)$. Letting $x_i = X_i/Z$, $y_i = Y_i/Z$ and completing the square in the numerator of λ, we obtain:

$$X_3 = 2FW \ , \quad Y_3 = R(G - 2W) - LFM \ , \quad Z_3 = 2F^3 \ , \tag{8}$$

where $U_1 = X_1Z_2, U_2 = X_2Z_1, S_1 = Y_1Z_2, S_2 = Y_2Z_1, Z = Z_1Z_2, T = U_1 + U_2, M = S_1 + S_2, V = (-1)^\delta(U_1 - U_2), N = (-1)^\delta(S_1 - S_2), E = M + V, F = ZE, L = FE, G = LT, R = T^2 - U_1U_2 + Z(aZ + N)$, and $W = R^2 - G$. Note that $\delta = 0$ when $S_1 + S_2 + U_1 - U_2 \neq 0$ and $\delta = 1$ otherwise (or a randomized choice of δ when both choices give nonzero values). This formula requires 16 field multiplications and 3 field squarings.[2]

5   Extending Walter's Attack

5.1   Conditional Modular Reduction Attack

Walter's original attack in Sec. 3.1 assumed that the conditional subtraction at the end of Montgomery multiplication could be detected. Under the same assumption that a conditional subtraction (or addition) can be observed, we note that such an operation at the end of a field addition (or subtraction) can be detected. For field subtraction as given in Fig. 1, the conditional addition is step 2.[3]

We will observe later in this section that there are some modular subtractions in the unified point addition algorithms where, in the case of a point doubling, the arguments are equal and hence the result of the subtraction is zero: when $c = d$, we compute $c - d \mod q$ as $c - d = 0$. In this case, a conditional addition in field subtraction is never performed. However, if we observe the occurrence of a conditional addition for the operation $c - d \mod q$, then it must be that $d > c$ and hence the operation in question must be a point addition.

---

[2] The multiplication by $(-1)^\delta$ in the computation of V and N can be implemented with conditional branching (`if` statement).

[3] In implementation, this is common. For example, the OpenSSL [14] library provides a function `BN_mod_sub_quick` which performs exactly the operations in Fig. 1, and similarly for field addition. When reduction is done using the Extended Euclidean Algorithm, as in OpenSSL's `BN_mod_sub` function, and the value to be reduced is strictly between $-q$ and q, the sequence of steps performed is effectively the same as Fig. 1 and includes a conditional addition.

5.2   Effect on Affine Formulæ of Sec. 4.1

The affine formulæ of Brier, Déchène, and Joye in (7) requires the computation of $y_1 - y_2$ and $x_1 - x_2$. If all of the coordinates are distributed uniformly at random, then the probability that a conditional addition is necessary in the computation of $y_1 - y_2$ is $1/2$, and similarly for $x_1 - x_2$. In this case, the probability that a point addition can be identified is $p_{\text{dist}} = 1 - (1 - 1/2)^2 = 3/4$.

We first note that even when additions and doublings cannot be distinguished, a side channel attack will reveal the number of operations performed in the point multiplication. If the key length is known, then knowing the number of operations gives the number of additions (since the number of doublings is fixed by the key length). To simplify the analysis, we assume that the attack can only be successful for keys of the most common length. This does not mean that the attack cannot work for other key lengths, but rather that it is more difficult to bound the work required to determine the key.

If q is between $3 \cdot 2^{r-1}$ and $3 \cdot 2^r$, then the most common key length is r and occurs for $p_{l=r} \geq 1/3$ of the keys (integers) between 0 and q. This probability is maximal if q is close to 2^{r+1}, in which case $p_{l=r} \approx 1/2$ of the keys have length r. If there are k additions of which k_1 are not identified, then we can consider the key-space to search as the set of sequences of $r - k$ "zeros" and k "ones". These sequences are combined with the identified additions of the double and add sequence to give a list of possible keys (the substring structure will often remove a number of sequences). The number of possible keys is then bounded by $\binom{r-k+k_1}{k_1}$, which in turn is bounded by $\binom{r}{k_1}$ (this estimate is usually very pessimistic, but it has the advantage of being independent from the value of k).

If we assume that all keys of length r are possible (which is true if $q \geq 2^{r+1} - 1$), the probability that a key of length r uses k additions is $\binom{r}{k}\frac{1}{2^r}$. Given a key with k additions, the probability that k_1 of them are not identified is $\binom{k}{k_1}(p_{\text{dist}})^{k-k_1}(1 - p_{\text{dist}})^{k_1}$. The probability that exactly k_1 additions are not identified in a key of length r is therefore

$$
\begin{aligned}
p_{k_1} &= \sum_{k=k_1}^{r} \binom{r}{k}\frac{1}{2^r}\binom{k}{k_1}(p_{\text{dist}})^{k-k_1}(1 - p_{\text{dist}})^{k_1} \\
&= \sum_{k=k_1}^{r} \frac{(1 - p_{\text{dist}})^{k_1}}{2^r}\binom{r}{k_1}\binom{r-k_1}{k-k_1}(p_{\text{dist}})^{k-k_1} \\
&= \frac{(1 - p_{\text{dist}})^{k_1}}{2^r}\binom{r}{k_1}\sum_{i=0}^{r-k_1}\binom{r-k_1}{i}(p_{\text{dist}})^{i} \\
&= \binom{r}{k_1}\left(\frac{1 - p_{\text{dist}}}{2}\right)^{k_1}\left(\frac{1 + p_{\text{dist}}}{2}\right)^{r-k_1}.
\end{aligned}
\tag{9}
$$

Although the average number of unidentified addition is $(1 - p_{\text{dist}})r/2 = r/8$, some keys will have fewer additions remaining to be identified.

For our 192-bit prime field example curve, we have $r = 191$ and we get an average of 23.9 additions remaining to be identified, so the search space is still quite large. This analysis assumes that the additions in a point multiplication are independent. This is not strictly true as x_1 and y_1 (the x and y coordinates of the base point) are the same for all the additions.

In $1/m$ of point multiplications sP, the x-coordinate of the base point P will take on a value between 0 and $\frac{1}{m}q$ and will have an average value of $\frac{1}{2m}q$. We take the notation that in the double-and-add point multiplication algorithm the fixed base point P is the first argument of the unified point addition formula. In the computation of $x_1 - x_2$ in (7), we assume that, over the course of a point multiplication, x_2 will behave as if it is uniformly distributed. Thus it is expected for $1 - \frac{1}{2m}$ of the point addition operations that $x_2 > x_1$ and a conditional addition occurs. We do not put any condition on the y-coordinate of P and assume that the size of y_1 can be considered independent from the size of x_1. In this case, the probability that a point addition can be distinguished is the probability that a conditional addition occurs in either the computation of $x_1 - x_2$ or $y_1 - y_2$:

$$p_{\text{dist}} = 1 - \left(1 - \left(1 - \frac{1}{2m}\right)\right)\left(1 - \frac{1}{2}\right) = 1 - \frac{1}{4m} \tag{10}$$

Using p_{dist} in (10) with $1/m = 1/8$, the expected number of additions in our example remaining to be identified decreases to 2.99. We can then conclude that a significant proportions of keys of length r will be left with at 3 or fewer unidentified additions (using the distribution in (9), we find that 1 in ≈ 24.6 of all keys satisfy that condition). The number of possible keys is then bounded (loosely) by $\binom{191}{3} \approx 2^{20.1}$, for which an exhaustive search is quite feasible.

5.3   Effect on Projective Formulæ of Sec. 4.2

Just as for affine formulæ, there are two operations in the projective formulæ of (8) where we can take advantage of the ability to detect a conditional addition in a field subtraction. Without loss of generality, suppose $\delta = 0$. Consider the calculations $V = U_1 - U_2$ and $N = S_1 - S_2$. In the case of a point doubling, $U_1 = U_2$ and $S_1 = S_2$, so no conditional addition will occur in the calculation of either V or N. However, in the case of a point addition, we assume that U_1 and U_2 will behave as if they are independent and uniformly distributed over $0, \ldots, p-1$. So, with probability $p_{\text{add}} = \frac{1}{2}$, $U_2 < U_1$ and a conditional addition is needed in the computation of $V = U_1 - U_2$ (similarly for $N = S_1 - S_2$). Moreover, we also assume that the occurrence of a conditional addition in the computation of V is independent of the occurrence for N. If a conditional addition is observed in at least one of these computations, then the operation is known to be a point addition, revealing the key bit. The probability of distinguishing a point addition is again $1 - (1 - p_{\text{add}})^2 = 3/4$. It should be noted that taking advantage of base points of a special form is not possible here as U_1, U_2, S_1 and S_2 all depend on both of the points of the addition, so for all practical purposes the probabilities of identifying point additions are independent from each other.

If the field is implemented using Montgomery representation, Walter's original attack [9] on detecting conditional subtractions in Montgomery reductions still applies to this projective formula. The detection of a conditional subtraction is used to distinguish a point addition from a point doubling in the computation of U_1 compared to U_2, and of S_1 compared to S_2. We can combine the two sources of information (conditional additions in the field subtractions and differences in conditional subtractions in the Montgomery reductions) to increase the probability of success.

We now have four different conditional events which distinguish a point addition from a point doubling:

1. conditional subtraction in computation of one of U_1, U_2 but not the other,
2. conditional subtraction in computation of one of S_1, S_2 but not the other,
3. conditional addition in computation of $V = U_1 - U_2$, and
4. conditional addition in computation of $N = S_1 - S_2$.

Under the assumption that these events occur independently, the probability of detecting a point addition given that the operation was a point addition is

$$p_{\text{dist}} = 1 - (1 - p_{\text{add}})^2 (1 - p_{\text{diff}})^2 \ . \tag{11}$$

In practice, the coordinate values observed during a point multiplication do seem to behave as if they are sufficiently uniformly distributed and, with respect to the four conditional events above, sufficiently uncorrelated.

If we assume no special knowledge on the base point of the point multiplication, i.e. $p_{\text{add}} = 1/2$ and $p_{\text{diff}} \approx 3/8$, we get $p_{\text{dist}} \approx 231/256 \approx 0.902$. For the distribution obtained in (9), we average $\approx 0.049r$ unidentified additions.

If we look for base points of a special form as in Walter's attack for the formulæ of Brier and Joye, the increase in the probability of success is relatively small. With a point of the form $\sim \left(\frac{1}{16}q, \frac{1}{16}q, \frac{15}{16}q \right)$, we get $p_{\text{diff}} \approx 0.93$ and the expected number of unidentified addition decreases to $\approx 0.035r$. This decrease is small considering that we have to restrict ourselves to 1 in 512 points. In this case, it is much more practical to consider all base points and take advantage of the variability. For example, for a field of 192 bits, 15.4% of all point multiplications have 6 or less unidentified additions, while the special base points (1 in 512) have 6.7 unidentified additions on average.

Table 1 gives estimates for the attack at various field sizes. At each field size, we give the average number of additions remaining to be identified. We give a probabilistic analysis of the best sample we expect to find in the trace of 512 random point multiplications.[4] In the probabilistic analysis, we determine an upper bound on the number of unidentified additions for which the attack will be considered successful, requiring a probability of success of at least 1 in 512. For each case, we give a (loose) upper bound on the keyspace and a better estimate using the approach described in Appendix A.

We also evaluate the costs of the attack when we give a bound on the maximum number of additions remaining to be identified before the key is attacked (with 3

---

[4] While the theoretical analysis in Section 5.2 only considers traces in which the key has the most common length, the "best of 512" analysis takes into account keys of all lengths (assuming failure of keys of length other than r).

as an example). In this case, we give the expected number of point multiplications that must be observed before finding such a key and a (loose) upper bound on the size of the remaining keyspace. It is interesting to note that for the 521-bit case, the expected number of keys required to obtain 3 unidentified additions approximately balances the bound on the keyspace giving, in some sense, an overall minimized complexity of attack. We also compare our results with those of Walter [9]. We assume that general points are considered, so $p_{dist} \approx 0.902$, that half the keys have size r (that is, $q \approx 2^{r+1}$) and that an attack on a key of size different from r is always considered unsuccessful.

Table 1. Expected number of operations using conditional modular reduction attack, using p_{dist} as in (11)

Field size in bits $(r+1)$	160	192	224	256	384	521
Average missing additions per point mult.:	7.76	9.33	10.89	12.45	18.70	25.43
Sampling best trace from 512 samples:						
k required for prob. of success $> 1/512$:	2	2	3	4	8	13
Upper bound on keyspace for this k:	$2^{13.6}$	$2^{14.1}$	$2^{20.8}$	$2^{27.4}$	$2^{53.2}$	$2^{84.5}$
Estimated keyspace (Appendix A):	$2^{9.03}$	$2^{9.67}$	$2^{14.3}$	$2^{18.9}$	$2^{37.2}$	$2^{59.4}$
To obtain at most 3 unidentified additions:						
Expected number of keys required:	22	67	217	746	$2^{17.1}$	$2^{25.2}$
Bound on keyspace:	$2^{19.3}$	$2^{20.1}$	$2^{20.8}$	$2^{21.4}$	$2^{23.1}$	$2^{24.4}$
Walter's attack [9]:						
Average missing additions:		19.2	23.0	26.6	41.5	57.9
Bound on keyspace (no restrictions):		$2^{33.2}$	$2^{42.8}$	$2^{52.4}$	$2^{91.4}$	$2^{134.3}$
Bound using substring restrictions:		$2^{17.6}$	$2^{24.0}$	$2^{30.4}$	$2^{56.0}$	$2^{84.2}$

Just as in Walter's analysis it may be possible to decrease the key space remaining to be searched, for example by using substring restrictions on the possible sequence of point additions and point doublings. This approach has only a limited impact in our case, since the operations remaining to be identified consist in a large number of doublings and a few additions.

5.4 Countermeasures to the Conditional Modular Reduction Attack

The success of the Conditional Modular Reduction attack depends on information leaked on the size of intermediate values which is observed based on the field subtraction having a conditional addition. If the field subtraction were to have constant runtime, for example by inserting a dummy addition to offset the conditional addition, then the attack would not apply. However, inserting dummy operations may create additional risks in the setting of differential side-channel attacks.

A nicer countermeasure would be to program the subtraction of $c - d \mod q$ as $(2q + c - d) - mq$, where $m \in \{1, 2\}$ depends on the value of $2q + c - d$, so the time required for a field subtraction is constant. For the field addition, one would replace $c+d \mod q$ by $(q+c+d)-mq$ where $m \in \{1, 2\}$, and similarly for Montgomery reduction (replacing $c+d$ by the value of the Montgomery reduction at the moment the conditional subtraction is used). These countermeasures still require a conditional operation to be performed, based on the appropriate value of m, but may have less of a detectable difference.

A third countermeasure consist in taking the field reductions (both Montgomery reductions and addition/subtraction of a multiple of q) as independent operations from the multiplications, squarings, additions and subtractions and rewrite the unified formulæ in consequence. This means we will accept that some of the values used during the computations may be greater than q. Although this approach removes any danger of an attack based on variations in the field arithmetic, it may have a negative impact on the efficiency, in particular when the field size is close to a multiple of the word size.

At this point we should also note that choosing $\delta = 0$ or $\delta = 1$ requires the comparison of two field elements, so at least these two must be fully reduced. Since repeated operations or even a change from addition to subtraction could potentially lead to an attack, we choose δ to ensure that $\frac{1}{2}(x_1 + x_2 + y_1 + y_2) \neq x_{2-\delta}$ instead of $y_1 + y_2 + (-1)^\delta(x_1 - x_2) \neq 0$ (the two conditions are equivalent, but the computations required for the first test are more uniform).

For simplicity, we will assume the field is in Montgomery representation. We distinguish Montgomery reductions and q-reduction where multiples of q are added/subtracted. In an attempt to avoid possible extensions of the attack, we err on the side of caution and implement the field operations as follows:

- Products (and squares) are not reduced unless stated.
- Sums are not reduced unless stated.
- Subtractions never contain a conditional addition (a fixed multiple of q is always added to the first operand before doing the subtraction).
- If an integer is to be fully reduced, then it is at least as large as q.
- For the affine formula, inversion accepts any integer between 1 and $6q - 1$ and coprime to q and returns an integer between 1 and $q - 1$.
- Montgomery reductions are allowed to return an output between 0 and $2q-1$. They accept inputs between 0 and $6q^2$ for affine coordinates ($R > 6q$) and between 0 and $16q^2$ for projective coordinates ($R > 16q$).
- The multiples of q used in the formulæ are precomputed.

For the projective formula, we let the X, Y and Z coordinates be in the range $[0, 2q - 1]$. Note that by construction $(x_1 + x_2)^2 \geq x_1 x_2$.

6   Timing

The timings in this section were performed on a 900 MHz UltraSPARC III using the multi-precision integer and elliptic curve libraries from NSS 3.9 [15] with no optimized assembly code. To obtain high-resolution timings, we used the Solaris `hrtime` C library, which has a resolution of 100 ns. We use the 160-bit prime field curve `secp160r2` [16].

On our test system, the average time of a 160-bit prime field modular subtraction $a - b \mod q$ when $a > b$ is about 320 ns. When $a < b$, and hence when a conditional addition is required, the average time is about 550 ns.

Table 2 gives performance timings for point operations using the unified point addition and doubling formulæ from Section 4 as well as other schemes. Point multiplications for all fomulæ except Jacobian projective and modified Jacobian wNAF use the double-and-add technique. The timings in the table are the average of 10^5 operations.

Table 3 gives average timings and standard deviations for point additions and point doublings in the course of a single point multiplication. The results were obtained by recording the time of each addition or doubling in a single point multiplication using the double-and-add algorithm.

Table 2. Average point operation timings for `secp160r2` curve

Formula	Addition	Doubling	Multiplication
BDJ affine	126.5 μs	126.2 μs	29.03 ms
Affine	115.7 μs	118.4 μs	27.89 ms
BDJ projective	58.9 μs	58.5 μs	13.99 ms
BJ projective	49.8 μs	49.5 μs	11.76 ms
Jacobian projective			7.95 ms
Modified Jacobian wNAF, $w = 5$			6.22 ms

Table 3. Individual point operation timings from a single point multiplication for `secp160r2` curve

Formulæ	Operation	Average	Standard Deviation
	unified addition	126.528 μs	4.094 μs $\approx 3.2\%$
BDJ affine	unified doubling	126.155 μs	3.700 μs $\approx 2.9\%$
	difference	0.373 μs $\approx 0.3\%$	
	unified addition	58.992 μs	0.474 μs $\approx 0.8\%$
BDJ projective	unified doubling	59.307 μs	0.448 μs $\approx 0.75\%$
	difference	0.315 μs $\approx 0.53\%$	

In the top half of Table 3, timings are given for point addition and doubling using the affine formulæ of Brier, Déchène, and Joye. A unified doubling takes slightly less time than a unified addition on average, but difference between the two operations (0.3%) is one-tenth the size of the standard deviation of either operation, so the timings of the two operations cannot be reliably distinguished.

In the bottom half of Table 3, timings are given for point addition and doubling using the projective formulæ developed in Sec. 4.2. A unified doubling takes slightly more time (0.53%) than a unified addition. The standard deviation of either operation, at 0.8% for addition and 0.75% for doubling, is less than twice difference.

For both the affine and projective formulæ of Brier, Déchène, and Joye in Table 3, the average difference in timing between a point addition and point doubling is too small compared to the standard deviation to be of practical use on its own. However, we do not dismiss the fact that this information could be helpful when combined with other side-channel information.

7   Future Work

The major drawback with our approach for the analysis is that we concentrate on keys with a minimal number of unidentified additions, not necessarily on keys for which the remaining keyspace is minimized. In general, binary keys where the zeros only appear in small groups in the key are much easier to break than keys with large groups of consecutive zeros since the first and last doubles coming from a string of zeros in the binary representation are likely to be identified and this is almost the same as identifying one of the zeros. For example, the 521-bit key $10101\cdots0101$ with 16 unidentified additions has a much smaller remaining keyspace than the 521-bit key consisting of 261 ones followed by 260 zeros for which only 8 of the additions have not been identified, even though the number of additions remaining to be located is divided by two in the second key.

A cost analysis that includes this idea would require a study of the distribution of strings of zeros in the binary representation of the key, taking into account the effect of unidentified additions. This is clearly beyond the scope of the work presented here.

Acknowledgments. The authors wish to acknowledge the assistance of I. Déchène of the University of Waterloo, N. Gura and S. Chang of Sun Microsystems Labs, and the anonymous referees.

References

1. Koblitz, N.: Elliptic curve cryptosystems. Mathematics of Computation **48** (1987) 203–209
2. Miller, V.: Use of elliptic curves in cryptography. In Williams, H.C., ed.: Advances in Cryptology – Proc. CRYTPO '85. LNCS, Vol. 218. Springer-Verlag (1986) 417–428
3. Kocher, P.: Timing attacks on implementations of Diffie-Hellman, RSA, DSS, and other systems. In Koblitz, N., ed.: Advances in Cryptology – Proc. CRYPTO '96. LNCS, Vol. 1109. Springer-Verlag (1996) 104–113
4. Kocher, P., Jaffe, J., Jun, B.: Differential power analysis. In Wiener, M., ed.: Advances in Cryptology – Proc. CRYPTO '99. LNCS, Vol. 1666. Springer-Verlag (1999) 388–397
5. Agrawal, D., Archambeault, B., Rao, J.R., Rohatgi, P.: The EM Side-Channel(s). In B.S. Kaliski Jr. and Ç.K. Koç and C. Paar, eds.: Cryptographic Hardware and Embedded Systems – CHES 2002. LNCS, Vol. 2523. Springer–Verlag (2003), 29–45
6. Coron, J.S.: Resistance against differential power analysis for elliptic curve cryptosystems. In Çetin K. Koç, Paar, C., eds.: Cryptographic Hardware and Embedded Systems (CHES) '99. LNCS, Vol. 1717. Springer-Verlag (1999) 292–302

7. Montgomery, P.L.: Modular multiplication without trial division. Mathematics of Computation **44** (1985) 519–521

8. Brier, É., Joye, M.: Weierstraß elliptic curves and side-channel attacks. In Naccache, D., Paillier, P., eds.: Public Key Cryptography – PKC 2002. LNCS, Vol. 2274. Springer-Verlag (2002) 335–345

9. Walter, C.D.: Simple power analysis of unified code for ECC double and add. In Joye, M., Quisquater, J.J., eds.: Cryptographic Hardware and Embedded Systems (CHES) 2004. LNCS, Vol. 3156. Springer-Verlag (2004) 191–204

10. Izu, T., Takagi, T.: On the Security of Brier-Joye's Addition Formula for Weierstrass-form Elliptic Curves Technical Report, Technische Universität Darmstadt, Available online:
    http://www.informatik.tu-darmstadt.de/TI/Veroeffentlichung/TR/

11. Brier, É., Déchène, I., Joye, M.: Unified point addition formulæ for elliptic curve cryptosystems. In Nedjah, N., de Macedo Mourelle, L., eds.: Embedded Cryptographic Hardware: Methodologies and Architectures. Nova Science Publishers (2004) 247–256

12. Hankerson, D., Menezes, A., Vanstone, S.: Guide to Elliptic Curve Cryptography. Springer-Verlag (2004)

13. National Institute of Standards and Technology: Recommended elliptic curves for federal government use (1999) Available online:
    http://csrc.nist.gov/CryptoToolkit/dss/ecdsa/NISTReCur.pdf.

14. OpenSSL Project: OpenSSL v0.9.8 (2005) Available online:
    http://www.openssl.org/.

15. Mozilla Foundation: Netscape Security Services (NSS) v3.9 (2005) Available online:
    http://www.mozilla.org/projects/security/pki/nss/.

16. Certicom Research: SEC 2: Recommended elliptic curve domain parameters (2000) Available online: http://www.secg.org/.

17. Hankerson, D., Hernandez, J.L., Menezes, A.: Software implementation of elliptic curve cryptography over binary fields. In Çetin K. Koç, Paar, C., eds.: Crytpographic Hardware and Embedded Systems (CHES) 2000. LNCS, Vol. 1965. Springer-Verlag (2000) 1–24

A   Cost Estimates

A.1   Zeros in the Binary Expansion

As our attack looks for keys with few unidentified additions, it introduces a bias in the expected number of zeros of the binary representation of successful keys (increasing its value). This is because keys with fewer ones need fewer identified additions to be successful, which makes them more likely to work then keys that have more ones.

The solutions is to go back to the probabilities of Section 5.3 and to compute the expected number of zeros under the condition that the attack is successful. Computations for the key sizes considered in Table 1 show the increase to be less than 5% of $r/2$ (the average expected value).

Also, the attack is considered successful for keys with fewer than k unidentified additions, so the expected number of unidentified additions is slightly lower than k, and once again the expected value can be found by going back to the probabilities. Both of these numbers (which also give the expected number of identified additions) are taken into account to produce the estimated keyspace.

A.2 Unidentified Substrings

To estimate the number of unidentified doublings, we introduce an approach that could also be used to detail the lengths of the unidentified substrings.

We will consider the probabilities that would occur for a key of infinite length that has the same proportion of zero bits and identified additions as our finite key. These proportions will give us an estimate on the number of identified (and unidentified) doublings in the finite key.

We use a state diagram consisting of six states, illustrated in Figure 2.

- The first three are doublings coming from moving from one bit of the key to the next: D_* (unidentified), D_1 (identified, preceding an identified addition), and D_2 (identified, following but not preceding an identified addition);
- The remaining three correspond to bit operations (that is, depending on the value of the bit): A (identified addition), A_* (unidentified addition), and V (absence of addition, for the bit "zero").

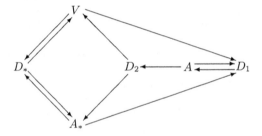

Fig. 2. State diagram

To estimate the number of identified and unidentified doublings, we must find which proportion of the doublings (r in total for the finite key) are in states D_1 and D_2. Every time we are in state D_1, the next state must be A, so the time spent in D_1 is the same as the time spent in A, that is, it corresponds to the number of identified additions. The only way to enter state D_2 is from state A, and the probability of moving to D_2 when leaving A is the probability that the next bit does not correspond to an identified addition.

If the r-bit key has m identified additions, then we can estimate the number of identified doubling as $\left(1 + \frac{r-m}{r}\right) m$ (the 1 is for moving from D_1 to A and $\frac{r-m}{r}$ is the probability of moving to D_2 when leaving A). The estimated costs in Table 1 are then straightforward to obtain.

Read-Proof Hardware from Protective Coatings

Pim Tuyls, Geert-Jan Schrijen, Boris Škorić,
Jan van Geloven, Nynke Verhaegh, and Rob Wolters

Philips Research Laboratories, The Netherlands

Abstract. In cryptography it is assumed that adversaries only have black box access to the secret keys of honest parties. In real life, however, the black box approach is not sufficient because attackers have access to many physical means that enable them to derive information on the secret keys. In order to limit the attacker's ability to read out secret information, the concept of Algorithmic Tamper Proof (ATP) security is needed as put forth by Gennaro, Lysyanskaya, Malkin, Micali and Rabin. An essential component to achieve ATP security is *read-proof* hardware. In this paper, we develop an implementation of read-proof hardware that is resistant against invasive attacks. The construction is based on a hardware and a cryptographic part. The hardware consists of a protective coating that contains a lot of randomness. By performing measurements on the coating a *fingerprint* is derived. The cryptographic part consists of a Fuzzy Extractor that turns this fingerprint into a secure key. Hence no key is present in the non-volatile memory of the device. It is only constructed at the time when needed, and deleted afterwards. A practical implementation of the hardware and the cryptographic part is given. Finally, experimental evidence is given that an invasive attack on an IC equipped with this coating, reveals only a small amount of information on the key.

1   Introduction

Secure key storage is an important problem from a theoretical point of view as well as from a practical point of view. Recently, the theory of this topic started to develop in [1]. In the traditional cryptographic setting the attacker has only *black box* access to the secret information (keys) of the honest parties. In [1] this assumption was removed and the impact on the algorithmic aspects was investigated. It was observed that this problem is highly non-trivial and that in the most general setting no security can be guaranteed. The authors introduce the notion of *Algorithmic Tamper Proof* (ATP) security and show that this can only be achieved if the device has *read-proof hardware* together with a self-destructing capability and some hardwired data which can not be tampered with (Tamper Proof Hardware).

Read-proof hardware is hardware from which an enemy can not read any information on the data stored in it. Tamper-proof hardware contains data that

L. Goubin and M. Matsui (Eds.): CHES 2006, LNCS 4249, pp. 369–383, 2006.

can not be changed by an attacker. Clearly, to approach the black-box setting of cryptography as closely as possible, the (secret) keys have to be stored in read-proof hardware while public information such as algorithms and public keys have to be stored in tamper-proof hardware.

In this paper, we focus on the practical implementation of *read-proof* hardware. An attempt to translate the theoretical definition of read-proof hardware into a practical realisation shows that the theoretical definition has a rich variety of practical aspects. More specifically, it has been shown that there are many practical ways for *reading* out information from storage media, and read-proof hardware has to be resistant against all those methods. At a high level one can distinguish between *invasive physical attacks* [2], side channel attacks [3], and *fault induction attacks* [4]. An invasive physical attack is defined as an attack where the enemy physically breaks into the device by modifying its structure. A non-invasive physical attack is one where the attacker performs physical measurements without modifications to the device's structure. If the memory is not protected, a non-invasive physical attack (*e.g.* optical scrutiny) suffices to read out the memory. If the memory is covered with a protective layer, the attacker may attack invasively, *e.g.* by chemically etching away the layer, drilling a hole, or using a Focused Ion Beam (FIB), and then applying a microprobe. Once an attacker is able to open up a device and investigate its memory (EEPROM, ROM) he can (with reasonable efforts) obtain the keys. One of the main reasons that this readout is possible, originates from the fact that the key is stored in digital form as a string of zeros and ones. Since the state of a physical system representing a zero is distinguishable from the state representing a one, the key bits are observable.

We develop *read-proof* hardware resistant against invasive physical attacks, and non-invasive optical attacks. In order to make read-proof hardware, we build further on the idea of Physical Unclonable Functions introduced in [11] and further extended in [17]. A Physical Unclonable Function consists of a physical object that is inherently unclonable (since it contains many uncontrollable parameters during production). When a stimulus (usually called *challenge*) is applied to the object, it reacts with a *response* that can be measured. This challenge-response behaviour characterizes the structure completely. Furthermore the structure is tamper-evident, meaning that if the structure is physically damaged (by an attack), its challenge-response behaviour changes noticeably. Our solution for read-proof hardware is built on *coating* PUFs which can easily be integrated with an IC. In contrast to the usual setting of PUFs, where it is assumed that there is a huge number of challenge-response pairs, we only require one challenge-response pair. It is clear however how our construction is extended to many challenge-response pairs.

Read-Proof hardware in general and our construction in particular can be applied for secure key storage in Smart-Cards, SIM-Cards, TPMs (Trusted Platform Modules), DRM (Digital Rights Management) systems and in RFID tags [16].

1.1 Model

In our model, we build an IC equipped with read-proof hardware and ordinary memory (ROM or EEPROM). The secret key K of the cryptographic algorithm is extracted from the read-proof hardware only at the point in time when needed. All other required cryptographic components (algorithms, public keys) are stored in tamper-proof hardware and can not be changed by an attacker (but can be read) [1]. The enroller of the IC is considered to be trustworthy. He has a private key sk with which he certifies the data in the IC. The attacker can get hold of the device when it is in the field and can apply physical methods (invasive and non-invasive) to investigate the device and try to retrieve information on the secret key K.

We consider an adversary who has access to optical and invasive methods,

- Optical inspection equipment to look into memory cells (ROM).
- Etching methods (*e.g.* chemical) to remove protective layers.
- Focused Ion Beam to make holes in protective layers and allow for probing (of *e.g.* buses, memory).

1.2 Contributions

We have the following contributions:

- We state the requirements for practical read-proof hardware. Additionally we derive principles to satisfy these requirements. The main idea is not to store a key in digital form in a memory, but to extract it from an unclonable physical structure only at the point in time when needed. In this way the *time* that the *digital* key is present in the device (and hence susceptible to attack) is minimized.
- We describe a Coating PUF in detail (both the physics and the measurement circuit) and argue that it is opaque and chemically inert.
- It is shown how a Coating PUF has to be integrated with an IC and the required cryptographic primitives to meet the abovementioned goals. In particular, we present a new information reconciliation protocol on analog data to derive a unique fingerprint from the coating in a reliable way.
- Experimental evidence is given which shows that protection against invasive attacks is indeed obtained.
- Finally, when the read-proof coating hardware is combined with tamper-proof data and with a self-destruction capability, our solution additionally provides protection against *fault attacks*. This statement is based on the analysis performed in [1].

1.3 Related Work

Since invasive attacks are sometimes performed by carefully removing protective layers of the IC (*e.g.* by etching), the smart-card industry is working on protective

---

[1] In this paper, we do not develop a hardware solution for tamper-proof hardware.

layers and coatings that are difficult to remove (*i.e.* removing the layer implies removing part of the IC, which renders the IC unusable). Additionally, sensors are sometimes built into the IC to check for the presence of the protective layer. If removal is detected, the IC will stop functioning and hence prevent an attacker from learning its secrets through playing games with the device. Although such coatings make life more difficult for the attacker, it turns out that in practice an attacker can often still successfully remove a coating (and possibly fool the sensors) and get access to the ICs interior. This is especially the case when the attacker has access to Focused Ion Beam (FIB) equipment, which makes it possible to reconnect wires in the interior of an IC [20]. The FIB is used to influence the (yes/no) signal that indicates the presence of the protective coating.

A more secure form of protective coatings, which has the potential to protect even against these sophisticated attacks, is the 'active coating' that was first introduced in [13] and further investigated in [14]. Our solution extends this work from the hardware point of view as well as from the cryptographic and design point of view. Additionally, we provide experimental data that show that our coating also provides protection against FIB attacks.

Another technology that is used to protect sensitive information stored in a memory is *memory encryption* [21]. This technology protects information from being exposed to an attacker who gets access to the memory. However, a key is still needed to encrypt and decrypt that information. The problem is then reduced to the secure storage of that secret key.

2   Read-Proof Hardware: Design and Requirements

2.1   Hardware Requirements

In order to protect stored keys against invasive physical attacks, we propose that *no key shall be stored in digital form in the memory of a device*. Since there is no digital key in the memory, it can not be directly attacked. Instead, we propose to generate the key K only at the time when it is needed. The key is extracted from a *tamper evident* physical structure, integrated with the IC, by applying a challenge, measuring the response and carrying out the reconstruction phase of the helper data algorithm. In our case we extract the key from the protective coating, which behaves like a PUF (see Section 3). Additionally, we assume that the device has some memory where the public information (algorithms, public keys) is stored in a tamper proof way. Furthermore it has registers/RAM for storage of the key K at the time when needed. In order to be resistant against physical attacks, such a physical structure has to meet the following requirements:

1. 'Inscrutability' including 'opaqueness'. Measurements (both destructive and non-destructive) must not reveal accurate information about the composition of the physical structure.
2. The structure has to be *unclonable*. This requires two properties.
   - Physical unclonability. It should be hard to make a physical copy, even given accurate knowledge of the structure's composition.

- Mathematical unclonability. It should be hard to construct a mathematical model that has a non-negligible probability of correctly predicting responses, even given accurate knowledge of the structure's composition.
3. The structure has to be tamper evident. Physical damage should significantly change the challenge-response behaviour of the structure.

Additionally, in order to be practically feasible, the following properties are required.

- It has to be easy to challenge the structure and to measure its response.
- It has to be cheap and easy to integrate the structure in an IC.
- From a robustness point of view, it should additionally have excellent mechanical and chemical properties, so that it cannot be detached from the IC (without causing damage to the coating and the IC).

2.2 Required Cryptographic Primitives

As mentioned before, the key is extracted from measurements on the coating. Since measurements on a physical structure are inherently noisy, the responses of such a structure can not be directly used as a secret key. This implies that we need a helper data algorithm/fuzzy extractor [10,8] for reconstruction of the secret keys. A fuzzy extractor consists of a pair of algorithms (G, W) and two phases: an *enrolment* and a *reconstruction* phase. We will use the following notation: x denotes the measurement value of a response during the enrolment phase, while y denotes the corresponding value during the reconstruction phase. During enrolment, the key K is created for the first time. The helper data algorithm $W(.,.)$ is used during the enrolment phase and creates the helper data w based on the measurement value x during enrolment and the randomly chosen key K. The algorithm $G(.,.)$ is used during the key reconstruction phase for reconstruction of the key K as follows: $K = G(y, w)$.

As a second primitive, we need a standard signature scheme SS: $(\text{SK}_g, \text{Sign}, V)$, where SK_g is the secret-key generation algorithm, Sign the signing algorithm and V the verification algorithm. The enroller runs SK_g and obtains a secret-public key pair (sk, pk). (This is a one-time action). The public key pk is hard-wired in each IC (*i.e.* tamper-proof memory). With the secret key sk, the enroller signs the helper data w and $P(K)$ (where P is a one-way function). The signatures $\sigma(w)$ and $\sigma(P(K))$ are then stored [2] in EEPROM memory of the IC together with the helper data w.

2.3 Procedure for Generation and Reconstruction

Creation and reconstruction of the secret key is done as follows. First, the global statistical properties (noise level etc) of the behavior of the physical structure are

---

[2] Instead of storing $\sigma(P(K))$, it is more secure to store $\sigma(P(K), \tilde{x})$ where $\tilde{x}$ is additional unpredictable key material that is obtained from the PUF (if necessary derived from the response of a second challenge). We have chosen not to include this in the notation throughout the paper for the sake of transparency.

determined. In particular, the entropy of the output of the physical structure is estimated and the secrecy capacity $C_S = \mathbf{I}(X; Y)$ (mutual information) of the channel describing the noisy observation is estimated [3]. This can be done using the methods described in [18]. These parameters determine the choice of an appropriate helper data algorithm/fuzzy extractor (G, W).

Enrollment. This phase consists of two steps.

1. Generation of a key $K \in \{0, 1\}^k$ and helper data w by running the enrolment phase of the helper data/Fuzzy Extractor pair (G, W) on the measurement outcome $X : (K, w) \leftarrow \text{Enrollment}(X)$.
2. The IC interprets K as a private key and generates the corresponding public key $P(K)$. Then the IC outputs $(w, P(K))$. The enroller signs these data and stores the signatures $\sigma(w)$, $\sigma(P(K))$ in the IC's EEPROM.[4]

Reconstruction. The IC performs the following steps.

1. It retrieves $w, \sigma(w)$ from EEPROM and checks the signature $\sigma(w)$ by running V on w and $\sigma(w)$. If the signature is not ok, the IC shuts down permanently. Otherwise, it continues.
2. The IC challenges its physical structure and obtains the measurement value y (note that typically $y \neq x$ due to noise).
3. The data w and y are processed by the helper data algorithm G. This yields the key $K' \leftarrow G(y, w)$.
4. The IC computes $P(K')$. Then it runs V on $P(K')$ and $\sigma(P(K))$ using the public key pk. If the signature is ok, the IC proceeds and K can be used as a private key. Otherwise, the IC shuts down permanently.

3   Physical Unclonable Functions

In this section, we describe the physical component of read-proof hardware. Opaque physical systems that are produced by an uncontrollable production process, *i.e.* one that contains uncontrollable randomness, turn out to be good candidates for PUFs.

3.1   Coating PUFs

Coating PUFs are PUFs in the form of a protective coating that covers an IC. The coating consists of a matrix material which is doped with random dielectric particles. By random dielectric particles we mean several kinds of particles of random size, shape and location with a relative dielectric constant ϵ_r differing from the dielectric constant of the coating matrix. This is depicted in Fig. 1.

---

[3] This is a one-time event that is performed during a pre-processing step.

[4] Alternatively, K is used as a symmetric key. The IC outputs K and the enroller stores $\sigma(P(K))$ in the EEPROM. The circuit that outputs K is destroyed after this procedure.

We used a mixture of TiO_2 and TiN particles in a matrix of aluminophosphate. This composition of the coating gives it the following properties. (i) The TiN-particles absorb light (from infrared up to ultraviolet) and hence make the coating opaque. Moreover they are conductive and very hard. (ii) The TiO_2-particles also absorb UV-light. (iii) The aluminophosphate matrix is very hard and chemically relatively inert. From this material the coating gets its protection against chemical substances. We note that the coating can be easily sprayed on top of the IC.

The top metal layer of the IC contains an array of sensors that are used to measure the local capacitance values of the coating. An example of a comb-shaped sensor structure is depicted in Fig. 2. Sufficient randomness in the measured capacitance values is obtained only if the dielectric particles are not much bigger than the distance between the sensor parts. The measurement circuit is integrated on the IC, so the measurements are done from within the IC. The measured capacitance values form the responses of this system and are protected against inspection from outside by the coating. Measuring the Coating PUF from the outside gives different capacitance results since the measurements are very sensitive to the precise locations of the dielectric particles. It is derived from the entropy formula in [5], that a coating PUF contains 6.6 bits of entropy per sensor.

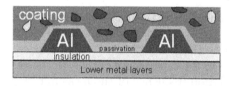

Fig. 1. Schematic cross-section of a Coating PUF IC. The upper metal layer contains aluminium sensor structures (Al) that are used to measure the local capacitance of the coating.

Fig. 2. Top-view microscope image of a single comb-shaped sensor structure (aluminum) in the top metal layer of the IC

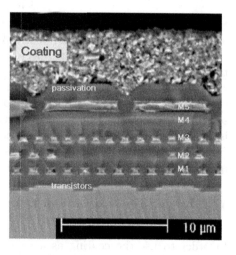

Fig. 3. Cross-sectional microscope image of a coating PUF IC. The sensors are located in metal layer 5 (M5).

4 Robust Fingerprint Extraction: Information Reconciliation

In this section, we describe the algorithmic part of our architecture. In order to derive secure keys from a physical source two steps are typically needed:

Information Reconciliation and Privacy Amplification. The Information Reconciliation phase is basically an error correction step. The Privacy Amplification step guarantees that the extracted key is highly secure [6]. In this Section, we focus on the Information Reconciliation procedure. Since the capacitances obtained from a measurement are analog values we present an Information Reconciliation protocol for the analog case. This leads to a unique digital fingerprint that characterizes the coating.

4.1   Measurement Method

We have developed an on-chip measurement circuit that measures capacitance values at several sensors. The measurement principle is based on a period-modulated oscillator circuit, similar to Smartec's commercially available Universal Transducer Interface (UTI) [15], in which the oscillating frequency depends on the capacity at the sensor. A multiplexer circuit allows for the selection of one of several sensors. In order to derive measurement results that are insensitive to temperature and supply voltage variations, a 'three signal technique' is used (see also [15]). Based on this technique, we calculate a relative capacitance value at sensor i as follows:

$$\frac{C_i - C_0}{C_{\text{ref}} - C_0}. \tag{1}$$

Here, C_i with $i = 1, \ldots, M$, is a counter value that corresponds to the number of clock cycles that has occurred within 1024 oscillations of the measurement circuit when the i-th sensor is selected (note that M is the number of capacitance sensors). This counter value is related to the capacitance of the i-th sensor since this capacitance determines the oscillation frequency of the measurement circuit. The value C_0 is a reference counter value that is measured when no sensor is connected to the measurement circuit. Hence, the difference $C_i - C_0$ is proportional to the capacitance of the coating directly above the i-th sensor. The C_{ref} is a counter value from a (pre-defined) reference sensor. By taking the quotient (1) we remove temperature and voltage fluctuations.

4.2   Fingerprint Extraction: Information Reconciliation on Analog Data

In order to use the coating as a source of cryptographic keys, we start with an information reconciliation phase to derive a unique fingerprint $K \in \{0,1\}^k$ from the noisy measurements of the coating. In order to extract highly secure keys, it is advantageous to have the distribution of those fingerprints as close to the uniform random distribution on $\{0,1\}^k$ as possible. In order to extract noise-robust and highly random fingerprints at the same time from the analog coating measurements, we first apply a histogram equalisation to the analog data, making the distribution almost uniform. Then, the 'helper data' are defined in the transformed domain.

Notation and Assumptions. We define the i.i.d. real stochastic variables $F_i := C_i - C_0$ and $F_{\text{ref}} := C_{\text{ref}} - C_0$, which are a property of the coating alone. Numerical instances of F_i are denoted as f_i.

The randomized manufacturing process of the coating gives rise to a probability distribution $\rho(F_i)$ for a capacitance value F_i at location i. Note that ρ is the 'true' capacitance distribution, *i.e.* without any noise. We incorporate temperature effects by postulating that F_i represents the true capacitance at a fixed reference temperature T_0. For any different temperature T, the capacitance changes to $F_i \cdot m(T)$, where m is a function satisfying $m(T_0) = 1$.

The distribution ρ has an average μ and a standard deviation σ. We assume that ρ is public knowledge and hence available to attackers. In order to equalize the distribution ρ, we define the cumulative distribution function q as

$$q(f) = \int_0^f \mathrm{d}x \rho(x). \tag{2}$$

Note that the stochastic variable $q(F) \in [0, 1]$ is uniformly distributed. A noisy capacitance measurement at temperature T and location i results in a stochastic variable F_i', $F_i' = F_i m(T) + N_i$, where the noise N_i is independent of T, i and F_i and also independent of previous measurements. We assume that N_i is gaussian with zero mean and fixed variance $\sigma_N \ll \mu$.

In order to deal with the noise, we define quantisation intervals as follows. The f-axis is divided into L equiprobable parts with boundaries at t_j, $j = 0, \ldots, L$. The boundaries are placed according to $t_j = q^{-1}(j/L)$. Here q^{-1} is the inverse function of q.

Enrolment. Enrolment occurs under tightly controlled circumstances. The temperature is T_0. For each IC the following steps are performed.

- The capacitance values f_i for $i = 1, \ldots, M$ and f_{ref} are measured. The value f_{ref} is stored in the IC for later use as a normalising factor.
- For each capacitance f_i ($i = 1, \ldots, M$) the quantised value $I_i \in \{0, \ldots, L-1\}$ is determined, $I_i = \lfloor L\, q(f_i) \rfloor$.
- Helper data W_i is computed as follows, $W_i = I_i + 1/2 - Lq(f_i)$. The helper data $\{W_i\}$ is stored in the EEPROM of the IC.
- From the set $\{I_i\}$ a codeword in an error-correcting code is created as follows. We will assume that L has the form $L = 2^a$. In this case it is advantageous to assign to each quantised value $I_i \in \{0, \ldots, L-1\}$ a code word from a binary Gray code. The Gray code has the nice property that the Hamming distance between two neighbouring code words equals one. In this way a measurement error $I_i' = I_i \pm 1$ has the effect of flipping only a single bit in the code word. By concatenating the Gray codes from all the sensors a string X is obtained of length $n = M \log L$. A secret $K \in \{0,1\}^k$ is randomly generated. Then, using the 'XOR-trick' as described in [9,16] a codeword $c_K \in \{0,1\}^n$ of an error-correcting code $\mathcal{C}$ is computed. Further helper data w called 'conversion data' are derived that map X onto c_K. The conversion data w are stored in the IC's EEPROM.

– The total set of helper data that has to be signed and stored in EEPROM is given by, $(\{W_i\}, w, f_{ref})$.

Key Reconstruction. At a later time, the IC reconstructs the key from noisy capacitance measurements combined with the enrolment/helper data. The temperature is not controlled.

– The IC measures noisy values f_i', $i = 1, \ldots, M$ and f_{ref}' and looks up the values f_{ref}, $\{W_i\}$ and w from memory.
– For each $i = 1, \ldots, M$ the IC computes a reconstruction of I_i as follows,

$$I_i' = \left\lfloor Lq(f_{ref}\frac{f_i'}{f_{ref}'}) + W_i \right\rfloor . \tag{3}$$

– From the values I_i' the IC constructs a string Y by concatenating Gray codes in the same way as was done during enrolment. Then it applies the mapping w to Y. Finally it performs the decoding step of the 'XOR-trick' (for details see the extended version). This yields the secret key K, provided that the number of measurement errors does not exceed the correction capacity of the error-correcting code $\mathcal{C}$.

Properties of the Method. The helper data method described above has the following properties (for details we refer the reader to the extended version of this paper).

– The noise in I_i' is linear in L, leading to a practical bound on the number of quantization intervals. To reduce the probability p_E of a quantization error to 10%, we need $L < 8.8$ in our experimental ICs.
– The maximum length of a secret key extracted from the coating is $M \log L \cdot [1 - h(p_E)]$.
– As long as the attacker does not have better knowledge of ρ than the manufacturer, the helper data $\{W_i\}$ do not leak any information about the key K.

5   Experimental Results

We have produced a batch of ICs containing the coating and the measurement circuit of Section 3. The top metal layer of the IC contains 31 sensor structures. Each sensor structure has a capacitor area of $120 \times 120 \ \mu m^2$. The top of the ICs is covered with a coating. The coating consists of a mono-aluminum phosphate matrix that is doped with TiN and TiO_2 particles.

5.1   Capacitance Measurements

We have measured the capacitances from 36 different ICs. On each IC, one of the 31 sensors is used as a reference sensor which leads to the value C_{ref}. The C_0 value comes from an internal measurement in which the measurement circuit is not connected to a sensor. The measurements at the 30 remaining sensors form the C_i values. We compute the stabilized capacitance value B_i of sensor i as follows:

$$B_i = f_{\text{ref}} \frac{f'_i - (\frac{1}{M} \sum_{i=1}^{M} f'_i)}{f'_{\text{ref}}} \tag{4}$$

Note that this method differs slightly from Eq. (1). In Eq. (4) we subtract the average of f'_i over the IC in order to compensate for unwanted coating thickness variations that are caused by the manufacturing process.

Fig. 4 shows the B_i measurements [5] of 30 sensors, measured at 6 different ICs. In the extended version of the paper, we show the influence of temperature variations on the values of f'_i and B_i.

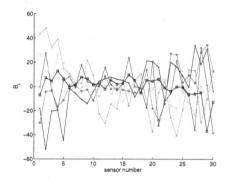

Fig. 4. Measured stabilized capacitance values B_i at 30 sensors of 6 different ICs

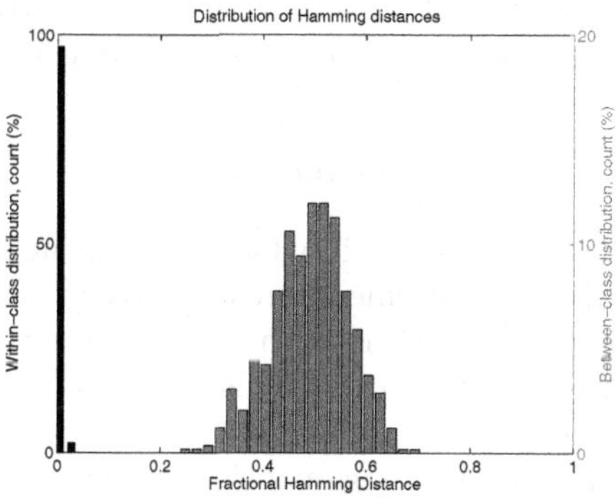

Fig. 5. Histogram of fractional hamming distances between fingerprints derived from the same IC (within class) and between fingerprints derived from different ICs (between-class)

The capacitance measurements show an average within class standard deviation of of $\sigma_N = 0.97$ and an average between class standard deviation of $\sigma_{B_i} = 18.8$. In our practical setup we derive 3 bits per sensor, which gives the best results w.r.t. robustness.

5.2   Fingerprints

By way of example, we show key extraction from our experimental data according to the method of Section 4.2 . First the distribution ρ was estimated empirically by measuring all 30 sensors on 36 ICs. The interval $q(f) \in [0,1]$ was divided into $L = 2^3 = 8$ intervals. We used a Gray code to make a 3-bit encoding of

---

[5] Note that B_i is dimensionless since f_i is the difference between two counter values (see section 4.1). Measurements of similar coating and sensor structures with a Hewlett Packard 4192 impedance analyzer show that the average capacitance value is around 0.18 pF (*i.e.* corresponding to $B_i = 0$ in Fig. 4).

each integer I_i. In this way we derived fingerprints of 90 bits. Histograms of the fractional Hamming distances between the extracted fingerprints for both the within- and between-class distribution are shown in Fig. 5. The between-class distribution is centered around a fractional Hamming distance of 0.5, which means that the fingerprints derived from 2 different ICs will on average differ in 50% of the bits.

It turns out that bit strings derived from the same IC (within-class distribution) have fewer than 4 errors. Hence, an error-correcting code that corrects 4/90 of all bits is suitable in this case. Using an optimal error correcting code (*i.e.* one that achieves maximal key length), one would get a key length of approximately $k = 66.4$ bits. In practice one can *e.g.* use a BCH code which turns 63 bits of the 90 into a key of 45 bits. The remaining bits can be turned into additional key material with a second error-correcting code. The practical choice of the error-correcting code has to be optimized. This is not the subject of this paper.

5.3   Attack Detection

Physical attacks in which the coating is damaged are detected from the capacitance measurements. A well-known method for getting access to internal circuit lines of an IC, is by making a hole through the IC with a Focused Ion Beam (FIB). Afterwards the hole is filled with metal such that a surface contact is created. This can be used by the attacker for easy access to an internal line (*e.g.* for eavesdropping on a signal). In Section 5.3, we show the effect of a FIB attack with gallium particles.

A FIB was used to create two holes in one of the Coating PUF ICs by shooting gallium particles on two areas of size $100\mu m$ x $100\mu m$ and depth of around $1.5\mu m$ in a coating of thickness $6\mu m$, see Fig. 6.

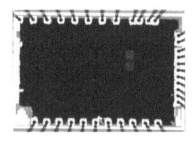

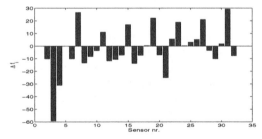

Fig. 6. Top view of a Coating PUF IC in which two holes have been shot with a Gallium FIB

Fig. 7. Differences in capacitance f_i' between measurements of Coating PUF IC 89 before and after the Gallium FIB attack

Fig. 7 shows the effect of the FIB attack on the measured capacitances f_i'. After the FIB attack, several sensors measure a significant change in capacitance value. This is due to the fact that ions are implanted into the coating, which

Table 1. Change of capacitance measured by the sensor lying under the area of impact of the beam

Beam type	Hit area	Depth	Δf
Gallium	$100\mu m$ x $100\mu m$	$1.5\mu m$	-40
Gallium	$15\mu m$ x $15\mu m$	$4\mu m$	-34
Argon	$100\mu m$ x $100\mu m$	$1.5\mu m$	-28

changes its behaviour non-locally. The derived fingerprint after the FIB attack differs in 14 of the 90 bits. Table 1 summarizes the direct effect of Gallium FIB and Argon beam attacks on a single sensor.

6 Security of the Coating: Experimental Evidence

Since the coating is opaque, optically looking into the digital memory is very hard without damaging the coating. Furthermore, since the coating is tough and chemically inert, it is very hard to remove mechanically or chemically. Next, we discuss some more advanced attacks and show the resistance of the coating against these attacks.

6.1 Impact of FIB Attack on the Keys

We discuss an attack, where the attacker first uses a FIB to make a hole in the coating. Then, he makes the IC start the key reconstruction phase described in Section 2.3. During the reconstruction phase, he uses his micro-probe(s) to retrieve the key bits. We denote the measurement values after the FIB-attack by a random variable Z and the key extracted after the FIB-attack by K'. During step 4 of the reconstruction phase, the IC checks whether the extracted key K' is correct by running the algorithm V on $P(K')$ and $\sigma(P(K))$. If the signature is not ok, the device is destructed. Hence, the attacker gets the information that the extracted key K' is incorrect. We assume furthermore that the attacker can capture the noisy measurement Z by using his microprobe [6] (note that this is a worst case assumption). It is natural to investigate how much uncertainty there still remains about the original key K.

In the extended version, we construct a model that represents the FIB damage as an additional bit error rate ϵ on top of the already present bit error rate α due to measurement noise, with $\epsilon > \alpha$. This effectively leads to a noisy channel $X \to Z$ with combined error rate $\chi = \alpha(1 - \epsilon) + \epsilon(1 - \alpha)$ as seen by the attacker. The amount of uncertainty he has about K can be expressed as a number N_c of 'candidate' keys, which turns out to be of order

$$N_c = \mathcal{O}\left(2^{n(h(\chi) - h(R\alpha))}\right),\tag{5}$$

---

[6] Since he also gets the helper data w from the ROM, this implies that he can reconstruct K'.

where R is a constant larger than 1 and the function h is defined as $h(p) = -p \log p - (1-p) \log(1-p)$. With the ICs that we have, the parameters α, $R\alpha$ are given by $\alpha = 1/30$, $R\alpha = 4/90$. The values for ϵ range from $\epsilon = 8/90$ to $\epsilon = 14/90$. Therefore we take an average value $\epsilon = 11/90$. In practice one would like to have a key of length 128 bits. Given these error rates that would require $n = 174$ (then $\mathbf{I}(X;Y) = 128$). Substituting this value of n into Eq. (5), we obtain $N_c = 2^{51}$.

7   Conclusions and Future Work

In this paper we have given an implementation of read-proof hardware. The main idea is: "thou shalt not store secret keys in digital memory". The key should be derived from a protective coating containing a lot of randomness. The key is obtained from capacitance measurements on the coating. In order to extract the key from the measurement values, we have developed a secure helper data algorithm that is implemented on the IC. We have provided experimental evidence that our construction is secure against invasive physical attacks such as attacks with a Focused Ion Beam.

One of the main open questions that remains is the resistance of this construction against side-channel attacks. In order to thwart those attacks, the cryptographic part has to be implemented in a side channel resistant way (which can be done with existing methods). Currently, it is being investigated whether the measurement circuit itself is susceptible to side-channel attacks such as Electromagnetic Analysis, Power Analysis and Timing analysis. Although no leakage has been reported yet, countermeasures against leakage of the measurement circuit are being considered.

Another open question is to investigate whether this technique can also be applied at the back of the IC to provide protection against backside attacks.

References

1. R. Gennaro, A. Lysyanskaya, T. Malkin, S. Micali and T. Rabin, *Algorithmic Tamper-Proof Security: Theoretical Foundations for Security against Hardware Tampering*, In Theory of Cryptography, First Theory of Cryptography Conference, TCC 2004, Cambridge, MA, USA, February 19-21, volume 2951 of LNCS, pages 258-277, Springer-Verlag.
2. R. Anderson and M. Kuhn, *Low Cost Attacks on Tamper Resistant Devices*, In M. Lemmas et al., editor, Proceedinggs of Security Protocols, 5th International Workshop, volume 1361 of Lecture Notes in Computer Science, pages 125-136, Paris, France, April 1997, Springer-Verlag.
3. P.C. Kocher, J. Jaffe, B. Jun, *Differential Power Analysis*, Proceedings of the 19th International Conference on Cryptology, Advances in Cryptology, volume 1666 of LNCS, pages 388-397, 1999, Springer Verlag.
4. E. Biham and A. Shamir, *Differential Fault Analysis of Secret Key Crypto Systems* Advances in Cryptology, Crypto 97.

5. B. Škorić, S. Maubach, T. Kevenaar, P. Tuyls, *Information-theoretic analysis of coating PUFs*, http://eprint.iacr.org/2006/101, accepted for publication in the Journal of Applied Physics.
6. C.H. Bennett, G. Brassard, C. Crepeau, and U. Maurer, *Generalized Privacy Amplification*, In IEEE Transactions on Information Theory, vol 41, 6, pages 1915-1923, 1995.
7. H. Bar-El, *Known Attacks Against Smartcards*, Discretix Technologies Ltd. http://www.infosecwriters.com/text_resources/pdf/Known_Attacks_Against_Smartcards.pdf
8. Y. Dodis and M. Reyzin and A. Smith, *Fuzzy Extractors: How to generate strong keys from biometrics and other noisy data*, In C. Cachin and J. Camenisch Editors, Proceedings of Eurocrypt 2004, volume 3027 of Lecture Notes in Computer Science, pages 523-540, Springer-Verlag
9. A. Juels and M. Wattenberg, *A fuzzy commitment scheme*, 6th ACM Conference on Computer and Communication Security, pp.28-36, 1999.
10. J.P. Linnartz, P. Tuyls, *New Shielding Functions to Enhance Privacy and Prevent Misuse of Biometric Templates*, AVBPA 2003, LNCS 2688, pp.393-402.
11. R. Pappu, *Physical One-way functions*, Ph.D. thesis, MIT, 2001.
12. R. Pappu, B. Recht, J. Taylor, N. Gershenfeld, *Physical One-way functions*, Science Vol.297, 2002, pp.2026-2030.
13. R. Posch, *Protecting Devices by Active Coating*, Journal of Universal Computer Science, vol.4 no.7, 1998.
14. G.A. Kamendje, R. Posch, *Intrusion aware CMOS Random Pattern Generator for Cryptographic Applications*, In Peter Rossler and Andreas Dorderlein Editors, Proceedings of Austrochip 2001, Vienna, Austria, 12 October 2001 ISBN 3-9501517-0-2.
15. Smartec, *Universal Transducer Interface evaluation board*, Specifications v3.0, http://www.smartec.nl/pdf/Dsuti.pdf .
16. P. Tuyls, L. Batina, *RFID tags for Anti-Counterfeiting*, RSA 2006 conference, San Jose, USA, Feb. 13-17, 2006.
17. P. Tuyls, B. Škorić, *Secret Key Generation from Classical Physics*, In Mukherjee et al. editors, AmIware, Hardware Technology Drivers of Ambient Intelligence, Philips Research Book Series, Kluwer, pages, 421-447,2005.
18. T. Ignatenko, G.J. Schrijen, B. Škorić, P. Tuyls, F. Willems, *Estimating the Secrecy-Rate of Physical Uncloneable Functions with the Context-Tree Weighting Method*, accepted at ISIT 2006
19. M. Witteman, *Smart card security analysis*, IPA Spring Days on Security, Kapellerput, Heeze, April 18-20, 2001. http://www.win.tue.nl/ipa/archive/springdays2001/witteman.ppt
20. M. Witteman, *Advances in Smartcard Security*, Information Security Bulletin, July 2002, pp.11-22. http://www.riscure.com/articles/ISB0707MW.pdf
21. J. Yang, L. Gao, Y. Zhang, *Improving Memory Encryption Performance in Secure Processors*, IEEE. Trans. Computers, vol 53, 5, 1-11, 2005.

Path Swapping Method to Improve DPA Resistance of Quasi Delay Insensitive Asynchronous Circuits

Fraidy Bouesse, Gilles Sicard, and Marc Renaudin

TIMA Laboratory, 46 avenue Félix Viallet F38031 Grenoble, France
Fraidy.Bouesse@imag.fr

Abstract. This paper presents a Path Swapping (PS) method which enables to enhance the security of Quasi Delay Insensitive Asynchronous Circuits against Power Analysis (PA) attack. This approach exploits the logical symmetries of the QDI asynchronous blocks, particularly its data-path redundancies, to make all electrical curves used when implementing a PA attacks useless. Indeed, the idea is to average the electrical signatures of a block by randomly exchanging its data-paths during processing. To be able to implement this approach, we adopted a formal model of QDI circuits. Firstly, this formal model enables the designer to formally verify the symmetry of all paths in order to apply a path swapping method. Secondly, it offers the possibility to model the electrical signature of QDI asynchronous circuits. Finally, applying DPA on this formal model allows us to evaluate, in an early phase of the design, the circuit's sensitivity to the relevancy of the approach. Electrical simulations performed on a DES crypto-processor confirm the efficiency of the technique.

Keywords: QDI Asynchronous circuits, Power analysis, Path Swapping (PS).

1 Introduction

One of the most difficult task when designing secure systems is to protect devices from so-called side-channel attacks such as power analysis attacks (DPA, SPA), electromagnetic attacks, timing attacks and differential fault analysis. Since the discovery of these attacks, self-timed circuits have demonstrated their inherent capabilities to increase the security of chips. In fact, the Differential Power Analysis attack, firstly introduced by Paul Kocher [1], uses the correlation between the data processed by the circuitry and an observable power consumption to reveal the confidential information. Secret keys are retraced from the device by observing and monitoring the electrical activity of a device and performing advanced statistical computations.

Additionally to its absence of clock signal which demonstrates the practical way to eliminate a global synchronization signal, self-timed logic is well-known for its ability to decrease the consumption and smooth the current profile. Simon Moore et al. described in [2] techniques for improving chip security against side channel attacks. Their approach to improve chip DPA resistance is focused on the use of an alternative data encoding scheme such as one-hot data encoding (*1-of-N* codes). In the same design context, the Balsa synthesis system was modified to generate circuits with enhanced security against side-channel attacks [3]. The countermeasures that

L. Goubin and M. Matsui (Eds.): CHES 2006, LNCS 4249, pp. 384–398, 2006.

used Self-timed circuit properties are all focused on balancing the operation through special DI Coding scheme. Moreover, Paul Kocher also developed some countermeasures based on the same properties [4], and a new design concept has been presented in [5] by Danil Sokolov et al. who used standard dual-rail logic with a two spacer protocol working in a synchronous environment. The results obtained by exploiting Self-timed logic have been reported in several papers. J. Fournier et al. evaluated and demonstrated in [6] that Speed Independent asynchronous circuits increase resistance against side channel attack and the concrete results of the effectiveness of the QDI asynchronous logic against DPA has been reported in [7].

However, all these papers concluded in terms of DPA that there still exists some residual sources of leakage which can be used to succeed an attack. These residual sources of leakage that are still observable when implementing a DPA attack on balanced QDI asynchronous circuits are addressed by G.F. Bouesse et al. in paper [8]. They show that, the residual sources of leakage of a balanced QDI circuits come from the back end steps which introduce some electrical dissymmetries, especially through the routing capacitances. The solutions implemented in paper [8] and also mentioned in paper [2] in order to remove electrical dissymmetries, consist in constraining the placement and routing. They defined a place and route methodology which enables the designer to control the net capacitances. Contrary to the previous proposed countermeasures mentioned above, the approach described in this paper does not try to get rid of these residual sources of leakage, but instead makes it not exploitable by the DPA attack.

The PS (path swapping) method takes advantage of the structural symmetries that exist in QDI asynchronous circuits or those proposed in [2][3]. In fact, in such circuits many identical structures called paths exist that can be alternatively used to compute a given function. Therefore, the idea is to randomly choose one of the possible paths to compute the function which hence averages the electrical signature over all the paths. The issue lies in succeeding to do so with minimum overhead.

The paper is organized as follows. Section 2 recalls the asynchronous properties that are used to increase DPA resistance, especially the N-rail Quasi Delay Insensitive asynchronous logic together with the four-phase protocol. Section 3 introduces the path swapping technique and section 4 presents the formal approach chosen to implement this technique. The specification of the formal model adopted to represent the circuits is first described, and then formal DPA resistance criteria at logical and electrical levels are defined using this circuit model. It enables us to formally justify the path swapping technique. The approach is validated with the case study described in section 5 and results obtained using electrical simulations are reported in section 6. Section 7 concludes the paper.

2 Previous Works: QDI Circuits and Security

QDI asynchronous circuits represent a class of circuits controlled by the data themselves. In fact, an asynchronous circuit is composed of individual modules communicating to each other by means of point-to-point communication channels. Therefore, a given module becomes active when it senses the presence of incoming data. It then computes them and sends the result to the output channels. Communications through channels are governed by a handshaking protocol which requires a bi-directional signalling between senders and receivers (request and acknowledge). Among the main classes of handshaking protocols [9] we only consider and describe the four-phase protocol (fig.1) which has an interest in security.

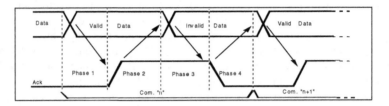

Fig. 1. Four-phase handshaking protocol

The four-phase protocol protocol requires a return to zero phase for both data/requests and acknowledgements. Contrary to synchronous circuits where the shape of the current (current peaks) depends on the previous states and data values, QDI asynchronous logic using a four-phase protocol re-initializes all previously activated nodes before processing a new data. This behaviour enables the designer to precisely control the transitions involved in a given computation. Moreover, because it is based on hazard free logic QDI asynchronous circuits eliminate all current variations caused by glitches.

The implementation of a four-phase handshaking protocol requires sensing the presence of data in phase 1 and their absence in phase 3. In order to do so, dedicated logic and special encoding are necessary for sensing data validity/invalidity and for generating the acknowledgement signal. Considering that one bit has to be transferred through a channel using the four phase protocol, one has to encode three different values: invalid, valid at '1', valid at '0'. Two wires (A0, A1) are then required to encode the three states. This technique is called dual-rail encoding. The acknowledgement signal is generated by taking advantage of the data-encoding. As depicted in figure 2, a Nor gate is usually used to sense the dual-rail encoding output for generating the completion signal.

Dual-rail encoding is easily extended to N-rails. It is called *1-of-N* encoding. This encoding data scheme is useful to reduce the number of electrical transitions involved in a given computation. For the sake of DPA resistance, *1-of-N* encoding ensures that the same number of transitions is required to encode the values *0* to *N-1* and guarantees a constant Hamming weight.

As an example, consider the xor function. Figure 2 shows a dual-rail xor gate implementation. All computations of this dual-rail xor gate involve a fixed and constant number of transitions regardless of the input data. Hence, the opportunity to have data independent power consumption i.e. not correlated to the processed data seems achievable and this is exactly the goal pursued.

However, the QDI implementation of a function is not always balanced. In such cases, the gate structure is modified to ensure that all data-paths and control paths can be balanced and do involve a constant number of transitions [2].

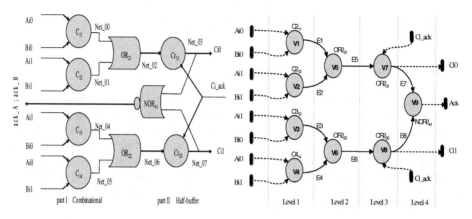

Fig. 2. Dual-rail gate with four-phase protocol (Cr = Muller gate with a reset)

Fig. 3. Annotated directed graph $G_{Xor}=(V,E)$ of the Dual-rail Xor gate of fig.2

To summarize, the use of QDI logic together with a four-phase protocol and *1-of-N* data encoding enables:

o   to control the current by removing all spurious transitions (hazard free logic).
o   to equalize the number of transitions using a constant hamming weight representation of data.
o   to control the type of all transitions.
o   to reduce the dependence between data and power consumption using symmetrical structures of data and control paths.

As described in [2][4] all these properties are suited to implement secure chips against DPA. The design methodology developed in this paper is based on these properties of QDI asynchronous logic, particularly the data path symmetries. They are exploited to randomly average electrical signatures so that the electrical dissymmetries described in [8] and amplified after the back end steps become useless. We now analyse this point by introducing the path swapping method.

3   Contribution: Path Swapping Method

The goal of this new design approach is to eliminate the electrical effects which enable to succeed the DPA attack on QDI circuits. To do so, we do exploit the circuit structure which exhibits a lot of symmetries. Indeed, in the blocks of such circuits there exist many identical physical paths from their primary inputs to their primary outputs. The idea is to randomly choose one of the possible paths to compute the function. More formally, let's define n_c as the number of output channels using *1-of-N* data encoding. Each output channel i has N rails. We can represent the logical equation of each rail by $f_{ij}(A_x)$ and its dynamic current profile by $P_{ij}(t/A_x)$ when the input value A_x is computed. The value A_x is one element of E_i, the set of all possible input values which activate the channel i. The indexes i and j identify the channel number and the rail number respectively. For each rail there is a data-path from the primary output rail considered to the primary inputs (N data-paths).

If all data-paths are logically symmetric, it means that:

$$\forall \; A_x \in E_i \quad \Rightarrow \quad f_{i1}(A_x) = ... = f_{iN}(A_x)$$

$$and \quad P_{i1}(t \,/\, A_x) \neq ... \neq P_{iN}(t \,/\, A_x) \tag{1}$$

This equation (1) shows that for any input value A_x of a QDI asynchronous block we can acquire N different electrical signatures, corresponding to the same computed logical function. The principle of this new design method is to randomly choose among the possible f_{ij} functions and therefore their corresponding electrical signatures in order to make the DPA attack inefficient. To illustrate this, let's now consider the simple xor function and the implementation depicted in figure 2. First, note that this circuit is balanced in the sense that the computation of the xor function always involves the same switching sequence of gates.

$$gate\;C \rightarrow gate\;Or \rightarrow gate\;C_r \rightarrow gate\;Nor$$

Besides, the structure is symmetric in the sense that there exist two identical logical paths between the outputs and the primary inputs.

- first data path :   - second data path :

$$\left.\begin{array}{l} gate\;C_{11} \\ gate\;C_{12} \end{array}\right\} \rightarrow gate\;Or_{21} \rightarrow gate\;Cr_{31} \qquad\qquad \left.\begin{array}{l} gate\;C_{13} \\ gate\;C_{14} \end{array}\right\} \rightarrow gate\;Or_{22} \rightarrow gate\;Cr_{32}$$

Moreover, each path can be split into two execution-paths which represent an exclusive path that can be used to process a rail.

* execution - paths of the first output rail   * execution - paths of the second output rail

- gate C_{11} → gate Or_{21} → gate Cr_{31} - gate C_{13} → gate Or_{22} → gate Cr_{32}

- gate C_{12} → gate Or_{21} → gate Cr_{31} - gate C_{14} → gate Or_{22} → gate Cr_{32}

Therefore, as shown in figure 4, different sets of inputs and outputs can be applied in such a structure. For the sake of DPA resistance, it is worthwhile to observe that for constant values at the inputs four different electrical signatures can be obtained using inputs and outputs permutations. We call this method path swapping because interchanging the inputs and/or outputs leads to swap the execution from logical paths to other logical paths inside the circuit.The realization of this technique requires the use of multiplexers/demultiplexers and a random number generator (RNG). Multiplexers/Demultiplexers are used to permute inputs/outputs and are controlled by the random number generator. The use of a random number generator guarantees an equiprobable and unpredictable distribution function of inputs/outputs. Considering the example illustrated in figure 5, if M data have to be computed, the random number generator must ensure to randomly activate each execution-path $M/4$ times. The specifications of the random number generator and of the Multiplexers/ Demultiplexers blocks are addressed in section 4.6. The path swapping method can only be efficiently implemented with design logic which offers an opportunity to implement symmetrical and balanced circuits as it is the case with QDI asynchronous circuits. This type of logic enables to implement the PS method with a minimum area overhead and by slightly changing the performance of the circuit.

To apply this technique to QDI asynchronous circuits, we have specified a formal design approach which enables us to formally verify the symmetry of the circuit and formally verify at each design level the relevancy of the path swapping approach. This design approach is based on a formal representation of QDI circuits.

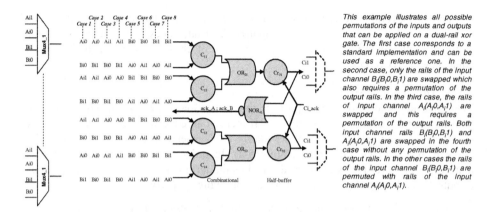

This example illustrates all possible permutations of the inputs and outputs that can be applied on a dual-rail xor gate. The first case corresponds to a standard implementation and can be used as a reference one. In the second case, only the rails of the input channel $B_i(B_i0,B_i1)$ are swapped which also requires a permutation of the output rails. In the third case, the rails of input channel $A_i(A_i0,A_i1)$ are swapped and this requires a permutation of the output rails. Both input channel rails $B_i(B_i0,B_i1)$ and $A_i(A_i0,A_i1)$ are swapped in the fourth case without any permutation of the output rails. In the other cases the rails of the input channel $B_i(B_i0,B_i1)$ are permuted with rails of the input channel $A_i(A_i0,A_i1)$.

Fig. 4. Path Swapping method applied to the Dual-rail Xor gate

4 Formal Model of QDI Asynchronous Circuits

The formal model we have adopted to automate and verify at each design phase all QDI properties described above is based on the digraph (directed graph) theory.

4.1 Digraph of QDI Asynchronous Circuits

A digraph is a graph in which the edges are directed from the initial vertex *(a)* to the terminal vertex *(b)*. If $G=(V,E)$ is a digraph, then V and E are respectively the set of vertices and the set of edges of the digraph G. For the purpose of representing the QDI asynchronous circuits as a digraph, we define the two following rules:

* *All gates of the circuit are considered as the elements of the set V (vertices).*
* *All interconnections are considered as the elements of the set E (directed edges).*

For example let's consider the block of figure 2. Its representation in the form of a digraph $G_{Xor}=(V,E)$ is presented in figure 3. Each vertex (V_i) and directed edge E_i are respectively annotated by the name of the corresponding gate and interconnection. All dotted lines represent primary inputs and outputs of the block.

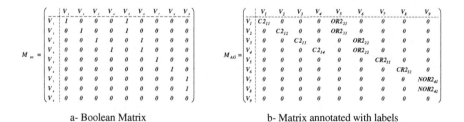

a- Boolean Matrix   b- Matrix annotated with labels

Fig. 5. Matrix of the digraph $G_{Xor}=(V,E)$

There are several different ways to represent a graph. The two common ways are as an adjacency list or as an adjacency matrix. The adjacency list is appropriate for software implementations. However, for the sake of clarity, we use in this paper an adjacency matrix representation.

4.1.1 Adjacency Matrix

The adjacency matrix of a digraph G is the n-by-n matrix $(M_G(n,n))$ where n is the total number of vertices of the graph G. If there is an edge from vertex (a) to vertex (b), then the element $((a),(b))$ of the matrix is 1, otherwise it is 0. It is called the boolean matrix of G $(M_{BG}(n,n))$ (figure 5-a). In order to represent in the Boolean matrix the input vertices which are defined as the terminal vertices of all input edges (inputs dotted lines in fig. 3), we define the following property:

> * For any element (a) of the set V, if ((a),(a))=1, then the vertex (a) is considered as an input vertex.

From this boolean matrix of the digraph G, we can associate an annotated matrix $(M_{AG}(n,n))$ of the annotated digraph G, where the directed edge between vertex (a) and vertex (b) are represented by the name of the terminal vertex as illustrated in figure 5-b. The number of elements in each row "i" gives the number of elements connected to a vertex (V_i) and the number of elements in each column "j" gives the number of inputs of the vertex (V_j), except for the output vertices. In fact, output vertices which generate the output signals are differently labelled in the matrix (in bold) in order to facilitate their identification. This makes easier finding the sub digraphs which compute each output rail of the block, and then to evaluate their data-path symmetries.

4.2 Logical Symmetry of Data-Paths

The data-path symmetries are analyzed by extracting in the digraph all subdigraphs that generate each output rail. This extraction is done by the exploration of the matrix of the block. The exploration starts by the identification of all output vertices, then collecting for each identified vertex, all its ascendant vertices. Each vertex output is then considered as an anti-root of the tree towards which directed edges are oriented. Let's consider the matrix of the digraph of figure 5-b. The matrix of the subdigraph $G_{Ci0}=(V_{Ci0},E_{Ci0})$ of rail $Ci0$ and the matrix of the subdigraph $G_{Ci1}=(V_{Ci1},E_{Ci1})$ of rail $Co1$ are presented in figure 6.

$$
M_{AGC\alpha} =
\begin{pmatrix}
 & V_3 & V_4 & V_6 & V_8 \\
\hline
V_3 & C2_{13} & 0 & OR2_{22} & 0 \\
V_4 & 0 & C2_{14} & OR2_{22} & 0 \\
V_6 & 0 & 0 & 0 & CR2_{32} \\
V_8 & 0 & 0 & 0 & 0
\end{pmatrix}
\qquad
M_{AGC00} =
\begin{pmatrix}
 & V_1 & V_2 & V_5 & V_7 \\
\hline
V_1 & C2_{11} & 0 & OR2_{21} & 0 \\
V_2 & 0 & C2_{12} & OR2_{21} & 0 \\
V_5 & 0 & 0 & 0 & CR2_{31} \\
V_7 & 0 & 0 & 0 & 0
\end{pmatrix}
$$

a- rail Ci1   b- rail Ci0

Fig. 6. Matrix of the subdigraph of the digraph G

To be able to define the symmetry of the data-paths between N-rail of the encoding bit, let us introduce the notion of execution-path.

* The execution-path is defined as any exclusive path that can be used to process one output rail.

One property of the QDI asynchronous logic is to offer the opportunity to use convergence gates. At each cycle, these gates guarantee the exclusivity of one of its inputs, i.e only one input of the convergence gate is activated. This property enables us to deduce the execution-paths by the exploration of the matrix. The OR gate of both subdigraphs is used as a convergence gate. It means that for each output rail there are two execution-paths described by the subdigraphs and their equivalent matrices in figure 7.

$E_{GC}(1)=(G_{E1},E_{E1})$ with $G_{E1}=\{V_1,V_5,V_7\}$ and $E_{E1}=\{E_1, E_5\}$
$E_{GC}(2)=(G_{E2},E_{E2})$ with $G_{E2}=\{V_2,V_5,V_7\}$ and $E_{E2}=\{E_2, E_5\}$
$E_{GC}(3)=(G_{E3},E_{E3})$ with $G_{E3}=\{V_3,V_6,V_8\}$ and $E_{E3}=\{E_3, E_6\}$
$E_{GC}(4)=(G_{E4},E_{E4})$ with $G_{E3}=\{V_4,V_6,V_8\}$ and $E_{E3}=\{E_4, E_6\}$

$$M_{EGC(i)} = \begin{array}{c|ccc} & V_j & V_k & V_l \\ \hline V_j & C2 & OR2 & 0 \\ V_k & 0 & 0 & CR2 \\ V_l & 0 & 0 & 0 \end{array}$$

Fig. 7. Subdigraphs $E_{GC}(i)$ and their equivalent matrices $M_{EGC(i)}$. $(V_J,V_k,V_l) \in [(V_1,V_5,V_7);$ $(V_2,V_5,V_7);(V_3,V_6,V_8);(V_4,V_6,V_8)]$

One way to formally analyze the data-path symmetry is to analyze the symmetry of each execution-path, by processing the digraph isomorphism.

4.2.1 Isomorphism of a Digraph

Two digraphs G_1 and G_2 are isomorphic if there is a one-to-one correspondence between their vertices and directed edges. If there is a directed edge between two vertices of G_1, then there is a directed edge between the two corresponding vertices in the digraph G_2. More formally,

* For any directed edge ((a),(b)) of G_1, G_2 is isomorphic to G_1 if and only if $F((a),(b))$ is a directed edge of G_2 (F is an isomorphic function).

In terms of matrices, if A_1 and A_2 are respectively the matrices of G_1 and G_2, the digraph G_1 is isomorphic to the digraph G_2 if there is a classification of the vertices of G_2 such as the boolean matrix of A_1 and A_2 are equal.

* If $A_1=A_2$ then G_1 and G_2 are isomorphic

Thus, the analysis of the data-paths symmetries is equivalent to determinate the isomorphism of block subdigraphs (each subdigraph represents one execution-path of the block).

* Data-paths are symmetrical at logical level if and only if their digraphs are isomorphic

Therefore, blocks are balanced if their data-paths are symmetric. If not, the module is said unbalanced. From the previous example, as the matrices $E_{GCo}(1)$, $E_{GCo}(2)$, $E_{GCo}(3)$ and $E_{GCo}(4)$ are equal, then their digraphs are isomorphic, so that the digraph $G_{XOR}(V,E)$ is a balanced structure. However, the QDI implementation of a function is not always balanced, in such a case, the digraph is analyzed and modified to ensure that all data and control paths are balanced [2][10]. The directed graph representation adopted in this design flow is well suited to formally analyze the design symmetries. It offers the opportunity to formally analyze the data-paths symmetries of the design and then balance the asymmetric data-paths if necessary. After that, we apply the path swapping method and formally verify that the structure of the circuit is still well balanced at the logical level.

Let's then apply the DPA attack on this type of circuit in order to evaluate the chip's DPA sensitivity. This starts by defining the electrical model of balanced QDI asynchronous logic.

4.3 Electrical Model of Balanced QDI Asynchronous Logic

The electrical model of balanced QDI asynchronous circuit used in this paper is based on the model developed in [8]. It proposes a current model of QDI block implementing a fix number of logical transitions regardless of the input data. As it represents about 85% of the CMOS gate power dissipation, the paper only considers the Dynamic power dissipation (P_d) which is defined as the power required to charge and discharge the capacitive load of the gates. Hence, the block dynamic current profile is expressed by:

$$P_{dc}(t) = \sum_{i=1}^{N_c} \left[\sum_{j=1}^{N_{ij}} I_{ij}(t_i) \right] + P_{dn}(t) \quad \text{with} \quad I(t) = C \frac{dV}{dt} \tag{2}$$

$I_{ij}(t_i)$ represents the dynamic current dissipated by the *jth* gate of level i and P_{dn} is a dynamic noise function. N_c is the number of gates along the critical data-path. It represents the maximum number of gates in series in the execution path of the block and also corresponds to a number of logical level used to divide a block in N_c logical levels as illustrated in the digraph representation (figure 6). N_{ij} is the number of gates switching at each logical level (N_c). The values N_c and N_{ij} are determined by a simple analysis of the block digraph representation. C is the total charge of the output gate node, defined by: $C=C_l+C_{par}+C_{sc}$ in which C_l represents the load capacitance (gate and routing capacitance), C_{par} is the parasitic capacitance, and C_{sc} is the Short-circuit equivalent capacitance. Let's again consider the block of figure 4. We deduce through the digraph exploration the values of N_c and N_{ij}: $N_c=4$; $N_{11}=N_{21}=N_{31}=N_{41}=1$.

Therefore, the block dynamic current at each phase (evaluation phase and return to zero phases) is given by:

$$P_{dc\ xor}(t) = \left(I_{1j}(t_1) + I_{2j}(t_2) + I_{3j}(t_3) + I_{41}(t_4) \right) + P_{dn}(t) \tag{3}$$

Equation (3) represents, in a first approximation, the profile of the dynamic current of the Dual-rail Xor gate.

This formal current modelling can be extended to all balanced QDI asynchronous block. Its application enables to evaluate with high accuracy the effectiveness of our new secure design approach on balanced QDI asynchronous circuits.

4.4 Applying DPA on the Formal Model

We have adopted the formalization proposed by Thomas S. Messerges et al. in [11] to apply DPA on this formal model. Before that, let's first review the basis of the attack.

DPA attack is performed by computing M random values of plain-text-input (PTI_i). For each of the M plain-text-input, a discrete time power signal S_{ij} and cipher-text-output are collected. The index i of power signal S_{ij} corresponds to the PTI_i that produced the signal and the j index corresponds to the time of the sample. According to a DPA algorithm, the S_{ij} are split into two sets by a separating function D.

$$S_0 = \{S_{ij}|D = 0\} \qquad\qquad S_1 = \{S_{ij}|D = 1\} \tag{4}$$

The average power signal of each set is given by:

$$A_0[j] = \frac{1}{|m_0|}\sum_{i=1}^{n_0} S_{ij} \qquad\qquad A_1[j] = \frac{1}{|m_1|}\sum_{i=1}^{n_1} S_{ij} \tag{5}$$

Where $|m_0|$ and $|m_1|$ represent the number of power signals S_{ij} respectively in set S_0 and S_1. The DPA bias signal is obtained by:

$$T[j] = A_0[j] - A_1[j] \tag{6}$$

If the DPA bias signal shows important peaks, it means that there is a strong correlation between the D function and the power signal. Selecting an appropriate D function is then essential in order to guess a good secret key.

Let us apply this DPA attack to a balanced QDI asynchronous design without activating the path swapping technique. Choosing an XOR for the D function implies to analyse the electrical signature of an Xor gate [8]. Then, the average current signal of both sets of equation (5) is written as follows:

$$A_{xor\,0}[t] = \frac{1}{2}\big(I_{11}(t_1) + I_{12}(t_1) + I_{21}(t_2) + I_{31}(t_3) + I_{41}(t_4) + I_n(t)\big)$$
$$A_{xor\,1}[t] = \frac{1}{2}\big(I_{13}(t_1) + I_{14}(t_1) + I_{22}(t_2) + I_{32}(t_3) + I_{41}(t_4) + I_n(t)\big) \tag{7}$$

Where $I_n(t)$ is a noise signal. The electrical signature is given by:

$$S[t] = T[t] = \left(C_{11}\frac{dVout_{11}}{dt_{11}} + C_{12}\frac{dVout_{12}}{dt_{12}} + C_{21}\frac{dVout_{21}}{dt_{21}} + C_{31}\frac{dVout_{31}}{dt_{31}} + C_{41}\frac{dVout_{41}}{dt_{41}} \right) -$$
$$\left(C_{13}\frac{dVout_{13}}{dt_{13}} + C_{14}\frac{dVout_{14}}{dt_{14}} + C_{22}\frac{dVout_{22}}{dt_{22}} + C_{32}\frac{dVout_{32}}{dt_{32}} + C_{41}\frac{dVout_{41}}{dt_{41}} \right) \tag{8}$$

as $\dfrac{dVout_{ij}}{dt_{ij}} \cong \dfrac{\Delta V}{\Delta t_{ij}}$ this expression becomes

$$S[t] = \Delta V.\left(\frac{C_{11}}{\Delta t_{11}} + \frac{C_{12}}{\Delta t_{12}} - \frac{C_{13}}{\Delta t_{13}} - \frac{C_{14}}{\Delta t_{14}}\right) + \Delta V.\left(\frac{C_{21}}{\Delta t_{21}} - \frac{C_{22}}{\Delta t_{22}}\right) + \Delta V.\left(\frac{C_{31}}{\Delta t_{31}} - \frac{C_{32}}{\Delta t_{32}}\right) \tag{9}$$

Δt represents the physical time taken by the gate to charge/discharge its output node. This time also depends on the value of C. Recalling that $C = C_l + C_{par} + C_{sc}$.

Contrary to synchronous design where the DPA attack reveals path dissymmetry of the attacked bit (C_i), DPA on the balanced QDI asynchronous design reveals path dissymmetry of all rails that are used to encode the attacked bit. The DPA on dual-rail xor gate requires comparing the electrical behaviour of paths which compute rail C_{i0} and rail C_{i1}. As it is shown in equation 9, the main dissymmetries of such a balanced

QDI structure are located on load capacitances which involve gates delay variations between their different paths. Let's now apply the same DPA attack on a dual-rail Xor gate implementing the path swapping. As all data-paths are used to compute outputs, the average current signal of each set of equation (5) contains all gates' currents of the structure. Then, its expression is given by:

$$A_{xor0}[t] = A_{xor1}[t] = \frac{1}{4}(I_{11}(t_1) + I_{12}(t_1) + I_{21}(t_2) + I_{31}(t_3) + I_{13}(t_1) + I_{14}(t_1) + I_{22}(t_2) + I_{32}(t_3) + I_{41}(t_4) + I_n(t)) \quad (10)$$

This nullifies the electrical signature of the dual-rail Xor gate.

$$S[t] = \approx 0 \quad (11)$$

Equations (10) and (11) clearly demonstrate that the differential power analysis on such a symmetric data-paths is completely unusable when using the path swapping method.

4.5 The Swapping Function

As illustrated above, implementing a DPA attack on bit encoded with 1-of-N encoded data, means analysing the electrical difference between its N data-path rails. This fact enables us to reduce the number of possible permutations which are useful to implement the path swapping method. Indeed, let's consider the attacked bit C_i of a selection function D encoded with 1-of-N. E_i represents the set of input values which activate the rail i of C_i and m_i represents the number of these input values (elements) in each set E_i. There are two possible approaches to implement the swapping function: a nondeterministic approach and a deterministic approach.

- The nondeterministic approach: in this approach the number of possible input permutations for each input element is computed by the following expression:

$$P_{PE} = \sum_{i=1}^{N} m_i \qquad \begin{array}{l} P_{PE}: \text{ number of possible permutation of one} \\ \text{input element} \end{array} \quad (12)$$

This number highlights two points: first, the elements of the same set E_i can be permuted between them and second, this approach requires for each input element A_i of E_i ($A_i \in E_i$), the use of P_{PE} P_{PE}-to-1 multiplexers (P_{PE} inputs and 1 output). Hence, the number and the type of multiplexers required for the bit C_i is given by:

$$N_{C_i} = P_{PE}^{2} \quad (P_{PE} - to - 1) \; Multiplexers \quad (13)$$

This number can be reduced if the permutations inside each set E_i are proscribed:

$$N_{C_i} = \sum_{i=1}^{N} \left[m_i \left((\sum_{j=1; j\neq i}^{N} m_j + 1) \rightarrow 1 \right) Multiplexers \right] \quad (14)$$

If all m_i are equal (each set E_i has the same number of elements), then:

$$N_{C_i} = P_{PE} \quad (P_{PE} - m_i + 1) \rightarrow 1 \; Multiplexers \quad (15)$$

For example, if $N=2$ and sets E_0 and E_1 have respectively $m_0=2$ and $m_1=2$ as shown in figure 4, we obtain 4 4-to-1 multiplexers which can be reduced to 4 3-to-1 multiplexers.

- The deterministic approach: the goal of this approach is to constrain the permutation function in order to optimize the use of multiplexers and to guarantee the security. The idea here is to permute one element of set E_i with one element of each of the other sets. Therefore, each element can be permuted N times (as we have N sets) and it requires for the bit C_i, P_{PE} N-to-1 multiplexers:

$$N_{C_i} = P_{PE} \quad N-to-1 \ Multiplexers \tag{16}$$

Considering the previous example, we obtain 4 2-to-1 multiplexers.

Even if the swapping function is known, it does not affect the efficiency of the approach because it is randomly executed. In fact, the choice of data-path used to process the data remains random. This point enables us to considerably optimize the use of multiplexers. In addition to this, some optimizations can be applied according to the regularity and the symmetry of the architecture. It is not necessary to implement multiplexers with each block of the architecture (see the case study on paragraph 5). These analyses are also available when using some demultiplexers and can be extended on all data-paths.

4.6 Discussion

Nevertheless, the security brought by this new design approach is fully efficient if and only if these two conditions are fulfilled:

* *Randomizing the path swapping*: the objective is to ensure unpredictable apportionment of path swapping inside a block. The attack is still possible if the hacker knows the random function generator. Indeed, the analysis can be focused on set of data that are processed by the same random value. For example, if the random function is always switching between two cases (case 1 and 2 as described in figure 4). Performing the attack on the first case is equivalent to attack a balanced QDI asynchronous circuit (without path swapping). The situation is the same if one output rail of the bit attacked is always computed in the same data-path. Then, the random generator must be an unpredictable and equiprobable function. The implementation of such a random function is out of the scope of this paper.
* *Implementing multiplexers and demultiplexers in the architecture*. One way to break the random function generator is to apply DPA attack on these blocks. For example, if the multiplexer of channel Ai (encoding with two rails: $Ai0$ and $Ai1$) presents a significant signature when its rails are swapped, the random function which controls this multiplexer can be predicted. A particular care must be done when implementing these functions [12].

5 Case Study: DES Crypto-Processor

A chosen example to validate this design approach is a DES algorithm. The asynchronous DES crypto-processor is implemented using a four-phase protocol,

1-of-N encoded data and balanced data-paths. The architecture used is an iterative structure, based on three self-timed loops synchronized through communicating channels: one loop for the ciphering data-path, the second loop for the key data-path and the third one for the control data-path (a finite state machine) which controls the data-paths along its sixteen iterations (figure 10).

The implementation of multiplexers/Demultiplexers in each block of the architecture could significantly increase the chip's area. This can be done efficiently by taking advantage of the implemented algorithm. As the DES algorithm uses only four simple types of functions (permutation, Xor, Substitution, Expansion and reduction functions), we only need to implement Multiplexers/Demultiplexers on registers and on the Substitution box (blocks in bold on figure 8). The Substitution function (SBOX) is selected because it is a surjective function (irreversible function).

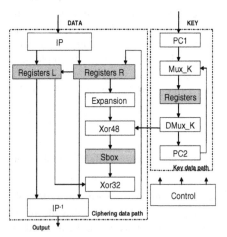

Fig. 8. DES architecture

Table 1. A new ordering of the SBOX1

Output values	Input values				Sets
0	14/0	0/1	15/2	13/3	E0
15	5/0	1/1	8/2	0/3	
1	3/0	7/1	1/2	6/3	E1
14	0/0	4/1	2/2	11/3	
2	4/0	5/1	6/2	3/3	E2
13	2/0	6/1	4/2	15/3	
3	8/0	14/1	12/2	10/3	E3
12	11/0	10/1	9/2	1/3	
4	1/0	3/1	0/2	4/3	E4
11	6/0	11/1	7/2	9/3	
5	12/0	13/1	14/2	8/3	E5
10	9/0	8/1	13/2	12/3	
6	10/0	9/1	5/2	14/3	E6
9	13/0	12/1	13/2	12/3	
7	15/0	2/1	11/2	7/3	E7
8	7/0	15/1	3/2	2/3	

Column number
↓
Cx / Rx
↓
Row number

Indeed, because it is a one way function, it is difficult to trace the information when its inputs/outputs are permuted. Each Substitution Box (SBOX) of the DES algorithm receives 6 bits (64 possible values) in their inputs and generates 4 bits on their outputs (16 possible values), so that, one output value can be selected by 4 different input values [13]. With the dual-rail encoding of the data for each SBOX, we have 8 sets (output rails) of 32 input elements. Applying a nondeterministic permutation, leads to implement 64 64-to-1 multiplexers which is not efficient in terms of area. We used a deterministic implementation exploiting the maximum redundancy of the Substitution function. Let's consider the first substitution box of the DES algorithm. To be able to efficiently swap data-path rails of the SBOX1, we gathered in the same set all input values which generate an output value and its opposite value. For example all input values which generate the output value '0' and its inverse output 'F' are gathered in the same set E_0 as illustrated in table 1.

This representation enables us to observe that, it is only possible to permute in each set, the input values which have the same row number. Therefore it requires 32 2-to-1 multiplexers which increases the SBOX1 area by 30%.

6 Validations: Electrical Simulations

The technology used for implementing the design is the HCMOS9 (0.13μm) from STMicroelectronics. All electrical simulations are performed with *Nanosim* with an asynchronous DES gate Netlist.

The electrical simulation offers the possibility to analyze without disturbing signals (noise), the electrical behaviour of the design with more details. Hence, the number of necessary messages (M) is minimal. In order to easily evaluate the relevancy of this new countermeasure, the path swapping method is only implemented in the first Substitution function (SBOX1) and to four bits of Register L (figure 8). These four bits are combined with the output bits of the first Substitution function (SBOX1) by an Xor function in block Xor32. To reproduce the effects of back end steps during simulations, a dissymmetry is introduced between rails which compute the fourth bit of the SBOX1. In fact, the load capacitance (C) of the first rail ($S_4(0)$) is set to 32 femto-farads. This value includes the gate, the routing, the parasitic and the short-circuit capacitances. It has been estimated after a pre-place and route step with Silicon Ensemble. The defined D function for processing the attack is as follows:

$$D(C_4, P_6, K_0) = SBOX1(P_6 \oplus K_0)$$

The attack is done on the fourth bit of the SBOX1 with 64 curves (64 plain-text-inputs). As a reference, the attacks were realized without activating the countermeasure by switching off the random number generator. The results of the attack are displayed in figure 9. The DPA bias signal (S) is clearly observable when the correct key is guessed.

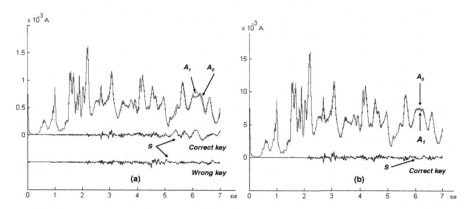

Fig. 9. Electrical Signature when performing DPA attack on bit 4 of the SBOX1. Loading charge difference of both rails of this bit is 32 femtoF. Only the first round is considered. (a) – path swapping is not activated (b) – path swapping is activated.

The result of the attack when the countermeasure is activated is illustrated in figure 9-b. The DPA bias signal is completely removed as predicted by the equation (11).

All results present in this paragraph demonstrated the relevancy of using the path swapping method on QDI asynchronous circuits which have their data-paths balanced and symmetric.

7   Conclusion

This paper presented a new design technique for enhancing QDI asynchronous circuits' resistance against DPA attack. This design approach which is called Path Swapping exploits all properties of QDI asynchronous logic which are suited to design secure chips, particularly the logical data-path symmetries.

The results obtained from electrical simulations of a DES crypto-processor proved the efficiency of the Path Swapping method in terms of DPA resistance. Current works are focused on the realization of a prototype in order to perform analysis on silicon.

References

[1]   P. Kocher, J. Jaffe, B. Jun, "Differential Power Analysis," Advances in Cryptology - Crypto 99 Proceedings, LNCS Vol. 1666, M. Wiener ed., Springer-Verlag, 1999.

[2]   Simon Moore, R. Anderson, P. Cunningham, R. Mullins, G.Taylor, "Improving Smart Card Security using Self-timed Circuits", Eighth International Symposium on Asynchronous Circuits and systems (ASYNC2002). 8-11 April 2002. Manchester, U.K.

[3]   L. A. Plana, P. A. Riocreux, W. J. Bainbridge, A. Bardsley, J. D. Garside and S. Temple, "SPA - A Synthesisable Amulet Core for Smartcard Applications", Proceedings of the Eighth International Symposium on Asynchronous Circuits and Systems (ASYNC 2002). Pages 201-210. Manchester, 8-11/04/2002. Published by the IEEE Computer Society.

[4]   J. Joshua, P. Kocher, J. Benjamin, Balanced Cryptographic computational method and apparatus for leak minimization in smartcards and others Cryptosystems, EP1088295/WO9967766.

[5]   Danil Sokolov, Julian Murphy, Alex Bystrov and Alex Yakovlev,"Improving the Security of Dual-Rail Circuits", CHES 2004, LNCS 3156, pp 282-297, 2004.

[6]   J. J. A Fournier, Simon Moore, Huiyun Li, Robert Mullins, and Gerorge Taylor,"Security Evaluation of Asynchronous Circuits", CHES 2003, LNCS 2779, pp 137-151, 2003.

[7]   F. Bouesse, M. Renaudin, B. Robisson, E Beigne, P.Y. Liardet, S. Prevosto, J. Sonzogni, "DPA on Quasi Delay Insensitive Asynchronous circuits: Concrete Results", DCIS 2004 Bordeaux, France, November 24-26, 2004.

[8]   G.F. Bouesse, M. Renaudin, S. Dumont, F. Germain, « DPA on Quasi Delay Insensitive Asynchronous Circuits: Formalization and Improvement », DATE 2005, Munich, p.424.

[9]   Marc Renaudin, "Asynchronous circuits and systems: a promising design alternative", Microelectronic for Telecommunications : managing high complexity and mobility" (MIGAS 2000), special issue of the Microelectronics-Engineering Journal, Elsevier Science, Vol. 54, N° 1-2, December 2000, pp. 133-149.

[10] F. Bouesse, M. Renaudin, F. Germain, "Asynchronous AES Crypto-processor Including Secured and Optimized Blocks", the Journal of Integrated Circuits and Systems (JICS), Volume 1, ISSN 1807-1953,March 2004.

[11] T. S. Messerges and E. A. Dabbish, R. H. Sloan, "Investigations of Power Analysis Attacks on Smartcards", USENIX Workshop on Smartcard Technology, Chicago, Illinois, USA, May 10-11, 1999.

[12] P. Maurine, J.B. Rigaud, F. Bouesse, G. Sicard, M. Renaudin, "Static Implementation of QDI Asynchronous Primitives", 13th International Workshop on Power and Timing Modeling, Optimization and Simulations, PATMOS2003.

[13] NIST, Data Encryption Standard (DES), FIPS PUB 46-2.

Automated Design of Cryptographic Devices Resistant to Multiple Side-Channel Attacks

Konrad Kulikowski, Alexander Smirnov, and Alexander Taubin

Department of Electrical and Computer Engineering, Boston University,
8 Saint Mary's Street, Boston, MA 02215, USA
{konkul, alexbs, taubin}@bu.edu

Abstract. Balanced dynamic dual-rail gates and asynchronous circuits have been shown, if implemented correctly, to have natural and efficient resistance to side-channel attacks. Despite their benefits for security applications they have not been adapted to current mainstream designs due to the lack of electronic design automation support and their non-standard or proprietary design methodologies. We present a novel asynchronous fine-grain pipeline synthesis methodology that addresses these limitations. It allows synthesis of asynchronous quasi delay insensitive circuits from standard high-level hardware description language (HDL) specifications. We briefly present a proof of concept differential dynamic power balanced micropipeline library cells that are approximately 6 times more balanced than the best (differential dynamic) cells designed using previous balancing methods. An implementation of the Advanced Encryption Standard based on these balanced cells and synthesized using our tool flow shows a 6.6 times throughput improvement over the synchronous automatically pipelined implementation using the same TSMC 0.18μm technology synthesized from the same HDL specification.

1 Introduction

Strong cryptographic algorithms have been designed to withstand rigorous cryptanalysis. However, if the overall cryptographic system is considered, including the physical implementation, the strong notions of security are far from guaranteed. Numerous attacks have been developed that exploit physical properties of implementations and information leaked through *side channels*, i.e. channels other than the data channel. By exploiting the information leaked through side-channels an attacker, with the help of statistical methods can quickly compromise the system. Side-channel attacks (and especially a combination of several such attacks) are often much more powerful than classical cryptanalysis.

In this paper we present a design methodology and a practical commercial quality Electronic Design Automation (EDA) flow which addresses the current practical and physical limitations. Our methodology provides tool support for the complete design cycle of secure cryptographic hardware which is capable of eliminating practically all sources of non-invasive side-channel information while allowing for very high performance of the implementation as well as low design time. It is based on asynchronous fine-grain pipelining with power-balanced cells

L. Goubin and M. Matsui (Eds.): CHES 2006, LNCS 4249, pp. 399–413, 2006.

to combine high performance with the best available power analysis resistance and excellent fault attack countermeasures. Our tool flow is based on off-the-shelf commercial EDA tools and does not require any specialized asynchronous design training or modifications of the original specification. Our flow is customizable through library approach to use various micropipeline implementations. Area and performance can be tuned as in other commercial quality synchronous synthesis flows.

The benefits of our methodology stem from two critical differences from previous implementations and are a direct consequence of the fine-grain structure of the final implementations. Fine-grain micropipeline cells are suitable for automatic ASIC synthesis from HDL specifications. Efficiently implemented using dynamic differential dual-rail circuitry micropipelines make it possible to automate normally custom power ballanced circuits design.

Using our methodology we have designed a complete hardware implementation of Advanced Encryption Standard (AES) [1]. Our AES implementation was synthesized for balanced library using our EDA tools. It combines differential power analysis (DPA) attack resistance with high performance. To satisfy the tight time-to-market and ease of design constraints our EDA flow accepts standard HDL input behavior specifications. Our design flow is complete. It incorporates off-the-shelf industrial tools with our scripts and reimplementation engine.

In this paper we first (Section 2) review previous work and some weaknesses and limitations of existing approaches. In Section 2 we also shortly introduce the key concepts of asynchronous design. The next two sections describe the keys for the success or our approach. Section 3 describes the main idea behind asynchronous fine-grain pipelining, implementation basis and automated design flow which allows asynchronous design using standard methodologies currently used in practically all automated synchronous design flows. Section 4 describes some details of the design and considerations of a dedicated balanced library cells for asynchronous fine-grain pipelining which are easily customizable and can be adapted to many existing balanced gate styles. Section 5 shortly describes performance characteristics of AES implementation and Section 6 presents short conclusions and future tasks.

2   Motivation

2.1   Dynamic Logic and Security

Some of the most promising methods for DPA resistance are based on specially designed balanced dynamic gates like those from [2]. Recent results on DPA resistance based on special power-balanced cells [2,3] show a significant reduction in the power consumption fluctuations. Specially designed custom cells have great potential since instead of masking or hiding they remove power related sources of side-channel information that can be used for an attack.

However, most of gate-level approaches, such as those from [2,3] have no countermeasures against glitch and fault-injection attacks and require additional protection. More importantly, since differential and dynamic (DD) approaches from [2,3] require dynamic (domino) logic cell design. The usage of DD gates is limited to custom or semi-custom design that greatly limits the perceived universality of DD based circuitry. The following are two major reasons why EDA support of dynamic logic based design is very difficult for synchronous methodology [4,5]. First, each synchronous dynamic gate requires a clock input and uses both levels of clock signal – it means that from the point of view of EDA tools each gate behaves like a flip-flop. Second, due to early/late arrival, charge sharing, clock distribution problems with small clocking granularity and uncertainty about worst case delay makes *static timing analysis* (STA) of dynamic circuits very problematic. STA is core part of any synchronous EDA approach. As a result no EDA tool support is available for synchronous design based of dynamic logic. As these problems make power balanced dynamic circuitry practically unavailable for rapid ASIC development the researchers resort to less secure (e.g. less balanced) but easier to implement solutions based on standard static non-balanced gate libraries (see e.g. motivation to use WDDL from [6]).

Our approach incorporates dynamic gate balancing techniques and methods with asynchronous design principles to address the timing and clock related problems associated with current and future balanced dynamic gate designs and to enable their use in automatic standard-cell based design flow.

2.2   Asynchronous Circuit Design

Many of the properties which many designs try to artificially add to synchronous designs are natural in some styles of asynchronous circuits. Some of the benefits previously noted include:

− Electromagnetic (or power) signature is strongly reduced by replacing a synchronous processor with an asynchronous one (no clock harmonics). Removing clock results in significantly flatter noise and electro magnetic interference (EMI) spectrum across the frequency domain (10dB drop according [7]).
− Absence of clock hardens triggering data detection at specific points of the data processing flow.
− With no clock glitch attacks are infeasible.
− In synchronous implementations, power supply fluctuations are used to force the circuit into an erroneous state allowing the use of differential fault analysis (DFA) attacks. Asynchronous circuits are much less sensitive to DFA attacks since the supply voltage drop gracefully slows down the circuit rather than leading to errors.
− Recent research suggests that asynchronous implementations have better resistance to power analysis and fault injection than synchronous counterparts. However, known implementations are still susceptible to information leakage both in power signature [8] and under fault injection. Contrariwise, balanced dual-rail domino with completion detection library - cell design that we chose for implementation of asynchronous fine-grain pipelining eliminates a side-channel for DPA [8,9].

- Comparison of electromagnetic analysis (EMA) results for synchronous and asynchronous implementations indicates that synchronous devices have data dependent EM emission, while non-pipelined asynchronous devices have data dependent timing visible with differential EMA (DEMA) [10].
- Asynchronous multi-dimensional (e.g. 3D) pipelined array architectures [11] can eliminate data dependent timing and thereby secure implementations against DEMA and differential timing analysis (DTA).

Various asynchronous design styles differ in the tradeoff between locality of timing assumptions and design cost (see e.g. [12]). *Quasi-delay-insensitive* (QDI) circuits [13] partition wires into critical and non-critical. Forks on critical wires are considered safe if they are isochronic – the skew is less than the minimum gate delay.

Universality and flexibility along with ease of design is a critical requirement necessary for the integration of any approach. QDI implementations appear to be the most appropriate – class of asynchronous circuits that can be synthesized automatically from large high-level behavior specifications. Return to zero hand-shaking protocol with dual-rail one-hot data encoding that switche the output from data to spacer and back regardless for every data portion is the most common QDI implementation. The most efficient QDI implementations are based on differential dynamic logic. That makes it easy to incorporate existing dynamic domino style power balanced structures in the QDI templates.

2.3   EDA Support for Asynchronous Design

QDI based approach developed by TIMA group [14] is based on complex static library cells (built from basic gates like *C-elements* [15] etc.). These cells are not compatible with e.g. SABL [2]. In addition, TIMA tool flow [16] uses a non-standard language extension (channels) of HDL that require rewriting of design specifications.

Most importantly, none of known asynchronous EDA tools address fine-grain asynchronous dynamic logic pipelining which is of major importance for security and high performance. Fine-grain asynchronous pipelining seems to be the only way to move most promising DPA resistant (differential dynamic well balanced gates like SABL) into engineering practice since it seems to be the only way to provide EDA tool support for dynamic logic based styles.

In a summary, differential dynamic well balanced gates seem to be the best choice to design secure hardware resistant to side-channel attacks. Because of the time-to-market pressure without a solid EDA support any methodology for secure hardware design is likely to remain unused. QDI implementation methodology is able to play a key role by making dynamic cell libraries acceptable for EDA. Fine-grain asynchronous pipelining is a way to develop commercial quality tool support for QDI cell libraries. It becomes possible based on synchronous-to-asynchronous directed translation (SADT) approach. The main idea of SADT is to start from conventionally synthesized synchronous circuit, and directly re-place the global clock network with a set of local handshake circuits. This way synthesis is performed by commercial synthesis tools originally developed for synchronous circuits. Since in dynamic logic each gate is a subject of clocking, fine-grain asynchronous pipelining by inserting local handshake control on the level of inter-gate communication (gate level pipelining) leads not only to convenient assimilation of differential dynamic balanced cell designs but also to high throughput solutions. In the next sections we explain how these necessary components lead to fine-grained structures and how they allow synthesis and other tool support.

3   Asynchronous Micropipelines Synthesis

Register Transfer Level (RTL) synthesis model simplified the clocked circuits' design and allowed design automation driving VLSI progress for more than a decade. Synchronous-to-asynchronous directed translation (SADT), we believe, is as important for asynchronous design automation as RTL for synchronous EDA. With RTL design dominating the industry SADT model is especially beneficial since (1) it offers support for existing specifications and (2) it is easily incorporated into contemporary design flow using the best available RTL synthesis engines. The handshake implementation and data channel organization is thereby hidden from the designer. Like in RTL it is customizable through a cell library approach.

Contrary to known approaches [16,17] which use HDL for *micropipeline* [18] synthesis, our method is not an attempt to express asynchronous formal models in terms of HDL. Our synthesis flow uses an off-the-shelf RTL synthesis engine as a front-end to support regular HDL behavior specifications and the same engine as a back-end to provide support for the variety of netlist specification formats used by post-synthesis tools in ASIC design flow.

The main contribution of RTL model to EDA is based on a separation of optimization and timing (all sequential behavior is in an interaction between registers, all synthesis and optimization are only about combinational clouds). RTL model (Fig. 1a) is based on global synchronization and timing assumption (computations are complete in every stage before the next clock edge). During every clock cycle every latch undergoes two phases: pass and store. Master-slave flip-flop organization where master latch is clocked by one edge of clock signal and slave latch by the opposite edge prevents the register from being transparent at any given time. Similarly to pass and store of latches dynamic gates go through: *evaluate* and *precharge* (reset). These stages map to asynchronous four-phase handshake protocols [12] where the four phases are data request-acknowledge (evaluate) and request-acknowledge reset. (Fig. 1b).

In addition to separation of optimization and timing SADT model contributes separation of set and reset phases: for example each gate in Null Convention Logic (NCL) [19] is sequential but can be presented as combinational – separately in set and reset phases. As a result in SADT flow logic optimization remains separate from sequential behavior – the reason why SADT flows can be based on standard synchronous RTL compilers. Likewise sequential behavior

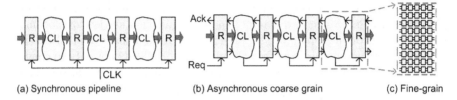

Fig. 1. Synchronous-Asynchronous Direct Translation: from synchronous (a) to desynchronized (b) and fine-grain pipelined (c) circuits

synthesized in RTL remains the same in a micropipeline. Only its implementation is changed from globally synchronized using global timing assumptions to local handshake with none or local timing assumptions. This low-level sequential behavior implementation is done automatically and does not affect the design specification. Final implementation (and this is the main difference from RTL) will provide the result as soon as it can – not at the predetermined time as with synchronous RTL. It will signal the data availability and wait for the environment to acknowledge the data receipt to output the new result.

SADT flows differ in pipeline stage granularity. Inter-register handshake insertion approach where clock connected to registers is substituted by handshaking between the registers placed at the same points in the circuit (Fig. 1b) is used by NCL [19] and De-synchronization [20] flows.

The main distinctive feature of our approach [21] is that in addition to replacing global synchronization with local self-timed control we also remove functionally unnecessary synchronization and alter the granularity of pipelining (usually significantly decrease it down to the gate level Fig. 1c).

There are several reasons for gate-level pipelining: overcoming parameter variations, lower completion detection overhead (see section 3.2 for details on completion detection) etc. Particularly, we would like to mention that lower pipeline granularity is a way to improve performance. For security related applications gate level pipelining allows development of small power balanced gates (as explained in section 4) that can be used to automatically synthesize DPA resistant implementations.

The asynchronous mechanisms (including handshake communication) are hidden from the end circuit designer in the ***micropipeline cell library*** leaving the handshaking implementation to the library designer.

3.1   RTL to Micropipeline Re-implementation in Our Synthesis Flow

Micropipeline synthesis (as a particular case of SADT methodology) consists of *three main stages: RTL synthesis, re-implementation and final mapping* explained as follows.

RTL implementation consists in synthesizing a synchronous implementation from HDL specification provided by the designer by a standard RTL synthesis tool. The only difference from standard RTL synthesis is that virtual library (imaginary) cells are used for synthesis. This step determines the implementation architecture. It can be tuned the same way it would be for RTL synthesis to trade-off area, performance and dynamic power consumption.

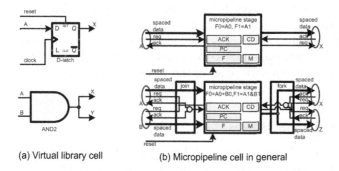

(a) Virtual library cell   (b) Micropipeline cell in general

Fig. 2. Micropipeline synthesis examples: clocked latch (top) and AND2 gate with a fork (bottom)

Re-implementation takes the RTL netlist obtained in the previous step. First, *RTL functionality is identified*. Every combinational gate or a clocked latch (g_i) is represented with a library cell (see examples in Fig. 2). Clocked flip-flops are considered as pairs of sequentially connected latches (master g_{mi} and slave g_{si}) with alternative clock and are represented as two cells each. Every data wire (any wire except for clock and reset) is mapped to a cell connection. This way no additional data dependencies are added and no existing data dependencies are removed. Initial state of state holding gates (D-latches and D-flip-flops) is guaranteed by appropriate reset.

The algorithm is substitution based linear complexity assuming that for every virtual library cell there exists a **micropipeline library** cell or a previously synthesized module implementing functionality represented by the cell. This assumption is satisfied by targeting RTL synthesis to the virtual library that is functionally equivalent to the micropipeline library and by bottom-up synthesis of hierarchical designs

Next deadlock freedom is ensured and the **micropipeline netlist** is optimized using *slack matching* [22,23] and other optimizations.

Fig. 2 presents identification and micropipeline synthesis examples for a clocked latch with fan-out of 1 and an AND2 gate with fan-out 2. The latch (Fig. 2a top) is connected to reset with its preset pin meaning that it is initialized to '1' in RTL implementation. During micropipeline synthesis an identity stage is chosen from the library that is initialized to dual-rail value of logical '1'. The combinational gate labeled with function A&B is implemented by a micropipeline stage with equivalent dual-rail functionality. The gate output depends on both inputs therefore the inputs must be synchronized by a *join* module. Likewise the output is split to X and Y what makes it necessary to synchronize the feedback acknowledgements with a *fork* module.

The nets not identified as special nets are treated as channels. Fig. 2 shows the general case of channel expansion using request (*req*), acknowledgement (*ack*) and dual-rail binary data wires. The join and fork module implementations are protocol dependent.

We have proved that asynchronous fine-grain pipelined circuit generated by our flow is live, safe and *flow-equivalent* to original specification (we borrow the notion of flow-equivalence and a method of proof from [20]). Flow-equivalence means that for each stage that corresponds to a latch in RTL implementation, the value stored at the i-th pulse of the control signal is the same as the value stored at the i-th cycle of the synchronous circuit.

3.2   Micropipeline Stages

Numerous protocols and implementation styles have been developed for asynchronous micropipelines. The protocols fall into two groups [12]: *bundled data* using delay element to match the delay of data propagation through combinational logic and *completion detection* based. The latter encode data to include a *spacer* (no data value) in addition to logical '1' and logical '0' (e.g. like in dual-rail domino with data values "01" and "10" and the reset state "00"). Such an encoding along with monotonic transitions makes it possible to distinguish data from reset state by looking only at the data itself.

Data/spacer detection is called *completion detection*. For the above data encoding it can be implemented with a NOR gate per data channel. For multiple channels synchronization of single channel completions is implemented by a latch with the function $g = x1 \cdot x2 + g \cdot (x1 + x2)$, known as a Muller's C-element [15] shown on Fig. 3 as a circle with "C" inside. With no global synchronization a stage determines the time to precharge/evaluate by observing the feedback from data consumers. It can precharge when all consumers evaluated and evaluate when all of them precharged.

An example of dynamic implementation of a micropipeline stage cell implementing the AND2 function is shown on the Fig. 3. (This particular example illustrates the Reduced Stack Precharge Half-Buffer (RSPCHB) template from [24]. Note that RSPCHB is not balanced. It was not targeted to secure applications.) Block implementing the stage logical function is F. The rest of blocks are typical for most of the stages. *LReq* and *LAck* are left and *RReq* and *RAck* are right request and acknowledgement, *ACK* – handshake implementation, *PC* – phase (precharge/evaluate) control, *CD* –completion detection and *M* stands for memory. '*Staticizers*' (or *keepers*) formed by adding weak inverters as shown in Fig. 3, store the stage output value for an unlimited time eliminating timing assumptions. At the same time keepers solve the charge sharing problem and improve the noise margin of precharge style implementations. The *req* line is used in some protocols to signal data availability to the following stages while the *ack* – to indicate that the data portion has been consumed. Depending on the communication protocol, some or all of the handshake events can be transmitted over the data lines so *req* and/or *ack* lines may not be needed.

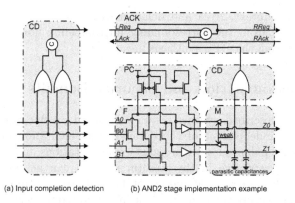

(a) Input completion detection   (b) AND2 stage implementation example

Fig. 3. AND2 micropipeline stage dynamic implementation example

A *dedicated micropipeline library* with each cell representing an entire micropipeline stage localizes in-stage timing assumptions and power balancing inside the cell thereby leaving it to the library designer. With delay-insensitive inter-stage communication the implementation functionality no longer depends on place & route. Note (Fig. 3) that memory and logic function implementation are of the same cost and speed as synchronous dual-rail domino counterparts. The main sources of area overhead are the Muller C-element for handshake control implementation (ACK), completion detection circuitry (CD) and ack/req synchronization (can be seen in Fig. 2).

3.3   Design Flow and EDA Support

Our synthesis flow consists of a reimplementation engine and a set of scripts responsible for implementing the user interface (commands) and interaction with the RTL synthesis tool. The engine incorporates VHDL and Synopsys Liberty parsers/generators to interface the design and library specifications with industrial tools. The RTL synthesis tool currently used in the flow is Synopsys Design Compiler®. This set of tools is targeted at micropipeline synthesis but it also automates some library installation tasks.

Library installation is executed once per library or every time the library is modified. This step is essential for the flow flexibility to use variety of micropipeline libraries. The flexibility is achieved through abstracting from particular micropipeline style(s) by defining a stage-cell as a pre-designed module implementing one or more functions of its inputs. Every data input or output is considered as a channel consisting of encoded data and zero or more handshake lines. On the example on the Fig. 2b a channel consists of dual-rail data, request and acknowledgement lines.

Virtual library is an imaginary single-rail synchronous RTL library functionally equivalent to the micropipeline library. The virtual library is generated from the micropipeline library during its installation. Cell AND2 on the Fig. 2a is a virtual library cell generated for stage AND2 implementation (Fig. 2b) found in micropipeline library. Area and delay characteristics of the virtual library cells are mapped from the corresponding micropipeline library cells to make optimization during the RTL synthesis meaningful.

4   Cell Customization and Security Benefits

The previously described synthesis approach based on fine-grained templates is in large part independent of the detailed implementation of the template cell. Unlike other balanced asynchronous implementations and flows [14] which are much more restrictive in the structures which can be used, this general template is much more flexible and adaptable. Libraries optimized for balance, performance, power, or overhead can all be incorporated to meet the security and other design goals. Since the basic templates are based on differential dynamic cells almost all of the existing or novel dynamic circuit structures can be easily incorporated into an asynchronous standard-cell library. New circuit structures do not have to be redesigned or invented for a particular application in order to be incorporated into the flow, thus allowing reuse of intellectual property and further decreasing development time and time-to-market of complex designs.

For example, SABL gates [2,3] can be easily adapted to the cells preserving all of their balance properties and enhancing their fault resistance and robustness. Addition of asynchronous control removes the clocking and timing difficulties normally associated with the gates and enhances their security applications due to the benefits of asynchronous behavior as mentioned in sec. 2. The function and operation of the additional asynchronous wrapper is almost completely data independent and only the completion detection of wrapper requires a trivial power balancing consideration which can be easily met with two additional minimal size transistors [9]. By simply using an unmodified SABL gate as the functional block of the asynchronous template and using the handshake circuitry of the template (like that presented in section 3.2 and shown on the Fig. 3) for the generation of the clock signal for the SABL gate as shown on the Fig. 4 a fully QDI balanced gate results. The resulting gate has identical balance to that of the original SABL gate.

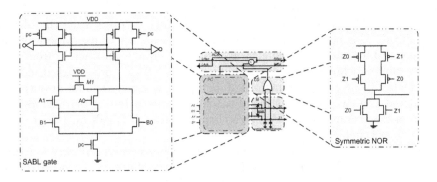

Fig. 4. Incorporation of a SABL gate into the QDI template

Additionally, the explicit synchronization and completion detection of the asynchronous template allows for fewer restrictions on the design of the balanced functional block. Restrictions such as elimination of early propagation effect [25] which need to be explicitly considered in synchronous implementations are automatically satisfied. Explicit input completion can be incorporated to the design which coupled with the C-element will prevent evaluation until all of the input data has arrived and is ready.

Furthermore, the timing and voltage tolerance of the QDI implementation allows for more aggressive dynamic designs which can achieve better balance than previous designs. A balanced library designed specifically for the fine-grained asynchronous template called Balanced Symmetric with Discharge Tree (BSDT) gates was fully incorporated into the flow. The gates showed approximately 6 times better balance than the synchronous SABL implementations (Fig. 5) [9].

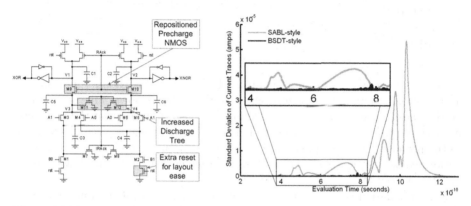

Fig. 5. BSDT-style XOR and the Standard Deviation of the evaluation phase of SABL and BSDT implementations

Current versions of the balanced library cells based on existing balanced dynamic functional blocks still require balanced routing considerations. However, due to gate level asynchronous QDI nature of the method the resulting implementations are very tolerant of process/voltage variations. The natural tolerance of the template can allow more aggressive dynamic balancing techniques which can allow for routing independent gate design. We are currently developing a balanced library design which does not require balanced routing considerations.

In addition to allowing a more robust design for dynamic balanced function blocks the asynchronous handshake protocol and template adds natural fault resistance to the design. For the balanced asynchronous gates presented in [9] out of all the possible transistor level single stuck-at faults inside and outside of the complete asynchronous gate not a single fault changes the Boolean function of the gate. Almost 80% of the faults result in a pipeline stall which naturally prevents further data processing and creates deadlock within the pipeline (Tab. 1). That is the faults prevent or stop the necessary four phase handshake protocol between each gate thereby stalling the communication between dependent downstream gates and preventing any further data processing. To resolve the deadlock the pipeline requires an explicit reset which will clear all intermediate faulty data values inside the pipeline removing the possible source of fault attack information. Synchronous based balanced dynamic logic gates have no comparable property. This additional property should make it much harder to use invasive or semi invasive attacks on a circuit since almost all of the tampering would be detected by a pipeline stall. Additional error detection based on other high level fault-tolerant methods (i.e. error-detecting codes) [26] can be added easily due to the HDL synthesis support. Only a modified HDL specification incorporating fault-tolerance needs to be generated.

Table 1. Effects of stuck-at faults in asynchronous dual-rail gates

	Pipeline stall	No Logical effect on function	Created an alarm state
Buffer	75%	21%	4%
AND	73%	16%	10%
XOR	73%	16%	11%

We are currently performing a full analysis of the side-channel information leakage from sample implementations. Initial simulated power analysis attacks on the Sbox of the Data Encryption Standard (DES) indicate that the beneficial properties of the balanced dynamic gates and asynchronous circuits translate to the proposed implementations. The DPA was applied similarly to the attack performed on our previous balanced library implementation [8] and shows similar simulation results.

Since the design is based on components of previously evaluated methods and designs (i.e., QDI asynchronous design, dynamic balanced gates) it is expected that the good properties of the individual components should be preserved as indicated by the results of initial DPA simulations. Therefore with respect to power, fault and EMI channels the methodology is expected to be as secure, by construction, as the individual components prior to integration. We are currently evaluating the details and possible weaknesses resulting from the combination of the countermeasures but up to this point none have been found.

5   AES Implementations Comparison

To estimate efficiency of our flow [27] we compare performance of automatically synthesized synchronous and asynchronous balanced and unbalanced fine-grain pipelined implementations using our simple dynamic logic based micropipeline libraries using TSMC 0.18μm technology (obtained through MOSIS). One of the libraries – BSDT is a power balanced library implemented with minimum transistor sizes. Another – MPCHB (modified PCHB from [24]) optimized for performance.

The same RTL Electronic Code Book mode (unfolded 10-round) HDL specification of the AES has been used for all implementations. Synchronous RTL implementation was synthesized with the Artisan Sage-X^{TM} [28] standard cell library using the same (TSMC 0.18μm) technology. The non-pipelined implementation shows performance of 16MHz. Automatically pipelined (with Synopsys Design Compiler® "pipeline_design –period 0" command – maximum performance setting) synchronous implementation – performed at 45MHz.

Our asynchronous fine-graine pipelined implementations exceeds 35Gbps (298MHz*128bit where 128 bits is the input and cipher text word length) for balanced and over 62Gbps (482MHz*128bit) for unbalanced implementations.

Compare these performance numbers with commercial ASIC implementations like one from [29] available on the market today (25Gbps the word length of 256 bits – that scaled down to 12.5Gbps for the word length of 128 bits) or the best known academic custom (manual) design (546MHz) [30]. Note that in both cases there is no side-channel attacks protection. High performance and protection level results cost significant area overhead – the area of protected gate-level pipelined implementation approaches 30mm^2. Thanks to resistance to variation inherent to asynchronous micropipelines the implementation can operate at lower voltage with lower speed and lower power consumption.

Finally, we would like to note that both the MPCHB and BSDT libraries are under development and in the current stage feature logic gates (stages) up to 2 data inputs as well as the identity function (to be used for initialization and slack matching) micropipcline stages along with synchronization cells and a minimal set of standard logic cells. Design characteristics can be improved with better optimized and richer micropipeline library.

6   Conclusions and Future Tasks

The lack of industrial quality electronic design automation flow has limited the use of the most promising side-channel resistant circuit techniques: dynamic style balanced gates and asynchronous circuits. We have implemented a design methodology based on dynamic asynchronous micropipelines which allows full industrial quality EDA support without requiring additional training in asynchronous design. Moreover the methodology allows easy incorporation of existing synchronous dynamic gate designs and circuit structures. The combination of asynchronous operation and balanced dynamic gates allows automated standard-cell library based design highly resistant to side-channel attacks.

We recently discovered a new Combined Differential Power Analysis/Fault Injection (DPA/FI) attacks (or power attacks on faulty hardware) [31]. Our experiments indicate that this attack is potentially extremely dangerous since even Differential Power Analysis resistant (power balanced) implementations are vulnerable to DPA/FI attacks. No previous countermeasures have been specifically considered against this type of attacks. However, methodology based on asynchronous fine-grain pipelined power-balanced library is the approach which could provide for a high level of resistance against these new attacks.

Acknowledgements

This work was partially funded by Omnibase Logic Inc.

References

1. Fips pub 197: Advanced encryption standard, http://csrc.nist.gov.
2. Kris Tiri, Moonmoon Akmal, and Ingrid Verbauwhede. A dynamic and differential cmos logic with signal independent power consumption to withstand differential power analysis on smart cards. In *28th European Solid-State Circuits Conference (ESSCIRC 2002)*, 2002.
3. Kris Tiri and Ingrid Verbauwhede. A logic level design methodology for a secure DPA resistant ASIC or FPGA implementation. *Design Automation and Test in Europe Conference (DATE 2004)*, 2004.
4. David Chinnery and Kurt Keutzer. Closing the Gap between ASIC & Custom. Tools and Techniques for Gigh-Performance ASIC Design. Kluwer Academic Publishers, 2002.
5. David Harris. Skew-Tolerant Circuit Design. Morgan Kaufmann Publishers, 2001.
6. Kris Tiri, Wei Hwang, Alireza Hodjat, Lai Bo-Cheng, Yang Shenglin, P. Schaumont, and I. Verbauwhede. Prototype IC with WDDL and differential routing - DPA sesistance assessment. In *Chyptographic Hardware and Embedded Systems - CHES*, pages 354–365, Edinburgh, 2005. LNCS3659, Springer.
7. J. McCardle and D. Chester. Measuring an asynchronous processor's power and noise. In *SNUG*, 2001.
8. Konrad J. Kulikowski, Ming Su, Alexander Smirnov, Alexander Taubin, Mark G. Karpovsky, and Daniel MacDonald. Delay insensitive encoding and power analysis: A balancing act. In *Proc. International Symposium on Advanced Research in Asynchronous Circuits and Systems*, pages 116–125, 2005.
9. Daniel Jay MacDonald. A Balanced-Power Domino-Style Standard Cell Library for Fine-Grain Asynchronous Pipelined Design to Resist Differential Power Analysis Attacks. Master of Science Thesis, Boston University, 2005.
10. H. Li, A. Markettos, and S. W. Moore. Security evaluation against electromagnetic analysis at design time. In *Workshop on Cryptographic Hardware and Embedded Systems (CHES)*, 2005.
11. A.Taubin, K. Fant, and J. McCardle. Design of delay-insensitive three dimension pipeline array multiplier for image processing. *ICCD*, 2002.
12. Jens Sparsø and Steve Furber, editors. Principles of Asynchronous Circuit Design: A Systems Perspective. Kluwer Academic Publishers, 2001.
13. Alain J. Martin. Programming in VLSI: From communicating processes to delay-insensitive circuits. In C. A. R. Hoare, editor, *Developments in Concurrency and Communication*, UT Year of Programming Series, pages 1–64. Addison-Wesley, 1990.
14. G. F. Bouesse, M. Renaudin, S. Dumont, and F.Germain. DPA on quasi delay insensitive asynchronous circuits: Formalization and improvement. In *DATE*, 2005.
15. David E. Muller and W. S. Bartky. A theory of asynchronous circuits. In *Proceedings of an International Symposium on the Theory of Switching*, pages 204–243. Harvard University Press, April 1959.
16. M. Renaudin, P. Vivet, and F. Robin. A design framework for asynchronous/ synchronous circuits based on CHP to HDL translation. In *Proc. International Symposium on Advanced Research in Asynchronous Circuits and Systems*, pages 135–144, April 1999.

17. Catherine G. Wong and Alain J. Martin. High-level synthesis of asynchronous systems by data-driven decomposition. In *Proc. ACM/IEEE Design Automation Conference*, pages 508–513, June 2003.

18. Ivan E. Sutherland. Micropipelines. *Communications of the ACM*, 32(6):720–738, June 1989.

19. Michiel Ligthart, Karl Fant, Ross Smith, Alexander Taubin, and Alex Kondratyev. Asynchronous design using commercial HDL synthesis tools. In *Proc. International Symposium on Advanced Research in Asynchronous Circuits and Systems*, pages 114–125. IEEE Computer Society Press, April 2000.

20. J. Cortadella, A. Kondratyev, L. Lavagno, and C. Sotiriou. De-synchronization: synthesis of asynchronous circuits from synchronous specifications. *IEEE Transactions on Computer-Aided Design*. (To appear).

21. A. Smirnov, A. Taubin, and M. Karpovsky. An automated fine-grain pipelining using domino style asynchronous library. In *ACSD 2005: Fifth International Conference on Application of Concurrency to System Design*, St.Malo, France, 2005. IEEE CS Press.

22. Peter A. Beerel, Mike Davies, Andrew Lines, and Nam-Hoon Kim. Slack matching asynchronous designs. In *Proc. International Symposium on Advanced Research in Asynchronous Circuits and Systems*, pages 184–194, March 2006.

23. Piyush Prakash and Alain J. Martin. Slack matching quasi delay-insensitive circuits. In *Proc. International Symposium on Advanced Research in Asynchronous Circuits and Systems*, pages 195–204, March 2006.

24. Recep O. Ozdag and Peter A. Beerel. High-speed QDI asynchronous pipelines. In *Proc. International Symposium on Advanced Research in Asynchronous Circuits and Systems*, pages 13–22, April 2002.

25. K. Kulikowski, M. Karpovsky, and A. Taubin. Power attacks on secure hardware based on early propagation of data. In *12th IEEE International On-Line Testing Symposium*, 2006.

26. K. Kulikowski, M. Karpovsky, and A. Taubin. Robust codes for fault attack resistant cryptographic hardware. In *Fault Diagnosis and Tolerance in Cryptography, 2nd International Workshop*, pages 1–12, Edinburgh, 2005.

27. Weaver: GTL synthesis flow. http://async.bu.edu/weaver/.

28. TSMC 0.18μm process 1.8-volt Sage-X standard cell library databook, September 2003.

29. High performance AES cores for ASIC - http://www.heliontech.com, 2005.

30. A. Hodjat and I. Verbauwhede. Area-throughput trade-offs for fully pipelined 30 to 70 Gbits/s AES processors. *IEEE Transactions on Computers*, 55(4), 2006.

31. K. Kulikowski, M. Karpovsky, and A. Taubin. DPA on faulty cryptographic hardware and countermeasures. In *Fault Diagnosis and Tolerance in Cryptography, 3nd International Workshop*, 2006.

Challenges for Trusted Computing

Ahmad-Reza Sadeghi

Horst Görtz Institute for IT Security, Ruhr-University Bochum
sadeghi@crypto.rub.de

The Trusted Computing Group (TCG), an alliance of a large number of IT enterprises, has published a set of specifications aiming at cost-efficient extensions of conventional computer architectures with security-related features and cryptographic mechanisms. The TCG core specification concerns the Trusted Platform Module (TPM) that acts as a root of trust of a computing platform and provides cryptographic primitives which can be used to realize more sophisticated security services. Currently, TPMs are implemented as dedicated chips mounted on the motherboard of a computer and many vendors already ship their platforms equipped with TPMs.

Trusted Computing (TC) is an emerging technology and several prominent research and industrial projects are investigating trustworthy IT systems based on TC with promising results. Nevertheless, for the employment in practice various challenging technical and research problems are still to be solved including:

TPM complexity: The TPM specification contains a large number of commands and parameters and seems unmanageable. A thorough analysis is still missing to determine the minimal/essential set of functionalities for the TPM.

TPM compliance: Recent efforts show that the majority of TPMs available on the market are non-compliant to the TCG specification. Currently, users of TCG-enabled platforms have no efficient means to test the trustworthiness of their TPM and/or its compliance.

Maintenance: Recovering sealed data and backups in case of modified platform configurations as well as the migration of TPM states among platforms (with possibly different trust level) demand for more satisfactory solutions.

Trust infrastructure: Distributed trusted computing needs an appropriate framework for handling trust in practice (platform certificates, trusted channels, attestation kernels, etc)

Attestation: Existing TCG attestation is not satisfactory and may need rethinking. In particular it discloses the system configuration raising privacy concerns. A more general concept is property-based attestation that requires attesting whether a computing platform (or an application) has the desired security properties instead of attesting measurements (hash values) of the corresponding binaries as proposed by the TCG. However, one still needs to define and efficiently determine reasonable properties.

Trustworthy systems demand for a careful design and security analysis of trusted computing components and their interfaces to provide multilateral security that is essential in multiparty computation scenarios in practice such as home banking, eGovernment, Grid computing, virtual data centers, etc.

L. Goubin and M. Matsui (Eds.): CHES 2006, LNCS 4249, p. 414, 2006.

Superscalar Coprocessor for High-Speed Curve-Based Cryptography*

K. Sakiyama, L. Batina, B. Preneel, and I. Verbauwhede

Katholieke Universiteit Leuven / IBBT
Department Electrical Engineering - ESAT/SCD-COSIC
Kasteelpark Arenberg 10, B-3001 Leuven-Heverlee, Belgium
{ksakiyam, lbatina, preneel, iverbauw}@esat.kuleuven.be

Abstract. We propose a superscalar coprocessor for high-speed curve-based cryptography. It accelerates scalar multiplication by exploiting instruction-level parallelism (ILP) dynamically and processing multiple instructions in parallel. The system-level architecture is designed so that the coprocessor can fully utilize the superscalar feature. The implementation results show that scalar multiplication of Elliptic Curve Cryptography (ECC) over $GF(2^{163})$, Hyperelliptic Curve Cryptography (HECC) of genus 2 over $GF(2^{83})$ and ECC over a composite field, $GF((2^{83})^2)$ can be improved by a factor of 1.8, 2.7 and 2.5 respectively compared to the case of a basic single-scalar architecture. This speed-up is achieved by exploiting parallelism in curve-based cryptography. The coprocessor deals with a single instruction that can be used for all field operations such as multiplications and additions. In addition, this instruction only allows one to compute point/divisor operations. Furthermore, we provide also a fair comparison between the three curve-based cryptosystems.

Keywords: Superscalar, instruction-level parallelism, coprocessor, curve-based cryptography, scalar multiplication, HECC, ECC.

1   Introduction

Public-key cryptosystems form an essential building block for digital communication. Unlike secret-key algorithms that allow for a fast encryption of a large bulk of data, the importance of Public-Key Cryptography (PKC) is to have secure communications over insecure channels without prior exchange of a secret key. In addition, PKC enables digital signatures as an important cryptographic service. Diffie and Hellman introduced the idea of PKC [1] in the mid 70's.

Implementing PKC is a challenge for most application platforms varying from software to hardware. The reason is that one has to deal with very long numbers in conditions that are often constrained in area and power. For the choice of the implementation platform, several factors have to be taken into account.

* Kazuo Sakiyama and Lejla Batina are funded by FWO projects (G.0450.04, G.0141.03). This research has been also supported by IBBT-QoE and the EU IST FP6 projects SCARD, SESOC, ECRYPT.

L. Goubin and M. Matsui (Eds.): CHES 2006, LNCS 4249, pp. 415–429, 2006.

Hardware solutions provide the speed and more physical security, but the flexibility is limited. For that property software solutions are needed, but a pure software solution is not a feasible option in most resource-limited environments. Hardware/software co-design potentially allows an efficient design platform that explores trade-off between cost, performance and security.

The most popular and most widely used public-key cryptosystems are RSA [2] and ECC [3,4]. In embedded systems, ECC is considered a more suitable choice than RSA because ECC obtains higher performance, lower power consumption, and smaller area on most platforms. Another appealing candidate for PKC is HECC. Recently many good results appear for software and hardware implementations of HECC at the same time more theoretical work has shown HECC to be also secure in the case of curves with a small genus [5].

A considerable amount of work has been reported on improving the performance of Elliptic Curve (EC) scalar multiplication. The work can be classified into following categories: First of all, mathematical investigation has been done for various types of elliptic curves such as Koblitz curves. Secondly, various algorithms for scalar multiplication have been proposed and criteria for improvements include performance as well as side-channel security. One of the best-known examples that meet requirements for both is the Montgomery's powering ladder [6]. Lastly, architecture-level improvements can be considered from a hardware implementations' point of view. Our interest in this paper mainly lies at this level.

The contribution of this paper is in accelerating curve-based cryptosystems by deploying a superscalar architecture. The solution is algorithm-independent and can be applied for any scalar multiplication algorithm. Some previous work reported parallel use of modular arithmetic units for accelerating scalar multiplication [7,8,9,10,11,12]. In those papers, point/divisor doubling and addition are reformulated so that they can take advantage of the parallel processing. One original contribution is that our proposed architecture embeds an instruction scheduler that explores the best level of parallelism and assigns tasks for the processing units in an optimal way. In this way the parallelism within the operations can be found *on-the-fly* by *dynamically* checking the data dependency in the instructions. We provide also a fair comparison between three cryptosystems, ECC, HECC and ECC over a composite field. Namely, it is known that for HECC of genus 2 one has the ability to work in the field of a size two times smaller than the one for ECC obtaining the same level of security. On the other hand using ECC over $GF((2^p)^2)$, we end up with the same field arithmetic as HECC. In this way, another contribution of this paper lies in the system architecture of three curve-based cryptosystems enabling one to use the same amount of area.

The remainder of this paper is as follows. Section 2 gives a survey of relevant previous work for curve-based cryptography implementations. In Section 3, some background information on ECC and HECC is given. In Section 4 the architecture for our proposed coprocessor is explained. The details of our implementation are introduced in Section 5 and the results are shown for various implementation options in Section 6. Section 7 concludes the paper.

2   Previous Work

This section lists some relevant previous work. As already mentioned, there is a considerable amount of work done on hardware implementations, especially for ECC [13,14], but more recently also some on HECC. Recent improvements on HECC divisor operations' formulae [15,16,17] resulted in several hardware implementations featuring efficient HECC performances [18,11]. The first result showing that HECC performance is comparable to the one of ECC is the work of Pelzl *et al.* [19].

In 1989 Agnew *et al.* reported the first result for performing the elliptic curve operations on hardware [20]. Since then a substantial amount of work dealt with hardware implementations of ECC, the majority of that over binary fields. In 2000 Orlando and Paar proposed a scalable elliptic curve processor architecture which operates over finite fields $GF(2^n)$ in [13]. Gura *et al.* [14] have introduced a programmable hardware accelerator for ECC over $GF(2^n)$, which can handle arbitrary field sizes up to 255.

There is not much previous work on hardware implementations of HECC. The first complete hardware implementation of HECC was given by Boston *et al.* [21]. They designed a coprocessor for genus two curves over $GF(2^{113})$ and implemented it on a Xilinx Virtex-II FPGA. The algorithm of Cantor was used for all computations on Jacobians. On the other hand, the work of Elias *et al.* [18] used Lange's explicit formulae. The results reported were the fastest in hardware at the time. Wollinger *et al.* investigated an HECC implementation on a VLSI coprocessor. They compared coprocessors using affine and projective coordinates and concluded that the latter should be preferred for hardware implementations [11].

While ECC applications are highly developed and widely used in practice, the use of HECC is still mainly for research purposes. Previous work on exploring the parallelism between the point/divisor operations has been done for both ECC and HECC. Smart [7] showed that up to three field operations could be executed in parallel for Hessian form of an elliptic curve. On the other hand, the work of Mischra investigated parallelism between divisor operations [10], both purely on algorithmic level.

3   Curve-Based Cryptography

Here, we consider some background information for curve-based cryptography over binary fields; for hyperelliptic curves we are interested only in genus 2 curves. We mention the basic algorithms and the structure of the operations. Good references for the mathematical background are [22,23,24].

The main operation in any curve-based primitive is scalar multiplication. The general hierarchical structure for operations required for implementations of curve-based cryptography is given in Fig. 1(a). Point/divisor multiplication is at the top level. At the next (lower) level are the point/divisor group operations. The lowest level consists of finite field operations such as addition, multiplication and inversion required to perform the group operations. The only difference

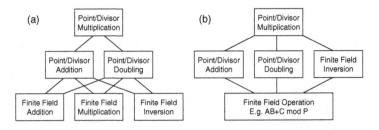

Fig. 1. Scheme of the hierarchy for ECC/HECC operations

between ECC and HECC is in the middle level that in this case consists of different sequences of operations. Those for HECC are more complex when compared with the ECC point operation, but they use shorter operands. One can perform inversion also with a chain of multiplications [25] and only provide hardware for finite field multiplication and addition. The corresponding hierarchy is illustrated in Fig. 1(b). We use this structure for our proposed coprocessor.

3.1   ECC over a Binary Field

ECC relies on a group structure induced on an elliptic curve. A set of points on an elliptic curve (with one special point added, the so-called point at infinity $\mathcal{O}$) together with a point addition as a binary operation has the structure of an abelian group. As we consider a finite field of characteristic 2, $i.e.$ GF(2^n), a non-supersingular elliptic curve E over GF(2^n) is defined as the set of solutions $(x, y) \in$ GF(2^n)×GF(2^n) of the equation: $y^2 + xy = x^3 + ax^2 + b$, where $a, b \in$ GF(2^n), $b \neq 0$, together with $\mathcal{O}$.

3.2   HECC

Let $\overline{\text{GF}}(2^n)$ be an algebraic closure of the field GF(2^n). Here we consider a hyperelliptic curve C of genus $g = 2$ over GF(2^n), which is given with an equation of the form:

$$C : y^2 + h(x)y = f(x) \quad in \quad \text{GF}(2^n)[x, y], \tag{1}$$

where $h(x) \in$ GF(2^n)$[x]$ is polynomial of degree at most g $(deg(h) \leq g)$ and $f(x)$ is a monic polynomial of degree $2g + 1$ $(deg(f) = 2g + 1)$. Also, there are no solutions $(x, y) \in \overline{\text{GF}}(2^n) \times \overline{\text{GF}}(2^n)$ which simultaneously satisfy the equation (1) and the equations: $2v + h(u) = 0, h'(u)v - f'(u) = 0$. These points are called singular points. For the genus 2, in the general case the following equation is used $y^2 + (h_2x^2 + h_1x + h_0)y = x^5 + f_4x^4 + f_3x^3 + f_2x^2 + f_1x + f_0$.

A divisor D is a formal sum of points on the hyperelliptic curve C $i.e.$ $D = \sum m_P P$ and its degree is $deg(D) = \sum m_P$. Let Div denotes the group of all divisors on C and Div_0 the subgroup of Div of all divisors with degree zero. The Jacobian J of the curve C is defined as quotient group $J = Div_0/P$. Here P is the set of all principal divisors, where a divisor D is called principal if $D = div(f)$, for some element f of the function field of C $(div(f) = \sum_{P \in C} ord_P(f)P)$. The discrete logarithm problem in the Jacobian is the basis of security for HECC. In practice, the Mumford representation according to which each divisor is represented as a pair of polynomials $[u, v]$ is usually used. Here, u is monic of degree 2, $deg(v) < deg(u)$ and $u|f - hv - v^2$ (so-called reduced divisors). For implementations of HECC, we need to implement the multiplication of elements of the Jacobian $i.e.$ divisors with some scalar.

3.3   ECC over a Composite Field

With respect to cryptographic security it is typically recommended to use fields $GF(2^p)$ where p is a prime. As an example we consider the case where $p = 163$. As already mentioned, HECC on a curve of a genus 2 allows one to work in a finite field where bit-lengths are shorter with a factor 2, when compared with ECC. That means, for the equivalent level of security we should choose $GF(2^{83})$. A similar situation we get when considering ECC over a field of a quadratic extension of $GF(2^{83})$, so $GF((2^{83})^2)$ $=GF(2^{83})[y]/g(y)$ and $deg(g) = 2$. In this way one can obtain a speed-up and benefit even more from the parallelism. The reason is that in composite field each element is represented as $c = c_1t + c_0$ where $c_0, c_1 \in GF(2^{83})$ and the multiplication in this field takes 3 multiplications and 4 additions in $GF(2^{83})$ [26].

3.4   Algorithms for Our Implementations

In our implementations scalar multiplication is achieved by use the NAF algorithm [23]. In this way the scalar is decomposed as a NAF and scalar multiplication is done with a series of addition/subtractions of elliptic curve points. We also use projective coordinates for all implementations.

Furthermore, we have rewritten the formulae from [23,16] for EC point operations and HECC divisor doubling, respectively to obtain an optimal usage of our new datapath. We use the same approach to get the formulae for HECC divisor addition in the case of mixed coordinates. Our datapath performs one basic operation, $AB + C$ or $A(B + D) + C$ over a binary field. This operation can be used for the sequence of point/divisor operations. For example, by using $A(B + D) + C$ operation the formulae for HECC divisor addition include 48 instructions instead of 44 multiplications and a lot of additions.

4   Architecture of the Curve-Based Coprocessor

4.1   System Architecture

The proposed architecture of the curve-based cryptosystems is composed of the main controller, several Modular Arithmetic Logic Units (MALUs) and the coprocessor memory that shares intermediate variables between the MALUs ($i.e.$ the so-called shared memory). The block diagram of the cryptosystem is

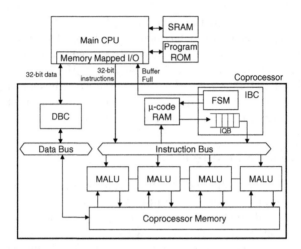

Fig. 2. Block Diagram for the system architecture with the curve-based coprocessor

illustrated in Fig. 2. The configuration of the coprocessor is flexible to provide from the smallest to the fastest implementation depending on a target application. Some components can be added or removed as will be explained next.

The main CPU communicates with the coprocessor through memory-mapped I/O (*e.g.* SRAM interface) and has three types of 32-bit in- and outputs; one of them is a signal that tells the controller to stop sending instructions when the instruction buffer is full. A 32-bit input/output passes data back and forward between the main CPU and the coprocessor and a 32-bit output is used to send instructions. The data transfer between the main CPU and the coprocessor is controlled by a Data Bus Controller (DBC). When using SRAM attached to the main CPU for storing intermediate variables for HECC/ECC operations, the coprocessor can be constructed without use of the coprocessor memory. Alternatively, for the purpose of reducing the I/O transfer overhead, the data memory can be embedded in the coprocessor. In this case, the path through the DBC is only activated when an initial point and the parameters of an elliptic curve are sent to the RAM, or when the result is retrieved.

Instructions are sent to the MALU either from the main CPU or from pre-set micro codes in the μ-code RAM. When the main CPU is in charge of dispatching instructions, the IBC block can be detached from the coprocessor. In this case, it occurs that the throughput of issuing instructions is not high enough for the MALU(s) to be utilized effectively. On the contrary, when the μ-code RAM is used for assisting the main CPU, the Instruction Bus Controller (IBC) can handle one instruction per cycle. For instance, the sequence of point doubling is stored in the μ-code RAM and the main CPU calls it as an instruction. Thus multiple MALUs can be activated in parallel without any instruction stalls. During point multiplication, the IBC keeps on reading instructions from the μ-code RAM and stores them to an Instruction Queue Buffer (IQB) unless the IQB is full. The IBC checks if there is instruction-level parallelism (ILP) by

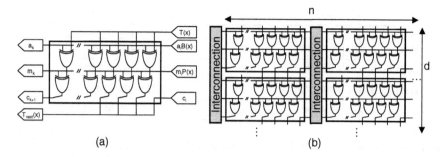

Fig. 3. Reconfigurable datapath for $GF(2^n)$ operation. (a) MSB-first bit-serial polynomial-basis multiplier. (b) Scalability of the MALU.

checking the data-dependency of instructions in the IQB and forwards them to the MALU(s) (see Section 4.2 and 4.4).

4.2 Modular Arithmetic Logic Unit

In this section the architecture for the MALU is briefly explained. The datapath of the MALU is an MSB-first bit-serial polynomial-basis $GF(2^n)$ multiplier as illustrated in Fig. 3(a). This is a hardware implementation that computes $A(x)B(x) + C(x) \bmod P(x)$ where $A(x) = \sum a_i x^i$, $B(x) = \sum b_i x^i$, $C(x) = \sum c_i x^i$ and $P(x) = \sum p_i x^i$. The proposed MALU computes $A(x)B(x) + C(x) \bmod P(x)$ by following the steps: The MALU sums up three types of inputs which are $a_i B(x), m_i P(x)$ and $T(x)$, and then outputs the intermediate result, $T_{next}(x)$ by computing $T_{next}(x) = (T(x) + a_i B(x) + m_i P(x))x + c_{i-1}$ where $m_i = t_n \oplus a_i b_n$. By providing T_{next} as the next input T and repeating the same computation for n times, one can obtain the result. The detailed explanation is also discussed in [27]. Moreover, by providing $B(x) + D(x)$ in place of $B(x)$, an operation, $A(x)(B(x) + D(x)) + C(x) \bmod P(x)$ can be also supported. This operation requires additional XORs and selector logics for registers storing the coefficients of $B(x)$ or $(B(x) + D(x))$.

The proposed datapath is scalable in the digit size d (in vertical direction in Fig. 3(b)) which can be decided by exploring the best combination of performance and cost. The field size n is determined by the key-length. It can be achieved also by interconnecting several MALUs in horizontal direction. Hence, various implementation options can be chosen with the MALU. For instance, the coprocessor can support arbitrary field sizes up to 335 when using four sets of the MALU whose field size is 83.

4.3 The MALU Instruction

Here, a new instruction called $MALU_n$ is defined. It is worth mentioning that this is the only instruction that operates on the datapath.

$$MALU_n(A, B, C, D) = A(x)(B(x) + D(x)) + C(x) \bmod P(x). \qquad (2)$$

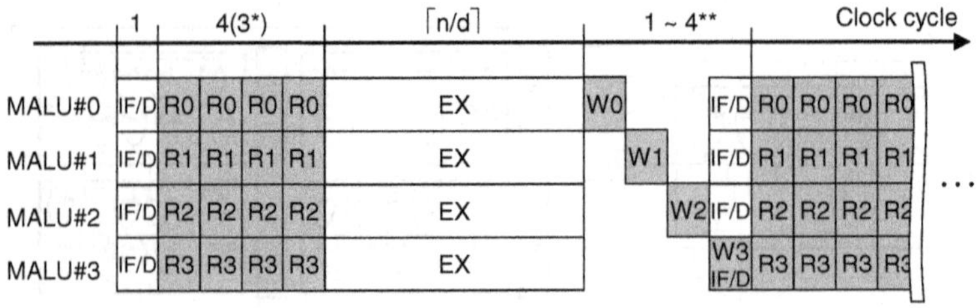

Fig. 4. Example of four parallel issue of instructions in case of allocating four MALUs. (IF/D: Instruction Fetch/Decode, EX: Execution of MALU, R/W: Read/Write from/to the coprocessor memory). *The read cycle differs from the type of operation. **The write cycle depends on the number of instructions issued in parallel.

When using $A(x)B(x) + C(x) \bmod P(x)$ operation, one can ignore $D(x)$ as $D(x) = 0$. The whole procedure to execute $MALU_n$ starts from an instruction fetch and decode (IF/D). Then, variables for $A(x), B(x), C(x)$ and $D(x)$ are loaded via RAM (R) for the succeeding execution stage. The result is stored to RAM (W) in the last step. Note that the data at different addresses can be read in parallel for the different MALU by replicating RAM (*i.e.* four clones of single-port RAMs in case of using four MALUs). The write cycle is determined by the number of instructions that can be issued in parallel. When using multiple MALUs, the write operations from every MALU are done at the different cycle to escape memory-write conflicts. This is illustrated in Fig. 4.

4.4 Dynamic Scheduling

ILP is exploited for all instructions as long as two or more instructions are buffered in the IQB. Here, we introduce our strategy to find ILP. A $MALU_n$ instruction has four source operands and outputs the result to RAM, *i.e.* $MALU_n$ deals with five types of addresses in the case of operating $A(x)(B(x) + D(x)) + C(x) \bmod P(x)$. Here, let A, B, C, D be the addresses for four inputs and R be the address where the result is stored. They are expressed as follows:

$$MALU_n : R = A, B, C, D. \tag{3}$$

The $MALU_n$ also refers to $P(x)$ that is stored in RAM. Including out-of-order execution, the following two types of dependencies are possible between two instructions, $MALU_n^i$ and $MALU_n^j$ (i and j are labels indicating order of instruction in the IQB). By checking the following two dependencies for all i and j that satisfy $i < j < ILP_D$, where ILP_D is the size of the instruction window, one can determine the number of instructions to be issued in parallel.

Read-After-Write (RAW) Dependency check for in-order execution ($R^i = A^j$, $R^i = B^j$, $R^i = C^j$, $R^i = D^j$)**:** If the result of the instruction $MALU_n^i$, R^i is input for the following instructions, the instruction $MALU_n^i$ cannot be issued until the preceding instruction completes the operation.

Table 1. Primary instructions for the coprocessor

INSTRUCTION	DESCRIPTION	OPERATION
STORE(@dst)	Data storing to the coprocessor	R@dst <= din;
LOAD(@src)	Data loading from the coprocessor	dout <= R@src;
MALU(@dst,@src1-4)	Operate MALU$_n$	R@dst <= MALU(R@src1-4)
HECCPD()	HECC divisor doubling	P <= 2P

RAW Dependency check for out-of-order execution ($R^j = A^i$, $R^j = B^i$, $R^j = C^i$, $R^j = D^i$): In case that all conditions are not true, the instruction MALU$_n^j$ cannot be issued until the instruction MALU$_n^i$ finishes. The example using the actual sequence of EC point doubling is shown in the Appendix.

The proposed architecture needs no check for Write-After-Read and Write-After-Write dependencies contrary a general superscalar machine. This is because MALU$_n$ is a fixed-length multi-cycle instruction and hence we can skip those dependencies in the sequence of point/divisor operations. Suppose the size of the instruction window is ILP_D, the number of conditions to check becomes $4(ILP_D - 1)^2$. The hardware complexity for ILP expands with a large ILP_D, but instead further parallelism can be expected.

5   Implementation

5.1   Instruction Sets for the Coprocessor

Table 1 shows some of the primary instructions for the co-processor. The input registers of the MALU are set via data-bus ports. In case of using a 32-bit CPU such as the ARM, setting a register whose address is src1 requires three STORE(@dst) instructions for HECC over GF(2^{83}). After all operands are set in corresponding registers, a MALU(@dst,@src1-4) operation is executed. When using the μ-code configuration, it is possible to define an instruction that consists of a series of MALU(@dst,@src1-4) operations. In this paper, point/divisor operations are all composed of the MALU instruction (see the Appendix).

5.2   System Configurations

The system configurations are explored in two steps. First, in order to make the best use of the superscalar coprocessor, four different coprocessor configurations are explored as listed in Fig. 5(a). This is the so-called vertical exploration of the hardware/software co-design. Secondly, the performance comparison is made with HECC, ECC and ECC over a composite field by changing the number of MALUs. Thus the coprocessor is also investigated from a parallel processing point of view (horizontal exploration).

5.3   Design Environment

The proposed design is constructed on GEZEL hardware/software co-design environment with the ARM Instruction Set Simulator (ISS) [28].

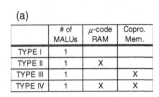

(a)

	# of MALUs	μ-code RAM	Copro. Mem.
TYPE I	1		
TYPE II	1	X	
TYPE III	1		X
TYPE IV	1	X	X

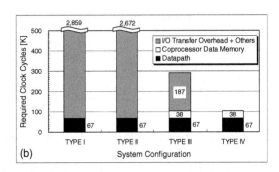

(b)

Fig. 5. (a) Coprocessor configurations for the vertical exploration. (b) Required clock cycles of HECC scalar multiplication for different coprocessor configuration ($d = 12$).

The platform provides cycle-accurate simulations for various hardware/ software system configurations. As mentioned in Section 4, the coprocessor is attached to the memory-mapped interface of the ARM. Thus, various types of system configurations are examined to verify the functionality and estimate the performance in a system-level. The GEZEL codes are automatically translated into VHDL codes that can be used for an FPGA prototype.

6   Results

6.1   Vertical Exploration of System Architecture with Coprocessor

Fig. 5(b) compares the performance of HECC scalar multiplication for different system configurations. For the case of the TYPE I and II, the I/O transfer overhead between the main CPU and the coprocessor is the majority of the cycles (about 97%). The reason for this is that the temporary data variables are stored in the memory of the main CPU and travel through the CPU to the coprocessor for processing. As for the TYPE III, the I/O transfer overhead is reduced significantly due to the effect of the data memory allocated in the coprocessor. However, the I/O overhead is still dominant because the main CPU issues instructions via the slow communication channel. The parallel processing feature is hence useless to improve the performance in such system settings. Note that the ratio of the I/O transfer overheads is reduced ostensibly by introducing smaller d since the datapath performs in more clock cycles. In this way, it is important to find the best digit size, d that can hide the I/O transfer overhead with the TYPE III. This paper, however, focuses on the TYPE IV for a deeper investigation of the parallelism in order to obtain high performance. Because the TYPE IV assures the highest parallelism regardless of the value of d.

6.2   Performance Comparison Between Three Cryptosystems

Fig. 6 shows the required cycles for various implementations based on the TYPE IV configuration. The building block of the datapath is the MALU whose field

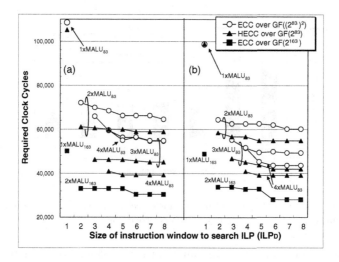

Fig. 6. Required clock cycles of scalar multiplication for different ILP_D $(d = 12)$. (a) Operation form is $AB + C$. (b) Operation form is $A(B + D) + C$.

size is 83 or MALU_{83}. Up to four clones of the MALU_{83} are embedded in the coprocessor to observe the performance improvement with the superscalar architecture. For ECC, a pair of MALU_{83} is equivalent to one MALU_{163} in terms of hardware cost. The overall performance improves as increasing the number of MALU_{83} for both of the operation type. Also a large ILP_D helps exploiting more parallelism and leads to a higher performance. The results show the effectiveness of an operation whose form is $A(B + D) + C$ especially for the ECC over a composite field. In our case, the performance of ECC is better than others on equivalent hardware resources. The results are also summarized in Table 2.

In order to investigate the performance bottle-neck of HECC and ECC, the required clock cycles in scalar multiplication is split into two factors; one is for the memory access and another is for the data processing of the datapath. As can be seen from the Fig. 7, operation form, $A(B + D) + C$ introduces more memory accesses while the data can be processed in less clock cycles. Overall

Table 2. Required clock cycles of scalar multiplication for $d = 12$ and $ILP_D = 6$. Figures in parenthesis are the speed-up ratio based on the smallest configuration.

Coprocessor Configuration	Operation: $AB + C$			$A(B + D) + C$		
	HECC $\text{GF}(2^{83})$	ECC $\text{GF}(2^{163})$	ECC $\text{GF}((2^{83})^2)$	HECC $\text{GF}(2^{83})$	ECC $\text{GF}(2^{163})$	ECC $\text{GF}((2^{83})^2)$
$1 \times \text{MALU}_{83}$	105,237 (1.00)	–	108,603 (1.00)	98,856 (1.06)	–	98,688 (1.10)
$2 \times \text{MALU}_{83}$ $= 1 \times \text{MALU}_{163}$	58,917 (1.79)	50,112 (1.00)	66,193 (1.64)	54,909 (1.92)	48,849 (1.03)	61,941 (1.75)
$3 \times \text{MALU}_{83}$	45,606 (2.31)	–	56,267 (1.93)	42,029 (2.50)	–	49,849 (2.18)
$4 \times \text{MALU}_{83}$ $= 2 \times \text{MALU}_{163}$	39,247 (2.68)	30,396 (1.65)	56,437 (1.92)	39,115 (2.69)	27,981 (1.79)	43,594 (2.49)

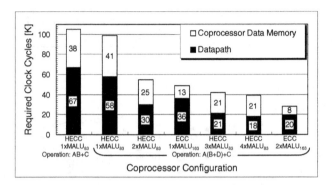

Fig. 7. The profile graphs of the required clock cycles in ECC/HECC scalar multiplication for different hardware settings of the coprocessor $(d = 12)$

the proposed superscalar feature can reduce the clock cycles in both of the coprocessor memory access and the datapath operation. The memory accesses of HECC become dominant as introducing more parallelism. On the other hand the memory accesses in ECC is less than 30 % of the total clock cycles. This fact explains the reason that scalar multiplication of HECC is eventually slower than that of ECC on equivalent hardware resources.

6.3   Prototype Results on FPGA

Based on the performance observation, the coprocessor is prototyped with the system configuration of $d = 12$ and $ILP_D = 6$ on Virtex-II PRO (XC2VP30). The operation that the MALU supports is $A(B + D) + C$. The the coprocessor memory consist of several 32×84-bit single-port RAMs and each RAM is assigned to each MALU$_{83}$. The μ-code program is implemented as an LUT ROM. As

Table 3. Performance Comparison of HECC/ECC implementations on FPGAs

Ref. Design	Field	Target Platform	Area [slices/gates]	f_{max} [MHz]	Perform. [μsec]	Polynomial $P(x)$	Comments
HECC							
This work	GF(2^{83})	Virtex-II Pro	2,446		989		1×MALU$_{83}$
			4,749	100.0	549	Arbitrary	2×MALU$_{83}$
			6,586		420		3×MALU$_{83}$
[11]	GF(2^{81})	Virtex-II Pro	4,039	57.0	787	Fixed	2×MULT,1×INV
			7,737	60.7	387		3×MULT,2×INV
ECC							
This work	GF(2^{163})	Virtex-II Pro	4,749	100.0	488	Arbitrary	1×MALU$_{163}$
			8,450		280		2×MALU$_{163}$
[14]	GF(2^{163})	Virtex E	19,508	66.5	1,554	Arbitrary	López-Dahab
					143	Fixed: $x^{163} + x^7$ $+x^6 + x^3 + 1$	scalar mult.
[13]	GF(2^{167})	Virtex E	3,002 (+ 10 BRAMs)	76.7	210	Fixed: $x^{167} + x^6 + 1$	López-Dahab scalar mult.
[29]	GF(2^{191})	Virtex E	19,626 (+ 26 BRAMs)	9.99	59.26	Fixed: $x^{191} + x^9 + 1$	López-Dahab scalar mult.

shown in Table 3, our HECC results show a better trade-off between cost and performance than the previous work. With regard to ECC implementation, our result is based on the IEEE-P1363 compliant sequence [23] and is not as fast as some previous work [13,29]. However considering the flexibility in our proposed coprocessor, the difference can be regarded as small.

7 Conclusions

This paper introduced a superscalar coprocessor that could deal with three different curve-based cryptosystems. The implementation results showed that scalar multiplication of ECC over $GF(2^{163})$, HECC of genus 2 over $GF(2^{83})$ and ECC over a composite field, $GF((2^{83})^2)$ was improved by a factor of 1.8, 2.7 and 2.5 respectively compared to the case of a basic single-scalar architecture. This speed-up was achieved by vertical and horizontal exploration of the system architecture to exploit parallelism in curve-based cryptography. In our design, ECC showed better performance than others on the same amount of hardware resource. All operations in three curve-based cryptosystems were performed with only one instruction that could be flexibly defined as $AB + C$ or $A(B + D) + C$.

Acknowledgement

The IBBT - QoE project is co-funded by the IBBT (Interdisciplinary Institute for BroadBand Technology), a research institute founded by the Flemish Government in 2004, and the involved companies and institutions [30].

References

1. W. Diffie and M.E. Hellman. New directions in cryptography. *IEEE Transactions on Information Theory*, 22:644–654, 1976.
2. R.L. Rivest, A. Shamir, and L. Adleman. A method for obtaining digital signatures and public-key cryptosystems. *Communications of the ACM*, 21(2):120–126, 1978.
3. N. Koblitz. Elliptic curve cryptosystem. *Math. Comp.*, 48:203–209, 1987.
4. V. Miller. Uses of elliptic curves in cryptography. In H. C. Williams, editor, *Advances in Cryptology: Proceedings of CRYPTO'85*, number 218 in LNCS, pages 417–426. Springer-Verlag, 1985.
5. N. Thériault. Index calculus attack for hyperelliptic curves of small genus. In C. S. Laih, editor, *Proceedings of Advances in Cryptology - ASIACRYPT: 9th International Conference on the Theory and Application of Cryptology and Information Security*, number 2894 in LNCS, pages 75–92. Springer-Verlag, 2003.
6. P. Montgomery. Speeding the pollard and elliptic curve methods of factorization.
7. N.P. Smart. The Hessian form of an elliptic curve. In Ç.K. Koç, D. Naccache, and C. Paar, editors, *Proceedings of 3rd International Workshop on Cryptograpic Hardware and Embedded Systems (CHES)*, number 2162 in LNCS, pages 121–128. Springer-Verlag, 2001.

8. M. Joye and S.-M. Yen. The Montgomery powering ladder. In B.S. Kaliski Jr., Ç.K. Koç, and C. Paar, editors, *Proceedings of 4th International Workshop on Cryptographic Hardware and Embedded Systems (CHES)*, number 2523 in LNCS, pages 291–302. Springer-Verlag, 2002.
9. T. Izu and T. Takagi. A fast parallel elliptic curve multiplication resistant against side channel attacks. In D. Naccache and P. Paillier, editors, *Proceedings of 5th International Workshop on Practice and Theory in Public Key Cryptosystems (PKC 2002)*, number 3027 in LNCS, pages 280–296. Springer-Verlag, 2002.
10. P. K. Mishra and P. Sarkar. Parallelizing explicit formula for arithmetic in the jacobian of hyperelliptic curves. In J. Hartmanis G. Goos and J. van Leeuwen, editors, *Proceedings of ASIACRYPT 2003*, number 2894 in LNCS, pages 93–110. Springer-Verlag, 2003.
11. T. Wollinger. *Software and Hardware Implementation of Hyperelliptic Curve Cryptosystems*. PhD thesis, Ruhr-University Bochum, 2004.
12. A. Hodjat, L. Batina, D. Hwang, and I. Verbauwhede. A hyperelliptic curve crypto coprocessor for an 8051 microcontroller. In *Proceedings of The IEEE 2005 Workshop on Signal Processing Systems (SIPS'05)*, pages 93–98, 2005.
13. G. Orlando and C. Paar. A high-performance reconfigurable elliptic curve processor for $GF(2^m)$. In Ç.K. Koç and C. Paar, editors, *Proceedings of 2nd International Workshop on Cryptograpic Hardware and Embedded Systems (CHES)*, number 1965 in LNCS, pages 41–56. Springer-Verlag, 2000.
14. N. Gura, S.C. Shantz, H. Eberle, D. Finchelstein, S. Gupta, V. Gupta, and D. Stebila. An end-to-end systems approach to elliptic curve cryptography. In B. Kaliski Jr., Ç.K. Koç, and C. Paar, editors, *Proceedings of 4th International Workshop on Cryptographic Hardware and Embedded Systems (CHES)*, LNCS 2523, 2002.
15. T. Lange. Formulae for arithmetic on genus 2 hyperelliptic curves. *Applicable Algebra in Engineering, Communication and Computing*, 15(5):295–328, 2005.
16. B. Byramjee and S. Duquesne. Classification of genus 2 curves over F_{2^n} and optimization of their arithmetic. Cryptology ePrint Archive: Report 2004/107.
17. T. Lange and M. Stevens. Efficient doubling on genus two curves over binary fields. In H. Handschuh and M.A. Hasan, editors, *In Selected Areas in Cryptography: SAC 2004*, volume 3357 of *LNCS*, pages 170–181. Springer-Verlag, 2004.
18. G. Elias, A. Miri, and T. H. Yeap. High-performance, FPGA based hyperelliptic curve cryptosystem. In *In Proceedings of the 22nd Biennial Symposium on Communications*, 2004.
19. J. Pelzl, T. Wollinger, J. Guajardo, and C. Paar. Hyperelliptic curve cryptosystems: Closing the performance gap to elliptic curves. In C. Walter, Ç.K. Koç, and C. Paar, editors, *Proceedings of 5th International Workshop on Cryptograpic Hardware and Embedded Systems (CHES)*, number 2779 in LNCS, pages 351–365. Springer-Verlag, 2003.
20. G.B. Agnew, R.C. Mullin, and S.A. Vanstone. A fast elliptic curve cryptosystem. In J.-J. Quisquater and J. Vandewalle, editors, *Advances in Cryptology: Proceedings of EUROCRYPT'89*, number 434 in LNCS, pages 706–708. Springer-Verlag, 1989.
21. N. Boston, T. Clancy, Y. Liow, and J. Webster. Genus two hyperelliptic curve coprocessor. In B.S. Kaliski Jr., Ç.K. Koç, and C. Paar, editors, *Proceedings of 4th International Workshop on Cryptographic Hardware and Embedded Systems (CHES)*, number 2523 in LNCS, pages 400–414. Springer-Verlag, 2002.
22. N. Koblitz. *Algebraic Aspects of Cryptography*. Springer-Verlag, first edition, 1998.
23. I. Blake, G. Seroussi, and N.P. Smart. *Elliptic Curves in Cryptography*. London Mathematical Society Lecture Note Series. Cambridge University Press, 1999.

24. A. Menezes, Y.-H. Wu, and R. Zuccherato. *An Elementary Introduction to Hyperelliptic Curves - Appendix*, pages 155–178. Springer-Verlag, 1998. N. Koblitz: Algebraic Aspects of Cryptography.
25. T. Itoh and S. Tsujii. Effective recursive algorithm for computing multiplicative inverses in GF(2^m). *Electronics Letters*, 24(6):334–335, 1988.
26. R. Lidl and H. Niederreiter. *Finite fields*, volume 20 of *Encyclopedia of Mathematics and its Applications*. Cambridge University Press, second edition, 2000.
27. K. Sakiyama, B. Preneel, and I. Verbauwhede. A fast dual-field modular arithmetic logic unit and its hardware imlementation. In *Proceedings of IEEE International Symposium on Circuits and Systems (ISCAS'06)*, pages 787–790, 2006.
28. P. Schaumont. Gezel version 2. http://rijndael.ece.vt.edu/gezel2/.
29. Nazar A. Saqib, Francisco Rodríguez-Henriquez, and Arturo Díaz-Pérez. A reconfigurable processor for high speed point multiplication in elliptic curves. In *International Journal of Embedded Systems 2005*, volume 1, No. 3/4, pages 237 – 249, 2005.
30. https://projects.ibbt.be/qoe/.

A   Dynamic Scheduling for EC Point Doubling

The first two instructions have a RAW dependency with t_1. ECDB04 has no RAW dependency upon the first three instructions in in order and out-of-order execution, and therefore it can be issued prior to the first three instructions.

Table 4. Example of parallelized out-of-order instruction sequence for EC point doubling in case of three consecutive point doublings (*i.e.* $P \Leftarrow 2^3 P$, where $P(X_1, Y_1, Z_1)$). The ECDBs in italic are instructions from preceding and succeeding point doublings.

Original Sequence						Parallelized Out-of-order Sequence
	Address: R	**A**	**B**	**C**	**D**	
ECDB01:	MALU$_n$(t_1,	X_1,	X_1,	0,	0)	*ECDB08* & ECDB04
ECDB02:	MALU$_n$(t_2,	t_1,	t_1,	0,	0)	*ECDB09* & ECDB06
ECDB03:	MALU$_n$(t_4,	Y_1,	Z_1,	t_1,	0)	*ECDB10* & ECDB01
ECDB04:	MALU$_n$(t_3,	Z_1,	Z_1,	0,	0)	ECDB02 & ECDB03
ECDB05:	MALU$_n$(Z_1,	X_1,	t_3,	0,	0)	ECDB05 & ECDB07
ECDB06:	MALU$_n$(t_5,	d_6,	t_3,	X_1,	0)	ECDB08 & *ECDB04*
ECDB07:	MALU$_n$(t_3,	t_5,	t_5,	0,	0)	ECDB09 & *ECDB06*
ECDB08:	MALU$_n$(X_1,	t_3,	t_3,	0,	0)	ECDB10 & *ECDB01*
ECDB09:	MALU$_n$(t_1,	X_1,	Z_1,	0,	t_4)	*ECDB02* & *ECDB03*
ECDB10:	MALU$_n$(Y_1,	t_2,	Z_1,	t_1,	0)	*ECDB05* & *ECDB07*

Hardware/Software Co-design of Elliptic Curve Cryptography on an 8051 Microcontroller

Manuel Koschuch, Joachim Lechner, Andreas Weitzer, Johann Großschädl,
Alexander Szekely, Stefan Tillich, and Johannes Wolkerstorfer

Institute for Applied Information Processing and Communications,
Graz University of Technology, Inffeldgasse 16a, A–8010 Graz, Austria
{manuel.koschuch, joachim.lechner, andreas.weitzer}@student.tugraz.at
{jgrosz, aszekely, stillich, jwolkers}@iaik.tugraz.at

Abstract. 8-bit microcontrollers like the 8051 still hold a considerable share of the embedded systems market and dominate in the smart card industry. The performance of 8-bit microcontrollers is often too poor for the implementation of public-key cryptography in software. In this paper we present a minimalist hardware accelerator for enabling elliptic curve cryptography (ECC) on an 8051 microcontroller. We demonstrate the importance of removing system-level performance bottlenecks caused by the transfer of operands between hardware accelerator and external RAM. The integration of a small direct memory access (DMA) unit proves vital to exploit the full potential of the hardware accelerator. Our design allows to perform a scalar multiplication over the binary extension field $GF(2^{191})$ in 118 msec at a clock frequency of 12 MHz. Considering performance and hardware cost, our system compares favorably with previous work on similar 8-bit platforms.

1 Introduction

Embedded systems made up of hardware and software components constitute the fastest growing segment of the semiconductor industry with products ranging from mobile phones over MP3 players to automotive braking systems. The traditional design techniques (i.e. separate treatment of hardware and software) do not cope with the complexity of today's embedded systems and the steadily increasing time-to-market pressure. Sloppily speaking, "building a machine and seeing whether it works" is not feasible due to unpredictable design times when heterogeneous applications are getting integrated to create a complex system [23]. A promising approach to deal with the complexity of modern embedded systems is *hardware/software co-design*, i.e. the concurrent (or simultaneous) design of hardware and software components with the goal to meet system-level objectives [5]. This includes the analysis of different boundaries and interfaces between hardware and software and the evaluation of design alternatives in a reasonable amount of time [8].

Hardware/software co-design is gaining in importance since the boundary between hardware and software becomes more and more blurred. One factor

L. Goubin and M. Matsui (Eds.): CHES 2006, LNCS 4249, pp. 430–444, 2006.

behind this trend is the advent of flexible architectures that combine general-purpose processors with custom, customizable, or reconfigurable logic. In recent years, major FPGA vendors started to offer special devices consisting of a processor core, on-chip memories, peripherals, and large amounts of reconfigurable logic for the implementation of application-specific hardware. In addition, some of these devices contain application-specific building blocks like fast multipliers for digital signal processing (e.g. Altera Stratix). Therefore, devices consisting of a processor core, application-specific parts, and reconfigurable logic are an ideal co-design platform for heterogenous embedded systems that may comprise several applications domains such as signal processing, networking, and security. Recently, the security domain has attracted particular interest since more and more embedded devices store or transmit sensitive data. This makes a strong case for applying hardware/software co-design techniques to the implementation of cryptographic primitives [20,21].

In this paper we investigate the co-design of *elliptic curve cryptography* on embedded 8-bit platforms, in particular on the 8051 microcontroller. Elliptic curve cryptography (ECC) is highly computation-intensive as it involves arithmetic operations in finite fields of large order (typically about 160 bits) [3]. The results from previous work [12,16,24] show that a "pure" software implementation of ECC does not allow to reach sub-second performance on a standard 8051 clocked at 12 MHz. Therefore, some kind of *hardware acceleration* of the performance-critical operations carried out in ECC is necessary. Elliptic curve cryptography offers a multitude of implementation options for both field and curve (group) arithmetic, respectively [13]. In addition, a number of different boundaries between hardware and software are possible, which allows a system designer to find the proper trade-off between performance and silicon area. One could, for instance, implement the point addition/doubling in hardware and the rest in software [15]. An alternative approach is to implement the field arithmetic in hardware and the curve/point arithmetic in software [1,2,7,14]. Furthermore, hardware acceleration at the granularity of instruction set extensions for the finite field multiplication has also been investigated [6,11,17]. Besides the hardware/software boundary, the *interface* between hardware accelerator and host processor is essential for the system performance, especially for "low-cost" accelerators without local storage since they require a high number of data transfers.

We have co-designed an elliptic curve cryptosystem over binary extension fields using the Dalton 8051 [22] as host controller which executes the software part of our design. The hardware part consists of an *elliptic curve acceleration unit (ECAU)* and an *interface with direct memory access (DMA)* to enable fast data transfer between the ECAU and the external RAM (XRAM) attached to the 8051 microcontroller. Our design goal is to achieve a maximum of performance with a "minimalist" hardware accelerator—the ECAU—composed of a bit-serial multiplier for binary extension fields of order ≤ 192 bits and a supporting register infrastructure. The ECAU allows to perform a full scalar multiplication over the field $GF(2^{191})$ in about 118 msec, assuming that the Dalton 8051 is clocked with 12 MHz. A scalar multiplication over the field $GF(2^{163})$ takes less than 100 msec, which is more than 25 times faster than the co-design for hyperelliptic curve cryptography (HECC)[1] presented by Batina et al. at CHES 2005 [2]. The hardware cost of the ECAU and the DMA controller is 12,65k gates altogether when synthesized with a 0.35 μm standard cell library.

1.1   Improvements over Previous Work

During the past five years, numerous papers dealing with the hardware/software co-design of (hyper)elliptic curve cryptography on 8-bit platforms (e.g. AVR or 8051) have been published [1,2,6,7,14,15,17]. However, the co-design approach for ECC presented in this paper differs from previous work in two important aspects. First, we pay special attention to the efficient implementation of the data transfer between the hardware accelerator and the external RAM attached to the 8051. Second, our approach uses a (limited) scalable hardware accelerator able to perform field arithmetic in all binary fields $GF(2^m)$ with $m \leq 192$ and not just in a single field.

The efficiency of the *data transfer* between ECAU and XRAM impacts the overall performance since the ECAU is a low-cost hardware accelerator, which means that it does not contain local storage for intermediate results. Consequently, all intermediate results occurring during a scalar multiplication have to be transferred between the ECAU and the XRAM[2]. Unfortunately, a standard 8051 only provides 8-bit I/O ports and a serial interface for the communication with the "world outside," both of which are rather slow. There are two principal options to alleviate the communication bottleneck. One possibility is to equip the ECAU with local storage for the intermediate results. The second option is to design a dedicated interface with direct memory access (DMA). We opted for the latter since the former would entail a considerable increase in silicon area. In addition, we have also integrated an I/O register into the ECAU which allows to overlap data transfer and computation phases.

A second point in which our co-design approach differs from previous work is *scalability*, i.e. the ability to process operands of any size without the need to modify or re-design a given implementation [19]. The ECAU contains a 192-bit multiplier that can be used for any binary extension field $GF(2^m)$ of degree up to 192, e.g. for the field $GF(2^{191})$ or $GF(2^{163})$. This means that our system is limited scalable similar to the cryptographic processor described in [9], but does not provide the high scalability of the ECC hardware from [19]. We emphasize that attaining scalability in hardware/software co-design affects all abstraction levels and layers between hardware and software (including the operand transfers), and is not a "pure" hardware design issue as in [19]. For instance, when

---

[1] Batina et al. presented a hyperelliptic curve cryptosystem of genus 2 over the field $GF(2^{83})$. The security level of this HECC system is approximately 166 bits, and thus it is comparable to the ECC system over the field $GF(2^{163})$ that we have used.

[2] We store the intermediate values in the XRAM since the internal RAM of a standard 8051 microcontroller has a size of only 128 bytes (see Appendix A).

using a "small" field like $\mathrm{GF}(2^{163})$, only 21 bytes per operand need to be transferred between ECAU and XRAM. Furthermore, all software routines have an additional parameter specifying the degree m of the field. To the best of our knowledge, this paper presents the first hardware/software co-design approach for elliptic curve cryptography providing a certain level of scalability.

2   Elliptic Curve Cryptography

Elliptic curve cryptography (ECC) has a number of advantages over the traditional public-key cryptosystems based on the integer factorization problem or the discrete logarithm problem in finite fields. The most important advantage is the absence of a subexponential-time algorithm that could solve the discrete logarithm problem in a properly selected EC group. As a consequence, elliptic curve cryptosystems can use much shorter keys, which results in faster implementations and lower memory and bandwidth requirements [3].

Formally, an elliptic curve cryptosystem operates in a group of points on an elliptic curve defined over a finite field. Most practical ECC implementations use special types of finite fields to improve performance; among these special field types are binary extension fields $\mathrm{GF}(2^m)$, prime fields $\mathrm{GF}(p)$, and optimal extension fields (OEFs), i.e. extension fields $\mathrm{GF}(p^m)$ whose characteristic p and extension degree m are specifically selected [13]. The latter two field types allow for efficient software implementation, especially on processors equipped with a fast integer multiplier. For hardware implementation, on the other hand, binary extension fields $\mathrm{GF}(2^m)$ are generally the better choice. Therefore, we shall only consider binary extension fields in the rest of this paper.

An elliptic curve over a binary field $\mathrm{GF}(2^m)$ can be defined as the set of all solutions $(x, y) \in \mathrm{GF}(2^m) \times \mathrm{GF}(2^m)$ to the (affine) Weierstraß equation

$$y^2 + xy = x^3 + ax^2 + b \quad \text{with} \quad a, b \in \mathrm{GF}(2^m) \tag{1}$$

A tuple $(x, y) \in \mathrm{GF}(2^m) \times \mathrm{GF}(2^m)$ satisfying Equation 1 is called a *point* on the curve. The set of all points, together with a special point $\mathcal{O}$ (referred to as the "point at infinity"), allows to form an *Abelian group* with $\mathcal{O}$ acting as identity element. The group operation is the addition of points, which can be performed through arithmetic operations (addition, multiplication, squaring, and inversion) in the underlying field $\mathrm{GF}(2^m)$ according to well-defined formulae [13].

A basic building block of all elliptic curve cryptosystems is *scalar multiplication*, an operation of the form $k \cdot P$ where k is an integer and P is a point on the curve. In its simplest form, a scalar multiplication can be realized through a sequence of point additions and doublings, respectively. There exist a number of advanced algorithms for point multiplication; one of the most efficient was proposed by López and Dahab in [18]. Their algorithm requires to carry out $4\lfloor \log_2 k \rfloor + 6$ additions, $2\lfloor \log_2 k \rfloor + 4$ multiplications, $2\lfloor \log_2 k \rfloor + 2$ squarings and $2\lfloor \log_2 k \rfloor + 1$ inversions in the underlying finite field $\mathrm{GF}(2^m)$ to obtain the result of $k \cdot P$ [18, Lemma 4].

Table 1. Overview of arithmetic operations when using LD projective coordinates

Operation	# Field Add	# Field Mul	# Field Sqr	# Field Inv
Point addition (Madd)	2	4	1	0
Point doubling (Mdouble)	1	2	4	0
Conv. affine to proj. coord.	1	0	2	0
Conv. proj. to affine coord.	6	10	1	1
Scalar multiplication $k \cdot P$	$3\lfloor \log_2 k \rfloor + 7$	$6\lfloor \log_2 k \rfloor + 10$	$5\lfloor \log_2 k \rfloor + 3$	1

Inversion is generally the most demanding—and hence slowest—arithmetic operation in $GF(2^m)$. Therefore, it is prudent to use an algorithm for scalar multiplication that minimizes the number of inversions. If the points on the curve are represented in *projective coordinates* [3], then the inversion operation can be almost completely avoided at the cost of additional field multiplications and some extra storage for auxiliary variables. Only one inversion is needed for the re-conversion from projective to affine coordinates. The point addition and doubling in López-Dahab (LD) projective coordinates can be calculated as shown in Algorithm Madd and Mdouble in [18, Appendix A], respectively. Table 1 specifies the overall number of field arithmetic operations for point addition, point doubling, re-conversion from projective to affine coordinates, and a full scalar multiplication. A special property of the LD scalar multiplication algorithm is the fact that it performs exactly one Madd and one Mdouble operation for each bit of the scalar k. Consequently, the total number of Madd/Mdouble operations depends only on the bitlength of k, but not on its Hamming weight, i.e. the number of "0" and "1" bits in the binary representation of k. This property helps to prevent certain *side-channel attacks* like simple power analysis (SPA) attacks and timing attacks [13].

The elements of a binary extension field $GF(2^m)$ can be represented by binary polynomials of degree up to $m - 1$. Addition in $GF(2^m)$ is simply a logical XOR operation, while the multiplication of two field elements is performed modulo an *irreducible polynomial* p of degree m. Hardware multipliers for $GF(2^m)$ produce the product of two field elements by generation and addition of partial products as well as generation and addition of multiples of p. Squaring in $GF(2^m)$ is a special case of multiplication and can be implemented in hardware in one clock cycle when p is fixed and has a low weight. Finally, the inversion can be realized either by using the extended Euclidean algorithm (EEA) or with help of Fermat's theorem by calculating $a^{-1} = a^{2^m - 2} \bmod p$, which results in a sequence of field multiplications and squarings, respectively. Therefore, a "minimalist" hardware accelerator should be able to perform addition and multiplication in $GF(2^m)$.

3   Hardware/Software Boundaries and Trade-Offs

Efficient software implementation of ECC on 8-bit platforms is a challenging task, in particular if the order of the underlying field is beyond 160 bits. Recent research has shown that highly-optimized software implementations can reach sub-second performance on the ATmega128 [12], but not on a standard 8051 microcontroller, at least not if the order of the finite field is 160 bits or more [12,16,24]. The main reason is the rather poor performance of a standard 8051 in relation to the ATmega128 (see Appendix A). Hardware/software co-design offers numerous possibilities for speeding up ECC at the cost of a moderate increase in silicon area. A survey of the recent literature allows to identify three basic co-design approaches for enabling ECC on 8-bit processors. In this section we discuss the different hardware/software boundaries and analyze the pros and cons of these approaches.

One way to partition between hardware and software is to assign a full point addition/doubling operation to the hardware part and the rest to the software part. A concrete implementation following this approach was reported by Janssens et al. in [15]. They implemented the field arithmetic operations in hardware, together with local RAM for storing intermediate results and dedicated state machines to control the point addition/doubling operations. While this approach is very fast (there are no operand transfers during a point addition/doubling), it suffers from high hardware cost. Furthermore, implementing the point addition/doubling in hardware does not allow to respond to progress in ECC, e.g. when more efficient addition/doubling formulae are developed.

A second way to draw the line between hardware and software is to offload the field arithmetic operations from the host processor and execute them in a dedicated hardware accelerator like a co-processor. All other operations, i.e. point addition/doubling and scalar multiplication, are implemented in software and executed on the host processor. In general, this approach offers high flexibility, including the ability to integrate the latest countermeasures against side-channel attacks into the algorithm for scalar multiplication. On the other hand, this approach may entail a significant communication overhead, especially when the accelerator hardware does not provide local storage for auxiliary variables. The fastest implementations following this approach have been reported by Ernst et al. [7] and Aigner et al. [1]. The latter implements all field arithmetic operations in hardware (including squaring and inversion) and uses affine coordinates. Other implementations are described in [17] and in [2,14], whereby the latter two are based on hyperelliptic curve cryptography (HECC). Detailed performance figures of all these works can be found in Table 5 in Section 5. Our co-design for ECC presented in the next section also follows this approach.

Finally, the boundary between hardware and software can also be defined at the level of custom instructions that are specifically designed to accelerate the field arithmetic, most notably the field multiplication [11]. Hardware/software co-design at the granularity of instruction set extensions provides the highest flexibility and requires the least amount of extra hardware of all approaches discussed in this section. It was demonstrated in [6] that instruction set extensions enable an ATmega128 to execute a scalar multiplication over $GF(2^{163})$ in 290 msec (at a clock frequency of 8 MHz). However, it is highly questionable whether similar performance can be reached on a standard 8051 microcontroller where one instruction cycle takes 12 clock cycles (see Appendix A).

4   Implementation Details

In the following, we describe the hardware accelerator that we implemented to enable fast ECC on the Dalton 8051 microcontroller [22]. We begin with a system overview. Then, the Elliptic Curve Acceleration Unit (ECAU), the interface to the external RAM (XRAM), and the system software are presented.

4.1   System Overview

The overall system structure is depicted in Figure 1. It consists of four major parts: The Dalton 8051 microcontroller core, the Elliptic Curve Acceleration Unit (ECAU) with a separate datapath and control unit, and the DMA interface to the XRAM.

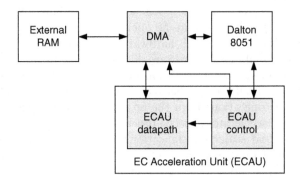

Fig. 1. System block diagram

The control unit inside the ECAU is responsible for generating appropriate control signals for the ECC datapath and provides busy signals to the DMA interface. The ECAU and the DMA interface support operand lengths of up to 192 bits, but can be configured at runtime for smaller operands.

4.2   Elliptic Curve Acceleration Unit (ECAU)

Figure 2 shows the internal architecture and the I/O interface of the ECAU. The heart of our EC accelerator is the $GF(2^m)$ arithmetic unit, which consists of a bit-serial polynomial multiplier with interleaved reduction and several registers for operands and the result. Furthermore, the $GF(2^m)$ arithmetic unit can also be used for the addition (i.e. XOR) of two field elements.

The I/O register decouples the ECAU from the DMA interface, which makes it possible to transfer data while the unit is performing a multiplication. The DMA interface shifts data in and out of the I/O register in blocks of 8 bits each. All other registers are accessed via the I/O register and support parallel data transfer through an internal 192-bit bus.

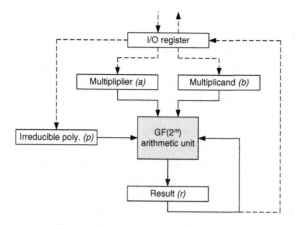

Fig. 2. Elliptic Curve Acceleration Unit

The datapath of the $GF(2^m)$ arithmetic unit, shown in Figure 3, is based on the structure proposed in [10]. It supports addition and multiplication in binary extension fields $GF(2^m)$ with $m \leq 192$ and puts no restriction on the form of the irreducible polynomial, i.e. it works with any irreducible polynomial. The control signal $\overline{add}/mul$ allows to switch between addition and multiplication mode.

In order to perform an addition, the first operand must be present inside the result register. This is almost always the case during a scalar multiplication since one of the two operands is the result of the previous arithmetic operation (addition or multiplication). The second operand needs to be stored in the multiplicand register b. The $GF(2^m)$ arithmetic unit operates in addition mode if the $\overline{add}/mul$ signal is set to 0 and the *multiplier bit* input is 1. This selects the upper inputs of the multiplexers and disables the reduction modulo the irreducible polynomial p. The addition in $GF(2^m)$ is nothing else than a simple bit-wise XOR of the coefficients and the sum is written back to the result register.

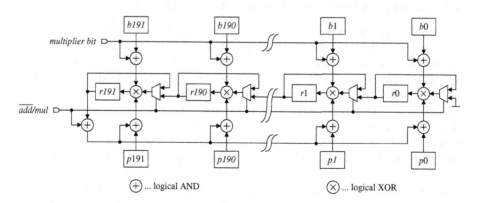

Fig. 3. Datapath of the $GF(2^m)$ arithmetic unit for operands up to 192 bits

The multiplication in $GF(2^m)$ is realized through an MSB-first bit-serial multiplier with interleaved reduction modulo the irreducible polynomial. Before a multiplication can be started, the result register must be cleared and the two operands need to be present in the multiplicand and multiplier register, respectively. To enable the multiplication mode, the $\overline{add}/mul$ signal must be set to 1. The control logic then causes the multiplier register to perform a 1-bit left-shift operation in each cycle, which delivers one bit of the multiplier polynomial a to the *multiplier bit* input, starting with the most significant bit a_{m-1}.

The partial products are calculated by a bit-wise logical AND operation between the *multiplier bit* and each bit of the multiplicand polynomial b. To get the final result of the multiplication, a total of m partial products need to be summed up. Together with the generation and addition of partial products, the bit-serial multiplier performs 1-bit left-shift operations and reduces the intermediate result modulo the irreducible polynomial p in each cycle. The reduction modulo p is performed by adding p to the intermediate value stored in the result register whenever its most significant bit (MSB) is 1. An MSB of 1 means that the intermediate result would have a degree of m after the next 1-bit left-shift operation, and therefore the irreducible polynomial p must be added to reduce the intermediate result to a degree of at most $m - 1$ (see [10] for details). Note that the addition of the partial product, the 1-bit left-shift operation of the intermediate result, and reduction step (i.e. the conditional addition of p) are taking place simultaneously in each clock cycle. After the final coefficient of the multiplier polynomial has been processed, the result of the multiplication resides within the result register (after m clock cycles).

Because a required reduction is detected by checking if $r191 = 1$, all arguments in the registers need to be left aligned. For example, if the field $GF(2^{191})$ is used, then all operands need to be shifted left by one bit, and for $GF(2^{163})$ by 29 bits. However, these shift operations have to be carried out only once at the beginning of the scalar multiplication. All field arithmetic operations during a scalar multiplication are performed with the shifted operands.

4.3   Interface with Direct Memory Access (DMA)

The 8051 itself has too little internal RAM to hold the operands and auxiliary variables needed during a scalar multiplication. Since the Dalton 8051 needs 17 clock cycles for each instruction cycle, it would require at least $17 \cdot 192/8 = 408$ cycles to transfer one 192-bit operand from XRAM to the ECAU and another 408 cycles to transfer the result back into XRAM (assuming only one instruction cycle for XRAM access). This is unreasonably slow compared to the m clock cycles needed for a multiplication in $GF(2^m)$ and the single-cycle execution of a field addition. Therefore, we propose to use a DMA controller to facilitate fast data transfers between the ECAU and XRAM, bypassing the slow 8051.

In order to load a whole 192-bit operand, one just needs to provide the start address of the argument in the XRAM and then start the DMA controller. The controller transfers the whole operand byte by byte in 85 clock cycles to the

Table 2. ECAU instructions and their execution times

Command	Cycles	Description
MUL	$m + 4$	Result ← Multiplicand × Multiplier mod p
ADD	4	Result ← Result + Multiplicand
LOAD_IOR	4	I/O register ← Result register
CLEAR_RR	4	Result ← 0
LOAD_MDR	4	Multiplicand ← I/O register
LOAD_MR	4	Multiplier ← I/O register
LOAD_IPR	4	Irreducible Polynomial (p) ← I/O register

I/O register. If operands shorter than 192 bits are used (e.g. 163 bits), then the interface automatically clears all unused bits in the I/O register and aligns the operand to the most significant byte. However, bit-wise alignments have to be done in software.

4.4 Software

To control the ECAU, three special function registers (SFRs) are used. The degree m of the binary field is set via the bitlength register. The status register provides feedback about the current operation status of the ECAU and the DMA interface. A third SFR is used to send instructions to the ECAU. Table 2 shows all implemented instructions and their respective timings.

In order to take advantage of the additional hardware, the software must be adapted accordingly. We have developed assembler-optimized functions that use our hardware extensions. Wherever possible, data transfers to the I/O register are interleaved with ECAU operations. By careful examination of the dataflow during a scalar multiplication, transfer delays can be reduced to a minimum.

5 Implementation Results

In order to determine the size of the new hardware units, we have synthesized the extended Dalton 8051 with a 0.35 μm standard-cell library from Austria Microsystems. The targeted delay for the critical path was set to 83 nsec (12 MHz). The minimal possible critical path delay is about 13 nsec (77 MHz), whereby the critical path is located within the ALU of the Dalton 8051. Our additional units (DMA, ECAU) could be clocked at significantly higher frequencies than the microcontroller.

Table 3 lists the size of the original Dalton 8051 microcontroller, the DMA unit, and the components of the ECAU (control logic, datapath logic, as well as datapath flip-flops). The size is given in absolute values in μm^2 as well as in gate equivalents (GE). The GE count has been derived from the absolute size of the component divided by the size of a NAND gate with the lowest driving strength from the used library.

Table 3. Hardware size and maximal clock frequency of the extended system

Component	Size μm^2	Size GE	Max. Freq. MHz
8051 core (excl. IRAM, ROM)	272,145	4,984	77
8051 IRAM (as flip-flops)	647,574	11,860	
DMA	56,202	1,029	
ECAU control	39,203	718	333
ECAU datapath logic	228,246	4,180	
ECAU datapath FFs	366,912	6,720	
Total	1,610,282	29,491	77

Table 4. Execution times of operations for scalar multiplication over $GF(2^{191})$

Operation	Cycles
Transfer of one 191-bit operand	85
Addition in $GF(2^{191})$ excluding operand transfers	4
Multiplication in $GF(2^{191})$ excl. operand transfers	195
Point addition (Madd) including operand transfers	2,623
Point doubling (Mdouble) incl. operand transfers	2,623
Full scalar multiplication over $GF(2^{191})$	1,416,000

Note that the internal RAM (IRAM) of the 8051 has been implemented as flip-flops for our synthesis. In practice a part of the IRAM could be implemented with SRAM macros in order to save silicon area. The enhanced 8051 microcontroller has a size of about 30,000 GEs. The additional components for ECC are about 75% of the original Dalton 8051's size and account for about 43% of the extended system.

Table 4 shows the execution times for diverse arithmetic operations with 191-bit operands. Table 5 compares the performance of ECC multiplication with related work. Systems built around an AVR microcontroller are faster than systems using an 8051, which is caused by the generally better performance of AVR devices (see Appendix A). The work by Aigner et al. uses affine coordinates and has an additional squaring and inverter unit which can perform a squaring operation in one clock cycle and an inversion in $2m$ clock cycles.

Batina at al. use in their work a HECC system of genus two over the field $GF(2^{83})$, which provides roughly the same level of security as 163-bit ECC. Our work reaches significantly better performance compared to Batina et al. mainly due to efficient operand transfer between ECAU and XRAM thanks to direct memory access. Hodjat et al. try to circumvent the performance bottleneck by using a local storage unit of 256 bytes, which needs additional silicon area.

Table 6 compares our implementation with related work in terms of hardware and code size. Our work needs more silicon area than the design by Batina et al., but achieves a 16-fold better area-delay product. Also our code size is considerable smaller, which directly translates into savings in silicon area when the program code is stored in on-chip ROM.

Table 5. Performance comparison with ECC/HECC scalar multiplication of related work. The first six table entries refer to "pure" software implementations and the rest to hardware/software co-designs.

Reference	Target Platform	Security Level	Field Type	Freq MHz	Performance msec	cycles
Woodb. [24]	8051 (SLE44C24S)	ECC 134 bit	$GF(p^m)$	12.00	1,830.0	21.96M
Kumar [16]	8051 (CC1010)	ECC 134 bit	$GF(p^m)$	3.69	2,999.8	11.06M
Gura [12]	8051 (CC1010)	ECC 160 bit	$GF(p)$	14.74	4,580.0	67.53M
Gura [12]	8051 (CC1010)	ECC 192 bit	$GF(p)$	14.74	7,560.0	111.48M
Gura [12]	AVR (ATmega128)	ECC 160 bit	$GF(p)$	8.00	810.0	6.48M
Gura [12]	AVR (ATmega128)	ECC 192 bit	$GF(p)$	8.00	1,240.0	9.92M
Ernst [7] [a]	AVR (AT94K)	ECC 113 bit	$GF(2^m)$	12.00	1.2	14.40k
Kumar [17]	AVR (AT94K)	ECC 163 bit	$GF(2^m)$	4.00	113.0	452.00k
Janssens [15]	AVR (AT94K)	ECC 192 bit	$GF(2^m)$	10.00	45.0	450.00k
Eberle [6]	AVR (ATMega128)	ECC 163 bit	$GF(2^m)$	8.00	290.0	2.32M
Aigner [1] [a]	8051 (SLE66CX)	ECC 191 bit	$GF(2^m)$	10.00	44.3	443.86k
Batina [2]	8051 (Dalton)	HECC 166 bit	$GF(2^m)$	12.00	2,488.0	29.86M
Hodjat [14]	8051 (Dalton)	HECC 166 bit	$GF(2^m)$	12.00	656.0	7.87M
This work	8051 (Dalton)	ECC 163 bit	$GF(2^m)$	12.00	99.2	1.19M
This work	8051 (Dalton)	ECC 191 bit	$GF(2^m)$	12.00	118.0	1.42M

[a] Estimated performance figures.

Table 6. Comparison of hardware cost, code size, and XRAM requirements

Component	Size (norm.)	Area-delay product Size (norm.) × msec	Code size Bytes	XRAM Bytes
Dalton 8051	1.00			
Batina [2]	1.15	2,861.2	11,524	936
This work (163 bit)	1.75	173.6	2,568	384
This work (192 bit)	1.75	206.5	2,568	336

6 Conclusions

In this paper we have presented a hardware/software co-design approach for enabling ECC on 8-bit platforms using a minimalist hardware accelerator. We have demonstrated the importance of a thorough analysis of the overall system performance to remove bottlenecks. Communication overhead due to operand transfers has been minimized by integration of a small DMA unit and through the inclusion of an additional I/O register into the hardware accelerator. With the help of our simple and fast finite field arithmetic unit, we can support scalar multiplication over binary fields of degree up to 192. At the cost of about 12.65k gates in hardware, ECC scalar multiplication requires 118 msec over $GF(2^{191})$ and 99.2 msec over $GF(2^{163})$ on our enhanced 8051 system when clocked with 12 MHz. Considering performance gain in relation with hardware overhead, our solution relates very well to previous work on comparable 8-bit platforms.

Acknowledgements. The research described in this paper was supported by the Austrian Science Fund under grant P16952-NO4 "Instruction Set Extensions for Public-Key Cryptography" and in part by the European Commission through the IST Programme under contract IST-2002-507932 ECRYPT. The information in this paper reflects only the authors' views, is provided as is and no guarantee or warranty is given that the information is fit for any particular purpose. The user thereof uses the information at its sole risk and liability.

References

1. H. Aigner, H. Bock, M. Hütter, and J. Wolkerstorfer. A low-cost ECC coprocessor for smartcards. In *Cryptographic Hardware and Embedded Systems — CHES 2004*, LNCS 3156, pp. 107–118. Springer Verlag, 2004.
2. L. Batina, D. Hwang, A. Hodjat, B. Preneel, and I. Verbauwhede. Hardware/software co-design for hyperelliptic curve cryptography (HECC) on the 8051 μP. In *Cryptographic Hardware and Embedded Systems — CHES 2005*, LNCS 3659, pp. 106–118. Springer Verlag, 2005.
3. I. F. Blake, G. Seroussi, and N. P. Smart. *Elliptic Curves in Cryptography*. Cambridge University Press, 1999.
4. J. Catsoulis. *Designing Embedded Hardware*. O'Reilly Media, 2002.
5. G. De Micheli and R. K. Gupta. Hardware/software co-design. *Proceedings of the IEEE*, 85(3):349–365, Mar. 1997.
6. H. Eberle et al. Architectural extensions for elliptic curve cryptography over $GF(2^m)$ on 8-bit microprocessors. In *Proceedings of the 16th IEEE International Conference on Application-Specific Systems, Architectures, and Processors (ASAP 2005)*, pp. 343–349. IEEE Computer Society Press, 2005.
7. M. Ernst et al. A reconfigurable system on chip implementation for elliptic curve cryptography over $GF(2^n)$. In *Cryptographic Hardware and Embedded Systems — CHES 2002*, LNCS 2523, pp. 381–399. Springer Verlag, 2002.
8. R. Ernst. Codesign of embedded systems: Status and trends. *IEEE Design & Test of Computers*, 15(2):45–54, April-June 1998.
9. J. R. Goodman. *Energy Scalable Reconfigurable Cryptographic Hardware for Portable Applications*. Ph.D. Thesis, Massachusetts Institute of Technology, 2000.
10. J. Großschädl. A low-power bit-serial multiplier for finite fields $GF(2^m)$. In *Proceedings of the 34th IEEE International Symposium on Circuits and Systems (ISCAS 2001)*, vol. IV, pp. 37–40. IEEE, 2001.
11. J. Großschädl and G.-A. Kamendje. Instruction set extension for fast elliptic curve cryptography over binary finite fields $GF(2^m)$. In *Proceedings of the 14th IEEE International Conference on Application-specific Systems, Architectures and Processors (ASAP 2003)*, pp. 455–468. IEEE Computer Society Press, 2003.
12. N. Gura et al. Comparing elliptic curve cryptography and RSA on 8-bit CPUs. In *Cryptographic Hardware and Embedded Systems — CHES 2004*, LNCS 3156, pp. 119–132. Springer Verlag, 2004.
13. D. R. Hankerson, A. J. Menezes, and S. A. Vanstone. *Guide to Elliptic Curve Cryptography*. Springer Verlag, 2004.
14. A. Hodjat, D. Hwang, L. Batina, and I. Verbauwhede. A hyperelliptic curve crypto coprocessor for an 8051 microcontroller. In *Proceedings of the 19th IEEE Workshop on Signal Processing Systems (SIPS 2005)*, pp. 93–98. IEEE, 2005.

15. S. Janssens et al. Hardware/software co-design of an elliptic curve public-key cryptosystem. In *Proceedings of 15th IEEE Workshop on Signal Processing Systems (SIPS 2001)*, pp. 209–216. IEEE, 2001.

16. S. S. Kumar et al. Embedded end-to-end wireless security with ECDH key exchange. In *Proceedings of the 46th IEEE Midwest Symposium on Circuits and Systems (MWSCAS 2003)*, vol. 2, pp. 786–789. IEEE, 2003.

17. S. S. Kumar and C. Paar. Reconfigurable instruction set extension for enabling ECC on an 8-bit processor. In *Field Programmable Logic and Application — FPL 2004*, LNCS 3203, pp. 586–595. Springer Verlag, 2004.

18. J. López and R. Dahab. Fast multiplication on elliptic curves over $GF(2^m)$ without precomputation. In *Cryptographic Hardware and Embedded Systems*, LNCS 1717, pp. 316–327. Springer Verlag, 1999.

19. E. Savaş, A. F. Tenca, and Ç. K. Koç. A scalable and unified multiplier architecture for finite fields GF(p) and GF(2^m). In *Cryptographic Hardware and Embedded Systems — CHES 2000*, LNCS 1965, pp. 277–292. Springer Verlag, 2000.

20. P. Schaumont and I. Verbauwhede. Domain specific tools and methods for application in security processor design. *Design Automation for Embedded Systems*, 7(4):365–383, Nov. 2002.

21. P. Schaumont and I. Verbauwhede. Domain-specific codesign for embedded security. *Computer*, 36(4):68–74, Apr. 2003.

22. University of California at Riverside. Synthesizable VHDL Model of 8051. Available for download at http://www.cs.ucr.edu/~dalton/i8051/i8051syn/.

23. W. H. Wolf. Hardware-software co-design of embedded systems. *Proceedings of the IEEE*, 28(7):967–989, July 1994.

24. A. D. Woodbury, D. V. Bailey, and C. Paar. Elliptic curve cryptography on smart cards without coprocessors. In *Smart Card Research and Advanced Applications*, pp. 71–92. Kluwer Academic Publishers, 2000.

A   8-bit Architectures for Embedded Systems

Most previous work dealing with co-design of ECC for embedded systems used either an 8051-compatible microcontroller or an AVR-based processor to execute the software. Both the 8051 and the AVR platform possess a significant share of the worldwide smart card market and other security-critical segments of the embedded systems industry, e.g. sensor nodes.

A.1   The 8051 Microcontroller

The 8051 is an 8-bit microcontroller originally developed by Intel for use in embedded systems. After its launch in 1980, the 8051 has quickly gained popularity in the 1980s and early 1990s, and is today generally considered as the most widely used microcontroller of all times. There exist more than 20 independent manufacturers of 8051-compatible microcontroller cores; among these are leading semiconductor vendors like Atmel, Infineon, and Philips.

A typical 8051-compatible microcontroller includes 128 bytes of internal data RAM (IRAM), 4 kB of internal program memory (ROM), four 8-bit I/O ports and a serial port, two 16-bit timers/counters, and optionally an extended data

RAM (XRAM). Numerous enhanced variants of the "original" 8051 have been developed during the past 25 years. For instance, the 8052 features 256 bytes of internal RAM instead of 128 bytes, 8 kB of ROM instead of 4 kB, and a third 16-bit timer. Other 8051 derivatives, such as the Infineon SLE44/SLE66 families of smart card controllers, have additional 16-bit instructions and extended addressing modes for smart card applications. Both the SLE44 and the SLE66 are referred to as 16-bit smart card controllers in the data sheets, but they are fully opcode-compatible to the original 8051.

The 8051 has probably the widest range of derivatives of any embedded microcontroller on the market today, and, as a consequence, the performance of the different 8051 devices varies significantly, even when running at the same clock frequency. Each instruction executed on an original 8051 microcontroller takes either 1, 2, or 4 instruction cycles to complete, whereby a single instruction cycle corresponds to 12 clock cycles. Therefore, the original 8051 is rather slow as it can execute at most 1 million instructions per second when clocked with 12 MHz. Newer variants of the 8051 run at six, four, two, or even one clock cycle per instruction cycle, and are able to operate at clock frequencies of 100 MHz or even more. For example, the Infineon SLE66 executes instructions at a rate of two clock cycles per instruction cycle, and thus it is up to six times faster than a standard 8051 at the same clock frequency. On the other hand, the Dalton 8051 [22] requires 17 clock cycles per instruction cycle, which means that the Dalton is even slower than the original 8051 developed some 25 years ago.

A.2   The ATmega128 Microprocessor

The AVR is an 8-bit RISC architecture with 32 general-purpose registers and separate memories for program and data (Harvard architecture). All instructions have a fixed length of 16 bits. The AVR instruction set is more regular than that of the 8051, but not completely orthogonal. Arithmetic/logical instructions have a two-operand format and allow to carry out operations between two registers or between a register and an immediate (constant) value.

The AVR implementations by Atmel, such as the ATmega128, feature a two-stage pipeline and execute most instructions in a single clock cycle. Multiply instructions need a second cycle to complete. Any access to RAM requires two cycles, while reading from program memory takes three cycles. The ATmega128 has 4 kB SRAM, 128 kB Flash memory, and 4 kB EEPROM. It can be clocked with frequencies of up to 16 MHz and achieves throughputs approaching 1 MIPS per MHz. Thus, the ATmega128 outperforms the original 8051 by more than an order of magnitude at the same clock frequency. It was stated in [4] that, for certain applications, an AVR core can be a whopping 28 times faster than an 8051 running at the same clock frequency. This must be taken into account when comparing the execution times of elliptic curve cryptosystems on these two platforms. Furthermore, the ATmega128 has certain architectural features (e.g. large number of general-purpose registers, two-cycle multiply instruction) which facilitate the efficient software implementation of long integer arithmetic operations used in ECC.

FPGA Implementation of Point Multiplication on Koblitz Curves Using Kleinian Integers

V.S. Dimitrov[1,*], K.U. Järvinen[2], M.J. Jacobson, Jr.[3],
W.F. Chan[3], and Z. Huang[1]

[1] Department of Electrical and Computer Engineering, University of Calgary, 2500
University Drive NW, Calgary, Alberta, Canada T2N 1N4
(dimitrov, huangzh)@atips.ca
[2] Signal Processing Laboratory, Helsinki University of Technology, Otakaari 5A,
02150, Espoo, Finland
kimmo.jarvinen@tkk.fi
[3] Department of Computer Science, University of Calgary, 2500 University Drive
NW, Calgary, Alberta, Canada T2N 1N4
(chanwf, jacobs)@cpsc.ucalgary.ca

Abstract. We describe algorithms for point multiplication on Koblitz curves using multiple-base expansions of the form $k = \sum \pm \tau^a (\tau - 1)^b$ and $k = \sum \pm \tau^a (\tau - 1)^b (\tau^2 - \tau - 1)^c$. We prove that the number of terms in the second type is sublinear in the bit length of k, which leads to the first provably sublinear point multiplication algorithm on Koblitz curves. For the first type, we conjecture that the number of terms is sublinear and provide numerical evidence demonstrating that the number of terms is significantly less than that of τ-adic non-adjacent form expansions. We present details of an innovative FPGA implementation of our algorithm and performance data demonstrating the efficiency of our method.

1   Introduction

In 1985, Koblitz [1] and Miller [2] independently proposed the use of the additive finite abelian group of points on elliptic curves defined over a finite field for cryptographic applications. The Koblitz curves [3], or anomalous binary curves, are

$$E_a : y^2 + xy = x^3 + ax^2 + 1 \tag{1}$$

defined over $\mathbb{F}_2$, where $a \in \{0, 1\}$. The number of points on these curves when considered over $\mathbb{F}_{2^m}$ can be computed rapidly using a simple recurrence relation, and there are many prime values of m for which the number of points is twice a prime (when $a = 1$) or four times a prime (when $a = 0$). Five Koblitz curves are recommended for cryptographic use by NIST [4].

The main advantage of Koblitz curves is that the Frobenius automorphism of $\mathbb{F}_2$ acts on points via $\tau(x, y) = (x^2, y^2)$ and is essentially free to compute. Because τ satisfies $(\tau^2 + 2)P = \mu\tau(P)$ for all points $P \in E_a(\mathbb{F}_{2^m})$ where $\mu = (-1)^{1-a}$, we can consider τ as a complex number satisfying $\tau^2 - \mu\tau + 2 = 0$,

* Chan, Dimitrov and Jacobson are supported in part by NSERC of Canada.

L. Goubin and M. Matsui (Eds.): CHES 2006, LNCS 4249, pp. 445–459, 2006.

i.e., $\tau = (\mu + \sqrt{-7})/2$. Thus, computing kP, where $k \in \mathbb{Z}$ and $P \in E_a(\mathbb{F}_{2^m})$, can be done using a representation of k involving powers of τ instead of the usual binary representation using powers of 2, yielding a point multiplication algorithm similar to the binary "double-and-add" method in which the point doublings are replaced by applications of the Frobenius [3,5]. Solinas [5] shows how the non-adjacent form (NAF) and window-NAF methods mentioned earlier can be extended to τ-adic expansions. The resulting point multiplication algorithms require on average $(\log_2 k)/3$ point additions or $(\log_2 k)/(w+1)$ point additions using width-w window methods requiring precomputations based on P. A recent result of Avanzi et. al. [6] reduces this to $(\log_2 k)/4$ at the cost of one additional point halving, but the practicality of this method has not yet been demonstrated.

Recently, double-base integer representations have been used to devise efficient point multiplication algorithms [7,8,9]. For example, it can be shown that the number of terms of the form $\pm 2^a 3^b$ required to represent k is bounded by $O(\log k / \log \log k)$. These representations can be computed efficiently and the resulting point multiplication algorithms are the only known methods for which the number of required point additions is sublinear in $\log k$.

In this paper, we extend the double-base idea to τ-adic expansions for point multiplication on Koblitz curves by representing k as a sum of terms $\pm \tau^a (\tau-1)^b$. Our algorithm requires no precomputations based on the point P, no point doublings, and fewer point additions than τ-adic NAF (τ-NAF) for the five recommended Koblitz curves from [4]. Our algorithm for computing the double-base representation of k is very efficient; it requires only the unsigned τ-adic expansion of k plus a few table-lookups. A precomputed table of optimal representations for a small number of τ-adic integers is required, but these are independent of the multiplier k and the base point P. We have developed a novel FPGA implementation of both the conversion and point multiplication algorithms that demonstrates the efficiency of our method.

We conjecture that the average density of our representations is sublinear in $\log k$, and provide extensive numerical evidence showing that the density is lower than that of τ-NAF expansions. Although we do not have a proof that the number of point additions required by our algorithm is sublinear, we provide a proof that sublinearity is obtained using similar expressions involving three bases of the form $\pm \tau^a (\tau-1)^b (\tau^2 - \tau - 1)^c$. This work represents the first rigorously-proven sublinear point multiplication algorithm using complex bases.

Avanzi and Sica [10] have reported independently on a provably sublinear point multiplication algorithm using bases τ and 3. However, it is not clear how their algorithm performs in practice, and their proof has been shown to have a gap [11].

The remainder of the paper is organized as follows. In Sec. 2 we present our provably sublinear point multiplication algorithm. We present a similar algorithm using only two complex bases in Sec. 3. Although we cannot prove sublinearity for this algorithm, we conjecture that the density of the representations is in fact sublinear, and provide numerical evidence in Subsection 3.2 indicating that the density of our representations is lower than that of τ-NAF representations. A description of our FPGA implementation and numerical data demonstrating its efficiency are presented in Sec. 4. Finally, we conclude with an outlook on possible directions for further research.

2   Multi-dimensional Frobenius Expansions

We start with the following three definitions:

Definition 1. *A complex number,* ξ *of the form* $e + f\tau$, *e, f-integers is called a Kleinian integer* [12].

Definition 2. *A Kleinian integer* ω *of the form* $\omega = \pm\tau^x(\tau - 1)^y$, $x, y \geq 0$ *is called a* $\{\tau, \tau - 1\}$-*Kleinian integer.*

Definition 3. *A Kleinian integer* ω *of the form* $\omega = \pm\tau^x(\tau - 1)^y(\tau^2 - \tau - 1)^z$, $x, y, z \geq 0$ *is called a* $\{\tau, \tau - 1, \tau^2 - \tau - 1\}$-*Kleinian integer.*

The main idea of the new point multiplication algorithm over Koblitz curves is to extend the existing and widely-used τ-NAF expansion of the scalar to a new form which will speed up the computations. The improvements obtained in the paper are based on the following representation, which we will call two-dimensional or three-dimensional Frobenius expansions (or $\{\tau, \tau - 1\}$-expansion and $\{\tau, \tau - 1, \tau^2 - \tau - 1\}$-expansion, for short):

$$k = \sum_{i=1}^{d} s_i \tau^{a_i}(\tau - 1)^{b_i}, \quad s_i = \pm 1, \quad a_i, b_i \in \mathbb{Z}_{\geq 0}, \tag{2}$$

$$k = \sum_{i=1}^{d} s_i \tau^{a_i}(\tau - 1)^{b_i}(\tau^2 - \tau - 1)^{c_i}, \quad s_i = \pm 1, \quad a_i, b_i, c_i \in \mathbb{Z}_{\geq 0} . \tag{3}$$

Such representations are clearly highly redundant. If we rearrange the summands in the above formula, then, using two bases, we can represent the scalar k as

$$k = \sum_{l=1}^{\max(b_i)} (\tau - 1)^l \left(\sum_{i=1}^{\max(a_{i,l})} s_{i,l} \tau^{a_{i,l}} \right) \tag{4}$$

where $\max(a_{i,l})$ is the maximal power of τ that is multiplied by $(\tau - 1)^l$ in (2). Using three bases, we can represent k as

$$k = \sum_{l_2}^{\max(c_i)} (\tau^2 - \tau - 1)^{l_2} \sum_{l_1=1}^{\max(b_i)} (\tau - 1)^{l_1} \left(\sum_{i=1}^{\max(a_{i,l_1,l_2})} s_{i,l_1,l_2} \tau^{a_{i,l_1,l_2}} \right) \tag{5}$$

where $\max(a_{i,l_1,l_2})$ is the maximal power of τ that is multiplied by $(\tau - 1)^{l_1}(\tau^2 - \tau - 1)^{l_2}$ in (3).

Algorithm 1. Point multiplication using $\{\tau, \tau - 1\}$-expansions.

INPUT: k, P
OUTPUT: $Q = kP$
   $P_0 \leftarrow P$
   $Q \leftarrow \mathcal{O}$
   for $i = 0$ **to** j **do**
      $S \leftarrow r_i(k)P_i$ {One dimensional τ-NAF corresponding to $(\tau - 1)^l$ in (4)}
      $P_{i+1} \leftarrow \tau P_i - P_i$
      $Q \leftarrow Q + S$

Alg. 1. computes kP given a $\{\tau, \tau - 1\}$-expansion of k. The corresponding algorithm for $\{\tau, \tau - 1, \tau^2 - \tau - 1\}$-expansions will be described later, along with a proof that the number of point additions is sublinear in $\log k$. Essentially, kP is computed via a succession of one-dimensional τ-adic expansions.

The representation of k given in (4) is the cornerstone of our algorithm, so some comments on it are in order.

1. The multiplications by $\tau - 1$ cost one Frobenius mapping (free in our computational model) and one point subtraction. The multiplications by $\tau^2 - \tau - 1$ cost two Frobenius mappings and two point subtractions. Therefore, the total number of point additions/subtractions, $AS(k)$, is given by

$$AS(k) = d + \max(b_i) - 1$$

in the case of $\{\tau, \tau - 1\}$-expansions and

$$AS(k) = d + \max(b_i) \max(c_i) - 1$$

in the case of $\{\tau, \tau - 1, \tau^2 - \tau - 1\}$-expansions. The smallest possible value of $\max(b_i)$ and $\max(c_i)$, 0, corresponds to the classical (one-dimensional) τ-NAF expansion, for which it is known that the expected number of point additions/subtractions is $(\log_2 k)/3$. It is clear that by allowing larger values for $\max(b_i)$ and $\max(c_i)$ one would decrease the corresponding number of summands, d. Therefore, it is vital to find out the optimal values for $\max(b_i)$ as a function of the size of the scalar.

2. Finding an algorithm that can return a fairly short decomposition of k as the sum of $\{\tau, \tau - 1\}$-Kleinian integers is absolutely essential. The most straightforward idea seems to be the greedy algorithm described in Alg. 2.. A greedy algorithm for computing $\{\tau, \tau - 1, \tau^2 - \tau - 1\}$-expansions is an easy generalization of this algorithm.

The complexity of the greedy algorithm depends crucially on the time spent to find the closest $\{\tau, \tau - 1\}$-Kleinian integer to the current Kleinian integer. Unfortunately we were not able to find a significantly more efficient method to do this than precomputing all Kleinian integers $\pm\tau^x(\tau - 1)^y$ for x, y less than certain bounds and finding the closest one using exhaustive search. In the next subsection, we present an efficient algorithm for computing $\{\tau, \tau - 1\}$-expansions

---

Algorithm 2. Greedy algorithm for computing $\{\tau, \tau - 1\}$-expansions.

INPUT: A Kleinian integer $\xi = e + f\tau$
OUTPUT: $\{\omega_1, \ldots, \omega_d\}$, a $\{\tau, \tau - 1\}$-expansion of ξ
   $i \leftarrow 1$
  while $\xi \neq 0$ **do**
     Find $\omega_i = \pm\tau^{a_i}(\tau - 1)^{b_i}$, $a_i, b_i \geq 0$, the closest $\{\tau, \tau - 1\}$-Kleinian integer to ξ.
     $\xi \leftarrow \xi - \omega_i$
     $i \leftarrow i + 1$

---

with slightly more weight than those produced by the greedy algorithm and an algorithm for computing $\{\tau, \tau - 1, \tau^2 - \tau - 1\}$-expansions with weight provably sublinear in $\log k$.

2.1 Comparison to Double-Base Number Systems

The similarities between (2) and the double-base number system (DBNS), in which one represents integers as the sum or difference of numbers of the form $2^a 3^b$, a, b non-negative integers (called $\{2, 3\}$-integers), are apparent. In the case of DBNS, one can prove the following result:

Theorem 1. *Every positive integer, n, can be written as the sum of at most $O(\log n/\log\log n)$ $\{2, 3\}$-integers and (one) such representation can be found by using the greedy algorithm.*

The key point in proving this theorem is the following result of Tijdeman [13].

Theorem 2. *Let x and y be two $\{2, 3\}$-integers, $x > y$. Then there exist effectively computable constants, c_1 and c_2, such that*

$$\frac{x}{(\log x)^{c_1}} < x - y < \frac{x}{(\log x)^{c_2}} \ .$$

The proof of Theorem 1 uses only the first inequality.

Theorem 2 provides a very accurate description of the difference between two consecutive $\{2, 3\}$-integers. More to the point, it can be generalized easily to any set of $\{p_1, p_2, \cdots, p_s\}$-integers if p_s is fixed. The proof depends on the main result of [14] from the theory of linear form in logarithms.

Theorem 3. *Let $a_1, a_2, \cdots, a_k$ be nonzero algebraic integers and $b_1, b_2, \cdots, b_k$ rational integers. Assume $a_1^{b_1} a_2^{b_2} \cdots a_k^{b_k} \neq 1$ and $B = \max(b_1, b_2, \cdots, b_k)$. Then the following inequality holds:*

$$\left| a_1^{b_1} a_2^{b_2} \cdots a_k^{b_k} - 1 \right| \geq \exp(-C(k) \log a_1 \log a_2 \cdots \log a_k)$$

where $C(k) = \exp(4k + 10k^{3k+5})$.

The constant $C(k)$ is huge, even in the case of linear forms in two logarithms, approximately $\exp(6 \cdot 10^9)$. By using some results aimed specifically at the case of two logarithms [15], one can reduce $C(k)$ to $\exp(10^7)$, but this is still enormous. However, practical simulations suggest that this constant is likely to be much smaller, perhaps less than 100.

There are two very essential points that are often overlooked in the formulations of the above theorems [16]:

1. the estimates are correct if the algebraic numbers used are real,
2. if the algebraic numbers are complex, then the estimates provided remain unchanged if one of them, say a_1, has an absolute value strictly greater than absolute values of the other algebraic numbers.

The latter point is what prevents us from applying Tijdeman's Theorem 2 to the case of $a_1 = \tau, a_2 = \tau - 1$. Thus, we are not in position to trivially extend the proof of Theorem 1 to the case of $\{\tau, \tau - 1\}$-expansions of Kleinian integers. Nevertheless, extensive numerical simulations (by using several attempted optimizations of Alg. 2.) has led us to the following conjecture:

Conjecture 1. Every Kleinian integer, $\xi = a + b\tau$, can be represented as the sum of at most $O\left(\log N(\xi)/\log\log N(\xi)\right)$ $\{\tau, \tau - 1\}$-Kleinian integers, where $N(\xi)$ is the norm of ξ.

A very recent paper by Avanzi and Sica [10] contains a proof that Conjecture 1 is true if one uses $\{\tau, 3\}$-Kleinian integers under the unproven but reasonable assumption that the irrationality measure of $\log_2 3$ and $\arg(\tau)/\pi$ is 2. Unfortunately, the proof, even with the assumption on irrationality measures, has a gap [11]. The use of two complex bases, used in this paper, increases the theoretical difficulties in proving the conjecture, but provides much more practical algorithms.

However, in the case of *three* bases we can prove without any assumptions the following:

Theorem 4. *Every Kleinian integer $\zeta = a + b\tau$ can be represented as the sum of at most $O(\log N(\zeta)/(\log\log N(\zeta)))$ $\{\tau, \tau - 1, \tau^2 - \tau - 1\}$-Kleinian integers, such that the largest power of both $\tau - 1$ and $\tau^2 - \tau - 1$ is $O(\log^\alpha N(\zeta))$ for any real constant α where $0 < \alpha < 1/2$.*

Proof. We assume that $b = 0$; otherwise, one applies the same proof for the real and imaginary part of ζ, which leads to doubling the implicit constant hidden in the big-O notation.

Let α be a real constant where $0 < \alpha < 1/2$. We determine the τ-adic representation of a, the real part of ζ, using digits 0 and 1. The length of this expansion is $O(\log N(\zeta))$. We break this representation into $\lceil \log^{1-\alpha} N(\zeta) \rceil$ blocks, where each block contains $O(\log^\alpha N(\zeta))$ digits. Each of these blocks corresponds to a Kleinian integer $c_i + d_i\tau$, $i = 0, 1, \ldots, \lceil \log^{1-\alpha} N(\zeta) \rceil$, where the size of both c_i and d_i is $O(\log^\alpha N(\zeta))$. Now, we represent each integer c_i and d_i in double-base representation using bases 2 and 3. According to Theorem 1, these numbers will require at most

$$O\left(\log^\alpha N(\zeta)/(\log\log^\alpha N(\zeta))\right) = O\left(\log^\alpha N(\zeta)/(\log\log N(\zeta))\right)$$

summands of the form $2^x 3^y$ where $x, y \geq 0$ and $x, y \in O(\log^\alpha N(\zeta))$. Using the fact that $2 = \tau(1 - \tau)$ and $3 = 1 - \tau - \tau^2$, we substitute the 2's and 3's in the 2, 3-expansions of c_i and d_i to obtain $\{\tau, \tau - 1, \tau^2 - \tau - 1\}$-Kleinian integer expansions of each $c_i + d_i\tau$, $i = 0, 1, \ldots, \lceil \log^{1-\alpha} N(\zeta) \rceil$. To obtain the expansion of $\zeta = a + b\tau$, we multiply each term of the form $\pm\tau^x(\tau - 1)^y(\tau^2 - \tau - 1)^z$ by τ^i where i is the index of the corresponding block. Note that $x, y, z \in O(\log^\alpha N(\zeta))$. Since the number of blocks is $\lceil \log^{1-\alpha} N(\zeta) \rceil$ and each block requires $O(\log^\alpha N(\zeta)/(\log \log N(\zeta)) \{\tau, \tau - 1, \tau^2 - \tau - 1\}$-Kleinian integers, we conclude that the overall number of Kleinian integers used to represent ζ is

$$O\left(\frac{\log^\alpha N(\zeta)}{\log \log N(\zeta)} \log^{1-\alpha} N(\zeta)\right) = O\left(\frac{\log N(\zeta)}{\log \log N(\zeta)}\right).$$

The exponents of $\tau - 1$ and $\tau^2 - \tau - 1$ are bounded by $O(\log^\alpha N(\zeta))$.   □

Theorem 4 is in fact constructive and leads to the following sublinear point multiplication algorithm (Algorithm 3.).

Algorithm 3. Point multiplication algorithm using $\{\tau, \tau - 1, \tau^2 - \tau - 1\}$-expansions.

INPUT: An Kleinian integer ζ, a point P on a Koblitz curve, a real constant α with $0 < \alpha < 1/2$

OUTPUT: $Q = \zeta P$

Compute in succession for $i = 0, 1, \ldots, \lceil \log^\alpha N(\zeta) \rceil$ the points $P_i^{(1)} = (\tau - 1)P_{i-1}^{(1)}$ and $P_i^{(2)} = (\tau^2 - \tau - 1)P_{i-1}^{(2)}$ where $P_0^{(1)} = P_0^{(2)} = P$.

Compute the points $Q_{i_1, i_2} = P_{i_1}^{(1)} + P_{i_2}^{(2)}$ for $i_1, i_2 = 0, 1, \ldots, \lceil \log^\alpha N(\zeta) \rceil$.

Compute a $\{\tau, \tau - 1, \tau^2 - \tau - 1\}$-expansion of the form (5) using Theorem 4.

Apply in succession τ-NAF based point multiplications based on (5) to compute Q.

The analysis of Alg. 3. is simple. Step 1 requires $O(\log^\alpha N(\zeta))$ point additions and Step 2 requires $O(\log^{2\alpha} N(\zeta))$ point additions. Because $\alpha < 1/2$, the total number of point additions for Steps 1 and 2 is $o(\log N(\zeta))$. According to Theorem 4, Step 3 requires $O(\log N(\zeta)/(\log \log N(\zeta)))$ point additions. The total number of point additions for Alg. 3. is therefore $O(\log N(\zeta)/(\log \log N(\zeta)))$. Thus, one can compute kP in $O(\log k/(\log \log k))$ point additions by computing $\zeta \equiv k \pmod{(\tau^m - 1)/(\tau - 1)}$ and applying Alg. 3. to compute ζP.

Note that the first two steps of Alg. 3. are independent of k. If a fixed base point P is to be used, the points Q_{i_1, i_2} may be precomputed.

The parameter α can be chosen in a variety of ways. The total number of point additions required by all three steps is roughly $\log^\alpha N(\zeta) + \log^{2\alpha} N(\zeta) + 2 \log N(\zeta)/(\alpha \log \log N(\zeta))$; for $163 < N(\zeta) < 571$, taking α such that $0.365 < \alpha < 0.368$ minimizes this quantity. Smaller values of α reduce the number of points Q_{i_1, i_2} that must be precomputed and stored at the cost of increasing the number of point additions that must be performed in Step 3. On the other hand, larger values of α decrease the number of point additions in Step 3 at the cost of having to precompute and store more points.

3   A Practical Blocking Algorithm

Although, as proved in Theorem 4, using $\{\tau, \tau - 1, \tau^2 - \tau - 1\}$-expansions does lead to a sublinear point multiplication algorithm, the resulting algorithm is likely not suitable for practical purposes. Nevertheless, assuming the truth of Conjecture 1, we can devise an efficient algorithm that computes $\{\tau, \tau - 1\}$-expansions with sublinear density of Kleinian integers. This algorithm is based on the following theorem.

Theorem 5. *Assuming Conjecture 1, every Kleinian integer, $\xi = a + b\tau$, can be represented as the sum of at most $O\left(\log N(\xi)/\log\log N(\xi)\right)$ $\{\tau, \tau - 1\}$-Kleinian integers such that the largest power of $\tau - 1$ is $O\left(\log N(\xi)/\log\log N(\xi)\right)$.*

The proof, omitted for brevity, is quite similar to that of Theorem 4. The τ-adic expansions of a and b are broken into $\log\log N(\xi)$ blocks and the conjecture is applied to each block. In fact, this observation gives us an efficient method to compute $\{\tau, \tau - 1\}$-expansions with sublinear density under Conjecture 1. The idea, described in Alg. 4., is to apply the blocking strategy described in the proof and compute optimal $\{\tau, \tau - 1\}$-expansions for each block.

Algorithm 4. Blocking algorithm for computing $\{\tau, \tau - 1\}$-expansions.

INPUT: A Kleinian integer $\xi = e + f\tau$, block size w, precomputed table of the minimal $\{\tau, \tau - 1\}$-expansion of every Kleinian integer $\sum_{i=0}^{w-1} d_i\tau^i$, $d_i \in \{0,1\}$

OUTPUT: List L of $\{\tau, \tau - 1\}$-Kleinian integers representing $\{\tau, \tau - 1\}$-expansion of ξ

  $L = \emptyset$

  Compute the τ-adic expansion of $\xi = \sum_{i=0}^{l} d_i\tau^i$, $d_i \in \{0,1\}$

  for $j = 0$ to $\lceil l/w \rceil$ **do**

    {Process blocks of length w}

    Find minimal $\{\tau, \tau - 1\}$-expansion of $\sum_{i=0}^{w-1} d_{i+jw}\tau^i$ from the precomputed table

    Multiply each term of the expansion by τ^{jw} and add to L

There are four important points regarding the implementation Alg. 4.:

1. All powers of τ can be reduced modulo m, as $(\tau^m)P = P$ for all $P \in E_a(\mathbb{F}_{2^m})$.
2. The bit-string $d_{w-1} \ldots d_1 d_0$ corresponding to any block can be used as an index into the table of minimal $\{\tau, \tau - 1\}$-expansions.
3. One can choose the size of the blocks based on available memory. The larger the block size, the lower the density of the $\{\tau, \tau - 1\}$-expansions produced.
4. If the block size is not too big, one can precompute the minimal $\{\tau, \tau - 1\}$-expansion of every Kleinian integer of the form $\sum_{i=0}^{w-1} d_i\tau^i$, $d_i \in \{0,1\}$, thereby ensuring as low a density as possible. This precomputation can be done using exhaustive search and need only be done once per elliptic curve, as it does not depend on k nor the base point P.

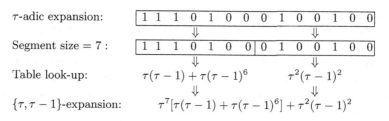

Fig. 1. Expansion of $-104 + 50\tau$ using Alg. 4.

3.1   Example

Consider the representation of 6465 into a $\{\tau, \tau - 1\}$-expansion by using the two different algorithm we have described. Assume that we intend to compute $(6465)P$ for some point $P \in E_1(\mathbb{F}_{2^{163}})$, so $\tau = (1 + \sqrt{-7})/2$. As in the case of computing the τ-NAF expansion, we first do a partial reduction of 6465 modulo $(\tau^{163} - 1)/(\tau - 1)$ as in [5], yielding $\xi = -104 + 50\tau$. The greedy algorithm, Alg. 2., returns

$$\xi = \tau^8(\tau - 1) + \tau^2(\tau - 1)^2 + \tau^8(\tau - 1)^6 \ .$$

The blocking algorithm, Alg. 4., using a block size $w = 7$ returns the same representation.

Fig. 1 illustrates the idea behind the blocking algorithm. The τ-adic expansion of ξ is $\tau^2 + \tau^5 + \tau^9 + \tau^{11} + \tau^{12} + \tau^{13}$. This 14-bit expansion of ξ is broken into two 7-bit blocks. The right block corresponds to $\tau^2 + \tau^5$, and $\tau^2(\tau - 1)^2$ is its optimal $\{\tau, \tau-1\}$-expansion. The left block corresponds to $\tau^2 + \tau^4 + \tau^5 + \tau^6$, and $\tau(\tau - 1) + \tau(\tau - 1)^6$ is its optimal expansion. Finally, multiplying the expression for the left block by τ^7 yields the $\{\tau, \tau-1\}$-expansion of ξ.

To see the usefulness of this idea, notice that the $\{\tau, \tau-1\}$-expansion obtained is very sparse. Of the 63 possible terms that could occur, assuming τ^8 is the maximum power of τ and $(\tau - 1)^6$ is the maximum power of $\tau - 1$, only three actually occur in the expansion. Furthermore, note that when computing kP using this representation, each power of $\tau - 1$ corresponds to a one-dimensional τ-adic expansion, and that each of these is very sparse.

3.2   Numerical Evidence

In this section, we present results from software implementations of Alg. 2. and Alg. 4. The objective is to compare the density of the $\{\tau, \tau - 1\}$-expansions computed by our algorithms with τ-NAF expansions. Our algorithms and the algorithm for computing the τ-NAF [5] of k were implemented in C, using the GMP library for multi-precision integer arithmetic. Tests were run on an Intel Xeon 2.8 GHz CPU running Linux.

Theorem 5 states that our conversion algorithm outputs expansions of k with sublinear density even if the maximum power of $\tau - 1$ is bounded by some constant $\max(b_i)$ as long as any sublinear expansion exists. For practical purposes, we need to know what value of $\max(b_i)$ gives us minimal weight expansions on average. We computed the average number of point additions required to compute kP using a $\{\tau, \tau - 1\}$-expansion of k, i.e., the number of non-zero terms in the expansion plus $\max(b_i) - 1$. For each size of k between 160 and 600 bits, the optimal value of $\max(b_i)$ starts at 4 and increases to 12 as the bit length of k increases. As shown in Sec. 4.4, $\max(b_i) = 3$ turns out to be optimal for our FPGA implementation of point multiplication on $E_1(\mathbb{F}_{2^{163}})$.

In Table 1 we list the average number of point additions required to compute kP on the five NIST-recommended Koblitz curves [4] when using τ-NAF, our greedy $\{\tau, \tau - 1\}$-expansion algorithm (Alg. 2.), and our blocking-based Alg. 4. using block lengths of $w = 5, 10, 16$ and $\max(b_i) = 6$. In all cases the data are taken as the average over 500000 random values of k. Our algorithm requires significantly fewer point additions than τ-NAF in all cases.

Table 1. The average number of point additions required to compute kP for the five Koblitz curves in [4]

		Alg. 2.	Alg. 4. (blocking)		
$\log_2 k$	τ-NAF	(greedy)	$w = 5$	$w = 10$	$w = 16$
163	54.25	36.37	47.86	40.00	37.22
233	77.59	49.31	66.23	54.96	50.76
283	94.25	58.64	79.37	65.66	60.49
409	137.12	81.84	113.64	93.63	85.68
571	190.25	111.90	154.98	127.21	117.04

4   FPGA Implementation

An FPGA implementation was designed in order to investigate the performance of the new algorithm in practice. The design implements kP on the NIST curve K-163 defined by (1), where $a = 1$, over $\mathbb{F}_{2^{163}}$ [4].

As the number of zero coefficients in a $\{\tau, \tau - 1\}$-expansion is large, a normal basis $\mathbb{F}_{2^m}$ was selected. In a normal basis, an element $A \in \mathbb{F}_{2^m}$ is represented as $A = \sum_{i=0}^{m-1} a_i \alpha^{2^i}$ where $a_i \in \{0, 1\}$ and $\alpha^{2^i} \neq \alpha^{2^j}$ for all $i \neq j$ and $\alpha^{2^m} = \alpha$. Thus, it is obvious that the squaring operation A^2 is a cyclic right shift of the bit vector $(a_0, a_1, \ldots, a_{m-1})$ which is fast if implemented in hardware.

Affine coordinates, $\mathcal{A}$, and López-Dahab coordinates, $\mathcal{LD}$ [17], are used for representing points on $E_a(\mathbb{F}_{2^m})$. In $\mathcal{A}$, a point P is represented with two coordinates as $P = (x, y)$, and, in $\mathcal{LD}$, with three coordinates as $P = (X, Y, Z)$. The $\mathcal{LD}$ triple represents the point $(X/Z, Y/Z^2)$ in $\mathcal{A}$ [17]. Three elements $x, y, \bar{y} = x + y \in \mathbb{F}_{2^m}$ are required to represent P and $-P$ in $\mathcal{A}$. A point addition in $\mathcal{A}$ is performed as presented, e.g., in [18], and its cost is $\mathsf{I} + 2\mathsf{M} + \mathsf{S} + 8\mathsf{A}$ where I, M, S, and A denote inversion, multiplication, squaring, and addition in $\mathbb{F}_{2^m}$, respectively. A point addition in $\mathcal{LD}$ is performed as presented in [19], and it requires $13\mathsf{M} + 4\mathsf{S} + 9\mathsf{A}$. A point addition $Q + P$, where Q is in $\mathcal{LD}$ and P in $\mathcal{A}$, is called the mixed coordinate point addition, and it requires only 9M + 5S + 9A [20]. If the curve is fixed and both P and $-P$ are available, one multiplication and one addition can be omitted resulting 8M + 5S + 8A. The $\mathcal{A} \mapsto \mathcal{LD}$ mapping does not require any operations in $\mathbb{F}_{2^m}$ while $\mathcal{LD} \mapsto \mathcal{A}$ requires I + 2M + S. The cost of a Frobenius mapping is 3S in $\mathcal{LD}$ and 2S in $\mathcal{A}$. An inversion in $\mathbb{F}_{2^m}$ is computed as suggested by Itoh and Tsujii in [21]. The Itoh-Tsujii inversion requires $m - 1$ squarings and $\lfloor \log_2(m - 1) \rfloor + H_w(m - 1) - 1$ multiplications, where $H_w(m - 1)$ is the Hamming weight of $m - 1$ [21]. Hence, I = 9M + 162S if $m = 163$.

Different coordinates are used in Alg. 1. as follows: the point addition in $\mathcal{A}$ is used in computing P_i so that the point addition in mixed coordinates can be used in $S \leftarrow S \pm P_i$ computations. Because the results of row multiplications are in $\mathcal{LD}$, the point addition in $\mathcal{LD}$ must be used for $Q \leftarrow Q + S$ computations.

The implementation was designed especially for Xilinx Virtex-II family FPGAs. The implementation includes a field arithmetic processor (FAP) for arithmetic in $\mathbb{F}_{2^m}$, control logic for controlling the FAP, and a converter for converting k to a $\{\tau, \tau - 1\}$-expansion. The FAP is considered in Sec. 4.1, the control logic in Sec. 4.2, and the conversion unit in Sec. 4.3.

4.1   Field Arithmetic Processor(FAP)

The FAP includes a multiplier, a squarer, an adder, a storage element and control logic. A storage element for m-bit elements of $\mathbb{F}_{2^m}$ is required in order to store points and temporary variables during computation of kP. As Xilinx devices offer embedded memory blocks which can be used without consuming logic resources, the storage element is implemented in BlockRAMs. One dual-port BlockRAM can be configured into a 512×36-bit mode. All m bits of an element must be accessed in parallel in the FAP architecture. Hence, $\lceil \frac{m}{36} \rceil = 5$ BlockRAMs are required. Write and read operations require both one clock cycle, i.e. W = R = 1.

The squarer is a shifter which is capable of performing operations A^{2^d}, where $A \in \mathbb{F}_{2^m}$ and $0 \leq d \leq d_{\max} = 2^6 - 1$,. Thus, A^{2^d} operations can be performed with a cost of S. Addition in $\mathbb{F}_{2^m}$ is simply a bitwise exclusive-or (xor). Both squaring and addition are performed in one clock cycle, i.e. S = A = 1.

Field multiplication is critical for the overall performance. The multiplier is a digit-serial implementation of the Massey-Omura multiplier [22]. In a bit-serial Massey-Omura multiplier, one bit of the output is calculated in one clock cycle and, hence, m cycles are required in total. One bit c_i of the result $C = A \times B$ is computed from A and B by using an F-function. The F-function is field specific, and the same F is used for all output bits c_i as follows: $c_i = F(A_{\lll i}, B_{\lll i})$, where $\lll i$ denotes cyclical left shift by i bits. [4,22]

In a digit-serial implementation, D bits are computed in parallel. Hence, $\lceil \frac{m}{D} \rceil$ cycles are required in one multiplication. In this FAP, $D = 24$. The F-function is pipelined in order to increase clock frequency by adding one register stage. As loading the operands into the shift registers requires one clock cycle and pipelining increases latency by one clock cycle, the latency is M = $\lceil \frac{163}{24} \rceil + 2 = 9$.

4.2   Control Logic

Logic controlling the FAP consists of a storage for k, a control finite state machine (FSM) and a ROM for control sequences.

The implementation handles k in a coded form. The coding is performed using $\kappa : \{s, d\}$ symbols, where $s \in \{0, \bar{0}, 1, \bar{1}\}$ and $0 \leq d \leq d_{\max}$. $\bar{0}$ is a symbol reserved for a row change not -0. Coding is started from the first non-zero signed bit of the first row and it proceeds as follows: s is the signed bit starting a symbol and d is the number of Frobenius mappings following s, i.e. the number of consecutive zeros plus one (the Frobenius map associated with the start bit of the next symbol). If the run of consecutive Frobenius maps is longer than $d_{\max}$, the run must be divided into two symbols and, for the latter one, $s = 0$. Each κ, with the exception of the row change symbol, transforms into an operation $S \leftarrow \tau^d(S + sP)$ on $E_a(\mathbb{F}_{2^m})$. Let $Z(k)$ denote the maximum number of consecutive Frobenius mappings required by k. Then, the number of κ-symbols, e, required to represent k, is given by $e \geq H_w(k) + j$, with equality if and only if $d_{\max} \geq Z(k)$.

Control FSM takes κ-symbols as input and, according to s and d of κ, it sets addresses of the control sequence ROM. The control sequences controlling the FAP consist of successive FAP instructions directly controlling the FAP. There are separate control sequences for $P_{i+1} \leftarrow \tau P_i - P_i$ computation (Frobenius map and point addition in $\mathcal{A}$), point addition and subtraction (point addition in the mixed coordinates), Frobenius map, row change (point addition in $\mathcal{LD}$), and $\mathcal{LD} \mapsto \mathcal{A}$ mapping. They are all stored in a ROM implemented in a BlockRAM.

If implemented so that, for each operation, the operands would be first read from the memory, then the operation calculated and finally the result saved to the memory, the latency of an operation would be the latency of the operation (M, S or A) plus two clock cycles (R + W). However, different operations can be performed with the same operands without reading the operands more than once, and the operands of the next operation can be read while the previous operation is performed if the result is not required in the next operation. When the control sequences were carefully hand-optimized, different operations have the following latencies: point addition in the mixed coordinates $\mathsf{L}_{\mathcal{M}} = 98$, the Frobenius map $\mathsf{L}_F = 6$, row change (point addition in $\mathcal{LD}$) $\mathsf{L}_{\mathcal{LD}} = 153$, the computation of P_i $\mathsf{L}_{P_i} = 182$, and the $\mathcal{LD} \mapsto \mathcal{A}$ mapping $\mathsf{L}_{\mathcal{LD} \mapsto \mathcal{A}} = 160$. The first point addition of each row is simply $S \leftarrow \pm P_i$ and the first row change operation is given by $Q \leftarrow S$. Both of these operations have a latency of $\mathsf{L}_C = 6$. In the beginning, an initialization including, e.g., the transferring of P into the FAP, needs to be performed. The latency of the initialization is $\mathsf{L}_I = 10$. Thus, it follows that the latency of the computation of kP becomes

$$\mathsf{L}_{kP} = (H_w(k) - (j+1))\mathsf{L}_{\mathcal{M}} + (j+2)\mathsf{L}_C + (e-j)\mathsf{L}_F + j(\mathsf{L}_{\mathcal{LD}} + \mathsf{L}_{P_i}) + \mathsf{L}_I + \mathsf{L}_{\mathcal{LD} \mapsto \mathcal{A}} \quad (6)$$

and, by assuming that $d_{\max} \geq Z(k)$, i.e. $e = H_w(k) + j$, (6) simplifies to

$$\mathsf{L}_{kP} = 104\, H_w(k) + 243\, j + 84. \quad (7)$$

4.3   Conversion Unit

The conversion unit, which converts an integer k into a $\{\tau, \tau - 1\}$-expansion, is a straightforward implementation of Alg. 4., our blocking-based method.

The main part of this unit is an ALU, which has two integer multipliers, each of which makes use of one 18-bit by 18-bit embedded multiplier to create 102-bit by 102-bit products. The ALU also includes adders, shifters and the rounding function required by the partial reduction algorithm [5]. The conversion unit uses the ALU and two intermediate registers for reducing every integer k to an equivalent $r_0 + r_1\tau$, then gets the τ-adic expansion by a shift-and-add circuit, which produces one bit per cycle, from the least significant bit to the most significant bit.

For our implementation, we selected a block size of 10, so every 10 bits of the τ-adic expansion are used as an index into a look-up table. This table has one entry for each possible index $(b_9 b_8 \ldots b_0)$, $b_i \in \{0, 1\}$, where each entry is the optimal $\{\tau, \tau - 1\}$-expansion of $\sum_{i=0}^{9} b_i \tau^i$ allowing a maximum exponent of 6 for $\tau - 1$. At most 3 terms of the form $\pm \tau^a (\tau - 1)^b$ are required for each representation, so each entry in the table consists of three tuples of the form (d_n, i_n, j_n) representing $d_n \tau^{i_n} (\tau - 1)^{j_n}$. Hence, each entry requires 27 bits and the whole look-up table requires 27 KB RAM. Note that, according to the data in Sec. 3.2, using a block size of 5 would still give us a significant improvement over τ-NAF and in this case the table would require less than 1 KB.

Because integer operations are slower than the $\mathbb{F}_{2^m}$ operations in the FAP, the conversion unit will be the bottleneck if the two units use the same clock. So a dual-port RAM is used in order to separate these units into different clock domains. The look-up results are written into the dual-port RAM using one port, and the ECC processor will read them out from the another port later.

4.4   Results

The FPGA design was written in VHDL and implemented on a Xilinx Virtex-II XC2V2000-6. The design was synthesized with Synplify Pro 8.0 and Xilinx ISE 6.2 was used for the place & route. The design (excluding the converter) requires 6,494 slices and 6 BlockRAMs on the XC2V2000-6, and it operates at a maximum clock frequency of $f_{\max} = 128$ MHz. The converter requires 2251 slices, 2 BlockRAMs and 2 multipliers. The maximum clock frequency is 88 MHz. It takes 335 clock cycles, or 3.81 μs to convert one 163-bit integer.

Average timings of the design are presented in Table 2. The latency L_{kP} is given by (7), and timings are calculated using $f_{\max}$. The time consumed in the conversion is neglected. Table 2 shows that the best performance is achieved when $j = 3$ which is smaller than estimated in Sec. 3.2, because the latencies of point additions differ. In Sec. 3.2, all point additions were assumed equal.

Numerous publications considering implementation of elliptic curve cryptography on FPGAs have been published, e.g., in [23,24,25,26]. To the best of the authors' knowledge, the only FPGA-based implementation using τ-NAF expansions was presented by Lutz and Hasan [26] where a kP operation on $E_1(\mathbb{F}_{2^{163}})$ was reported to require 75 μs on a Xilinx Virtex-E XCV2000E.

Table 2. Performance calculations of the FPGA implementation on a Xilinx Virtex-II XC2V2000-6 with different values of j. $H_w(k)$ for $j > 0$ are based on empirical data. The numbers of point additions in the mixed coordinates, in $\mathcal{A}$ and in $\mathcal{LD}$ are denoted as $\mathcal{M}$, $\mathcal{A}$ and $\mathcal{LD}$, respectively.

j	$H_w(k)$	$\mathcal{M}$	$\mathcal{A}$	$\mathcal{LD}$	L_{kP}	Time (μs)
0	54.33	53.33	0	0	5735	44.80
2	39.47	36.47	2	2	4675	36.52
3	36.18	32.18	3	3	**4576**	**35.75**
4	34.74	29.74	4	4	4669	36.48
5	33.42	27.42	5	5	4775	37.30
6	32.22	25.22	6	6	4893	38.23

5   Further Work

Our results demonstrate that $\{\tau, \tau - 1\}$-expansions lead to a competitive point multiplication algorithm for Koblitz curves when the base point P is not fixed. Nevertheless, there are a number of aspects we are continuing to explore.

The latency of a point multiplication using our FPGA implementation could be significantly reduced at the expense of larger area requirements by computing each row in parallel. This possibility will be studied in the future. In addition, alternative choices of the bases, or even using three bases, may lead to further improvements.

Our point multiplication algorithm does not require any precomputations involving the base point P nor storage of additional points, and hence is well-suited to applications where P is random. We are investigating the possibility of generalizing window methods, using two-dimensional windows, to our algorithm in order to obtain further improvements when precomputations involving P are permitted.

Although our numerical data suggests that the density of the $\{\tau, \tau - 1\}$-expansions obtained by our conversion algorithm is sublinear in the bit length of k, we do not yet have a proof of this fact. In addition, our conversion algorithm requires a modest amount of storage. These precomputed quantities are independent of both the base point P and multiplier k and can be viewed as part of the domain parameters. Nevertheless, we continue to search for an efficient memory-free conversion algorithm.

References

1. Koblitz, N.: Elliptic curve cryptosystems. Math. Comp. **48** (1987) 203–209
2. Miller, V.: Use of elliptic curves in cryptography. In: CRYPTO '85. Volume 218 of Lecture Notes in Computer Science (LNCS). (1986) 417–426
3. Koblitz, N.: CM-curves with good cryptographic properties. In: CRYPTO '91. Volume 576 of LNCS. (1992) 279–287
4. National Institute of Standards and Technology (NIST): Digital signature standard (DSS). Federal Information Processing Standard, FIPS PUB 186-2 (2000)

5. Solinas, J.: Efficient arithmetic on Koblitz curves. Designs, Codes, and Cryptography **19** (2000) 195–249
6. Avanzi, R., Heuberger, C., Prodinger, H.: Minimality of the Hamming weight of the τ-NAF for Koblitz curves and improved combination with point halving. In: SAC 2005. Volume 3897 of LNCS. (2005) 332–344
7. Dimitrov, V., Jullien, G., Miller, W.: An algorithm for modular exponentiation. Inform. Process. Lett. **66** (1998) 155–159
8. Ciet, M., Sica, F.: An analysis of double base number systems and a sublinear scalar multiplication algorithm. In: Mycrypt 2005. Volume 3715 of LNCS. (2005) 171–182
9. Dimitrov, V., Imbert, L., Mishra, P.: Efficient and secure elliptic curve point multiplication using double-base chains. In: ASIACRYPT 2005. Volume 3788 of LNCS. (2005) 59–78
10. Avanzi, R., Sica, F.: Scalar multiplication on Koblitz curves using double bases. Technical Report Number 2006/067, Cryptology ePrint Archive (2006)
11. Sica, F.: Personal communication. (2006)
12. Conway, J., Smith, D.: On quaternions and octonions. AK Peters (2003)
13. Tijdeman, R.: On integers with many small prime factors. Compos. Math. **26** (1973) 319–330
14. Baker, A.: Linear forms in the logarithms of algebraic numbers IV. Mathematica **15** (1968) 204–216
15. Mignotte, M., Waldshmidt, M.: Linear forms in two logarithms and Schneider's method III. In: Annales Fas. Sci. Toulouse. (1990) 43–75
16. Tijdeman, R.: Personal communication. (2006)
17. López, J., Dahab, R.: Improved algorithms for elliptic curve arithmetic in $GF(2^n)$. In: SAC '98. Volume 1556 of LNCS. (1998) 201–212
18. Doche, C., Lange, T.: Arithmetic of elliptic curves. In Cohen, H., Frey, G., eds.: Handbook of Elliptic and Hyperelliptic Curve Cryptography. Chapman & Hall/CRC (2006) 267–302
19. Higuchi, A., Takagi, N.: A fast addition algorithm for elliptic curve arithmetic in $GF(2^n)$ using projective coordinates. Inform. Process. Lett. **76** (2000) 101–103
20. Al-Daoud, E., Mahmod, R., Rushdan, M., Kilicman, A.: A new addition formula for elliptic curves over $GF(2^n)$. IEEE Trans. Comput. **51** (2002) 972–975
21. Itoh, T., Tsujii, S.: A fast algorithm for computing multiplicative inverses in $GF(2^m)$ using normal bases. Inform. Comput. **78** (1988) 171–177
22. Wang, C., Troung, T., Shao, H., Deutsch, L., Omura, J., Reed, I.: VLSI architectures for computing multiplications and inverses in $GF(2^m)$. IEEE Trans. Comput. **34** (1985) 709–717
23. Bednara, M., Daldrup, M., von zur Gathen, J., Shokrollahi, J., Teich, J.: Reconfigurable implementation of elliptic curve crypto algorithms. In: IPDPS 2002. (2002) 157–164
24. Leong, P., Leung, K.: A microcoded elliptic curve processor using FPGA technology. IEEE Trans. VLSI Syst. **10** (2002) 550–559
25. Eberle, H., Gura, N., Shantz, S., Gupta, V.: A cryptographic processor for arbitrary elliptic curves over $GF(2^m)$. Technical Report SMLI TR-2003-123, Sun Microsystems, Inc. (2003)
26. Lutz, J., Hasan, A.: High performance FPGA based elliptic curve cryptographic co-processor. In: Proc. of the Int'l Conf. on Information Technology: Coding and Computing. Volume 2. (2004) 486–492

Author Index

Lecture Notes in Computer Science

For information about Vols. 1–4144

please contact your bookseller or Springer

Vol. 4191: R. Larsen, M. Nielsen, J. Sporring (Eds.), Medical Image Computing and Computer-Assisted Intervention – MICCAI 2006, Part II. XXXVIII, 981 pages. 2006.

Vol. 4190: R. Larsen, M. Nielsen, J. Sporring (Eds.), Medical Image Computing and Computer-Assisted Intervention – MICCAI 2006, Part I. XXXVVIII, 949 pages. 2006.

Vol. 4189: D. Gollmann, J. Meier, A. Sabelfeld (Eds.), Computer Security – ESORICS 2006. XI, 548 pages. 2006.

Vol. 4188: P. Sojka, I. Kopeček, K. Pala (Eds.), Text, Speech and Dialogue. XIV, 721 pages. 2006. (Sublibrary LNAI).

Vol. 4187: J.J. Alferes, J. Bailey, W. May, U. Schwertel (Eds.), Principles and Practice of Semantic Web Reasoning. XI, 277 pages. 2006.

Vol. 4186: C. Jesshope, C. Egan (Eds.), Advances in Computer Systems Architecture. XIV, 605 pages. 2006.

Vol. 4185: R. Mizoguchi, Z. Shi, F. Giunchiglia (Eds.), The Semantic Web – ASWC 2006. XX, 778 pages. 2006.

Vol. 4184: M. Bravetti, M. Núñez, G. Zavattaro (Eds.), Web Services and Formal Methods. X, 289 pages. 2006.

Vol. 4183: J. Euzenat, J. Domingue (Eds.), Artificial Intelligence: Methodology, Systems, and Applications. XIII, 291 pages. 2006. (Sublibrary LNAI).

Vol. 4182: H.T. Ng, M.-K. Leong, M.-Y. Kan, D. Ji (Eds.), Information Retrieval Technology. XVI, 684 pages. 2006.

Vol. 4180: M. Kohlhase, OMDoc – An Open Markup Format for Mathematical Documents [version 1.2]. XIX, 428 pages. 2006. (Sublibrary LNAI).

Vol. 4179: J. Blanc-Talon, W. Philips, D. Popescu, P. Scheunders (Eds.), Advanced Concepts for Intelligent Vision Systems. XXIV, 1224 pages. 2006.

Vol. 4178: A. Corradini, H. Ehrig, U. Montanari, L. Ribeiro, G. Rozenberg (Eds.), Graph Transformations. XII, 473 pages. 2006.

Vol. 4177: R. Marín, E. Onaindía, A. Bugarín, J. Santos (Eds.), Current Topics in Artificial Intelligence. XIII, 621 pages. 2006. (Sublibrary LNAI).

Vol. 4176: S.K. Katsikas, J. Lopez, M. Backes, S. Gritzalis, B. Preneel (Eds.), Information Security. XIV, 548 pages. 2006.

Vol. 4175: P. Bücher, B.M.E. Moret (Eds.), Algorithms in Bioinformatics. XII, 402 pages. 2006. (Sublibrary LNBI).

Vol. 4174: K. Franke, K.-R. Müller, B. Nickolay, R. Schäfer (Eds.), Pattern Recognition. XX, 773 pages. 2006.

Vol. 4173: S. El Yacoubi, B. Chopard, S. Bandini (Eds.), Cellular Automata. XV, 734 pages. 2006.

Vol. 4172: J. Gonzalo, C. Thanos, M. F. Verdejo, R.C. Carrasco (Eds.), Research and Advanced Technology for Digital Libraries. XVII, 569 pages. 2006.

Vol. 4169: H.L. Bodlaender, M.A. Langston (Eds.), Parameterized and Exact Computation. XI, 279 pages. 2006.

Vol. 4168: Y. Azar, T. Erlebach (Eds.), Algorithms – ESA 2006. XVIII, 843 pages. 2006.

Vol. 4167: S. Dolev (Ed.), Distributed Computing. XV, 576 pages. 2006.

Vol. 4166: J. Górski (Ed.), Computer Safety, Reliability, and Security. XIV, 440 pages. 2006.

Vol. 4165: W. Jonker, M. Petković (Eds.), Secure, Data Management. X, 185 pages. 2006.

Vol. 4163: H. Bersini, J. Carneiro (Eds.), Artificial Immune Systems. XII, 460 pages. 2006.

Vol. 4162: R. Královič, P. Urzyczyn (Eds.), Mathematical Foundations of Computer Science 2006. XV, 814 pages. 2006.

Vol. 4161: R. Harper, M. Rauterberg, M. Combetto (Eds.), Entertainment Computing - ICEC 2006. XXVII, 417 pages. 2006.

Vol. 4160: M. Fisher, W.v.d. Hoek, B. Konev, A. Lisitsa (Eds.), Logics in Artificial Intelligence. XII, 516 pages. 2006. (Sublibrary LNAI).

Vol. 4159: J. Ma, H. Jin, L.T. Yang, J.J.-P. Tsai (Eds.), Ubiquitous Intelligence and Computing. XXII, 1190 pages. 2006.

Vol. 4158: L.T. Yang, H. Jin, J. Ma, T. Ungerer (Eds.), Autonomic and Trusted Computing. XIV, 613 pages. 2006.

Vol. 4156: S. Amer-Yahia, Z. Bellahsène, E. Hunt, R. Unland, J.X. Yu (Eds.), Database and XML Technologies. IX, 123 pages. 2006.

Vol. 4155: O. Stock, M. Schaerf (Eds.), Reasoning, Action and Interaction in AI Theories and Systems. XVIII, 343 pages. 2006. (Sublibrary LNAI).

Vol. 4154: Y.A. Dimitriadis, I. Zigurs, E. Gómez-Sánchez (Eds.), Groupware: Design, Implementation, and Use. XIV, 438 pages. 2006.

Vol. 4153: N. Zheng, X. Jiang, X. Lan (Eds.), Advances in Machine Vision, Image Processing, and Pattern Analysis. XIII, 506 pages. 2006.

Vol. 4152: Y. Manolopoulos, J. Pokorný, T. Sellis (Eds.), Advances in Databases and Information Systems. XV, 448 pages. 2006.

Vol. 4151: A. Iglesias, N. Takayama (Eds.), Mathematical Software - ICMS 2006. XVII, 452 pages. 2006.

Vol. 4150: M. Dorigo, L.M. Gambardella, M. Birattari, A. Martinoli, R. Poli, T. Stützle (Eds.), Ant Colony Optimization and Swarm Intelligence. XVI, 526 pages. 2006.

Vol. 4149: M. Klusch, M. Rovatsos, T.R. Payne (Eds.), Cooperative Information Agents X. XII, 477 pages. 2006. (Sublibrary LNAI).

Vol. 4148: J. Vounckx, N. Azemard, P. Maurine (Eds.), Integrated Circuit and System Design. XVI, 677 pages. 2006.

Vol. 4147: M. Broy, I.H. Krüger, M. Meisinger (Eds.), Automotive Software – Connected Services in Mobile Networks. XIV, 155 pages. 2006.

Vol. 4146: J.C. Rajapakse, L. Wong, R. Acharya (Eds.), Pattern Recognition in Bioinformatics. XIV, 186 pages. 2006. (Sublibrary LNBI).

Vol. 4145: L. Moreau, I. Foster (Eds.), Provenance and Annotation of Data and Processes. XI, 288 pages. 2006.